The

New Russian Thought

The publication of this series was made possible with the support of the Zimin Foundation

Vladimir Bibikhin, *The Woods*

Boris Kolonitskii, *Comrade Kerensky*

Sergei Medvedev, *The Return of the Russian Leviathan*

Maxim Trudolyubov, *The Tragedy of Property*

The Woods
(*Hyle*)

Vladimir Bibikhin

Edited by
Artemy Magun

Translated by
Arch Tait

polity

First published in Russian as *ЛЕС (hyle)* by Наука (Nauka), 2011.
Copyright Vladimir Bibikhin © 2021
This English edition © Polity Press, 2021

This book was published with the support of the Zimin Foundation.

Polity Press
65 Bridge Street
Cambridge CB2 1UR, UK

Polity Press
101 Station Landing
Suite 300
Medford, MA 02155, USA

ISBN-13: 978-1-5095-2586-7 Hardback
ISBN-13: 978-1-5095-2587-4 Paperback

A catalogue record for this book is available from the British Library.

Typeset in 10 on 11 pt Times New Roman MT by
Servis Filmsetting Limited, Stockport, Cheshire
Printed and bound in Great Britain by CPI Group (UK) Ltd, Croydon

For further information on Polity, visit our website:
politybooks.com

Contents

Contents

Foreword

This is the first book-length translation into English of the work of the Russian philosopher Vladimir Bibikhin (1938–2004). Bibikhin is recognized by many (myself included) as the most important Soviet/Russian thinker of the second half of the twentieth century. In the 1990s, his public lecture courses enjoyed immense popularity, the lecture hall was packed, and almost every course was later published as a solid philosophical treatise. Within some fifteen years, Bibikhin created an impressive oeuvre on the scale of a philosophical encyclopaedia. This work was 'marked' (to use his term) and remarkable for many reasons, including a virtuoso Russian style, freely flowing in unpredictable directions to express an original thought, to connect a foreign word to a Russian word, a metaphysical formula to the spirit of the times and to the lived experience of contemporary politics and everyday life. Bibikhin's was a free, original philosophy of genius which, nevertheless, was based on great erudition, some bibliographical research, and, as is clear with hindsight, was moving towards becoming systematic.

Bibikhin did not have a conventional academic career, and always characterized himself as a bit of a radical or rebel. In high school, he wrote something subversive in an informal school 'wall' newsletter, got a negative personal reference from the school principal, and for that reason failed to be admitted to the department of philosophy of Moscow State University. Instead, he served his time in the Soviet Army (from which most university students were exempted), then joined the department of foreign languages and spent his early life learning, with great proficiency, an impressive number of them: German, English, French, ancient Greek, Latin, and even Sanskrit. These studies, during which he met and studied under Andrey Zaliznyak, subsequently a renowned Soviet linguist, enabled him to develop an original hermeneutic theory of language, which he summarized in his dissertation (1977) and in his book *The Language of Philosophy* (1992). In the late 1960s, when a period of political freedom in the Soviet Union came to an end, as did the enthusiasm for Marxist doctrine, Bibikhin increasingly turned to religion and the Russian religious tradition, supported in this by that great survivor from early twentieth-century Russian philosophy, Alexey Losev, at that time better known as an authority on classical Greek culture. He befriended such key Russian Orthodox intellectuals of the late Soviet period as Sergey Horuzhy and Sergey Averintsev, both open-minded and interested in the high culture of Western Europe. In the 1970s and 1980s, Bibikhin worked at translating numerous philosophical texts, from Aristotle and Nicholas of Cusa, to Heidegger, Arendt, and even Derrida. He developed his own virtuoso style of hermeneutic translation, seeking to make foreign thought, faithfully translated, as intelligible and organically Russian as possible.

Most of his translations of twentieth-century non-Marxist authors, as well as critical digests of their work, were published in a limited number of copies for 'special use', under restricted access. As Bibikhin himself explains, the communist authorities were considering whether to switch their ideology from Marxism to something more realistic and nationally orientated (as their heirs eventually did in the 2000s). They therefore engaged intellectuals to critically review European and American non-Marxist philosophy (which ironically helped convert these intellectuals to liberal or conservative ideas).[1] Only during Perestroika in the USSR (1985–91), during a reform of university teaching in the humanities, did Bibikhin, who at that time was best known as a Heidegger specialist, begin teaching at the philosophy department of Moscow State University. This soon ended, in 1993, because of a conflict with the more positivistically minded senior members of the department, and also Bibikhin's scatter-gun manner of teaching and researching. From then on and for most of the 1990s, Bibikhin did not have a university post. He obtained a position at the research-orientated Institute of Philosophy, and would just come to Moscow State University, since access to the building was then open, and teach in a lecture hall which happened to be unoccupied. He usually attracted a full house of students from all over the city. It was at this time that Bibikhin produced most of his numerous books, because he fully wrote his lectures out in advance and then read them to his audience. He spoke in a detached manner, in a rather high-pitched voice, creating the impression of a medium through whom the lecture was transmitting itself. It gradually became evident that the linguist and philosophical autodidact, who at first appeared simply to be rephrasing Heidegger, was actually an original philosopher in the process of creating his own philosophical system. He lectured on the world, the Renaissance, property, time, Wittgenstein, truth, wood, energy, and many other subjects. Importantly, Bibikhin was not a religious zealot remote from everyday life. His lectures were well spiced with irony and mundane examples. He drove a car (a rare thing at that time in the USSR for an academic), built his own wooden house in the country, married late for a second time, and was the father of

---

[1] Vladimir Bibikhin, 'Dlia sluzhebnogo pol'zovania' ['Restricted'], in: *Drugoe Nachalo* (SPb: Nauka, 2003), pp. 181–207.

four young children. Sadly, he contracted a cancer which killed him at the relatively early age of sixty-six.

To summarize Bibikhin's ideas without tracing their organic development and historical context is inevitably to do him a disservice. I must, however, follow the rules of foreword writing and attempt to do so. Bibikhin was extraordinarily well read, but I see him as influenced primarily by two philosophers: Martin Heidegger and Alexey Losev. Both were approximately contemporary, both were conservatives cherishing the classics above all else, but the former achieved fame while the latter was barely allowed to survive by the Soviet authorities, and concealed himself behind volumes on 'classical aesthetics'. In his thirties, Bibikhin worked as Losev's secretary (in 1970–2), and this left its mark on his style and attitudes, even though he rarely quotes his former boss (apart from in his early *The Language of Philosophy* and in a special autobiographical book dedicated to his conversations with Losev). As for Heidegger, Bibikhin became interested in his work, as, belatedly, did many other Soviet intellectuals, in the mid-1970s, when the German philosopher of 'being' was all but banned in the USSR.[2] Bibikhin became one of Heidegger's first Russian translators, with his rendering of *Being and Time* (1996) as a crowning achievement. This was after the fall of the Soviet system, at which time Heidegger became fashionable. When Bibikhin first started lecturing towards the end of the 1980s (late in life), the philosophical establishment had formed a stereotypical image of him as a 'Russian Heidegger'. This was gradually seen not to be the case: if some of Bibikhin's Russian concepts are close to Heidegger's ('the world', 'the event'), others are not. For one thing, Bibikhin is not particularly interested in 'being', 'death', or 'anguish'. He most readily takes from Heidegger everything related to event, particularly, the term 'other onset' from the *Introduction to Metaphysics*,[3] which became the title of one of Bibikhin's own books, devoted to the historical destiny of contemporary Russia. The entire tonality of Bibikhin's thought is different, however. In contrast to the ultra-serious and edifying ontological prose of Heidegger, I see his philosophy as centred rather on aesthetics, or, more precisely, on the aesthetic interpretation of phenomenology. This is a direct effect of Losev's teaching. Losev, after being politically persecuted for his philosophical work, camouflaged it under a multi-volume *History of Classical Aesthetics*. There was method behind this choice of disguise. For Losev, symbolic expression was the indispensable culmination of ontology. In retrospect, it seems clear that he had much more influence on Bibikhin than did Heidegger (whom Bibikhin read only as a mature adult). Bibikhin's notes on his conversations with Losev were published during his lifetime, with discussion of topics such as the primacy of aesthetics,

---

[2] Ibid.

[3] Martin Heidegger, *Introduction to Metaphysics*, 2nd edition, tr. Gregory Fried and Richard Polt (New Haven: Yale University Press, 2014).

the holistic act of linguistic utterance, the role of etymologies, the value of harsh authoritarian systems from a philosophical point of view, and the philosophical relevance of colour. These topics later featured in Bibikhin's own oeuvre.

Subjectively, there was a third figure of major importance for Bibikhin, and that was Ludwig Wittgenstein. However, in my view this is less a case of following a tradition and more a case of an interpretation, and idiosyncratic reading, of the Vienna–Cambridge philosopher in an existential-phenomenological context. Bibikhin read Wittgenstein in his own way, disregarding most of the reception history and context of Anglo-American neopositivism. Wittgenstein is important for Bibikhin as a philosopher of intuition, of the this-ness of things, and of the inaccessible, aesthetic self-showing of the world. Wittgenstein's 'aspect change', a sudden Gestalt switch, is understood as the formula of a phenomenological event close to a conversion.

This said, Bibikhin's system of thought boils down to the following. There is an event, the 'lightning', which suddenly reveals the world in a new light and mobilizes the living being for near-to-impossible achievements. (In contrast to Heidegger, death is barely mentioned.) The event is thus a pure, festive effect whose ontological content consists primarily of unravelling and separating the contrasting aspects of being (the regular and the chaotic, the light and the matter, the masculine and the feminine). The event 'captivates' humans, entrances them, and forms a mission that gives them meaning. The event of captivation is not under our conscious control. We only become conscious of it retrospectively, which gives a special role, in the process of knowledge, to attention: the moment we notice something is the moment when our relation to the world, our mission, is decided. Captivation also allows the human being to capture things and lands, which grounds 'property'. Property, however, works both ways: things captivate people who capture them. (Before there was private property, there had already been property as such, where a thing opened itself up to a human in its uniqueness and its essential possibilities.) 'Energy', which the contemporary world exploits and longs for, comes from the capacity for a standstill, or an idle celebration (the 'energy of rest'). Against Modern activism, Bibikhin values careful attention to the event, which must come before any serious activity.

The event is, however, not all there is. It plays out the contrasting poles of the world which, taken together, constitute what he calls the 'automaton' of the world (Aristotelian spontaneity or the Leibnizian machine of machines) and equates it with 'Sophia', the central concept of Russian religious philosophy. Being rather critical of Russian religious philosophy, and particularly of its recent, nationalistically motivated, resurrection in Russia, Bibikhin nevertheless accepts and esteems Sophia: in Orthodoxy, a force of facticity and plurality in God. The rhythmic automaton of the world is Sophia, because it is a way of gripping contraries together, and because it is, and should be, beyond human control or calculation.

Both Sophia and the event have, for us, two faces: the freedom that inspires enthusiasm, and the iron, authoritarian law that governs the essentials. Bibikhin is consistently attentive to, and sympathetic towards, the phenomena of law, discipline, and grammar, which he derives from the 'harshness' (*zhestkost'*) of the event's imperativeness. He therefore values the Western culture of 'early discipline' (rightly understanding that the difference of Western culture from Russian is its respect for law) and contrasts it with an anarchic unpreparedness but attentiveness to an event, which he attributes to Russian culture. However, even in the Russian and similar cultures, there are 'harsh' phenomena, such as *krepost'* (a system of peasant serfdom) or, later, 'totalitarianism', which Bibikhin understands, neutrally, as a society with an unusual level of regulation and control. Thus, in the present book also, the irrational element of 'the forest', or matter, a phenomenological form of being, not a thingly substance (a reading which reminds us of Losev's Neoplatonic '*meon*'), only makes sense in interaction with the harsh, iron formatting of the gene-based '*eidos*'.

What does this all mean in the present historical context? Bibikhin started his public teaching, and most of his writing, in a revolutionary period when the Soviet Union was undergoing democratic reforms, before collapsing and heading into a period of neoliberal changes led by a weakened state. This revolutionary situation created a space of freedom for new ideas and initiatives, and hunger for new, unofficial and non-Marxist, philosophy. (Marx and Lenin are barely mentioned in Bibikhin's writings.) This is the window of historical opportunity which provided Bibikhin with his platform and his mission. But the ideological content of the revolution and the reforms was an alloy: liberal and democratic ideas were mixed, often in the same media and books, with a conservative and even traditionalist message. This is reflected in Bibikhin's thought: without ever designating his ideological stance, it is clear that, politically, he is navigating somewhere between liberalism and conservatism. Property (in things and industries) and energy (of oil and of creative labour), even if they are deduced back to their onto-aesthetic origins, are the words of the day, a concern of the new economy and new lifestyle. The interest in Wittgenstein (and, in the present book, in Darwin) reflects Bibikhin's deep empathy with Western rationalism. There are, however, obvious conservative elements too. Bibikhin writes *The Law of Russian History* and, later, *An Introduction to the Philosophy of Law*, in which he discusses and essentializes a specifically Russian historical trajectory and destiny. Orthodox religion, understood in a philosophical way as a religion of an absent God beyond rational discourse, is very present in his writings, particularly in the present book, where the Cross becomes an epitome of the forest. Bibikhin also shares Heidegger's disdain for activism. Conservative, and typical of the time in Russia, are his views on gender (where he values a contrast between a marked masculinity and marked femininity).

Bibikhin's main interest was in German philosophy, but he also knew and cherished the contemporary French tradition. He read, and even translated, Jacques Derrida, arguing against some of his interpretations. His strategy of writing books in the form of lecture courses targeted at a wide audience may have been a conscious emulation of the strategy of such great French public intellectuals as Lacan and Derrida.

Accordingly, when Bibikhin addresses the current moment, he refers to it, in awe, as a 'revolution' or 'renaissance'. Reminiscences of Peter the Great's reforms, or of the Italian Renaissance in the fifteenth–sixteenth centuries, help him understand a time of changes in Russia. It is always the extreme effort, the openness of freedom (beyond traditional morality), and festive colour that open everything up. In the Italian Renaissance, erroneously thought by some conservatives (including Losev) to be the beginning of a nihilistic sceptical age, 'the human essence reduced itself, in philosophical and poetic anthropology, to a few simple traits: selfless love, tireless activity (mostly of the higher faculties of the soul), informed attention to the world.'[4] Extreme ambition was characteristic of that age: 'Dante reports [...] that the task of his great poem was nothing less than to "lead the living out of their misery to the condition of happiness."'[5] It is the scale of the ambition that is important.

However, in every case there comes a default, or a breakdown (*sryv*) after the event, mostly due to the hubris of human subjects who put all their faith in themselves and disregard the pressures of history, which leads to an avalanche of violence. The description is reminiscent of the German 'conservative revolution', only this time combining the liberal and conservative elements.

Bibikhin himself was a 'Renaissance Man', with unbelievable energy and willpower (in the 1990s, he produced two book-length lecture courses each year), and an anarchic disdain for convention. The first impression he made was of a slightly lunatic intellectual with a posture of exaggerated humility. This was wrong on both accounts. As mentioned, he was not just a professional translator but also a competent manual worker. And he displayed impressive personal ambition and originality in his philosophical projects.

When we read Bibikhin's book today, we will probably appreciate his genius, but we need also to be aware of the historical distance, short as it still is. We need to remember that Soviet culture was isolated from Western culture to a greater degree than the 'normal' isolation of different cultures such as British and French. American, British, and French books were available, but:

• only to a closed academic elite
• there was a long delay before they became known

---

[4] Bibikhin, *Novyi Renessans* (Moscow: Nauka, 1998), p. 321.
[5] Ibid., quoting Dante, *Letters*, pp. 15, 39.

• only intellectual blockbusters were available, not routine intellectual discussion.

Libraries had very restricted collections of Western literature on the social sciences and humanities, and the access to some of that was further restricted for ideological reasons. In the 1970s, Bibikhin worked at INION, the Soviet Academy of Sciences' Institute of Scholarly Information on the Social Sciences. This institution engaged, as mentioned above, in digesting Western literature in the social sciences and humanities, in Russian, by trusted experts, in very small print runs and accompanied by ideological criticism. Bibikhin thus had privileged access to Western scholarship, though he regretted that he heard of Heidegger so very late. His experience at INION put him and his colleagues in the curious position of disengaged observers (which corresponded to his philosophical notion of the 'energy of rest'). This gave them an odd, decentred, outsider view of twentieth-century Western culture. It is hardly surprising that certain interpretations (like Bibikhin's reading of Wittgenstein) seem often really quite strange. He studied the reception literature only afterwards: the first encounter of Russian thinkers with Western thought was without critical context.

Conversely, the West knew very little about Russian intellectual life. There was a discrepancy not just in the scholarship, but also in the general approach of critically thinking intellectuals, which was libertarian (anarchic/conservative) in Russia, and ethical, rights-orientated, and left-leaning in the West.

After the collapse of the USSR in 1991, the situation did not change overnight and, lacking the Internet, Bibikhin in the 1990s was still proceeding in a bibliographical vacuum, with limited knowledge of intellectual concerns outside Russia. This did not prevent him from addressing the theme of environmental, biological philosophy in the present book. As you may see, many references in the book come from the *Encyclopaedia Britannica*. This might seem unprofessional, but we need to bear in mind the situation and genre of the work, the fact that Bibikhin did not live to prepare it for printing, and to see that he did, nevertheless, get some key things in contemporary biology right.

Let me turn to the present book in more detail. There is little point in rehashing a work in a foreword, but perhaps a few words about Bibikhin's methodology, implicit assumptions, and conclusions here will be apposite. This volume contains one of his most coherent, extensive, and wide-ranging lecture courses, and includes most of his concepts and philosophical preoccupations. That is why it was singled out for translation.

Bibikhin's book has in fact two subjects, one logically following from the other. The first one, as announced in the title, is the concept of matter, '*materia*', or in Greek, *hyle*. Because the word derives etymologically from wood or timber, Bibikhin enacts a phenomenological reconstruction of the notion by referring it not to an inanimate stuff that we master, but to the element of woods that surround and even entrance us. We are captivated

by the forest, but we have learned to carve a space for form within it. We
return to intoxication with the forest when, for instance, we smoke and
drink. Thus, Aristotelian 'matter' does not exist by default but is an important, substantial element of the world.

> [F]or humans there is no other law; because they are faced with sub-
> stances in which they drown. Matter as the power of the forest, the
> potency of its materiality: the smoke of tobacco, the wine of Bacchus,
> narcotics, intoxication, ecstasy. The wood of the forest is the matter
> from which all else derives; it is not the timber of the carpenter but
> like passion, the race, the grove of Aphrodite, the smoke, the aroma
> of tobacco, the inebriation of Bacchus, of Dionysos, the intoxication
> of coca. The forest, then, is conflagration, the fire of passion. (This
> edition, p. 16)

Thus, matter is primarily living matter, which allows Bibikhin to spend
most of the book discussing the essence and evolution of life, again from
the phenomenological point of view. The phenomenology is backed, first,
by a lengthy hermeneutic reading of Aristotle's *The History of Animals*,
which takes seriously, in a philosophical way, Aristotle's descriptions
of animal life, which have normally been treated as irrelevant mistakes.
Secondly, Bibikhin reads some classical literature in evolutionary biology
(Darwin, Tinbergen, Lorenz, Dawkins, as well as the great Russian evolutionary thinker Lev Berg).

The main questions Bibikhin poses here concern the reasons for the
emergence of sexual reproduction, and, related to it, the reasons for the
dual nature of life, split between the self-reproducing genes and the proteins. Bibikhin brilliantly summarizes the complex biological findings into
a dualistic picture of the world, torn between strict repetition (the form)
and free plasticity (of the matter), in the same way that the matter itself is
relatively segregated into the light and the particles.

Sexual reproduction, says Bibikhin, has an aesthetic explanation. It is a
mechanism of inducing polar contrasts, which is not necessary per se for
the preservation of an organism, but turns life into a complex and interesting gamble. The need for sexual activity, again, entrances animals, puts
them into a state of what Bibikhin calls, with a Greek word, 'amekhania',
loss of mind and of the capacity to move. But the condition is a clear-cut
contrast, and the result, a strict law of repetition. When we then go into
structural matters, we see a cruel, 'harsh' law of form, which governs the
protein being and imposes a discipline, which then repeats itself in the law
of instinct at the behavioural level (examples of birds and ants as captivated by cosmic tasks). There is thus a form found within matter itself
(if we count life as an extended forest), and, moreover, I would suggest,
based on Bibikhin's argument, a certain dialectic of trance and law. Form
imposes itself on matter under the condition of a hypnotic *amekhania*,
through a fascinating game of contrasts.

Again, this argument is not only backed by extended exegetic exercises but also illuminated by strokes of subtle observation and virtuoso interpretations. In addition, it has an ethical aspect pertaining to what Bibikhin calls the 'automaton' of life, its spontaneous energy. No need to meddle with this automaton, let it work while it works; there is a need only to fine-tune it and to respect the iron laws which it at times imposes. However, the automaton, alias Sophia, captivates humans and sets before them a task of extreme and ambitious effort. The book was written at a time of violent primitive accumulation of capital in post-Soviet Russia, and while feeling no great empathy with its protagonists, Bibikhin nevertheless tried to do them justice.

Captivation and capture, captivation by capture, wit and wiliness are the only thing that works. Someone who can captivate and be captivated, capture the world and be captured by the world. [Darwinian] [a]daptation is essentially capturing the world in both these senses, and not necessarily only here on earth but also more widely. (This edition, p. 309)

This book by Bibikhin is perhaps his most overtly theological. Despite being a devout Orthodox Christian, he usually avoids explicitly speaking of God in his philosophy, treating him as something 'unapproachable', but here he makes an exception and actually discusses religion at some length. The forest, with its trance, is a site of natural religion, of a devout attitude to the mystery of life; it is also the site of the Cross, which was made of wood. The law of nature is, the author says, an immediate form in which grace is manifest. Life is sanctified and sanctioned by energy, of which a human ethical effort, a 'yes' to the world, is a part. The Russian word 'saint' (*svyatoy*) has a telling pre-Christian etymology of phallic tumescence.

One could say that Bibikhin's book is a lengthy commentary on Baudelaire's 'Nature is a temple where the pilasters/ Speak sometimes in their mystic languages.'[6] However, when finally considering God, Bibikhin says, after Feuerbach, that he is simply the human him/herself, but taken as the hidden Other in the human being.

By way of short commentary, I think that this book was partly an attempt to repeat and surpass the gesture of Heidegger, who in 1929–30, in *The Fundamental Concepts of Metaphysics*,[7] decided to ground his existential phenomenology in biology, but ended up reasserting a sharp divide between humans and animals which Bibikhin here, in contrast, seeks to undermine. The phenomenological conversion of matter, from a

---

[6] Charles Baudelaire, 'Correspondences', in *Selected Poems*, tr. Joanna Richardson (Harmondsworth: Penguin, 1975), p. 43.

[7] Martin Heidegger, *The Fundamental Concepts of Metaphysics: World, Finitude, Solitude*, tr. William McNeill and Nicholas Walker (Bloomington: Indiana University Press, 2001).

thing to environment, methodologically reminds us of Gaston Bachelard's poetics of the elements.[8] The task of addressing the natural sciences from a philosophical point of view is extremely important, particularly now, with positivism on the rise in the life sciences. There are not that many authors who have done this. However, Bibikhin does not refer to the most famous of them, Henri Bergson. Sometimes his argument comes close to Bergson's *élan vital*, to his serious consideration of the rational nature of instinct. Bergson, however, does not yet know genetics and does not make an aesthetic argument. The lack of engagement with Heidegger or Bergson, like the rudimentary nature of some of the notes, has to do with the fact that Bibikhin died early and, as I mentioned, did not have time to prepare the manuscript for publication.

This volume is the first book-length edition of Bibikhin to appear in English. I think we chose one of his best works for translation. It contributes to our understanding of the meaning of life: a fascinating spectacle set up in a cosmic amphitheatre for the potential audience of humans and gods-in-humans. It sets itself the ethical task of rehabilitating the scale of human ambition as a sanctioning instance of being. It contains an important discussion of genetic Darwinism and natural selection in the spirit of Continental philosophy.

In all this, it may leave a foreign impression on the English-speaking reader, not only because of its impressionistic methodology and ethical pathos (common in both contemporary Russian and French philosophy), but also because of its conservatism and the extent to which it is embedded in twentieth-century Russian thought. I think this is a 'great book', in terms of its ambition, of the richness of its content, of its brilliant style, and of the popularity of its author at the time of its public delivery. Even though written recently, it must be seen both as a contribution to current debates and as a monument of its own time and space, on which it bestows the sanction of memory, and even a certain grandeur.

Artemy Magun
Department of Sociology and Philosophy,
European University at St Petersburg, Russia

---

[8] Gaston Bachelard, *Psychoanalysis of Fire*, tr. Alan C.M. Ross (New York: Beacon Press, 1987); and *Water and Dreams: An Essay on the Imagination of Matter*, tr. Edith R. Farrell (Dallas: Institute of Humanities and Culture, 1999).

Introduction

The ancient Greeks' awareness of wood as a versatile substance which could be consumed by flame to produce different forms of energy ensured that the term ὕλη (*hyle*, wood, timber, forest) should be adopted to designate matter. Facilitating its adoption was the use of the term in ancient medicine, hence in biology. With its non-metric space (notions of the biological cell as a tropical forest), through imaginings of a primaeval, hairy human living in the forest, through the mythopoiesis of the World Tree, through the return of our contemporaries (who have turned their backs on nature) to such surrogates of the forest as wine, tobacco, and narcotics, *hyle* is far more present in the daily reality of modern humans than we care to admit.

The powerful presence of the forest is underappreciated. It is to be found in the philosophical concept of *hyle* (matter) in religion and theology (the Cross as World Tree), and in poetry (in images of the tree, the bush, and the garden). We are surrounded by the forest, and what seems so personal to us, our own thinking, is no less affected by it than are our bodies. The forest is all around.

Modern science's periodically renewed interest in the biological treatises of Aristotle and his school is fully justified. We shall find that in his biology, *hyle* is not viewed as being in contrast to form, *eidos*, whose opposite is 'formlessness'. The female principle of matter is found to contain the entire potential for development. We need to link the so-called spontaneous generation of living things in Aristotle to his interest in parthenogenesis. To *eidos* as the male principle he ascribes the role of the historical, purposeful meaning of motion, its dynamic supported by the material, female, and maternal principle.

The topic of *matter* is one of the most difficult in Aristotle. The difficulties are of two kinds: first, having propounded one thesis, Aristotle does not always feel obliged to be consistent and may later propound a contradictory one; and the second difficulty, for Aristotle himself, is that primary matter should not just be 'such', because then a different kind of matter would be conceivable. There could be two kinds of primary matter, or more, whereas primary matter must be primary. At the same time, Aristotle emphatically refuses to remove matter from the category of things and see it as separate from them. Just as there is no donkeyness, other than purely imaginary, without a particular donkey, so matter is always 'just this'. Current trends in biological research have heightened interest in the practice, common in the classical world, of placing humans on a scale of living beings, in respect of morphology, physiology, and ethics.

The cosmic unity of life, or, more broadly, its unifying sensitivity (Tsiolkovsky, Vernadsky), complicates discrimination between inanimate and living matter.[1] (Neo-)Darwinism as a principle of systematic replacement of life forms needs to be reconsidered in the light of adverse selection and non-stochastic development (nomogenesis). Overall, the views of Lev Berg, compared with those of Darwinism, lose out by failing to take into account the importance of a gathering, concentrating, focusing, extreme element which is critical for life.[2] Berg leaves this role to natural selection, but only as a means of maintaining the *norm*. He discerns a significant role for deviations from the norm. Berg does not argue that the status quo of a constant natural dispersion of variants and deviations is preserved within a species, but that, although in every generation there is invariably a large dispersion, there is, through the action of Darwinian selection, a thinning out, a testing for vitality. Marginal forms are eliminated and the species reverts towards the norm. Berg quotes Karl Pearson's research into generations of poppies to the effect that every race is much more a product of its *normal members* than might be expected on the basis of the relative numbers of its individual representatives.[3] The same applies in human society: the dispersion of deviants, degenerates, and alcoholics is great in every generation, but in each subsequent generation, children, on the whole, again begin within the norm. If the number of children in poor health increases, then it is to a lesser extent than among adults. Typically, children are more normal than their parents. The opposite is less common. Attention needs to be paid to Berg's thesis. By itself, natural selection does not change the norm; for that to happen, other factors are needed. There is a great need to clarify the concepts of improvement, adaptation, fitness, and survival. When Darwinism, or selectionism, talks of survival of the fittest, if by 'the fittest' is meant only those most able to survive, we are looking at a pleonasm. This awkward fact has been noticed, but it is one of those instances where a striking expression takes on a life of its own.

In reality, 'survivors' and 'the fittest' are not synonyms and are even, in some respects, opposites. It would not be wholly absurd to say that the miracle of life is that the fittest do actually survive. Darwinism does more than present a picture of stray individuals, some of whom happen to be selected. We need to recognize that this array, this spread and these degrees of possibility are *objective*. It is *not* the fittest that exist and there is, moreover, no need to wait for the extinction of individuals or a species before concluding who does. Already in their behaviour, in their every movement and the profile of every living creature, the divergence between the fittest and the rest is obvious.

Researchers often naïvely judge success in terms of what they would see as success for themselves: that is, having a full stomach, being in good health and fertile. Clearly, however, other criteria are possible. Life is contingent on possibility and selection, where the criteria are uncertain. There are at least two of these, survival and fitness, and the correlation between them is uncertain. Only a total absence of fitness precludes survival, but the opposite does not follow: total retention by a savage beast of its savagery in the presence some hundreds of thousands of years ago of human beings led to extinction. When, after the radiation death of this planet, only the rats remain, their survival will not in any customary sense prove they were the fittest. Although logical analysis of premises is a rarity and everything is allowed to remain on the level of intuition, academic biologists might be surprised to know how often in assessing fitness they are applying a criterion that Konstantin Leontiev used for arguing against positivism. This was the criterion of 'flourishing complexity', which, while not excluding protracted observation, does not require it, relying less on observation than on sympathy and empathy.[4] We can also note, dotted around in the economy of nature, pre-existing niches of fitness, hospitable locations to which life forms are attracted and into which they are drawn. That 'strokes of luck' are a possibility in our world deserves to be considered alongside the observation by physicists that our part of the universe is itself a stroke of luck because of the clear segregation here of energy and matter. In respect of the attraction of life forms to fitness, it should be noted that in the behaviour of herds, including the human herd, we do not find a stochastic distribution of more and less successful forms of behaviour from 0% to 100%. Technically, according to mathematical probability theory, this could be the case, but life seems from the outset to be predisposed to hitting the target. In view of all this, it is proposed that Darwin's term 'fitness', in the sense of successful adaptation, should be replaced with the term 'goodness', in Russian *godnost'*, 'to be good for something'. In the Indo-European languages, this word is in good company. The word for 'weather' in Russian is *pogoda*; in Slovenian, a related word means 'timeliness', 'ripeness', 'festivity', 'anniversary'; in Latvian, it means 'to hit the target', 'to gain'; in Lithuanian, 'honour', 'glory'; in German, there is *gut* and in English 'good'; in Greek, αγαθόν, *agathón*, 'good'.

For a life form to be good for something does not necessarily mean only that it is successfully adapted to a purpose: it may indicate that it is a celebration, a glory. There is a great deal of controversy surrounding selectionism and Darwinism's concept of natural selection, which we can sidestep by defining fitness as 'goodness'. We have no grounds to oppose the idea that the spread of possible forms of life, including forms of behaviour, is enormous, or that which of these are 'good' becomes evident *post factum*. We must not, however, overlook the fact that even *ante factum* a 'taste' for goodness, either immediate or after trial and error, determines or tends to determine the behaviour of living creatures (as evidence from ethology tells us). It resembles such things as joy and celebration, and dictates not the content of behaviour but purely the form, in terms of gesture, brilliance, and beauty. This is born of anticipation that a pleasing action is possible in our world. We do not have to reject Darwinism and its random mutations and imagine that God has stored up a set of forms for future content into which life preforms itself. There are no ready-made anticipated forms, but something that argues in favour of an attracting, anticipatory effect of goodness is the absence of intermediate species in the gaps between those that have been successful. Darwin supposed they had just not yet been found. 'The explanation lies, as I believe, in the extreme imperfection of the geological record.'[5] Now it is almost conclusively clear that these intermediate forms have never existed. Nature can be compared to an artist whose works always find a place in the exhibition. 'Nowhere do we find monstrous forms such as would indubitably have occurred in the event that limitless variability was the rule' (Berg).[6] This makes it all the more pressing to find an explanation for the succession, and abandonment, of hundreds of millions of its forms in the course of life's history on earth.

The polarities of life are reflected in science in the contrast between the processes of feeding and reproduction; of proteins and nucleic acids; of symbiosis, inquilinism, parasitism, and xenobiosis; in the hypothesis of two lives; and in the 'tyranny of genes'. It appears helpful to view the cell as an anthill, a colony of lower physiological units, in the light of the fact that absolutely all organisms are in fact colonies and communities, and that life is fundamentally 'sociogenic'. All life is drawn towards other life and either assimilates or collaborates with it (symbiosis, inquilinism, parasitism, xenobiosis). The guiding principle is not so much the struggle for survival as an organism's ability to find its place, to compromise, to serve the interests of unity and of other organisms in a kind of 'egoistic altruism'.

Myrmecology, the study of ants, provides an opportunity to observe collective organisms. It opens up perspectives for understanding, on the one hand, the interaction of cells in an organism and, on the other, that of communities of living beings, including human beings. It also shows how expedient many processes in fact are which, if not closely examined, might lead to superficial conclusions. In ant colonies, we can observe age groups, a calendar, castes and caste-based laws, purposeful organization, training in personal hygiene, social education of the young, collaboration, mutual care, division of labour, general education, ethics, etiquette, taboo foods, donation, greeting, rituals of personal care, hygiene, incest taboos, language, care of larvae, medicine, metamorphosis rituals, honeymoon trips, deference to a leader, warrior castes, surgery, tool making, commerce, visiting, and meteorology.

This study reveals the importance of distinguishing between the true, living automaton and the mechanical automaton or robot; between genetic programming as against planning; of focusing on the distinctive features of the true automaton and how it copes with a situation of crisis, extreme stress, uncertainty, and *amekhania* (*aporia*). We find a degree of complexity that is not adequately observed using modern techniques of close study, and a great subtlety in phenomena ranging from the 'unity of the geno-type' to the compaction of the genetic programme of a large organism into a vanishingly small cell.

Ethology, the study of animal behaviour, especially in extravagant breed-ing behaviour, offers the prospect of a convergence of the humanities and biology. Rehabilitating the classical world's location of human beings in the animal realm enables us to review in a new, down-to-earth manner the history and purposes of the development of life on earth.

Analysis of geological, biological, and philosophical knowledge relevant to the history and current situation of life on the planet gives a clearer understanding of the prospects for human theory and practice to con-tribute positively to the process of life. These prospects are seen less in the area of global planning than in recognition by individuals and the human species at large of their potential role in moving life on earth in an auspi-cious direction.

Lecture 1, 2 September 1997

This autumn's semester is a direct continuation of the spring semester course on Principles of Christianity. There we sought to show what is intimate and personal to us in faith. There is always the wretched possibility that faith will be left a notional concept of merely historical interest, a construct in the science of theology, whereas what we are interested in is a fundamental hermeneutics or phenomenology, in the sense of Husserl and Heidegger, or a grammar in the sense of Wittgenstein.[1] In order to avoid any risk of straying into mental constructs and lexical exercises, of failing to notice what we are drowning in and merely enumerating concepts, we are going to take a large step backwards to first principles, until, like the defenders of Moscow, we can retreat no further.

Those words, 'behind us lies Moscow', whether or not uttered in 1941, were no less applicable in 1812.[2] Then Moscow was captured, but it caught fire or was deliberately set ablaze. Moscow was built mainly of wood, the most readily available material, intimately familiar, particularly in those years when the forests of Russia were all but untouched. For a Russian, for a Muscovite, the burning of that wood, that '*hyle*', was something personal. Leo Tolstoy tells us that a wooden township that has been abandoned cannot but catch fire; that is just something it will do. What is our attitude towards *hyle*? It continues to be very personal. Today we have a standing column of smoke over Moscow from the daily combustion of 10,000 tonnes of petroleum products. In this city alone, 30 million tonnes of fuel will be burned in a decade.

The origin of our main modern fuel is organic, mostly prehistoric 'floating forests', planktonic, free-floating algae, of which there were vast quantities in the water basins from 500 million years to about 30 million years ago. We heat ourselves and our homes and light our world with a bonfire of petroleum and coal; its combustion beneath pistons in cylinders moves mechanisms that catch fish for us, plough our fields, reap the harvest, and deliver the grain to our bakeries.

Just as humankind sat around a campfire in the forest in ancient times, so today it warms itself at a campfire diligently replenished (because who can bear to stand back and watch a fire go out?) with some 5 million tonnes of coal and oil, which will add up to around 15 billion tonnes in a decade. We are starkly reminded that this is necessary by the fact that thousands of people die every day from not being close enough to the fire. Humanity, the greater part of which has managed to find a place more or less near the fire, does sometimes reluctantly glance across to those hapless others, and is acutely aware of those who have failed to find a place there. It sensibly, prudently, takes special care to keep the fire fuelled.

People say humanity will find other sources of energy, but the fact remains that by far the greater part of our needs is supplied today, as in the distant past, by burning the forest: no longer the forest around us, because that was all burned long ago, but faraway forests. Faraway not in terms of space, because those forests, too, have been felled, but from far back in time, from the millions of years before humanity appeared and after it appeared. At that time the forest was still close to human beings, not only in the sense that they lived in it, but also in the fact that they were themselves covered with abundant growth, a forest of hair. The forest encroached so intimately upon them that it comprised their very skin, their very bodies. There was far less need then to burn the forest because human beings were kept warm by this fur which covered and was part of their body. Was this the only way they were related to the forest?

A close relationship with the forest seems to continue among the so-called primitive tribes who live there now and whose abhorrence of tree felling is so deeply ingrained that, even when their communal ways are taken from them, for example when they are brought into civilized society, they never become loggers, will not work with chainsaws, on trailing tractors and the like. Violation of the forest is tantamount, as far as they are concerned, to violation of their own body, although no surviving furry human beings are known to science today. The hairy yeti still stalks our minds and inhabits folklore, close to modern humans. The yeti has no place near the fire either, but his is a different kind of distance from that of the unfortunates who would be glad of a place.

Just as modern humans are almost devoid of hair, so the earth today is losing its forests. More important, though, than the visible forests for fuelling the fire humans cluster round are those invisible forests from half a billion years ago now so tangibly present in the form of coveted coal and oil. Is there not, however, another way in which the forest is even more germane to how we exist today? There is indeed, and when we recognize that, several doors immediately open. For now, we shall only peep through them while deciding which one to enter. We are in a hall of mirrors.

Let us consider a burning wood fire. In his latest, as yet unpublished, work, Andrey Lebedev examines the etymology of *hyle*, the word for 'wood', 'forest', in ancient Greek and concludes that fire and conflagration are inherent in it; the etymology suggests flammability and burning.[3] Since the point is still under debate, let us leave it for now and pursue a different avenue of inquiry.

Besides today's forests, which are all but exhausted, and the ancient forests, which are half-exhausted, one of the most significant sources of energy must surely be nuclear energy. Atomic energy can also be seen as a product of combustion, but of what? Even highly specialized knowledge will take us only so far here because of issues science has yet to resolve. We can, and commonly do, represent an atomic reaction as a kind of burning, an explosion, a fast-developing fire or a process of slow decay. But a burning of what? In autogenous welding, the elements of hydrogen and oxygen combust, combine, become a molecule of a different compound, water, cease to exist autonomously but remain unchanged as water. A thermonuclear reaction, too, involves elements – uranium, plutonium, hydrogen – but something transformative is done to the elements themselves. We are talking about changes not to elements but to matter itself: the transformation of matter into energy. That is, what is 'burning' is not wood, petroleum, or coal, not compounds of elements. In a thermonuclear reaction, what is burning is matter itself.

How curious that the original meaning of the word for 'matter' in ancient Greek philosophy is wood, forest. The word '*materia*' is Latin and its original meaning is primal matter. In Cicero, it is the matter of the world, of which everything consists and in which everything exists: *materia rerum ex qua et in qua sunt omnia*. This Latin philosophical term is a translation of that Greek philosophical term, ὕλη, *hyle*, whose primary meaning is 'wood'. It is entirely possible that the official, technical meaning of *materia* in Latin, then meaning 'matter' as it now does in Russian and English, only became primary within official culture, while in popular culture the main meaning continued to be combustible material and, more specifically, wood in the sense of fuel, firewood. That is, before it was squeezed out there, too, by the philosophical usage. In Latin, felling timber is *materiam caedere*. In one of the Romance languages, this expression became *madeira*, whose primary meaning is simply *forests*.

In atomic energy, then, in a thermonuclear reaction, if we want to avoid a lot of specialist terminology, we can say more or less accurately that what is being burned is actually *wood*.

Unexpectedly, our own philosophical language is telling us that what is burned in the promising new thermonuclear energy reactions is the matter of the world: 'wood'. In the light of this discovery, we shall exercise caution before deciding that *hyle*, meaning 'an area of land covered with trees' or 'timber', should take precedence over the classical philosophical meaning of 'matter'. Language in general does not arise from adding sememes together; its origins are as deep as dreaming. In the word 'wood' it refers to trees, to fuel, and to the matter of the world. Let us not, therefore, be in too much of a hurry to decide which meanings are original and which are derivative. May not the use of *materia* in philosophy as well be, not a departure from the original meaning of 'wood', but a return to it? For now it seems that, as soon as we get into the forest, we lose our way.

Let us approach the forest from a different angle. This other aspect has long been present and all we need to do is look at it attentively. There is nothing new about comparing the world to a living being. No European figure has articulated such comparisons more comprehensively and clearly than Leonardo da Vinci, whom we will need to study closely. In this simile, the forests of the earth would correspond to the hair or fur on the body of a living creature. Here is one context:

> ... *potrem dire, la terra avere anima vegetativa e che la sua carne sia la terra; li sua ossi sieno li ordini delle collegazioni di sassi, di che si compongono le montagni ... il suo sangui sono le vene dilli acque; il lago del sangui, che sta di torno al core, è il mare oceano: il suo alitare è il crescere e decrescere del sangue ... e il caldo dell' anima del mondo è il foco, ch'è infuso per la terra ...*

So then we may say that the earth has a spirit of growth, and that its flesh is the soil; its bones are the successive strata of the rocks which form the mountains; its cartilage is the tufa stone; its blood the veins of its waters. The lake of the blood that lies around the heart is the ocean. Its breathing is by the increase and decrease of the blood in its pulses ... and the vital heat of the world is fire which is spread throughout the earth ...[4]

The human body nowadays is not completely covered with hair. I cautiously say 'nowadays' in order not to be drawn into the debate over whether early human beings were or were not covered with hair. For the theory of evolution, the issue is not crucial because there are other hairless animals – elephants, for example. What is phenomenologically important for us is to note that in our minds, our myths, and our fiction, the bigfoot, the furry anthropoid, the child born covered with hair, *caesariatus*, recur regularly and are evidently dear to us. We are intrigued by the idea that human beings can be hairy. It makes them either frightening, like the *Leshiy*, the Russian wood demon, or auspicious, as suggested by *caesariatus* in Latin, covered with hair, having long hair.

What is not speculation but fact is that the parts of the body covered with hair are prominent, most notably the head, hence the mind. If the most distinctive feature of humans is intelligence, then the locks on their head are an indication of that. They are like a microcosm. The beard clearly has a demarcation function: men have beards and women do not, so, in a manner still under debate, that is an indication of gender. Science tells us that chest hair betokens the presence of androgens, while underarm hair suggests a vestigial role for odour in the life of the species.

In folklore, mythology, and poetry, hair in that part of the human body directly serving procreation may be called a grove, a forest, or a meadow in the forest. In a recent article, Andrey Lebedev analyses a passage about the Naassenes in that great work by Hippolytus (born before 170 AD, died 235), *Refutation of All Heresies*.[5] 'Naassenes' is the Hebrew name for the Ophites, of whom there were several varieties in the second century. The belief they held in common was that Jehovah had created only the material world, transient and illusory, and that man would have been left mired in it and blundering about for eternity but for the revelation of the serpent, ὄφις, of which in the first book of the Pentateuch of Moses it is said that it first opened man's eyes to the abyss of the spiritual, by enabling him to discriminate between good and evil.[6] The serpent, however, did not show the way, and it was for this that Christ came, the Light of the material world. Refuting the Ophites, Hippolytus paraphrases their teachings about mystical descents to earth which, incidentally, follow the paths of Aphrodite and Persephone.

It seems to me intuitively – and that is all one can say until Lebedev's new etymologies of the forest are published – that wood-as-fire points us in a direction we need to think about. In his second article, while agreeing with attribution of the fragment about the sacred grove of Aphrodite to Empedocles, I would have argued with Lebedev's approach. In my opinion, it is a dead end when it separates the physiological, embryological, and anthropogenic realities in the thought of Empedocles from the philosophical and poetic metaphor: Lebedev thinks that scientific positivity requires remaining down to earth, and believes that, in talking about the meadows and groves of Aphrodite, Empedocles 'is describing metaphorically the female genitals'.

The tenacious, supposedly objective scholarly distinction between physical realia and poetry is neither self-evident nor factual. It proceeds from a questionable academic mythology that tries to distinguish what is a legitimate object of scholarly study from what is not. For example, the poetic. The delusion that anything properly scholarly and technical must be readily open to study betrays a blindness scholars allow themselves. We are not going to indulge in this blindness. [...][7] The supposed encompassing of the world by science and technology encompasses nothing. Their victory is a myth, and the scholarly euphoria over the triumphs of technology is no better than the delight of one of Leo Tolstoy's characters, a three-year-old girl who sets fire to hay in her log hut and invites her little brother to admire the splendid stove she has managed to light.[8] All will be restored to what is dismissed as 'poetic', to the 'gentle power of thought and poetry'.[9]

The meadow, the sacred grove, the forest in folklore and mythology, in poetry and philosophy, are in no way a mere metaphor for coyly referring to vulgar realia. We *first* understand the forest in industrial and aesthetic terms, and are then unable to find a better way of understanding the grove of Aphrodite than as a metaphor, a discreet euphemism, perhaps veiling with a fine phrase a nakedness we find embarrassing. Art has the ability to show nakedness in a way that makes it neither metaphorical nor physiological. Can words be similarly used to name the intimate? Indeed they can, and are, using metaphors like grove and meadow, ἄλσος and λειμῶν, between which Lebedev and other writers he refers to see 'a close association . . . in sacral contexts'. For Empedocles, a grove is not a metaphor for Aphrodite because, as Lebedev himself points out, he sees that the earth itself is a uterus, the womb of humankind. Lebedev mentions Empedocles' enthusiastic cult of Aphrodite. The grove or meadow of Aphrodite is not some 'biological referential signifier' for us, and neither is *alsos* a 'metaphor for the reproductive organs in general conceived as a "holy precinct" with a walled temple-uterus inside', but rather quite the opposite. The biological referent, if present at all, is referring to the forest as something primal, as matter, as something maternal. Lebedev speaks of the sacred Temple of Nature in pre-Platonic thought, when its sacramental mystery is the formation of the embryo, the focal secret of life and of nature. It is a secret hidden from the profane gaze of ordinary men, but not from the probing insight of the philosopher proceeding along the path of mystical initiation. I would like to read in its entirety the remarkable conclusion of this article, which, as is often the case with Lebedev, opens up much broader perspectives than the primitive positivism about which I have been complaining.

> For our present purpose, it is important to notice that typologically *alsos Aphrodites* represents a variation on the theme of *Templum Naturae*, a recurrent topos in pre-Platonic thought. Here it probably connotes ἄβατον ἱερόν: the formation of the foetus conceived as a mystery of life is hidden from the sight of the *polloi*, but not from the intellectual eye of a philosophical *epoptes*. Thus the mystery initiation motif, *prima facie* eliminated from the fragment together with the Gnostic interpretation, is eventually restored as authentic, though in essentially different form: it has nothing to do with the mysteries of Persephone and Diesseits-Hades of the Naassenes, but relates to the philosophical rite of passage. The metaphorical complex of secret knowledge is well attested in *Peri physeos*. As a philosophical mystagogue, Empedocles leads Pausanias to the innermost sanctum of nature: the embryological treatise to follow upon the prefatory verses on the anatomy of the female genitals and reproductive organs will reveal to Pausanias the secrets of birth no mortal eye has ever seen. And the same metaphor conveys the fundamental idea of the holiness of life inherent in Empedocles' philosophy of cosmic Love.[10]

So it will be difficult for us, too, as we enter into our new topic of the forest not to follow the mass of the *polloi*; we shall proceed with caution.

Perhaps the first objection we anticipate, and to which it is important and helpful to respond, is that scientific positivism, whether secondary or not, is what we are familiar with. However, to see the grove and the forest as something sacred and mysterious, we need a trained, discriminating eye. Seeing the forest other than from a commercial or aesthetic viewpoint would not seem to call for preliminary training. People talk about getting lost in the forest. We have the saying that someone 'could get lost among three pine trees'; or, when baffled, we talk of being 'in a dark forest'. May the explanation of this – that you cannot see far in a forest, that there are no familiar landmarks – be only a rationalization of an experience that in various guises many people have probably had, namely that being in a forest takes us out of metric space? The presence of trees, being among them, instils, or induces, or lulls us into a sense of – the range of vocabulary itself points to the singularity of the experience – something that does not lend itself to description. What the forest says to us – and the expression 'trees can talk' is yet another attempt to characterize the experience – causes a person to become confused and disorientated in more than a narrowly geographical sense.

Looking ahead, I will mention another way of talking about this osmotic quality of the forest: it is said to act like a drug, sometimes more, sometimes less powerful, depending on the experience. This power of the forest can be intimidating, and I will mention here a literary example to which we shall return: nausea, or perhaps more the sense of disorientation at sea, which the narrator of Sartre's *La Nausée* experiences in the vicinity of a tree or of tree bark.[11] Another example is the experience described by Vasiliy Belov, where a great pine tree evokes a sense of reverence in the person felling it.[12] We need not enumerate other instances because everybody has felt them at one time or another. There is nothing contrived or artificial about these; on the contrary, they are unexpected and amazing, but feel out of the ordinary only because our habitual ways of looking at the forest are utilitarian or aesthetic. How we came to develop that habit we need not go into, because much more interesting is how insecure it is, how ready to be displaced and to yield to the amazing experiencing of the forest.

A constant feature of the experience of the forest is how intimate it feels, even while it seems intimidating, as in Sartre or as in the figure of the wood demon. The fear that grips us in the forest is not of a kind that we can take practical measures against; it is too much a part of us. We find the demon seems to be within us and that what we fear in him is ourselves, different, altered. When the spirit of the forest is something we desire and are seeking, it feels near and dear to us.

The experience we have of our relatedness to the forest might seem to be pointing us towards the secrets of the sacred grove, through which initiation into the mysteries begins, and there is no call for us to rush to decide which interpretation, the philosophical or the gnostic, is better. Of one thing we can be sure, and that is that every interpretation will be lame, will flounder, which is precisely why *a plurality* of interpretations is needed. That is why I am so lacking in confidence when I say that the signs might seem to be pointing in a particular direction, and why I believe it is better to indulge that uncertainty. One thing that is clear is that Empedocles, and the ancients generally, were far more at home with and had a much better understanding of the forest than we do, and that their thinking may well include insights we will be hard pressed to keep up with. May these reflections on our experiencing of the forest serve for the time being only to let us see how *un*artificial this unfamiliar way of seeing, or intuiting, the forest is.

The second doubt hanging over our choice of topic, which some have already voiced, is why particularly wood, the forest, should be singled out. Why not also the meadow, the more so when there are studies on the links between the forest and the meadow? Or why not take as our topic water, earth, sky, the sea? Experiencing the sky or water is no less of an issue for us. We are captivated by the starry sky. Come to that, just about everything captivates us no less than the forest. The first answer is that the earth which Xenophanes saw as infinite, the water which Thales saw as the first principle, could have established themselves in philosophical thought as primal matter, *materia*, but did not.[13] The fact is that it was wood, *hyle*, the forest, that was adopted, and it is another question whether that came about before or after Aristotle. Perhaps it was an accident and came about simply because Aristotle, while lecturing, was looking for an example of what material *eidos*, form, is made of and took the nearest object to hand, which happened to be a wooden table. He had a concept for which he needed a name. The name reaches out towards the concept and acquires content. Content is the giving of form to the formless or, in this case, since wood is not formless, to something whose form is of no importance and can be used to provide a foundation for form that is of importance. Form puts its *imprint* on what it will, on a basis of matter: you can saw a piece of wood and form from it anything you like. This is a traditional and ostensibly philosophical commonplace, but we are about to say goodbye to it forever, because the much-vaunted *indefiniteness* of matter is going to prove to be its fundamental *indefinability*.

It is intriguing that the choice of wood to designate primal matter is at least partly due to a connectedness with the forest that we do not have with water, sky, or earth: that we seem, not so long ago in geological terms, to have been covered in vegetation but are so no longer. Something akin to deforestation has happened to us, and it is the destruction of the forests that is presently so alarming us on our planet.

Quite apart from whether the human species really is Desmond Morris's 'naked ape',[14] whether it ever was hairy and, if so, when it stopped being hairy, what is phenomenologically of value to us is that the experience of being hairy is simultaneously inaccessible to us and very close. We can readily imagine what it would be like to be hairy, although, if we imagine ourselves hairy, it is *ourselves* we are seeing as hairy, our real selves except, perhaps, for our consciousness.[15] The original hairy human's consciousness must surely have been different, *primal*, although the primitive mind was not necessarily crude and underdeveloped, something to be despised. On the contrary, we are curious and feel it is relevant to us. We can see that in the anthropology of Lévi-Strauss, in William Faulkner's *The Sound and the Fury*, and in all our scientific and artistic reconstructions.[16]

There is no need for us, in the interests of the integrity and reliability of our work, to start vexing ourselves over whether humans were ever hairy, or speculating about the nature of primitive consciousness. What is of significance for us, though, is the presence in the human experience of primitive tribes, their presence in the thinking of people like Jean-Jacques Rousseau, in the arts, in writing (for example, in C.S. Lewis, who imagined a sweet-natured, hairy primal human being, a wise superman – the snow man in the American film *Bigfoot* evidently draws on Lewis), an *alternative* human being whom we find familiar and acceptable, who is more a creature of the forest than we are, partly because of his hairiness, partly because of his categorical refusal to fell trees, and partly because he lives in the forest.

Today's urbanized and technologically minded people keep the forest at a distance, enjoying its wonders in measured doses that pose no risk to health: enjoying the countryside, going for a stroll in the park. The forest, however, precisely because it is pushed back, eats its way into humanity ever more vengefully and irrevocably. It is as if humankind has failed to make its peace with the forest and now it is payback time. I do not think it unreasonable to see tobacco, wine, and drugs as the forest's revenge, tightening with its juices, poisons, and smoke the grip it has on humanity. The modern city has no escape from the forest, which reaches out after it through the power of its alcohol, tobacco, and cocaine. With these so much in evidence, we can see that the ancient religions and civilizations have lost none of their power. In using cocaine, individuals tear down the fence artificially separating them and surrender to their authentic element, the forest, to shamanism and fire. Of course, they are thereby desperately flinging themselves headlong into the fire, but that results from something that has built up over a long period during which they artificially separated themselves from the forest, from its *matter*.

I emphasize that we need to refrain, in the interests of good order, from any attempt to resuscitate the benign hairy human. Our focus is only on what there is today and constitutes our phenomenology. Whether we fear the hairy hominid or feel drawn to it, we are *different*. We are confronting a *different consciousness*, which it is impossible to imagine, reconstruct, or compute, but with which, in some strange way, it is entirely possible to conduct mental experiments.

What was the *faith* of this individual? 'Primitive.' The same as Michel Foucault describes in a child, a lunatic, or a poet.[17] There can be no end to replies of that kind, where we say much more than we have any business saying, more than is sensible or necessary. In attempting to answer the question, we will do better to behave like good phenomenologists and make notes and take readings of what we can see here and now.

And where does that leave us? Let us suppose someone believes in God. They go to church and profess their faith, but they can see within themselves a *different* faith. I invite you to look, and to see that all of us live believing in two faiths. In just the same way that, without being able to step outside the consciousness in which we live, we can easily feel our closeness to that other one, the forest dweller, with his primaeval consciousness which is no different from ours in content. The Fathers of the Church see the Church as beginning with Abel. The Roman Catholic theologian Bernhard Welte always associated the Abel of the Bible with the people who inhabited caves of volcanic origin on the Mount of Olives near Cologne 10,000 years ago. Is there anything we can know about their worship of God? Welte felt himself in a eucharistic communion with those cave dwellers. How is that possible if theirs was a different faith? Or can we indeed talk about a faith we share with cave dwellers from 10,000 years ago?[18]

St Paul invites us to recognize Abel's sacrifice as coming from unshakeable faith (Hebrews, 11: 4). St John Chrysostom, interpreting chapter 4 of the Book of Genesis, speaks of the right disposition of Abel's heart, compared with that of Cain. Cain's countenance fell because God did not respect his gift. 'And the Lord said unto Cain, "Why art thou wroth? and why is thy countenance fallen? If thou doest well, shalt thou not be accepted? and if thou doest not well, sin lieth at the door."' This is already a matter not solely to do with the offering of sacrifices; it concerns any act a person may perform. This can be a good deed, the person 'raises their countenance' and God looks upon them in response; or the promptings of their heart can go awry, the person's countenance becomes dark, confused, their eyes look downwards, and they become a prey to loneliness and are accursed. It is up to individuals to desire an open countenance for themselves and to be afraid of a fallen countenance, or to suppress that fear, as Cain suppressed the fear of his own disgruntlement and envy, and cast aside his concern about what the commentators call his 'inner disposition'.

We can imagine a person, a child, the hairy human, without this concern to retain their portion, to stay with God, not to be bereft, not to fall from his favour; or, if they already have, not to be a prey to anxiety about that fall, to be without irritation or envy, in a state halfway between, on the one hand, the raised face and open expression, and, on the other, that other state of degeneracy. We can imagine them vacillating between Cain, who was spurned, and Abel, who cheerfully raises his countenance and meets the gaze of God.

I want now to introduce a word I have avoided so far: the *law* of human beings or of human nature. It is a law without limitation, fundamental, and in fact the only law, because in everything else people are unbounded and free. For every person, no matter how they frame their faith, in any situation and condition and age, this is concern about their portion, concern in the sense of Heidegger's *Sorge*, their concern in terms of being endowed not dispossessed, of living in prosperity rather than wretchedness, and if in poverty, then in that ascetic poverty that is better than any prosperity.[19]

We are completely unable to read or articulate this law of concern, of εὐλάβεια, of right thought and piety, of God-fearing. It is probably operating before we have found any definition of it. Before we have any awareness of it, it is leading us, suggesting how we should act. Everything we do, we do in obedience to it. Can we privately choose not to conform to it? No, it only seems that it can be resisted. It can neither be rescinded nor made more lenient, although the approach of Cain is open to us, to declare, 'Then so be it: the worse, the better.' Our freedom here extends no further than to be or not to be in a place where we already are. It is only by recognizing this level of the universal law of human nature that religion can be understood.

Religion will always be found, within its culture, language, and way of life, to be a restoration of that unwritten law, of instinct. Religion is in its essence that same law. Religious discourse is consequently a matter of only secondary importance.

The instinct of piety, the need, second by second, to choose Abel, and the ever-present threat of Cain, is an innate law, and the word 'law' needs to have this meaning restored to it. Discriminating between secular and religious law, between civil law and canon law, is essential if the initial law is to remain unsullied. These two parallel systems of law, the secular and the divine, are complementary ways of capturing something it is impossibly difficult to formulate. Sharia and, in Orthodox Christianity, Palamism seek to be the unmediated expression of a single law and hence put the original law at greater risk.[20]

Having recourse to another of our mental experiments, one has no sense that in any ancient forest and/or hairy incarnation humans could ever have been formed without being creatures of the law of which I am speaking. It preserves the human species. That law is something that restrains us every moment.

Religion: the etymology of the word speaks, I believe, of mindfulness, concern, and piety, and it was formerly known as the Rule. Let us now rehabilitate this old word, whose primary meaning until quite recently, some 300 years ago, was 'faith, the profession of faith'.

Why do we so formally and superficially call the law of humankind 'εὐλάβεια', a cautious, attentive acumen? Because humans are open, their nature is freedom, and because what people are primarily dealing with, both in themselves and in the world, is indefinable: it is *the forest*. The forest, an abyss, the forest unexplored and indefinable, the forest that we find again in *tobacco* (you may recall the ritual tobacco, much stronger than ours, of the American Indians).

The law we have been talking about will need to be compared with Kant's categorical imperative. I repeat, because for humans there is no other law; because they are faced with substances in which they drown. Matter as the power of the forest, the potency of its materiality: the smoke of tobacco, the wine of Bacchus, narcotics, intoxication, ecstasy. The wood of the forest is the matter from which all else derives; it is not the timber of the carpenter but like passion, the race, the grove of Aphrodite, the smoke, the aroma of tobacco, the inebriation of Bacchus, of Dionysos, the intoxication of coca. The forest, then, is conflagration, the fire of passion. When Aristotle gave primal matter the name of 'wood', this was the forest he saw before him, the forest as we shall yet see it.

Lecture 2, 9 September 1997

We touched last time on the topic of the law and, without naming it, unceasing prayer. This is the central theme of *The Candid Tales of a Pilgrim to His Spiritual Father*, or *The Way of a Pilgrim.*[1] Among the collection of literature on asceticism of Hieroschemamonk Feodosiy of Karulia and of his disciple and novice Nikodim was a book titled simply *The Pilgrim*. Feodosiy was an elder living on the almost sheer cliffs in the south of Mount Athos and died on 2 October 1937. By the early 1980s, Nikodim was himself an extremely aged elder.

It is important for us to understand that prayer must be unceasing and synchronized with breathing and the beating of the heart. Unceasing prayer is considered to be not an act of human beings but a condition of grace. Nobody could stop the bleeding of the woman who had an issue of blood. The wandering of our thoughts, their flow and dissipation cannot be stopped by thought alone. They wander, and in the course of their wandering the desire arises to staunch the flow, but this desire itself is part of their straying. The woman's bleeding was stopped by the grace of God. What part must be played by the individual? It is essential that we should have faith: we must believe that the straying of our thoughts can be stopped. Today we shall need also to talk about what faith is. Faith means that a person must sincerely do their utmost to pray continually if its grace is to descend. There is a paradox here: I am doing my utmost to attain something I know is beyond my strength, but if I give up and tell myself it is all right to rest, the gift will not be given.

Again, there can be no question of progressing through the stages of spiritual life by experience. On the contrary, if it was a matter of experiencing ascetic practice, the so-called artistic praying of adepts, the τέχνη τεχνῶν, to use a very old expression of asceticism, that would make it impossible to talk about it. There would have to be some quite different way of passing it on. We are going to stay on the level of phenomenology and, in Wittgenstein's sense, of *grammar*. The task we are setting ourselves is not to learn how to do and practise something clever; our focus is on understanding how constant, unceasing prayer is profoundly relevant to all of us here and now, and how it is present in what we are saying. In other words, we are focusing our attention on something that is already here, right now. We are focusing strictly and solely on that. The extent to which that should be our mission is also part of today's topic because we cannot focus our attention on everything.

What we imagine we need to do is not necessarily what we genuinely must do. An error frequently encountered in theological writing is describing something as a matter for the *believer*: in other words, not for everybody because not everybody goes to church. To some extent, perhaps to a large extent, and we will need to decide for ourselves how large, these matters may be of importance for everybody.

By failing to distinguish between what is common to everybody and what is of relevance only to those within the faith community, theologians do immense damage. They professionalize what is common to all humanity, 'relieving' ordinary people of work that needs to be done, 'relieving' them of the Cross that is theirs by right, as if spiritual matters were the concern only of us, the church-goers and, more particularly, of the people who write books about theology. You can, however, oppress someone not only by imposing an unsupportable burden on them, but also by depriving them of a task, and the theologians who declare that sort of lockout are trying to deprive the large numbers of people who do not go to church of the employment that is of the greatest importance for a human being. That is one kind of harm. The other is the opposite: 'For they bind heavy burdens and grievous to be borne, and lay them on men's shoulders' (Matthew, 23: 4). The harm comes not from placing burdens on people's shoulders, since, as we read in Matthew, 11: 29, Christ himself is a yoke and a burden, but from the fact that the Pharisees tie the burden to be borne in the wrong way, perhaps even deliberately, with the intention of making it uncomfortable, δεσμεύουσι (δεσμός, binding and shackles): they bind it so as to fetter a person. Whereas the church should be a place of divine freedom, they make it a prison. It will be our job to unpick the granny knots they tie.

We read the theologian's instructions.

Before the commencement of prayer, arrange yourself reverently in the presence of God until you are conscious of his nearness, and kindle in your heart a living faith that God sees and is ready to hear you.

Make yourself mindful of who God is and who you are. He is the Creator, the lord and master of all. He is the One who holds in His hand your life on earth and in the hereafter. He is your Maker and, although you were created in His image, because of the Fall you languish in inner darkness and spiritual blindness. As one blind from birth, you pray to Him continually to give you sight, and thus you stand in ever growing godly fear before Him, filled with the pain of self-knowledge.[2]

Well, what is wrong with that? It is all true. Not a granny knot to be seen. Only, to whom is this being said? To a believer prior to prayer? Why not to me here and now? Is self-knowledge not my own task right now? I am not praying, not in church. Does that mean I don't need to bother with it at present? Has my obligation, which I should have assumed long ago, been taken from me and dumped on someone else, or on some *other* me, not the one who is here but one who is somewhere else?

There is a confusion surrounding the issue of unceasing prayer. There is a confusing of the focusing of the mind – which is the task and most important job of *every* human being, and is indeed what makes us human, something which is the continual obligation of all of us – and a highly specialized monastic practice, both Christian and non-Christian (in the case, for example, of Tibetan monks). This practice is extremely difficult and unusual, and achieved, according to a monk with a great deal of experience of prayer, by only a very few, perhaps one in a thousand.

Ladies and gentlemen, perhaps I really ought to be somewhere else, but the duty of mindfulness is upon me at this moment, and on however many me's there may be, and wherever I am. A cat goes out to a soft flower bed in the garden, does its business in a hole, and, using its two front paws alternately, it fills in the hole with loose soil, approaching it from different directions, then sniffs to make sure there is no longer any smell there. It brings its claws out a little further, adds a little more soil, again from different directions to ensure that the surface is level and that it has not formed another hole, then goes off reassured to lie down peacefully in the sun. It has done so not because it remembered that was the right thing to do, but because it is an automaton, in the sense in which Philo of Alexandria says that humans are incapable of creating an automaton; our present-day so-called robots are the exact opposite of real automata. The cat is in no danger of forgetting, because it does not need to remember; what you have never memorized you can never forget. It is the law without the need to remember it. Without going into what remembering and consciousness are, let us make one very plausible supposition, that the aim of the law, as indeed the overall goal, is not consciousness and remembering but salvation, redemption. The cat, when it has done everything in accordance with its own law, goes off a little smugly, with a sense of appropriateness and having done the right thing. If the situation were different, it might hastily skulk off. A question to check you are still awake: what has all this got to do with the forest? The cat is not, of course, in the forest, but domesticated animals are like the forest coming to visit us. In them the forest comes to us or into us. It comes very close.

Let us add here something to our understanding of the law. It faces us with the problem of our separation from grace. At first glance, we can see no difference: the law and grace are surely just the same thing; the law is part of grace. But, as Olga Sedakova notes, we find a complex, intertwined relationship between the law and grace in the writings of Hilarion, Metropolitan of Kiev in the mid-eleventh century.[3] Grace is more lawful than the law, just as Sarah is the lawful wife of Abraham as opposed to Hagar. Grace, according to Hilarion, takes precedence over the law, just as Sarah was already Abraham's wife before there was the law. The law is inspired by grace, just as Sarah, who for St Paul is the embodiment of grace, advised Abraham to have a child by her slave, Hagar. The law, we find, is wholly subsumed by grace, dictated by it and inconceivable without it. 'First there was law and after there was grace,' Hilarion says, speaking of time, but in reality the opposite is the case: grace came before there was law and only had to wait for the time to be right before it sent forth the apparition of itself, the law. 'Grace said unto God, "If it be not yet the time to send me down to the earth to save the world, go Thou down to Mount Sinai and give the Law.' That which casts a shadow, the law, must always rise previously since otherwise there would be nothing to cast the shadow. The law was sent down first by grace.

Let us adopt this inseparability of the law from grace from Metropolitan Hilarion, and thank Olga Sedakova for drawing our attention to it.[4] If, however, this portent of salvation, the law, always lies over us, if the law is in essence grace and is innate in us, why do we not see it, and why do we claim that human nature is freedom? It is because the law is too integral to us, and because it operates of its own accord, as an automaton, we do not notice it because that faculty we could notice it with is being used for purposes other than those for which the faculty was designed.

Olga Sedakova, to whom we will find ourselves referring increasingly, responded to a questionnaire sent out by *Lettres internationales*. The magazine was planning to mark the year 2000 by holding a contest for the best philosophical essay, analogous to the one that launched the career of Jean-Jacques Rousseau in 1750.[5] Sedakova responded to a request to suggest a title with, 'What We Have Forgotten About Humans'.

We clearly have forgotten something. When the pilgrim in *The Way of a Pilgrim* discovers his other, self-moving self, the automaton within him, he exclaims, 'Lord! What a mysterious thing man is!'[6] Forgetting is not necessarily a bad thing. It would be insane always to remember everything. 'How handsome you are, how intelligent, how healthy, how admirably you live your life, what a lot you know!' All that is no doubt true, but it might be a good idea to forget it. Is forgetfulness ever a disgrace? It can be. It was disgraceful for Russia to forget that religion is, quite literally, the law; and to forget that 300 years ago the primary meaning of 'the law' was 'faith', 'religion'. It would be different if human nature had changed in the intervening period, but it has not; it is still just the same. Attending to our salvation and redemption remains our law, fundamental, immediate and constantly at work within us, but that is something we have forgotten, and that is a disgrace.

If I have forgotten where I put the scissors and am looking for them, that is tiresome, even disgraceful; I am ashamed to be losing my marbles. If, however, I have forgotten that I owe someone money, I will not even be trying to acquire some. If the person who lent me the money is waiting, I really ought to go and see him. Better still, I should do the right thing, go and see him, ring his doorbell and tell him, very pleased with myself, that here I am and have brought the money I owe. But instead I have forgotten all about the debt, I am not where I should be, standing on my creditor's doorstep with a self-satisfied smirk, but am somewhere else. To make matters worse, nobody else in the world knows I am in the wrong place. My creditor continues to trust (*credere*, to believe) all is well, and supposes that if I have not come to see him it is probably because I am getting the money, earning it perhaps, and conscientiously making arrangements to repay the debt.

Perhaps a person is not where he should be, not because he has yet to find his place in life, but because he has never thought to look for it. I need to remember a phone number but can't, so I use a mnemonic technique, having taken Freud's advice and tried free association of ideas. What technique can I use, though, if I have forgotten what it is that I have forgotten?

The expression for this in asceticism we have already mentioned: the technique of techniques, τέχνη τεχνῶν. Just as asceticism, as the theologians rightly remind us, is by no means the same as monasticism – there is asceticism for the family and asceticism has a long history in philosophy – so self-discovery is for everybody. 'At the commencement of prayer, ask the Lord Jesus Christ for true self-discovery of your disastrous inner state, your spiritual poverty and complete inability to abide by your own efforts in virtue.... The path of self-perfection is a path of contrite self-discovery, awareness that you are blind, deaf, mute and naked.'[7]

This is so far common to all. Philosophy with its techniques does the same thing. We recall Wittgenstein's warnings that we are incurably blind. 'The aspects of things that are most important for us are hidden because of their simplicity and familiarity.' 'We are asleep. Our life is a dream, but we wake up sometimes, just enough to know that we are dreaming.' According to Plato, we are always just halves, symbols.

'Concentration is as essential for true prayer as a lamp is for light. Train your mindfulness; it is prayer better than anything else that keeps track of it.'[8] There is only one form of concentration, one form of mindfulness; if you have a church-going kind of concentration and a church-going attention span and they dissipate when you leave the church, you just need to pay more attention, until it ceases to squander itself on trying to distance itself from some other kind of mindfulness.

This is just a general guide to prayer, the commonplaces related to unceasing prayer. 'In order to concentrate the mind on the content of prayer, you must bring it into your heart.' Next, warmth. 'The heart will immediately respond to this concentration with a subtle feeling that is the beginning of inner warmth.'[9] There can, however, be the danger in warmth that it may prove to be sensual arousal.

The effort of concentrating is hard at first, but then it becomes the automatic self-movement of prayer. It addresses the automaton; it is the opposite of a mechanical response in which we are not participating, merely observing the automaton from outside, setting it going. On the contrary, we sink into the automaton.

On this path, there are many dangers: 'any vice may possess a man'. The very description of them is terrifying: 'the progeny of hell'; 'a soul covered in wounds descends in unendurable sufferings to the depths of despair'.[10] By now we may be wondering whether it was such a great idea to enter the dark forest, but this is an ordeal of purification, and those who pass through it are rewarded.

Let us turn to *The Pilgrim*. The Pilgrim (*strannik*) has revealed to him a strange person. We have called the divine wisdom and its automaton strange. In the landscape of strangeness, strangeness grows within Sophia, the divine wisdom. There is no other place where the cultural or spiritual or creative dimension is purified by the ideal processing and assimilating the material. Here there is no depressing experience of death, the death, say, of culture or education. Despair comes when we plan, when we hoped to do something good but as usual it did not turn out as we wished. 'As usual' is bad, and we wanted something better than 'as usual', something good. But let us ask why 'as usual' is bad and leaves us dissatisfied. It is precisely because our plans were for something different and things did not turn out in accordance with them. Our soul is anguished by the difference between how things are and how they should be. We see it only too clearly. There it is. We have work to do. We work on it.

In the landscape of *The Pilgrim*, there is nothing remotely resembling that gap. He is surrounded not by 'dead matter' (there is such an expression), but by the forest before it turns into matter. Metric space is absent, there are no signposts to guide us, and the only appropriate reaction is a combination of fear, mindfulness, and caution, εὐλάβεια. The goal is not to fulfil a plan, which does not exist and could not be carried out in the forest, but the difference between the frightening, alien entrancement of the forest and his own, redemptive entrancement. The forest has within it a potential both for danger and for redemption. In the dark forest, the only possibility is to become lost and disappear, but we have a choice between different ways of becoming lost. Fleeing from the forest into what merely appears through lack of insight to be dead matter is not an escape from danger to redemption, but fleeing from choosing between them back into the realm of plans. In place of εὐλάβεια, in place of the technique of techniques, the art of arts, there is only technology. Instead of engaging with the forest, we merely flee from it into the realm of artifice.

The opening of *The Pilgrim* reads:

By the grace of God I am a Christian man, by my actions a great sinner, and by calling a homeless wanderer of the humblest birth who roams from place to place. My worldly goods are a knapsack with some dried bread in it on my back, and in my breast-pocket a Bible. And that is all.

On the 24th Sunday after Pentecost I went to church to say my prayers there during the Liturgy. The first Epistle of St Paul to the Thessalonians, and among other words I heard these – '*Pray without ceasing.*' It was this text, more than any other, which forced itself upon my mind, and I began to think how it was possible to pray without ceasing. (15)

The commentator to the first Epistle to the Thessalonians, 5: 17, hastens to clarify that this means pray *spiritually* with ceasing. The Pilgrim is not up to dealing in such subtleties, thank God. Pray without ceasing means pray without ceasing. Full stop.

He treks through forests mainly, not as a spiritual being remote from the things of this world, but as a solitary human being. 'Thus once more I set out on my lonely way.... It happened at times that for three days together I came upon no human dwelling, and in the uplifting of my spirit I felt as though I were alone on the earth' (77–8). People want to help him and say, 'Here is a nice fellow-traveller for you.' 'God be with you and with him too,' said I, 'but surely you know that it is never my way to travel with other people. I always wander about alone' (86). Other people are constantly and powerfully present, but either as death, or murder, the abyss, stupefied by drunkenness, lust, malice, or, on the contrary, as charity, feeding him, loving him, discovering heaven and weeping with joy.

The guidelines of metric, calibrated space only confuse this man of the forest, who lives by the heart and breathing, not by the mind (if by that we understand something separate from the heart). His concern is so completely with the heart that he thinks no more about his mind than he does about bread: if there is none, there is none and it is time to die. If there is bread, that is a miracle. When deserting soldiers fall upon him in the forest, they decide there is no point talking to this incoherent wanderer and beat him senseless. When he regains consciousness, he is not in the least concerned about having been unconscious or the possibility of suffering from concussion: the brain is no more his than money, the body, or clothing. And accordingly his body, clothes, and mind serve him obediently and faultlessly.

The Pilgrim's breathing is like thought, his inhaling and exhaling a cautious probing of the world. We are reminded, to anticipate, of one point in pre-Socratic philosophy where the cosmic mind is absorbed through breathing. We guess why, in Leonardo's likening of the earth to a living creature, there is no mind, no consciousness, no brain: the breathing of the earth, the rising and falling of the tides, are how it senses the cosmos. Consciousness can add nothing to the way the earth absorbs the world into itself through this breathing, and might even detract from it: when a cautious, tentative probing of the world is taking place with every inhalation and exhalation, the whole world and all its wisdom, Sophia, is being sensed; not just one's own, limited mind but all minds.

Are humans dissolved, lost, in the world? How can we put it? They absorb the world and are absorbed by it, but to the extent that they meekly withstand and endure their own emptiness, impoverished and receptive, they become so unique that they alone stand out (in their solipsism, we can say after reading Schopenhauer, Wittgenstein, and Heidegger) from absolutely everything else.

There is here a curious contrast: total acceptance of everything and of any world, just as it is, no matter how it may conduct itself, obedience to it; indeed, dissolution, but that is because there is a power cast into the world that consists, as it were, of pure attentiveness, intent scrutiny. In the Pilgrim's intellectual baggage, as in his knapsack, there is only bread, never anything more than his daily bread. Christianity is not a system of knowledge but a craving, an attraction, and to what we shall shortly see. What corresponds to this state of emptiness, this pure bafflement about how unceasing prayer can be possible (since a person 'must practise other matters in order to support his life'), to this utter helplessness, is the very extremity of what he desires: divinity for his entire self, even when asleep: 'The continuous interior Prayer of Jesus is a constant, uninterrupted calling upon the divine Name of Jesus with the lips, in the spirit, in the heart; while forming a mental picture of His constant presence, and imploring His grace, during every occupation, at all times, in all places, even during sleep' (22). 'I sleep, but my heart waketh.' This is a huge demand, if you recall the tone of blissful happiness beyond measure with which these words are uttered in the Song of Solomon, 5: 2. This penniless wanderer is anticipating just such an encounter, in which everything will be fulfilled.

The Pilgrim succeeds in this. He begins with the unceasing prayer to Jesus, which at first he pronounces out loud, forcing himself: '... repeat only the following words constantly, "Lord Jesus Christ, have mercy on me." Compel yourself to do it always,' he is told by a holy man (26). We can readily imagine that, pronouncing these words of the prayer 3,000 times, then 6,000, then 12,000 times a day, forcing himself at first, he would eventually learn to do so from habit and find it easier.

> To begin with, this ceaseless saying of the Prayer at first brought a certain amount of weariness, my tongue felt numbed, I had a stiff sort of feeling in my jaws. I had a feeling at first pleasant but afterwards slightly painful in the roof of my mouth. The thumb of my left hand, with which I counted my beads, hurt a little. I felt a slight inflammation in the whole of that wrist, and even up to the elbow, which was not unpleasant. Moreover, all this aroused me, as it were, and urged me on to frequent saying of the Prayer. For five days I did my set number of 12,000 prayers, and as I formed the habit I found at the same time pleasure and satisfaction in it. (28)

But this was only like the starter motor turning over the engine. The serious business began when the engine started. This is not an inappropriate metaphor. Let us remember that the mover, movement of a mover by another mover, and prime mover are important philosophical terms. Like any metaphor, it takes us only so far before failing, and where it fails is where we encounter something that is impossible in mechanics. Perpetual motion is an impossibility and there cannot be a motionless prime mover. An automaton is a mechanical impossibility.

The praying which the Pilgrim learned is called self-moving, self-acting prayer. It came as a greater surprise than if he gained something: a new skill, for example. It was a different kind of enrichment from what he was looking for, and it was not something he acquired: he found himself. He discovered that this self-mover, this automaton, was something he had always been.

There is *all* the difference, all the interest (*inter-esse*), between what had become an agreeable habit, a mechanism, something that had become a settled pious practice after some initial compulsion involving skill, and what was vouchsafed the Pilgrim. His holy man, his *starets*, said,

> Be thankful to God that this desire for the Prayer and this facility in it have been manifested in you. It is a natural consequence which follows constant effort and spiritual achievement. So a machine to the principal wheel of which one gives impetus works for a long while afterwards by itself.... You see what feelings can be produced even outside a state of grace in a soul which is sinful and with passions unsubdued. (29)

This is all mechanics, but it is quite different when 'God is pleased to grant the gift of self-acting spiritual prayer' (ibid.).

The receiving of this gift of self-activating or self-moving prayer was accompanied by good signs. 'If I happened to meet anyone, all men without exception were as dear to me as if they had been my nearest relations.... My lonely hut seemed like a splendid palace' (30). 'Everybody was kind to me, it was as though everyone loved me' (31). For the time being, there were only signs, as if the Pilgrim were being drawn almost against his will into a vortex, a whirlpool, and he found that strange.

> I have become a sort of half-conscious person. I have no cares and no interests. The fussy business of the world I would not give a glance to. The one thing I wish for is to be alone, and all by myself to pray, to pray without ceasing; and doing this, I am filled with joy. *God knows what is happening to me!* (32)[11]

A sense of danger, of dizziness, because one has been caught up by forces immeasurably greater than oneself. An auspicious craziness, and yet one is not even at the threshold, only on the far-off approaches. 'Of course, all this is sensuous, or as my departed *starets* said, an artificial state which follows naturally upon routine' (ibid.).

This is joy at the ending of blistered feet and weariness, the gliding along of human existence; it is the free soaring that is sometimes mistaken for the full measure of the freedom conferred upon the Pilgrim. This man has taken on a yoke; he is engrossed every minute in the issue of salvation or perdition, and that is already a change he will prefer to any other lot. He is, though, still unimaginably far away from what is to come.

'In this blissful state I passed more than two months of the summer. For the most part I went through the forests and along by-roads' (35). In the forest, though, there was nothing to eat, and he went hungry. In the dark forest, there can be robbers, and he was robbed. 'When I came to I found myself lying in the forest by the roadside robbed. My knapsack had gone: all that was left of it were the cords from which it hung, which they had cut' (35–6). But he thanks God. He needed this to calm him down, to ensure even further that he had no possessions of his own. You may ask, was that so as, in return, to gain something especially valuable? That is how we are used to thinking, but it seems it would be mistaken here. The truth is evidently that the Pilgrim needed to yield, to give up absolutely every-thing. But surely he must at least have something to hold on to, something to keep him alive? No, nothing; and if his life goes on, then this is purely through grace and, actually, by a miracle.

The experience of the Pilgrim is needed in order to show that humans *can* in fact not cling to anything. Perhaps only such a person can be granted unconditional liberation, and in his condition he received it not only for himself – he was half-crazy and unable to define and delimit himself – but, as it were, for himself and on behalf of all people. This was, perhaps, not yet total liberation, but a liberation it clearly was.

> And when with all this in my mind I prayed with my heart, everything around me seemed delightful and marvellous: the trees [he is in the forest, his immediate environment is trees, *Bibikhin*], the grass, the birds, the earth, the air, the light, seemed to be telling me that they existed for man's sake, that they witnessed to the love of God for man, and that all things prayed to God and sang His praise. [The trees spoke to him, *Bibikhin*.] Thus it was that I came to understand what the *Philokalia* calls 'the knowledge of the speech of all creatures,' and I saw the means by which converse could be held with God's creatures. (45)

The forest becomes ever more dense around him until he eventually walks for three days without coming upon any village at all.

> My supply of dried bread was used up, and I began to be very much cast down at the thought I might die of hunger. I began to pray my hardest in the depths of my heart. All my fears went, and I entrusted myself to the will of God. My peace of mind came back to me, and I was in good spirits again. (46)

In the very depths of the forest, he stayed and lived with a forester who had kept watch over it for ten years. The forester lived on bread and water and, moreover, wore penitential chains weighing over 30 kg next to his skin, and was, accordingly, practising his asceticism even more strongly than the Pilgrim. 'I never swear, drink neither wine nor beer, I never quarrel with anyone at all, and I have had nothing to do with women and girls all my life' (48–9).

But this is not the Way. 'Unless you have God in your mind and the ceaseless Prayer of Jesus in your heart', all will be in vain (50). The only way is to cleave to Christ in all his dear sweetness, warmth, and peace.

Here, in the very depths of the forest, the Pilgrim finally learned to trust himself and began looking for 'ceaseless self-acting prayer in the heart' (51). He found it, again accompanied by auspicious signs. 'Sometimes my heart would feel as though it were bubbling with joy, such lightness, freedom and consolation were in it' (55).

One note, though, about techniques of prayer: in stark contrast with the simplicity and naturalness of the 'self-movement' that the Pilgrim will come to, his techniques of twelve thousandfold repetition of a seven-word phrase, of sitting in a special posture while praying, of focusing his attention on the heart, are not just manifestly not 'self-moving' but are, as he himself admits, manifestly compulsive. They are methods applied specifically to the body and emotions, while what he is seeking is neither specific nor constrained. The Pilgrim's transition from mechanical to self-acting prayer has a glaring and intentional paradox at its heart. We can find passages, not one but several, that manifestly illustrate this dichotomy or paradox, right there in the text of the Pilgrim. He is teaching a blind man, who already engages in unceasing prayer but has not yet discovered *how* 'the mind finds the heart' (114) (or what Feodosiy of Karula calls 'the place in the heart').[12]

> *[Y]ou can imagine with your mind and picture to yourself*[13] [note that imagine and picture! *Bibikhin*] what you have seen in time past, such as a man or some object or other, or one of your own limbs.... *Then picture to yourself your heart in just the same way, turn your eyes to it just as if you were looking at it through your breast, and picture it as clearly as you can. And with your ears listen closely to its beating, beat by beat*[14] ... with the first beat say or think 'Lord,' with the second, 'Jesus.' ... Thus, as you draw your breath in, say, or imagine[!] yourself saying, 'Lord Jesus Christ', and as you breathe out again, 'have mercy on me.'

That is on p. 115, and in the same paragraph he continues, 'But then, whatever you do, be on your guard against imagination and any sort of visions. Don't accept any of them whatever, for the holy Fathers lay down most strongly that inward prayer should be kept free from visions, lest one fall into temptation.'

Are we really to suppose that whoever wrote *The Pilgrim* failed to notice this lexical absurdity: 'Picture! Imagine!' 'Guard against imaginings, pictures!'? Perhaps he did, but wrote it anyway, as if he had not noticed. The paradox is almost thrown in our face. Does that make the incongruity, which is unquestionably important and even crucial, only all the clearer and more splendid? Has anyone already decided?

Let me make it easier by giving two examples of 'picturing'. During the course of these conversations, the Pilgrim and the blind man are wandering in the forests of Siberia ('we were walking through a forest,' 116). 'Suddenly he said to me, "What a pity! The church is already on fire; there, the belfry has fallen." "Stop this vain dreaming," I said, "it is a temptation to you. You must put all such fancies aside at once."' It was exactly what the Fathers of the Church had denounced, was it not? A call to sobermindedness, a warning against daydreams. The blind man meekly obeyed, fell silent, and continued his praying. When they had gone twelve versts, they entered the town and saw several burnt houses still smouldering and the collapsed belfry. The blind man had seen it just as it was falling.

The purpose of the interdiction of imagining and picturing is to liberate a different kind of imagining and picturing, to restore the vision of *the seer*. Does that mean those techniques of compulsion serve to liberate? What is liberated is nothing less than the prophetic, intelligent human being from the rot and the filth of coagulated putrefaction.

> The human soul ... can see even in the darkness, both what happens a long way off as well as things near at hand. Only we do not give force and scope to this spiritual power. We crush it beneath the yoke of our gross bodies, or with our haphazard thoughts and ideas. (116–17)

That 'or' is preceded by a comma, meaning that the yoke of our bodies includes the haphazardness of our thoughts. Let us recall the bonds in the Gospel according to St Matthew. The body becomes gross not when it is given freedom – of itself the body is wise – but when by perfidious bonds it is entangled by our thoughts. The Pilgrim's whole purpose is to collect and preserve himself every minute, every second; in this way, the body returns to the body and the mind is returned to the mind. This important part of the text is marked out, unexpectedly and inconspicuously, by the fact that the language is transformed into good, classical Russian philosophical discourse. That is not something that comes without real mental effort, the only way words can be chosen so felicitously. 'But when we concentrate within ourselves, when we draw away from everything around us and become more subtle and refined in mind, then the soul comes into its own and works to its fullest power' (117).

In the course *Know Thyself*, and later in *Wittgenstein*,[15] and again, if only briefly, elsewhere, we have touched on, or rather been touched by the angelic wing of, the topic of 'the double'. This is a topic so personal to me that I have yet to make up my mind whether or not to go public on it. But here too, following on from the paragraph from which the last quotation was taken, on the soul's coming into its own, the topic seems once more to sear me in passing and disappear. The soul's breaking out of its prison continues to be discussed:

> [T]here are people (even such as are not given to prayer, but who have this sort of power, or gain it during sickness) who see light even in the darkest of rooms, as though it streamed from every article in it [this is the same as the *logos* of things discussed in earlier lectures, *Bibikhin*], and see things by it [their invisibility means that they are radiating their essence]; who *see their doubles*[16] and enter into the thoughts of other people. (117)

The soul released from prison lives in a state of stable, constant celebration.

> I felt there was no happier person on earth than I, and I doubted if there could be greater and fuller happiness in the kingdom of Heaven.... Everything drew me to love and thank God.... Sometimes I felt as light as though I had no body and was floating happily through the air instead of walking. Sometimes when I withdrew into myself I saw clearly all my internal organs, and was filled with wonder at the wisdom with which the human body is made. Sometimes I felt as joyful as if I had been made Tsar. And at all such times of happiness, I wished that God would let death come to me quickly, and let me pour out my heart in thankfulness at His feet in the world of spirits. (118)

This part of the text would arouse the ire of Olga Sedakova, who is repelled by the Pilgrim and scents the 'stench of death' coming from him.[17] She is disturbed that his tales seem to be turning into something akin to scripture.

It is difficult to discuss the nature of the change that comes over the Pilgrim because it is again connected with the theme of the double, which has been little researched. They '*see their doubles* and enter into the thoughts of other people'.

> The self-acting prayer in my heart never hindered things, nor was hindered by them. If I am working at anything the Prayer goes on by itself in my heart, and the work gets on faster. If I am listening carefully to anything, or reading, the Prayer never stops, at one and the same time I am aware of both[!] just *as if I were made into two people, or as if there were two souls in my one body*.[18] Lord! what a mysterious thing man is! (56–7)

This discovery of the two became possible precisely because they had come into harmony. Otherwise they would not have seen each other and would not have been surprised to find they were different. The double is, in fact, no less strange and remote, we read in the continuation of that paragraph, than a wolf in the forest. Deep in the forest, a wolf attacks the Pilgrim but runs away because it feels the contact with the change that has occurred in him; it can feel its power. The double is as inaccessible as the wolf in the forest.

Is it possible to reach the double through compulsion, as it is possible to force oneself to repeat a prayer 12,000 times a day? There is a distinct and comprehensive answer. The double, my double, simply *will not* compel himself to do that or anything else, any more than the wolf in the forest. Unceasing prayer is something *very* different from an exercise.

Lecture 3, 23 September 1997

If unceasing prayer is the unearthing, the digging down to something that already exists in everybody ('There is no need to learn it, it is innate in every one of us,' *The Way of a Pilgrim*, p. 61, *Tr.*), integral to breathing, the beating of the heart, eating and moving, then a simple understanding of faith reveals itself to us: it is trusting what already exists. The law of our being is religion in the sense of attentiveness. (*Re-ligio* means attention.[1]) Our primary bond (our belonging, our relationship) is with God. That means we need look no further than within ourselves (there is no need to consult an encyclopaedia or ask anyone else) to know what God is. That is tantamount to asking someone else who I am. It is within us always, although most often in privation, while we are paying dearly in various ways for straying from where our religious nature always is.

Faith is like an exposing of things unseen. We are usually quite unaware of the fact that we are breathing, that our heart is beating, or of eating. If we then decide to regulate our breathing, or our heartbeat, or to follow a special diet, to subordinate them to our conscious mind, that implies emphatically that we are only now making a start, that up till now we have not been doing any of these things. That, needless to say, is a double-dyed, blatant untruth, as if we are trying to get in our alibi in advance. 'No, no. Where I was – that wasn't me; I've only just now turned up where I am. The reality is that when I was born I, as a human being, cried from fear of breathing, was comforted when my breathing became regular, and fell asleep; then I cried again in a panic when I became hungry, but calmed down when I was given milk.'

But all that was not yet in metric space; it was still in the forest, inside matter and, before that, inside my mother. Respiratory gymnastics and dietary concerns already belong to metric space. An unnecessary binding, an overly metric approach to the things of the forest, a complicated entangling that fetters mind and body – they all have a beginning, so they will all have an end. The practising of unceasing prayer does not fetter but unfetters our breathing. It does not unfetter it in the sense of some ridiculous 'expansion and liberation of breathing', which is only going to lead to hyperventilation of the lungs and ultimately to deranging the way they work, but in the sense of leaving the body to do what the body does well. The God with whom people converse in prayer is, after all, that same God who created the body the way it is. We do not know exactly how that is, but we know that *as it is* we can offer it to the service of God. We are not conversing with God in order to convey our thoughts to him, because he undoubtedly already has plenty of thoughts of his own, but in order to make our confession, to offer ourselves sincerely: look, this is me. People speak to God with their whole being, just as they are, with their whole existence, their very presence. So they do, ladies and gentlemen.

I repeat that what is important for us is that in the school of unceasing prayer there is a clear boundary, a stage beyond which seeking becomes finding. The practitioners of unceasing prayer differ not by the fact that *starets* (elder) Vasilisk of Turov would remain motionless in prayer for twelve hours at a time and say the Jesus Prayer on a rosary 12,000 times a day, while *starets* Zosima Verkhovsky, founder and father confessor of the cenobitic convent of the Virgin Hodegetria near today's Naro-Fominsk, did even more,[2] and that now we can compare them with the spiritual proficiency of Arseniy Troyepolsky, the Hieromonk of the Pafnutiy of Borovsk monastery, who died in Nara on 7 July 1870.[3] What is important is the discovery that all that matters is faith, not in humankind, but in the fact that humans as they are have the capacity as part of their being, not by chance, or some fluke, or by a stroke of luck, but *of necessity*, for unceasing prayer: prayer tied to their breathing, to their heartbeat, to the food they eat and their eating, but as something integral to their body, which is also called attentiveness.

Secondhand information strikes us as unreliable, and those actually praying say little directly about it and remain serenely reticent. The Pilgrim, as he is known from our reading, might seem to be a fictitious figure, irredeemably anonymous, so perhaps a mere legend leading us in the opposite direction from reality. But he is *Russian* literature and, moreover, an important *event* in Russian literature through whose miracle the Pilgrim becomes direct and conclusive testimony, a primary source on unceasing prayer. The fact that he somehow additionally embodies almost every tradition of Russian thought – the Siberian tradition through Zosima Verkhovsky; the tradition of the followers of St Ignatiy Bryanchaninov through Arseniy Troyepolsky;[4] the official, 'synodal' tradition through his final and definitive editor, Feofan the Recluse;[5] and, indirectly, that of the Optina Pustyn monastery through the attention, if not uncritical, he pays to the experience of Vasilisk of Turov, the teacher of Zosima – that makes the Pilgrim all the more impressive, confirming something everybody in any case senses: that he is *authoritative*.

If unceasing prayer was achieved in the forest, in the backwoods (Zosima Verkhovsky when he came to the Moscow region from Siberia – and it is through Siberia that the Pilgrim mostly travels – sought out the most obscure and marshy of locations), we need to ask whether it is even possible without raw experience. It is not an intellectual matter but brings us back down to the earth of the heart, to primal matter, to the void at the beginning of the Book of Genesis; since otherwise how does it produce its sobering effect?

Unceasing prayer comes from an encounter with the intimate, real God, and leads us to silence. The strictness of divine attentiveness rules out easy solutions and leads us to confront the irresolvable. And indeed, it is not for humans to define their relationship with something more powerful than themselves. Humans can decide only not to run away, to show fortitude when something comes so near, because returning to the truth of the forest, to the heartbeat, to breathing, is to come closer to the fire. As already in the twentieth century, in the Prayer Diary of the *starets* Feodosiy of Karulia on Mount Athos, in the entry for 3 September 1937, a month before his death on 2 October, we read,

> A heat began ... to flare from the heart in my bosom, and became so strong that my heart seemed aflame ... and became agitated by this great heat, which began to spread from my bosom down to my lower abdomen ... although with great effort I managed not to abandon my prayer, trusting in God, during this time of temptation. The flame in my heart and in all my body gradually passed from this heat.[6]

Returning to the physical is risky; indeed, dangerous.

We may define spirituality as a return to the body, only not to a concept of the body that never advances beyond the fantasy of an inappropriate fusion of mind and body but to the body as our unapproachable double that forbids any flirtation, any commerce of the mind with it.

The woman's bleeding could be healed suddenly, not by human efforts but by the approach of the divine presence, which always occurred. We read in Psalms, 16: 8, 'O my soul, thou hast said unto the Lord, Thou art my Lord: my goodness extendeth not to thee.' The Creator does not move, he is eternally close; neither does the one who sees him move. Does this eternal relationship apply only to the Church, and not to everyone? What is vast attracts by its very weight. If the sun with its storms and flares came close to us, it would certainly be frightening, but not as frightening as the approach of God. 'The fear of God, bringing about unceasing worshipful prayer to God and ensuring observance of Christ's commandments, leading to reconciliation with God, when fear is transformed into love and the anguish of prayer, transformed into sweetness, fosters the flowering of enlightenment ... the knowledge of God's mysteries.'[7] Faith is believing that this precisely is the way everything stands with humankind. One is returning to oneself. From whence? Folly and stupidity say, from freedom to the yoke of unfreedom. No! From the void into history.

Unceasing prayer reveals, then, humanity's ancient task, through which alone what is truly occurring is revealed. Those who have had faith, those who have achieved unceasing prayer, returning to humankind like seeds of the present, of real history, these are the markers of the history of our land. Those who retreated into silence, who began to envisage their destiny in terms of the moment they would stand before the eternal, the unchanging – St Seraphim of Sarov, Vasilisk of Siberia, the Pilgrim – are more assured in their plotting of the course of history than Russia's writers within the literary process, although these, too, are toiling in the workshop, their work, too, is illuminated by inspiration. These holy men are guiding stars no less than the earliest sages of the ancients.

> The silent contemplatives are like pillars supporting the devotion of the Church [and perhaps not only of the Church, *Bibikhin*] by their secret continuous prayer: Even in the distant past one sees that many devout lay-folk, and even kings and their courtiers, went to visit hermits and men who kept silence in order to ask them to pray for their strengthening and salvation.[8]

What I would like is to put an end to the separating of faith from philosophy and, more broadly, of faith from culture. Also, of course, of one faith from another. All that is different about them is their different languages. Anyone who claims their faith is 'better' than others is a pagan who has not yet noticed that theirs is not the only language in the world, who imagines that the world does not extend beyond their village, their *pagus*. Whether such benighted people like it or not, everything of significance in their language springs from the same soil as that from which other languages grow. There is no reason to repudiate one's own language, but not to listen to someone else just because they speak a different language is to be deaf also to one's own language and, indeed, to oneself, because every person, every day of their life, has their own language. People's laziness and weariness cause their language to ossify ridiculously even as they cling to it. It only seems that loose language is the opposite of pedantic language. In fact, both have that same inertia, that same parochialism.

The threshold of silence stops bleeding, stops the spattering of blood, assuming, of course, that is what the woman with an issue of blood wants, and is not deliberately spattering it around in the belief that this is somehow a 'flight of intellect' or 'freedom of thought and expression'.

Because genuine philosophy has crossed this threshold of silence and mindfulness, it is the same as unceasing prayer. Mindfulness is also silence. One of the lessons of the Pilgrim: 'Mindfulness, in order always to keep your heart free from intention, even if it should seem good.'[9]

The Pilgrim talks about mindfulness as faith and religion. One of the narrators, a professor, relates, 'For five years I was a professor and I led a gloomy dissipated sort of life, captivated by the vain philosophy of the world,[10] and not according to Christ. Perhaps I should have perished altogether had I not been upheld to some extent by the fact that I lived with my very devout mother and my sister, who was a serious-minded young woman' (199–200).

'Serious-minded' is used here as a synonym for pious, and on the following page we read, '[M]y sister was preparing to dedicate herself to monastic life' (201). Serious-minded attentiveness, too, is no different from unceasing prayer. Christian asceticism adopted the philosophical school of attentiveness, and began also to call itself 'philosophy', accepting the goal of self-knowledge, in the sense of standing perpetually, not in front of the mirror, but before God.

Christianity is aware that asceticism is identical both in philosophy and in religion, whether it admits that it adopted the philosophical school or claims that philosophers took everything from the Bible. The friends and enemies of the philosophers within Christianity alike accept that the Bible's 'Beware that there be not a thought in thy wicked heart' (Deuteronomy 15: 9) is the same as the Delphic 'Know thyself'. Unfortunately, this convergence of philosophy and faith in the matter of attentiveness has been forgotten. We are reminded about this in *The Pilgrim*: 'Even the most elementary sages have recognized the value of silence. The philosophical school of the Neoplatonists, which embraced many adherences under the guidance of the philosopher Plotinus, developed to a high degree the inner contemplative life which is attained most especially in silence' (250).

We can resolve the issue of unceasing prayer by noting something to which its belated critics do not always pay attention (calling it 'technique', 'physiology', 'primitive', 'navel-gazing', 'an impoverishment of prayer'). Unceasing prayer in the sense of Psalms, 16: 8, 'I have set the Lord always before me: because he is at my right hand, I shall not be moved,' is an old and obligatory philosophical discipline (which can have a variety of methods), both of monastic and of non-monastic ascesis. Its encompassing of a person's whole being, their body, mindfulness, breathing, the beating of their heart, cannot but bring about a real, rapid, and miraculous change in them, halting the issue of blood. (Mindfulness of the heartbeat and at the same time the heartbeat itself, as also breathing in the sense of a careful entering, a careful probing of matter, primal matter in the earthly forest, in which, moreover, it is impossible not to sense God's presence. The heartbeat itself, the breathing becomes this forest, although pure mindfulness remains a separate Sophia unlike anything else – and thereby lets in everything else.) A different mission for a changed person is revealed, in effect the only true mission. Here any would-be criticism of unceasing prayer is simply fatuous and shows up the critic for someone who does not understand the issue.

But precisely because other habits than unceasing mindfulness have emerged and become ingrained, in the sense of growing accustomed to the bleeding (and the woman in the Gospel had not just accepted it, she wanted to be healed), because of the unfortunately widespread neglect of discipline, those who return to themselves, the mindful, may face problems. Just because the return to yourself in mindfulness is light and easy ('Take my yoke upon you ... for my yoke is easy, and my burden is light,' Matthew, 11: 29, 30), it may take a long time for this new spirit to overcome old and ingrained habits.

We need to discriminate. The discrepancy between the promise that unceasing prayer is easy (just a few days of practice will be sufficient) and the lifelong commitment called for by monastic life is only superficially beguiling. Of course, mindfulness should come quickly and easily if it is to come at all. It does not have to be created through exercises: real mindfulness needs only to be recalled. It is of a kind with the way our breathing and rate of heartbeat are changed in the presence of something vast and awe-inspiring like mountains, the sky, beauty, and all the more so the beauty of a human with a body and heart, of humankind, of God incarnate in Jesus Christ. For unceasing prayer all that is needed is to *notice* where and who we are. Prayer is primal: it does not need practice, it is what we start with. Regrettably, editors excised from the original *Pilgrim* his clear protest against the notion that special preparation is needed before we can turn to God. There is a powerful section early in the manuscript where the Pilgrim states that, quite the contrary, without *prayer* it is not possible even to begin. 'From all the prayers found in the Bible it is evident that they were offered for absolution of sins, and that no absolution of sins was needed prior to prayer.'[11] This is accompanied by a quotation from the Bible: 'And I will give them one heart, and I will put a new spirit within you' (Ezekiel, 11: 19). In *any* human situation, the first thing to do, the first priority, like clutching at the banisters, is to turn, if you have deviated, to unceasing prayer, to mindfulness. '[A]fter every fall and sinful wounding of the heart the thing to do is immediately to place it in the Presence of God for healing and cleansing.'[12]

It is monastic philosophy that seems most relevant to this primary, groundbreaking task, which is why the beginnings of Russian philosophy should be sought in *The Pilgrim* and in Vladimir Soloviov,[13] to the extent that he, too, is a pilgrim. In the light of *The Pilgrim* and his unceasing, obligatory praying, most discussions on philosophical topics seem like homeless orphans.

Unceasing prayer, philosophy, and faith in each individual is ontology. The difficulties that the light yoke of work encounters, and the complications it produces, is biography.

Emerging into the presence of the divine is the beginning of the history of the real freedom conferred by the yoke, which is horror at our blindness, at our fear and penitential burden of guilt and shame, and amazement at how free we have become!

Who are people exposing when they pray? Primarily, of course, themselves, the *I* that is speaking; next, their neighbour, and what is closer to you than your breath, your heart, and that strange, unknown but so intimate thing, your body. Picture *not* thoughts about your body ('See how filthy I am, how sensual'); picture *not* the positions of the body: praying, kneeling, prostrated on the ground, emaciated by fasting, exhausted by sleep deprivation, in the posture of a believer, making the sign of the Cross.

All such facilitating postures of the body are prescribed, defined by detailed rules and considered necessary until not flighty but pure prayer of the heart is achieved. When by the favour and grace of our Lord Jesus Christ you attain this, then, leaving behind many and varied doings, you will be united beyond words with the Lord in pure and not flighty prayer of the heart, without need of these facilitating devices.[14]

What is offered is just the body: see, the heart is beating, the blood invisibly circulating, the lungs breathing. Bid your thoughts farewell, abandon them; you no longer have need of them, or of your concerns about yourself, your body, about the world or about God. No one has need of them. You have no need of them if you are genuinely, honestly standing before God; no need even of other people's thought, other people's prayers. 'When betimes prayer in all its purity comes to you of its own volition, you must in no way ruin it with your rules for verbal prayer' (ibid.). Prayers are also a means: as penitential chains are for the body, so they are for the mind, for exercising it. When, however, real physical work begins, the building of a church, say, the chains should be set aside, your hands need to be free to work. In the same way, for the heart to work it should be equally free both of intentions and of prayers. Mindfulness means 'keep your heart free from intention, even if it should seem good' (ibid.).

Standing pure before God is like being undressed, naked before him. Oh, if silence meant only not to be speaking, not to be expressing our thoughts, it would be such a small matter, something everyone already does when seeking to conceal their thoughts. But it is more: we need to still our thoughts. 'Retaining awareness while invoking Jesus Christ entails looking constantly into the depths of the heart and ceaselessly keeping thought silenced; even, I would say, trying to be empty of intentions that seem good, or of any other intentions, lest felonious thoughts be lurking beneath them.'[15] As they assuredly will be, ready to rob us the minute we stray out of that pure mindfulness in which even our own thoughts surprise us and seem to belong to somebody else. The value of intentions is only that they, too, may be presented, offered, exposed.

Moving away from thoughts and intentions to pure mindfulness is also the teaching of an old school of philosophy (νοῦς). How is it that in our time it has survived only in the form of unceasing prayer, and virtually only in the monasteries at that? That is cause to be grateful to the Church and something that makes the Church indispensable. Is this discipline not now being diminished by being separated from the totality of human experience, the experience of other languages of faith, by becoming specialized and isolated from philosophy and the experience of poetry and music? And similarly, is secular culture not also diminished to the extent that it lacks understanding of the school of unceasing prayer, has not studied but has instead squandered it? It is as if the storehouses and their watchmen were in different places: the storehouses full of fabulous riches but unlocked; the guard incorruptible, competent and vigilant, only nowhere near the storehouses.

How are we to return the storehouses once more to their guards, and return the guards to their storehouses? Neither prayer nor faith can be perfect if the person praying has first decided to be this way or that, and only then to turn to God. There was good reason why this first, and perhaps most important, thesis of the Pilgrim was excised by those who edited him. Unfortunately, the specialization of faith, the transformation of religion into a profession, is a fact. Ecumenism, stripped down to its essence, would do well to remember that the real Church, the Church of faith in the divine, has existed not for 2,000 years, but since the days of Abel and, according to Bernhard Welte, we are in eucharistic communion with the cave dwellers of the Mount of Olives near Cologne.

> The natural man arrives naturally at the knowledge of God. And, therefore, there is not, and never has been, any people, any barbarous tribe, without some knowledge of God. As a result of this knowledge the most savage islander, without any impulse from outside, involuntarily raises his gaze to heaven, falls on his knees, breathes out a sigh which he does not understand, necessary as it is.... Universally the essence or the soul of every religion consists in *secret prayer*.[16] (*The Way of a Pilgrim*, p. 237)

Faith is the same in every paganism; religion and devout mindfulness are one.

A human being's most important job is to be mindful. Work? 'Every hour and every moment let us with utmost diligence guard our heart against all manner of intentions dimming the spiritual glass in which it is meet that Jesus Christ alone should be impressed and imprinted.'[17] Against all manner of intentions: that is, we must fall again and again.

Phenomenology is the showing of what is. To whom? To whomsoever or whatever is manifested, to the extent that they are manifested. Beyond that showing, we should have nothing in mind. Husserl's phenomenology is pure mindfulness as novelty. A further interpretation and application, in passing, on the value of philosophy: only from this pure standing in the Presence can there arise not power but emptiness and a measure of amazement, of wonder, from which alone one can bypass all traditions and find an absolute starting point. 'Pray, and do not labour much to conquer your passions by your own strength. Prayer will destroy them in you' (230). And further,

> The man who lives in silent solitude is not only not living in a state of inactivity and idleness; he is in the highest degree active, even more than the one who takes part in the life of society. He untiringly acts according to his highest rational nature; he is on guard; he ponders; he keeps his eye upon the state and progress of his moral existence. (248)

There is a sober awareness that we have no power over the forest, the wolf, and the double. With our body, our heart, our food, merely by eating every day, we belong to the forest, the world's matter. Presenting ourselves in unceasing prayer just as we are, we present ourselves as creatures of the forest, our own forest. Like the forest, we are created, but as creatures presenting ourselves, as pure mindfulness, as phenomenologists, we are apart from the forest: we are divine. At such a time, what we are doing with the forest is what God wanted. Of course, in order to find out what at that time we are doing, we must try to see what, in religion, we may be.

Why does mindfulness release wonder? Because, of course, it is simply wondrous that I, mindful and observing, am somehow related to my neighbour here, my body that is here and nowhere else, standing and doing what it is doing, breathing and thinking.

Together with my neighbour, my body, I am immediately back in contact with the global forest it is growing into, as are other bodies with which every body is linked in essentially the same way as the parts of one body are linked: in the way bodies are linked to each other, through kinship, relationships, breathing the same air, being irradiated by the same rays, visible or invisible. There is nothing fundamentally different from the way the head is linked to, say, the hand. In St Paul's comment that the community is like a body, in his addressing it as 'brothers and sisters', there is nothing in the least metaphorical. If this kinship has been rejected by the mind, forgotten as an ideal, it is not the kinship we need to worry about. It is not going anywhere, it will simply carry on being what it is. Perhaps, though, we need to be worrying about the mind, what it is and whether, perhaps, it has not gone a bit off the rails and might need to be put right in some essential.

That is why it is not self-centred to seek redemption for oneself. Redemption of one's neighbour is, first of all, redemption of one's body, which, through its universal interconnectedness, is at once salvation for all bodies. Any movement, through interconnectedness, moves all matter.

Redemption, that is, putting the mind right, begins with fear, with horror, and that is another merit of a remarkable note passed to me at the lecture on 9 September, which I read too hastily and which deserves better: 'I have set the Lord always before me: because he is at my right hand, I shall not be moved.'[18] Fear of the Lord is the beginning of wisdom. But is always setting God before us (not imagining him), the seeing of him before us that the prophet David speaks of ... is that not something reserved exclusively for the souls and minds of believers rather than for just anyone? For the believer, this is the way out of the forest. God is always before you. The forest, dark, terrifying, dismal, is the condition of any soul, with or without faith. (The soul, according to Tertullian, is 'in its very nature Christian.') 'I entrusted myself to the will of God. My peace of mind came back to me and I was in good spirits again' (46). Theology teaches us how to find our way out of the forest, and it does so on the basis of past experience. There is no universally accepted image of God or of faith in him (and any imagining of God is idolatry). Imagination is a temptation, when the individual forces himself to picture the heart, the kidneys, veins and fat (things he considers necessary); it is a different matter when in a mysterious way something quite else is revealed to him. He does not know why, and perhaps until his dying day he never will.

Redemptive fear is the most terrifying. People are afraid of fear. One character in *The Pilgrim* is straying but unable to take the decision to turn to mindfulness. 'I thought that directly I began to pray God would destroy me' (187). Fear, or Heidegger's '*Angst*', will cripple, destroy, sweep away, only all the familiar, inessential links between body and mind, will cast the body back to the body, and return the mind to pure mind.[19]

People remark on how few prayers there are in the Gospels. There seems to be a straightforward explanation for this. Perhaps, speaking of prayers strictly in the traditional sense, there is not a single one, but that is just how it should be: the Gospels are in their entirety a school of mindfulness, of *unceasing* prayer. I probably do not have to explain further that by that I mean *real* constant mindfulness and not, of course, repeating the same words a thousand times over. St Feofan the Recluse contemptuously styled such practitioners 'whisperers', muttering their prayers meaninglessly; and those who mechanically synchronized their breathing to the words he called wheezers who snuffled through their prayers. For him, these were both senseless external techniques. In *The Pilgrim*, too, the Gospel is primarily a school of prayer. '[The] Gospel bids unceasing prayer. To other acts of piety their own ties are assigned, but in the matter of prayer there are no off times. Without prayer it is impossible to do any good and without the Gospel you cannot learn properly about prayer' (193).

Mindfulness interrupted ceases to be mindfulness. If prayer is not unceasing, it becomes something *entirely different*, a ritual.

For the Pilgrim the dark forest was initially frightening and oppressive, but he came to feel at home there and rejoiced in the wilderness: 'The silent forest is like a Garden of Eden in which the delightful Tree of Life grows in the prayerful heart of the recluse' (240). The silent forest is the familiar, Russian body of the Pilgrim. Just because it is so boldly, so completely itself, all that is remote from him becomes the Pilgrim's own. (The dichotomy propounded by Lotman and Uspensky between what is one's own and what is alien is simply wrong.[20] It is based on a loose, conventional understanding of ownership. What is truly one's own includes everything that is genuine.) The Russian forest merges with the Garden of Eden into a single Tree of Life, which is also the wood of the Cross.

Here we will only touch lightly on this theme, but moving on from *The Pilgrim* we will need to talk more precisely about the Russian forest.

Mountains, by which I mean high mountains rising above the tree line, pierce heights where, because the air is rarefied, one feels the coldness of space. The sun shines more brightly than down below but the thin air already has almost no mass, and there is no medium to conduct the heat from a blazing hot rock. If a short-sighted alien were to come close to the earth in a mountainous region devoid of forest, he would find the planet no different from a sterile asteroid. He would be unable to understand why there should be air and water lower down, and even more puzzling would be the meadows and forest. The earth might have been an asymmetrical lump of rock if wind, and water expanding in cracks when it froze, had not dragged the mountain peaks down to the plains. The soil settling there from mudslides became almost as smooth as the water that had brought it down. One could imagine that the rocks and mountains were thrown, sprayed at the earth from above, while its roundness resulted from slow erosion by wind and water. The earth may have been thoroughly angular, a hotchpotch of bits of the asteroids which bombarded it over billions of years. How did those bare bones come to be covered in organic tissue? That is an interesting question, but not one we are called upon to answer. The question for us is, could it be that, just as the thing closest to us, our body, almost never comes into our field of vision, so the same is true of the entity on which we exist. Our body is viewed from the outset – we are after all spiritual, conscious, intelligent beings – as a means of attaining ends: for example, by working. May the same not be true of the earth? We have only to frame the question in those terms for the answer to be obvious.

The summits of mountains are snowy, icy, or bare, as if the earth were still being buffeted by the solar wind. It is much the same at both poles. Then suddenly, below a height of four kilometres, the forest begins, it descends from there along with the streams, and would continue down into the valleys but for people. In regions levelled by water, half the forest has been cut down, or more than half, or all of it. Leonardo da Vinci was right: the mountains have been levelled by wind and water. It seemed to him there was something wrong about that: something must have happened to the earth and it seemed to be bleeding to death. The water, draining away, left plains.

Nowadays, great cities stand on those plains in which, thanks to their dwellings, electricity, mains water, and sewerage, a different metabolism has been created. A different luminary shines round the clock and there is a different habitat. Only, as it is so elegantly put, nowadays that habitat is in a state of 'environmental disequilibrium'. In other words, the city cannot exist without further ploughing up of the soil around it, and further pollution of the soil, air, and water. A major city stands out on the plain like a rash of eczema or an allergy. The forest has been felled so that the plain can be ploughed up so that the city can be fed. In exchange, the city belches out chemicals, radiation, and gases. The mountains are being eroded and levelled to make way for the forest, while the forest makes way for people. As people proliferate, they cut their primal environment down and plough it up. The mismanagement is causing degradation of the soil. Just as the deserts of Arabia and North Africa were caused by protracted human 'management', so people nowadays are making a global desert for themselves. Neglect the ecology of the fields and you get a desert.

Using the level ground and the forests in this manner, there is clearly something people have not thought through. Proliferation of great cities has been a mistake, as their planners are themselves forced to admit. It seems that in this respect, too, there is no topic more important than the forest.

The number 2000 appeared only on the pages of newspapers and on screens. Looking down from the air, looking at the great cities spilling over the plains, the number appeared to herald nothing whatsoever. Unless perhaps a glimmer of hope that humans might wake up, at least partly, and open their eyes. What people love – old churches, castles in the mountains – shows that a different way of treating the earth is possible, but they appreciate these things aesthetically, and enjoy holidays in the countryside only then to return to their globalism. To encompass the world 'globally' seems now to be the aim of almost everything anybody does, but that focus does not mean any more attention is being paid to the earth itself. On the contrary, it is lost behind plans and screen images as never before. Globalism is a sick imitation of paying attention to the earth, just as the main aim of the comprehensive studying of 'humankind' is not to notice what the Pilgrim discovered when he decided to become mindful. He discovered the nature of his own breathing, of his heartbeat, of the way he ate. He noticed what he ate, and how he related to other bodies.

In globalization, a mindful attitude towards the earth is the last thing we can hope for. People are as blithely unaware of the nature of this living entity as they are of the animal that they are themselves, and they will pay no heed to it until it revolts. They regress back to the forest in their tobacco smoking, wine bibbing, and drug taking; the forest, so long dispossessed, thus cruelly avenges the injury directly in the big city centre.

Even a less striking overpopulation in the classical world brought the Trojan War down on humankind, and the earth's vengeance on the big city will be infinitely more terrible. A return to religion, that is, to philosophy – but not by any stretch of the imagination to that sick counterfeit, religious philosophy – seems almost certain.

Trains, planes, and cars encompass not matter but a pre-identified business segment. Tourists imagine they are broadening their narrow horizons and seeing the world, but in reality they are mere exploiters, blissfully unaware that they are only tightening the grip of industrialization. There is good reason to refer to their activities as the tourist *industry*. Criticism of civilization, by keeping it in the headlines, only serves to consolidate it.

There is something strangely hopeful and offbeat, something almost of the holy fool, about the lands of Russia and the way that here the sprawling of our standardized cities over the plains is dysfunctional, tentative, as if subverted in advance by our nervous haste, the provisional nature of almost all decisions, and the manifest absence of any trustworthy, long-term strategy such as we find, for example, in America. There is no call for us to envy America its strategy, with its centuries-long perspective (in the conservation of forests, in the *deliberate* limiting of arable land, and its preference for buying in oil rather than extracting it locally). By contrast, our own strategy seems short of breath, not to say suffocating. Why? Because where exploitation of the earth is concerned it is better not to have a strategy than to have one. The only right approach is to recognize that what matters is not know-how or the lack of it, but awareness that the world's Sophia is not to be found in technology, however ultramodern and sophisticated. In the absurd rootlessness of our technological invasion of the forest, of which a glaring and literal example is the ridiculous building of opulent villas in Moscow province by people unfortunate enough to have picked up all the money they found lying at their feet (just as the communists had the misfortune to seize power that was theirs for the taking), we seem to believe that, because of a drowsy awareness that it will not be human intelligence that puts everything back in place, all attempts to behave rationally should be shunned.

Lecture 4, 30 September 1997

Something very notable is our widespread, distraught nostalgia for the forest, our hopeless dream of somehow still being able to escape back into it: for example, by concealing upmarket residential estates in its depths. That is about as sensible as trying to get back to nature by swimming or sunbathing on the beach.

The desire to gain a suntan, or to move out of the city, or to agonize about the environment, all point to the fact that our present way of life is manifestly unsustainable, 'marked' in the sense of structural linguistics. Ask anyone why it is unsustainable, since when and, most importantly, to what end. One person may say that human life on earth has always been stressful and under threat. Maybe so. That certainly seems to be the case today. For us, all that is noteworthy about this is that the voices around us vehemently assert that 'today it is clearer than ever before', or that this or that 'continues to be crystal clear', or that humankind needs to do one thing, was wrong to do another thing, will have to pay if it does not do something else, or has really got it coming to it this time. Stress is difficult to bear without talking fearfully. Our definition of the core of human nature as being religion and philosophy, as unceasing mindfulness, and, in response to stress, even more mindfulness, tells us to be wary of all clichés but pay attention to everything people say. What is, is: what is not, is not. We may perhaps even agree that the earth is sick, not because we have made a diagnosis, but simply because that is what a lot of people are saying and there seems to be no great harm in it. Or is there? At all events, science by its very nature will be unable to reach any conclusion about that because it has no experience of diseases of cosmic entities. Well, unless Mars is a precedent.

Let us draw a slightly curious conclusion, probably uncontroversial, but which we shall shortly need. The state of the forest, the terrestrial forest, and of matter, the global forest, the birthplace of humanity, is extreme but indefinable. This unexpectedly brings us back to an old paradox in the history of philosophy: for Aristotle, and effectively also for Plato, matter plainly exists but no less plainly is very elusive; it is important because it occupies a place at the opposite end of the spectrum from something as important as form, *eidos*, but that is precisely why it is indefinable.

The situation is 'marked', and loudly proclaims, demonstrates, that *eidos* and matter are coupled, but *eidos* does not magisterially dictate its form to matter merely because matter is elusive and indefinable. *Eidos* is intertwined with matter in such a way that all matter is predisposed to certain forms and not to others, as if it were already charged with *eidos*. The *eidos* of a statue, for example, can be dictated to bronze but hardly to air; a statuette of the human figure might be carved from bone and a bust might be made of marble or clay but hardly of water.

We find this complex interweaving of *eidos* and matter being considered already in Plato's dialogue *Timaeus*, where the place we now expect to find occupied by matter is occupied by χώρα, *khora*, which is also *eidos*, only a darker, more complicated and elusive *eidos* because it is wide enough to accommodate many different concepts of *eidos*.[1] *Khora* is all-accepting nature which knows no birth or emergence. It is obscure and problematical and, needless to say, also needs to be treated with caution.

At our first approach to Aristotle's concept of matter, we obtain a result that is reassuringly trivial. There is general agreement that the concept of matter was 'introduced' by Aristotle: that is, he heard the word, took the risk of using the term, and was so successful that it has been found useful by everybody since, right up to the present. We are shocked by the use made of materialism in Russia, by the way people of the worst kind wielded it as a weapon and a bludgeon to crush and smash everything. We are reluctant now to use it ourselves, just as we would shrink from picking up an executioner's axe, even if it was much needed, if it was covered with blood and we knew it had been used for beheadings. Even if it was made of good steel, even if it had been rinsed clean. We would much prefer to take a different axe, and point out that executioners are not the only people who use axes.

Everything we find ourselves ignorantly handling has properties, and these are not just something we attribute to it. We have talked in an earlier lecture series about property and ownership.[2] That, however, was about property, and if we now look in more detail we will find that we are short of words to distinguish between what we think of as owned by us and what someone else may think of as owned by them. That is why I said then that the formulation proposed by Yury Lotman and Boris Uspensky, 'our own/of others', is incomplete. 'Our' Leonardo da Vinci is ours because we have mentioned him, but as I was writing that I was reminded of Pavel Florensky, who thought and felt his way so deeply into substance that he seemed to become immersed in it, as if he were no longer writing about substance but taking down dictation from it.[3] For a true artist or musician, the colour or the sound are his own; he himself is the colour and sound, the mood. A craftsman begins by feeling his way into his material, the wood or the clay, and we constantly see that, for those who fail to do so, nothing comes out quite right. The Russian word '*khaltura*', hack work, is derived from a word meaning a funeral wake (which is also '*chałtury*' in Polish). A funeral is a hallowed occasion at which all are fed. They may be asked to eat rice, raisins, and honey, *kut'ya*, food for the dead. Hack work, too, is dead; it is what Heraclitus meant when he said that what was dead should be thrown out even before what was insanitary.[4]

We can rest content for now with finding that our similes for the forest have one thing in common: they give the lie to the idea that there is such a thing as 'lifeless nature'. We can never be too sensitive in seeking to understand *materia*. We should quote so many agreeable cultural clichés that no genuine theoretical physicist will insist there is a boundary between his own science and the humanities.

But these are all, as I say, agreeable clichés that only seem to be important. All the positive attitudes of thoughtful, humane, artistic people towards the world we live in will remain no more than hot air, because what will decide not only the fate of things, not only what people do with them, but their very emergence will be mindfulness. 'You look at the forest from the sidelines,' a certain knowledgeable and sympathetic person told me. In fact, however, we are looking at it from the standpoint of mindfulness, which is crucial.

There are different kinds of mindfulness. A hack is attentive: he pays attention to where and how there is dead money to be made. Investigative, probing attention will see what needs to be seen in the forest by someone who is assured of three good meals a day in comfortable surroundings and whose priority is to ensure that situation continues.

Mindfulness is not a tool to be used by humans but a state into which they can and should fall. It is not targeted at the forest. Let us instead attempt a provisional conjecture about how it is that the forest captivates us and lifts us out of metric space. It is in fact possible for mindfulness and the forest, two polar opposites, to come together. Nicholas of Cusa's *coincidentia oppositorum* develops something that Aristotle all but explicitly spells out.[5] We are moving towards our reading of Aristotle with a working hypothesis that for him matter, like that of Plato, will prove to be *eidos*.

Before we read them, let me dictate this to you: we expect to find in Plato and Aristotle conclusions that we have arrived at ourselves. What arrogance, to attribute our own concepts to distant classical authors! For anyone inclined to that view, let us add insult to injury by saying that not only do we expect to find our own viewpoint in Aristotle but that, if he does not confirm our hypotheses, we will consider there has been no point in reading him.

To anyone complaining that this is a departure from the proprieties of the history of philosophy and philology, we can and will argue that, on the contrary, it is the only proper way to read Aristotle. The history of thought, and history in general, will crumble and I will find myself a New Russian in the most deplorable sense of the word if we do not insist that the most important occupation of humans has never changed: it is working on themselves, digging down to their true self. All our talk about the classical world will prove empty (the 'Axial Age', the 'beginnings of our civilization') if we fail to notice that these were different times, when the air was purer and visibility was better. The millennia act as a filter, so that in our modern, murky, unfiltered thinking we can presently only have conjectures as to what we *will* find there, in the classical world, taken as if it lay in the future. We shall be capable of rising to the challenge of the future, of modernizing, only if we lose no time in rising to the challenge of the classical world, and before we can do that we must once and for all repudiate the mentality that avers 'they had not yet ...'. If there is something we talk about now that we do not find in them, that means only that we for some reason are still talking about something they long ago gave up talking about. Their silence is not because they have nothing to say: it conveys a more important message.

One such thunderous silence is Plato's doctrine of physical bodies. They are, he tells us, composed of geometrical shapes, so that, for example, fire is composed of tetrahedra.[6] Did Plato really not know that a point, a line, a triangle, a plane surface, have no volume? That they are abstractions and that the ideal tetrahedron will never be found? That we can spend the rest of time trying to establish the exact line of its perfect edge, just as Achilles will never catch up with the tortoise? Not only the edge but the ideal tetrahedron in its entirety is wholly elusive. What has happened to matter? Where is it? Well, that's just philosophical idealism for you! It needs to be fixed with materialism!

Let's try to fix it. Let's point out to Plato: you have failed to understand, you have failed to notice that there is matter in this tetrahedron we have drawn. There is the wood of the blackboard, the chalk, even the energy used in drawing the lines: these are all material. We find your tetrahedron bewildering, but we do understand chalk on a blackboard (materialism deals with tangible things). But these soon melt away, along with the Platonic solid! The blackboard, the line, the classroom, the 'solid', are all clear and easy to understand until we come to mindfulness. When we come to mindfulness, we find, to our amazement, that we must take our leave of metric space, and these material things become no more familiar and comprehensible to us than they would be to someone who was drunk out of their mind. We can have absolutely no doubt that Plato managed to do what we can do: namely, he crossed the threshold of unceasing mindfulness which grinds up the material objects of traditional perception.

Plato's silence in response to our bewilderment, our indignant 'Where has matter gone?' and 'How can they burn, these ideal tetrahedra nobody has ever seen?', firstly results from his reluctance to chop logic with us in the delusive space of traditional thinking and, secondly, delivers a message we are not yet ready, not yet mature enough, to hear. In the forest, there is not only indefinability, a superseding of images, a silencing of thought, wonder and horror. There is also *geometry*. More than that, there is actually nothing there *but* geometry. There is a sign at the entrance that reads:

'Anyone Who Has Never Studied Geometry: Keep Out!'[7] Geometry is our introduction to philo-sophy, the love of wisdom.

This is all the more unexpected because the first thing we noticed about the forest, and it is the reason we chose it as the topic for these two semesters, is what it inspires and instils by propelling us out of metric space. Of course, in the forest there is none of the geometry of lines and projections such as get drawn on a blackboard. The ungeometrical nature of the organic was noted some time ago, if by geometry we understand nothing beyond diagrams. So, is there another geometry, and is the forest pushing us out of metric space in order to make us finally understand *geo*-metry? Geometry as taking the measure of the earth? What would that be? It would be pre-Euclidean geometry, in the sense of not giving Euclid what he is asking for (or demanding) in his postulates and, first and foremost, not accepting his points as something that can be determined or found. Let us again follow the path of our heuristics, of expecting something we already surmise. The point in this early geometry will be Parmenidean and Zenonian, an unattainable focus on precision extending to everything. There is only one point and it coincides with everything. The small difficulty that my work on points in various courses about porosity and Wittgenstein has not been published[8] will be put right shortly, so I will not repeat myself, and anybody interested can look up the coincidence of opposites, of the absolute minimum and absolute maximum in a point, in my index to the two-volume collection of the works of Nicholas of Cusa.[9]

Given that our concern is not with the problems of geometry, we need go no further than the 'point'. The more so because the fundamental issue, which we should never have forgotten, is that Euclid *asked* to be conceded his point, that it was a convention. We conceded it and promptly forgot all about it. The result is that now that point seems to have as much right to exist in reality as a cup of coffee. We ought to have remembered, as Euclid himself always did, that the point on which all his geometry is based is only a convention. That, thank God, was finally recalled in the twentieth century.

Toward the end of the nineteenth century the keenest thinkers in the field of geometry became increasingly concerned about the lack of true rigour in Euclid's presentation. Undoubtedly, the invention of non-Euclidean geometries did much to spur the search for a correct and complete treatment of classical geometry. The most notable work of the new type was Hilbert's *Grundlagen der Geometrie* [*Principles of Geometry*], published in 1899.[10] David Hilbert (1862–1943) began by stating 21 axioms involving six primitive or undefined terms. [Chief among these was the point, *Bibikhin.*] He once made a famous comment (not actually published until 1935) to emphasize the importance of keeping the undefined terms totally abstract, that is, devoid of preconceived meaning: 'One must be able to say at all times – instead of "point, line, and plane" – "tables, chairs, and beer mugs."' Such a viewpoint was not widely accepted until well into the twentieth century and, of course, had never occurred to Euclid or his followers.[11]

That is a good rule for keeping the debate on the ground. We should take a beer mug and place it on a table that extends as far as another beer mug. This would be the best way to talk until such time as we actually know what a point is, and that becomes less clear every time we encounter one. Up until the present day, the 'point', as well as other geometrical terms, has existed only thanks to our ability to grasp and hold an object. It was not the point we could see and hold; all we had was our ability to grasp and hold, and the thing we did that to most often, and with great gusto, we called a point or something derived from a point.

Everything about geometrical constructs is beautiful and indisputable, but the elements of geometry are floating in thin air. The fact that they are mere conventions is blindingly obvious, and they hold true only because people have agreed to believe that they should. In Euclid's original definition, a point 'is that which has no part'. The ungraspability of a point is established with a deliberate paradox. I say it was deliberate, because in the classical world it was a commonplace that something that has no parts has nothing with which to have contact with anything else. If it merged with something else, it would add nothing to the whole of that other, or, if it entered as a constituent part of that other, it would rend it apart, because nothing in the other would be able to be in contact with a thing that had no part.

Whether it is easy, difficult, or impossible to obtain a point, the only way it can be done is by concentration. The still unresolved paradoxes of Zeno and Parmenides show that concentration of the mind alone is insufficient. I have no time to repeat what has been said in earlier lectures, and would ask those who are thinking about this for the first time to take on trust, without ifs or buts, that in the most literal manner, in the problem of the point, the basis of geo-metry, we come back to mindfulness. All the observations on the relationship of the point to time, about the point as the present, according to Aristotle and Hegel, which has also been previously discussed in detail, provide the context of what we need now to engage with. Our topic is Plato's unexpected geometry where we would have expected to find matter, the geo-metry of the forest, the forest as geo-metry without Euclidean metric space. Here is what a modern historian of thought has to say about Plato's 'eidetic atomism', which means that in place of the expected atoms of matter we encounter pure *eide*: '*Diese kühne und in ihrer Weise großzügige Theorie der Materie ohne Prinzip der Materie hat weder im Altertum noch später Nachahmung, ja auch nur Verständnis gefunden.*' 'This bold and, in its way, ambitious theory of matter without the actual principle of matter was not taken up, or even understood, either in classical times or subsequently.'[12]

Whether or not it was understood, whether it is easy or difficult, we need to buckle down. As Plato says in *The Epinomis* (992a), '[T]his is the way, this the nurture, these the studies, whether difficult or easy, this the path to pursue.'[13] The *Epinomis* here is a legacy, bequeathing the law of bliss, the law in the sense we have been speaking of, the law of humankind, of its nature; happiness in the sense that it was experienced by the Pilgrim when he discovered unceasing prayer, constant mindfulness. The whole history of thought speaks with striking unanimity of the happiness of humanity when it returns to the law. We read the final pages of *The Epinomis*, and this is so similar to the joyous pages of *The Pilgrim*. When he comes back to the law, to religion and faith, Plato tells us, a man will be freed from his distress (which we referred to, following the Gospels, as 'the issue of blood'):

> And the man who has acquired all these things in this manner is he whom I account the most truly wise: of him I also assert, both in jest and in earnest, that when one of his like completes his allotted span at death, I would say if he still be dead, he will not partake any more of the various sensations then as he does now, but having alone partaken of a single lot [i.e. he will be vouchsafed wholeness, unity, *monasticism, Bibikhin*] and having become one out of many, will be happy and at the same time most wise and blessed. (992b)

We shall need to return to *The Epinomis*, because our main themes of the law, religion, constant mindfulness, and the forest in the sense of matter come together there really very clearly. But we shall remain firmly focused on what has just intrigued us most: matter as number; the forest whose very breeze, we cannot doubt, despatches metric space; and geography, which, according to Plato, has pure geometry as its law. We are not ready for this, to proceed by way of clues and glimpses, such as one that has been suggested to us, of seeing the pillars of a mosque, symbolizing the pillars of the universe, as a forest, as trees, and in some way subordinate to the sacred number of '17'. We can, if so inclined, link anything to anything else, any idea to any other. We, however, will prefer to admit failure, inability, rather than rush to associate the forest with a number, or agree with the majority of historians of thought who believe Plato was getting a bit carried away here, coming up against the limitations of idealism, or even, as Alexey Losev manages to claim in line with his preoccupations, that Plato was a man of his time who 'lived and worked' in slave ownership, with the result that he projects the callousness of a slave owner on to the world of ideas, and that his geometry is based on heartlessness. 'Because number, devoid of qualities or indifferent to them, is precisely his basic principle, lacking any personal or "spiritual" dimension. Accordingly it is entirely predictable that Plato's philosophy, having developed as far as its limitations allowed, ends up with the doctrine that his eternal and divine forms are numbers.'[14]

This is sad. I do not think Marxism was the cause of this blunder. More probable is what Nicolai Hartmann noted: that matter as number is such an amazing leap in Plato's thinking that it has not been understood to this day.[15] If Losev effectively passed on this, preferring to say nothing, that is because in his curious formulation he only hinted at a strict, harsh discipline, also to be found in the structure of the ancient *polis*, which succeeded in binding in slavery anybody unwilling to accept the risk of being free and taking responsibility for themselves. It was a degree of disciplining of thought that we have forgotten, but which is no less unyielding than mathematics. We have worked our own way round to the discipline and school of constant mindfulness. There is, of course, plenty about that in Plato. It is clear that without schooling, without strict discipline, it will be impossible for us to understand the riddle and mission of Plato, namely matter as number. Discipline is undoubtedly a necessary condition here, but is it a sufficient condition? We may not have enough vision.

Does anybody know why the forest is digital?

The forest is wood, and wood is fuel. We take heat and light from fire, the burning of matter. Fire, according to Plato, is a tetrahedron. Not something in the form of a tetrahedron, not a tetrahedron filled up with something, just a tetrahedron. It is not that somewhere baffling processes are taking place with the primary elements in attendance and the tetrahedron is a kind of assembly or abstract function signalling or symbolizing them.

To our difficulties, deadlock actually, must be added the fact that if Plato understands the element of number, the one, in what is called a substantialist way, as a simple concentration, a happy totality, as a blessed fulfilment of *everything*, how is he to get anything out of such a one, which is clearly singular and clearly equivalent to the maximum integer of the universe? How is he to construct anything with it when a tetrahedron requires at least four different points? We land ourselves in the problem of the difference between the substantialist so-called Pythagorean number and the arithmetical number, which are completely different things. A lot of care has been needed to avoid getting burned by this distinction.

Again the admirable Nicolai Hartmann warns us:

> The theory of *Timaeus* represents, in terms of its content, a synthesis of atomism and the doctrine of forms, which should be considered impossible in view of the natural antithesis of these two doctrines. There has to this day been no thorough investigation of this historical topic. This is one of the numerous gaps in classical historiography of philosophy in the last hundred years that result from its deficient understanding of the problem.[16]

That is, the problem is not in the method and apparatus, but in too much understanding: everything is immediately abundantly clear to the researcher, just as the slave-owning undertow of Plato's idea was, unfortunately, only too clear to Losev. Hartmann sees no problem where Plato did, and is perhaps even a little smug at having been able to sort it out as

Plato, unable to resolve the contradictions between materialism and idealism, failed to.

Owing to the fact that the 'contradictions' between Plato and Aristotle have by and large been invented, it is even constructive to read the two philosophers as, on the contrary, complementary to each other. There is the brilliant, characteristic, and generally accepted denial by Aristotle of the existence of species and genera – 'the animal in general' exists only in the imagination, the species of donkeys perhaps a little more but still not really – and all that really exists is this particular donkey, and another one over there. He places a taboo, in other words, when inspecting this particular donkey, with those particular ears and those big eyes, on hypostasizing donkeyness; a taboo on extending it any further than this particular donkey. Or, if you like, we can eliminate donkeys altogether by counting them as one, two, and three but remembering while doing so that we are counting something that does not exist, and take full responsibility for the fact that we are doing, operating, something that does not exist. That makes all applied mathematics a risky business when, if you forget when counting 'one thing, two things, three things', no matter what they may be, it has already slipped into the realm of things that are not there.

And what if applied mathematics is calculating without including what is being counted after the number? The number will have reality if we see it as counting 'this thing here': that is, if we are viewing the donkey, not abstracting the number back to a general species or genus. At this point, Aristotle seems unable to help us further and it looks as though (although there can always be a surprise in store) we need to go back to Plato, to see the number itself no less specifically, as 'thisness' (*haeccaeitas*), than the donkey. Can we see the number, can we look straight at it in the same way we can look a donkey straight in the eyes?

Yes, we can, and, oddly enough, the experience will affect us more directly and strongly than our encounter with the donkey.

This experience is not possible with a denumerable number, an element of mathematical operations, because any number there as an element of a set of integers must be abstract and generalized, totally indistinguishable from any other number, since otherwise the set will fall apart. But actually, to our relief, we find we are not being called upon to distinguish between a number with which a close encounter is possible and a mathematical number, because modern mathematics gets by perfectly well without the concept of number and deals instead with structures and processes. In other words, just as geometry repudiates the indefinable and undefined concept of the point and is entirely willing, according to Hilbert, to talk instead about a beer mug, so modern mathematical terminology does not include the concept of number. Philosophy was all for donating number to mathematics (at least, general and philosophical reference books say that number is 'one of the basic concepts of mathematics'), but now mathematics is returning the gift and philosophy will have to return to it, which is something else for us to look forward to.

Aristotle has experience of encounters with 'this thing here', Plato of encounters with forms or, later, with numbers. Just as 'this thing here' cannot be part of a calculation, since otherwise it will cease to exist, so Plato's forms cannot be counted in terms of one, two. This is what I call moving out of metric space. Let us tentatively, without becoming prematurely confident, say that by moving out of the space of counting, auditing, and structuring, we are returning to the early geometric number. I am setting myself that as a task for the future. Just as Plato has long been urging us to think more thoroughly about number, so he is also calling upon us to review geometry. I am merely accepting the challenge which, as an old man, he left at the very end of *The Epinomis*.

In order to train minds capable of mastering this knowledge,

> one must teach the pupil many things beforehand, and continually strive hard to habituate him in childhood and youth. And therefore there will be need of studies: the most important and first is of numbers in themselves; not of those which are corporeal, but of the whole origin of the odd and the even, and the greatness of their influence on the nature of reality. (990c)

I understand this to mean the invariable symmetry of all that exists, which is called real number.

> When he has learnt these things, there comes next after these what they call by the very ridiculous name of geometry ... and this will be clearly seen by him who is able to understand it to be a marvel not of human, but of divine origin. (990d)

Numbers themselves, like geometry itself rather than the ridiculous way in which it may be understood, are an invitation and a task for us. Let us initially try to approach this task from a fairly easy and uncontroversial direction. A confident counting of things, 'one window, two windows', or, which is essentially the same, of numbers, 'one number, two numbers', is possible because the generalizations are, as it were, ready and, indeed, waiting for content. Let us imagine a pit that we want to fill up. Who dug the pit, and how, into which the set of natural numbers is thrown? The series can be very long, but the pit is invariably bigger, as if anticipating and inviting it in. Counting things such as the stars in the sky will surely run into difficulties, not because of any lack of space, but only because it is difficult to count them.

Now at this point there is something to which I want to draw your attention, namely what might be called the 'lure of the pit', or 'the lure of the heap',[17] which seems to have a will of its own to grow bigger, to accumulate, and which, if we did not keep our eyes open, did not protest and resist, would level things down even more. A random example: 300 years ago, a census of the population, conducted as it is nowadays, would have been impossible. The difference between a working man and a woman seemed just too great, and this was even more true of an old man or a child, so the count was based on households or smallholdings. In a modern census, all classes of the population are, as it were, lumped together, levelled out. What is causing this virtually limitless trend towards generalization? Obviously, the fact that ultimately everything belongs to one primal category, the totality of all that exists, is, as it were, sucking everything into itself, demanding enumeration, and avidly seeking to be filled up. Moreover, we know in advance that there is no danger of the categories running out of space, that there might not be a receptacle to count everything into. Everything – and that is a lot of stuff – belongs ultimately to the One, to one world, one universe. We have always enumerated too little, ascribing things to the universe. Everything always fits into it. It has room. Everything ultimately can be generalized by the very fact of belonging to one and the same universe.

This power of unity, of wholeness, encompassing, drawing in, clearly can never be captured by counting. The universe is of a size that, no matter how much you put into it, there will still be room for more. Trying to put more and more into One is clearly an inadequate, negative, or deluded response to the challenge of unity. We can see that the numerical series gets its power from its infinity, from the negative knowledge that the power of unity cannot be exhausted by endless listing. The origin of number is thus negative. A numerical series, infinite counting, are based on a tacit assumption that we *can* safely engage in endless enumeration because unity *is* strong enough to accommodate that. We enumerate all the constituent parts and abilities of a human being, but then realize that they can be further subdivided, and that there are others yet to be discovered, not yet investigated.

We encounter something analogous with time: its infinity stems from our own irremediably late arrival on the world scene, from our being late for the event of the world. No matter how many years we add to our own lifespan or to that of humankind, we can be reassured by our intuitive certainty that the event of the world has infinite room to draw on. A supply of unified, official time is reliably provided by our lateness; it can, and should, never end.

Just as, apart from official, levelled-down time, there is being-time, so, apart from the negatively defined unit of arithmetic, there is a unit or unity in the experience of the whole, but as a unit of *experience* we are much more directly affected by it. More directly, I would say, than the live donkey in front of us: the latter affects us on a living and organic level, but the experience of unity is, by definition, everything, integral. The experience of unity is the same as of the point as concentration, of mindfulness, of prayer as the submission of everything to the one who is no part of being, no part of anything, and yet has the most intimate and direct relationship to everything of anything.

For the time being, we do not see how *this* all-encompassing unit can move, create order, a set or calculation, and yet the Pythagoreans and Plato talk of substantial *numbers*, not a substantial unit.[18] This difficult question we shall address next time.

A request for papers, on this topic, or more general. A competition is to be announced nationally. Those submitted now will be eligible.

Lecture 5, 7 October 1997

I am trying to resolve the riddle set by Plato, of having pure geometrical shape in place of matter. We spend a lot of time trying to guess things. Averintsev once said that Russians may not be particularly sharp-witted, but they are good at guessing.

It would be better if I did not try to guess. Without guesswork, of course, it is difficult to know where you should look, and, more importantly, there may just be no point in looking because it is unlikely you are going to find anything. The real problem with guesswork, though, is that you are more likely to start trying to fit your solution to the answer you want to get. My guess is that Plato gives himself over body and soul to the forest: that is, that he ceases to see himself as separate from the forest and intuits that everything, through the air, water, food, the race, is entirely part of everything else. He ceases to ask himself questions about why everything is just as it is, why the sky is above and the earth below, and becomes intoxicated, like the Pythagoreans and Parmenides, with the suchness of everything, that everything is precisely as it is. Everything he sees, everything he thinks, fuses into an ultimate, reassuring experience, an experience of serenity and peace that everything that is, is just as it is, and that everything that has been was just as it was, and that everything that will be, however it turns out, will be just as it will. This experience is at once moral, an acceptance of all that is, and it is mystical, because it opens a channel to ultimate, final, full divine knowledge at the outer limit. When God at the beginning of Genesis says, 'Let there be light: and there was light. And God saw the light, that it was good,' and the same is repeated with everything else, that 'Let there be' is not design, not engineering. Light is not being given a definition, a specification, a description, to which what appears is to conform. Light already is, since what is said is, 'Let there be light.' God himself is taken by the ecstasy of identity.

This merging not only does not lead to any blurring of distinctiveness but, on the contrary, creates a structure of things being identical to themselves, of sameness, of thisness and suchness (*immennost'*). In other words, we, and we are again guessing here, having been swallowed up by the forest, find ourselves in the realm of logic. But are the foundations of logic identical to those of mathematics? It would be good to find that was the case, but we are suddenly faced with a problem. Wittgenstein warned that there would be difficulties with identity, and the difficulty begins with the trap that there seems to be no problem. I also need to bear in mind the additional problem of how identity relates to unity and unity to number, but when we get down to starting to grapple with this, we find that guesswork is no longer helpful.

Or it is, indeed, distinctly unhelpful in the case of the clue of the Cross. The Cross is the tree. Well, obviously, well-informed people will tell us; indeed, it is also the well-known World Tree of every mythology in the world. So it not only relates to the forest but in fact itself is the forest.

> Of all relic discoveries the most impressive was that of the True Cross (the cross upon which Jesus was crucified, found in September 335 or in 326, according to other accounts).... [Prompted by a dream, Helena, mother of the emperor Constantine, *Bibikhin*] located the place where the Cross lay buried and had the wood unearthed.... The power of the Cross, the history of the wood, and the story of its discovery became legendary. [In Christian myth this relic of Christ's death dated back to the mortal origins of humanity. Innumerable cures attested to the authenticity of the Cross, *Bibikhin*.] Through the symbolism of the Cross early Christian imagery perpetuated, and at the same time transformed, the myths of the World Tree. The sacred drama of Christ's birth, death, and resurrection participates in the rejuvenating rhythms of the fecund cosmos. Early Christians identi-fied the Cross of Christ as the World Tree, which stood at the centre of cosmic space and stretched from earth to heaven. The Cross was fash-ioned of wood from the tree of knowledge of Good and Evil which grew in the Garden of Eden. Below the tree lies Adam's buried skull, baptized in Christ's blood. The bloodied cross-tree gives forth the oil, wheat, grapes, and herbs used to prepare the materials administered in the sacraments that revitalize a fallen world. The Italian Renaissance painter Piero della Francesca later depicted the myth of the True Cross in his frescoes in Arezzo, Italy. They portray the death of Adam, fallen at the foot of the Tree that provides wood for the crucifix on which Jesus is slain. The wood of the cross becomes the instrument of salvation and the holiest matter in Christendom, and the cross itself became the focus of tales of fantastic historical episodes.[1]

Let us continue this brief excursion into the World Tree, a myth of pri-maeval humanity, and since we are not primaeval but have progressed, we can accordingly look down condescendingly on the forest and the World Tree. We note from the heights of our scientific understanding that there are two types of World Tree, one vertical, the other horizontal. Admittedly, the distinction is more for convenience of description and classification, and in the World Tree the horizontal and vertical are interwoven and merge. In Genesis, we find both trees: the Tree of Knowledge is vertical and enables contact with the gods, its sanctity impugned only by a taboo, a moral nuance optional in the mythology. What the Ophites, serpent-worshippers, did was simply to remove the moral veneer, the tinge of transgression, from the biblical story and restore the vertical tree to its eternal role of linking the earth below with the divine world above, of ascending to ultimate knowledge and wisdom, the knowledge of good and evil. The horizontal tree is the heavenly tree of life, the source of fertility. It, too, has a taboo attached: it may not be cut down if procreation and abundance are not to end. A fairly recent television interview with one of the few remaining primaeval sages indicated that for him Europeans, with all their pretensions, their manners and clothing, were no longer people of the forest; as far as he was concerned, they were the dead and the harbingers of death.

In Norse mythology, Yggdrasil (in old Norse, they said *mimameidr*), the giant rowan tree, sank its roots down into three worlds: Niflheim, the lower world of darkness; Jotunheim, the world of giants; and Asgard, the city of the Æsir gods.[2] Similarly, there are three keys by the roots of the World Rowan Tree: Urðarbrunnr is the key of prediction; Mimisbrunnr is the key of wisdom; and Hvergelmir is the key of passion. The Boiling Cauldron is where a monster, Níðhöggr, resides which is engaged in gnawing at a root of the World Tree. Applying our basic classification, this is, of course, a vertical tree. As in the Bible, there are the Norns, who live by Yggdrasil near Urðarbrunnr, and they are associated with good and evil. As in Socrates, they assist at childbirth.

When the world comes to an end with Ragnarök, the gods, too, may die, as in Wagner's *Götterdämmerung*, but the World Tree, the tree of the cosmos, although damaged, will remain and will give birth to two beings, Líf (life) and Lífþrasir (lover of life), from whom humankind will be reborn. The tree is more enduring than the gods. As in the Ophite reading of the Bible, God creates only the horizontal tree of matter, while the vertical tree that hints at limits of the divine is not and could not be revealed by God.

Traditionally, the tree pierces and simultaneously links different tiers of life. In Siberian religions in the Altai Mountains, a tree is installed in the hole in the roof of the tent. It is beneath the roof in the human world, but above the roof in the cosmic and divine world; smoke from the stove inside, entwining the tree, rises to the upper tiers. The shaman himself then climbs the tree in the direction indicated by the smoke, ascending to the higher world up the World Tree. By doing so, he is of course also taking the risk of dying on the tree for humankind.

The shaman clings to the tree, merges with it, or, we might say, is crucified on it, because he is taking a terrible physical and spiritual risk. This cleaving of the shaman to the tree brings to mind the relationship of the Crucified to the wood of the Cross. The wood raises him and they become one. Rather than repudiate the Cross as an instrument of execution, Christ clings to and connects with it. This theme of merging, even of identification of Christ with the Cross, is evident in an unusual 1939 sculpture in elm by Ossip Zadkine.[3] Born in 1890 in Smolensk, he died in Paris in 1967 and is best known for his 1951 sculpture *The Destroyed City* in Rotterdam, which depicts a broken human figure with arms outstretched in horror. Zadkine's elm Christ appears to be convulsed, but his arms are like bare tree branches. This merging with the Cross is more evident in the earliest extant crucifixes, in which Christ does not have his eyes lowered in mortal anguish but is alive, with his eyes wide open. The Cross seems more the place where his divinity is made manifest, and he seems to be reaching out with his arms intentionally.

This corresponds to something about the Cross which is now almost overlooked and which Pavel Florensky (1882–1937) in his thinking about the divinity of the Cross needed to reconstruct: the wood of the Cross itself has features of divinity.[4] It is life-giving. That is, the Cross itself is a tree, like the body of the god. The Cross was absolutely the most important of all the relics of Christianity as a result of the awareness of this fusion of the deity with his tree.

In the Cross, people see both trees, and often refer to its horizontal as representing the human world and the vertical as humanity standing before God, which is not apart from but rises above the horizontal. A variety of pious and pleasing interpretations are possible. Out of this range of interpretations, meditations, mythologems, and other kinds of mystical understanding, what matters for us, what we are reaching for, is just one thing: the Cross unexpectedly points in the same direction as Plato with his tetrahedron in place of the first element of matter, fire. The Cross is wood, it is the World Tree, and it is geometric. An easy and rather widespread notion is that the wood is matter and the Cross is form brought to and superimposed on matter. If we settle for that, we will have got one problem out of the way and can move expeditiously on to the next. The trouble is that, having adopted that approach, we can no less expeditiously deal with any other difficulty and will end up in the unenviable position of the cultural historian, a historian of thought whose sole mission is to 'assimilate and present' his or her material. Well, who cares anyway that, if we stubbornly refuse to acknowledge the dualism of matter and form, we will have to wave goodbye to all traditional history of philosophy and culture? Away with them! So we'll be empty-handed. Sooner that than find ourselves with a museum on our hands and playing the part of museum attendants. We're better off out in the open and empty-handed.

Well, actually, no. We are not going to make the obvious mistake of thinking that Plato chose one pole on the materialism–idealism spectrum and then made sure everything he said conformed to it. The materialism–idealism divide dates from long after Plato, and is a great deal shallower than his profundity. His conundrum that matter is pure geometry *exactly* reflects the mystery of the Cross. The Cross is not a philosophical construct, a primitive representation or abstraction of the World Tree: the Cross *is* the forest. It is not the Cross that needs to be explained in terms of the World Tree but, on the contrary, if we are to understand anything about the World Tree at all, the only possibility is by way of the Cross.

So, it will be better if we again mill around on the spot where we stumbled. The dark, primaeval forest, the later forest of the megapolises, tobacco, alcohol, and drugs, all liberate us from metric space. In the forest, you are disorientated. The forest is in the Cross just as pure geo-metry is in the tetrahedron. We find our way through by distinguishing number from number, ontological number from arithmetical number. It transpires that mathematics does not know what number is and surrenders it to philosophy. So much the better; that only makes things easier for us. It means we now have to construct a theory of number. The commonsense theory is clear: the generalizations derive from experience. We supposedly count our fingers, or sheep, then look away from our fingers, or the sheep, and arrive at pure numbers. Let us discard that out of hand as a piece of nonsense that can only trip us up. In the first place, before we can start counting fingers or sheep we need to standardize them: that is, they need to have been strong-armed into the realm of arithmetic. Abstract counting, then, was there first, before specific counting. Secondly, if counting were an abstraction from specific counting, where did the infinite set of natural numbers come from?

After all, in practice no one has ever counted up to infinity, and the total number of objects in the entire world is most probably finite, so that in practice we have no grounds at all to believe in an infinite set of numbers. It has come from a different source, which we started thinking about last time.

We talked about the alluring, attractive power of the whole: it wants to be named, enumerated, although we know in advance that it cannot be exhausted through enumeration. We can sense enumeration's inadequacy in the face of the whole at every step. For example, there are so many members in a collective. We immediately add that, of course, the team is more than the mechanical sum of its members: it has an extra quality. Has this quality been added because quantity has been transformed into quality? This is a bad law of dialectical materialism that results from poor eyesight: the new quality derives not from some quantitative addition but because the set under consideration has, barely perceptibly, unexpectedly, been drawn towards unity. The whole is beginning to shine in it more strongly.

It would be more precise to say that the way of viewing it has switched; there has been a change of viewpoint from one unity to a different one. The inclusive, attractive power of unity cannot be encapsulated by enumerating its components. The universe is a heap, and no matter how many components you throw on to it, there will still be room for more. And that is true of virtually any unity. Behind the family, we detect the genus, and here is where we need to seek the cause of the inexhaustible bounty of nature. We cannot construct a cell from its constituents because it is a unity. Why it is a unity is a separate matter, and it is as difficult to find an answer to that as it is impossible to create a unity, a wholeness: it has to be found, intuited; it has to give itself away. It is impossible to detect elementary particles, neutrinos or quarks; it is impossible because of the 'natural' method of physics. The reason it is called natural science is because it is unable, is not supposed to, has never learned how to, deal with anything that is not a whole. Any whole, any unity, cannot by definition be mechanically assembled from parts. That is a peculiarity of the structure of any unity in nature.

The issue of the elusiveness of wholeness in nature is different from the issue of wholeness in technology, where, for example, there is no difficulty in enumerating how many parts a wheel consists of, and I cannot raise it here. Some other time.

For now, let us hold on to our thread of how and why the forest proves to be geometry. It is so tempting to try to fill up unity with quantity, because we feel the need to respond to it in some way. It challenges us, but perhaps the purest way to redeem thought is to leave unity alone.

So leave it alone we shall, but whether we worry at it or leave it alone and in peace, it remains unassailable. Nevertheless, we understand the origin of numbers and their strength: their infinite reserves. We know negatively and not necessarily consciously, perhaps intuitively, that mere enumeration will never exhaust the power of unity. So let us rest assured that there will be no end to our enumeration.

The origin of number is, then, negative. Numbers with their infinite counting have as their base the hidden intuition that it is *possible* to carry on safely enumerating till the end of time: unity is strong enough to cope with any amount of enumeration. We have enumerated all the constituent parts and capabilities of the cell, but that is not the end: there are more fragmentary parts, newly discovered, unresearched. We encountered something similar in the computation of mechanical time. Its boundlessness is explained by our ineradicably late arrival in the occurrence of the world. No matter how many years we add to ourselves or to humankind, we can do so secure in the knowledge that, precisely because of our secret awareness that we know nothing of its origin, the event that is the world will be sufficient for us to draw on it indefinitely. The steady movement of unified or official time is reliably ensured, again negatively, by our late arrival, by the fact that the world was already there when we arrived. It can never come to an end.

Just as, separate from the official, standardized time of negative origin there is positive being-time, so, separate from the negatively founded unit of counting, there is the unity of the whole. To use Wittgenstein's expression, any unit of counting is a test or a measure of the unassailable whole. We approach it this way and that, calling it our experimental number. The more we operate with these measures, these tests of unity, the more the experience of unity recedes into the unfamiliar, something we do not know how to deal with. Plato needs to remind us that the experience of number affects us more directly and fully than, say, the experience of our encounter with the donkey. The latter concerns, let us say, the living, the vegetative in us, and even then not always; while the experience of unity affects us always and completely. The experience of unity is at the same time both very rare and definitive, like the full stops we put at the end of every sentence. We can put them anywhere and everywhere, but do not even notice the charge of a full stop, the experience of concentration, because we have become completely used to operating with them. Prayer as the exposing of everything to what is nothing out of everything is something we undertake very rarely; we are usually busy with something else. In reality, though, we are showing ourselves constantly, always posturing, only we have become confused about who we are, and who it is that we are posing in front of. For a child, for example, the face of the person to whom it tells everything and before whom it poses, until emancipated from the family, is identified with the face of the parent, simply because the parent is constantly imposing a particular agenda. God does not impose himself.

So, number is a measure of unity as a whole, and not the other way round. Unity is not the measure of number. The dimensional number comes from a different, negative, space than unity. The shadow takes its orientation from the tree and not vice versa. But, even while recognizing this, we do not see for the present how all-embracing unity can move, or count, give form to order, a series. For now all we see is one unity, and yet the Pythagoreans and Plato speak of substantial *numbers*, not only about a substantial unit. I understand one wholeness. Two wholenesses, however, by virtue of there being two of them, will immediately cease to be joint or separate wholeness. Or am I wrong?

Substantial numbers are a difficult issue, and I have no confidence at all we will be able to resolve it; there may not be enough mindfulness, our attention may stray to other matters. It is tempting to say that there simply are no such numbers. The main problem is that we have no idea how to set about resolving this issue. For the time being, therefore, I will skirt round it. Actually, I do have a negative hypothesis, so here it is. Aristotle says clearly and distinctly that number is matter: ἀριθμὸν ... ὕλην τοῖς οὖσι (986a, 16–17), but in the context of criticizing the Pythagoreans and Plato. Number and *eidos* seem to be the same thing for him and he uses the terms interchangeably in *Metaphysics* A6 and elsewhere.[5] Or so, at least, people say. It is said that if we listen attentively, as we did, to Plato's idea that the forest is number, we will find Aristotle among our critics.

This problem really is one we are going to have to face up to here and now. It would be highly distasteful to try refereeing philosophers' opinions: 'In this instance, we agree with Plato and oppose Aristotle.' We need either to agree with Aristotle's criticism of Plato or to disagree with it. We are really not going to start haranguing Aristotle along the lines of progressivist scholarship: 'He committed the error of ... failed to take account of, did not understand ...' It would be just too grotesque to 'referee' in this manner a thinker who lived 2,300 years ago. The only respectable and elegant way out of our predicament over Aristotle's criticism of Pythagoreanism is either to manfully jettison everything we have said about number within the forest, about the forest as number, or find precisely that same thought in Aristotle: the forest as number; the forest as the Cross, pure geometry.

Immediately, as if for our boldness, we are rewarded, although matter is one of the most difficult topics in Aristotle. The difficulties are of two kinds. Aristotle does not tie himself down: having propounded one thesis, he does not consider himself disqualified from later putting forward a different one. His truth is on the move. The second difficulty, which is a difficulty for Aristotle himself, is that primal matter must not be 'like this here', because then it would be possible to imagine a different kind of matter, meaning there were two or maybe more. There needs to be just one kind of primal matter, but if that is so, where does the difference between substances come from? From different structures of the primal matter? But if we are saying that there are within it proto-structures with the potential for further formation, we are back to dealing with structures, and we wanted to be dealing with pure matter. Certainly, we find different kinds of matter in Aristotle, but the difference comes about from the depth of our scrutiny of it: the immediate matter for illness, for example, is humankind, but humankind itself is *eidos*, and matter is placed at one remove.

One thing Aristotle is predictably definite about is his refusal to accept that matter can be located anywhere beyond the boundaries of things and separate from them. Just as there is only imaginary donkeyness separate from this particular donkey in front of us, so matter, too, will either be here in front of us or it will be a mental construct. We can understand from this why Aristotle should emphatically object, as he does at the beginning of Book 2 of *On Generation and Corruption*, that 'those thinkers are in error who postulate, beside the bodies [four elements, *Bibikhin*] we have mentioned, a single matter – and that a corporeal and separable matter'.[6] Aristotle's immediate objection is that this matter would duplicate the already known elements: it would either be light like air and fire, or heavy like earth, and so on. It might perhaps be even more basic than the elements, but certainly not of a different kind from them.

Why? Was Aristotle really incapable of imagining imperceptible matter? We are only too good at that, in the case of radiation, say. Ultraviolet and infrared rays are imperceptible. Quantum leaps are imperceptible. Why is it that for Aristotle a body, and any primary matter will be a body, 'cannot possibly exist without a "perceptible contrariety"'? (329a). Because his perception was more refined. Radiation, owing to its effects on the body, would definitely be considered perceptible: the boundary of perception extended to include that. The same would be true of ultraviolet light: that 'different' light, or 'different', 'higher', ethereal fire was perceived, so to speak, as a change of mood before it was noticed that it caused a suntan. We are mistaken also in thinking that quantum mechanics as an intellectual (which is not the same as a mathematical) system was not elaborated by classical thinking in the topic of the automaton and spontaneity: there *was* an intellectual system of analogous complexity in the teaching about the soul.

When Aristotle talks of 'perception by the senses', he includes intuition and mood; at all events, he includes more than just direct impingement on the sensory organs. If the soul is in some way everything, then everything in a specific way will affect it. Today we have a foreboding that somewhere, in some dark, still place, someone – aliens, the government, the mafia, an international conspiracy – is up to something we cannot detect, do not know about, cannot perceive, cannot influence; or that in the bowels of substance, processes beyond our ken are brewing. Aristotle would have called that induced, superstitious. Everything affects me in one way or another; I react effectively to it in my own individual way, and can influence it just as long as I do not close my eyes or numb myself with noise.

Aristotle's objection to Plato's geometrical matter is precisely that such matter would be separate from what affects me personally, just as abstract values do not affect me. But we have already said that identity and unity affect *all* of me more than some random passing donkey. Again we are back with the problem of so-called substantial numbers. So that is the root of the difficulty! For Aristotle, numbers are apart, like geometric shapes. That is why, without explanation, he rails against Plato's tetrahedrons again and again. It is impossible for abstract planes to be the wet-nurse (i.e. primary matter) (329a). Being is complete being, the being of things, which means that 'things' must be understood differently. And that is how Aristotle does understand them; they are not peeled away from *eidos*. And that is where we need to look for what we are surmising in Aristotle: ontological numbers, number as being? Almost certainly.

For the present, if Aristotle says something 'exists', he is automatically conferring fullness of being on it. He does not look for 'existence' among intellectual abstractions. 'Our own doctrine is that although there is a matter of the perceptible bodies (a matter out of which the so-called "elements" come-to-be), it has no separate existence, but is always bound up with a contrariety' (329a).

With great aplomb, taking a good swing, Aristotle approaches the topic of matter at the beginning of his *Physics*, and the examples he gives there for matter, or the substratum, the underlying *hypokeimenon*, speak volumes.[7] The examples are of education and formation: first the becoming of a musical man from a not-musical man; and then the forming of an image, a statue from bronze. We can say, from being not-musical, the man becomes musical. Was being not-musical the substratum underlying the musical man? No, because the condition of being not-musical ceased to be, and the substratum is so called because it continues to lie beneath. On the other hand, we do not say from being a man he came to be musical. That would imply that we had in mind that a man is always unmusical. That is something we do not know. He may be as yet not-musical, but it is not necessarily the nature of man to be unmusical. Another example: we speak of 'a statue coming to be out of bronze'. A form out of something formless? Here we need to differentiate. Just as it is not necessarily the case that before becoming musical a man was unmusical, so bronze before a sculptor gives it form is not necessarily formless. It is only carelessness that makes it seem so to us. Formlessness is no more the natural state of bronze than being a sculpture is, and in just the same way it is not necessarily formless. Formlessness is not the substratum of the statue: bronze is.

Note that a person is not entirely neutral, not wholly indifferent to becoming musical; it is not meaningless to say that people want to be, are attracted to being, musical. Matter is not chaos. It is not meaningless for a sculptor to say that the bronze wants to be a statue. Aristotle's third example of a substratum clarifies this situation (190b). There is always something that underlies, from which that which comes to be proceeds: for instance, animals and plants from seed. In this third example, it is quite clear that the substratum has a reserve of movement in it. A person reaches out for the art of music the way a seed reaches out to develop into a living being. In order to understand how bronze reaches out to be a sculpture, we must remember that the Greeks were not at all interested in the microscopic world: for them the world they knew was their microscope and telescope. The bronze reaches out to the sculpture ... we need now to return to this idea of Aristotle's, to seek to penetrate it with the aid of the theories of modern physics about self-organization. We shall ask, however, as physicists cannot: what do we mean by 'self-'?

I shall read out, to reprise and consolidate what has already been said, a long quotation from the *Physics* (190b), the point of which is that it introduces nothing new. 'Thus, clearly, from what has been said, whatever comes to be is always complex. There is, on the one hand, (a) something which comes into existence, and again (b) something which becomes that – the latter (b) in two senses, either the subject or the opposite. By the "opposite" I mean the "unmusical", by the "subject" "man"' (190b, 10).[8]

To repeat: the 'matter' for becoming musical was, make no mistake, not the chaos of 'unmusical' but human; the chaos of unmusical is the contrary of musical and, paradoxically, it is lodged not in the person but in the musical: until the aim of becoming musical was formulated there was no unmusical; 'the absence of shape or form or order are the "opposite", and the bronze or stone or gold the subject"' (190b, 15). We tend to think that the matter itself was chaos and that it is overcome by *eidos*. Not a bit of it. Before *eidos*, matter is not chaos. As soon as *eidos* comes on the scene, the absence of shape or form or order also appears.

Now, just as the seed wants to develop, does every substratum contain this movement within it? Exactly so, we read in the *Physics*, Book 1; and in Book 2 we find matter and movement placed side by side (200a, 31). Matter and its movements, the forest and its history. If the forest is like the seed, it, too, will have its history of development.

Lecture 6, 14 October 1997

The subject and the contrary, ὑποκείμενον and ἀντικείμενον: we are invited to distinguish between these two things. Why on earth would we want to do that? That is the question, and the more abrasively we ask it, the better. Why do we do anything anyway? (God knows, we are always doing something. Anything.) What are you doing? I am studying, doing that something that is studying. And since I am doing it, it means that what I am doing does not yet exist. That would seem to mean I am making my something out of nothing. But, no, it is not being made out of nothing; it is only God who creates out of nothing. So what is it that I am making my something out of? From some other something. I am wrestling; I am trying to conquer my ignorance, overcoming it and becoming a scholar. Scholarship is light: unscholarliness is darkness – *per aspera ad astra*, 'Through hardships to the stars.' But what are we saying? All Russia is overcoming its backwardness and studying.

Ladies and gentlemen, Aristotle stops us in our feverish activity, not some time in the future but right now, because if you did not have that idea in your heads, then your lack of education would not exist. Every one of you is obsessed with the idea of studying, and that is why you find yourselves having to overcome the darkness of ignorance; you will carry on trying to overcome it for the rest of time, because it was there before there was studying, and it will only be pushed back a little by study, will not go away, and will forever continue to be present. You are confusing two things: the contrary and the substratum. The contrary of studying is posited by studying itself. Before there was studying there was no ignorance, and there will be none after studying. The *real* substratum, which was there before studying, remains there all the time you are studying, and will remain after it, and it is human matter, the human forest. It is the substratum of both ignorance and culture. That is to say, it is *equally* the basis of both. The forest can simultaneously be alien to itself; it can be frightening, dense and dark, yet dear to us; it can be good or bad. The Russian word for 'healthy', '*zdorovyi*', etymologically means 'of good wood, good timber'. Seeing the 'human matter'.

Before we read the important ending of Book II of the *Physics*, Chapters

7–9, we will see once again, from Aristotle's description of his method at the very beginning of the *Physics*, that he will never, unlike, say, Euclid, *ask* us to do anything. He will always first draw our attention to something we are *already* doing, and will note something we had not yet noticed but which more than anything we needed to notice. This is a more radical phenomenology than that of Husserl. The pure phenomenology of Heidegger takes us back from Husserl to Aristotle, limpidly and deliberately. I remember the look of amazement I got from Professor Chanyshev[1] when I called Heidegger Aristotle's most faithful interpreter. More deserving of his amazement is one of Heidegger's earliest courses, in the winter semester of 1921–2, titled *Phenomenological Interpretations of Aristotle.*[2] There is absolutely none of the standard exposition of Aristotle there. It is pristine Aristotle. For example, when we find 'life' in place of 'existence', we find it immediately followed by 'life = being'. The entire landscape of *Being and Time*, life and world, care, event, inclination. 'Lightness' is proposed as an Aristotelian term, but immediately turns up in the structure of concern as the omission of sameness, like Aristotle's 'movement' in the context of distancing, removal of distance, then collapse, which will become a falling – and since it seemed to me myself as I first casually leafed through it that the young assistant lecturer had got carried away from his set topic into enthusiasms of his own, many others will probably make the same mistake, and not all of them will find the time to look more closely and see that this is the *only true account* of Aristotle there is.[3]

The fact that Aristotle introduced the concept of the forest is associated with his return to phenomenology (that is not a slip of the tongue). No matter where we stop to focus our attention, we find so much that we never get round to constructs. In the midst of such riches, why would we bother to introduce our own lame maxims? They would be needless, absurd. It is an understatement to say 'such riches'. We would do better to say we could never exhaust these riches, because, wherever we turn, we find beneath them, in the substratum, what they are made of.

In ὕλη, we find the elements of a standard, first attempt at e-ducation: we form, build, draw, bring up (educate), while nature, too, is occupied, in broad terms, with the same thing as our 'technology'. What are our materials? We look around. For a teacher, the material is the student, but a teacher will not educate every student with equal enthusiasm. Each case is different. Plato calls matter '*khora*', a receptacle, a midwife, a mother. Is it indifferent to what it contains? Actually, probably not. But does the material, the substratum, our forest, dictate what is to be done? Everything – our experience, intuition, and our authorities – suggests that is not the case.

Accordingly, we find ourselves with a negative asset on our hands and must make the best of it. We are forbidden by the *right* to think that the ideal, *eidos*, the idea, the form, are only waiting for us to have the tenacity to 'realize' them. We will get nowhere if we pay no attention to the matter, to the primaeval forest. In other words, it is not true, as I recently heard in the speech of an amiable Italian, that 'the spirit will prevail over matter'. The spirit will never prevail over the substratum, which underlies and always will; the most we can say is that the spirit will prevail over its opposite, the absence of spirituality. But matter, undefinable, is as much bereft of spirituality as a bearer of it. By the *left* we are forbidden to think that we have to wait for the substratum to speak in us. Elsewhere I quoted the diary of a heavy drinker.[4] 'I can't see anything,' he announced, and went off deeper into the forest. 'I still can't see anything,' he declared, and drank some more, until he was no longer capable of declaring anything else. Prohibitions from the right and the left leave us with nowhere to go, which means everything is just fine, we are in *aporia*, a hopeless situation, in other words we are precisely where we should be.

Incidentally, the absence of clear starting points, of abscissas or ordinates in the writings of Aristotle, is just a different aspect of the same situation. Unfortunately, [...] historians of philosophy mainly occupy themselves with the needless and misleading business of proposing just such starting points: mistaken, of course, because they base them on currently fashionable and supposedly easily graspable concepts. The scene of Aristotle changes with every change of perspective and view and, as we know from Wittgenstein and Plato, viewpoints and doxas change ceaselessly. It is a true, that is, a spontaneous, automaton, like the statues of Daedalus.

I hope that those of you who looked at Aristotle's *Physics* in preparing for today's lecture did not go straight to Book II, Chapter 7 without reading the beginning, with its notes on methodology. The essence of the first chapter of Book I is, 'In the science of Nature, as in other branches of study, our first task will be to try to determine what relates to its principles.'[5] It is a defining gesture, like slamming a door. We've had enough, this has gone on too long. Physicists only confuse everything, representing their knowledge as primary and fundamental; they do not seriously engage with the bottomless, the abyss, the mysterious. They go no further than causal chains; the real, basic philosophy is, in fact, meta-physics, and in order to sober the physicists up, even if their works do have a few metaphysical insights woven into them, we are going to view their science as limited to cause-and-effect, much like mechanics. We are going to slam the door to metaphysics in their faces. The opening of *Physics* says, you have only yourselves to blame; here is what you have always been trying to limit yourselves to: not pure examination or pure phenomenology as in metaphysics but a doctrine of causes, principles, and elements.

In that same brief first chapter of Book I, Aristotle continues no less irascibly to develop that idea. What did you expect? To proceed from the wisdom of the gods? Nobody can proceed other than from their own knowledge. What need do we have of sciences and methods to attempt to proceed from our current knowledge, which is closest to us, to knowledge of how things are 'by nature'?

This sober reasoning, that we have what we have and that there is nothing else to hand, deflated some fairly idiotic speculations about what we ought to rely on: the *doxa* of popular prejudice or true knowledge, and whether Parmenides was positively or negatively inclined towards the doxa. Needless to say, he was positively inclined. True knowledge might well be a good thing, but what choice do we have, because all we have at our disposal is the changeful doxa. Whether it is good or bad, we have nothing else to go on, and the only sure knowledge we have is the doxa of what knowledge is true, which is one aspect of it.

Aristotle goes on to say what I myself said last time, without acknowledgement to him: our vision is such that we first take in whole things, unities. We do not need to consider whether this is a good or a bad thing: that is how it is, and debating the matter is pointless. If anyone is able to see or hear something that is *not* whole, not a unity, please let me know. We can confidently say that this is a feature of the human eye because, from an early age, human babies seem unable to see other than by fishing out, extracting large whole things from the world. They have a single word to designate all flying and everything that flies, from a mosquito to an aircraft; the words 'two-four' encompass everything countable, numbers, repeating objects like the steps of a stair, money, and *all official documents and forms*, which children also recognize as adding up and listing.

There is something quite brilliant and enchanting about this way children have of seeing things. When it can be retained, it gives rise to the kind of archetypal vision Goethe and Dante had.

At about five years of age, according to Freud, something happens to a human being. There is a major break. This is something we surmised but about which we now have further clear confirmation. Children's wholeness of vision, so wonderful, so extraordinary, does not change but suddenly spoils. It breaks down. Little children 'initially', πρῶτον – and it does not matter whether this stage lasts for long or not – 'call all men "father" and all women "mother", and only later distinguish who their fathers and mothers are' (ibid.). Again, it is unimportant when: what matters is that the early generalization breaks down, as it is right that it should.

This example of Aristotle's is cool, real Attic wit, like when someone makes up a bed in a seemingly innocent manner, soft and comfy, but you cannot sleep because it is unbearably hard. Really, to be calling everybody 'father' is completely scandalous and provides a foundation for the most foul-mouthed Russian swearing. What Greek philosophy was actually like is something we can read about in the above-mentioned course of lectures by Heidegger, or deduce from the fact that we find this outrageous and scandalous situation right at the heart of Greek epistemology. Knowledge was divided into the legitimate, where the father was known, and the illegitimate, where the father was unknown, when nobody knew where knowledge came from. From the end of the first short chapter of the *Physics*, we are referred straight back to its beginning and the issue of the culprit, the principle.

It is a disgrace not to know which man was your father, but the knowledge is so intimate that even modern biology is unable to establish the fact with 100 per cent certainty. Today, as in the days of Aristotle, the matter rests on intimate knowledge. Wittgenstein tells us that family likeness does not lend itself to official purposes. It can be sensed, but what does it consist of? From a first impression to a final belief, everything is down to feelings; for precision, you might add, as Aristotle does, *intelligent* feeling. In intelligent feeling, we have the ultimate reality, or, as Aristotle might say, being.

So, where does that leave us? It is quite right, indeed inevitable, that we grasp first, indeed always, the whole. Somehow, though, that breaks down into 'by and large', τὸ ὅλον on τὸ καθόλον, the very superior bird's-eye view from above down on to the disgraceful, or indeed the most disgraceful thing possible, the rubbish tip, the συγκεχυμένα (184a, 22) where all fathers are jumbled together. This rubbish tip is what we invariably find ourselves dealing with and we live on it. According to Aristotle, the earth is the rubbish tip of the cosmos on to which everything is thrown and where it gets jumbled together. This is our starting point, and we need to 'progress from the general to the particular'. To put it more simply, do try to identify your father among other men, your real father, naturally by trusting your mother implicitly.

So far, registering Aristotle's rigorous strictness, we do not seem to have lost our way, even if we do not yet see our goal. Our goal is, you will remember, as it is traditional to say in the history of philosophy, to 'reconcile Aristotle with Plato'. In terms of our topic, that means finding acceptance in Aristotle of matter-as-number. As yet Aristotle, making a distinction between formless chaos and matter, noting that the rubbish tip is not matter but a thing in our perception, preparing us to search for the particular, is leading us in the direction we are seeking.

He is also leading us in the expected direction about matter, the substratum. Those of you who have read the beginning of the *Physics* will remember that, after the analysis of opinions as to what is most reliable and ancient, which he evidently believes to be the same thing, Aristotle is left with three principles: 'The idea that oneness and excess and defect are the principles of being also seems to have a long history' (189b, 11–13). Excess and defect are unstable states contingent on each other: they arise from oneness and return to oneness. Here an overly bold interpretation of this passage would suggest that the substratum, matter, is the oneness which becomes unbalanced but then returns to equilibrium. For that interpretation, I presently lack the courage, and, even if I do decide that I have finally understood this passage, I will not know what to do with my understanding. For the present, I, like Aristotle, see clearly that for everything that arises, in technology or in nature, there is something 'out of which', and that that 'out of which' and that 'which arose' are different things but not opposites.

What has arisen is simple, or at least simpler. It is definite, it can be pointed to: 'there is a statue', 'there is a bed', 'there is an educated man'. The statue may be made of bronze, but calling it 'bronze' leaves unclear what kind of bronze: a lump of bronze, several pieces melted together? Wood is less definite than a bed. What is an ordinary person, as distinct from an educated, refined person like Socrates? Aristotle warns us that matter is *not* formless chaos. Does that mean it is halfway between the undefined and the defined, that it is semi-defined? Is matter something half-finished?

We do not find Aristotle belittling matter as some kind of misunderstanding. It is both oneness and being, only not in the sense of τὸ τόδε τι: that is, something of which it can be said, 'See what kind of thing this is.' We are being confidently recommended to see wholeness in matter, only somehow in a different way. But how? Aristotle may not have known that himself, or may not have thought about it. Do we have the right to think that matter is fully fledged being, only not quite the same being as we usually mean? That is what is said at the end of Book I of *Physics*: ἐγγὺς καὶ οὐσίαν πῶς, 'matter [and, let us add in the manner of the mediaeval commentators, the forest, *Bibikhin*] is a thing that coincidentally is not, and it is in a sense very close to being [substance, *AM*]' (192a, 6).

'Clutch it as you may, still it slips away.' Matter is oneness, but in its own way; it is being, but only after a fashion. It is the underlying, the continuing co-principle, remaining itself even when arising, of the form of what is arising (the other principle being *eidos*), ὑπομένουσα συναιτία. Aristotle, too, wants to understand the forest, but what does he do? He just gives another name for the forest: 'mother'. Just as the Latin for wood is *materia*, so Aristotle, as if remembering, reproduces, recreates in his own language, something that in it, unlike in Latin, did not show through. Aristotle again emphasizes that the female element is confused with evil because of a misunderstanding, when one fails to notice the difference between the substratum and the contrary. What harms *eidos*, the 'culture' of *eidos* and form, is not matter at all but ugliness. Ugliness is not attracted to shapeliness but matter, the female, is, just as the wife is attracted to her husband.

Only do not be in too much of a hurry to celebrate, to understand matter as woman-the-mother who is attracted to maternity, with *eidos* as the male principle. This is only a sketchy metaphor and it is not going to take us very far. Aristotle himself will cut it short. *Eidos* is entelechy and energy, that is, fullness, and fullness has no need of anything. It is not attracted towards the female. It is a strange sort of maleness. And matter is woman-as-mother, but only by 'coincidence', that is, only in respect of its being needed for the appearance of form. Either the extended metaphor is not extending very far, or we do not know what Aristotle means by the maternal and female. Most probably, it is the latter. There is good reason for us to be thinking of the forest as the mother.

Let us trample round on the spot for the present, even if we are empty-handed. Let us look back to where we started: that the main thing that is puzzling about the forest is that it can be frightening. That goes for such modern forms of the forest as drug addiction. *Eidos*, on the other hand, for Aristotle just as for Plato, is good, a fullness of bliss and insight, of something created, and existential perfection. Accordingly, something is going to have to be done to matter which, insofar as it possesses a blurred

ambiguity, cannot be eternal but can be completely burned up, irradiated
by *eidos*, to which it is itself attracted. But in another respect, matter will
remain the substratum *forever*, even under *eidos*, which means that, like
eidos, it neither perishes nor arises, ἄφθαρτος καὶ ἀγένητος (192a, 23). That
is, it is the equal of *eidos*. There will never be *eidos* without matter. Only
for *eidos* is matter comprehensible, as if the forest is pure, and demonstrating that disorder is not characteristic of it. The forest as paradise, or like
Boccaccio's Renaissance forest, or a park. Or the earth as a garden. But
this vocation of the forest to be a paradise and a park is something we
somehow seem already to have known. Ours, however, is a different task.
Through eternity the forest has come closer to the Idea, but does that perspective really demonstrate that the forest is a number? Or have we stumbled upon the answer already, and just not noticed?

When Aristotle speaks of an impulse, an attraction, and about what is
aspired to, ἐφετόν, he does not stop to ask whether the aspiration is for
good or evil: it is impossible to aspire to anything other than good. All
aspiration is, by definition, to θεῖον, to ἀγαθόν. There is no evil in aspiration, but precisely because there is aspiration, and that it is to the good,
it is possible that there could be no aspiration. This possibility creates
ἀντικείμενον. The contrary, to put it technically. It will perhaps be well at
this point to recall the etymology of the word Satan: the Gainsayer. Like a
shadow: behind every 'yes', the 'no'.

Then, does the contrary also lay claim to matter? Is matter the place
where, if it is not the cause, it is at least the place where good and evil are
separated: not in the sense that matter is evil, but in the sense that without
the forest, there would be no evil? If matter is a woman, is there a fight over
the woman? If so, why do all those delightful speculations about the eternal
feminine say nothing about this fight? This is another instance where I am
obliged to let go of what little I have grasped. I have no idea.

We shall have to mark time, and again console ourselves with the modest
satisfaction of moving aside one source of muddle, the common confusing
of matter and nature.

Of course, here, too, we can just readily agree with Aristotle. It only
seems that nature and matter are the same thing if we do not take the time
to consider the question carefully. We have made a bed out of new wood,
abandoned it in the orchard, it settles in the loose soil, gets rained on, and
the wood in the bed sprouts in the ground; what sprouts from the bed is
not another bed but a tree. The tree is clearly nature, so does that mean the
matter the bed is made of and nature are the same thing?

No. What sprouted was not the matter of the bed; the wood sprouted
precisely when it forgot it was the matter of the bed. What sprouted was
not the potential of a tree to be used as matter by a carpenter, but the
actual form of the tree. Nature would not allow, more precisely, will never
allow, a bed to be made out of a tree. Nature is one thing, while matter
adapts to whatever purpose it is required for.

But then, our forest, too, is not the same as nature. We see it earlier, as it were, than we see nature. It is full of sounds, dark and indefinite. Indeterminacy, in some way, being, undefined being – that is another of Aristotle's definitions of matter. Like Aristotle's ὕλη, our forest is always in a state of not yet having taken shape.

Aristotle's ὕλη is unquestionably being (οὐσία, in translation, essence), but we have yet to see of what kind. For him, nature is almost exemplary being, without ifs or buts. There is no need to subject it to scrutiny, and Aristotle becomes angry if people are too blind to see that nature, a self-moving automaton, *is*. In other words, that it is a fully fledged being. Using a single word, Aristotle says that nature moves. 'Moves' means much more in Aristotle than it does for us: changes, grows, and generally has a history of its own. If the word 'development' had not become so tarnished in contemporary discourse, that would have been the way to translate Aristotle's κίνησις. He uses the same word or expression to say that nature is known and recognized, γνώριμον, of its own accord and through itself (193a, 5). That is, just use your eyes and nature will show itself and make itself known and tell all about itself. It is obtuse, wilful blindness not to see the obvious fact that all around us, in front of our noses, and indeed within us, everything is almost self-moving, an automaton, and to think that is open to debate. That is like blind people wanting to discuss colour. The issue is the transparency of nature, but for the present we are not discussing the topic of the automaton. We just need to bear in mind that the automaton is real and spontaneous. We should not assume that procreation is preordained to be endless repetition of exactly the same form. A genus of nature can change swiftly; it seems capable of removing itself from the scene completely, giving up its place to others; in other words, of fitting itself into the automaton that is the world. It appears capable of innovation.

We are hunting the forest and that is our sole topic, but for Aristotle it is only one of many. We have the excuse that, as yet, the forest is the only thing we can see. There is no question of looking to find support in the forest as materialists, or trying to find an opposition between the forest and reason. We have no inclination to be distracted by miscellaneous hypotheses about the Russian forest, about femininity or maternity in the Russian soul, and suchlike aesthetics. The only hypothesis we are testing is the notion that the indeterminacy of the forest somehow coincides with the rigorousness of mathematics, geometry, or logic. Let us repeat our task more explicitly. We are seeking to understand Plato, for whom matter is number. In Aristotle, we found that exact same formula and wrote it up on the blackboard but, critically, tongue in cheek. We have declined to make a choice between their 'different points of view'. We were obliged to accept Aristotle's objection, but our hypothesis compelled us to look to see whether, despite their different terminology, there was latent agreement between Plato and Aristotle in their thinking.

But then we did succeed in finding what we were looking for when we read in Aristotle about the desire of matter, the mother, for the divine. (In Losev, if anyone has looked at his volume on Aristotle in connection with our course, there is a lot about matter, but there is a telling slip: the substratum alongside form, *eidos*, is the joint cause of what arises, 'like matter'.[6] This is meaningless and should read 'like the mother'. In other words, *eidos* is like the father and matter is like the mother.) The forest desires the good, the godly. That is, in its desire, Aristotle's matter is the same as Plato's divine ideal. *Quod erat demonstrandum*.

Unfortunately, this solution only poses new problems (but, after all, for Plato, too, matter is obscure). We shall need to think again about the Beautiful Lady, the Eternal Feminine, and this is how: we seem always to have assumed that it only attracts and captivates us, but Aristotle talks about her being drawn to the male. Are we really to understand the words at the end of the Second Part of Goethe's *Faust*, 'Das Ewig-Weibliche zieht uns hinan,' 'The Eternal Feminine draws us on,' as meaning that the Eternal Feminine draws us into its striving? There is a further problem: are the Feminine and the Maternal the same thing?

Having unexpectedly and so easily reconciled Plato and Aristotle, we had better nevertheless finish reading Book 2 of the *Physics*, as we said we would. Always bearing in mind that the automaton of nature is directed by a teleological principle and not hustled towards its next condition by local factors, Aristotle adduces the same powerful argument as modern critics of vulgar Darwinism: if you say that chance provides the distribution of mutations of which the fittest survive, show me the dispersion between, say, two closely related species. We see the species, but the intermediate forms that were unsuccessful are nowhere to be found in the fossil record and not to be observed today. There is another argument we hear nowadays, although it is deployed only rarely: technology imitates nature in many respects, and it is purpose-driven; does not the very fact of its being able to imitate nature mean that nature itself is reaching out to objectives (199a, 15)? And again: technology can fall flat because it is not dictated by the past and the future, that is to say, by what does not exist, but jumps across non-being and non-knowing and breaks the chain of continuity. But in nature, too, we see failures, because monstrosities are clearly mistakes rather than experiments by nature in her quest for new, better adapted forms. If anyone is concerned that in nature there is no discussion of goals, if we look more closely at technology, we see that there, too, there is no discussion and its drive towards goals comes rather through intuition, surmise, and the swing of the pendulum between the dead end of despair and inspiration (i.e. an unaccountable breakthrough).

We are talking here about nature, but this applies to every impulse towards a goal, towards a teleological principle, including in matter (200a, 6). The saw arose not because metal under the influence of certain processes turned into sharp teeth, but because there was a need to saw, and if the saw was to come into being, then strong, sharp (i.e. iron) teeth needed to come into being. Similarly, animals' teeth appeared not because certain chemical conditions were created which caused them to form, but because animals needed to have something for biting off pieces of food.

But first, surely, there had to be matter, so that teeth could be formed out of it? Doubtless so, but we can view this another way. It is by no means absurd to say that the iron was created by its purpose, the saw, rather than that the saw was created out of metal. The saw and suchlike was called forth by the need to cut things; the goal required metal, and otherwise, in all probability, there would not even be metal. The saw as a goal for sawing with found for itself, elicited, demanded, drew forth from oblivion, metal. A house is needed, and the goal of having a house finds for itself, identifies, for the first time, extracts, discovers the matter, the building materials needed (200a, 24). Of ourselves we can say that, just as a husband looks for a wife and *creates* her, because, if there were no such thing as a husband, there would be no such thing as a wife, a woman is created as a mother. The mother, the matter, is created by him who set himself that purpose.

Absolutely all matter is identified, selected, and indeed created by a purpose. If there were no purpose, there would be no 'what for?', there would be no 'what of?'

Conversely, of course, if there were absolutely, in principle, nowhere, ever, any material with the potential to aspire, no goal would ever be attained.

'The purpose is the principle of matter,' Aristotle specifies. Matter arises from the attraction of its purpose. All arising is attracted to being.

Thanks to Aristotle, we notice that for us, too, our matter, the forest, arose in the light of its purpose, the purpose of finding our place in the world.

If matter has for a very long time (it is eternal) been attracted to perfecting the particular, how can there still be any 'not-yet' now, in our time? There has been so much time, matter should surely by now have been transformed completely into *eidos*? The forest should have become a garden, a paradise.

This is not the fault of things that have not been perfected but something more unforgiving: the contrary that we have mentioned. It is not in matter and neither is it in *eidos*, but in the fact that the creation of all beauty of form instantly contrasts itself with formless ugliness, and thereby brings ugliness centre stage! The good, the divine, the fullness of life, the radiant and defined, brings its contrary in its wake. You might almost wish it had never arisen in the first place. Only what remains apart remains safe. The contrary appears long before any attempt to put something into practice. No matter what you think of, contrariety, objections, immediately arise. It could put you off ever moving a whisker. As the Russian saying goes, 'Do no good and there will be no evil.'

Or are we again missing something? Can it really be that in the course of all the time that has passed, perfection was not in fact reached in nature long ago? Does nature not encompass everything? Was matter, the forest, say, not a living forest before it was turned into problematical timber? Something perfect and ultimate must in all that time surely have succeeded in being drawn to *eidos*. All nature is precisely that successful attraction to *eidos*. Nature was that success, and that is why it is beautiful.

What was not realized then, not achieved, what is still 'not-yet'? Let us take as an example, or no, actually, not as an example but as the crux of the matter: a physician and an architect. We say they are two experts, two professionals. What is the difference between them? We are not talking about the fact that one restores health while the other builds houses and that these are different professions. There is a much more important difference.

It is that, if the physician stops his work, the patient may get better anyway, while if the architect stops his work, there is absolutely no way the house is going to end up built. The physician *attends* as health is restored, the architect *attends* as the house is built, but he cannot say, as the physician can, 'That's it. Things can now be left to take care of themselves.' He will get nowhere if he says, 'That's it. The house can be left now to finish itself.' While the physician is doing his work, the restoration of health comes not from him but from nature itself; he is only facilitating that. The architect, however, is not merely facilitating the building of the house. Both are dealing with matter. The physician is restoring natural good health, while the architect is realizing the desire of his wood, but in nature movement, change, comes from within, like an *automaton* (1034a, 10) at its own urging, spontaneously, 'and *within matter, from within matter*', whereas in technology change is coming from outside, from a different element.

If the art of architecture were innate, inherent in the stone, the wood, the lime, in the same way that nature inheres in the body, and all were identically desiring to perfect their form, then, just as the sick, weary body recovered, so the scattered stones and trees, the cement and sand, would spontaneously assemble themselves and grow into a house. That would be no problem. There is always matter and form.

In nature, arising is the province of the automaton, the true automaton that never wearies, never breaks down, that renews itself. The automaton is somehow inherent in nature; the automaton is *Sophia*, the wisdom of the world.[7] But what of technology? It 'comes from a different element'. What different element? Has it invaded from somewhere? Why is not everything what we are familiar with? How come we take leave of ourselves? Where has this other element come from? Plato had no answer, so in his *Parmenides* he introduced it as one of the first principles, which just *are*.

The topic of matter as the mother in Aristotle brings us back to the *Timaeus* (49a etc.).

I repeat my invitation to you to submit right now papers for a competition for the best philosophy essay of the Russian Federation at the end of the millennium.

Next time, after some more remarks about Aristotle's views on matter, we shall move on to the *Timaeus*.

Lecture 7, 21 October 1997

Let us go back for a moment to the *Physics*, Book 2, Chapter 8. 'Moreover, whenever there is an end, the whole prior sequence of actions is performed with this end as its purpose. Now, unless something intervenes, how an action is done corresponds to how things are in nature, and vice versa' (199a, 8). Here is a question for you: why should intelligent action follow nature and do precisely what is characteristic of each thing? What is behind this coincidence of the working of human action and nature?

It is the presence of an end that dictates that. You will remember from the last lecture that the end is so powerful that it is the cause of matter. Everything is determined by attraction towards the end, so that the difference between nature and human action pales away: nature and action behave in exactly the same way in terms of conducing to the end.

> For example, a naturally occurring house – supposing such a thing were possible – would happen in exactly the same way that a skilfully made house does; conversely, if naturally occurring things were made by skill as well as by nature, they would still happen in exactly the same way as when they occurred naturally.... And in general human skill either completes what nature is incapable of completing or imitates nature. If artificial products have some purpose, then, natural things obviously do too, since in both cases the relation between the later stages and the earlier stages is the same. (199a, 13)

In the light of this diktat of the end, it is very easy for Aristotle to imagine a house or ship that builds itself. If a house is really needed, it will lay its own foundation, assemble its materials, and virtually build itself. From this, Aristotle arrives at his definition of art. Art is something that, like nature, imitating nature or completing nature, draws in material, matter, and gets it into shape. Anyone who has done something not just intellectually, theoretically, but because it was really needed, for example building a house, will remember the strange presence of the house from the very beginning when, in some sense, you can 'see' it, and working backwards from its final completion the parts are thought out and the materials, the concrete, the boards, the tools, and, most importantly of all, the time are brought together. When once the end has been accurately formulated and visualized, you have a strange feeling that it is impossible for the house not now to be built; it is ready even before it has been completed and is truly being drawn towards the end, the goal. It is building itself.

But is that right, or is there something missing?

Well, yes, there is just one little thing missing. There are, after all, masses of architectural projects that never get beyond the design stage and remain only on paper. In the architecture of the Italian Renaissance, there was a whole genre or style of designing palaces and even entire cities that got as far as drafting, that were examined and exhibited in that form. Almost all Leonardo's engineering projects got no further than the design stage, including the steam engine and even the bicycle.

In nature, too, not all projects, indeed only a tiny proportion of them, reach the stage of 'entelechy'. Entelechy is the greatest imaginable perfection, completeness. The word ἐντελέχεια contains the root τέλος, and, conversely, *telos* implies entelechy. See what happens then: we discover that we have been wrong in trying to differentiate between a realized and an unrealized project. The distinction is dispensable. The end is already the ultimate perfection without needing anything added to it. The end cannot not be realized.

In nature, however, as in art, there are many embryos, most of which perish. Only the fittest, we say, attain their end, those that most actively fight for life. Thus, architects have to fight if they are to see their architectural projects realized, to win a competition, show their superiority, to elbow aside their competitors. Similarly, in nature, wild antlered beasts must fight other males for access to the female. Following this line of thought, or observation (and is it untrue?), I almost said that the end really will implement itself and draw in to itself the matter it needs, given sufficient resolution.

This is perfectly correct, but we also observe a trance-like state, *amekhania*, both in nature and in art precisely when we reach the stage of realization, entelechy. Perhaps you have observed how a sexually excited dog behaves: he is persistent, so preoccupied that he forgets about food, ceases to obey his master, but, when he is drawn to a bitch in heat, where is his aggression, his bark, his fangs? You can chase him, push, beat him; he seems not to notice anything and leaves himself terribly vulnerable to attack. Tomcats become totally exhausted during their mating period; on their more domestic example we can see that the fights between males over a female are caused not by aggressiveness, but by entrancement, by *amekhania* again. Just as in nature, so in art, we find the very 'action' Aristotle refers to. The behaviour of our architect can be described as a struggle for first place in the competition, but in the case of a real architect, someone with a serious prospect of getting placed in the competition, his behaviour is also entrancement by the idea, the concept, the job; he is bewitched, totally captive: he forgets about food and sleep, and all the more so about the social and administrative actions needed to actually enter the competition.

Telos, entelechy, complete realization in nature and art are surrounded by an aura of *amekhania*. The prime mover is motionless.

Which is just as it should be. Let us view the matter from a different perspective. Let us suppose that what is realized in nature did not have to pass through the filter of entranced, cataleptic motionlessness, of absolute *amekhania*. Let us suppose that from genus to genus and from generation to generation, in nature as in art, for the generations inventing machines, what was being devised did not first have to be immersed in serenity. Nature and art would become weary. They do not because, at crucial moments in their story, they are released, escape into a void, blossom in an entranced liberation.

I almost said that, in addition to setting a goal, resolution was needed, but then focused on this strange release, this opening out around the fullness of achievement, and on the word 'resolution' with its connotations of dissolving, untying, unfolding.

Our forest is like that: entrancing, burgeoning. Plato's matter, *khora*, allows for the same kind of entrancement.

Bringing art and nature together, Aristotle says that art, *techne*, does not reason. (This is the origin of Heidegger's 'science and technology do not think'.[1]) In the relaxed state of *amekhania*, the house is always self-building. In the entranced serenity of 'creativity', art and nature are one and the same.

That entranced serenity is a filter which, if we pass through it, gives access to the automaton, the true automaton that never wearies, not just in the sense that it can maintain itself – that is something programmed, mechanical automata can also do – but also in the sense that *it recreates every time not itself but the act of recreation, something more than itself.* The natural, spontaneous automaton can recreate itself, but it can also move in a new direction, because the state of release, of permissiveness, is fertile. In the spring waters of *amekhania*, everything is allowed. Matter is pure possibility, the inviting *khora* of Plato.

Among those who dreamed of being admitted to the realm of the true automaton were, for example, the theoreticians of automatic writing during and immediately after the First World War. Freud, at least according to his own account, allowed himself the practice of automatic writing, plunging into a state of semi-somnolence in the last part of *The Interpretation of Dreams*, and there are claims he routinely used cocaine to keep himself on the verge of automatism.

In the Russian village, in its style, the nineteenth-century Polish poet Adam Mickiewicz saw an extension of the forest, as if the forest almost invited itself to assume the form of huts of this shape.

But here and there, one sees a rough-cut fall
Of timber leant-to in haphazard dome,

A strange mass, which recalls a roof and walls,
With folk inside. This thing they call a 'home'.[2]

All this with barely a mention of people, because every detail of the village is described, including the smoke hanging above the chimneys, and only then are we told, 'I've met the people.'[3] In this vein, Mickiewicz describes the organic nature of Russia's wooden village architecture, in comparison with which the architecture of almost all the cultures of the East European Plain seem a violation which the forest, matter, is reluctant to accept.

Art (*techne*), then, is either a possible or a necessary part of the automaton; it is what the Sophia of the world requires in the automaton of human art. We have talked previously about this in the lecture course on Wittgenstein. Human searching, stumbling, the so-called travails of creation, uncertainty, hopelessness, bewilderment, and despair are the certain signs of inner, intimate membership; of a person's admission, as it were, to the world Sophia. (The delusion that action can be smooth and 'go like clockwork' indicates that something has been overlooked: it will most assuredly be noticed in the end.) There is always a risk that *amekhania* and powerlessness may strike the automaton at a crucial moment.

Thus, crossing this threshold, art, like nature, has to force its way ahead, always facing the risk of seizing up permanently into immobility, striving towards truth, richness, and relevance. It seems likely that nature itself knows no other route to take than that of passing through the filter I have mentioned. Where did the idea come from that nature acts more confidently and reliably than art?

Was it solely from not knowing something that we now do know, because of violence, not allowing ourselves to be 'resolute' because of a defective understanding of resoluteness that made us mistake it for its polar opposite? Is it because, when the forest, the World Tree, becomes the Cross, we need to stay motionless on it, and not resort to frenetic activity out of fear? Plotinus says that we resort to activity from psychasthenia, from spiritual lassitude.[4] And Osip Mandelstam says, 'There is a lechery for labour and we have it in our blood.'[5]

The forest invited us in, enchanted us, and led us away from metric space. It invited us to join it and become an automaton. The degenerate or late forms of the forest – tobacco, alcohol, and cocaine – lure the user towards automatism. The semi-somnolent practice of automatic creativity is an oversophisticated, sly sampling of automatism. A different lure of the – Siberian – forest was experienced by the Pilgrim, to whom we shall need briefly to return today in a particular connection. The luring of Goethe by the Eternal Feminine, his entrancement by it, has the suggestion of a return to *amekhania*.

Students of Freud pay little attention to the connection between sex and *amekhania*, but it is an important aspect. Freud was semi-somnolent when finishing his book about dreaming. For him, dreams are a path into the unconscious, and it is not without significance that the unconscious operates in the realm of repressed sex. The inscrutability of sex and the unconscious is one and the same. They are the same in the sense that they are a filter, a barrier of entrancement. Sex is a junction, a climactic moment, an act of 'resolution' (releasing, relaxing, when the race recklessly gives itself over to complete automatism, which *is* the unconscious at its peak).

Another facet of what we are talking about is the already mentioned double, and I have, of course, warned you off dallying with it. In our double, it is as if we have left, forgotten all our other selves, but all we need to do is to remember the fact that we have forgotten, to recall our forgetfulness without trying to remember what we have forgotten. What we have forgotten about human beings is that they are mortal; they are not God. Such efforts to access the unconscious as automatic writing are like the half that is 'us' trying to restore, to reconstruct, our other half. Cloning experiments in biological engineering come under the same heading, trying to obtain an immortal being from a mortal one. That is possible, and that being will surpass the conventional human being in the same sort of way that a programmed, mechanical automaton, a robot, never lapses into *amekhania*, which is part of the very essence of the true automaton. It is all about finding ways of avoiding risk, of staying safe.

Sometimes, for example in a dream, we notice strange, unfathomable stirrings of our double. In our dreams, he moves away from us just as independently as the nose of Major Kovalyov in Gogol's story *The Nose*.[6] Major Kovalyov's nose, as it drives around the city, parades its independence of Kovalyov just a little too ostentatiously; it is just a little too sure of its separate identity. In the same way, dream images are suspiciously just too strange, too independent and separate from us. It is too deliberate. The independent, uncontrollable actions of someone *like* me which I see in my dream are so *deliberately* foreign because they are so entirely mine, and my double is perhaps even more real than me in my waking hours. Only these are the actions of a me from the dark side of the moon. My double is my twin.

Both dreams and Freud's cocaine are an entrance to the same strangeness, the same 'other side'. Freud is absolutely right to remind us that the day, which, according to the clock, the diary, the routine, the newspaper, or the television, is completely smooth, is actually perforated with gaps and, so to speak, pointedly directing us towards night-time. Freud can be rash, building up our hopes of being able to rationalize our relations with the unconscious. Or is his rationalism only a way of sobering us by reminding us of death?

The departure from metric, measurable space into free space is imperceptible. It is like falling accidentally, like Thales, down a well and immediately becoming unobservable. This is the basis for tales of invisibility and the invisible man who becomes visible. The most striking thing about the invisible man is how spectacularly unsuccessful he is in remaining unnoticeable. In Pasolini's film *Theorem*, an entire prosperous family falls out of its measurable space for no apparent reason, unexpectedly entranced by a visitation from, in the context of some of Pasolini's other works, a strange, mysterious, god-like young man.[7] They are happy in their entrancement. They remain entranced and drop out of their routine lives and highly remarkable events begin to happen to them in this place formerly ruled by routine. They seem immediately to burn up in a place where, until then, they had existed securely. They become automata, but of a different kind from other people in their civilization. They burn up like meteorites entering the atmosphere. That Pasolini's film is true, and the fact that his knowledge of this entrancement, this dropping out, and the impossibility of resolving the theorem by human means, was not cerebral but had come from lived experience is demonstrated by his death. He was murdered, apparently on the beach at Ostia near Rome.

The Cross on which anyone lured in by the forest finds themselves motionless is reminiscent of the strictness, the geometry, into which consciousness is to be transformed: the focus, the concentration in a single point. Mathematics in the midst of passion, enthralment, entrancement: is this what Plato and Aristotle have to teach us? We shall have to think about that.

Christ as a new redeemed and redemptive Adam brings back also the Garden of Eden, but now under the aspect of the Cross. The Garden of Eden of the New Testament is the Cross. The old garden is long gone and there will never be another like it.

The conclusion we came to last time was that Aristotle sees potential *eidos* in matter, a garden in the forest; just as Plato sees no obstacle to matter smoothly becoming – lock, stock, and barrel – number, harmony. Dante is both a Platonist and an Aristotelian when he talks about it being the mission of humanity to transform the earth into a flowerbed or a garden. Actually, he is a Thomist Aristotelian. Thomas Aquinas does certainly seem to see the mystery of the Cross and to understand the form the Old Testament paradise has now assumed. The Garden or the Cross? We do not sense anything intrinsically absurd about this, just as Olga Sedakova in 'The Wild Dogrose' sees that the divine Garden of Eden can wound and is harsh and wild.

But what common ground is there between the Garden and the Cross? The heavenly lightness felt after their divine visitation in Pasolini's *Theorem* infects his characters to the point where it is impossible for them to go back to their routine lives. *Amekhania* in one case can be no more than immobility, fixity, the absence of something; in another case, however, along with the immobility there is entrancement, not from the absence of something but rather from an intense presence that gains supernatural force. In both cases, however, life is impossible; there is a lack of the adaptability essential for simply continuing to exist. It is the same for the character of the lady who retains the ability to move but, as in a dream, mechanically picks up young men in her car as she drives along and mindlessly gives herself to them wherever she can, until she, too, smoothly exits life. Undoubtedly, however, the most alarming breakdown is that of the strongest character, the intelligent, strong-willed factory owner. He breaks down straightforwardly in the middle of a business trip, at the railway station in the middle of a crowd. He strips naked, and strips himself bare in another sense when he surrenders his large factory to the workers and goes off into the wilderness. The film ends as he stands barefoot and naked among the slag heaps, uttering a terrifying feral shriek, less like a cry of remorse over what he has done than of horror at being abandoned: it is total *amekhania*, which is the impossibility of lifting a finger in this divine state of crucifixion, and the equal impossibility of living on this unexpected Cross.

The experience of cycling varies, of course, depending on the quality of the bicycle, of the road, on who is cycling, but as an event it is always the same and wholly satisfying for as many people as you can imagine. There is the tendency to fall off sideways, where in walking you tend to fall forwards; the quiet speed, the gliding – an impersonal experience and, as it were, non-situational. Anyone who is into cycling understands any other cyclist, irrespective of barriers of nationality or time. There is the same reality in the experience of trauma, which is truly as strictly geometric as a theorem. Trauma is the closest neighbour of *amekhania*. Anatoly Akhutin has shown this in classical tragedy: *amekhania* or, in Aristotle's terminology, catharsis, purging, coincides with the peripeteia, the tragic turn of events.[8] The proximity of purity and anguish is something wholly analogous with cycling. In a completely different country and environment, in the Siberian forest, a Russian knows how an encounter with God will end: entrancement, enthralment, and spiritual anguish. One of the characters in the first story of *The Pilgrim Continues His Way* tells us,

'[F]ear and horror often used to come over me and now I only have to remember what I suffered in that dream for the agony and exhaustion to begin again and such torture that I don't know what to do with myself.... Then I could neither eat nor drink nor sleep because of this suffering. I was worn to a ravel.' ... 'Dear Brother, during the time of that fear and agony you ought to have prayed to God.' ... 'Not on your life!' he said to me. 'I thought that directly I began to pray God would destroy me.'[9]

That is, his terror was greater than the fear and horror when he could neither eat nor drink nor sleep and was 'worn to a ravel', because this was all suffering in human terms, but the anguish (and this we could perhaps compare with the withdrawal symptoms of a drug addict, but for that we would need specialized medical knowledge), the real anguish when it comes, replaces these human travails, which are, after all, tolerable, as hunger can be endured, with something fundamentally different, which begins like a dead calm out at sea.

The Cross: geometry, a tree from the forest in the Garden of Eden (you recall, it is all the same sort of wood), the sense of being fettered by immobility, *amekhania*, and death.

We cannot say that the Garden of Eden becomes the Cross only in the Gospels. In Plato, the forest is already pure geometry; and for him, too, enthralment is associated with spiritual anguish and aching (people's eyes ache when, after looking at a screen, they start looking at pure light) and with death. The real life of someone who has seen the light becomes invisible to people who watch screens. They do not understand it and they kill, as Socrates was killed, fettered by his demon as if to the Cross, when it would have been only too easy to run away or deliver a speech not of indictment but of self-exculpation.

The rigidity of these circumstances, their pure, elegant, deadly geometry, creates the style of Aristotle. He is already beyond the bounds of that knowledge after adopting silence, and the school of conducting himself on the far side of the impossibility of making the least movement.

Transformation of the forest. The forest will be transformed. Now, I crave your attention, we shall read Aristotle.

Eidos is first and foremost – and it will do no harm to suppose that it is exclusively and invariably – a thing, any thing that has achieved the fullness of its perfection. Accordingly, another name for *eidos* is 'dominance', 'abundance', 'wealth', and the name of its contrary is στέρησις, from στερέω, 'to deprive', for example of property. Property, fullness, wealth, are words for being. The difference between *eidos* and deprivation is like that between yes and no, good and evil, and it concerns humankind. A human being can at least take the trouble to notice, if not to live, the difference between perfection, good quality, fullness, and error and failure. Does the difference matter all that much? It is not even visible, but that distinction is Aristotle's primary concern. His metaphysics defers to ethics, the supreme science.

The fullness of perfection is given only to God, not to humankind. For human beings, deprivation is always there, like a shadow, immediately next to *eidos*. If I say I see, in reality I do not, because the full range of possible vision is not revealed to mortals. If I am good, in reality I am not good, and so on. Eyesight and goodness are only being used illustratively here, but what is the difference, for example, between success and failure for an artist? It is not anything that can be named and categorized: Phidias worked in gold and ivory, while Polykleitos only worked in bronze. It is *impossible* to define what perfection consists of, and one inevitably falls back on what can be counted or enumerated. But we ought not to. What interests the ancient Greeks, what makes the whole difference, what alone is acceptable, is perfection. That is the only thing that matters, and somebody else can be left to worry some other time about everything else. Does that come as a surprise? If it were not for this insane, exclusive focus on *ariston*, there would be no 'classical antiquity' and no reason for us to study history.

What is so major about failing to register the difference between perfection and something that does not quite make the grade? Ladies and gentlemen, it implies there is no difference between matter and *eidos*, or that it is vanishingly small. We will fail to miss the finishing touch that would have perfected a work of art. Before that final touch of the pediment and the roof, the house is not quite finished, and then, suddenly, it is; or, if it is just not quite finished but good enough, is it unfinished? The house is *eidos* but, until it gets that final touch, it is just matter. That last, elusive touch makes it *eidos*, a perfected house, and without it, it is imperfect, indistinguishable from, no different from, matter. 'We do not describe the completion of a house as an alteration (since it would be ridiculous for the coping-stone and the tiling to constitute an alteration, or for the house to be altered rather than completed by being coped and tiled' (*Physics*, 246a, 18).

Eidos is not content but is completeness. The perfection of the world itself – this is my example – breaks down into an incoherent multiplicity of parts, but that same world is seen by the artist or heard by the musician as harmony. All right, my example is pathetic. Aristotle's is better.

Aristotle speaks of the body. The body, he tells us, is the matter of the soul. What does the soul add to the body to make it a living person? It very obviously adds something, and perhaps it adds something that is supremely important but that we cannot detect by studying the body. We cannot detect the difference between *eidos* and matter here well enough to observe and register it.

Woman, in Aristotle, is matter. This, unexpectedly, abruptly, down-grades the role of men: when giving birth, the woman herself produces the whole person. The role of man is only to provide the finishing touch, to add the final detail. Human beings give birth out of human beings; the whole human being is already there in the human matter, the mother (*mater*). Woman bears the whole person, who, in their entirety, is him- or herself, but completed. When people claim that Aristotle sees the woman as merely a nutrient medium, with *eidos* coming from the man, this is just a lot of unsavoury nonsense.

More detail about the topics of the body and woman. The beginning of Book 2 of *On the Soul*. The body is substance; the living body has the power of self-nourishment, of independent growth and decay. This living, self-moving body is matter; it is as yet still substratum. To become soul, the body must become *eidos*. Does that mean it is formless and needs to take on form? Nothing of the sort. Nothing in its form will change: the same, already formed, living body will remain, only now perceptive, full of mindfulness. What that means is clarified: it is not the daily, careful watching of the world and itself, but the sensitive attention we find in dreams and in intoxication. Although unconscious, it is nevertheless mindfulness, the fullness of a human being when the soul is somehow everything in the world. In someone asleep or intoxicated, the soul is receptive to the whole world. That is the *eidos* of the body. The body, I repeat, was and remains alive; it does not suddenly sprout additional arms and legs. This receptiveness is knowledge in the sense that, even when asleep, I know the multiplication table. 'Here sleeps someone who knows the multiplication table.' Absolutely. They will wake up and will teach and explain it, and there will appear that ultimate way of seeing that is accessible to human beings, *theory*; but until then the mass of knowledge in the sleeping teacher is primary in relation to what that knowledge will develop into, theory, which will be secondary. The actuality, the receptive fullness, of the soul possessing knowledge is entelechy, the perfected *eidos* of the body, for which the body was all along intended.

Or was the body perhaps not intended for θεωρία? No, in θεωρία there is fullness of happiness. The soul, however, is not yet the fullness of happiness; it is only at the first stage of knowledge and is, accordingly, only the first entelechy of a living body. Once more, how is such a soul to be differentiated from the body, from matter? Aristotle takes as his example an axe. 'Suppose, for example, that ... an axe were a natural body, its axeity would be its substance, would in fact be its soul. If this were taken away, it would cease, except in an equivocal sense, to be an axe.' But what it is and whether it 'is' at all is something we have to decide while its being, that it is, is not evident. As if this were not enough, Aristotle gives another example: the eye 'is the matter of eyesight' (412b, 20).[10] Here is the eye. It is alive, it is looking, but it is not *seeing*. Looking but not seeing. Does it differ materially from the seeing eye? No, they are exactly the same, but it remains matter in the sense that for the present it has only the potential to see: that capacity has not yet become entelechy. Until it has, the eye is no better than an eye sculpted in stone or painted in a picture. But such an eye will surely never be able to see? Who knows?

What we do know is that almost all living eyes look but do not see. Why? Is the matter in them faulty? No, it is exactly the same as those in eyes that see. The eye remains matter for eyesight, which will eventuate only if it can outweigh, eclipse, all privation or στέρησις of sight. Why, instead of the fullness of eyesight, of vision, is there the privation of it? Why has eyesight not eventuated? Why has it failed? Just because it did not work out. There could have been eyesight; all the matter needed for it was present, it just did not happen. What is missing? Probably knowledge. Of course, because hasn't Aristotle just said that the soul, the first entelechy of the body, is like knowledge? So teach soul to people. If anyone is in the dark after psychology, read the passage in *Physics*, Book 7, Chapter 3:

> The original acquisition of knowledge is not a case of generation or alteration, because it is when the thinking part of the mind has come to a rest and is not active that we are said to know and understand [*episteme* is for both Plato and Aristotle a coming to a standstill, *Bibikhin*] and generation never has rest as its end-point since ... change in general is not subject to coming into being. Moreover, when someone has passed from being drunk or asleep or ill to the opposite condition, we do not say that he has become knowledgeable again, despite the fact that he was incapable of making use of his knowledge before; by the same token, we do not say that he has become knowledgeable when he first acquires the state, because understanding and

knowledge come about as a result of the mind quietening down from its natural disturbance. (247b, 9)

It may be that for Aristotle the difference between matter and *eidos* is only this minimal distinction, but that it is also maximal. In fact, that is not only possible but anything else would be downright boring, both for him and for us. The difference is between what is, for now, still *recumbent* and what is moving. What moves has history.

This is the body. The woman gives the body. That is, she herself gives the whole person. The difference between matter and mother is not at all the difference between raw material and the processing of it. In the mother, the whole person is already present. We need to note something important that will come in very useful later: that matter is the mother (we read that in Aristotle's *Physics*). Now for another term, τὸ θῆλυ. Its synonym is the notion that the male relates to the female as *eidos* to matter. 'The Female is χώρα and ὑποδοχή' (both terms Plato uses for matter).

The female provides the body. Does the male give it form? Not at all: what we now know about the body is that it is already the complete, living body, with the female providing the whole person. What comes from the male is *eidos*, the element of motion, while from the female comes the matter and the body. That means that the male makes the body soul, in the sense of having perceptiveness, asleep and awake, of the whole world, and makes the body become historical. '[T]he male always completes the business of generation – it implants sentient Soul, breathes, ἐπιτελεῖ τὴν γένεσιν, ἐμποιεῖ τὴν αἰσθητικην ψυχην' (741b, 5).[11] '[J]ust as the ability to see does not get perfected without eyes, nor the eye without the ability to see' (766a, 9). The body, however, is already wholly present without the male.

This is unfamiliar, unusual genetics but gives no impression of being outdated, if only because it has yet to be fully understood. It deals with the mystery of birth and says that the ultimate fullness of what has become – not some supplementation of the physiology, all of which is complete and has come from the female – is given by the male, but what he gives is analogous to the difference between imperfection and perfection, between which it is as difficult – Umberto Eco says impossible – to discriminate as between a masterpiece and a skilful forgery. The male gives the new being something like his passion, his worship.

I urge someone to check, as I am unable to, whether in certain instances where Aristotle is describing the appearance of beings as the result of decay he is really talking about parthenogenesis. Although perhaps it is not all that important. What points in the direction of parthenogenesis and its associated issues is what I have just described, the role of the male in bringing to completion something which is fully ready. Jacques Loeb (1859–1924), an American biologist of Prussian origin, successfully brought about artificial parthenogenesis of the eggs of sea urchins. These and other biological data show that the role of the male in gestation is curious and, in the case of some invertebrates, non-existent. There are species where parthenogenesis is the norm and where males can be dispensed with until a change in environmental conditions, probably unfavourable, sees them beginning to be produced again, still through parthenogenesis. Similarly with bees: the fertilized queen lays only female larvae. When, towards the end of the season, her stock of sperm finishes, she ceases bisexual reproduction and proceeds by parthenogenesis to produce only male drones.

So the role of the male is, to say the least, peculiar. Everything has already been completed without him. Modern biology tells us that the male seed, when it enters the ovum, enhances the difference between parent and offspring, *may* affect the sex, and stimulates the ovum's development. It 'stimulates the ovum's development': this expression from modern biology is identical in meaning with Aristotle's 'completes the business of generation'. Moreover, in parthenogenesis experiments, it proved possible to trigger development of the egg both by sperm from the male and by other chemical methods.

Because the role of the male is somehow not technical, the male element is adding a kind of perfection, a kind of non-physiological fullness to the new birth, and this dimension, with which Aristotle was familiar, is the reason we feel genetic engineering experiments like cloning are – and they are – immoral. This is tantamount to saying that the masculine element introduces, precisely as Aristotle suggests, something like morality into the new birth. If the male role was purely technical and genetic engineering had found alternative ways of performing that purely technical function, it would simply have found ways of breaking through the defence mechanisms of the female body, which, for some reason, does not allow itself to give birth without male involvement, or would have found other ways of stimulating an ability the female always had. The offensiveness of cloning sheep and, later perhaps, human beings is that science and technology have learned to dispense with something that, from a chemical and biological viewpoint, is not actually necessary, but is needed in some other respect for which I will use Aristotle's words: 'to implant sensitive Soul', since otherwise there will be a body and life, a living body lacking that elusive final touch, indefinable but necessary for fullness, for *eidos*.

But who needs that final touch, who needs masterpieces if they cannot in any case be distinguished from forgeries?

Who needs it? An example. For Aristotle, the word is matter, it is the 'body' of sense. In the dictionary, words seem completely viable, but they will be dead within a year, even within a month, after ceasing to be used in coherent speech. Matter does not only have meaning: matter *exists* only as a potential for perfection, for a valuable fullness. *Eidos* creates matter. There is a mother only if there are intelligent sons. When human beings no longer come out of her body, there is no longer a mother, only a female. History creates matter.

That is why, in Aristotle, history is implanted in the form (*eidos*) of the male semen into the woman, into the mother, the matter and 'completes the business of generation', imparting to the matter the purpose of attaining fullness. We will now think differently about the myth that begins with a birth. The Christian myth of God's giving birth to God, through matter, through a mother who already personified humanity in full measure, through love.

In a human nature – only in one, that of the Mother of God – there was already all of humanity, all that is human. Quite irrespective of whether human parthenogenesis is possible or not – and in the light of its widespread incidence in the living world in general it most likely is – the truth about 'immaculate conception' among humans or the rest of the animal realm is that the male element is *strange*, and marginal.[12] It comes from far away and seems like a visitation, a visitor, with whose very remoteness history begins.

Lecture 8, 28 October 1997

Parthenogenesis is possible only in invertebrates. If we have read Aristotle correctly, and the male is the element of the historical, eidetic, and logical, then we need have no qualms about the fragility of this 'idealism' of Plato and Aristotle: it is inserted, introduced into human existence with the same rigorous firmness with which, for continuance of the race, the male is introduced because the female alone will not suffice.

Then again, the firmness of this union of matter and meaning is guaranteed by the fact that matter of its own accord desires *logos* and *eidos* (for the present we can bracket them together, although we may later need to differentiate them). We need to talk about this because understanding matter as the passive contrary of active *eidos* is a common mistake. After all that I have said and quoted here, my listeners may object, 'No, in Aristotle *eidos* and matter are very much contraries.' I will repeat. They are not contraries at all: matter is the substratum, not the contrary. Matter is *eidos* in potential, not in the sense that *eidos* can be made out of it, but in the sense that it wants to become *eidos* and is itself attracted towards meaning. Among the latest works on Aristotle's understanding of matter is the thousand-page, in effect, philological and philosophical encyclopaedia by Heinz Happ, *Hyle. Studien zum aristotelischen Materie-Begriff.*[1] After detailed consideration, his main conclusion about the *Vollkommenheitsstreben der Hyle* ('*hyle's* aspiration to perfection') is:

> One wonders why these well-known individual features of Aristotle's *hyle* have not long since corrected the stereotypical image of a 'passive' Hyle, or indeed how that image could ever have come about.... The Hyle of Aristotle is a metamorphosis of the 'pre-Socratic' principle of matter, applied to the problems Aristotle is dealing with and woven into new contexts, but full of unimpeded power.[2]

Strato, Eudemus, the Stoa,[3] Alexander of Aphrodisias, Avicenna, and Averroes in particular 'were by no means wrong in their very dynamic interpretation of Aristotle's matter'.[4]

It seems to me, only seems because it is difficult to pronounce on this definitively here, that 'we' modern people reading Aristotle are concerned that there may be too much matter; too much in the sense of too much to bear, and we would like to moderate it, or somehow tame it, perhaps by comprehending it. And naturally, since we have that intention, we also have in us its contrary, the fear that we have done too much ordering, that we have overdone the systematization, and need accordingly to give substance and the world their head. In this respect, we swing like a pendulum, now in time to the beat of the organization of energy, we decide firmly, 'This is so, let this be so'; at another time, more liberally, 'but maybe that is actually not the case. We'd better look at it again, and think about it some more.'

'We'd better', or even, 'Quick! Quick!', or 'At all costs!', set the tone in both our assertive and hesitant modes. Aristotle sets a different tone: 'Everything has already happened.' In his understanding, all the matter in the world has already been encompassed by the world in a serene and perfect way. Heinz Happ draws our attention to Aristotle's proof in *On the Heavens*, Book 1, Chapter 9, that the world is one and that it already contains all matter that exists anywhere. 'The world as a whole, therefore, includes all its appropriate matter, which is, as we saw, natural perceptible body. So that neither are there now, nor have there ever been, nor can there ever be formed more heavens than one, but this heaven of ours is one and unique and complete.'[5] Aristotle produces his evidence in that chapter, and it is integral to all his thinking. The most important thing about his message is its almost musical tone.

We have no business arguing over whether the tone is right or wrong, critical or uncritical, because in both the assertive and the hesitant swings of our attitude to the world we find that same fullness, only with the addition of 'should', testifying to our failure to understand that any real 'should be' in philosophy invariably already is. From that 'is' we have lapsed to 'should be', just like Aristotle's pupil Alexander the Great, for whom living with the fullness of the world was his main idea, but who stopped seeing the fullness of the world as something that already is and imagined it as something that should be, and would be, just as soon as the Hellenic Army crossed the Ganges and put behind it the modest distance remaining to the 'ends of the world and the Great Outer Sea'.

Matter is also matter in the sense of a subject, an object, and (until the concepts of object and subject were inverted in modern times) matter was a subject, a sub-ject, subject to definition. It is something subject to pronouncements, categorization, and judgement. The principle of matter is 'that out of which', including the sense of 'over which you are having an argument'. Not 'because of what': that would be a different, formal principle; not 'because of whom', who first started everything, another mover; not 'for the sake of what', purposive, but precisely 'out of what'.

Classical, or indeed any powerful, thinking so much dislikes indirect, calculated moves, so much dislikes lagging behind what it sees in front of it, that it is not in the least shocked by what so shocked Alexey Losev, when he was editing Aristotle's volume, in the quote, 'Out of what? Out of

matter [in Russian *materia, Tr.*].' He decided to 'correct' it. No, make that
'Out of a mother [in Russian *materi, Tr.*].'⁶ That will cause no trouble; that
will be sobering. It will be enlightening to say that everyone was literally
born of a mother. When you say, when you look at, that, you can see there
is something really not quite appropriate about asking a question like,
'What is matter?' 'What is mother?' Mother is what gave birth to us. Let us
take a look at ourselves, at what we are. Mother is what was there before
us so that we could be born. The anthropic so-called principle is applicable
here to a self-evidently special case: if the mother from whom we came is,
naturally, such that we can be as we are, then the mother of the mother and
the first mother, or matter, from which we came is, of course, such that we
could be as we are.

The definition of matter, of mother, here, needless to say, acquires a
sense not of an inquisitive attempt to find out what kind of interesting
object, outside of us, our mother is, but something quite different: to discover how, being as we are outside our mother, we should behave. To know
how we should live given that we are what we are, outside our mother.
How, then, to behave? The definition is not motivated by any cognitive
interest – imagine a son taking a cognitive interest in his mother – but is
part of the big question addressed by all thinking, one that animates it so
constantly that it is not even made explicit: how should we be?

We come out of a mother. But are we because of the mother and for the
purposes of the mother? The initiative was taken and the goal set by the
father. The father determined, for better or worse, that the mother should
give birth. So is the father the definition of mother, is the *logos* paternal?
Busying ourselves with defining matter, the mother, we are doing the job
of the father. We say the father 'knew' the mother, in the interests not of
satisfying scientific curiosity but of determining her in the sense of 'we
have to sort this out'. The male decides. He 'takes' the female as his wife, he
'releases' her, leaves her. If it is the woman who leaves, it is she who decides
and determines. Besides patriarchy, matriarchy is possible: determining
and deciding by the female. We are not familiar with that order today, at
least, but suppose it did exist long ago. In fact it is really not important for
us here and now whether it did or did not exist. What is important is what
the controversy about it, whether it is possible, whether it ever existed,
emphasizes: the conspicuous, special, eidetic (*eidos* meaning in the species)
position of the male is prominent, 'marked'. The topics of matriarchy and
of feminism only serve to underline even more the special, conspicuous
position of the male. The louder the voices of the feminists, the more glaringly obvious does the status not of the female but of the male become.

The male, defining, and decisive role of the *logos* in classical philosophy
is nowadays being called phallo-logocentrism or phallogocentrism: that is,
placing the phallus, the penis, and the *logos* centre stage. This term is in
the thick of an extremely animated controversy in contemporary thinking.
Fighting is nearly always over a woman.

The term phallo-logo-centrism has resonance because of its blunt truth:

that is exactly the way it is. The *logos* as the male, defining element is introduced by Aristotle with assertive masculine firmness into the body, into matter, into the female. From what little we know about Aristotle, it seems unlikely that he is introducing it unintentionally or surreptitiously, like a naïve adolescent incapable of talking about anything other than his penis, but entirely deliberately, in the clear light of day. More than that: he talks of a *duty* to determine it. Yes, the male should take the initiative and occupy centre stage. It seems that Aristotle is quite consciously advocating phallogocentrism.

Is Jacques Derrida then doubly correct? Actually, his exact thesis is well summarized by Geoffrey Bennington:

> This complication of the empirical and the transcendental marked by the prefix 'quasi-'– which would perhaps, if such a formulation were still possible, be Derrida's contribution to the history of philosophy, what would make him a 'contemporary' – disallows on the one hand that philosophy relegate sexual difference to the status of an object of a regional science on the pretext of a transcendental neutrality which in fact has always veiled a privilege of the masculine (whence 'phallogocentrism'), and on the other hand that we attempt simply to unseat this masculine transcendental to replace it with a feminine.[7]

For Aristotle, the male and female are not relegated to the margins. As *eidos* and matter-mother, they stand in plain sight, but this does not undermine Derrida's position. The majority of metaphysicians behave in precisely this manner, otherwise Vladimir Soloviov, for example, would not have represented his writing on the male–female theme as something new.[8]

But let us now move away from this official language of philosophy and listen to Derrida speaking for himself, on the lower half of the page, in the additions he makes against a grey background under the columns of an expository book about him, in highly intimate autobiographical notes which twenty years previously he never intended to show to anyone. Let us really just *listen* to Derrida, since otherwise what point would there be in approaching him? He truly feels words, and because of that the inattentive reader will make a fool of himself literally at every step. I invite you to translate a crucial sentence: *Dès qu'il est saisi par l'écriture, le concept est cuit.*[9] *Cuire*: to cook, but also to fire, as bricks are fired; and to ready, to bring to readiness. *Cuit*: ready, cooked, but also fired as in *face cuite*. The matter is closed, 'in the bag', uses the same word: *c'est du tout cuit*. But also to 'land in it', to be lost, perish, fall for something, is *être cuit*. There is quite a difference, is there not, between 'brought to readiness', 'in the bag', and 'lost'? What does Derrida mean? What is the translator to do? What, for the translator, is just different meanings, *différence*, is something for which Derrida invents a new word in the French language, *différance*, 'differentiation and deferral': any word, as soon as it is uttered, immediately founders, melts in front of your eyes, becomes charred, and there is nothing you can do about that, you can't 'deal with' it, can't transfix it. We try to catch something in a word, but what we are trying to deal with is in motion.

Writing, then, arrests (one of the meanings of *saisir*) a concept, or roasts or 'fires' it. Is that a good or a bad thing? It is either very bad or simple necessity, just as, in order to make a pot, you have to fire the clay. Does that make it all right?

No sooner has the male, phallogocentrism, appeared on the scene than it differentiates, just as mention of patriarchy immediately suggests an earlier matriarchy. Derrida does not use the words 'woman' and 'mother' to designate something opposed to 'male', ladies and gentlemen, and that is just the same as in Aristotle. This is one of those cases where any thought, if it is real, is integral, or rather it is a whole complicated situation in which an opposition, or different oppositions, can arise. How is that possible? I shall tell you, but first I need to make two comments. When Derrida says 'woman', he is not naïvely forgetting the mother, and when he says 'mother', he is not forgetting woman; he is here in the biblical tradition which gives the name of 'Eve' (a word whose approximate meaning is 'the mother of all that lives') to the wife, the woman of Adam. Derrida does not forget the maternal when speaking of the feminine: he obliges us to ponder the distinction. My second comment: on page 192 of the Bennington–Derrida book the *surnoms* '*femme*' and '*mère*' in the upper, unshaded section of the page correspond roughly in the lower, shaded, intimate commentary by Derrida to 'Sultana Esther Georgette Safar Derrida', the full name of Jacques Derrida's mother.[10] This entire lower section of the book consists of entries about the days and months of her long illness and her death in a clinic in Nice. She is being written about by someone who emerged from her. 'Mother' means primarily this, something close out of which everything else comes.

In Derrida, 'mother' is the name for 'already', *déjà*, and for 'text'. Text is what lies at the base of all the work of deconstruction, the 'matter' of Derrida's thought. Deconstruction is not inquisitiveness, a seeking for definition; it is primarily a revelation of that 'differentiation' mentioned above. So it is not that 'mother' is used to clarify what 'text' or 'tissue' are, but this act of naming raises the question of what female and maternal are. This 'mother', matter raising questions, is anterior to the opposition of good–evil, male–female, or truth–lie. It is important to emphasize, and to remember, that *anterior*. That is, it is not something slippery and questionable, maybe true or maybe false, but the task of scrutinizing, pondering, and seeing what the categories of good–bad are inapplicable to.

This non-relativeness of maternal-female is not negative. Towards good–evil it again corresponds precisely to the pre-contrariety of Aristotle's substratum. Derrida, however, does not notice this correspondence, and in principle is incapable of doing so, because as soon as he takes the texts of Aristotle and Plato, more often of Plato, and pores over them, he is already conditioned to see in them the conventional opposition of male to female, that is, phallocentrism; and of speech to writing, that is, logocentrism. Unfortunately, going along with the deconstructed metaphysics of classical authors, with the loud mainstream of French thought, is already a given, and to go against that critical, revolutionary pose would mean to find oneself with only a minority of readers. Derrida manifestly sides with the majority.

But we have better things to do than try to catch Derrida out where he misreads his authors. Nietzsche did not even get round to misreading them, and contented himself with how they were paraphrased in reference books. *This is not the point.* If the readers, he is saying, who are reading about me on that bright top half of the book only knew what my life consists of: unceasing prayer and tears – 'for like SA I love only tears, I only love and speak through them'[11] – and a wish to die, not from weariness but rather because he cannot bear the slipping away of fullness, the impossibility of understudying, of reliving life.[12]

What in September we identified as the indispensable, primary, essential condition of any thinking is prayer as an offering of oneself:

[T]o God, the only one I take as a witness, without yet knowing what these sublime words mean, and this grammar, and *to*, and *witness*, and *God*, and take, take God, and not only do I pray, as I have never stopped doing all my life, and pray to him, but I take him here and take him as my witness, I give myself what he gives me, i.e. the *i.e.* to take the time to take God as a witness.[13]

Let God be the witness of all that is clear and all that is unclear in oneself. From the impossibility of understudying the moment comes the constant thinking about putting an end to his life, not in the sense of acting out a suicide, but in the sense of gambling one's entire life and death as a stake, a price one will willingly pay for the luxury, the happiness, of an enduring moment. It is because of this that Derrida since his childhood, when the grown-ups amused themselves with how easy it was to make this child cry for no apparent reason, loves those who cried easily: Rousseau, Nietzsche, or St Augustine.[14]

Because of the impossibility of understudying or photographing 'now', I am already dead – and that is the source of tears: I am mourning myself, simply continuing the lamentation of the mother over her sick, and perhaps dying, child, just as she wept over two other sons who died, two brothers of Derrida, a continuation of his mother's tears as a continuation of life from within her.

Standing in the presence of God is not by any means describing oneself to him, as if He did not already know; it is not a matter of truthfulness, genuineness, sincerity of communication, but an outright soliciting of the gift, *don*, that was and is in all that has being. Or, and this is the same thing, asking for forgiveness, *pardon*, begging for everything to be left as it is; together with a begging for forgiveness for being unable to repeat or retain what has been given. Then everything that happens, one's autobiography, becomes theology. Along with the unbearable sense of fullness slipping away and the constant longing for death, the lamentation and unceasing prayer, Derrida finds that he is 'interested in the bedsore, not in writing or literature, art, philosophy, science, religion or politics but only memory and heart, not even the history of the presence of the present'.[15]

Begging for forgiveness, something I cannot give but God can, begging a confirming repetition of the gift of everything, confident only of the affirmation, the identification of what is, that it is what is, as it is, does not by any means indicate that anything is known of what I, God, the gift or forgiveness, are. What, then, can your body be? That, too, is unknown, and will seemingly remain unknown even after the accumulation of immense amounts of knowledge in biology. Not everything is lost in the darkness of the dark, indefinable forest. One fact cuts through the darkness, the tears and the bafflement, one indubitable, monstrous fact, always present before Derrida's eyes, also inexplicable, perhaps, but absolutely, incontrovertibly certain. That fact is that, on the seventh day after the birth of this mysterious creature, the writer who, according to official documents, bears the name Jacques Derrida but whose secret name is Elijah Derrida, his uncle, also called Elijah, firmly held his body in his lap and, spreading his knees, being a person, a *mohel*, with authority from who knows how far back in history, performed with a stone knife on his small infant body the operation of circumcision.

Why? Whatever for? Those questions would take us far back into the history of religions and mythology and they are as nothing against the indisputable, observed fact that an operation was performed on that body by the people gathered there, moreover on the particular part of that body required for procreation, namely the penis, the phallus, the operation of cutting off the ring of foreskin. The extremely special, multi-layered nature of this event was stressed by the fact of what deliberately and emphatically was not carried out during the ritual, but whose very absence brought to mind that it had been performed in other instances, in other times: the mother had sometimes in the past had to eat the severed ring of foreskin; and furthermore, until the abolition in 1843 of the practice as unhygienic, and even then only in Paris, the *mohel* had to suck the blood from the penis washed with wine after circumcision in the ritual of *mezizah*, thereby combining a sacred rite of cannibalism (which gave rise to the myth that Jews ritually ate babies) with an equally ritual religious consecration of fellatio or giving head.

These themes have long been surfacing in various books by Derrida. They might not be considered particularly significant, but he himself wrote in his diary on 20 December 1976:

> Circumcision, that's all I've ever talked about, consider the discourse on the limit, margins, marks, marches, etc., the closure, the ring (alliance and gift), the sacrifice, the writing of the body, the *pharmakos*

excluded or cut off, the cutting/sewing of *Glas*, the blow and the sewing back up, when the hypothesis according to which it's that, circumcision, that, without knowing it, never talking about it or talking about it in passing, as though it were an example, that I was always speaking or having spoken, unless, another hypothesis, circumcision itself were merely an example of the thing I was talking about, yes but I have been, I am and always will be, me and not another, circumcised, and there's a region that is no longer that of an example, that's the one that interests me and tells me not how I am a case but where I am no longer a case, when the word first of all, at least, CIRCUMCISED, across so many relays, multiplied by my 'culture', Latin, philosophy, etc., as it imprinted itself on my language circumcised in its turn, could not have not worked on me, pulling me backward, in all directions, to love, yes, a word, *milah*.[16]

'*Milah*' means a word. The root is the same as in *mohel*.

And the fact that Algerian Jews, under the soothing influence of Catholic French culture, called circumcision 'baptism' and, instead of Bar Mitzvah, spoke of 'communion' only served to repress all the more deeply a sense of guilty involvement in a covert ritual murder, making them secretly admit it and binding them more tightly in a chasm of shame, concealment, and a need to justify themselves.

Derrida feels bound to what he writes by the secret, private urge to untie the knot that has been tied by his circumcision, but it is too late to untie it. And then, it is not enough to read his text, his material, his matter – it needs to be eaten, to be sucked like the foreskin, the severed ring – because in Hebrew the word for 'word' is '*milah*', cut off, circumcised.[17]

Tied up in that knot is Derrida's attitude to his father, whose ring Derrida lost after the old man's death. At the same time, he began to think of writing a book about circumcision, that shadowy, behind-the-scenes world of scars and sores, of cutting off and cannibalism, of birth in flowing blood, through sucking and eating. The same link of flesh, of the body, as a direct continuation of the pain of circumcision, 'the phantom burning, in my belly, irradiating a diffuse zone around the sex, a threat which returns every time the other is in pain, if I identify with him, with her, even', like the threat of castration;[18] the visceral empathy with any pain, '*sympathie algique autour de mon sexe*',[19] felt clearly for the first time in early childhood at the sight of blood when his seven- or eight-year-old cousin Simone's genitals were wounded by a scooter (ibid.).

If we dig up, open up, this tangle which, with a single bloody connection, links generations, Derrida's most personal and secret pain, the circumcision and the severed foreskin, the word – if we look into this dark dungeon, we will discover what seems like a new, hitherto unknown language. A secret Elijah, patron of circumcision, will peep out through the Jacques everyone sees and the walls will be broken down. This was dangerous and difficult. He had to decide to become

the only philosopher to my knowledge who, accepted – more or less
– into the academic institution, author of more or less legitimate writings on Plato, Augustine, Descartes, Rousseau, Kant, Hegel, Husserl,
Heidegger, Benjamin, Austin, will have dared to describe his penis, as
promised, in concise and detailed fashion, and as no one dared, in the
Renaissance, paint the circumcised penis of Christ on the incredible
pretext that there was no model for it.[20]

The word should be tied to the belly like that, by simultaneously the most
intimate, the most sacred and intimate connection: '[W]hat happens in
circumcision, what is done, outside language, without a sentence, the time
of a proper name, the rest is literature.'[21] But the urge to know oneself
suddenly leads you away from yourself to a strange twin or double who,
precisely to the extent that he is totally me, for just that reason is completely separate, cut off from me, peeled off. When Derrida noted this,
as if reminding him of the inaccessibility of his twin, Jean, his son, said
to Marguerite, his wife, on 17 July 198(?) that 'he had dreamed he had
a double' and 'he is grammatical'.[22] Because of the unfathomable depth
his circumcision had cut into him, Derrida makes desperate, highly risky
movements, exposing himself, exhibiting his most secret, intimate, and
personal secrets. He wants to *write*

> the mixture on this incredible supper of the wine and blood, let people
> see it how I see it on my sex each time blood is mixed with sperm or
> the saliva of fellatio, describe my sex throughout thousands of years
> of Judaism, describe it (microscopy, photography, stereophototypy)
> until the paper breaks, make all the readers drool, wet lips, high and
> low, stretched out in their turn on the cushions, right on the knees of
> 'godfather' Elie.[23]

Fellocircumcision, autofellocircumcision, one's own *mohel* doubled up –
and this is a rite or a supreme act of his unique and personal religion.[24]

> [T]he constancy of God in my life is called by other names, so that I
> quite rightly pass for an atheist, the omnipresence to me of what I call
> God in my absolved, absolutely private language being neither that of
> an eyewitness nor that of a voice doing anything other than talking to
> me without saying anything.[25]

Ladies and gentlemen, this is completely frank, explicit, pronounced phallocentrism. Accordingly, the critic of phallocentrism needs to choose not
between phallocentrism or no phallocentrism, but between naïve, concealed, covert phallocentrism and phallocentrism brought centre stage. Do
not ask where it has come from: it just *is*. Just as the mother and the father
are, out of whom I came. If anyone has forgotten that, they are not a Jew
who, at his father's funeral, had a button ritually torn from his shirt by the

Rabbi, a second circumcision and a reassertion of the Rabbi's association with the authority of the father.[26] That all this focus on the organ of procreation, of sex, is not a personal autobiographical peculiarity of Derrida, he asserts defiantly: all this is my confession, certainly, but more than that I am taking the confession of others, probing their most embarrassing secrets, of which I am the involuntary heir.

What happens when the supreme goal is reached and an end comes to circumcised writing and uncircumcised writing begins, now without the assistance of the seemingly always present father? Will all these real details go off somewhere and something else move into the limelight? Perhaps, but which something else? Will it be made clear what circumcision is and what it signifies? Or will the body change and the mark of circumcision vanish? What is it all about anyway? Why is the body attacked, precisely this part of it, and the foreskin severed from it? Why is it so terminally marked? It is obviously a castration substitute, deployed in the most violent way. Or is it a vaccination, a sign of the unconditional and final abolition of castration? The act is at the very least a lurid way of drawing attention to sex and procreation – but how and why?

A man sees his own circumcision, on *his* body. It may have been undergone by others; it has not only been visited on him but, like his death, it belongs exclusively to him and not to him as one of many. I am dying and my death is not just one more, not one in a succession. Death is not distributed like work to the many. In the same way, my circumcision is always exclusively mine, not in some statistical sense but in the most intimate way imaginable. Talking about it is the only thing that is really interesting, but whom to communicate with about it, and what to communicate, apart from the fact that I have been violently, sexually assaulted in the most vulnerable and sensitive part of my body?

Phallocentrism, the phallus in the centre of attention, and of gossip with a woman and a mother imagining a fantasy circumcision where the exaggerated operation, with a spilling out of all the innards, enormously painful, coincides simultaneously with fellatio and orgasm, so that semen is mixed with blood, unbearable pain with unbearable delight.[27]

In this phallocentrism, keyed up to the limit, it becomes very clear how it differs from Aristotle's, which is also as plain as can be imagined (up to a limit, clearly). The dual operation on the phallus, performed by a woman, makes it doubly a topic for discussion, an issue, startling in its indeterminateness and the extent to which it is unknown. For Aristotle, the phallus is not a topic but a role: assuming leadership, taking the historical initiative with the risk, of course, of making mistakes. This strong leadership, this risk, Derrida does not take upon himself.

Accordingly, criticism of phallocentrism is by no means repudiation of phallocentrism; indeed, on the contrary, the phallus is in the spotlight as never before, precisely as material for deconstruction. Circumcision is understood not as vaccination against castration but as a real castration. Derrida did not submit his own children to circumcision. He is 'the last

Jew'; Judaism ends with him. Repudiation of his own circumcision is rejection of the confident imperative to do what is 'proper', a bafflement as to why it is proper, and indeed of why anything at all should be considered 'only proper'. All reason, every goal, is understood as a construct, and a construct that should be taken apart.

Without saying a word about postmodernism or about deconstruction, we need to seek Jacques Derrida in our *forest*, outside the metric space to which he insistently bids us to return, not believing, refusing to believe, in the geometry of the forest or in its Cross. Now, when we are very close to arriving at an answer, or at an intuition, which may not happen, it is important to refrain from highly strung decisions, like his rejection of the male role. Rejecting the imperious gesture does not call for abandoning the male role. To decide to terminate the tradition of circumcision, despite the belief that a Jew who refuses to be circumcised is doomed to eternal Gehenna; to remain a Jew and accommodate the God of St Augustine; to choose for all time, with total commitment, a life of prayer and tears – is a definitive and very major action. Not to name your God, to keep him in a private place no one else is permitted to enter – that, too, is an important, definitive gesture. Note that in all this there is courage and resolution, in which we recognize the discipline of philosophy.

We have said that all genuine seeking that does not weary passes through a phase of *amekhania*, obscurity, and bafflement. Derrida's attitude to the word, to the text – the word when he deconstructs it breaks down into letters, melts into similar words, spellings, and these transitions lead his thinking – is supported by a phase when a word 'freezes'. He suddenly sees a word – one spring morning in 1990, it was the word 'cascade' (a cascade of troubles and upsets was what started him off) – as if for the first time. That happens frequently. Each time he stares senselessly, vacantly, uncomprehendingly, at the word with the same lack of the least response as he saw in his mother in the last year of her life, recognizing nobody, understanding nothing, not knowing her son or responding to his greeting. And every time this freezing of the word proved to be the beginning of a new love, the discovery of a new land. Every time this freezing of a word occurred, it was like the beginning of a cascade of love for *all* words. That both these things should happen, that the word should become detached from the lexical grid and become unapproachable, but then open out with fresh, alluring charms, is not something the individual can arrange, or even hope for. Both things just have to happen by themselves and it always comes as a surprise.

As with the word, so with everything else. We have quoted Derrida telling us how everything – literature, politics, philosophy – comes to an end. Nothing matters, nothing is interesting. Just like that word, everything freezes in a state of neglect and deceit. Everything just irritates and induces impatience and despair. You can say nothing; whatever you say is stupid and falls flat, of no interest to anyone. But then that very moment of impotence suddenly, again of its own volition, transforms into a completely fresh captivation and interest in everything in the world: language, literature, philosophy, and then, incoherent with happiness, Derrida writes:

> I have not met anyone, I have had in the history of humanity no idea of anyone, wait, wait, anyone who has been happier than I, and luckier, euphoric, this is a priori true, isn't it?, drunk with uninterrupted enjoyment, *haec omnia uidemus et* bona sunt ualde, *quoniam tu ea uides in nobis.* ['We see all these things, and they are very good, because thou seest them thus in us.' *Tr.*][28]

This is submission to the scrutiny of God, allowing God to see through us what he saw at the very beginning of His new creation, achieved by letting go, by the emptiness of being blocked, by the *resolve* to give in to the sense of having been abandoned, to being 'constantly sad, deprived, destitute, disappointed, impatient, jealous, desperate, negative and neurotic'.[29]

Abandonment, emptiness, and *amekhania* are not accidental but the primary and most important reality. It is *unclear* why Derrida's mother cast him out into the world, why she did not let him stay with her, why she forced him to attend a harsh school rather than allowing him to stay at home. But she also bequeathed him a redeeming, life-saving heredity,

> for her capacities for silence and amnesia are what I share best, no arguing with that, that's what they can't stand, that I say nothing, never anything tenable or valid, no thesis that could be refuted, neither true nor false, not even not seen not caught, it is not a strategy but the violence of the void through which God goes to earth to death in me.[30]

In this implacably defensive posture, he will never surrender. From there, from that impregnable ferroconcrete silence, nothing can get through, nothing can make itself heard to Derrida, as nothing could get through to his mother as she lay unconscious and dying. She had never read a word of what he wrote, had never so much as glanced into any of his books.

> [T]he unforgettable power of my discourses hangs on the fact that they grind up everything including the mute ash whose name alone one then retains, scarcely mine, all that turning around nothing, a Nothing in which God reminds me of him, that's my only memory.[31]

One of the subtleties of dead silence is that you can speak with imperturbable coldness about tragic things, putting quotation marks round them, as if parsing them.

Who actually am I and what do people want from me? I'm the little Jew who understood nothing when he came into the world. Derrida still understood nothing when, at the age of twelve, with top marks in everything, he was expelled from his school in Algeria. Why? He had no place in a European French school; he belonged to Africa, so let him speak Hebrew or Arabic. In 1981, he was arrested in Prague and sent to prison. Was that for drug trafficking? Between that expulsion and this prison, or more broadly, between his birth, between being thrown out into the cold and the unknown and death, what could he rely on that would not betray him? Where am I between necessity and chance, what is there in me that is necessary and what is random? It seems to be only *me* that does not know what is what; everything around me is full of that knowledge, from the confidence of the French administration in Algeria that a Jew should know his place to the confidence of the authorities in Czechoslovakia that some Frenchman cannot be just allowed to conduct an unauthorized seminar in Prague. To the confidence of that knife-bearing hand that rose to hack off a baby's body part. Around, everything is full of *logos*, sound reasons, sense, and everything invites him to understand them, to think about them, to agree to them. He is on the verge of agreeing. He is prepared to understand, to think about it, to consent.

Lecture 9, 4 November 1997

Around, everything is full of *logos*, sound reasons, sense, and everything invites Derrida to understand them, to think about them, to agree to them, compelling him to disagree, to be complicit, to go along with this and that: for example, to come together and inflict circumcision on the body of a seven-day-old baby as is only proper. He does not know how to protest and is on the verge of agreeing with the dictates and the accusations. He is prepared to understand, to think about it, to consent. The individual is just too roundly besieged by the empires of propriety. A weak person, he begins to blame himself for everything, even to the point of agreeing with someone at one of his lectures who accused him of not having done enough during the Second World War to help suffering Jewry. Perhaps he really was in some way to blame for the persecution of the Jews, if only by himself being a Jew.

Derrida stands out in the world as a prophet who clearly has a mission. There is plainly a reason why he is writing, being published, and lecturing. He has been saddled with a mission which he must carry out personally. He would be only too glad to pass it over to someone else. Here, take my celebrity, take in my place these hundred-strong audiences. I give you my listeners. They will not transfer to someone else. It is my duty. But what is the mission? It would be good to know that but no one has told me. It is a mission 'whose undecipherable letter arrives only at himself who understands it no better than anyone else'.[1]

What is he guilty of? Why is this taciturn little Jew being persecuted, this intimidated boy at the top of his class in a good French school in Algeria who gets expelled, the would-be drug dealer crushed by the burden of his guilt for every conceivable crime, highly strung, frozen with fear like some small furry animal?

[T]he innocent child [an in-fant, unable to speak, *Bibikhin*] who is by accident charged with a guilt he knows nothing about ... cadaver carrying himself ... he runs he flies so young and light futile subtle agile delivering to the world the very discourse of this impregnable inedible simulacrum.[2]

Only it seems as if in fact this writer and speaker *does* know, or at least knows more than other people. As he complains that he has no guidelines, Derrida can repeat: this is not my confession, it is *yours*; the only difference between us is that I am confessing now while you have not got round to it yet. If we remove, if we scrape away, the layer of imposed meanings passed down from who knows where or when, such as circumcision, such as a quota for Jews in higher education, such as a system of strict taboos – justified when and by whom? – on peddling drugs, if we disassemble the superstructure of dictatorial reasons that we have called prescriptiveness, and this disassembly is what deconstruction is all about, we shall find the busi-ness-free, 'forest' condition of every human being, of every living thing, bereft of guidelines in the midst of the forest. The bright, clear world of prescriptiveness, of the screen, is a snare and a delusion. Derrida is and always will be a thousand times right in his deconstruction. In *reality*, genuinely, there is only the distressed, confused, abandoned (in Heidegger's sense), living being in the midst of the dark forest.

> [A]nd here he is bending beneath the burden, he takes it on without taking it on, nervous, worried, hunted, cadaverized like the beast playing dead and melding with the foliage, literature in short, to escape the murderers or their pack, cadaver carrying himself.[3]

Let it not seem strange to anyone that we have reduced the whole vast discourse of culture, of the entire civilized world of screens and scripts, which constantly scripts and screens everything imaginable, which never takes a step without a roadmap, when every possible step that could be taken has been scripted and mapped, to something that lacks only anything to which it might tether the principal terms and values of its system, so that they are suspended, frozen, above an abyss. Suppose we notice it is dangling and allow the empire of handed-down meanings to go to the fate it deserves, into the realms of illusion, dream and emptiness, what will remain? A small, bewildered furry animal hiding from hunters among the leaves at the top of the trees.

There is valour in not falling asleep in the mechanical, prescriptive motion of civilization, in disassembling the superimposed schemes of meanings – taking them apart in every sense, to read them carefully and see what lies behind them. Behind them there is always a strange space, an inviting void, like circumcision, a mishandling of the organ that serves procreation of the species. The law goes far back to times *immemorial*, it comes from some distant place past and above the rationalizations, more or less comical, the hygienic explanations and all the rest; it is like tree roots going deep down into the soil, while official explanations are like planks, planed and processed. But before you can trim and machine it, the wood has to have been a tree, rooted in the soil. After that you can take it and make whatever you want from it, but, Aristotle reminds us, if we neglect this rational artefact and it is sucked back into the soil, what will grow will be not a replica of the product, but a new, natural tree.

Deconstruction, disassembly, is like planting artefacts in the ground, returning them to where they came from, and the truth they unfailingly demonstrate is that what is actually alive is not the artefact itself, but the forest. Only the forest has a life of its own and can live it. Even if some cannot see beyond the prescriptive schedule, the calculations, the distribution, the management, at the beginning and end of all the planning and calculating there is the forest. In broad daylight, in the middle of an intense discussion, Derrida comments and admits that he is only a small furry animal hiding, camouflaging itself in the foliage. His forest is literature.

We have heard what we have heard. Now we have to decide whether Aristotle surrendered in panic, in a fit of nerves, of blindness to the world of *logos* or the phallocentric empire of rationality. We find the answer almost immediately. Derrida himself helps to provide it, and is the best introduction to classical thought – as Heidegger is its soundest commentator and heir. Aristotle's thought is like that of the other classics, like any genuine thinking in that unknown, measureless space that Derrida has outlined for us through his determination to break free of prescriptiveness, to stop the tradition of circumcision and retire with his hidden God to complete defensive silence. We need to shake off the habit of reading philosophy within the grid of established tradition, to *accept* the preparatory school of Jacques Derrida, and see classical thought *in its forest*.

Derrida took a decision and put it into practice. He is to be the last in his family to be subjected to the millennial practice, extending back over hundreds of generations, of inflicting circumcision. Henceforth the operation on the male organ that serves procreation will not be conducted in his family. He is the last Jew.

The corollary of this action is that the schedule of human biography is struck out and there opens before us an unscheduled, measureless unknown. Man reverts to the small furry animal hiding in the forest from the whole gang of hunters.

Of the extant works of Aristotle, the longest is his *A History of Animals*, which might more accurately be titled 'What We Know About Animals'.[4] Why should there be interest in collecting information about living beings? Because we are ourselves in the midst of living beings and are embedded or hidden in the forest, like Derrida's small animal. Humankind in its essence is first among living beings. It is so deeply and inextricably embedded among earth's creatures that, to Aristotle's vision in *Physics* (that if nature possessed the art of building, then the trunks of trees, the rocks and clay would assemble themselves into houses and the houses would grow spontaneously), there is a corresponding section in *The History of Animals*. Animals imitate human beings: swallows build nests in imitation of human homes, parent birds jointly feed their young. In other words, humans are even more firmly and securely rooted in the world forest with their art than some of the animals with their instinct. The human has more comfortably, more harmoniously, found its place amidst substance. A human is a living being like any other but is, in addition, *political*. This place in *The History of Animals* has been misinterpreted to mean that humans are social animals. Individuality and independence are for Aristotle as characteristic of humankind as sociability; after all, bees are social creatures. In Aristotle, 'political' means moral, and accordingly we need to think some more about the meaning of 'moral'. By all accounts, moral does not mean prescribed in regulations (like circumcision). For Aristotle, moral means active, capable of making decisions and choices, and acting.[5]

The translation 'social animal' is wretched, terrible, and in fact just plain wrong. It is the work of 'wreckers'. The revolutionaries building a new society had good reason to battle against wreckers, winkling them out and neutralizing them. In human society, wrecking is a necessary evil. Almost all communal living is poisoned by wrecking, whether in a communal apartment or in the Supreme Soviet. Why is wrecking so rooted in human society? Because to do it you don't need to do anything. It does itself. Why, when the revolutionaries, new, fresh, and alert people, started building the new society, did they see wrecking all around, everywhere, almost within themselves, and were prepared to execute themselves for wrecking? Because humans are ζῷον πολιτικόν, not in the sense of swarming in a beehive or teeming in an anthill, although they are capable of that and even now are building termite states. They are, though, also capable of living a monastic life. There is a distinction between what people are capable of doing, what they can choose to do (or not do); to build a society, or not; a society as a termite state, or not; an iron ship, or not; what they decide and manage to do, or do not.

There is an accidental in a human being: they may know how to build, or they may not; they are substantially capable of learning and, naturally, it is accidental whether they learn all about something, or learn nothing at all. 'Substantially', but not just in the sense of having an ability which may or may not turn out well, but in the sense that there already is in every human being the potential to be 'political', to be an ethical living being. It is inherent in their nature, above all else, to choose to be good or bad, right or wrong, to see everything in the light of what should or should not be, to approve or disapprove, to accept and be glad, or not to accept and reject. Before anything else is awake in them, a human being will wail in protest: that first cry of a newborn baby is unambiguously, unerringly, recognized as discontentment and evokes a response that is also an ethical impulse, to give support, or to be confused, but something that, at all events, is recognizable as an existential response. Awareness of good and evil is more deeply instilled in a human being than life itself: a human being will not die in order to be part of society rather than alone, but will die so that things should be as they ought, rather than as they ought not, to be. They will die in full view in a war against the enemy, or in private, killing themselves quickly or, more often, slowly because in their own judgement they have found themselves not as they should be, 'unworthy', according to Aristotle.

Humans are political, ethical animals, meaning that everything is primarily orientated towards a purpose, towards making things better. *Logos*, the mind, takes its bearings from this better–worse dichotomy, without which, without purpose, it would have no meaning; it would be a computer with no tasks. As regards definitions of the human being as a 'political animal' that 'has *logos*', everything is as back to front as the traditional ranking of ethics and metaphysics in the system of philosophy: it is a standard mistake not to recognize that ethics takes priority. Ethics dominates.

Human nature, ethics, choosing the good, the kind, goods (i.e. property, being over the bad, over non-being, scarcity, want), is innate in the human body and is part of it, just as claws are part of a cat, and it is equally impossible, or at least far more difficult, to extract it. Concern over how society is arranged or ordered, or not, is wholly understandable, because people can arrange things well for themselves or not, and are capable of learning, but what they never need is to be taught the difference between good and bad. For some reason, people just do know that from the outset. We need not be anxious that people will like sweet things more than they like good things. They will like sweet things only to the extent that they see them as good. When someone tries to teach us what is good and what is bad, they are actually teaching us to see in a particular way what needs to be *considered* good. This is possible only because the place for the categories of good and bad is already there.

We have said that history (i.e. teleology, the attainment of perfection, of fullness, of being, of good) is as innate in a human being as distinguishing between male and female. Perfection is the task of human beings, the final touch, the *telos*. An abandoned small animal, knowing nothing, hiding among the foliage, Derrida knows, and it is the only thing he knows for sure, that he is the last Jew, and that with him circumcision will come to an end.

> I shall always have been eschatological, if one can say so, in the extreme I am the last of the eschatologists, I have to this day above all lived, enjoyed, wept, prayed, suffered as though at the last second in the imminence of the flashback end.[6]

As in all his confessions, here, too, he is admitting something everybody else will admit only later, and indirectly at that. He is living out, well or badly, his vocation, his destiny as a human being, and will, you can be sure, see it through. Today, or perhaps always, owing to a lack of understanding of ourselves, the most common and triumphant form of eschatology is the guiding principle 'the worse the better', a vicious and vindictive pushing of evil to the limit, in the belief, evidently, that good will eventually come out of it. 'When the suffering of the lower orders becomes intolerable, there will be a revolution and justice will be victorious.' It does not very much matter whether that is how it has always been or not – personally I think it has – and Parmenides gives us a timely reminder that 'Nothingness does not exist.'[7] Playing games with the hope of things getting worse is a diminution of being: we are toying with something that does not exist, not in the sense of the void and nothingness, since nothingness does not exist and therefore cannot be toyed with, but in the sense that toying itself does not exist: it only seems that, by deciding 'the worse the better', a person is following some sort of path. In reality, they just vanish, cease to be.

Humans, within being, are middling creatures. They are higher than other living creatures because they have basically everything that those have and, in addition, they are the perfection, entelechy, the purposive principle, again not in the sense that they are the best and the highest – 'there are other things much more divine in their nature even than man, e.g., most conspicuously, the bodies of which the heavens are framed'[8] – but in the sense that it is not they who are supposedly the wreath of creation, but through them that the wreath is attained. Man is present and is concerned about fullness and perfection, but, Aristotle stresses, 'in some respects, many animals are better, stronger, more keen-sighted than he'.[9]

Humans hide among the leaves in the forest like all the others, but they are by destiny, in their real essence, eschatologists, the artist putting the final touch. Otherwise they have nothing that is not to be found in other animals.

Do you recall something familiar – two already mentioned characteristics? Neither brings anything significant of its own, because everything is already present in matter, in the mother; and bringing the final touch, the ultimate fullness of *telos*, and of eschatology, are both *male* characteristics. Is Aristotle surreptitiously identifying the human with the male? Have we exposed his phallogocentrism? To put it crudely, is the female, the mother, not really human? Is she or is she not?

Well, actually, it would seem she is not. The nature of male and female is different. The female is only potentially human, potentially a 'political' animal. Only, are we to see this as a belittling of woman? It is interpreted as a humiliation of women by the present-day stereotype of matriarchy versus patriarchy, which has, built into it, a dimension of above–below, master–underling. This is once again (and no matter how many times we repeat it, it will be apropos) a contrariety, and in Aristotle the culminating fullness of *eidos*, or the male, is not at all the contrary of the female and matter, but that of diminution and privation. The contrariety is the contrary of perfection, while the female, on the other hand, is passionate about perfection and already bears within it all the 'matter' required for it; the male only 'conduces to fullness'.

The female, so to speak, 'enables' the male. The male, as it were, confirms, affirms, the female as it already is. The female, so to speak, invites fullness, because it already spontaneously desires it. The male is historical and political, because it resolves, allows, affirms, fulfils, what all matter is waiting for.

Only the male is human in the sense defined by Aristotle that he is as an adult distinct from the infant. It is not human morphology that links the human being with the forest in general: the most important thing, the defining factor, is concern for the fullness of perfection in absolutely everything he enters. The human being is such that it is he who must be asked what the essence and purpose of everything is. His vocation is not primarily to *know* that but to *provide* it, and only then to know it. Everything must be brought before him for confirmation.

Humankind's kinship with the animals, over and above its morphological, biological similarities, results from the unmediated sympathy it feels through its nature, that is, its 'politics', its ethics, for the perfection already existing in nature, just waiting for humankind to acknowledge and approve it, rather as a project has to be taken to the director for approval. This endorsing involvement of humankind is all the stronger and more direct because, even without it, its biological, morphological involvement with nature is all-embracing and self-evident. There is no question of any innate, 'racist' distinction here between the male and the female in what is simply a human function of selecting and deciding. In this the male is exactly the same as the female, only with the additional precarious obligation of beginning (or ending) history.

It is important that, apart from historical initiative, taking decisions, assessment, a kind of completion of the fullness of a perfection that already exists and is accomplished by nature no worse than by art (which is actually the role of the divinity, looking and seeing what is good), and apart from their presumption that they have the right to approve (the role of managers always comes down to no more than approving or blocking creative initiatives coming from below), human beings, and men as human beings, have little other purpose to serve (but this one function is exclusive to them). Accordingly, it is dizzying to see the ease with which Aristotle tosses the human species into the sea, the forest of living beings, so that it becomes indistinguishable, invisible apart from all the others, from those approximately 500 genera and species that Aristotle is inspecting. After all, Aristotle himself is human and, as a living being, ends up in that undifferentiated mass, just like Derrida, the little animal cowering in the leaves. Let us not forget, after all, who is writing and saying all these things!

> Further, some are crafty and mischievous, as the fox; some are spirited and affectionate and fawning, as the dog; others are easy-tempered and easily domesticated, as the elephant; others are cautious and watchful, as the goose; others are jealous and self-conceited, as the peacock. But of all animals man alone is capable of deliberation.[10]

There have long been discrepant readings of this important passage, corresponding to an old debate which continues to this day.[11] First, 'domesticated', ἥμερος. This word means 'tame, horticultural, cultivated', and its specific root and underlying meaning is 'amenable to hybridization', that is, breedable, enabling the creation and maintenance of a breed, like varieties of wheat or breeds of dogs. The mule comes into this category, and cannot be born without cross-breeding, while donkeys can be wild, as Aristotle would have known. In other lists, we find the donkey is replaced by humans, as if everyone would agree that humans are a domesticated, tame animal. Aristotle, however, immediately proposes a further distinction. There is no such phenomenon in nature as tame, reliably domesticated animals; all tame animals can also be wild. Wild horses, wild dogs, wild goats. Perhaps, then, there are only different degrees of wildness, and there is no such thing as absolute wildness. Possibly, although Aristotle does not say that. One has the impression, however, that leopards, for example, are firmly fixed at the extreme end of wildness and there seem to be few candidates for extreme tameness. Perhaps before selective breeding is undertaken, all animals are 'wild'.

But what about humans? It seems an odd idea that humans belong among the wild animals, and in some lists they have been taken out of the category of those who are sometimes wild, sometimes tame, and moved to the list of those who are always tame, evidently in the belief that Aristotle could not possibly have thought otherwise. In favour of the view that he could and did, there is an argument taken from modern biology. If humans had been tame and never wild, it should have been possible to realize a eugenics project through genetic engineering, such as creating an obedient Christian population as envisaged in Dostoevsky's 'Legend of the Grand Inquisitor', but nothing of the sort has been forthcoming.[12] Charles Galton Darwin, a biologist and the grandson of Charles Darwin and, by the distaff line, a grandson of the founder of eugenics, Sir Francis Galton, a cousin of Charles Darwin, draws attention to the fact that all the species of genuinely domesticated animals readily break down into breeds, each with a desirable feature bred into them and amenable to having that feature brought to greater prominence. Human beings also show signs of having such features: for example, there are musical families, but they do not develop into a separate breed of musicians. Even if we imagine that, under inhuman conditions of some description, breeding of humans proved possible, the people breeders would undoubtedly remain wild.[13]

Possibly, like dogs, there are tame and wild people. Viewing humans as firmly embedded in biology, Aristotle faces the question of who he, the researcher, is himself. He knows that no better than Derrida, but is clearer about his mission. He has it clearly defined, and can define himself back from it: he is an expert, an assessor, a judge.

When Aristotle peers into the eyes of a human being, a vulture, a goat, or a horse (491b–492a),[14] human eyes are on exactly the same level as those of any other living being. There is nothing at all in human eyes that would justify placing them in a separate category; they fit perfectly into a continuum in terms of the qualities of acuteness of vision and indication of greater or lesser moral qualities. Eyes 'are sometimes inclined to wink under observation, sometimes to remain open and staring, and sometimes are disposed neither to wink nor stare. The last kind are the sign of the best nature, and of the others, the latter kind indicate impudence and the former indecision' (492a, 8). Who is he talking about, a goat, a human being, a vulture? He is talking about all of them, because Aristotle sees no reason not to carry the signs of moral qualities over from human beings, who are the most readily observable, to the unblinking vulture or the blinking horse.

The exceptional feature of humans of being the judges of perfection is associated with their exceptional posture: standing vertically. Not always, of course, but when they grow out of infancy: '[M]an alone, as has been said, has, in maturity, this part uppermost in respect to the material universe' (494a, 32; 494b, 1).[15] Just as our compasses always point to the pole, so the main, the sole, the sufficient compass for Aristotle was 'up', in the direction of the stars, which showed marvellous regularity and constancy of movement, and in the direction of light and fire, that is, of spirit. No different, but the same compass is the norm of honesty and scientific accuracy. Does their upright posture, then, belong to humans as an attribute of their knowledgeability? No, because man is always a 'political' animal, able to distinguish good from evil even in early infancy when he 'creeps on all fours' (501a, 1–3).[16]

Given its strict phenomenology, classical thought takes little interest in the possibility that prehistoric humans might have been hairy. It does, however, note that in humans, in the first place, not all hair appears immediately: some only ten to fifteen years after birth, with growth and sexual maturing. In those who are infertile, this delayed hair never appears. In the second place, only humans *lose* hair, and that is gender-related because it is lost mainly by men.

A quick comment on the means of seeing, the eyes. Nowadays we commonly experience being in a crowd, even a dense crowd, in a big city. This is analogous to the experience in antiquity of being surrounded not by a crowd of humans but by a crowd of animals, namely birds. They, incidentally, are the majority of the 500 living beings Aristotle mentions by name, followed by fish, antelope, wolves, elephants, tigers, cows, sheep, dogs (an entire army is known from history to have been comprised mainly of dogs), camels (which were also used in warfare, when they were equipped with special shoes). These are only the creatures he knew about. All around were other, unknown and unnamed animals that were difficult to reach, either because of distance or of depth, like those in the sea.

Furthermore, there are some strange creatures to be found in the sea, which from their rarity we are unable to classify. Experienced fishermen affirm, some that they have at times seen in the sea animals like sticks, black, rounded, and of the same thickness throughout; others that they have seen creatures resembling shields, red in colour and furnished with fins packed close together; and others that they have seen creatures resembling the male organ in shape and size, with a pair of fins in the place of the testicles. (532b, 18–25)[17]

Of course, over 2,000 years ago, there were many more animals than Aristotle mentions. We would be amazed by just how many. It is, however, very mistaken of us, lazily imagining ourselves doomed, to delude ourselves that the living conditions then were completely different, natural, afforested, and gave people living in the classical age their classical breadth of vision, which we in our crowded cities can no longer aspire to. Thus we seek to excuse the poverty of our thinking. *We, too*, are living in close proximity to an abundance of living beings, only we do not deign to notice the myriad living beings around us. We try to push them away, or rather to imagine that we are squeezing them out. These are the billions of living beings inside us, the microflora or microfauna of the stomach and intestines. The scientists cannot make up their minds whether to call these fungi, bacteria, and viruses 'flora' or 'fauna'. There are fungi on the body, strains of pathogens of influenza, AIDS, and other diseases; there are microsporia, again fungi on various parts of the body, micro-organisms in our food, in the mouldering walls of houses, in the refuse, the dirt, on our house pets, and so on.

Here our discovery of the microscope has done us a disservice. Because with the naked eye we cannot see all this teeming life, we do not to this day really believe we are living in such proximity to this crowd, much closer than to the crowds in the city. We imagine that, through use of disinfectant, sanitation, and hygiene, we are managing, or will manage, to drive these throngs back from ourselves. 'They're so small,' we tell ourselves, 'we can easily deal with them. Probably.' In the first place, though, there are a lot more of them than there are of us; and in the second place, even after all our discoveries, we have identified only a part of this realm in the midst of which we live.

People in the classical world did not proceed down the route of the microscope, and we know why. For them, splitting items into pieces would have no end; the concept of mathematical finitude simply did not exist. In other words, someone undertaking to divide and fragment a value could be guaranteed to disappear without trace into the process, so they were not much bothered where exactly one drew the line. They did not need the microscope because what could be seen with the naked eye was microscopic enough. Any further degree of digging down would only uncover an identical abyss. If we remove a final value from infinity, we will again obtain infinity, of which it would be absurd to say that this second infinity was 'less' than the first.

The vision of a dense crowd of living beings all around us, and of humankind as simply another face in that crowd, did not derive from the quantity of animals inside an as yet little violated ecosystem, but from the sufficient implied microscope already in it and a disinclination to invent any further microscope or telescope. People in the classical world knew that what they could see was only what they could see with their eyes, and that many living things in the heavens remained unknown. They knew that the earth, whose boundaries were also unknown, was full of life but thought that, instead of speculating and trying to find what could not be seen, it was better to look closely at what could. What could be seen thereby became a plenipotentiary representative and illustration of what was not visible, and was all the richer for that. The impression of an incalculable richness of animal life in the classical world comes from this way of seeing; from a readiness, instead of delving into the microscopic and telescopic realms, and in reality into a bad infinity of fragmentation and immensity, to see what was in front of you and extrapolate the micro- and macrocosm from that.

An example of this kind of vision: the elephant and the tiniest, barely visible, fly for Aristotle have absolutely equivalent value. He ignores the difference of scale: for him it simply does not exist. Every animal is equal and takes up the full screen. As a result, humans, seen in the midst of this multitude of full-sized living beings, are in a very dense crowd. The discovery of the microscope would add nothing to this vision. On the contrary, oddly, by distracting attention, it would detract from the profundity of that vision.

And one more unusual feature of this way of looking at things. Because humans are so much a part of the animal world, their behaviour is taken as a no less observable fact than, say, the results of dissecting an animal. To test the hearing of aquatic creatures, Aristotle will first examine fish and dolphins to identify their organ of hearing, their 'ears', and after that how fishermen behave when catching them. He is primarily interested not in what the fishermen say, but in what they do. There is a premise that humankind has securely found its place in the animal world and, since it is closer to hand and easier to observe, its own reactions will reveal more about the animals than direct observation of the animals themselves.

> And, at times, when they want the fish to crowd together, they adopt the stratagem of the dolphin-hunter; in other words they clatter stones together, that the fish may, in their fright, gather close into one spot, and so they envelop them within their nets. (Before surrounding them, then, they preserve silence, as was said; but after hemming the shoal in, they call on every man to shout out aloud and make any kind of noise; for on hearing the noise and hubbub the fish are sure to tumble into the nets from sheer fright.) (533b, 22–8)[18]

Human contact with other animal genera resembles a game of catching them out by exploiting their vulnerabilities and predilections as a conjuror might catch an audience out on their naïve expectations and weaknesses.

> And the eel is caught in a similar way; for the fisherman lays down an earthen pot that has held pickles, after inserting a 'weel' in the neck thereof. As a general rule, fishes are especially attracted by savoury smells. For this reason, fishermen roast the fleshy parts of the cuttle-fish and use it as bait on account of its smell, for fish are peculiarly attracted by it; they also bake the octopus and bait their fish-baskets

or weels with it, entirely, as they say, on account of its smell. (534a, 20)[19]

The cunning of one animal genus, human beings, preys on the weaknesses of another, fish.

But humans are so different from the animals! Are we sure? Humans have language? What does that mean? Infants have no speech. In their speechless, four-legged infancy, humans are more immersed in the animal world, and standing upright and possessing speech seem secondary, later acquisitions. The definition of humans as 'animals possessing *logos*' cannot relate to the ability to speak, since all animals have language, φωνή – λόγος is speech-as-reasoning – and otherwise we would have to say a baby, an in-fant, and with it the mute, is not human. It must relate to the first, basic meaning of *logos* as taking, gathering, accepting. The baby with its first cry is not accepting the world. When it begins to breathe and to suck, it calms down and accepts it. And so, for the rest of their life, humans' first, simple, 'pre-conscious' urge is to function within this basic rhythm of acceptance and non-acceptance, of what exactly they will, if they can, later clarify, but initially it is a matter of acceptance or non-acceptance on the grand scale, of the world as a whole. Evaluating the whole world by the criterion of good/bad, as it should be/not as it should be. A tear-stained face and calm, peace; then the smile on the face. That is how human beings, before they can speak or walk upright, show the essence of their being, which is rational and political. This acceptance/non-acceptance of the world as a whole and evaluation of it as good or bad is something that animals, if they do it, keep very much to themselves, whereas humans flaunt it. As for everything else, humans are like any other animal.

Without this actually rather scary, not to say downright terrifying, rationality, which is taking the axe to the existence of the entire world, all its animals and other riches, without its twisting and overturning in liter-ally every sentence (you will be remembering we previously agreed to leave the German word '*Satz*' untranslated, with all its cavalier positing and categorizing of everything under the sun), virtually every animal is fully possessed of speech.

> Birds can utter vocal sounds; and such of them can articulate best as have the tongue moderately flat, and also such as have thin delicate tongues. In some cases, the male and the female utter the same note; in other cases different notes. The smaller birds are more vocal and given to chirping than the larger ones; but in the pairing season every species of bird becomes particularly vocal. Some of them call when fighting, as the quail, others cry or crow when challenging to combat, as the partridge, or when victorious, as the barn-door cock. (536a, 20–8)[20]

When Aristotle says that animals have a kind of language but not speech, he is referring to *logos*, logic, which is entirely based on identification: this dreadful issue I mentioned, the approval and acceptance of all manner of things when humans recognize in them something 'right'. Animals do not go in for that. They are risk-averse.

We find ourselves in a paradoxical situation which really is counter to all our traditions and expectations, and what is paradoxical about it is not what Aristotle says in *The History of Animals*, Book 4, Part 9[21] and in other places besides, but the fact that we have failed to notice something so obvious: all nature's creatures chatter away, but just one – and who would that be? – by nature cries or remains silent. Or babbles. All living creatures except humans are born in possession of language, in the sense of sign systems: only humans have to acquire language, and if it was not taught to them, they would not have it. The baby is an in-fant, devoid of language. Tertullian is right: the soul is born a mute Christian, the pagan argumentativeness comes only later, at school, from the ambient culture.[22] The *logos*, however, the acceptance or non-acceptance of the world, is something humans have from the outset, even before speech and language.

This is something Derrida remarked on: silence is closer to human nature than speech.[23] Humans immerse themselves in silence as into a completely familiar place, and hunker down in there with their secret, personal God. Animals know how to quieten down: being silent is something only human beings can do.

Lecture 10, 11 November 1997

It is easy to criticize, and difficult to say anything positive, but if you get stuck you can always criticize just in order to be doing something. Perhaps just keeping on the move, no matter in which direction, a new perspective will open up.

It is always a pleasure to bid farewell to an inaccuracy that has been plaguing one since childhood just because so little around us is pure. The natural metaphor for everything on earth is a rubbish tip, and to rise to a pure environment we need to rise at least seventeen times as high as the moon. Everything is better up there. You will be remembering, though, that in Aristotle's psychology the soul is the form of a thing. Extremes are like trees. They grow simultaneously upwards and downwards. That same strict precision we find above, very far away as it seems, is here down below, very close to us, inside us, 'in our bowels', when you think things through. High above, the tree absorbs the sun through photosynthesis in the chlorophyll of its leaves. Without these modern scientific terms, Aristotle, as we shall see, talks about the sun in biology. By the way, someone who was called a physician (and Aristotle was an Asclepiad, a descendant of Asclepius) was thereby a biologist. We can justifiably say that by experience and education Aristotle was a biologist. This is partly why he had an affinity for the word ὕλη: the forest had significance for him. A tree at its extremities breaks down into nothingness, detecting, sensing, the world, intertwining with it, so that where the tree ends is no longer tree but still its environment. It lives right on the verge of itself and its environment, metabolizing with the environment in just the same way that the soul lives, breaking away from itself, on the verge of itself. We should be prepared for everything here, as it were, to melt, to dissolve into something elusive. One minute everything is tangible and solidly based, the next it has changed and is flying away.

Something similar is the case with the so-called speech organs, which a careless and inattentive person will naïvely believe must exist because people talk about them; but those who talk about them are also careless and inattentive. Writers who think more carefully about language note that there are in fact no separate speech organs analogous to those of sight and hearing. Speech is not an organic part of the human body. This is interesting. So, Wittgenstein's 'Language is a part of the human organism' and Aristotle's 'Man is a living being that possesses the *logos*' are definitions not of a human being and the human body, or at least not primarily that, but more definitions of language and the *logos*.[1] A human being is better defined as a 'political animal'. What place politics actually occupies in Aristotle we can read at the beginning of his *Ethics*.[2] *Greater Ethics* begins: 'Since our purpose is to speak about ethics, we must first inquire of what moral character is a branch.... And as a whole it seems to me that the subject ought rightly to be called not Ethics, but Politics' (1181a, 24; 1181b, 26).[3]

And at the beginning of the *Nicomachean Ethics*:

Shall we not, like archers who have a mark to aim at, be more likely to hit upon what is right? If so, we must try, in outline at least, to determine what it is, and of which of the sciences or capacities it is the object. It would seem to belong to the most authoritative art and that which is most truly the master art. And politics appears to be of this nature; for it is this that ordains which of the sciences should be studied in a state, and which each class of citizens should learn and up to what point they should learn them; and we see even the most highly esteemed of capacities to fall under this, e.g. strategy, economics, rhetoric. (1094a, 24–1094b, 4)[4]

We could define politics as the science of what should or should not be done. This should be done, that should not. Humans live before they can talk. The situation in respect of speaking is paradoxical. All living beings possess language, in the sense of a sign-orientated system, while human beings have to *acquire* language, and if they were not taught it, they would not acquire it. All living things in nature talk uncontrollably: it would be absurd to imagine that some cockerel with a challenged personality might decide at five o'clock one summer's morning to remain silent. His very silence would convey a message that something was wrong. Humans are the creature able to be silent, to keep a secret, to break the chain of bruiting abroad, of incessant, universal talkativeness, to abstain from contributing to the soundtrack of biology. They are the exception in, at first, having no language, of being a non-talking in-fant.

The words of Tertullian, that the soul is born a mute Christian, have the further sense that infants become heathen only later in the school of culture, and then Christianity is needed as a reminder of its early religion. The reason why Christianity is difficult, and it always is a hard task, is because, much as Fyodor Tyutchev warned that 'a thought articulated is a lie', all religion puts things in words, and so it is from the outset a lie (irrespective of whether it calls itself Christianity or by some other name).[5] All religious education, every national church institution, will prove from the outset to be articulating a lie, and will have from that basis to make its way, or fail to make its way, to Christianity. This is apropos of early human life, in-fan-cy, and the simple landscape in which the soul dwells, between terror and salvation, acceptance and non-acceptance of an undifferentiated world.

We have read in Derrida about silence, that it is more characteristic, closer to us than speech. He immersed himself in silence as if into a completely familiar place, and hunkered down there with his secret God. No one knows how to be silent. Animals are capable only of being still: that is, in time of danger pausing the incessant clamour of their lives.

We need to learn to be more generous, to give animals their due, which, through a simple lack of attention, we have supposed to be our exclusive merit: articulate speech:

> Vocal sounds and modes of language (διάλεκτος) differ according to locality. Vocal sounds are characterized chiefly by their pitch, whether high or low, and the kinds of sound capable of being produced are identical within the limits of one and the same species; but articulate sound, that one might reasonably designate 'language', differs both in various animals, and also in the same species according to diversity of locality. (536b, 8)[6]

What is most interesting here is that Aristotle does not even add 'in the case of both humans and animals'. On this level, where what is being considered is articulate speech, the distinction between humans and animals in general has not yet appeared, so there is no call to talk about them separately. Actually, a distinction is made, but it is a different one: speech, '*dialektos*', is something birds and humans have in common but which other animals lack. Speech is less developed in humans because a lack of expertise in language in infancy is a hindrance. There are no *lexical* grounds to support claims of anything resembling exclusive or superior abilities for humans, or even something we regard as so specifically human as policy.

> Social creatures are such as have some one common object in view; and this property is not common to all creatures that are gregarious. Such social creatures are man, the bee, the wasp, the ant, and the crane.[7]

Similarly, Aristotle finds policy among animals in respect of the bringing up of offspring. (We are specifying animals because the conventional understanding and scientific definition of *hyle* include both flora and fauna.)

> Thus of plants that spring from seed the one function seems to be the reproduction of their own particular species and the sphere of action with certain animals is similarly limited. The faculty of reproduction, then, is common to all alike. If sensibility be superadded, then their

lives will differ from one another in respect to sexual intercourse, through the varying amount of pleasure derived therefrom, and also in regard to modes of parturition and ways of rearing their young. (588b, 24)[8]

So, if you insistently press me to state, in the light of this torrent in which humans are drowning among the animals, what the *specificum* of a human being is, if it is not even to be found in politics, I will reply, together with Jacques Derrida, that the more blurred, the more elusive and indefinable this distinctive characteristic becomes, the more unintelligible and impossible their mission, the more stubborn their will and determination is going to be. As I have said, humans are never more themselves and closer to Sophia the divine wisdom than in a state of anguish, schism, and suffering. This is their most natural and, strange to say, harmonious state. What is essential is sufficient resolve and irresolution. Viktor Molchanov is right: first there must be discrimination, and only then need one decide between what exactly.[9]

People said of Heidegger under National Socialism that he was very resolute, only he did not know what he was resolute about.[10] Much the same can be said of Derrida: that he is full of awareness of his mission, only he does not know what it is. That is how it must appear on the outside and it shows up very precisely the difference between Nazism and Heidegger. Of course, Heidegger picked up and imbibed all the energy of the determination that was the driving force of that revolutionary movement in Germany, since what else could he derive his strength from? The *topos* here is exactly the same as the way that in theology demons are considered to partake of goodness to the extent that they have being, will, and energy. But whereas the Party imagined in a state of mental aberration that it had been spared suffering and could make others suffer because it already knew the way ahead and could take charge, Heidegger redeemed Germany and the Party by being no less determined but not deciding anything.

We find ourselves in a similar quandary, uncertain what remains of a human being who completely drowns in the forest. But what of it? There will not be a problem if we never do understand anything, but there will if we understand too quickly, if we rush to be definite.

Our aim is not to 'study Aristotle', his 'concept of matter', the mother, or the forest, but to learn from him to see what, without him, we would not see: that we have not emerged from the forest. An independent human body, protected from bacteria by sanitation, from ultra-violet radiation by lotions, from ailments by a seaside tan, from radiation by a radiation counter, from AIDS by a condom, is something that exists solely on advertising hoardings. Nowadays, of course, Aristotle's biology, after the animal world has been almost destroyed, would have to be differently composed; the society in which the human body finds itself, now less agreeable since the invention of the microscope, does not consist of dolphins, deer, lions which stray casually into towns and may bite us or behave more charitably.

It consists of microbes, bacteria, viruses, of unknown 'pathogens' (what a word!) with which we may need to engage; but *essentially* the unity of all living things remains the same as that observed by Aristotle, and so, for the present, we should simply carry on reading *The History of Animals*.

We paused at the fact that, in their four-legged babyhood, human beings, while still *infants*, are closer to other living things and, *at the same time*, still free from what seems specific to man: from language (which Aristotle, always astutely discerning the nature of things, designates with the word 'dialect'), from standing erect, from social interaction. They are, as they say, a 'little child who does not understand', mute, without speech, but here the computer helps us to define their status by showing that having understanding, in the sense of even the most delicate and complex calculation, is not necessarily human. What can humans do before acquiring understanding? They immediately have the ability, and after acquiring understanding are less able, to laugh and cry: that is, instantly to reject or accept everything, the whole world.

Computers are described as devices that resolve calculations, but it is then added that humans have to resolve what to do with the calculations. In fact, in the sense of resolving that people usually have in mind at this point – that is, that on the basis of data we select one of a number of presented options – humans resolve issues less often than they still like to believe. We need also to remember that 'resolving' in this sense, of selecting and deciding, is no more than a human deciding whether or not to assess as true or false what a computer has resolved. The human is playing a fairly minor, secondary role. A more important and momentous decision is whether to sit down at the computer at all or do like Arnold Schwarzenegger in one of the *Terminator* films: hurl it to the floor and, in an elegant and full-blooded manner, trash it. This momentous decision has already been taken, in the computer's favour, by the child, who has accepted it. Children, in some manner and for some reason as yet unclear, have mysteriously and enigmatically made friends with the computer, adopting it into our civilization. This, however, is another topic, which I will mention only in passing: the integration of human beings and computers, about which there is already an extensive literature. Peeling away, establishing the boundaries of, which part of the brain, to what degree, and with which mental operations humans can do things a computer cannot do is a time-consuming, boring, and futile exercise, because what it cannot do today, or what the computer on our desktop cannot do, it probably can already do in the secret development facilities of Bill Gates. Computers can do anything except laugh and cry. Computers can do anything except formulate a policy about whether to fundamentally accept or reject the world.

Perhaps a computer cannot dream, or perhaps it can and 'sleep mode' is not just metaphorical. At all events, human beings and animals are equally at home in the realm of dreams. Aristotle points out that 'it would appear that not only do men dream, but horses also, and dogs, and oxen; aye, and sheep, and goats, and all viviparous quadrupeds; and dogs show their dreaming by barking in their sleep' (536b, 29).[11] In humans, dreaming comes on, Aristotle says, in most cases at about four or five years of age, and whether he is right or wrong about that, if we take a broad definition of dreaming, this is further confirmation that this is perhaps the crucial turning point in human consciousness, the transition from 'pre-school' to 'school' age. Before four or five, humans do not dream, although there is a dream state in the all-important sense that until the age of five there is no clear distinction between dreaming and non-dreaming. In some manner that we have forgotten, the person is speaking, watching, and acting 'unconsciously'. One small methodological observation. 'But dogs, not only people, also laugh and cry.' Perhaps I have not been clear and need to repeat that we *really* only have at our disposal very little. Everything that appeared to be taxonomy and classification has only been an identifying of problems. The way language is, we talk mud and rely not on vocabulary and terminology, but on what, in spite of words, glints through. That is what we need to hold on to. We simply do not know the difference between humans and dogs. We have said nothing about it and have nothing like an accepted classification of what it is. If we unintentionally drive our car into somebody else's garage, we need to back out fast, before we get roundly cursed. 'People cry' does not mean we know what a person is, or what crying is. Imagine someone drowning who is clinging for dear life to a lifebelt which keeps slipping from their grasp and is in any case deflating and barely afloat. More certain than tears and more familiar is something else: a mood of total, mute rejection of the world in its entirety, the world becoming immersed in grey indifference. And the opposite mood. We are always dealing primarily with these and analogous moods. We have a right to say that these are human, rather than canine, moods only to the extent that we actually are people rather than dogs, even if we have been called subhuman, have been called dogs, but we have no special right to claim that we are unconditionally right rather than those who have called us that.

It is an uncomfortable situation, almost like playing croquet with hedgehogs instead of balls and live flamingos instead of mallets, but that is how it is with phenomenology if we do not want to lapse into constructivism, where more and more definitions snowball round a text, which by its second sentence becomes as impenetrable as mud. No amount of rigorousness can contain this exponential accumulation of explication. No, we know nothing and define nothing, but only try as best we can to catch glimpses of clarity. And so does Aristotle.

We need therefore to look not just at his vocabulary but at what he is saying. Not to catch him out when he says that children under four never dream – later on he himself says that they do – but to understand what it is he is getting at: there is always some one important thing that is of great concern also to us. Here it is our complete forgetting of the all-encompassing world of infancy.

Similarly, there is no need for us to catch him out with the fact that there is no instance of parthenogenesis among vertebrates.

With partridges, by the way, if the female gets to leeward of the male, she becomes thereby impregnated. And often when they happen to be in heat she is affected in this wise by the voice of the male, or by his breathing down on her as he flies overhead; and, by the way, both the male and the female partridge keep the mouth wide open and protrude the tongue in the process of coition. (541a, 27)[12]

One commentator waxes ironical on this point, but he and modern biology would do better to enquire what was happening here, why nature followed this path of pairs and pairing, which is in fact quite risky *because there might be no pair to mate with*, and we have discovered and experimentally verified the viability of cloning, so that it is possible in nature for conception to occur without the need for a mate and copulation.

Then we will discover to our surprise that courtship dances and ritual combat are by no means an epiphenomenon, a splendid accompaniment of the straightforward and prosaic supposed biological necessity of the union of two embryonic elements, and because it transpires that an organism could and can perfectly well arise from a single cell, it transpires also that these dances and mating rituals are the whole crux of the matter, and the singing of birds in the spring is not an aesthetic accompaniment to the biology in order to produce progeny but, strange as it may seem, the progeny, which could be brought forth without it, are brought in as a pretext for birds to sing in the spring. The forest is drawn towards being, the female to the male. Again we see the firm rooting of the male in the female. So it is not the sentiments that are an optional accompaniment to the sexual act but, on the contrary, it is the sexual act that is optional for nature (which could go ahead more directly through parthenogenesis and cloning or straightforward reproduction of cells as in a cancer tumour) and can be seen as an excuse for the polarization into male and female.

Nature could ensure continuation of the race without all that, but it seems to be gunning for something like anguish, separateness, distance, individuality: *not* contrariety but complexity. Partridges, let us admit it, are not 'really' induced to conceive by the aroused voice and hot breath of the male – they do not conceive as the result of a ritual flying of the male over the female – but what is true, and Aristotle is right, is that nature is playing a larger game, and it, and Sophia, needed mating in order that this extreme, indeed deadly, sporting should occur, and not vice versa. To use the phraseology of Pushkin and Leontiev, the 'complex flowering' is not to create life, but rather life is the pretext, the excuse for a complex flowering. Nature found it just too boring to generate a sheep by cloning and devised the interplay of the submissive ewe and the insistent ram. Scientists, for some reason, seem not, for the time being, to find it boring. Well, that will be something for the historians of science to write about. In the past nature found it boring, in the future it will doubtless also be found boring, but right now there is great interest in asexual reproduction. It is a puzzle.

Aristotle allows human beings, including himself, to be subsumed in this mass of life. If we look, for example, at the startling multifariousness of mating in the fifth book of *The History of Animals*, we see him presenting the animal as a whole, as a perfect, wonderful, harmonious, powerful mechanism. What is everything for? It is for the sheer joy of that power! Life is the very reason for existence: existence is not the reason for life.

We can finally work out what is going on with what all the textbooks with their superior knowledge condescendingly refer to as Aristotle's 'mistake' regarding the origination of animals from mould. My hunch the lecture before last was correct: he does indeed see an analogy between parthenogenesis and the generation of life from mould and decay. This is his answer, his surmise, as to why nature did not choose the path of parthenogenesis and cloning for reproduction but mating, even though it is more difficult and risky.

Conception without mating. Aristotle moves on to parthenogenesis and cloning, not, incidentally, distinguishing between them, in Book 5, Part 15 of *The History of Animals*, just after his description of the copulation of elephants.

> The female elephant becomes sexually receptive when ten years old at the youngest, and when fifteen at the oldest; and the male is sexually capable when five years old, or six. The season for intercourse is spring. The male allows an interval of three years to elapse after commerce with a female; and after it has once impregnated a female, it has no intercourse with her again. The period of gestation with the female is two years; and only one young animal is produced at a time, in other words it is uniparous. And the embryo is the size of a calf two or three months old. (546b, 6)[13]

'So much for the copulations of such animals as copulate.' Let us recall that Aristotle believes that whether animals reproduce by parthenogenesis or copulation depends on the climate and ecology. 'We now proceed to treat of generation both with respect to copulating and non-copulating animals [within a single species, *Bibikhin*], and we shall commence with discussing the subject of generation in the case of the testaceans.' Shellfish, snails, and shelled molluscs. 'The testacean is almost the only genus that throughout all its species is non-copulative.' You need to listen carefully to this next part. Porphyrae are whelks, testaceans that were the main source of red dye in antiquity. 'A king clad in purple' would have been wearing a garment dyed with the 'floret' of one of these molluscs.

> [They] gather together to some one place in the spring-time, and deposit the so-called 'honey-comb'. This substance resembles the comb, only that it is not so neat and delicate; and looks as though a number of husks of white chick-peas were all stuck together. But none of these structures has an open passage, and the porphyra does not

grow out of them, but these and all other testaceans grow out of mud and decaying matter. (546b, 18–24)[14]

Commentator: 'After describing the spawn of molluscs, Aristotle immediately bars to himself the way to a correct understanding of its nature.'[15] And indeed, it does seem perverse. Having seen and described this spawn, he sets it aside and goes out of his way to emphasize, '[N]one of these structures ... the porphyra does not grow out of them.' But why? Does it not seem natural that they would arise from something that came out of their own body? Why go looking for their 'spontaneous generation' out of mud?

It is not actually just mud. There need to be beings of the same species present alongside the mud and slime which somehow provoke the spontaneous generation of their own kind out of it.

> Such, then, of the testaceans as deposit the honeycomb are generated spontaneously like all other testaceans, but they certainly come in greater abundance in places where their congeners have been living previously. At the commencement of the process of depositing the honeycomb they throw off a slippery mucus, and of this the husk-like formations are composed. These formations, then, all melt and deposit their contents on the ground and at this spot there are found on the ground a number of minute porphyrae. (546b, 26)[16]

Everything is given its name, the spawning is described, and yet Aristotle is insistent that this is not how the molluscs are born. I cannot decipher this, I have no explanation, but there is clearly a message for us here. The one thing that is clear is that this is *not* a gaffe but a thought I cannot make sense of. It relates to the arising of all living things. As a phenomenologist, Aristotle feels he does not have the right to explain events by a past that has not been observed, so it makes no sense to say anything about them. This kind of sober methodological sense results in him having no historical perspective: everything, including the origination of life on earth, is happening right now, as if it must be observable right now or it does not exist at all.

Among modern hypotheses of the emergence of life is an influence from space. Just as Aristotle finds it impermissible to blur the given by bringing in historical perspective, so, too, he abjures wandering off beyond the visible. What has to be relied on has to come from the extreme, the ultimate boundary. The words 'sun' and 'wind' are used to name absolutely all the influences that can come from the far-off realm of the stars, not because Aristotle lacks the imagination or the instruments to picture or register them but because there exist no instruments capable of registering everything. We see the way new 'elementary particles' keep further dividing, in spite of all the power of our instruments, into those that have already been discovered and those that have not. Everything that exists should either be perceived (*aesthesis*), or thought (*noesis*), as suggested by *mimesis*, meaning the real, the pre-conscious. Talk of registered elementary particles, with the risk that the whole picture will change when new ones are discovered, is not the way of philosophy. The given either is the given in its entirety or it is nothing at all; in *this* sun and *this* wind is gathered all possible remote influence. Does that mean we should say that Aristotle's sun and wind are symbols? No, not if symbols are to be understood as signs or fragments of something else: Aristotle when he sees the sun perceives it as all the sun of the world, just as for him the matter of this world is all the matter there can be. There simply is no matter outside the world.

Here an accurate remark by the historians of religion in antiquity holds true. The names of the gods are not parts but aspects of the universe. A god is a god because he is everything, the whole world encompassed in that tone or, if you prefer, mood.

Lecture 11, 18 November 1997

In the same way – in a kind of philosophical religion, a hyphenated philosophy-as-religion – the wind is like a deity for Aristotle: that is, the *entire* cosmos in the aspect of the wind. This simple view – and it is simple in the sense of preceding the distinction between philosophy and religion – will prove useful to us for a later course on the beginnings of religion.[1]

When moving on to the invisible, Aristotle again takes care not to stray into hypotheses but finds a prop in the world as a totality incorporating absolutely all existent matter. Because classical thought has no historical or spatial perspective – everything is here and now – what has been is not gone but has been realized and thereby even consolidated for continuation, and what is far away, in the ether, is close by its very remoteness, and indeed is constantly impinging on us as a result of its searing absence. It is something real, reliable, and invisible in which there is no illusion.

Perhaps Aristotle needs the primal origination of life from mud in order to show life as an escape from the chaos, the rubbish tip, to the beginning of self-movement? To show all life as a kind of mould, a putrefaction that is simultaneously a breaking out of it owing to some instability in the putrefaction? Then the appearance in life of pairing and mating will be like a breakthrough of life into existence, a longing on the part of matter for *eidos*, for perfection and history.

An unresolved mystery is Aristotle's description of animals that appear and live in fire (552b, 10).[2]

Again, Aristotle on the link between parthenogenesis and emergence from mud: drones, he tells us, citing the view without objecting, are born without any involvement of the queen bee, while a new generation of bees cannot be born this way. There is indeed a distinction between the way in which worker bees and drones are born, the former resulting from a mating, while the latter appear through parthenogenesis, which Aristotle calls spontaneous generation. He draws the distinction unerringly, and it is a distinction modern biology accepts, while using different terminology.

It is again the polity of bees Aristotle uses to demonstrate the extent to which life is bound up with the cosmos as a whole, with the movement of the stars.

The honeycomb is made from flowers and the materials for the wax they gather from the resinous gum of trees, while honey is distilled from dew, and is deposited chiefly at the risings of the constellations or when a rainbow is in the sky: and as a general rule there is no honey before the rising of the Pleiads. The bee then makes the wax from flowers. (553b, 28)[3]

Many would now make bold to assert that honey is not distilled from dew deposited from the air and has no connection with the movement of the stars. Instead, they will adduce data provided by modern science. Bees and similar insects, they will explain, evolved at the same time as certain kinds of plants and flowers in whose life processes (and this again relates to the kinship of the flora and fauna of the forest) bees are essential for pollination. Here is a well-known example of this kind of dependence: Charles Darwin in one of his travels in equatorial regions predicted that there would be insects, as yet undiscovered, that had a 25-cm-long proboscis, because he had described orchids whose flowers had just such a narrow passageway to a place from which pollen needed to be taken for pollination. And, indeed, an insect of that kind was later discovered. The fact that it had not been observed lowering its proboscis into the flower of this orchid only tells us that science had something else yet to discover. For the time being, it puts a full stop, but the ancients, with their admirable good taste, instead inserted an illumination, usually depicting a starry firmament, or a rainbow and the constellation of the Pleiades playing their part in the collection of honey.

Beekeepers are naturally preoccupied with collecting honey and are, like their customers, inclined to forget that the role of bees, as an essential part of the mechanism of plant reproduction, as pollinators, is of infinitely greater value, even in purely economic terms, than the honey they produce. In other words, the pollen the bees do not bring to the hive, that they lose on their way back, is economically far more valuable. Here honey is a means of enticing humans to proliferate hives, blithely unaware that the considerable amount of money they make in the process is effectively payment for their contribution to supporting the main job of the bees. We are paid employees, hired to assist in this project. The bees for their part are actually also hirelings, enticed to undertake the work of pollination.

The cunning with which plants exploit bees amazes researchers. Thus, certain orchids have a system within their flower consisting of a special substance, not yet pollen, which makes the bee's little feet heavy, obliging it to take off abruptly. This guarantees that it will bump against a screen which will cause it to fall into a chalice containing a special fluid. The walls of the chalice are sheer, which means that with its wet feet it cannot climb out and can only escape along a tunnel leading out from the surface level of the fluid. The walls of this tunnel are covered with pollen, so the wet bee as it proceeds along this narrow corridor is sure to get pollen stuck to its body. Other orchids mimic the scent of a particular queen bee out of the hundreds of species of bees. There are bee species adapted to collect honey only from very specific flowers. This scent of the flower, and the structure of part of it which mimics the shape of the body of a female bee, provokes mating behaviour in the male bee, only not bringing it to the point of releasing its semen. These preliminary movements are, however, sufficient to send it further on its way, laden with pollen.

This complex strategy on the part of plants of enticing bees with lures and food to play their part in their life cycle, and on the part of bees in inducing humans to breed them, is only a tiny component of the universal interconnectedness of nature, only one of its ecosystems. And this despite the fact that reproduction is possible, as with cancer cells, by forming a compact living mass. This policy of nature can be seen as a definite strategy: an increase, despite increased risk, in boundary zones, in points of decision and choice, an increase in polarity or, to put it less accurately, in complexity.

We are freed by Aristotle from a burdensome waking nightmare proposing that the need to give birth is unavoidable, and around it, like a rainbow, there is an aura of idealization and ideals. In this connection, we shall yet have cause to remember that in biology the Platonic 'idea' has the meaning of both species and genus. We shall see that in nature the genus exists as a perspective on life, and in subspecies of the idea such as good (richness), truth (viable being that replicates itself), and beauty (the captivating, the alluring).[4]

Aristotle's biology continues to function, and indeed after the 'exposure' of its inaccuracies, it starts to work at its best. Let's face it, using a 2,000-year-old philosophical treatise in order to study animals makes about as much sense as using it as an aid to studying the language of ancient Greece. Rather than looking to Aristotle, we should just go and look at animals ourselves. After Linnaeus, after Darwin, when proper biological science has woken up again, it is perfectly well able to make its own observations and has no need to resort to what is in any case not of primary importance in Aristotle. The surprise is that it took so long, 2,000 years, for the world to get round to conducting fieldwork comparable with what we find in the biology of classical times.

We are, of course, currently witnessing an upsurge in scientific research unprecedented in history, and it is to be expected that we will soon be witnessing a change in the mentality, the entire intellectual structure, of humankind. For our limited purposes, it is all to the good that we are now free to read Aristotle as learning, as philosophy, and not as a notebook recording fieldwork. We are now in a position to see what is perhaps the insight running right through it: that nature does not shun effort, and indeed seems even to go in search of it. Take, for example, the behaviour of migratory birds, which could surely find themselves a nook nearer than 1,000 km away; or the wild animal that could submit to domestication and enjoy a secure existence, or human beings who make life difficult for themselves because they value something more than life itself. We will learn to look in a different way at savage peoples who obstinately decline to become civilized.

The so-called balance of nature cannot be disrupted: all manner of excesses, effort leading to extreme stress, are working towards the same goal as nature. Everything works in favour of the thief with good intentions: thieving, cunning, kidnapping, Sophia. We are looking at Hegel's view of the craftiness of the world spirit.[5]

In reality, nothing can be disrupted in nature other than the ratio between its wild and domesticated forms. It would seem that 'domesticated' here does not have the meaning of subservient to humans, living in proximity to or actually in the homes of human beings. Aristotle speaks of more domesticated and more wild wasps, not by any means in the sense that some are bred by humans while others are not. Wild wasps are larger, longer, and darker in colour. They are more aggressive than others, and their sting is more painful. What are the criteria for classifying wasps as 'wild' or 'more domesticated'? That their sting is less painful? Not only that, and not because they live in the proximity of humans. Because they are more orderly, then? They are tame, domesticated, placid, in the sense that *they* have a home, not that they live in or near ours. It is hard to tell, but it is as if, without any human agency, or perhaps through imitating what they have seen of humans, ants or bees accept a discipline like members of a community.

This domestication can be damaged and disrupted. Here is a minor instance, and more could be cited, of reversion to feral behaviour, which, in this case, resulted directly from human intervention. In Brazil in 1957, in the course of producing a superior breed of bees, an unsuccessful hybrid of killer bees, which were African bees only even more active and difficult to pacify, escaped and began to proliferate with the radius of their habitat increasing by about 300 km a year. By 1980, they had reached Mexico, having killed several hundred people.[6] The bees seemed to have gone mad. Something had gone wrong with their physiology, of course, but also with their morality. They had become wild.

The highly strung nature of bees, the vulnerability of the working equilibrium of the state, which can be disrupted by a communal sickness, was, interestingly enough, known to classical biology. Incidentally, when Heidegger says the bee population will never stray beyond the boundaries of what is possible, he means, as in Aristotle's biology, not that bees will never flout their own laws, but that they want discipline and support order. The young, who have yet to be initiated into this discipline, are up for hooliganism. There are young, inexperienced bees that build honeycomb 'crudely'. Hives may become ill: 'Another diseased condition is indicated in a lassitude on the part of the bees' (626b, 19).[7] This is a combination of chemistry (the system of communication and management) and physiology. It is a biological aberration but, accompanying sickness, caused by or in parallel with the sickness, it is also an aberration of mood. The bees, when they expel the sick, are rejecting both the contagion of their sickness and their mood. Beekeepers evidently recognize this serious-mindedness of bees. Anyone who has observed dogs, which are more accessible, will have noticed that, in addition to their ability to distinguish the obvious hunger–satiety, heat–cold dichotomies, their alarm at abrupt movements, running and commotion, they can discriminate between moods and temperaments.

So much for our own observations. Now, back to Aristotle. 'The little bees, as has been said, are more industrious than the big ones; their wings are battered; their colour is black, and they have a burnt-up aspect. Gaudy and showy bees, like gaudy and showy women, are good-for-nothings' (627a, 11).[8] 'Like gaudy and showy women' might seem to fall short of moral judgement, but in Aristotle both these explanations, the objective and the moral, invariably go together. It is not that he believes that, if they wanted to be good and industrious, the bees could change their nature or at least recover from their idleness. Aristotle does remember this sick, physiological, irremediable aspect, of course. Even in the world of humans, however, if we abjure the frivolous and superficial supposition that they are morally free and have free choice, although moral behaviour will be physiologically and chemically conditioned in a chain of causality, it still makes sense to talk about it being moral. It is better, therefore, to learn this sobering lesson by observing living creatures, as Aristotle does. Not only does the fact that they are automata not preclude morality, but a serious discussion of morality can begin only where supposedly free acts are impossible. The polity is order, the rule of law. Democracy and so on is rule by certain humans.[9] For Wittgenstein, for example, a pure, ethical attitude is revealed simultaneously with the realization that it is impossible to change, influence, or affect anything in the world in any way. We are like someone without arms or legs in a state of helpless immobility. Only at that point does ethics begin: that is, acceptance of this whole situation, along with our total inability to intervene in any way, or non-acceptance. There is no myth-making, there are no fairy tales about morality in animals, but only the knowledge that they are complete automata, in their own way without arms or legs. Shackled. Bees work within a shackled ecosystem, under the rigour of orderliness, unfree.

> As has been said, they differentiate their work; some make wax, some make honey, some make bee-bread, some shape and mould combs, some bring water to the cells and mingle it with the honey, some engage in out-of-doors work. At early dawn they make no noise, until some one particular bee makes a buzzing noise two or three times and thereby awakes the rest; hereupon they all fly in a body to work. By and by they return and at first are noisy; then the noise gradually decreases, until at last some one bee flies round about, making a buzzing noise, and apparently calling on the others to go to sleep; then all of a sudden there is a dead silence. (627a, 20)[10]

The polity as discipline.

This Spartan order is flimsy and easily disrupted. By sickness, of course, by physiology and chemistry – the 'idleness' of the bees is clearly a sickness – but along with the sickness it is unclear what is primary and what is secondary, what is cause and what is effect, the anguish of what from sloppy thinking, from habit, we might call a weakening or loss of the will to live. Everything somehow collapses at once; all desire is lost to continue to support all this complex orderliness; discipline falls away. Let us assume that moral fatigue, a decline of morality, would not occur without chemical changes in the hive, and moral decline might cause harmful chemical changes. *Mens sana in corpore sano.* Which is more important? That is the question. The likelihood is that neither body nor mind is more important, but that what matters most is not to lose sight of the problem – while hasty solutions are on offer all around, and the most common seems to be autosuggestion: by robust cheerfulness of spirit to influence the health of the body, and by exercising the body to maintain robust good spirits. The usual solution is to meddle with the relationship between body and mind, to intervene in it, and that is destructive and lethal. The right solution would seem to be, on the contrary, never, under any circumstances, to blur the distinction between body and spirit, to keep them as separate as they are.

> The hive is known to be in good condition if the noise heard within it is loud, and if the bees make a flutter as they go out and in; for at this time they are constructing brood-cells. They suffer most from hunger when they recommence work after winter. They become somewhat lazy if the bee-keeper, in robbing the hive, leave behind too much honey; still one should leave cells numerous in proportion to the population, for the bees work in a spiritless way if too few combs are left. They become idle also, as being dispirited, if the hive be too big. (627a, 27–627b, 1)[11]

And so they work, so they toil. It is hard and they can break down. Wild bees and wasps are also at work, but not in the same way as the hive bees, whose diligence reflects their incorporation into the affairs of men, in which, by and large, discipline is well established. Since bees evolved simultaneously with plants that need them for pollination and are part of one interdependent ecosystem, are human beekeepers part of the same system? Perhaps. Prehistoric people were at all events more integrated into the life of nature, and not in that old and mistaken sense that in order to preserve their tribal way of life they needed to have more contact with nature, but in a different sense that is in the process of being discovered, that they were part of a plan or part of the forest's aspiring to *eidos* as fullness, with fullness understood to mean perfection. Let us propose that the 'crown of creation' in respect of humankind needs, then, to be understood not in the sense that nature, through a process of trial and error, has attained formal perfection, but in the sense that now the most important work is being done by humankind. More than anyone else, it is humankind that is responsible for fullness, simple, integrated wholeness. Do not ask for the fullness of what. Let us say, of the species, that is, of *eidos*, or the Idea, of the idea as the ideal of completeness, of being as the radiance of fullness. Merab Mamardashvili writes well about this in his *Lectures on Classical Philosophy*:[12]

> Being cannot but appear. The Greeks believed that being is something that is in the open. It is entirely predictable that their first thinking about being is thinking about heroes in their acts and in the light of their renown, in which they continue to reside in all their fullness. The aura of renown, as it were, plucks the man out of darkness and keeps him fully in that light, like a halo, that symbol of holiness in Christianity and Buddhism. It is an old theme: glory as something that completely exhausts and defines life – its entire meaning. Understanding the ontological ideal in this way, the Greeks said, 'This is a real man; there is something of the philosopher in him.' Full performance of the glory of life. The Greeks saw that as – philosophy.

'Full performance of the glory of life.' That is *eidos*, the visible. Bees in the intensity of their toil, and then their buzzing as they work (like the sound of a taut string); they stretch out to the best of their ability that same fullness. Not the fullness of honeycombs, although that is part of it; not good pollination, though that is part of it too. Under poor conditions, there may be little honey and nothing much to pollinate, and then the sign of their fullness, strange to say, will be nevertheless their high quality as they conscientiously produce what Ross translates well as 'a prosperous hive' (627b, 3).[13] Physiology, aesthetics, ethics: a trinity in ontology.

Aristotle does not talk about wasps in terms of lethargy, the struggle against lethargy, the appetite for work. He does not disparage them: they distinguish themselves in other ways. For example, tenthredon wasps 'being epicures as to their food, they fly, one at a time, into kitchens and on to slices of fish and the like dainties' (629a, 30).[14]

The larger animals nearest to humans come tantalizingly close to the constant and major topics of human morality.

> The male camel declines intercourse with its mother; if his keeper tries compulsion, he evinces disinclination. On one occasion, when intercourse was being declined by the young male, the keeper covered over the mother and put the young male to her; but, when after the intercourse the wrapping had been removed, though the operation was completed and could not be revoked, still by and by he bit his keeper to death. A story goes that the king of Scythia had a high-bred mare, and that all her foals were splendid; that wishing to mate the best of the young males with the mother, he had him brought to the stall for the purpose; that the young horse declined; that, after the mother's head had been concealed in a wrapper he, in ignorance, had

intercourse; and that, when immediately afterwards the wrapper was removed and the head of the mare was rendered visible, the young horse ran away and hurled himself down a precipice. (630b, 31)[15]

If incest had not been a highly sensitive human topic, these observations would not have been made. Are human values being projected on to animals? No. Animals do have family relationships. The maternal concern of a bitch for her puppies is not being projected on to her. What we are observing is not self-delusion. There she is, and there are the flashes of pride, the serenity, the reordering of all her habits around her progeny, and the gradual decrease day by day of her maternal involvement as her puppies grow.

Aristotle has many commonly known stories about dolphins: they have a gentle and kindly nature, manifest a 'passionate attachment to boys', and take good care of young dolphins. But here is a similarity with humans about which Aristotle makes no further comment: the dolphins go down to deep waters in pursuit of fish,

> but, when the necessary return swim is getting too long, they hold in their breath, as though calculating the length of it, and then draw themselves together for an effort and shoot up like arrows, trying to make the long ascent rapidly in order to breathe, and in the effort they spring right over a ship's masts if a ship be in the vicinity. This same phenomenon is observed in divers, when they have plunged into deep water; that is, they pull themselves together and rise with a speed proportional to their strength. (631a, 8)[16]

This story from Aristotle has a place in modern discourse on the intelligence of dolphins, except that, instead of comparison and assessment, human intelligence itself, the thinking of a diver, is found in the dolphin, when it suits the dolphin. This is the sense also of Aristotle's last communication about dolphins. 'It is not known for what reason they run themselves aground on dry land; at all events, it is said that they do so at times, and for no obvious reason' (631b, 2).[17] That is, the suicide of dolphins is a free act, chosen by the dolphin like the unfathomable suicides of human beings from fullness of life and happiness.

The linking of body and soul is both taboo and useless in all attempts to control the body by mind or the spirit by physical efforts. Things like self-hypnosis or physical techniques *usually* lead to nothing but bewilderment, confusion, and dirt. The inability of body and soul to control each other, the fact that they do not intersect, clears a path for them to become mutually attuned through *fullness*. When they are left to their own devices, the less commerce there is between them and the more they become windowless monads, the greater the response, the stronger the summons. The fullness gathered in one, the body, evokes and provokes all the more fullness in another, the soul. This is not to say that the body acts on the spirit, or vice versa. It means that fullness, if it has come close, no matter in what way, is infectious. Only in the matter of fullness are they one, to the extent to which fullness is available for both body and soul.

> Just as with all animals a change of action follows a change of cir-
> cumstances, so also a change of character follows a change of action,
> and often some portions of the physical frame undergo a change, as
> occurs in the case of birds. Hens, for instance, when they have beaten
> the cock in a fight, will crow like the cock and endeavour to tread him;
> the crest rises up on their head and the tail-feathers on the rump, so
> that it becomes difficult to recognize that they are hens; in some cases
> there is a growth of small spurs. (631b, 5)[18]

The History of Animals is Aristotle's most inspired work.

The authenticity of the gynaecological ninth [*sic, Tr.*][19] and final book is disputed, although most scholars ascribe it to Aristotle. It could be an early, student work written in the course of his studies for his first profes-sion of physician, which it would have been natural for a capable young man from the house of Asclepius to pursue. Bearing in mind Aristotle's grounding in the medical profession, we can see how he would introduce in place of the Platonic term χώρα, receptacle, wet nurse, ὕλη, from the impor-tant medical terms for diet, nourishment, and excretion.

In Aristotle's gynaecology, woman is so identified with the survival of the race, with childbirth, and with the parts of the body that serve that purpose, that her duty, her vocation, dictates even what thoughts she should have during intimacy.

> For if it is true that the wife too contributes to the seed and the gen-
> eration, plainly there is need of equal speed on both sides. Therefore
> if he has completed quickly while she has hardly done so (for in most
> things women are slower), this is an impediment. This is also why they
> generate when united with each other but fail to generate in encoun-
> ters with partners who go with the same speed towards intercourse.
> For if the woman is excited and prepared and has thoughts that are
> appropriate[!], while the man is preoccupied with troubles and has
> become cool, then the result must be equal pace with each other.
> (636b, 16)[20]

What a subordination of woman, we may exclaim, to only one of her functions, even if it is the most important one. Where are the spiritual interests of woman? Is this not an instance of male chauvinism? Such a reaction says a lot about us and almost nothing about Aristotle, because anyone who so suspects him has overlooked the fact that dry, moist, warm, cold, are, in Aristotelian medicine, the most important criteria – both external during palpation, and internal in self-perception – of health, fer-tility, assessments of the correct or incorrect proceeding of intimacy and pregnancy. These are the primary elements and natures of the cosmos and, at the same time, of the moral world. It is only that we have forgotten how to listen to and understand this language. The reproductive organs are not *appurtenances*, parts of a woman's body: they are all of her. In her mood and thinking, the whole woman becomes a reproductive organ in perfect *fullness*, and this does not limit her but, on the contrary, through the fullness of her entry into the elements of warmth–cold, moistness–dryness, a woman grows to the size of a cosmic event, of a deity. So does the man, of course, but in a different sense.

We have already seen that the ideal, eidetic, historical, male adds to matter, to the mother, to the female, only an elusive something that Akhutin calls, with reference to Aristotle's *eidos*, the final brushstroke, just as an artist in some unfathomable way completes a painting with an elusive final touch. Paradoxically, in matter (both in the matter of a painting and in biological matter), everything is present, but without fullness. The fullness is under those circumstances not 'it', in the sense of 'that's finally it'.

Here is the place where Aristotle says that the female gives everything but is not 'it':

> For if a male is not present, she drops down under herself and becomes pregnant and lays wind-eggs, showing that she desires also to emit then, and that she does emit when she actually mates with the male. The others do this too, for there was a woman who made trial of the singing grasshoppers which she reared after catching them while still tender; and when they had grown they became pregnant spontaneously. It is clear from these things, then, that every female contributes to the seed (at least if this is seen to be the case in one kind). For there is no difference between the animal that is due to wind-pregnancy and this one, except that it fails to generate an animal. This one generates because it came from both parents too. Hence the male contributions too are not all found to be fertile, but some are infertile when there has not been the due harmonising of both contributions. (637b, 14)[21]

A wind animal, a mole, a growth in the uterus caused by 'the wind' without normal intercourse, is also an animal, if not quite, if not quite right. As always, Aristotle adheres strictly to observed phenomena and names three cases. The first is the unfertilized egg of a chicken, no different in appearance and composition from a fertilized egg, except that it is pointless trying to hatch it: no chick will emerge. The observation is based on 'only one species', but Aristotle legitimately concludes that this is not the only species of living beings in which the male and female are not equal contributors to the creation of progeny, and that, indeed, the female always brings *everything*, but in such a way that that is not 'it': fullness is not achieved.

What fullness? What are its features? In an unfertilized egg, we find the first and most important: the inability to reproduce. Aristotle notes that same telling and conspicuous feature in the mule, the offspring of a

mare crossed with a male donkey, and a hinny, the offspring of a stallion
and a female donkey, which are usually (although not always) sterile, and
supposes that, although there has been mating, the offspring has been
'unsuitably composed from the parents'. We cannot translate this into the
language of modern genetics and say, for example, that what is meant is
something along the lines of trisomy or some other deviation from the
normal number of forty-six chromosomes. A comparison with modern
biology is, however, possible, and I believe it should proceed from what
Aristotle says is not an animal but also not 'unsouled' matter:

> For when they are in this state, if the emission from both has not been
> mixed but the uterus could take in the emission from one of them, like
> the wind-egg, then there develops the so-called mole, being neither
> animal, because it has not come from both, nor soul-less, because it
> has been received, [perhaps conceived by itself, as might be said today,
> through parthenogenesis, *Bibikhin*] ensouled, like the wind-eggs.
> (638a, 23)[22]

It is important, though, not to rest content with the critique of Aristotle
who supposes this mole to be an unfertilized egg, but to reflect on the status
of something that is not alive but is ensouled: that is to say, the understanding of the living as an authentic, self-moving automaton capable of
reproducing by giving birth. He proposes this category of a non-living but
ensouled being or, in other words, of life that has not attained form, *eidos*.

Lecture 12, 25 November 1997

Our final topic last time was the intermediate state of beings that could be called biological mass, which contain all the necessary material but lack motion, so that they are unable to be a part of history, to be involved in fullness: which have everything but not 'it'. We will return to this in the middle of this two-hour lecture because there is more about it in another important biological treatise by Aristotle, *On the Generation of Animals*. For now, however, let us finish reading our way through *The History of Animals*.

I have twice used the word 'history'. The first time I mentioned it was in our sense of movement, development, where how issues develop is important to us, in which we take an interest, *inter-est*, where it is not all the same to us what happens, where there is a big difference at stake, and even where that difference is all that concerns us, where what kind of movement will go. This is κίνησις, *kinesis*. When we read in Zeno that there is no motion, then, just as we have said that warmth in classical biology also means passion (I'm getting a little ahead of today's lecture), so *motion* also means history and is the key word for history. Ἱστορία, *historia*, on the contrary, is just collecting up information, intelligence. The etymological root of the word, *histor-*, from Proto-Indo-European *wid-tor*, a wise man or judge, one who enquires, is the same as our Russian *vedat'* or English 'wit', knowing, knowledge. But since not all information gets collected, only that which clusters around *interest*, what captivates us, what we find engrossing and important, comes to be called ἱστορία, and that is our history.

In which case, should ἱστορία have κίνησις at its heart? Kinesis is that extra which the male brings to matter and to the mother, and without which the forest would be everything, but we could not say of it, 'that's finally it'. The forest would be full and everything would be full of the forest – and yet the one thing missing would be fullness. Male and female really is an important, perhaps the most important, topic in Aristotle's biology.

I leave it to you to read *The History of Animals*. It is wonderful. Only, let us take from it that holistic examination of every aspect of the behaviour of animals relating to their species and propagation of species which is such that any name I can give to it will only prove misleading, because we have become just too accustomed to dividing into separate disciplines and sciences something that Aristotle himself never separated out. If I read some quotations, you will immediately see that we, quite unlike Aristotle, have somehow come to adopt, perhaps in the last 100 years, after positivism, a division of everything into basis and superstructure, and become just far too used to that.

'The longest period of gestation is that of the species which some call a *marinus.*' There follows a list of various fish species.

The sargue conceives during the month of Poseideon (or December) and carries its spawn for thirty days; and the species of mullet named by some the chelon, and the myxon, go with spawn at the same period and over the same length of time. All fish suffer greatly during the period of gestation, and are in consequence very apt to be thrown up on shore at this time. In some cases they are driven frantic with pain and throw themselves on land. At all events they are throughout this time continually in motion until parturition is over (this being especially true of the mullet), and after parturition they are in repose. (570a, 30–570b, 7)[1]

What is translated here as 'suffer', πονοῦσι, from πόνος πένομαι, has three main meanings of 'work', 'torture', and 'birth'; there is a well-known etymological link between *labor* (labour) and *labo* (I slip, stagger, perish). There is also an etymological link with 'labile'. In other words, labour is not just hard, but so hard that I stagger under the weight of it. In Romanian, *muncă* (work) has the same derivation as the word for torment, torture. In English, 'labour' has the meaning of immense effort and again of the pangs of childbirth. In Aristotle's πονοῦσι, there is, similarly, labour, suffering, and giving birth. In Russian medical terminology, we refer to 'parturient effort', which of course reflects the ambivalent attitude in Russia towards any kind of effort.

Notice that Aristotle does not separate out the 'physiological' from the 'psychological'. We have a feeling that our own differentiation of this becomes ludicrous in the term 'parturient effort'. There seems to be something seriously wrong in our separation of the 'business' of physiology and the 'subjective state of mind'. We need to get back to classical simplicity.

The state of motion, the κίνησις, in which all fish find themselves at this time, encompasses the fact that they are rushing about, that they are aroused, but more importantly it points us towards that motion imparted to matter by the male, to history. At the same time, Aristotle is registering all this in his *history*: that is, it is important to him to communicate information about it. In the course of our reading, we will increasingly come to understand why it is so important. We will find that this is of more than mere cognitive interest, and that through this knowledge, and only through it, a person can enter that state of motion, that fullness. Not otherwise, as we shall see.

We have spoken about the behaviour involved in procreation – we have called it *amekhania*, our helplessness to voluntarily set mechanisms in motion – but we have not in the process spoken sufficiently about the handing over of the being in *amekhania* to the automaton that begins to decide everything, including even whether that being is to live.

Having dealt with the 'pairing, conception, and the like phenomena' of fish, birds, and reptiles, Aristotle moves on in *The History of Animals* to viviparous animals and humans. The first and most shared attribute he identifies is 'excitement', the greatest being 'the desire of one sex for the other and by the pleasure derived from copulation' (571b, 2).[2] Expressing himself cautiously, Aristotle touches on the weird and wonderful, the magical.

'Stallions at this period bite one another, throw their riders and chase them.' Wild boar are unusually fierce during the mating season, though usually enfeebled at this time as the result of copulation. They are as powerless as automata and

> fight with one another in an extraordinary way, clothing themselves with defensive armour, or in other words deliberately thickening their bodies by rubbing against trees or by coating themselves repeatedly all over with mud and then drying themselves in the sun. They drive one another away from the swine pastures, and fight with such fury that very often both combatants succumb. (571b, 11)[3]

This is most pronounced in human beings. Aristotle has in mind possible all-out war. Of the other animals, the mare is the closest to human beings.

> In fact, the mare is said to go a-horsing; and the term derived from the habits of this one animal serves as a term of abuse applicable to such females of the human species as are unbridled in the way of sexual appetite. The mare is said also about this time to get wind-impregnated [perhaps what is meant here is that, as with the partridge, it is impregnated by the hot breath of males, *Bibikhin*], and for this reason in Crete they never remove the stallion from the mares; for when the mare gets into this condition she runs away from all other horses. The mares under these circumstances fly invariably either northwards or southwards and never either to the east or west.

Note the link to the cosmos and the stars. There is no talk here of the compass or the earth's magnetic field. 'When this complaint is on them they allow no one to approach, until either they are exhausted with fatigue … ,' διὰ τὸν πόνον (572b, 19). It is the same word Aristotle uses for labour; in their rushing about, their motion, the wildness attending mating, there is already a hint, an anticipation, of the labour of

childbirth. We find him hinting at the same link again in a sentence
shortly before (571b, 10), Τὰ μὲν οὖν θήλεα χαλεπώτατα – 'The female is
most cross-tempered just after parturition,' ὅταν ἐκτέκωσι πρῶτον, οἱ δ
'ἅππενες περὶ τὴν ὀχείαν, 'or have reached the sea. Under either of these
circumstances they discharge a certain substance called "hippomanes",
and this is also the name given to the growth on a new-born foal; this
resembles the sow-virus and is in great request amongst women who deal
in drugs and potions' (572a, 18).[4]

Hippomanes, mares' madness. This is another substance firmly associated with the urge to copulate and childbirth; it is the name given to a
growth on the forehead of the newborn foal, and it has the same magic
power and was also in demand with pharmacists, people whose profession
was φάρμακον,[5] in which, too, no distinction was made between the power
of acting on the body and the power of invoking the madness of love. We
translate these words as 'love philtre', 'sorceress', but this purpose was not
separate from, say, 'heat' or 'cold', 'dryness' or 'moistness', and that could
cause a great deal of confusion.

> After parturition the mare at once swallows the after-birth and
> bites off the growth called the *hippomanes*. This growth is somewhat
> smaller than a dried fig; and in shape is broad and round, and in
> colour black. If any bystander gets possession of it before the mare,
> and the mare gets a smell of it, she goes wild and frantic at the smell.
> [Mania, *Bibikhin*.] And it is for this reason that vendors of drugs and
> simples hold the substance in high request and include it among their
> stores. (577a, 7)[6]

'Mares' madness' has matter the smell of which makes mares go mad.
This is not some magic combination of mind and matter: our distinguishing between those is still in the future. It is something quite different:
the madness, the racing about, the galloping of mares to north or south
but not to east or west, their madness is the same *motion* as mating, the
growing of the embryo, the appearing of the milk, all one complete reality,
a dark forest.[7]

Pigs have a similar physical madness, also eerie and sometimes sui-
cidal, and it, too, has an embodiment, καπρία, the sow-virus – postnatal
discharges different from the chorion, the placenta (573b, 2).[8] The word
derives from κάπρος, a wild boar, and not from the word κάπρα, a goat,
which is a later Greek borrowing from the Latin *capra*. To go berserk like
a wild boar about to mate is καπρᾶν καπρίζειν. I simply do not believe
that this meaning played no role in the formation of the Italian '*capric-
cio*', caprice. The derivation of 'caprice' from the capering of a she-goat
seems euphemistic. That there might be an earlier stratum, dating back
to the days when Italy was called Great Greece, throws doubt on the idea
that the late Greeks adopted κάπρα from the Latins, and suggests rather
that long before that the Latin-speaking Italians had borrowed the word

from the Greeks, changing the meaning from boar to goat. We can be fairly sure that, at the same time, καπρᾶν καπρίζειν, too, would have been adopted. The watering-down of antique rawness and strength is common in language. Furthermore, even if there were none of that ancient Greek madness about the word, it is only town dwellers who would apply *capriccion* to the normal gait of goats; for country people, it describes their behaviour during mating, which is also 'capricious'. Αἰγῶν δ᾿ ἡγεμόνα οὐ καθιστᾶσιν οἱ νομεῖς διὰ τὸ μὴ μόνιμον εἶναι τὴν φύσιν αὐτῶν, ἀλλ᾿ ὀξεῖαν καὶ εὐκίνητον, 'With goats the shepherds appoint no bell-wether, as the animal is not capable of repose but frisky and apt to ramble' (574a, 11).[9] I would look for parallels to these observations in Russian words evidently cognate with *kobyla* (mare), such as '*kobenit'sia*', to be stubborn, capricious; '*kobël'*, a formidable woman; '*kobyla*', an ungainly woman; and '*kob''*, sorcery, fortune-telling. In the etymological dictionary, instead of help I find: '*kobel'*, a measure of dry, free-flowing goods; '*kobenit'sia*', associated with '*skoba*', a bracket, thus, to get caught on a bracket.[10] Where something is terribly important, important and terrible, the classical mind was not afraid to look straight at it and contemplate it. Our minds have just an empty gap: we are too embarrassed.

I promised to show why, not just out of curiosity, we need real science, which we have lacked since classical times and still lack today. And that is because, I said, what has only begun in the last 200 years, and in which we are ahead of classical thinking, is only specialized observation and in no wise a philosophy of nature. The collapse in the philosophy of nature came about at the end of the classical period, and to this day there is still a gaping void where it used to be. Folk wisdom is, within its limitations, doing what it is supposed to do, to the extent that it can without access to libraries and printing presses, using the means available to it: language. Academic learning, puffed up with its own importance, is getting on with doing what it does: developing epistemology and theories of knowledge or consciousness. In this sense, Heidegger is only the first intimation of what the philosophy of nature in its next iteration is going to be, for the first time since classical antiquity.

Read Book 6 of *The History of Animals* for yourselves. I am going to move on to Book 7, on 'Man's Growth, First within His Mother's Womb', on the maturing of children, early habits, and what today is sometimes considered an innovation in courses and committees on sex education, in sex textbooks, and in science generally, and which simply is already all there in Aristotle. Here is a random example: nowadays, ridiculing the primitive quirks of the theory of evolution, people recall the deception when the human embryo was portrayed at different stages as replicating in ontogenesis a telescoped rerun of the development of the animal world from bacteria to invertebrates to fish, amphibians, and mammals. The truth of the matter is that the human embryo is human from the outset. Aristotle writes, 'At the fortieth day ... the embryo is revealed, as big as one of the large kind of ants; and all the limbs are plain to see, including the penis, and the eyes also, which as in other animals are of great size' (583b, 14).[11]

But I shall pass over this seventh book also, only giving another example of the fact that things we customarily (and I now state confidently, out of bad habit) divide into 'objective symptoms of pregnancy' and 'subjective symptoms of pregnancy' fit perfectly well in Aristotle into a single category and are not 'symptoms' of anything but are pregnancy itself.

> [S]ome women suffer (πονοῦσι) most at the beginning of their preg-
> nancy and some at a later period when the embryo has had time to
> grow; and in some women it is a common occurrence to suffer from
> strangury towards the end of their time. As a general rule women who
> are pregnant of a male child escape comparatively easily and retain
> a comparatively healthy look, but it is otherwise with those whose
> infant is a female; for these latter look as a rule paler and suffer more
> pain, and in many cases they are subject to swellings of the legs and
> eruptions on the body. Nevertheless, the rule is subject to exceptions.

That is, some have an easier pregnancy and varicose inflammation of the veins passes.

> Women in pregnancy are a prey to all sorts of longings and to rapid
> changes of mood, and some folks call this the 'ivy-sickness'. And with
> the mothers of female infants the longings are more acute, and they
> are less contented when they have got what they desired. In a certain
> few cases the patient feels unusually well during pregnancy. The worst
> time of all is just when the child's hair is beginning to grow. (584a,
> 17)[12]

In *A Writer's Diary*, Dostoevsky intercedes for a pregnant woman who is in court on a charge of theft, explaining exactly this: that in her condition the female of the species is not able to control herself fully, and this is not the same as surrendering to difficulties and slipping into vice: after childbirth everything will of its own accord return to normal, and that her strange desires are nothing to do with moral degeneration.[13] He has to explain this. If medicine had a term for the eccentricities of pregnant women, as the Greeks did, if there were not this absurd insist-ence that always, in every forest, human beings should maintain – what? The problem is that nobody knows. This 'norm and form' that 'society' demands of everyone has simply not been studied. Along came Stalin and showed that under coercion anybody can be made to buckle, and that was normal. The Stalin era has been dismissed as untypical, wrong, in order that people could continue to believe in a norm. Drug addiction shows that a few grams of chemical substances dissolve norms and forms. The war against drug addiction is conducted mainly to support the myth that a normal individual should be able to maintain a certain level of composure.

The figures we see on the screen and in advertisements have miraculous composure. Everybody knows about the whims of pregnant women, but medical science calls them 'subjective experiences'.

Aristotle shocks this prim and proper person – who regards his body as an animal which it is for reason to subjugate – by not leaving him a leg to stand on. Not even his upright gait. He lumps humans in with animals that walk on all fours, perhaps because he has been talking about infants and the very obvious way they crawl about on all fours. 'Women continue to have milk until their next conception; and then the milk stops coming and goes dry, alike in the human species and in the quadrupedal vivipara' (587b, 27).[14] When human beings are thus inserted into the animal world, or, rather, returned to it, their real specific characteristics become more important and significant than when they are on their own and set apart from the animals (thinking up ways in which they are different). One is puzzling:

> Now all other animals bring the time of pregnancy to an end in a uniform way; in other words, one single term of pregnancy is defined for each of them. But in the case of humankind alone of all animals the times are diverse; for pregnancy may be of seven months' duration, or of eight months or of nine. (584a, 31–584b)[15]

Now back to the topic of the role of the male. If wind eggs of various birds, not only domesticated, do not differ from fertilized eggs, they are clearly living matter, but without motion, without history. Aristotle confidently dismisses the idea that a hen continues to lay even without a cockerel because it still contains the remnants of an earlier fertilization. He is right. The egg is growing inside the chicken because that is the chicken's constitution. If it were to cease to lay, that would be an aberration and indicate sickness.

How Aristotle understands the role of the male we have seen in the example of the female partridge which already has an egg. Everything is in place for the emergence of the offspring: it has only to be flown over by the male and to catch his hot breath. This breath seems a slight thing, but without it the life matter will remain lifeless.

We can read more fully in *On the Generation of Animals* than in *The History of Animals*[16] about why it is that 'if it is the secretion of the female which is the material of the embryo, she needs the male besides instead of generating entirely from herself' (741a, 8).[17] But let us now, as always, read or at least browse through this, beginning at the first page.

[On the first page, *Tr.*] there is news which, although not unexpected, we should have been able to anticipate: 'The material of animals is their parts – of the whole animal the non-homogeneous parts, of these again the homogeneous, and of these last the so-called elements of all matter' (715a, 9).[18]

How are we to understand this, that the material of animals is their parts? The animal is the whole. It could not be a whole, it would make no sense to talk about a whole, if it were not composed of parts. Parts are essential if there is to be a whole, and the whole reaches out for the parts in order to be possible. There is a particular number of parts and they are as they are for the whole to be possible.

Did the whole arrange for, order, as it were, its own parts? Somehow it is so splendidly arranged that one part fits with another, and that there are just the right number of the right sort of parts to constitute the whole. When they were put together, did someone say, 'That's finally it!'? Fullness.

For this to happen, the part needed from the outset to be attuned to the whole. Matter is attracted to fullness, to *eidos*. It is so attracted that of its own accord, envisaging how the whole was to be, it provided all the parts needed for the whole to be. That is, the whole already was. It did not yet exist, but it was. This is interesting. It was and was not, being and non-being in one.

To put it another way, *eidos* is form, but it is not form. Structure and form are already there before *eidos*. Completely, entirely, only not fully. Without fullness.

The male, Aristotle tells us, gives motion and generation just like heaven or the sun, or, as he cautiously stipulates, other analogous things if they exist, having in mind all the influence exercised by heaven. The earth effectively provides everything: what comes from the sun is invisible, weightless, and does not appreciably add matter to the earthly (716a, 6).[19]

Let us not be in too much of a hurry to define distances: that could prove problematical because we would have to define and understand the distinction between the ordinary human world, a parlously thin membrane of air, land, and water, and the awe-inspiring dimensions of the depths of the earth and of outer space, but in purely formal terms we are within our rights in pondering the polarity of the space in which we have our being; and it will not be unreasonable to say it includes contrasts and is capable of accommodating great differences.

It is very clear, on a purely formal rather than a substantive level of speculative discussion, that we are privileged by the fact that definite boundaries run right through our world and us ourselves. Physicists say that our part of the universe is a very hospitable place, in that matter and energy are clearly separated, which is not the case everywhere: they can be fused, without any clear dividing line. The scientific, and indeed the naked, eye can see there is no incontrovertible reason why our circumstances should be as they are. Angles could be and may yet be different, the boundaries blurred or fewer. In discussions about entropy and the like, what carries most weight is the persistent, recurring sensation that we are in the presence of something, perhaps in a special place or a special space, but at all events in history, and not by any means only human history but the history of nature. It is nonsense to say that nature is indifferent and that it has no history.

The 'goldilocks' nature of our world, noted by physicists, is what

Aristotle calls wellness and purpose. Here is a very good example. Why among the higher mammals have the male sex glands been placed outside, almost separate from, the body (717a, 12 ff.)?[20] Nature makes everything either because it is necessary or because it is better. There is here no call for us to adopt a superior pose and lecture Aristotle to the effect that nature neither takes action nor sets goals but operates strictly in accordance with causality. In his own language, which we still have no grounds for declaring inferior to our own, he identifies something that for us, too, is a problem, and perhaps the main problem: why is there such evident complexity? Why is not everything subject to entropy? There is no unambiguous need for the dual testes of male mammals to be located outside the main part of the body: in fish and snakes, they are inside the body. Nature has again followed the circuitous route of increasing complexity. In fish, the milt is ejaculated directly during insemination, by the shortest route, whereas in mammals, ejaculation is circuitous and delayed, not delivered through a momentary clasping of male and female; it is more 'balanced' and there is more 'rationality' in it. That is, as I see it, there is more space for the application of reason. In place of the instant ejaculation of sperm of fish, there is greater scope for reflection and intention. One of the opportunities nature gives here, and which is exploited, is direct intervention: the castration of domesticated animals. Aristotle may have something else in mind when he several times points out that this arrangement of the testes extends the duration of intercourse.

The assertion that 'nature makes things better' is not dogmatic but *heuristic.* It reminds us, orders us, to observe that whenever the necessity for something in nature is not immediately evident (and sometimes it very clearly is), complexity, circuitousness entailing enhanced risks, free us from needless searching for some hidden necessity there. They oblige us instead to search and speculate and discover things that *nature itself may not know.* This is analogous to the instinct of the artist or the poet who does not by any means always know why some particular thing has to be done in a particular way. But there is more to this than just the trust of an artist, or indeed anyone else, in their own intuition. Nature follows its instinct and plainly also has confidence in it. Animals rely on instinct more than human beings do. What nature lacks, however, to support its intuition as the best course by deliberate choice and decision is that simple acceptance we talked about the time before last. Nature lacks policy and political decisions.

But the female, as female, is passive, and the male, as male, is active, and the principle of the movement comes from him. Therefore, if we take the highest genera under which they each fall, the one being active and motive and the other passive and moved, that one thing which is produced comes from them only in the sense in which a bed comes into being from the carpenter and the wood, or in which a ball comes into being from the wax and the form. It is plain then that it is not necessary that anything at all should come away from the male, and if anything does come away it does not follow that this gives rise to the embryo as being in the embryo, but only as that which imparts the motion and as the form; so the medical art cures the patient. (729b,12)[21]

This is more definite. It is from a cursory reading of passages such as this that it was believed that *eidos* is itself the structure of the body. But let us not forget what the matter of a living being is: it is the parts of its body, and that is all. Wax is mentioned only as a simile which does not take us very far. The female element is not in the sense of a piece of wax, but in the sense of wax already in the shape of a ball. It is a ball, but not yet a ball because there is something missing. Let us say for now that what is missing is someone who knows it is a ball.

Incidentally, we have here one of the problems of the theory of evolution. From the fossils of certain prehistoric people, we know, given the size of their brain (actually a very questionable parameter), that they could have been human. That is, in material terms, everything was there. But from that we cannot say, 'Right, that's it.' We need to see what they were making. If they were making tools, then, yes, they were already human; but if they were not, then no, they were not yet human.

What occurs in birds and oviparous fishes is the greatest proof that neither does the semen come from all parts of the male nor does he emit anything of such a nature as to exist within that which is generated, as part of the material embryo, but that he only makes a living creature by the power which resides in the semen. (729b, 35–730a, 3)[22]

Modern biology has lately been circling around this topic, which is in fact crucial, and not by any means because it is 'phallocentric'.

Lecture 13, 2 December 1997

Anatoly Akhutin in *The Concept of 'Nature' in Antiquity and in the Modern Age*[1] touches on the fact that our topic is the attraction of the forest *itself*, in its very essence, to fullness, to *eidos*, or, in the more familiar, understandable language of the Modern Age, to number and the Cross. The approach to Aristotle is encumbered by the stereotype of *eidos* as structure. It is a fair bet, therefore, that the approach to this subject in modern times will also be obstructed, and, sure enough, the term 'pantheistic nature philosophy' or 'pantheism' duly appears, with the connotation of a non-mainstream approach leading to a dead end and, what is worse, a connotation of something dreary which is not interesting to think about. Akhutin writes, 'Hermeticism seems to immerse itself in nature, it engages in trying to unlock its secrets and pursues practical goals. In fact, with its cyphers, secret links, and its entanglement of humans in this web, it in fact conceals and withholds nature and makes impossible a detached, curious relationship to it' (34). One can only agree. Akhutin notes several characteristic features. The cosmos in its animate unity replicates the unity of an intelligent world. This, as Giordano Bruno defines it [in his hermetic allegory *The Expulsion of the Triumphant Beast*, 39, *AM*], is the revelation of nature itself, 'because *Natura est Deus in rebus* – Nature is God in things' (ibid.). Nature is a single formative force. Nature in this context of Akhutin's is close to matter. Matter is a formative power: that is against a schematic understanding of Aristotle but in favour of the 'active' understanding of matter that he has and about which we have read in Heinz Happ. Akhutin also notes this 'pro et contra':

> To use Aristotelian language and polemicizing with the Peripatetics, Bruno expresses an idea that will be important later for a new understanding of nature. 'Certainly,' Bruno writes, 'Aristotle and his followers usually say that forms come out from matter, rather than that they are introduced into it, that they emerge from it rather than being absorbed into it.'[2] We should change our understanding of the material existence of nature, and rather see it as 'all-being' rather than nonbeing, because, as Bruno says, it seems to him that if nature draws all

forms from its bosom, it follows that it already has them. The matter of nature is defined as the enfolded universal possibility of forms unfolded into manifest nature.

'That [i.e. matter, *Akhutin*],' concludes Bruno, 'which unfolds what it possesses enfolded must, therefore, be called a divine and excellent parent, generator and mother of natural things – indeed nature entire in substance.' (Ibid.)[3]

This is good Aristotelian thinking, both on the part of Giordano Bruno and as paraphrased by Akhutin. We have ourselves come to it, but we are further interested in a topic that is present as a latent problem in the words Akhutin has quoted but which he does not take up and which remains unaddressed. Picture this: matter 'unfolding what it possesses enfolded', namely, all forms, in the sense of structures and bodies. It could have held and kept them forever, and God knows what else it keeps enfolded or why it began unfolding what it does. Aristotle: it was touched by the breath of *eidos*, of the attraction to fullness, and not in the least of form and structure. Why were forms and structures enfolded and did they then begin to unfold? Why did history begin? Why could mother matter not give birth on her own? Akhutin leaves this question in Aristotle's *Of the Generation of Animals* unanswered. Giordano Bruno does not, but right now it is not Bruno we are reading; we are reading him as quoted by Akhutin, which is not the same thing.

A second characteristic of 'hermeticism', 'pantheism', '*Naturphilosophie*' (is that the same as philosophy of nature or something else? Is it a good or a bad thing?):

The human being is a real microcosm, not just an analogue of the world, but a creature genuinely linked to everything – spiritual and material – in the world and potentially omnipotent. From the famous definition of the human being by Pico della Mirandola in his *Oration on the Dignity of Man*[4] to Jakob Böhme and Juan Luis Vives, the theme of the human is dominant in this tradition. Humans are not 'naturally' linked to anything, and yet at the same time they are magically woven into the fabric of the cosmos; they are 'this quintessence of dust', as Hamlet says, and the 'quintessence of the four elements of the cosmos', as Paracelsus defines them; they are Nothing and potentially Everything. (35)

We, too, have intuited this insignificance in humanity, but we ran into a problem that is present in these quotations but not raised and so not answered. *Which kind of human being are we talking about here, a man or a woman? 'Man' is described in a way that fits the definition of the male*, eidos. The whole, crucial problem is what in the clownish language of journalism is given the shadowy designation of 'phallogocentrism'. The human being is insignificant for Derrida, too, but this is a man scarred by circumcision who, out of his wordlessness, his know-nothingness, weakness, fear, his neurotic thoughts of relentless despair about his penis, is nevertheless, after the end of history, in a lacklustre period in the midst of spiritual decline, scraping together in his impotent poverty the strength, in spite of everything, to restart history, if only in the form of deconstructivism and postmodernism. Nothing and potentially everything. Between this 'being' and matter a stress field forms.

Akhutin almost touches on this concern of ours when he says, 'Hermeticism transfers the active principle into nature itself.' He is referring to matter, nature as matter. If hermeticism transfers the active principle into nature itself, that means it was external to nature, or it was in nature but, somehow, was not in nature. It was and was not. In nature, absolutely everything was in matter but that was not yet everything. There was everything in full, in full without exception, only fullness had not been achieved. Had it been achieved? It had and had not. 'Hermeticism transfers. . .', so once it has done so, does that mean all is well with nature? Everything is in it? Fullness is in it? Well, no. It transpires that for some reason it still has to suffer, and primarily at the point of the human being.

> Permeated with likes and antipathies, influences and aspirations, nature proves to be active or suffering in every part. This engenders an ineradicable and relentless unease, because to 'be' means to be present in history: to strive, to oppose, to prevail. To be means to manifest one's quality, that is, as Böhme puts it, to be tormented (*Qualität - sich quälen - die Qual*).

In other words, if matter is tormented in itself, it could equally successfully be tormented by non-matter. Akhutin: 'The perpetual transformation of the corporeal into the spiritual ... draws the human being into unceasing action and suffering' (35–6). Which human being – Nothing or Everything? The human being is suffering Nothingness? The question is again left hanging; one thing remains unchallengeable: the Cross.

Now, about the Cross, Böhme says that there is accord and harmony in nature, but to be means *sich quälen*.[5] Aristotle's πόνος. To say, 'Why suffer?' means to dream of returning to the forest, but it is no longer there: it has turned into the Cross. Whether it has done so for us or not is neither here nor there, because there is no way we can get back into the skin of those for whom that transformation has not occurred: it is obvious to us that it has occurred and that they just do not yet know that.

Πόνος and labour are needed because things have not yet been born; or they have been born but not yet completely, and they need to be born completely; or they have even been reborn but so far lack the imprimatur, the signature of approval of spirit, to say, 'That's finally it!' Humankind is included in nature through work, through the Cross.

Who was Jakob Böhme? He was of peasant stock, a shoemaker, and did not live even to the age of fifty. Half his years fell in the sixteenth century and half in the seventeenth. He was married and had six children. Unfortunately, he speaks a very rarefied language, which means it is as if we are having to study philosophy in Urdu. One of his strengths is the courage with which he examines forces in which he immediately drowns without any attempt to carve out an artificial independence for himself. Humans are within forces. The first chapter of *Aurora, or the Rising of Dawn* begins, 'Yet if a man will speak of God, and say what God is, then, a man must diligently consider the powers in nature, also the whole creation, heaven and earth, the stars, the elements, and the creatures that are proceeded from them; as also the holy angels, devils, and men.'[6] Böhme is a man not of schemata, but of colour and taste, and also he sees how thin the membrane of life is in which humankind is situated, when almost immediately next to him are infinite freezing or scorching regions. He calls elements 'qualities'; for him to be is to be present in history, to be tormented.

> A quality is the mobility, boiling, springing and driving of a thing. As for example, *heat*, which burneth, *consumeth* and driveth forth all whatsoever that cometh into it which is not of the same property; and again, it *enlighteneth* and warmeth all cold, wet and dark things; it compacteth and hardeneth soft things. Heat containeth likewise two other kinds in it, namely, (1) Light, and (2) Fierceness.... The light, or the heart, of the heat, is in itself a pleasant, joyful glance or lustre, a power of life, an enlightening and glance of a thing which is afar off, which light is a piece or source of the heavenly kingdom of joy. For it maketh *living* and moving all things in this world. All flesh, trees, leaves and grass grow in this world in the power of the light, and have their life therein, *viz.* in the good. Again, heat containeth also a fierceness or *wrath*, which burneth, consumeth and spoileth; this wrath or fierceness springeth, driveth and elevateth itself in the light.... The heat is *predominant* in all, in trees, herbs and grass, and maketh the water moveable, so that through the springing of the waters, herbs and grass grow out of the earth. Heat is therefore called a quality (*Qualität*) because it operateth, moveth and boileth (or welleth up) in all, and elevateth all.[7]

When we read in the 'pre-Socratics' about the existential fundamentals of heat and cold, it is as if the texts have faded. It is through Böhme that we understand for the first time what the ancients meant by heat. And here is what they understood by cold:

> *Cold* is a quality also, as well as *heat*; it qualifieth or operateth in all creatures whatsoever that come forth in *nature*, and in all whatsoever that move therein, in men, beasts, fowls, fishes, worms, leaves and grass. Heat is set in *opposition* unto it, and qualifieth therein, as if it were one and the same thing; but cold opposeth the fierceness or rage of the heat, and *allayeth* the heat. Cold containeth also two sorts

or species in it, which are to be observed, viz. It *mitigateth* the heat, maketh all things pleasant, and is in all creatures a quality of life; for no creature can subsist without cold; for it is a springing driving mobility in every thing. The other kind or species is *fierceness*; for where this getteth power it suppresseth all, and spoileth all, even as the heat doth; no life could subsist in it if the heat did not hinder that. The fierceness of cold is a destruction to every life, and the house of death, even as the hot fierceness also is.[8]

If only, having thus surrendered himself to 'qualities', to colour, Böhme had then waited patiently. He seems in too much of a hurry to bring order-liness to his forest, and harnesses God and the angelic powers (*Deus ex machina*) to the purpose. We do not learn from him how the forest itself comes to geometry, but *Aurora*, too, is recommended.

Among those most quoted by Akhutin in his book is Vladimir Vernadsky (1863–1945), a Russian geographer whose reputation is associated with the concept of the noosphere: that is, the complete application of the human mind to what previously was left to nature.[9] The noosphere (from the Greek, *noos*, 'mind') in theoretical biology is

that part of the world of life that is strongly affected by man's con-ceptual thought; regarded by some as coextensive with the anthro-posphere. The noosphere, as proposed by scientific theorists Pierre Teilhard de Chardin, Vladimir Ivanovich Vernadsky, and Edouard Le Roy, is the level of the intellect, as opposed to the geosphere, or non-living world, and the biosphere, or living world.[10]

Understood as a progressive mission – that is, as intervention by 'human conceptual thought' essential at this present stage in history in at least part of the living world – the noosphere goes directly against everything we have been saying about the attitude of the mind to the body and forest, and against that willingness to surrender oneself as a creature of the forest to the forest which we have found in Aristotle. The noosphere is a continu-ation, whether from fear or muddleheadedness, of that same itch to 'take measures' and try to impose plans on nature which invariably ends in a shambolic mess. The noosphere is, naturally, only possible where there is *noos*, and *noos* is only possible where it has admitted itself to the fullness of pure understanding: that is, has rendered to the forest all that rightly belongs to it. The noosphere has accordingly existed on the earth when, and only when, pure thought has existed, thought like that of Aristotle, which participates fully in nature because for the first time it lets nature be completely itself. The noosphere as, on the contrary, a purposeful, deliberate intention to give *noos*, human intelligence, a role in nature is the ultimate rift both with nature (matter) and with humankind; because quite clearly, despite all its valiant efforts to take over the management of nature, humankind will first cast off that strange, difficult means of participating in nature which is what true art and true thinking are. In the 'theory of the noosphere', these will have constructs substituted for them.

Another Russian cosmist is Konstantin Tsiolkovsky.

Born 5 September (17 September, New Style) 1857 in Izhevskoye, Russia. Died 19 September 1935, in Kaluga, USSR. A Russian research scientist in aeronautics and astronautics who pioneered rocket and space research and the development and use of wind tunnels for aerodynamic studies. He was also among the first to work out the theoretical problems of rocket travel in space.

> Tsiolkovsky was from a family of modest means. His father, Eduard Ignatievich Tsiolkovsky, a provincial forestry official, was a Polish noble by birth; his mother, Mariya Ivanovna Yumasheva, was Russian and Tatar. The boy lost his hearing at age nine as a result of scarlet fever; four years later his mother died. These two events had an important bearing on his early life in that, being obliged to study at home, he became withdrawn and lonely, yet self-reliant. Books became his friends. He developed an interest in mathematics and physics and, while still a teenager, began to speculate on space travel.[11]

Let us read from his article, probably dating from 1918, on the matter comprising the world.[12] Unfortunately, because he 'knows not what he doeth', we find him on one page with lofty, judicious nostalgia dispatching ancient mythology as a naïve, childish illusion, only immediately to propose another mythology more congenial to generalization and schematicism.

> Let us proceed from the properties of matter or substance.... Exact science as of now observes nothing other than a single substance of which all animals, plants and inorganic bodies consist. If indeed there are beings barely perceptible by our imperfect senses, the so-called spirits, there is nothing to stop us supposing that they are composed of the same material as the animals known to us, only more subtle and perhaps as yet unknown. This matter serves as the basis for the creation of substance of which the things we do perceive are composed. We think that everything there is in the cosmos has a single beginning in the primaeval substance from which everything is constructed. This very elementary philosophical view, which goes by the name of material monism or unity, is beguiling in its simplicity and is ever more firmly supported by science, that is, by the most intelligent and diligent people of past and present times. (138)

Everything about this is questionable, from the 'primaeval substance' to the supposed triumph of 'material monism' among the brightest scientists. It talks about 'facts' that have not been observed, and its beguiling simplicity is something convenient for theorizing rather than for philosophy. For philosophy, it would be de rigueur to ponder how this image of a homogeneous 'primaeval substance' has evolved in the human mind, what roots it has.

If we start from scratch, everything immediately becomes much easier. 'Let us begin, say, with astronomy. First gaseous nebulae appear. They existed previously but were not for the time being observable using even the most powerful telescopes' (139). The grammar underlying these sentences is 'What's the harm to us or you if we imagine stars materializing out of gas nebulae. It does not matter in the slightest whether celestial bodies really materialized out of primal nebulae; even if they did, Tsiolkovsky's speculation does not cease to be a construct, and it would not make a blind bit of difference if he was mistaken.' What makes sense is pure phenomenology. We did not observe the materialization of components of nebulae into spheres as a cosmogonic process whether it actually did or did not take place: in either case it remains the same construct. It is not a scientific fact.

'Every path leads us to the same conclusion: The universe consists of something homogeneous. This homogeneous something combines to produce everything we see. The integrity of the foundation of the cosmos prompts us to deny the existence of any other thing that is not composed of that universal foundation' (ibid.). This is putting the cart before the horse: because we would find it inconvenient for there to be things not composed of a universal foundation, we introduce the integrity of the cosmos.

This sole substance of the cosmos is called *matter*. It is homogeneous. 'Today all known matter, except the ether, is accepted as consisting of protons and electrons, that is, of positive and negative electricity. We can also say that it consists of hydrogen atoms' (ibid.).

Today, meaning around 1918, this is what matter consists of. With future scientific discoveries, understanding of its structure will change, but what really matters is that it is homogeneous. Tsiolkovsky declares openly why this is necessary: it is because, if the entire cosmos is not wholly permeated by one identical attribute, sensitivity, the cosmos, or at least its parts, would be locked, fettered, and that would not just be boring but senseless and unnecessary.

Everything is sensitive. A barometer is sensitive to air pressure, a thermometer to temperature, a hygroscope to humidity. Every inanimate instrument, every machine, is sensitive. Even every mineral is sensitive because it reacts, if barely perceptibly, to the influence of temperature, humidity, pressure, electricity, light, and the substance, around it. Every stone is permeated by gases and liquids; it changes chemically, emitting its own matter and absorbing external matter, etc. Animals are like machines, only more sensitive. That is, they respond more strongly, more noticeably, more clearly, in more complex ways to the external action on them of forces and substances. That is the only difference: it is quantitative and hence, to all intents and purposes, no difference at all[!] We can only say in this connection that all the bodies in the universe are sensitive – or rather irritable, responsive to a greater or lesser degree. Here by sensitivity we mean the human or animal sense of joy, pain, suffering, or serenity; exactly what is most precious for every being, what it is that gives value and meaning to life, the value of the cosmos. (140)

That is, just as for Böhme, colour, tone, taste. Colouration. Mood. Mood as the basic tone of being, as in Heidegger.

If the cosmos or its parts did not rejoice, what would be the point of it? In that case it would be as if it did not in fact exist. What use would it be to anyone? ... I would willingly replace the word 'sensitivity' with a different expression, but which? The sense of well-being? That barely sounds any different. (Ibid.)

It is hard not to feel that in Russia at the beginning of the century the floodgates opened for all manner of revelations. The 'parts of the cosmos' that rejoice are us. A life without joy, without happiness, would have no meaning. If joy and happiness, fullness and contentment were a private matter for humankind and not its participation in the cosmos, all talk of culture would have no more meaning than if it were being conducted between cockroaches averse to dialogue.

So, all the bodies of the universe are sensitive – the living and the dead, only to different degrees. The dead to a lesser degree, the living to a greater degree. But perhaps we cannot say even that. There are thermometers and barometers a thousand times more responsive even than human beings. So we can only say that all objects in the universe are responsive or sensitive ... capable of feeling joy or suffering, or of being self-aware. (Ibid.)

But in that case I am under no obligation to be concerned or worried about my own smallness. It is expanded by simply believing that everything that is most personal about my being, everything that is most intimate, is just the same in other people.

Actually, each of us can believe only in what we personally feel. We can harbour doubts about the feelings of other people: perhaps they are just automata that can talk but that have no feelings. However, we do believe in the feelings of other people. They can express, and even define, them more or less accurately through speech. The higher animals express their feelings with cries or movements and we believe them also. The lower animals have no voice and express their suffering by movement alone. People are beginning to doubt the sensitivity of bacteria, but everything is continuous and accordingly cannot disappear without trace. Just as there is no boundary between plants and animals, between dead and living matter, so there is no boundary between the feelings of organic and inorganic matter. (141)

Tsiolkovsky does not mention something because it is just too obvious: that those 'electrons' of which everything is made are also sensitive. That means that the so-called problem of the origin of life can be solved very simply. A certain sensitivity evolves in such a way that it becomes life, a sensitivity developed in a very special way. 'Dead matter can become animate. More precisely, its embryonic sensitivity can rise to the height of the sensitivity of animals, humans, and even more highly organized beings' (ibid.). He stops just short of saying, like Böhme, angels.

There is no mention of Aristotle and his biology, but we hear something familiar: matter comes to life by itself, by parthenogenesis. 'Every grain of matter periodically becomes animate,' but there is a very direct and swift path to life: 'There is a quick way of converting dead matter into living matter. It is an impulse or jolt in the form of organic matter. Quite simply: reproduction' (ibid.).

All matter is sensitive, but as if in a dream. Life is when matter wakes. Matter can wake up and find it is the entire cosmos, but that is not actually necessary, because the dream can be left to continue. It is only preparing awakening, because in any case the entire cosmos is encompassed by one unbroken sensitivity, and that can happen while you are asleep.

We are here on earth, where life is actually only just beginning, and it is bestial despite what we see and know. Life can develop anywhere like wildfire and will be characterized by joy and wretchedness. If the universe is linked by sensitivity, the infinity of its body, on our Ethereal Island and countless others, is not oppressive or confusing. Neither is infinity in time, nor the eternal recurrence of everything. Thus a person cannot be disturbed by the fact that of breathing in and out many times, or that their heart beats repeatedly.

> The earth and the Sun arise again many times, like a phoenix from the ashes, and along with them the life of the planets.... But Milky Ways too, arising many times and dying again, ultimately merge into one, as if dying. But they are resurrected again, forming the Ethereal Island numerous times. Beyond that, reason is silent. (147)

In what sense? We might think in every sense. What occurs is, so to speak, more profound than reason and concern over whether life on the planet will be preserved or not. Reason, ultimately, hurls itself into the history of the cosmos.

Tsiolkovsky, however, is aware that 'beyond that, reason is silent', yet at the same time, to his own surprise, finds himself saddled, right in the middle of developing his thought, with a puzzle that his reason is going to have no option but to solve, and you can guess what that is. He seems to be saying that the universal sensitive material of the cosmos enables its coming to life in its parts and as a whole. There would seem to be nothing to worry about, everything has been worked out nicely, to fullness. But no. Imperfections are seemingly to be found only on the earth.

> Almost all the bestial rudiments are still potent and bear their dreadful fruit in the form of self-destruction and all manner of disasters. Only human reason has shone out unilaterally, giving cognition to nature but not providing the strength needed to overcome bestial instincts. It is human reason that will elucidate them, then overcome and vanquish all the misfortunes. We must not, however, forget that not all of humanity excels in reason but only a millionth part of it, a few thousand individuals. A tiny percentage has fully adopted this movement. Some thirty per cent have subscribed to it with little real understanding, while the vast majority of humans are still in a primal state of total ignorance. (148)

Tsiolkovsky does not say it, but we should dot the 'i's for him: just as the entire universe is permeated by that sense of well-being, by sensitivity, so it is permeated also by this flaw, this earthly imperfection. So much for life, but if it is 'bestial', that, for Tsiolkovsky, is somehow bad and in need of *progress*. Everything is, but that is not the end of the story. Tsiolkovsky accounts for life, but presents it as something the universe might almost be better off without. Everything has already been done in countless worlds, but everything has yet to begin to be done and, moreover, from scratch.

We need to go to school.

> Knowledge will be disseminated. Everyone will receive as much information as their mind can accommodate. Knowledge of what is beneficial and what is harmful for humans will become obvious. Socialist ideals will be worked out and assimilated. The shortest and most natural way to them will be established. In the course of a few centuries, they will gradually be implemented. Humanity will merge into a single entity and be managed by a single elected reasoning mind. (149)

We can see that this is political advice to the leaders of the Russian Revolution to act in accordance with reason, but what a pathetic understanding of politics as mere management! Tsiolkovsky seems to be on the verge of designating politics as a priori acceptance or rejection of everything, but then slips up again fatally, almost pathologically fascinated by the thought that there is so much we can do with matter. He seems to forget it is already *sensitive*.

Lecture 14, 9 December 1997

'And the human species was not at all dependent on the climate: it was created as desired and required' (150). To put it in other words, human beings ceased to be savage: races of people were bred. 'There were no oceans and seas. Their depths were laid bare and huge deposits of ores, precious stones, fossil fuels, etc.' (ibid.). But this was not for the benefit of humanity: the living universe becomes active and prepares the earth for its future convenience, essentially in the same way that the plants use bees for their own pollination, and bees use humans in order to proliferate. 'An end was put not only to the suffering of human beings, but also of animals, which ceased to exist' (151). This was not cruel: extermination was evidently the only way to save defenceless animals from their suffering. 'The world ... of animals and their suffering terminated. Even sea creatures disappeared when light ceased to have access to the seas, and all the more so when the very oceans themselves evaporated' (ibid.).

This monstrous change to life on earth – with all life transferred to greenhouses and essential gases extracted like minerals – resulted from its environment being moved away from earth.

> In this way, over a short period of time, numerous solar systems were populated. The imperfect life forms in them were eliminated and replaced by the settlers' perfect forms. It was a kind of judgement; not a doomsday but a judgement merciful and benign for the imperfect: after their painless, natural extinction without offspring they rose again to better life. (152–3)

Eugenics, in the sense of breeding, was, of course, applied also to human beings.

> If minerals were transformed into a human, how could a human not rid himself of his flaws and attain a higher form? Even today, we see members of the human species who have outstanding characteristics: some never fall ill, while others live almost to 200 [*sic, Tr.*]; others again, brilliant people, create great inventions, discover truths, have

an extraordinary memory, have distinguished moral qualities, great beauty, intelligence, eloquence or other talents. We need only to put these people in favourable breeding conditions for them to populate the earth. (153)

Tsiolkovsky looks *billions* of years into the future. Everything has changed, but that means it can continue to change. Does that mean that all existent forms are only transitional? Everything is only provisional and will be replaced by something else. Yes, everything we see now, we shall see entirely different, entirely different suns, and we will see with different eyes or even entirely without eyes, but with new feelings. What will be left? A will, mutating, creating new races of men, sending them to other galaxies for millennia into the future. Needless to say, that will is not going to belong to an individual, a collective, or even to the entire human species, because the human species will change. It emanates from the totality of the sensitivity of matter and serves to increase sensitivity. Does that mean, itself? Another name Tsiolkovsky uses for sensitivity is the sense of self-awareness. It strives to attain the self.[1] That is something we, too, have been approaching from various directions when thinking about the automaton.

Who, then, is going to oversee this activity over billions of calendar years in time and thousands of light years in space, if all today's humanity, even if it were to focus its will, is no more than a grain of sand? Itself! Since matter itself was able to evolve life, matter itself will arrange it intelligently. The selfness of the subject of a sense of self-awareness, however, contributes precisely nothing substantial to the development of matter, and yet it contributes a lot: by asserting its identity, its suchness. Granting it, to use a fashionable expression, identity. Identity asserts precisely what is. Why is what is already there? Who authorized it? The answers we have heard are: *eidos*, the Idea, the male, the element of movement which is history. The supreme idea, the idea of ideas, the idea of blessedness, is interpreted as the notion of goodness, validity. This is the Platonic idea making its mark on Darwinism and genetics; in genetics as the stability of the race, in Darwinism as survival of the fittest. 'Fit' is more important and broader in meaning than 'adapted'. It does not necessarily presuppose an environment into which it fits, so a more original sense is 'fit for purpose, appropriate, ready, healthy'.

It seems to me that a line of holiness can readily, indeed necessarily, be woven into this Darwinian–Platonic idea of the 'fitness' of a species, as if it has successfully intuited, guessed, what is needed. It is fit not only because it has managed to fit into the environment, but somehow because of the transcendent nature of its sensitivity which accounts for its superiority. The species (or genus) fits well into a causal chain of phenomena, while at the same time refreshing and renewing 'fitness' all over again, and this makes its intuition transcendent. I have a feeling we will have a lot more to say about holiness. It is a corridor down which we can glimpse the ends of our topic. You will remember what they and that were.

We sometimes hear 'with the blessing of'. 'The conference has the blessing of the patriarch.' Sanctification. 'The apartment was consecrated.' A blessing added nothing to the proceedings of the conference. The consecration of an apartment brings nothing additional to the introduction of furniture. The signature of the director under a project was mentioned above. It adds nothing meaningful: the signature is not an order and does not guarantee the project will be realized, but perhaps, just because it does not add anything substantive, it introduces something more important than any content. In the Germano-Slavic languages, for example in the Scandinavian names Oleg and Olga, holiness is associated with health, with wholeness, and with healing. Etymologies prove nothing, but nowhere else will you find clues and hints as powerful as those in language. In the Russian word for holiness, *sviatost'*, Vladimir Nikolaevich Toporov finds something similar: the same structure, as it were, on different grounds. The concept of holiness we are familiar with nowadays grew long ago, before the coming of Christianity to Russia, out of the meaning of increase, swelling of physical matter, of mass, and at the same time of inner, fecund strength, spiritual energy, and, connected with it and proclaiming it, its external form, light (*svet*) and colour (*tsvet*):

> The appearance of colour as such, its differentiation into separate colours, arranging them in accordance with intensification, the occurrence of glowing and shining which at its most impressive captivates not only the eye but also the heart and soul of human beings.... For the Proto-Slavonic **svęt-* it appears possible to reconstruct the meaning already mentioned of 'to increase' or 'to swell'. To judge by the relevant contexts and typological analogies, the meaning was of bountiful increase and flourishing of some life-giving substance that conduced to the ripening of fruit as the culmination of previous development and a breakthrough to a new, higher state, eternal birth, maximum fertility and gain. This *sviatost'* (**svęt-*) as a vision of extreme abundance was most probably the substratum on which the concept of spiritual holiness, a superhuman state of prospering when working 'in the spirit', was based To some extent this is confirmed (at least hinted at) also by combinations of **svęt-* with nouns, which, classified with a sufficient degree of certainty as Proto-Slavonic, already display something more than purely physical (material) increase.[2]

Let us take this literally. In material increase, we already have – increase, *materia*. Toporov tells us that to this, like light (*svet*), colour (*tsvet*), consecration (*osviashchenie*), sanctification (from the Latin *sanctus* – holy), there is added – what? What Toporov calls 'expansion, burgeoning' was already there. Is what is added a significant *nothing*, *im*material holiness? Or is it nothing to such an extent that it cannot be described as immaterial? What Toporov is talking about is like joy, which would seem to be immaterial but has its own bodily accompaniment, an ecstasy that is far from intellectual but a jubilation of precisely what Bakhtin would call the 'bodily lower stratum';[3] something that can also be called 'wild' or 'mad' joy, despite the fact that the root of the Russian word for 'joy' (*radost'*) has stillness at its core, peace. An explosion of physical bounteousness is not incompatible with stillness. So is it material or immaterial? It is that *fullness* in which, as we have seen, in it and through it, two categories that do not merge and which are not to be confused, body and spirit, like parallel lines, converge in *fullness*.

It should be emphasized immediately and emphatically that the notion of material growth in these cases is *in no wise* diminished, but that at the same time a detached form of the idea of physical holiness combines, penetrates: holiness, as such, no longer in its deepest reaches dependent on the notion of material increase, as an element of evaluation using a different scale. The spring barley is 'holy' not because it grows and is fertile, but it grows and is fertile because it has been holy from time immemorial, by decree, in accordance with the supreme will.[4]

The topic of transubstantiation is being touched on here. Something new is happening to the barley or, on the contrary, holiness is not only in the barley but was there before it, caused it, not, again, substantively, but for the joy of finding it and including it in history. Was the barley in nature or not? It assuredly was, but became so fully through 'consecration'.

Given the way Toporov develops consecration, we will be justified, and even duty bound, to link with this holiness the fullness (richness) we find in classical thought. We have already said of fullness as an ideal that it is blessed. We have spoken elsewhere about the connection of blessedness with species and birth.

'All forms of realization of human activity are orientated towards holiness: one's own (potentially) and what emanates from above.' By this, Toporov means that initially, before official religion (e.g. imposed top-down by the state as in the reign of St Vladimir), holiness was an obligatory 'add-on' to everything humans did and what they were. Only, do not overlook how holiness was sensed: viscerally; and what testified to it was ecstasy, jubilation, beauty as a mood: that is, as a burst of colour associated with festivity and celebration (celebration as the essence of poetry – Olga Sedakova[5]). Festivity is associated with colour and colour is sufficient, mediated by matter – like in the music of Mozart, which, incidentally, has little matter of its own, as is true also of Pushkin. Just enough.

Tsiolkovsky: festivity, the celebratory element, in his discourse fuses inextricably with action and leaves behind it *nothing* beyond the act.[6]

Lecture 15, 16 December 1997

We would be better off if we were working to an agenda and clarifying its points. We cannot do so, not only because there is no language in which we could talk about the forest. (The technical language of forestry and the language of biology are no help.) The significance of timber in terms of the national economy and the recreational value of woodland in the system of public health (the recreational value of woodland is constantly increasing and can be measured and quite accurately valued in monetary terms through statistics of morbidity in communities which do or do not have the amenity of woodlands) require clear definition of what is understood by the nation and the economy; and here we should perhaps go to some lengths to clarify these concepts, not least because in various lecture courses, especially those on 'Property' and 'The World', to a lesser degree in 'The First Philosophy' and, as regards the foundations of understanding language, 'Wittgenstein', we have in fact already done so.[1] With the issue of what is meant by 'the national economy', the task is political. That is a depersonalizing area dealing with people in general, or citizens of the Russian Federation in general. The topic of the destiny, history, and law of history of the people, the people of Russia, was the focus of discussion at the end of our course on the language of philosophy; at the conclusion of the course 'Know Thyself', and particularly in the final part of the course on 'Time'.[2] We cannot allow ourselves the luxury of returning to these topics here.

The situation in respect of the basic concepts in biology is little better than in forestry. Again, we cannot concern ourselves with interesting specific problems of modern biological science because of the complete lack of clarification of its basic concepts, such as 'life' itself, 'evolution', and even 'gene' and 'sex'. There is a striking disparity between the purity and rigour of the best observations and experiments in biology, and the obscurity of the general concepts without which it cannot deliver its observations or experiments. We are indeed engaged in clarifying these concepts and cleansing and enriching the network of concepts that will define the syllabus of biological science, but as I have said, our main task is not the construction of language. In defining what our task is, science is helpful. It, too, of course, is only engaged in clarifying basic concepts as far as necessary, because it can get by using a defective system of concepts. Its bedrock is findings like the important technical discovery that for microscopic examination of the cell nucleus it is unnecessary to keep it under observation constantly, when virtually everything in the cell is almost indistinguishably merged, but to do so only at the moment of cell division, because it is at that moment, and only at that moment, that the chromosomes are revealed, emerging from non-observability and acquiring a clear structure. Cells display themselves at the moment of reproduction, but otherwise conceal themselves. We have noticed the same thing in the observed deviant, irrational, a-mechanical, ex-static behaviour of the living world around mating and birth, which is analogous. But we can only talk in this manner, only interpret, if there is something there. In other words, there needs first to be a 'find' (*nakhodka*), a clear observability of chromosomes at the time of cell division, and we realize that this discovery is so much more important than our interpretation of it that, where there is a discovery of this kind, even if it is a bare fact, we can do entirely without interpretation. A discovery or phenomenon speaks for itself, even if it says nothing about anything other than itself.

Accordingly, our aim is not to clarify concepts or construct a language for talking about the forest, but phenomenology, relying on phenomena that label (mark) themselves and everything around them. Unlike science in its modern sense, for example biology, we are aware that it is impossible to swallow whole chunks of raw, unexamined concepts. That is to say, we cannot use a rule book we did not ourselves compile, and it seems evident that, in the 'current situation' (and we will leave it to others to define what that is), we cannot use any rule book, and that is one of our own discoveries, that we have no use for one. We lose nothing by declining to act in accordance with so-called scientific method, where neither the method nor the science can be depended on. In philosophical phenomenology, in relying purely on discoveries, there is (or at least, there should be) no less rigour than in science.

The topic of the forest cannot be apolitical. The very fact of choosing it is political. The choice can be considered a continuation of the task Vasiliy Rozanov set himself when he wrote towards the end of the second 'basket' of his *Fallen Leaves*, 'The wild and forest particles in human beings are unlikely ever completely to disappear, and indeed it is hardly to be desired that they should entirely be smoothed out. Everybody in black tie like Skalkovsky – never! never!'[3] But Rozanov lived in a situation where programming was not an absurdity. He prescribes: that is, to existing sets of concepts he adds his own. Erasing what is wild and of the forest in human beings is not desirable. He shouts no and no again to any such erasure. In our time, perhaps because the air has become more rarefied, programming, re-programming, and fixed sets of concepts no longer make sense.

That does not, however, mean that we withdraw from politics, from taking decisions, that we leave all agendas undisturbed. Here is what is happening. If previously, for example at the beginning of the twentieth century, phenomenology could stay within the confines of a programme (for Husserl, this was analysis of consciousness; for the young Heidegger, clarification of being), nowadays there is no sign of any such opportunity or right, but on the other hand the energy that previously was expended on a programme and agenda can be put into the parameters of discoveries or, at least, reconnaissance.

Biology we will not engage with, let alone the philosophy of biology, but we will be needing biology, if not its theories (which are a derivative of the general philosophical beliefs of scientists and have not been properly thought through), then its *discoveries*. First and foremost, its discovery through observation, its heroic feat of attentive description of the incredible diversity of thousands and tens of thousands of species of living beings, their mobility and variability. When it might have seemed that everything in the animal world was fluid, in flux, another, opposite pole of the inflexible constancy of species was discovered; and just as the mobile variability seemed infinite, so the constancy of species seems infinite. We can go so far as to say that the species survives intact across any number of generations. You would have to be obtuse not to discern here the same polarity the classical world saw between matter and form, between the forest and geometry, the forest and the Cross; a polarity that links the pair of opposites more firmly than any similarity. On a purely formal level, confidently expecting the facts to confirm it, we can say that the plasticity of living things is underwritten by the rigidity of the species. Or, on the contrary, change is necessary for the species to remain unchanged. Or, changeability is a form of changelessness. And again, a similar, formal generalization: the species is variously protected, it is invulnerable because it is the inaccessible extreme. Everything closes ranks in every respect around the species, again polarizing in the amekhanical energy we talked about when, together with Aristotle, we were contemplating the behaviour of living things during mating and giving birth.

From Aristotle, we learned not to separate out our body from the mass of living things. On the crest, at the boundary, near the limit or the nadir, around sex and species there arise tone, colour, form, words, music, poetry, and painting, about which we know that they are apposite and that they more fully and purely engender amekhanical energy than science, which makes reputations. The polarity of matter and *eidos* presents a challenge for everyone, including us, and to the extent that we take on that challenge, to the extent that we discipline ourselves, we are included in the work of nature. We work at philosophy, poetry, art, and religion, which are well aware that there will always be a challenge (our Cross). Or at science, which does not always know that and may sometimes hope to find a mechanical way of slogging through difficulty, not believing that *aporia* and *amekhania* are an intrinsic law of life.

We could say that physics and biology are different subjects if we could see even approximately that these subjects are different not as human occupations but in themselves. That, however, is impossible *in principle*.

Quantum mechanics, thanks to its formal transparency, has explicitly confirmed the inevitability that matter will slip away, and has decreed that science will once and for all abandon the search for ultimate knowledge. The uncertainty principle has established, with mathematical formality, that we should give up all expectation that at some time in the future it will be possible to measure a particular magnitude. That is impossible and will always be impossible anywhere in the entire cosmos. In this respect, quantum mechanics classically conforms to the overall modern European refusal (since differential and integral calculus, since the introduction of the mathematical concept of limit) to scrutinize the ultimate.

It is absurd to imagine an electron having 'free will' before defining what is meant by freedom and will; but since we *define* the parameters of uncertainty, we have no right to say that the slipping away of nature, established by physics, is anything more than the indefinability of life confirmed by biology. *Here any assertion falls into the category of unverifiability: that is, it falls out of the category of scientific rigour.*

The fact that biology uses different tools than physics is no proof that they are different subjects. It is analogous not to saying that the pliers of a carpenter and a dental surgeon are different because a nail and a tooth are different, but to a situation where someone cannot get into their own house and one person tries to get in through the door while another tries to get in through the window: that does not mean that there are two different houses. It is the same house on the other side of the door and of the window, only neither has yet managed to get into it. Francis Crick (b. 1916), who, together with James Watson (b. 1928), proposed a model of the three-dimensional structure of deoxyribonucleic acid, in his book *Of Molecules and Men*, writes,[4] 'Thus eventually one may hope to have the whole of biology "explained" in terms of the level below it, and so on right down to the atomic level.' When they finally get into the room, the methods of physics and biology will merge. The opposing opinion is that they will never merge. All that stands behind that, at least for the time being, is only a feeling. It seems that, *naturally*, of course life is intimately close to humankind, and that *physics* is not, so that their methods never will merge. But that seems to be the case only to the uninitiated. The experience of beauty and order in the laws of nature can affect a mathematical theorist of physics more intimately than life itself affects a genetic engineer.

What we are coming to, which we want to wrestle with, is more difficult and interesting than many familiar, supposedly eternal and 'accursed' questions which are actually not even all that philosophical. For example, the supposed outrage of the mortality of human beings, of civilization and the universe. Does that mean there is no point in working, when everything is only for a limited time and destined to vanish? Tsiolkovsky's 'sense of self-awareness' or the 'holiness' of Vladimir Toporov are terms for being admitted, in ecstatic joy and a sense of simultaneously physical and spiritual fruitfulness, to 'fullness'. (Today we will introduce a more satisfactory term for that.) At that moment of admission to a backward- and forward-looking infinity, a spark passes, breaking through everything that seems dismayingly extended, all of time and space. Not some day but right now participation is attainable in the energy that holds all of nature together, in the certainty that the parameters of fullness in itself, as itself, are the same in everything. To the extent that it shares in that holiness, integrity, joy, and celebration, every human action, every wedding ceremony, sports contest, all poetry, philosophy, and dancing, is participation, divination of an event on a cosmic scale, a global event. Technology, in comparison with the non-progressing character of art, is growing inexorably and is bound to grow in proportion to how much it is denied ultimate fullness: for the present, the machine is not yet the emblem of a global machine; but it can see its final meaning only in terms of the law of being and fullness; and that is possible for technology only by achieving scale, amplitude, within the bounds of the cosmos through universal destruction. Technology will not rest until it has made a fairy tale come true. It will calm down only in something resembling the madness of amekhanical energy.

We can speak of the inanimate only relatively, bearing in mind the varying degrees to which matter is incorporated in an organism, but here, too, everything is determined by our seeing, not by an 'object'. We are not prepared to see the earth as an animal, but many people have, and then rocks and water were as confidently alive, bones and blood, as for us they are confidently inanimate. The only difference is where we draw the line defining an organism. As soon as our seeing changes and we see the forest not as timber but as a recreational amenity, the forest becomes 'the lungs of the city', it is reclassified as an organ, admittedly so far only metaphorically. The colours of the sunset, or of the sea, or the green of the forest, seemed to be something external to humankind, but when we learn that they are needed for vision to be healthy, then they are included in the body. Something that is really unhelpful is materialism, the utmost spiritual arrogance, which decides that it has no one to talk to and nothing to communicate. It stands aloof.

Behind the question of the origin of life is an implicit admission that the natural state is death and that life is the problem. Indeed life, modern life, is marked, labelled, and disturbs us; but we need to decide whether that is as an interesting object in our field of vision, or as a puzzle to be solved. The genuine, scientific study of life understands it as a message. The fact that there might have been no life is connected to the fact that we can do or not do something, and it matters, *inter est*, whether we do or do not do it. But in what is called science, efforts can be made, strenuous attempts, to represent as inevitable and essential something that might never have been.

Can we say that studying and clarifying something that exists but might not have is part of the effort as a result of which there is life? Let us leave the question hanging for now.

Just as we wonder about the origin of life, so we wonder about the origin of the world. It either solidified out of nebulae, the optimistic view that something compact will grow and something diffuse will decrease, or it once expanded out of something supremely dense, which is the pessimistic view because everything is then moving in the direction of entropy. It transpires that, oddly, we are asking ourselves the question in order to find out which mood is to prevail in us.

Is it true that, whatever the mood of the researcher, any methodology will point to an event that has already happened and ask how it happened? No. There is synchrony, as in Aristotle, without extending back into an unobservable past: for example, in the establishing by mathematical physics of cosmic constants, the invariable and ubiquitous way in which nature operates. But physics has a price to pay for the divergence between well-developed mathematical formalism and impure, if unavoidable, common terminology, surmising that at the very beginning of everything, at the time of the Big Bang, cosmic constants themselves went up in flames. They melted. The Big Bang happened a long time ago and very far away, at the ultimate limit. This and similar hypotheses are an awkward way of allowing a limit to exist in science. Philosophy needs to be able to resist carving out a convenient modus operandi of this kind, relegating the ultimate to somewhere outside it.

In an analogous manner, modern Europeans, imagining they were operating in an environment which they must combat and triumph over, surmised that nature and life functioned without us, and that our interaction with them was confined to educating ourselves with knowledge. In order to prove themselves wrong, and that human interaction with nature is more than mere observation, they needed to invent means to destroy nature and life. All of it. This absolute certainty is more trustworthy and durable, more tangible, than the old belief that humankind was somehow involved in everything, but instead, now protecting nature from itself, it starts unintentionally ascribing also to nature the goals of self-preservation and prolongation of life, and that is erroneous.

Everybody finds it acceptable to talk about nature having a *purpose*, but again, projecting their own moods into it, people most often imagine that its purpose is to preserve the miracle that is itself. That aim appears natural, but it is no more important to nature than preserving their masterpiece and becoming the museum curator of themselves is to artists of genius. For nature, failure, the big mistake, would not be death, just as the survival of the human species is not the purpose of humankind, and as its main aim is not to live at all costs as long as possible. On the example of moribund species of animals, we can see that their aim was not to survive, but something else, since otherwise wild animals would compromise their wildness, and this is not something we observe.

The human species cannot consecrate and gladden itself. That has to come as a *gift*. Consecration (*'osviashchenie'*: you will remember we introduced it as a biological term) is not a substantive addition, and is similar to illumination (*'osveshchenie'*). Light passes through our part of the universe as a constant reaffirmation of how fortunate we are with our precise differentiation of energy and matter. This differentiation occurred either during the cumulation of cosmic dust into strands and rings and threads, or during the explosion of an early clump where matter and energy were fused, or under some other cosmogony, but happen it did. Cognition corresponds to this differentiation of light and matter. It contributes nothing substantive to the thing perceived, but establishes its identity, its suchness, and in that sense generates it. Recognition of it, identification of it as a return to itself, is simultaneously a generation of it as a primal idea. The idea of blessedness passes through being like light–joy–holiness. It is that same essence of celebration, both as a return, as a birthday, and as leisure, liberation from hard work, because identification, recognition, of suchness is itself a liberation from labour.

As we consider this, we become used to the fact that in the repertoire of concepts, in the notionality of biology, there is confusion over the fact that life is not the purpose of life. Thanks particularly to Rozanov, it is clear that the goal of understanding (philosophy) is not life. It is more difficult to see that life is also not the purpose of life. Life as suchness, as precisely life itself, is distracted, drawn away by its suchness to pure self-identification with itself, not with *something*, where life proves to be neither ultimate nor self-explanatory.

Aristotle, yet again, makes it clear, prompts us: the goal is *en-ergeia*, fullness of fulfilment. Fulfilment of what? That question is secondary. Strictly speaking, it does not arise, because before asking it the impossibility of fullness, of wholeness of anything at all, should have been noted. For a living entity, wholeness is located beyond the threshold, firstly of its personal being (it needs the existence of the other sex); and secondly of death, because mating presupposes birth and hence death. Fullness, wholeness, have *aporia* as their mode of existence. Birth remains the way out of *aporia*.

When Darwinism, or selectionism, talks of survival of the fittest, if by 'the fittest' is meant only those most able to survive, we are looking at a pleonasm.[5] This awkward fact has been noticed, but it is one of those instances where a striking expression takes on a life of its own. People continue to use it even as they wonder why they are doing so. In reality, 'survivors' and 'the fittest' are not synonyms and are even, in some respects, opposites. It would not be wholly absurd to say that the miracle of life is that the fittest do actually survive.

Darwinism is not reducible to a picture of stray individuals, some of whom turn out to be the elect. We need to pay attention to the fact that the spread, distribution, and gradations of possibilities are a *given*. That is, that the non-fit exist too. There is, moreover, no need to wait for the end of the life of individuals or of species to conclude from the result who is who. Right now, both in the behaviour, in every movement, and in the appearance of the living creature, we must evidently suppose there is a difference between the fittest and the less fit. We just need not to be in too much of a hurry, and to ask ourselves how we define that difference. We judge success by human criteria, which usually involve satiety, good health, and fertility. The suspicion grows, however, that nature's criteria may be quite different.

Life is contingent on possibility and selection, where the criteria are uncertain. There are at least two of these, survival and fitness, and the correlation between them is uncertain. Only a total absence of fitness precludes survival, but the opposite does not follow: total retention by a savage beast of its savagery in the presence some hundreds of thousands of years ago of human beings led to extinction. When, after the radiation death of this planet, only the rats remain, their survival will not in any customary sense prove they were the fittest. Although logical analysis of premises is a rarity and everything is allowed to remain on the level of intuition, academic biologists might be surprised to know how often in assessing fitness they are applying a criterion that Konstantin Leontiev used for arguing against positivism. This was the criterion of 'flourishing complexity',[6] which, while not excluding protracted observation, does not require it, relying less on observation than on sympathy and empathy.

Perhaps now is the time to approach from a different angle and notice that dotted around in the economy of nature are pre-existing niches of fitness, hospitable locations to which life forms are attracted and into which they are drawn. That 'strokes of luck' are a possibility in our world deserves to be considered alongside the observation by physicists that our part of the universe is itself a stroke of luck because of the clear segregation here of energy and matter. In respect of the attraction of life forms to fitness, it should be noted that in the behaviour of herds, including the human herd, we do not find a stochastic distribution of more and less successful forms of behaviour from 0% to 100%. Technically, according to mathematical probability theory, this could be the case but life seems from the outset to be predisposed to hitting the target. In view of all this, it is proposed that Darwin's term 'fitness', in the sense of successful adaptation, should be replaced with the term 'goodness', in Russian *godnost'*, 'to be good for something'. It seems it will serve, and it has interesting relatives. It is somewhere in the background of weather, '*pogoda*', because '*nepogoda*' means weather unfit for something, although that overtone barely registers with us. 'A lively weather whips the waves' (from the song 'Sailing Down Mother Volga'). The weather is important and at this particular time it is fit. Other languages show the latent possibilities of *godnost'*. In Slovenian, the cognate word means 'the due time', ripeness, a festival, an anniversary; in Latvian, it means to hit the target, to gain; in Lithuanian, honour, reputation; and in German, '*gut*' is a link. '*Godnost''* is goodness. In Greek, ἀγαθός, βοὴν ἀγαθός is to shout 'Come on!' in battle. Plato's ideal of blessedness is the idea of ideas, letting everything be as it is, having the luck of being oneself. My own hypothesis is that '*god*', 'year' in Russian, is getting it right, a sunbeam falling in an ancient observatory exactly through the same slit as the previous summer; in major observatories it was possible to achieve accuracy to within minutes and even seconds.

For a life form to be good for something does not necessarily mean only that it is successfully adapted to a purpose: it may indicate that it is a celebration, a glory.

There is a great deal of controversy surrounding selectionism and Darwinism's concept of natural selection, which we can sidestep by defining fitness as 'goodness'. We have no grounds to oppose the idea that the spread of possible forms of life, including forms of behaviour, is enormous, or that those which are 'good' becomes evident post factum. We must not, however, overlook the fact that even ante factum a 'taste' for goodness, either immediate or after trial and error, determines or tends to determine the behaviour of living creatures. It resembles such things as joy and celebration, and dictates not the content of behaviour but purely the form, in terms of gesture, brilliance, and beauty. This is born of anticipation that a pleasing action is possible in our world. We do not have to reject Darwinism and its random mutations and imagine that God has stored up a set of forms for future content into which life preforms itself. Our own experience, observations, the experience of the artist, the inventor, the seeker, tell us that discoveries are not like mushrooms waiting to be found, that there is operating here a taste for getting it right, that there would not be a strange urge to *divine* something if there was not already something there to be divined.

Everybody agrees there are no ready-made anticipated forms, but something that argues in favour of an attracting, anticipatory effect of goodness is the absence of intermediate species in the gaps between those that have been successful. Darwin supposed they had just not yet been found:

> But just in proportion as this process of extermination has acted on an enormous scale, so must the number of intermediate varieties, which have formerly existed, be truly enormous. Why then is not every geological formation and every stratum full of such intermediate links? Geology assuredly does not reveal any such finely-graduated organic chain; and this, perhaps, is the most obvious and serious objection which can be urged against the theory. The explanation lies, as I believe, in the extreme imperfection of the geological record.[7]

Now it is almost conclusively clear that these intermediate forms have never existed. This means that nature can be compared to an artist of genius who made numerous studies and sketches, all of which proved viable, survived, and merit a place in an exhibition, not on the rubbish tip.

In favour of natural selection, or at least as a justification that its idea is based on an important and well-known human experience, is the fact that the creations of the human mind and inventions display an enormous spread which is on the scale proposed by Darwinism: that out of an incalculable multitude of unsuccessful creative efforts only a very few, produced by geniuses, prove to be of value. Perhaps nature has stopped creating now, but when it was doing so, successes, viable species, were as rare as successes are for humankind now that it is our turn to create. After a hundred, or even twenty years, of the entire mass of what has been invented, only a fraction of one per cent survives. It argues in favour of Darwinism that there is an optical illusion, roughly comparable with the way that today we see the whole mass of doomed, non-viable, unfit material all around us and imagine that in ancient times, on the contrary, almost everything was, fit: plainly of value. If human creativity came to a stop, then in a hundred years' time what remained, what was still sold and studied, would be only what had earned a place among the classics of its kind. At that an observer of *human* culture might be moved to say, 'Nowhere do we discover monstrous forms, which we would certainly be coming across if unconstrained changefulness had been the norm.'[8]

The Anti-Darwinists say, 'No matter how far back we trace the fossil record, we never come across ill-adapted plants but only plants adapted to conditions dissimilar to those existing today.'[9] But perhaps nature was long ago in the state of creative trial and error in which humanity finds itself today, and since its creative work ceased, we know only what has proved itself good.

In Book 5 of *De rerum natura*,[10] Lucretius Carus describes nature as a woman now past her prime, no longer fertile, although once she was *nova tellus*, new territory (5, 790). At that time, the ether, too, the male principle, was new. In various places, the fruit-bearing bowels of the earth were revealed. It gave birth incessantly. Then the creatures it had borne came suckling to it and nipples grew out of the earth, filled with a milk-like juice. Nowadays, however, it is not the earth but only women who do that.

> But, lo, because her bearing years must end,
> She ceased, like to a woman worn by eld.
> For lapsing aeons change the nature of
> The whole wide world
> and all things needs must take
> One status after other, nor aught persists
> Forever like itself. All things depart. (5, 826–30)

Lucretius paints a word picture of confusion.

> Then there were born
> monsters that upsprung
> with their astounding visages and limbs.
> The Man-woman a thing betwixt the twain,
> yet neither, and from either sex remote. (837–9)

Or creatures with:

> Some gruesome Boggles orphaned of the feet,
> Some widowed of the hands, dumb Horrors too
> Without a mouth, or blind ones of no eye. (840–2)

Quotation from Lucretius usually stops at this point, but observed deformities are listed, *vincta membrorum*, 'bulks all shackled by their legs and arms cleaving unto the body fore and aft' like Siamese twins. Nature did not allow monsters of this kind to mature and continue their species.

Less frequently mentioned is that Lucretius does not accept the possibility of intermediate species, and says as much in the strict terminology of anti-Darwinist genetics.

> Still that is nothing of a sign that then
> Such hybrid creatures could have been begot. (919–20)

We are even now surrounded by a multiplicity of plants, and the species are not confused.

> ... but each sole thing
> Proceeds according to its proper wont
> And all conserve their own distinctions based
> In nature's fixed decree. (922–4)

There is strict segregation.

Lucretius clearly distinguishes between deformity and intermediate forms. Creation produces pure forms or monsters, but rarely impure, ambivalent forms. It ensures that monsters soon die. There may possibly be countless numbers of them, as Darwin surmised, but within a very short time they no longer exist. The survivors do.

A more difficult question for Darwinism is why 'development', life, could all emerge in one form.

It would be convenient if all fossil humans, who have now been named *Australopithecus* (from 5.3 million years ago), *Homo habilis* (from 2 million years ago), *Homo erectus* (formerly known as *Pithecanthropus*, from 1.6 million years ago), and *Homo sapiens* (possibly from the end of the era of periodical glaciations alternating between ice and warming), could be lined up in an evolutionary series, but it seems that Neanderthal Man was also *Homo sapiens neanderthalensis* (several hundred examples) – a subspecies of humans. This is already our history, and it is difficult to claim that it is the fittest of us who have survived. What modern humankind has prepared itself for is the fate of the dinosaurs: it can no longer end other than in disaster. In this sense, Neanderthal Man departed this world by no means because he was less 'fit'. We shall explain why next time.

Lecture 16, 23 December 1997

When you think about the 500,000 years humans have been in Europe and of the probably 5 million years of fossilized human remains found in Africa, the 5,000 years of recent, recorded history seem a mere episode, the end of the story with technological humankind burning the remains of ancient plankton, accumulated in the earth's surface over hundreds of millions of years, and poisoning the air, the seas, and the land with God knows what kind of filth; and accumulating enough nuclear fuel to inciner-ate everything on the planet. You realize we are heading for catastrophe. It is, however, unlikely to be any worse than the great Ice Age, or than a burst of growth of vegetation such that the oxygen content of the atmosphere would be so high that a bolt of lightning could burn everything organic to a cinder. Or the explosion of the earth that caused the moon to separate from it and left a hole where today we have the Pacific Ocean. The glaciers of the Ice Age melted, the new Ice Age in the sixteenth century proved minor, and the dinosaurs helped us to cope. That sickness of the earth was not fatal, but it is no more logical to hope the earth will prove immortal, or the galaxy or the universe, than to hope for personal immortality. On the other hand, there is in the death of an individual or the demise of the sky, or a great conflagration or the collapse of the universe when, according to one hypothesis, fiery matter will cease to be so thinly scattered and will implode in on itself – there is, I say, as also in the birth of an individual or the universe from a piece of super-dense matter, a feature which is vari-ously defined. We have spoken about holiness and joy and ecstasy, but we can more easily give a formal, logical definition of this feature: it can be defined as 'yes', 'precisely', 'thus'. This is a timeless characteristic. It mani-festly runs through the entire cosmos and all time, and it does not depend on whether there is or is not me, because even when there is no me, this will still be 'precisely thus'.

Nikolai Timofeyev-Ressovsky is someone we hear about because in the Stalin era he was one of the few who escaped 'adverse selection'. That is an expression used by biologists and specifically by Timofeyev-Ressovsky and his teacher, Nikolai Koltsov, to denote a process where Darwinian selection is evident, possibly intensely so, but clearly in the wrong direction, not at all up the 'ladder of development'.[1] Those who survive are the worst, as in times of war or revolution. The phenomenon of adverse selection obliges us to distinguish between different meanings of the word 'fit', because those who survive are the best adapted but of least value. I am by no means convinced that adverse selection in our country ceased with the death of Stalin. In the last revolution, Perestroika, which began ten years ago and looks as though it must soon come to an end, we have a classic instance of adverse selection where adaptation and worthlessness are almost synonymous; the penalty for not fitting in was death, as is evident from the statistics on reduced life expectancy and the birth rate. Those punished were indubitably those who were the least fit because, by definition, if you are dead you were unfit, but they were not by any means less fit by a criterion of better or worse, or even of more or less perfect, higher or lower. Extrapolating from this, we cannot in good conscience assert that *Homo sapiens neanderthalensis* a quarter of a million years ago was less developed than that other, victorious, subspecies, today's *Homo sapiens*. We can safely say only that *Homo sapiens* proved better adapted, for example, to the conditions of periodic glaciations, but even that is a tautology if 'to adapt' is synonymous with 'to survive'.

Survival is not the purpose of living beings: life has a different aim. Biology naïvely, neglectful of philosophy, fails to think this hypothesis through, perhaps instinctively leaving itself room for development when its concepts are more carefully examined. The expression 'adverse selection' is not properly thought through because, although it is untrue that it is always only the best who survive, it is also untrue that the best can never survive. Highly restrictive conditions can pose a *positive challenge*. In those circumstances, it is doubly necessary to discriminate between different kinds of fitness. In the Pleistocene, in the midst of bouts of glaciation, an adverse selection was clearly also taking place: survival of those members of the human species who, for example, adapted by resorting to cannibalism. But, *at the same time*, over and above, on the basis of this adverse selection, through testing and examination, a *positive selection* was taking place, adaptation and survival of the best by virtue of their amelioration, not their deterioration. Adverse selection is in progress right now, as it always is whenever conditions deteriorate. During the war, the rat population in Moscow's granaries increased so much that on one part of the embankment the police closed the road off at a point where rats from the elevator at Setun formed a continuous carpet down to the river to drink. Who, after all, wants to live in a constant state of thirst? It was very clear which life forms were proving victorious in those trying times. That does not mean, however, that human reason was not then seeking a solution to the problem, and not solely because of a desire to live, but from a sense that this situation was not 'meet', that *godnost'*, goodness, meant this was unacceptable. Nowadays, on this earth with its population of 6 billion, survival of the fittest is in full swing and it is only too obvious which way the adapted human population is going: it is headed simply and straightforwardly for disaster. That does not, however, mean that we can say that through this adverse selection, on its own territory and because of it, there is not also a positive selection of qualities of quite a different human species.

For this different human species, and any other species of humankind, for all living beings and life itself, the purpose of life cannot be life, just as for a housewife who has received her housekeeping money for the month ahead the aim cannot be to keep those banknotes inviolate and uncrumpled to the end of the month. Timofeyev-Ressovsky was a biologist but also a very lively person, and the poetry he most liked to quote was two quatrains written by Derzhavin just three days before his death:

Time's torrent ever onward flowing
Bears off, away and downward flings
To drown in darkness and oblivion
All peoples, kingdoms, yea, and kings.

Though any thing be yet remaining
That lyre and flute did render great,
The eternal funnel downward draining,
Will drag it to the common fate.[2]

Celebration, in the sense in which Olga Sedakova sees the meaning of poetry in celebration and victory,[3] is not here in the gloating of a dying man that all things shall perish but in a festival of acceptance that everything is as it is: death and the all-devouring funnel of eternity are nothing. To love these verses and yet dedicate one's life to the living could only be for the sake of *science*. We detect the festivity that there is in science, in stubborn, rigorous knowledge, in connection with Derzhavin's devouring funnel of eternity when we read one of science's scenarios for the death of the universe. The scenario is rather dependent on the hypothesis of the Big Bang (which is by no means the only hypothesis and indeed has recently been seriously challenged) and another hypothesis, suggested by it, of a Big Crunch. I mention it not for any scientific interest. You are aware of the difference between a mathematical formulation developed on the basis of reference data, usually only partial and from the outset pre-prepared, and an attempt undertaken, sometimes by the same scholar but more often by another who is popularizing it, to imagine graphically what 'in reality' would correspond to that formulation. According to grand unification theory, when the temperature of a super-dense object collapsing under the influence of gravitation reaches 10 to the power of 28 degrees Kelvin, there is a transition to so-called unbroken symmetry of interactions. After the fire comes the cooling. The special vacuum formed is rapidly cooled. Radiation pressure is absent. [...] Gravity in the process is transformed into anti-gravity [...] Then the inertia of the Big Crunch causes an extremely rapid (10 to the minus 32nd degree seconds) decrease in the volume of the special vacuum by 10 to the power of 50 times: that is, the universe shrinks to microscopic size.[4] If the picture of the Big Crunch strikes anyone as just too depressing, we can only say that, just as the death of a particular individual is a necessary condition for the survival of humanity, so our universe would not exist if an unimaginable multitude of others had not perished. This picture, I repeat, is not scientific. It is interesting for its reiteration of Derzhavin's all-devouring 'funnel of eternity', and the juxtaposition of the individual and the universe: in an important sense, there is no difference between the death of one person and the death of everything.

The fact is that people talk often about the death of the individual (thus, one scholar recently made the 'discovery' that for Vladimir Soloviov 'human' and 'mortal' are synonyms[5]). People talk far more rarely about the death of the universe, and that is one of the more suspicious paradoxes of our time. I fear our forgetfulness regarding the end of the cosmos is to make adaptation appear necessary. The immortality of what we are adapting to would 'justify' the cosmos and provide grounds for hope that science and technology, growing into it, would partake of its immortality, and justify the adaptation of those who pay for it and serve it. Just as it is easier to obtain money from an institution that is stable, so it is pleasant to believe we exist in the big, eternal body of the earth or cosmos. But knowledge of the ultimate great conflagration does little for us on its own until we come to the understanding that life is not the purpose of life. With that insight it may be agreeable to believe that absolutely everything will be burned up with the death of the universe, rather as the owner of a market kiosk who has failed to keep his accounts in order and whose goods are of doubtful quality finds it agreeable to dream of a fire. Accordingly, while it is meet to remain mindful of the death both of the individual and of the universe, that should not be our main preoccupation. More important is to be aware that the purpose of life is not the mere continuation of life. The mystic and clairvoyant Eugène Ionesco envisages the end of everything in much the same way as Derzhavin and the author of the hypothesis of the Big Crunch: 'The world is heading for disaster.... The whole world is playing with apocalyptic danger. People are both tormented and at the same time seduced by this impending end, which they seem to want to bring on.'[6] In one of Ionesco's visions or waking dreams, the world first cools. It is significant that already today people are becoming possessed of an icy insensitivity. Then a raging heat melts the polar ice and the world is enveloped in an impenetrable hull of vapour. This eventually dissipates and beneath a radiant blue sky there remains not a trace of all the things that once disturbed the earth. Just like Derzhavin, Ionesco is more inclined to feel delight not at the destruction but at the purity and austerity of the event. The point of life is not just to live. Ionesco writes, 'I have the impression that people and writers who presently fear death from the nuclear threat or something similar ... are not very interesting because ultimately, if the immediate threat disappears, they will be able to live in peace.'[7]

The purpose of life is, at all events, not 'survival of the most adaptable' – life needs to be understood as redemption, and adaptation as *godnost'* in the sense of goodness. Ionesco:

> Behind visible reality there stands another reality, another volcanic universe ready at any moment to replace the first, to blow it up, to melt it. It is possible that ultimately that other world will supersede ours gradually, so that we barely notice it, without dreadful disasters, perhaps owing to a kind of slow metamorphosis, so that we find ourselves in different spaces without realizing it. The appearance of a new universe, a new Creation.[8]

Ionesco has seen what it will be like. Objects are bathed in an ocean of blue light for a few moments, while the state lasts. They seem distinct, delicate and elegant, unprecedented and yet unprecedentedly familiar. Most notably, they lose the significance usually assigned to them and are liberated to be just themselves. Not only do this sudden purification of the world, and joy, have no cause, but the secret of their captivating power is precisely that they manifestly do not have a cause. The logic of the joy is absurd; it is at once a joy and a riddle as to where it has come from and what it is for. It is itself the answer to the problem, the ultimate source of explanation.

> I feel right alongside the essence of things, of being when, surrounded by the radiant morning, it is as if the world had just appeared and I am opening my eyes for the first time in my life. Full of wonder, I ask myself, 'What is this? Where am I?' And yet, 'Why is this? Who am I? What am I doing here?' My question, of course, cannot be answered, but I am not expecting an answer. At the very moment when the question arises in me, I feel a boundless, groundless joy, and that joy, that rapture, seems the real answer to the question that arose in me.[9]

> At that moment I cannot even ask myself a question like, 'What is society?' or any other question like that, because I cannot move beyond the bounds of that first, most fundamental question and the hot, blinding light it evokes. Objects glowed and became transparent but their outlines were not wholly lost, did not disappear completely.... I seemed to have arrived at a frontier, a boundary of history [he could have said, of a new beginning of history, of its essence, *Bibikhin*] but I was still here, on the frontier of existence, very close to the place where objects dispense with their names and definitions, and where time stands still. I had that experience, I learned what it was to be beyond the boundary of history. This is achievable. This state of primordial surprise, astonishment, is inherent in human nature and can illumine anyone irrespective of their social circumstances, the era they live in, irrespective of any economic qualification. Not one of

these factors is relevant here; not one facilitates the coming of this experience or contributes to its disappearance.[10]

We have already been prepared by our reading of Toporov and Tsiolkovsky, and before that, of course, of Aristotle's biology and ethics, to recognize that here is that experience of *godnost'*, of wholeness, redemption, festivity, or fullness, which, according to our hypothesis, should prove to be the purpose of life, not at some hypothetical end of evolution, but from the very beginning, and now, not in time but in eternity. That is, in youth. Life (and we are not drawing any dividing line between animate and inanimate; the living is just more responsive, closer, and easier to discuss) is situated around youth. Holiness and light, colour, celebration, play (and that includes the propensity of youthful beings to play), are the element and purpose of living things. Biological science, we can confidently predict, will be obliged to return again and again to this element, because science finds it difficult or impossible to talk about it. Biology will not be up to the task and it, like physics, will only be able to boast of technological advances as spectacular as the atom bomb, like the breeding of artificial people. We can be sure that, as is most natural and common in the development of science, genetic engineering will bring nobody any joy, and probably attention will shortly switch from biology (just as at one time it drew the spotlight of attention away from physics) to psychology, to experimental and natural science, only studying not reactions of the mind but moods. I am not alone in making this prediction.

What hinders us from seeing global, or even quite 'unprecedented', 'game-changing' developments in recent centuries, decades, years, months, or days (e.g. exaggerating the importance of the latest computer and Internet novelties) is not a loss of interest in all that but a more profound sense that, through it all, or in spite of it all, underlying it all, and representing the real substance of all these innovations, is something more basic, something analogous to the youthfulness we have mentioned. No matter what discoveries science and technology make, no matter what the political news, the most important underlying fact is that human beings, through affirmation or denial – that is, through their 'politics' in the classical sense – are partaking of existence; and the discovery of religion, of the divinity of humankind, that it is made in the image and likeness of the Creator of the world, is of far more fundamental importance than all the power that science and technology can offer it. The real innovation in science is actually not something like satellite communications, but the return along the path of science and the naming in its language of things that have long been said in the language of tradition but have now lost their currency. This is evident when science recognizes, for example, and there is nothing specifically 'scientific' about the discovery, that humanity is not an external observer of the cosmos but embedded in it. Its entirely reasonable answer to the question, 'What is the cosmos like?', the more so since humankind would seem to be the closest observable part of it, is 'The nature of the whole cosmos is that it has humankind in it.' Or when science intuits that, when humanity observes the universe, it is as if the universe is so arranged that it can observe itself, and that this is part of its fullness, purpose, aim, so that our observing of the universe is making it real. 'Anybody who thinks of themselves as simply an observer, finds they are a participant. In a strange sense, this is participation in the creation of the universe.'[11]

We have several times talked in terms of what happened 5 million or 500,000 years ago. In the light of what we have said about youthfulness, it will be better not to blindly adopt these dates from science. They are problematical. We talk about the past, about development and the future, about evolution, and that means we are presuming to encompass an entire event which it is impossible for us to encompass in its entirety. As a result of that impossibility, we sense that the event in its entirety is something that cannot be encompassed. The impossibility of encompassing it, the first thing we know about the event, we immediately project on to time and promptly forget that that event is the way in which time originates. Because of this impossibility, we find it difficult to understand that the human species exists and 'develops' in calendar time only for us. In order to take this in, we do not necessarily have to refute Darwinism. Do species appear, prove 'fit', then disappear, become extinct, because everything has the purpose of advancing towards the goal, shall we say, of humankind? Or is it, in view of what has been said about adverse selection, that in evolutionary terms – and, incidentally, what do a couple of millennia count for in the context of 500 or 5,000 millennia? – that we are lagging behind the so-called ancient world in which, perhaps, the composition of the air was more favourable to memory and mindfulness. And Aristotle, if not indeed the Neanderthals, were ahead of us in fullness of being? The fact that the record of human history began 6,000 years ago as a history of illnesses is not a metaphor but a fact. It is a file in which symptoms and prescriptions are entered, like those of old people in clinics are entered in bulky medical records.

Perhaps the profligacy of life in reproduction needs to be thought through in terms of the purpose of life. If the purpose was not something beyond the immediate requirements of life, it would doubtless be possible to expend the resources more economically; thus prokaryotes, phytoplankton, and cyanobacteria, whose cells multiply by straightforward division, are, strictly, immortal beings. For eukaryotes, which have to give up cells, to separate them from themselves, it is more difficult to ensure that those do in their turn live, and they most often do it through pairing. This is never certain. Then they have to agree to die in order to help their progeny. They have to bring about the necessary encounter in order to draw into their circle, one is tempted to say their round dance, other beings in the vicinity. The eukaryotes are a step forward along a path that will ultimately lead to humankind encompassing everything with its science and becoming completely dependent on it. The human species will, in a very complicated way, continue its existence with a positively cosmic reach, but eventually in a highly risky manner, and proclaim its purpose to be not just life but the evolution of life. Indeed, since eternal life had already been attained in the prokaryotes, the goal of evolution is now complex, advanced life. That the goal of humankind now seems to be to create a base in space or the cosmos for supporting life might seem an advance on the prokaryotes, which would be unable, if the earth were to become uninhabitable, to move to other planets. The eukaryotes, with their rockets, will perhaps have that bolthole. There are a number of reasons why I find it difficult to endorse this strategy, and I will revise my opinion only when someone persuades me that the goal of life cannot be attained right here, right now, without waiting for another hypothesis, humanity, to start creating new universes. The real significance of communion, of oneness with the deity, is that it is already available to humans. We will come back to this meaning of the sacrament of communion when our course continues under the same title on 10 February 1998.

Of the many topics that suddenly demand to be addressed, I will choose today the polarization between soft and hard, which is absolute in living things, beginning with the polarity of adaptive protein and the nucleic acids, acids of the nucleus, RNA and DNA. These absolutely do not adapt or react to changes in protein, depending on the type of carbon and hydrogen compound in the base of the ribose or deoxyribose. Scientists talk solemnly about the inaccessibility of these acids of the cell nucleus, which, in the presence of sparse, rich, overheated, overcooled, traumatized, or cultivated protein, strictly dictate one and the same pattern of behaviour to everything proliferating, including the protein. In reality, the remarkable stability of genotypes (horsetails, ferns, brachiopods) over a period of hundreds of millions of years is very strange. One would expect that the errors inevitable in replication of the highly complex molecular chains of DNA and RNA, consecutively repeated innumerable times, would over this period have inevitably eroded the genotype. This highly complex bioinformatic structure has, however, as Erwin Schrödinger notes, been preserved, over an improbably long period. There is every reason to see in this genetic stability something of a different order from the restoration in physics of precisely the same structures after any mixing.[12] (You can do many different things with a water molecule but, given the chance, it restores itself to its initial condition.)

The template mode of action of the structures in the nucleus which deliver heredity naturally raises a question, because every template becomes worn with use. It is better to imagine the template as a numerical code or a geometric numerical code, which is the same thing. Its immutability over hundreds of millions of generations is then comprehensible. The reproduction of living organisms occurs not by relaying genetic information from generation to generation, with the inevitable accumulation of errors and erosion of the genotype that would entail, but by means of a single, inviolable template within the species. When we were discussing geometry, number, and the Cross in connection with the forest, we were already anticipating such confirmation from genetics. This immutability of the genotype, safeguarded by a code not of a mechanical but of a numerical, geometrical nature, can only be seen as a phenomenon analogous with Plato's *eidos* (form), which is also timeless.

With this perspective, we can look afresh at the order of a state, or of a rite such as the wedding ritual, at discipline and standardization in human society. There is an unconscious mimesis both of what there is in nature and of what there is in ourselves. In the punctiliousness of its order, which can be made even stricter and still appear insufficient, society imitates the way everything is arranged in nature and *how the human body itself is arranged*. The individual would never call the human behaviour in the wedding ceremony 'mimesis', but would explain it by saying only that this is how things have been done 'since time immemorial' (and have, indeed, been done since the beginnings of existence itself).

The world is turned inside out. It takes a look at itself, puts itself on display. Nature seems to need to exhibit itself in this way, to repeat itself, to manifest itself in terms of the world of human beings and, of course, not only of them. What for? The physicist surmises that the universe needs an observer, but that it no longer knows why. Why has nature employed us, lured us into acting out itself? Demurely, respectably, in the wedding ritual, which, undiluted, is very demanding, by implication, by unconscious mimesis, there is acted out what science would say occurs 'at the molecular level': a union of gametes to form a zygote. The same is true of the order in any society with authorities, or even just in the order imposed on traffic in the street. It is not usually asked to what lengths orderliness should be taken. We somehow just know, we sense, it will be taken to the ultimate limit. The very air we breathe, even, more precisely, we ourselves, in the digital template of the automaton of our cells, insist on extreme rigour. If it does nevertheless remain possible to breathe (in both the literal and the political senses), that is not so much because order has been undermined as because, alongside the digital geometry, there is the protein element, nurturing and, if you will, softer. Neither hardness nor softness overwhelms the other: they interact like two polarities.

In this context, the problem of consciousness fades irrevocably, dissolving into invisibility. Mimesis, the acting out of the micro- and macrostructure of everything by human concepts of order, is what? The 'self-consciousness of nature'? One detects that conscious action has no part to play in this, and the issue develops more widely into the issue of the role of humankind in the cosmos. Whether that role is major or minor appears to be undecided, the decision seems to be awaited. A living being endowed with reason can surely do absolutely anything? The world itself, which is stuck in the rut of the 'anthropic principle', according to one wild modern hypothesis, has been created by humankind, which has forgotten that fact. At the other end of the spectrum of divinity, humans are, according to Plato, puppets, playthings of the gods.

Whether humans are gods or puppets of the gods is not something we are going to learn from knowledgeable authorities. Heraclitus says war will decide who is a god and who is mortal, who is a master and who is a slave. It will be decided by extreme effort. Only super-powerful forces will decide. Let this stand as a note of where the issue of human consciousness can lead us if considered seriously.

In this note, we have not strayed too far from the topic of mimesis, and let us now return to it. Irrespective of whether the ape is the ancestor of human beings, or human beings are the ancestors of apes (and in certain countries of the world the language and folklore indicate confidently that apes are humans who have gone to seed), whether there is a direct genetic link or not, there is a *closeness*, and for the time being we need be no more specific. Apes are famous for their ability to imitate, so much so that 'to ape' means just that. Humans, it is said, are capable of imitating. One could say that the true extent of human imitation has not been noticed. Here Akhutin has just the right expression for this mimesis: 'closed consciousness'.[13] It really is closed, just because mimesis is so widespread that it encompasses absolutely everything. The ape, whether the ancestor or descendant of humankind, is only imitating the imitation humanity has made its own. To put it another way, given the plenteousness of the living world, all that has been left for the ape is to imitate. It is like a recoil, a step back, a mirror the universe has set up for itself. Humankind is, to an even greater extent, precisely such a mirror.

The elements of physics and chemistry are already *letters* in Plato. In respect of the genetic code, the discourse is all about 'letters', 'codes', and 'copying'. The sciences intuit that the structure of nature involves letters. That is open consciousness, but in closed consciousness, Schelling's 'unconscious production', with eyes closed rather as Homer was blind, through some Florenskian mimesis, these letters have appeared in human-kind. Even further back, before literacy, the human species was dreaming about language with the same literal (phono-logical, if you dislike literal) system, which later turned out to be the arrangement of a microcosm, and perhaps later of something else besides. There had been twenty-one or twenty-four phonemes in languages long before there were found to be twenty-three pairs of chromosomes in a cell.

Science is already on the threshold of cracking the mysteries of life by deciphering its 'code'. Immense forces have been thrown into completing one of the most ambitious scientific programmes of the twentieth century – sequencing the 'letters' in the text of the DNA molecules of human beings. Those involved in the project believe that when they have read this 'book' they will not only have understood the essence of life, but will also reveal the mystery of humankind.[14]

Whether or not they manage to read the letters, for it to be possible to find gene-letters in the chromosome, it was necessary for these letters to be a familiar part of human commerce. The 'legislators' and 'administrators' were enacted in human history long before biologists noticed the hierarchy of nucleic acid legislators and protein administrators within the cell.

Do nature and the universe need witnesses? What kind: sleeping or wakeful? Most probably they need questioning witnesses, witnesses who go off on the wrong track, who, with extreme effort, through *amekhania*, achieve rigour and purity.

It is not for us to say there were exceptional breakthroughs of life in the course of Darwin's natural selection, and that humankind was one of them, having perhaps at one time numbered only a few hundred specimens in the forest. It is, however, our job to note that, if there was some ill-defined battle, we need to consider further whether it can be called 'natural selection'. There is no need, alas, to further clarify the difference between war and peace. We should just know that. It seems likely that the human species was and will be different from what it is now. The earth is a living, changing being, and we need not be afraid that nature will be crushed by the intervention of technology. More likely, the sharp end of war will simply move elsewhere.

When I talk about mimesis and the acting out by the human world of the world event, I make no attempt to guess what the significance of that might be, or how deep it may go. All I can say with confidence is that our links with the forest are unimaginably far reaching. In the past, waves of change swept over the earth before they were detected, if, indeed, they were detected at all. A classic example of one that was detected is the 'Axial Age', a time that affected all the cultures of the world.[15] We have already mentioned that the Modern Age, after the Middle Ages, began in Europe at the same time as the so-called Little Ice Age, which ended at about the time of the French Revolution. This does not necessarily mean that the Little Ice Age caused a mutation in humans the way the great Pleistocene Ice Age did, when a third of the earth was covered with ice. We talk of human history, preceded by 'prehistory' or 'prehistoric times', not because there was no history of animals and humans taking place then, but because there was only 'closed', not 'open', consciousness. Everything started after the last great thaw, which occurred 10,000 years ago. Some historians of the earth periodize that as a boundary: before was the Pleistocene, meaning 'for the most part everything was new'. Afterwards, now, is the Holocene, meaning 'everything is completely new'. There is an alternative view that the Pleistocene is continuing, which is encouraging, given that we have ventured to surmise that humankind is very much woven into the life of the planet.

As regards the ostrich, some believe that it is on its way to being able to fly, and will do so after another few hundred thousand years. Its wings are just not ready yet but will develop. Others believe, however, that it is too big, has developed too much, and that the evolution of this species may be considered to be over. That is, it has got stuck. It could have evolved and been able to fly, but will not now have time to do so. What is important for us here is that observers of nature have no problem envisaging a creature which, for a million years, has been walking around with an underdeveloped organ. Everything is much less clear in the case of the octopus, which has a brain comparable in size to that of a human and more arms, or tentacles, than a human being. Do we have to believe that the ostrich and the octopus have got stuck on the path of evolution? They started out from somewhere but never arrived at their destination? Or does 'adaptation', can *godnost'*, fitness, stretch to include this case? Does as yet unrealized potential qualify as fit for something?

The ostrich has wings for flying but cannot fly. The octopus and human beings have large brains, but they use them much less than the computer is used in the office in the Moscow Philosophy Institute. The beauty of this huge excess can be considered as evidence of plenteousness, analogous to the wealth, abundance, prodigality, of reproductive capacity, an excess of life's fertility. If the brain is connected and united through bone marrow with the sex glands, then in both cases we have a similar kind of excess, an unthinkable excess of capacity over what is necessary.

The capacity to reproduce has been shown to be sufficient in the event of a cataclysm to enable a species to survive a disaster of the order of Noah's Flood. If just one mating pair survives, within a century the earth can be repopulated. For the present, it is unclear under which circumstances and for what purpose the entire monstrous potential of the brain can be used. Perhaps some day it will be.

There may early on have been a premonition of the power of the mind, not among Pleistocene engineers, Neanderthal hunters, or organizers of the extermination of elephants and rhinoceros in Europe, but precisely among the 'superstitious' mythologists with their intuition of God and the possibility of following God.

When we return in February to *De generatione animalium* and see Aristotle's discrimination between levels of life, it will become clearer that biology often recognizes life on only one of its levels: vegetative or plant forms.

So, on 10 February 1998, same place, same time, continuation of the same topic: Wood. *Hyle*.

*   *   *

[Continuation of the lecture course on 'The Woods (*Hyle*)'] [*O.E. Lebedeva*] The existence of the human species on earth. The Forest and the metric domain. Matter. The World Tree. The Tree of Life and the Cross. Geometry of the Cross. Aristotelian biology. Parthenogenesis. *Eidos*, the historical beginning. Plato's *Timaeus*. Logocentrism (Jacques Derrida). Topics in modern biology. Nomogenesis (Lev Berg). The purpose of life. Holiness (Vladimir Toporov).

Lecture 17, 10 February 1998

At the basis of biology, we find what Vladimir Toporov defines as *holiness*, in the sense of uplift, burgeoning, light and colour, which adds nothing measurable to matter but has the significance of sanction. It sanctions. Sanctification, consecration, serve to establish suchness. They do not impose a metric or plan on matter, but add an imprimatur, like approval by higher authority.

Life before that signature, before that sanction, will not be different by any measurable parameters from life after sanctification, approval, imprimatur, but we can sense that, despite their common starting point, divergence will begin to emerge between life that is losing its way and life that is historical. That will not be merely a matter of more attention being paid to historical life, as it might to legitimate or aristocratic or wealthy children, to thoroughbred puppies rather than to strays. The special attention paid to what is authorized is of secondary importance and sometimes misplaced: it can be the wild apple that grows better.

No, it seems more likely that holiness (in Toporov's sense) most effectively sanctions life by affecting its destiny, showing it a *redeemed* future in the same sense in which Tsiolkovsky talks of a dimension of sensitivity inherent in all matter. Holiness, in this sense, is inseparable from living matter, but we will do better to talk about it separately. It is not sanctification that gives life its perspective: life itself looks to the future.[1] Yet, for some reason, there is a need for ritual and ceremony.

Why is the future of genetic engineering so unpromising? Because although the new life forms it creates may be self-consecrating, science as a matter of principle lacks the gesture and tone for consecration, which matters if what we have said about sanctification is correct. Poetry and myth, which until now have gone hand-in-hand with life, do have the means, but genetic engineering lacks even basic support from the humanities. It has an unprecedented opportunity. It is performing an operation much as surgeons have done for thousands of years, manipulating living material and exploiting its ability to recover, but no operation before now could be carried out simultaneously on the whole of a body rather than only on a part of it. Operating on a cell, you are operating on the whole organism that will grow out of it, on all its cells, leaving none unaffected or able to resist the intervention. It is a way to multiply the effect of the surgery. A single cell is altered in a way that means the change will be stamped on all its successor cells.

There was something deeply disturbing about the reports on the killer bees which escaped from a laboratory in Brazil. They highlighted the possibility of an aberrant life form developing and led to demands that genetic engineering should be banned. Development needs to go in the right direction. To put it another way, we expect and demand consecration of new life. Darwinism was reassuring in this respect, coming on the scene just as the Church seemed to have forgotten about the sanctity of life. There was no cause for alarm because sanctification was ensured by extremely harsh rigorous selection, survival of the *fit* in an environment where clearly not everything could survive. Darwinism thus offered a quirky replacement for religion's function of consecration. Life was being consecrated by *natural* selection. In effect, the function of consecration was being performed by science, which promised that what it was saying was true, and that if things existed at all, they were as they should be.

In traditional faith, 'the whole creation groaneth and travaileth in pain'[2] and awaits sanctification from that radiant, male, and historical source that is the Saviour. One of his symbols is the fish, a phallic symbol. As something that sanctifies and consecrates the Saviour and his Cross, the geometry of the wood of the Cross is so completely male that within the story of the Gospel the Saviour needs no specifically male traits. Feminism, because it is blind to the consecrating mission of the male, attempts to take this mission upon itself and in the process itself becomes masculine. It finds in the Gospel Saviour all the features of the feminist ideal. In the transsexual, when what is usually considered male takes on the role of the female, and vice versa, what is really occurring is a recollection of the truly male as something historical and sanctifying. The challenge, contradictory, defiant, calls for restoration of the truly male in defiance as against its battered and eroded interpretations.

In the holy, there is overabundance, a fullness which has already been mentioned in the context of Aristotle's *eidos*, but today we need a different aspect of that, something impossible and ultimate. Being at the limit. That seems also to imply being lawless, outside the law, yet the impossibility of the ultimate does not violate the law of nature but refers us back to it and exalts it more than ever. That law becomes close and integral to us.

I should say now that I want to see in the 'idealistic', the impossible, the very essence of life's strategy. Compared to that, the set ways of the present are sclerotic and fossilized, rather like the durability of the skeleton of a living organism compared to the brevity of its life. Again, I do not want to draw a dividing line between the living and the inanimate. Something said to be inanimate – objects, rocks – may prove just as much the product or element of something living as bones. Modern chemistry and physics in their 'elementary particles' are finding their way to the animate as they become convinced of the impossibility of defining the 'inanimate'. This may sound strange, but it is true: only oversimplification can find anything 'inorganic'. Elementary particles are not plain to see and elude physics and chemistry. What we are dealing with, what we are capable of seeing, is all alive.

The strategy of nature, effectively of all living things, builds on the unheard-of, on what has never been. That is today's topic and this is how we are going to approach it.

What problem can there be with life and its self-preservation when its powers of proliferation and reproduction are such that Aristotle's self-spontaneous generation, physiologically, perhaps, inaccurate, is backed up by a more important truth? Life does, to all intents and purposes, generate spontaneously. It flares up so rapidly, like a bonfire, that it makes your head spin. Its exponential growth all but tends to infinity: the graph of a hyperbola soon ends in a lemniscate symbol. Aristotle's spontaneous generation of life is another way of saying that if there is a problem with life, it is, rather, how its increase can be halted.

An aside. Duality and symmetry in physics should perhaps be compared not only with cell division but also with reproduction. This is probably a topic for a new convergence of physics and biology. Proliferation is one of the hypotheses of the origin of matter, in the sense not that the moon gave birth to another moon, but that through gravitation any body presupposes and predetermines another body. The sun proliferates itself in a solar system. The earth splits and the moon breaks off it, continuing to be a continent of the earth projected into space while remaining firmly attached to the earth. The sun does not need to be imagined as an engine which can run out of fuel. There is no reason to suppose it may not be in an interactive system when the galaxy clearly is. It is a composite, unlike the extra-galactic void. All this is guesswork, not even for testing but just so that we do not lose sight of the fact that the history of the cosmos is one of convergence and divergence of bodies.

Another aside. Analysis of the nature of the world and the universe has no beginning and seems always to have been a work in progress. Cosmogony and cosmology were imposed on humankind even before they were imposed on science, and it is not immediately obvious why. Anticipation and preparation of results is not the only approach. Scientific elucidation of the foundations of the universe will come sometime, and it is clear that this activity is already having an effect on us.

Let us return to the text. It is not because they do not believe in religion that scientists stubbornly refuse to find a place in nature for will and reason. There are no fewer believers among them than there are among us here. Instead it is because of their *attentiveness*. If you read the universe using yourself, through yourself, then you are inadvertently taking as your guiding principle not will and reason, but the forest by which we are engulfed and the Cross into which the forest is being transformed. It is not necessary for science to name the Cross, but it has no choice but to bear it.

The options of scientific research include a non-mechanical approach. Our stereotype sees science as having a mechanical approach based on formal calculations, but this is not necessarily the case. To put it more simply and precisely, where the Cross is, that is where we should seek not only science but also the human. (The Cross as an indication of a focus.) We cannot say that the Cross appears only as an episode in history: the Cross is so central that everything emanates from it.

The Cross is wood, matter, and in this sense matter is, of course, primary, the central point of everything. Consciousness is secondary.

Accordingly, to put reason and will, as the farcical creationists do, at the beginning of everything is simply unscientific. Serious science will base itself on what it knows to be rigorous, imperative, and accurate, and that is the Cross, seen, of course, in the way science can view it, as geometry, topology, logic, and mathematics. Mathematics is, from what I hear, now returning, as in antiquity, from arithmetic and algebra to geometry.[3] Science is an honest reduction of the Cross to geometry, where the Cross is retained in all its rigour and acuity, but as an abstraction. And if there is no reduction? The fullness of the Cross is after all more than that: it is the forest. Is it made from the Tree of Life in the Garden of Eden? Here is an example for you of an admirable return, without losing the geometrical rigour, from mathematics as a reduction of being, to unreduced geometry, to what we may call the geometry of the Cross. This is the so-called axiomatic method in philosophy. Let us take as an example a case where (although it is not obligatory, since philosophy can dispense with such formalism) the schoolbook mathematical form of proof is retained, as in Spinoza. This is Proclus, *The Elements of Physics*.[4]

Like Euclid, he begins with definitions:

I. Indivisible are those whose edges are one.
II. Contiguous are those whose edges are together.

This could not be more precisely expressed: just try to define that more elegantly. There are few definitions; rather, as in Euclid, six. After them come the theorems. Again, let us take the first two:

1. Two indivisibles cannot touch each other.

No definition of an indivisible is given: that would be tautological. An indivisible is something which cannot be separated, right? Nothing to take issue with there. It could be objected that Proclus immediately begins to operate with something that does not exist. Indivisible things do not exist? Agreed?

But on what grounds are we to forbid Proclus what we do not presently forbid ourselves? 'This property is indivisible.' 'The territory of the state is indivisible.' 'Property cannot be divided.' 'An elementary particle is probably indivisible.' 'Personality cannot be dissected, it is one.' 'United and indivisible.' And so on ad infinitum. And at the same time the meaning we attach to this word is: some things we clearly do divide, but that means there should be some things that are indivisible.

Svetlana Mesyats notes: 'Hereafter we translate *amere* (literally, "not having parts") as "indivisible" (*atomoi*) because in the text of *Elements*, as in the corresponding passages from *Physics*, no distinction is made between *amere* and *atomoi*.'[5]

Proof of the theorem. 'Let us suppose that two indivisibles, A and B, are contiguous. But contiguity relates to two things whose edges are in one and the same place. This means that the two indivisibles have edges. Therefore, A and B are not indivisible.' Do not be suspicious of the elegance of the formulation. It works here and does not offend against the logic of the proof. And indeed, give me two indivisibles and they will not touch. Draw your own conclusions. The first conclusion: Euclidean geometry in its entirety is called into question, fundamentally! Because in it a point 'has no parts' – that is, it is indivisible – and hence points will be suspended, no matter how many of them there may be, in isolation in space, not touching each other anywhere. Line, surface, and volume will become a supreme enigma. If this annoys you and you decide to populate a space with an infinite number of points, so that they eventually occupy it totally, their infinity totally squeezing out everything else, we shall arrive at a mind-boggling picture of a total point, *one* total point, and after all that we will observe that it was meaningless from the outset to speak of *two* points, since they never can or will touch and hence it is meaningless to speak of their coming together, since there was evidently only ever one point in the first place.

The second theorem:

2. Two indivisibles cannot form anything continuous.

'Let us suppose we have two indivisibles, A and B, and that together they form a continuous unity. But all that is continuous is first contiguous. Therefore, A and B, despite being indivisibles, are contiguous with each other, which is impossible.'

Again, draw your own conclusions. For example, if elementary particles in an atomic sense really do exist, then all so-called bodies are problematical, an illusion, and we are in the thick of Hindu philosophy.

This is what a return from reductive Euclidean to ontological, existential geometry looks like. You will say, but where does that leave us, with no ground beneath our feet? That is, we find ourselves on the Cross, unable to move our arms and legs. But what did you expect? This is real philosophy. It immediately and brutally faces us with genuine difficulties. It immediately returns us to the forest, to matter and the Cross. To the material from the ideal.

Let us return to our proliferation with its geometric progression. The power of it surprises everybody every time. Seasoned biologists will repeat with their never-failing naïvety, and the budding future biologist, too, unable to get used to it, will say, 'All organisms tend to reproduce in such quantities that the entire surface of the earth would not be able to accommodate the progeny of a single pair.' Darwinism and Anti-Darwinism equally start from that fact.

Here we see the truth of Aristotle's spontaneous generation of life. We do not even have to make excuses for him by pointing out that by spontaneous generation he sometimes has parthenogenesis in mind. Proliferation of life is dizzyingly powerful. Life really does seem to flare up of its own accord. The problem is not how to kindle the fire of life but how to stop it. Or is this deluge of life, which is threatening to drown life, actually rarely, or even never, a threat? After all, fish do not drown in water, but for some reason the deluge of life is seen as a constant threat.

The history of life on earth, then, is the story of an extreme, a framework of the living Cross whose rigour and imperativeness are inherent in life's potential for proliferation. The earliest life form, which was still immortal, could, through the division of one old cell into two young ones, have turned the earth into a single, fused, living entity. Ontological geometry, the geometry of the Cross, prevented that. In the history of life on earth, what is special and extraordinary is not life, but constraining the flood of life forms within banks and borders.

Here is a panicky hypothesis: perhaps humans exist in nature to use their reason to bring order to this flood; were *Australopithecus* and Neanderthal Man needed to deal with the dinosaurs, mammoths, and lions in Europe, to stem the flood of life, to play a policing role?

It is a good phenomenological principle to say, 'That was a long time ago and it's not true.' Let Pelevin carry on fantasizing: we will stay with the facts.[6] And the fact is that humankind appears and is *amazed* at how well balanced everything is in nature. From the outset it finds itself *looking*, inspecting, researching. In other words, *extraneous*.

In a recent interview, Sergey Averintsev said, 'At the end of the twentieth century, humans are in the situation of someone who has lost their place.'[7] If at the end of the twentieth century they could lose their place, that means that from the outset they were the kind of creature which was capable of losing its place. Or, to put it even more bluntly, which was out of place. I am not criticizing, just stating a fact. Look at everything, your sense of self. The 'superfluous people' in Russian literature are just good phenomenology, manifestations of a fact: people are superfluous, I say without any criticism.[8] It would be absurd to say that the lion at the end of the twentieth century has lost its place. It has not: its place has been usurped.

Averintsev continues, 'When someone has no place, they have no resilience, no boldness, no rebelliousness, no fight.' The lion's invariable tonic, and undoubted, indisputable right, is to rend the flesh of other animals and drink warm blood. Humans in their ritual hack flesh and shed blood, offering them to their god and only from the god receiving their due. There is no tonic for those who are out of place. The fact that they are constantly looking for and finding tonics only proves that by nature, from the beginning and not just at the end of the twentieth century, humans have no boldness. They are outside the mechanism of the world; they are its observer. They are in a state of *amekhania*.

This points us in the direction of recognizing that the Cross was not invented, not introduced to history in some particular century: the Cross has been the essence of humans from the beginning; or it would be truer to say that a human is a superfluous being for whom a place has been found, always. At the end of the twentieth century, too, that place remains available, the human's place on the Cross. Averintsev's 'being in the situation of someone who has lost their place' is just another way of speaking about the geometry and topology of the Cross.

It is wrong to say that first, a long time ago and more recently, there was paradise, and afterwards the Cross. The Tree of Life is what the Cross is made of, which is to say that the Cross was already within the Tree of Life, unseen.

That is why the urge in human beings to impose order and 'take measures' is not inherent or even simply wrong, a mistake. The first impulse will not be, as in Martin Scorsese's film *The Last Temptation of Christ* (based on the novel by Nikos Kazantzakis), the temptation to come down from the Cross since you are invited to descend, and all common sense and all nature advise you to do so. A more genuine impulse – last only in terms of historical time but first in terms of human nature – is at all costs, if it is the last thing you do, as quickly as possible, to crawl, to climb, back up to your place on the Cross, driven by horror at the prospect of remaining someone who has lost his place, likely to be taken by people you want nothing to do with and used as you do not wish.

The problems of a human, a being out of place, are solved by his returning to his place on the Cross, to *amekhania*, *aporia*, to not resorting to mechanisms. There is no other solution in prospect. It makes no sense, it is bad phenomenology, or not phenomenology at all, to ask why things are that way. It is enough that we see that is the way they are.

*   *   *

As soon as we saw the Cross only in terms of geometry, reductively, as soon as we became distracted and decided to see only what was immediately visible – and how could that not be seen? ('Look, two straight lines at right angles, that's all there is to it') – we were already divided. We seemed to have taken the easy way out but only laid ourselves open to the question: what right do you have to turn the Cross into a design? It is sacred. Why in this secular university is there a Cross painted? What does it signify? Why is the Cross drawn incorrectly, not as a Russian Orthodox Cross? Anyway, why a Cross, rather than a Crescent, which would be more topical, or soon will be? In other words, drifting down what seemed like a well-kept path, we have found ourselves facing a whole lot of problems. So it would be better to see the Cross in all its fullness from the outset. We may find we then have too much on our hands, but at least there won't be this awkward split.

A real philosophical conversation always involves engaging with the geometry of the forest: that is, coming back from the design of the Cross to the Cross as the Tree of the World, the Tree of Life, and so on. We are in any case not going to move far away from the Cross, we will always be hovering around impossibilities, as there is right there in the forest Proclus's ontological logic of impossibilities and extremes. It is better just immediately to concede the non-mechanical, the impossible.

In this light, it is Darwin who is unquestionably right when people try to argue with him that life develops in accordance with a regular plan. Against any kind of metric, Darwinism is right to draw attention to the crucial, decisive situation. It sees the root of the matter in extraordinary tensions, extreme situations of a fight to the death.

Darwinism is wrong, however, when it resorts to reductionism; when for this extreme situation, for the Cross for which the Tree of the World, the Tree of Life, has been taken, it does not conjecture *impossibility*, in the sense of extreme, ultimate possibility. *Mechania* ends in *amekhania* but total *amekhania* suddenly transforms into every possibility. This transition is well present in the Greek ἀμήχανος, 'helpless, being in a difficult situation, baffled, in need', δρᾶν ἀμήχανος, 'incapable of doing, acting'. A second meaning of the same word is 'a person or thing against whom there are no resources, insurmountable': in the *Iliad*, 10, 167, ἀμήχανος ἐσσι, 'you are unconquerable', 'nothing can be done to resist you'; also 'inexplicable, amazing, incredible, immeasurably large, amazingly great'; ἀμήχανος κάλλος, 'incredible beauty'. There is this same twist in the Russian '*nevozmozhnyi*', impossible.[9] An example from the dictionary would be 'impossible heat', which, of course, does not mean 'heat it is impossible to withstand'.

Darwinism does draw attention to the critical situation of *impossibility* but looks no further into it, as if that is enough.

For reductive geometry or conventional ontology, a system of bodies always tends from a less probable to a more probable state. That is, it is eroded, it passes into entropy. Poincaré's principle of 'least action'.[10] Leibniz said that it was more natural and simpler for nothing to exist than for anything to exist, but it seems very much as if a view that sees entropy as inevitable is already reductive, Euclidean, and a schematization of the Cross.[11]

With life it seems likely that the situation is the reverse. Lev Berg writes, 'Every individual living being, insofar as it represents a totality of material particles, is, of course, subject to the same laws: it follows the path of least resistance.' One could say more precisely, a living being can be schematized, reduced to a mechanical specimen.

But this path is not at all characteristic of the process of evolution of a single individual (i.e. for ontogeny) or species or generally for *the direction of the evolution of life*. In contrast to what happens in the inorganic world, in the organic world development moves in the direction of creating organisms that will be able to produce not a minimum of work but a maximum. Life moves in the direction of what is *least probable*. Yet, nevertheless, everything that takes place in organisms occurs in accordance with the laws of physics and chemistry.[12]

Berg gives an example to illustrate this difference: a machine is built strictly in accordance with the laws of physics and mechanics, but something holds us back from saying that those laws foresaw the machine from the outset. For the future we shall need to try to explain why it is awkward to say that the machine was foreseen, pre-programmed by the laws of physics. Why? The laws of nature were from the outset such that a machine was possible. More broadly, is the anthropic principle wrong? Can one not say that the laws of nature were from the outset such that a human being was possible? I will not answer that question because others will answer it for me. Berg meanwhile continues:

> The whole extraordinary, unfathomable mystery of life is that everything in it occurs in exact accordance with the same laws as operate in inorganic nature. Or, in the words of Leibniz, in the body (of a human being) every detail of the processes takes place in such a way as if the sordid doctrine were true of those who, together with Epicurus and Hobbes, considered the soul to be something material. In other words, what if the human being was only a body or an automaton? He is a machine down to his most minute components.[13]

The animal organism is an automaton; there we can agree with Descartes. Berg agrees with Descartes, Leibniz, and Aristotle that life is a machine. 'One kind of machine is an organism.'[14]

There is a slight strangeness here: a living creature is a machine, but we swallow it, we accept it. Why? Because we somehow unintentionally all use the word 'machine' in two senses. The machine has split in two: into an automaton and into – an automaton, and for us the automaton split unambiguously and conclusively long ago. The difference, however, is not the one we have been using up till now because, although true, it is not what really matters. What really matters is not that the self-moving element in the true, living automaton is spontaneous, while in the mechanical automaton it would be preset and rigidly prescribed by its programming. That is, that everything the man-made automaton will do would already have been rehearsed in its program. Today, the difference between one kind of machine and another can be recognized more clearly: the living automaton includes a phase of *amekhania*, of 'freezing' or stumbling. For example, a living mammal passes through *amekhania* during mating; it is the shadow of death, and through it, the mammal throws itself into the species, which is no less immortal than those immortal creatures that reproduce by division of all their cells.

We need to get on with the basic job of scraping away mud that has stuck, to the effect that there should be a mechanism of the life of a species, and that important matters like the continuation of the species should be accompanied by 'subjective experiences', like when, on a rollercoaster, you find yourself travelling upside down and experience an intense thrill. (Maybe not, if you are very tough.) It is not the case during the phase of *amekhania* and alteration of the soul when ensuring continuity of the species that this is just a subjective accompaniment of physiological processes to which tough guys might be immune. It is not the case that the tougher someone is the less they will be moved when experiencing the moment of conception.

At those critical moments in the life of the species – birth, pairing, and death – each person replicates the leap life made when it dared to embark on the complex path of history and decided to part with immortality. Life did not have to choose this interesting path. It could have not done so. There was plenty of life around as it was.

It was never the case that life had instilled in it at some primal level the mechanisms for its functioning and continuation which subsequently, with the development of consciousness, began to be felt and experienced. It has always been the case that the genus has lived around the focal point of *amekhania*, something that encompasses both the physiology and 'experiences' of the psyche. The psyche was there from the outset.

The machine that is an organism (this idea is widespread and is, for example, elegantly developed by Merab Mamardashvili – the work of art as a machine)[15] includes that most wretched and infuriating feature of a programmed automaton: freezing, crashing, the inability to take the next step, mechanical breakdown. In Mamardashvili, this is the moment of creative inspiration. I have a feeling we shall yet encounter this issue of the machine and creativity, and will each time wonder how we could have imagined we understood either of them. For now, however, all we are interested in is this distinctive moment, this dead stop in the functioning of the living machine. How does the living machine come out of that dead stop by itself? Why in Hegel's triad does the synthesis revert to the thesis?

The first answer that comes to your mind and mine is, of course, the fuel supply. Burning coal heats water; inspiration powers the spirit and provides the dynamism for thought. You will appreciate that such an answer is phenomenologically invalid: it merely shifts the issue elsewhere – into the depths of the cosmos, perhaps, from where mysterious beams emanate. The primal energy would then come from the Big Bang, cascade down on us, and power the machine of the world.

We feel it is actually rather devious to focus on the fuel supply. If *amekhania* is partial, if the freezing is simply a temporary failure in the energy supply, if there are guarantees of a way out, then the Cross is a mere trick, an illusion, a piece of operetta. What we experience is that we are being abandoned not notionally, not with some safety net, but for real. It is not the case that the creation of the world from nothing, or whatever, happened long ago and that we are still living on the dividends. It is an integral part of the machine and, importantly, of the machine that is the world.

Berg writes, 'Life, we may say, is like a clock which you can wind up for an unusually long time, perhaps for eternity. Having been wound up at the dawn of the history of life, the clock manages to retain its supply of energy, passing it down from generation to generation.'[16] Unfortunately, this shunting back to 'the dawn of life' will not do. It is simply moving back a difficulty into the past, a typical academic technique for clearing a comfortable space. This technique, providing present convenience only later to get bogged down in the need for further terminological clarification, is the distinction Berg proposes between the living mechanism and the mechanical assembly. We will approach this as we always do: having registered the difference, we shall resign ourselves to the fact that, just as previously the automaton, so now the mechanism is a slippery place where different layers may unpeel.

Darwin, with the confident gesture of a Moses, pointed as if in a dream to the crisis of life forms. All nature is at war; the stronger, in the end, have the upper hand, the weaker are defeated.

All these results ... follow from the struggle for life. Owing to this struggle, variations, however slight, and from whatever cause proceeding, if they be in any degree profitable to the individuals of a species, in their infinitely complex relations to other organic beings and to their physical conditions of life, will tend to the preservation of such individuals, and will generally be inherited by the offspring. The offspring, also, will thus have a better chance of surviving, for, of the many individuals of any species which are periodically born, but a small number can survive. I have called this principle, by which each slight variation, if useful, is preserved, by the term Natural Selection, in order to mark its relation to man's power of selection. But the expression often used by Mr Herbert Spencer of the Survival of the Fittest is more accurate, and is sometimes equally convenient.[17]

In 'survival of the fittest', let us remember, the fittest are not those best adapted but those with most 'goodness'.

This makes it all the more curious why Darwin's confidently asserted term of 'natural selection' struck everyone as self-evidently true. Thomas Henry Huxley (1825–95) said, 'My reflection, when I first made myself master of the central idea of "The Origin", was, "How extremely stupid not to have thought of that!"'[18] It is all the more surprising because the idea goes back a long time and has had frequent recurrences. Heraclitus, for example, protests to Homer that his benign wish that 'Discord should vanish from among gods and men' is a recipe for the destruction of the world. It is a law of nature that everything should be pushed to the limit, to the brink of disaster. It is a law that all the most interesting things happen when tension is extreme.

Kant writes in his *Idea for a Universal History with a Cosmopolitan Purpose*,

> As gentle as the sheep they tended, such men would hardly have won for their existence a higher worth than belonged to their domesticated cattle; they would not have filled up with their rational nature the void remaining in the Creation, in respect of its final End.... Man wishes concord; but Nature knows better what is good for his species, and she will have discord. He wishes to live comfortably and pleasantly; but Nature wills that, turning from idleness and inactive contentment, he shall throw himself into toil and suffering.[19]

There is nothing evil about this. People, like trees in the forest, Kant says, grow tall and straight when they are constrained.

> [Nature] works through wars, through the strain of never relaxed preparation for them, and through the necessity which every State is at last compelled to feel within itself, even in the midst of peace, to begin some imperfect efforts to carry out her purpose. And, at last, after many devastations, overthrows, and even complete internal exhaustion of their powers, the nations are driven forward to the goal which Reason might have well impressed upon them, even without so much sad experience. This is none other than the advance out of the lawless state of savages.[20]

This does not 'betray the hand of a malevolent spirit', but is the work of a wise Creator. To Kant we can add here that there is such a thing as a good meanness (*zloba*, from *zlo*, evil), a competitiveness which leads to a positive, if unkind, outcome.

Darwin's thinking comes in at too late a stage. He identifies selection after it has taken place, but before that outcome there has been a fierce struggle to hammer out possible solutions to go forward and compete for that selection.

What is created out of that unremitting stress? With a sense of full responsibility, we reply: the unexpected, the *impossible*. This is not mere improvement of something useful. There is little room in *amekhania* for utility. The criterion is, in its broadest sense, goodness.

In other words, to quote Kant's seventh proposition in the same document: out of war, out of the general relentless struggle, there should be born an automaton. If gradual improvement leads to increasing complexity, then, out of *amekhania*, out of breakdown, a breakthrough is possible, and if it is possible, then only to an automaton which *retains the foundation of* amekhania.

Next we shall answer the question of why the anthropic principle is mistaken. Until next time.

Lecture 18, 17 February 1998

There are differences between automata: one I load up and switch on because I need what it does. For example, when the detergent is becoming less effective and before the tumbling of the washing, the machine *itself* does what is needed next. Strictly speaking, it is not the machine that has worked out when to do this, but the fact is that I no longer need to perform this action every time. *Scientifically*, that is, *ritually*, after undertaking various complicated computations, I have managed to free myself from having to wash dirty clothes and worrying about the water. I did not, of course, manage to free myself from worrying scientifically about the consequences of the release of detergent into the drainage system, the need to filter urban water, the effect of residual cleaning chemicals on my skin, the problem of finding something to do with the time freed up, provision of the entertainment now required, such as women's magazines, women's television programmes, and feminism generally – all this now looms over me and not only has it not been automated but, what is much worse, the prospects for total automation have receded to infinity. I am left with an accumulation of issues on my hands, of urban management, planning, equipping of residential accommodation, psychology, and ecology, and there is nowhere for me to dump these spiralling problems.

Kant wants society and the state to become an automaton, not in the sense – here again there is an important difference between one automaton and another – of someone programming society. The external programmer of Kant's automaton is the human being. (I am referring to 'The Natural Principle of the Political Order Considered in Connection with the Idea of a Universal Cosmopolitical History', Proposition 7.) The automaton is what human society will become in the plan of nature if not of humans (*'zwar nicht in der Absicht der Menschen, aber doch in der Absicht der Natur'*) and the human being will be *inside it*, as in Pelevin's story 'Prince of Gosplan'.[1] Unlike Pelevin's video game automaton, where people are being played with, Kant's automaton is free, but not in the sense that a component of an automaton can stop, leave the game for a time, and fix itself externally. Crashing is the most important, crucial, and indeed decisive feature of a true automaton (the rest of the time it functions smoothly). When the automaton freezes, it cannot instantly change its program. It finds itself in an impossible situation facing the jaws of the meat-grinder with no option to act.

What right do we have, apart from the desire to dream a little, to talk of impossibility in another sense, that of immensity? Something incredible may happen, but it is not mine and will not be the result of my own power. A divine hand intervenes, the keying of an unseen operator, unseen. The hypothesis of God or an operator we immediately reject, however, not because they do not exist but because it is uninteresting. A true automaton should, we feel, be able to get out of *amekhania* by itself. But it can do nothing while it is frozen. We are here coming to the mystery of consciousness. We agree, do we not, that an automaton does not need consciousness, but in *impossibility* there may be found a difference in *how* to go into the teeth of a devouring machine. This is likely to be the difference between 'let it be' and 'let it be', between acceptance and acceptance, a difference in the tone of letting fate happen.

Although we have already intuited that one cannot choose one's role but only whether to act it well or badly, we had not yet guessed that good or bad acting is of no consequence except in the one respect of whether it has been good or bad. The game will not change, the machine at the end of the escalator will, come what may, devour the person, but – Pelevin does not foresee this unexpected alternative but the ancient philosophical imagination did – there will be no continuation in a different game and situation. As they said, the cycle of rebirth will end.

Can we in this way approach the origin of species? For the time being, let us try a purely formal approach: evolutionism, or creationism, and the history of life in general associate the origin of species with 'goodness'; the degree of fitness must at all events be intuited for the species to emerge and develop. The criterion of that fitness, however, is not a comfortable fitting into an ecological niche, but relates to admission of a different kind. In Kant's automaton, choice and the arranging of niches is automatic; for Pelevin, and in his view this is his world, but also for other people, this is a field cleared for freedom where the most weighty and fascinating decisions are taken, precisely between one kind of absolution and another, between one kind of decision and another in that sphere or in the topology of *amekhania* where a person cannot lift a finger. I have written 'a person'. Perhaps, more generally, that should be 'life'. We shall need to come back to Aristotle's biology, where animals have morality, intelligence, principles, where bees, for example, can take measures against lethargy. We need to get used to the thought that any living being always somehow partakes of this goodness, this intuition, as it always proves to be, in order to survive.

Taking our leave of Pelevin: the automaton and operator within the automaton will participate in the goodness or unfitness of their role and of that of the automaton overall, and there will be natural selection in accordance with this principle. The question of goodness or unfitness will always be open not to a willed planning, but so early that goodness or unfitness will precede both planning and will.

Fit and unfit are the same as good and bad. Survival may be given as a reward to those who successfully adapt, or it may not. It makes no sense to say that dying pine trees are 'not adapted' to a certain percentage of carbon monoxide in the atmosphere and that is why they are dying out. Not all living things, as we have said, are fit. Fitness gives life a task it may grumble and complain about, like a Roman soldier complaining about his backpack with a half-hundredweight load. Life may rebel against the Cross, and in fact does so all the time.

Let us check the hypothesis that fitness is not needed by life and slips into adaptation, but becomes definitive when the automaton crashes and then escapes *amekhania* by distinguishing good from bad, which acts as a sanction or non-sanction, a sanctification or withholding of it. The operator in the automaton does not know how it works or what its purpose is and has no specific plan for himself, only a communal one, but in some way he has as much knowledge as the creator of the automaton or anyone else.

It is not true to say that, as far as life is concerned, it is good for a Roman to sunbathe in Baiae, while in terms of the Cross, it is good to carry a half-hundredweight load on your shoulders through the mountains, and that the different criteria just depend on your point of view. The One on the Cross had no conflicted calculation that what he was losing in biological terms he was gaining in terms of biography. The mystery of the Cross is that the Cross is victory unalloyed. Incidentally, the theory of natural selection does not indicate for what purposes the selection is being made. Why does it not divide the shape of the ostrich, which it classifies as successful, between two columns, one headed 'adaptation for flying in the air' and the other headed 'adaptation for swimming in water'? Why is 'adaptation' not structured but only described? Strong legs reach ... , feathers facilitate ... , the arrangement of the stomach allows ... I imagine the reason is that nature's species amaze the researcher on a naïve, human level as incredibly *clever*. Scientific observation enhances the pre-scientific experience of admiration, and constant repetition, confirmed by each new experiment, trains a scientist in what to expect. In each new being, fitness is waiting to be discovered and it remains only to unpack and interpret it.

It is good if the thought has just struck you that there is something not quite right about this. We have no honest, comprehensive grounds for thinking that different life forms do not strive to improve themselves as we do, or that the desire for goodness is equally present in all rather than, as Aristotle suggests, that a bee's life is 'better' than that of a wasp. That may seem a strange thing to say, so let us confine ourselves to a cautious negative: we do not know that the desire for goodness in the living world is confined to human beings. If we are speaking only about the desire for fitness, then most likely that desire is universal. Desire is perhaps not quite the right word here, and we will do better to resort to the more formal 'sanctification'. The operator of the true automaton is always within the field of sanction, which there either is or is not, and which can be recognized just as surely as holiness, wholeness, and fitness. Interestingly, sanctification can be recognized only as sanctification: it has no objective characteristics.

The so-called anthropic principle presupposes that it is possible to talk about 'humans' in general, but the deictic gesture falls flat as soon as we notice that we are indicating a good person, not a bad person.[2] A bad person has exactly the same physiology, so that is evidently not what is being indicated. Skipping several steps in the reasoning, because this is not too interesting or important, the result we obtain from the anthropic principle is that the universe was from the very beginning such that it could go in a good or a bad direction, and this characteristic, the potential for holiness, has evidently always been there. No matter what substantive parameters, such as intelligence, we project from humans on to the universe, we can always ask whether they are actually needed at all. Sanctioning them brings us back to holiness. It is clear where the anthropic principle came from: a mediocre scientific milieu, in order to be able to consider itself good because of its consciousness, paid the price by oversimplifying the criteria of goodness to the point of woolly liberalism and excessive tolerance.

That the criterion of fitness was fully present in ancient evolutionism is not always apparent, because, for example in *On the Nature of Things* by Lucretius Carus, it is enciphered by the poetic perfection of the treatise, which is deployed to describe the development of life.[3] Lexically, there would appear to be nothing about the sanctification of the victorious life forms, but they are elevated as something holy and victorious by the loftiness of the poetic language. Lucretius says of the disappearance of species:

> Beasts quite unfit by own free will to thrive
> And vain for any service unto us
> In thanks for which we should permit their kind
> To feed and be in our protection safe –
> Those, of a truth, were wont to be exposed,
> Enshackled in the gruesome bonds of doom,
> As prey and booty for the rest, until
> Nature reduced that stock to utter death. (5, 873–80)

This is not our current sadness over the extinction of species, perhaps because so many remained. Extinction itself is sanctified by the voice of sacred poetry. Poetry would be lying if it admitted something to its holiness without first having seen holiness in the essence of the matter.

All this 'nature of things' is displaced by Lucretius slightly into the past. His present world is reeling and is not sanctified by him. It is dark and is foundering. Like a ship on stormy waves, his times are taking risks and playing with disaster:

So man in vain futilities toils on
Forever and wastes in idle cares his years –
Because, of very truth, he hath not learnt
What the true end of getting is, nor yet
At all how far true pleasure may increase.
And 'tis desire for better and for more
Hath carried by degrees mortality
Out onward to the deep, and roused up
From the far bottom mighty waves of war. (5, 1432–8)

'The nature of things' in the world Lucretius inhabits must accordingly be seen as visions of paradise, akin to the Bible's description of the Garden of Eden. Poetry has the ability to see things with this kind of vision and is entitled to do so, just as childhood is. Usually the differences of lighting and perspective are preserved and there is no confusion. I have mentioned how the washing machine, although a convenience for the average unthinking housewife, actually generates a whole host of environmental problems. Here by way of contrast is the description of an analogous action, the washing, admittedly only of hands, but assuredly doubly or triply sanctified as an old pagan custom to mark the summer solstice, now in the Christian calendar as the day of John the Baptist, and also by being described by the twenty-nine-year-old Petrarch in 1333. He was travelling in Germany and reached Cologne, Agrippina Colonia,

which lies on the left bank of the Rhine, and is noted for its situation, its river, and its inhabitants. I was astonished to find such a degree of culture in a barbarous land. The appearance of the city, the dignity of the men, the attractiveness of the women, all surprised me. The day of my arrival happened to be the feast of St John the Baptist. It was nearly sunset when I reached the city. On the advice of the friends whom my reputation, rather than any true merit, had won for me even there, I allowed myself to be led immediately from the inn to the river, to witness a curious sight. And I was not disappointed, for I found the river-bank lined with a multitude of remarkably comely women. Ye gods, what faces and forms! And how well attired! One whose heart was not already occupied might well have met his fate here.

I took my stand upon a little rise of ground where I could easily follow what was going on. There was a dense mass of people, but no disorder of any kind. They knelt down in quick succession on the bank, half hidden by the fragrant grass, and turning up their sleeves above the elbow they bathed their hands and white arms in the eddying stream. As they talked together, with an indescribably soft foreign murmur, ... this was an old custom among the people, and that the lower classes, especially the women, have the greatest confidence that the threatening calamities of the coming year can be washed away by bathing on this day in the river, and a happier fate be so assured. Consequently this annual ablution has always been conscientiously performed, and always will be.[4]

Petrarch openly elevates what he has seen to the paradisaical and separates it from the topical. This automaton does not work genuinely, in any serious manner. (It is an automaton because it is a custom, ancient, joyful, observed with unflagging diligence, and has no reason of its own to cease for as long as the Rhine continues to flow.) He exclaims to his companions,

> Those who dwell by Father Rhine are fortunate indeed if he washes their misfortunes away with him; I fear that neither Po nor Tiber could ever free us of ours. You send your ills to the Britons, by the river; we would gladly ship ours off to the Africans or Illyrians. But I was given to understand that our rivers were too sluggish.[5]

At that present moment, the poetic philosophy of Petrarch continued to sanctify, but in a different dimension, glances and faces which meet, the geometry of intersecting glances and the meeting of frank and open faces, divine and human.

Why is there a problem with sanctification in science? In part, perhaps, it is because of a careless muddling of the paradisaical and the mundane, of the supposedly scientific 'hypothesis' and the 'fact', because of a failure to remain within the boundaries of phenomenology. In other words, there is a lack of light about the whole issue.

Something else that remains obscure to science is the extent to which the error is made of projecting backwards on to the past, for example the method of trial and error. Nature supposedly, if not now, then when everything was just beginning, sought in the same way that we do and made mistakes in the way that we make them. 'How many faulty or incomplete worlds,' Diderot wonders, 'have been dispersed and perhaps formed again, and are dispersed at every instant in distant regions of space ... but where motion continues, and will continue, to combine masses of matter until they have found some arrangement in which they may finally persevere?'[6]

Persevere. That is the key word. The problem is that what surrounds and is within the writer, in his body and his writings, what concerns and is available to him, is clearly not going to 'persevere'. He projects on to the unobserved past what he finds too disturbing. Diderot again:

> I may ask you, and Leibniz, Clarke and Newton, who told you that in the first instances of the formation of animals some were not headless or footless? ... that monsters mutually destroyed one another; that all the defective combinations of matter disappeared, and that only those survived whose mechanism was not deficient in any important particular, and who were able to support and perpetuate themselves?[7]

One senses the yearning for permanence.

Where do Leibniz and Newton get such an idea about the beginnings of things? From different experience, from the contrary experience of luckily, immediately hitting the target, of preservation which you do not have to wait to see confirmed because there is other evidence to support it in sanctification, in holiness. Thus for Goethe, who knew the secret of fortunately getting things right, there is nothing strange or unnatural in seeing nature as a super-lucky, easy-going creator:

Figure to yourself Nature, how she sits, as it were at a card-table, incessantly calling '*au double!*' [i.e. each time she wins calling for the stakes to be doubled, in order for her winnings to increase in geometrical progression, *Bibikhin*] i.e. exulting in what she has already won, through every region of her operations; and thus plays on into infinitude. Animal, vegetable, mineral are continually set up anew after some such fortunate throws of the dice; and who knows, whether the whole race of man is anything more than a throw for some higher stake.[8]

Our present task is not great, to decide whether nature attains its goal by luck, instantly, or only agonizingly. To note that in one case, and most often it is the case in so-called science, after false starts, unsystematically, often spread out over time and the supposedly (only because we do not observe it) gradual emergence of species, we do all the same become aware of a leap. Somewhere in the shadows, stealthily, there occurs the difference between a doomed try-out and a success, something 'preserved'. In another case, usually in polished poetry and philosophy like that of Goethe or the philosophical poets of the Renaissance, a line is clearly drawn between the discarded and the preserved (which is called 'redeemed'), and we find those key words, 'joy', 'happiness', 'success'. Goethe is bolder than science: he does not assume that the human species is (as the anthropic, or rather the anthropocentric, principle claims) the definitive creation. Perhaps it is only intermediate, but it is the ultimate delight of a rejoicing nature, as is always the case when nature scores a success. The mineral world was a success, the vegetable world was a success (and then some!). After that there was the animal world. Partaking of that joy which we, along with Toporov, call holiness, the human species may yet be unfinished business, not necessarily a culmination.

The figure of the automaton, not fully thought through, not yet fully clarified, strays through the literature of evolutionism. (Kant in his *Ideas* is also an evolutionist.) Diderot, *Pensées sur l'interprétation de la nature*, 1754: organic molecules are characterized by rudimentary consciousness (aversion, desire, memory, and intelligence).[9] This is, of course, a thousand times less than that of even the lowest animals. These views are similar to those of Tsiolkovsky. There is only one position appropriate for any organic molecule, which is where it best fits. Lucretius (in 5, 426) refers to 'immemorial aeons' during which 'primordials of things', 'many in many modes, astir by blows from immemorial aeons, in motion too by their own weights, have evermore to be borne along and in all modes to meet together and to try all sorts which, by combining one with other, they are powerful to create'. This is the crux: these *primordia rerum* suddenly 'meet at the last again', *coniecta repente*, and so become 'the commencements fit of mighty things – earth, sea, and sky, and race of living creatures'.[10] Diderot names that success more straightforwardly: tiny molecules, feeling something, seek, 'with the restlessness of an automaton', a comfortable, stable position, like animals turning over in their sleep until they find a suitable position. Diderot: the animal is 'a system of diverse organic molecules [i.e. with rudimentary consciousness, *Bibikhin*] which, under the influence of a sensation akin to a vague, dull sense of touch, with which they have been supplied by the Creator of all matter in general, combined until such time as each found the place best suited to its form and repose'.[11]

Why did the Creator, who provided molecules with the sense of touch, leave it to them to find their own form, when he could also have provided them with that? Because it is an observed fact that we seek preservation and salvation, or 'equilibrium', and why would we need something already innate in us from the outset? Because again it is an observed fact, now, that we enter that state of equilibrium suddenly, abruptly, as in Lucretius. And it is a fact that we have successfully landed in a pocket, as in billiards, and that that pocket must have been put there by somebody.

All this is also a long, twisting path to Aristotle's energy: that is, to Parmenides' being. Because Aristotle no longer has to depict how everything came to be what it is, his attention is released to focus on details. If intuition, if getting it right, is possible, then it is not all that crucial when that comes about, whether after a thousand attempts, or immediately. Establishing that is not a matter of dogma, it is a matter of fact.

We have talked about the automaton. There would seem to be no other support for it than this strange provision for getting things right, striking it lucky: that is, there is no guarantee that I will get something right but, if I do, there will be an encounter. We will find that a 'fit', a 'good' form, is *this*. If that is so, we need to be prepared to jettison evolution. Fitness, intuiting, could not be unconditional if they created something that still has to wait to be checked: intuiting is a one-off, its own success and sanctification. What is fit gets it right in the same way, and in fact is actually the same thing. It is natural to extend the analogy between nature and art to the point that, as in art, there is no development in nature. We cannot say that with the years Goethe was writing better when he was eighty: he evolved in a different sense. Making forms more complicated is no more growth, no more moving towards fitness, than the complexity of the baroque is a development of the Renaissance, or the unkempt, unstructured nature of postmodernism is superior to the structured nature of modernism. Development, if it does not have the sense of unrolling a bolt of fabric, can only be retrogression to what is already there. By and large, the increase in the world's population has dictated the history of recent times, the past

6,000 years. According to Tsiolkovsky, progress is for the human species to increase to trillions, but it will not be possible to say even that the task has become more complex.

The so-called 'Aristotle's ladder' (there are beings in the sea of which it is impossible to say whether they should be classified as plants or animals, an intermediate stage between higher and lower) needs to be projected on to time in order to become evolution from the highest to the lowest. 'First the lower, then the higher.' 'We should bear in mind that the modern idea of the course of evolution as a process of development of higher forms from lower forms *in time* was foreign to Aristotle. The notion of historical continuity of organisms is first outlined by French authors in the mid-eighteenth century.'[12] The notion that time is required for development was associated with *rejection* of the necessity of striking it lucky, and a revolutionary granting to oneself of permission to blunder and make mistakes. Permission was granted to oneself to act without sanction, and that was justified by progress. That is, a whole chain of unsanctioned actions was permissible because sanction would be forthcoming in the form of progress. In effect, of course, one was giving oneself permission always to act without sanction. For Aristotle, that was never permissible.

The revolutionary evolutionism of the eighteenth century is diametrically opposed to Aristotle's ladder, starting with just the opposite. The purpose of human history, this is particularly evident in Marx, was considered to be all-round development of capacities. For Aristotle, this is as absurd as teaching someone to play the flute solely because they have a flute. And human beings have plenty more than just a flute. First you define the goal, and then you muster the means to achieve it.

We have been descending into modernity down a staircase of dubious permissions which, in some strange way, are spoken of as achievements. Evolutionism as an analogue of laisser-faire in politics and economics, putting its faith in a rising graph to rescue us, relying essentially on the restorative power of nature, planetary and human: that is one of a series of permissions modern humankind has allowed itself – postmodernism is only a more extreme form of modernism in this sense – such as the introduction of limit into mathematical calculus, a liberty to operate with the limit and thereby skirt the problem of infinitely small and infinitely great values. Or, as with the car, allowing ourselves to take energy from nature without giving anything in return. These liberties are mass movements to which only a very few refuse to succumb.

The power and influence of Darwinism derives not from the novelty of its idea, which was already formulated by Aristotle, but from the novelty of the permission to wait for the battle between species itself to determine the fitness or unfitness of living beings, the permission to regard a living being as 'so far not quite' or 'no longer': that is, to pass over it as not in itself something ultimate and integral. As a justification of that permission, there is a great sense of the superiority of Darwinism primarily over Lamarckism. In 1802, Jean-Baptiste Lamarck introduced the term 'biology' at the same time as did the German naturalist Gottfried Reinhold Treviranus. He was 'the founder of animal psychology'. According to Lamarck, '[A]nimal and plant species are constantly changing, becoming more complex in their organization under the influence of their external environment and a certain inner drive to improvement possessed by all organisms.'[13] Animal psychology studies this self-motion of life. As in Aristotle, for Lamarck a person learns to play the flute not because there is a flute, but because when there is a need to play, they acquire or make a flute.

'[T]he constant use of any organ, accompanied by efforts to get the most out of it [Life makes an effort to change, to acquire a new instrument!, *Bibikhin*] strengthens and enlarges that organ, or creates new ones to carry on functions that have become necessary.'[14] From the outset, the goal, fitness, is present as an aspiration. Conversely, '[T]he disuse of any organ modifies, reduces and finally extinguishes it.'

> [T]he bird of the water-side which does not like swimming and yet is in need of going to the water's edge to secure its prey, is continually liable to sink in the mud. Now this bird tries to act in such a way that its body should not be immersed in the liquid, and hence makes its best efforts to stretch and lengthen its legs. The long-established habit acquired by this bird and all its race of continually stretching and lengthening its legs, results in the individuals of this race becoming raised as though on stilts.[15]

Again there is effort, but it is being made in the profound slumber of life, here, of a heron. It is done without consciousness, but no less effectively for that, and we should remember Plotinus remarking that consciousness only weakens the working of the will and thinking.[16] Without consciousness, the living body is more pliable, like clay which can be moulded.

Lecture 19, 24 February 1998

[W]hen the will guides an animal to any action, the organs which
have to carry out that action are immediately stimulated to it by
the influx of subtle fluids (the nervous fluid), which become the
determining factor of the movements required.[1]

(Jean-Baptiste Lamarck, 1744–1829)

This is a difficult and disturbing view. Inside the living organism, we find a
will and an extraordinary sculpting of itself. Hastening to give the masses
permission not to cudgel their brains over this, the *Soviet Encyclopaedia*
adds,[2] 'Lamarck did not, however, reveal the true causes of evolutionary
development', namely the three mechanisms: wide diversity of natural
variations; the firm fixing of variations through heredity; and the rejection
of unfit variations during 'natural selection', the extinction of the insufficiently adapted. 'In the pre-Darwinian period, the causes and driving
forces of evolution of the organic world were not yet known.'

Charles Darwin himself (1809–82), on the contrary, in 1876, expressed
regret in a letter to Moritz Wagner. Darwin was sixty-seven, his three major
books had been published, – *The Origin of Species by Means of Natural
Selection* (1859); *The Variation of Animals and Plants under Domestication*
(1868); *The Descent of Man, and Selection in Relation to Sex* (1871) –
arguing that man was descended from an ape-like ancestor. 'In my opinion
the greatest error which I have committed has been not allowing sufficient
weight to the direct action of the environment, *i.e.*, food, climate, &c, independently of natural selection.'[3]

Here Darwin is really not conceding very much. He remains stubborn
and intentionally one-sided. He seems to be leaving it to others to note
that even the aphids could effectively process a sufficiency of vegetation:
the horse has not only 'adapted' but provides life with a non-essential
(because the aphid could do the job) but complex and splendid transmutation of vegetation. Compost also plays a part in biology. Darwinism
which now borrows something from Lamarckism may be worse than
pure, one-sided Darwinism, which, in addition to its actual tenets, is animated by the energy of disputation, and tacitly implies that a living being,

a species, would be able almost to sense (we are deliberately speaking loosely and provocatively) that it is doomed by natural selection. There will be a psychological difference between a species with a future and one with none. The alternative is to suppose that life has a strategy from the outset.

The term *mutation* was introduced by the Dutch botanist Hugo de Vries (1848–1935). If Gregor Mendel (1822–84) had not conducted his experiments on the hybridization of pea varieties in 1856–63, we would talk not of Mendelism but would speak of de Vries, who rediscovered Mendel's laws around 1900 and published two large volumes about them in *The Theory of Mutation* (1901–3). He writes about something we will periodically encounter. What he took to be an instance of mutation in a plant, he subsequently found to involve a strange and complicated crossing of varieties. This does not, however, discredit what he thought he had found. (I am saying that this is a case or even a pattern not uncommon in science, not only in biology but also in physics, where theory and fact do not coincide but continue in parallel with each other. Theory never springs simply out of fact.) 'No indication of their appearance was noted in their parents. They came into existence at once, fully equipped, without preparation or intermediate steps. No series of generations, no selection, no struggle for existence was needed. It was a sudden leap into another type, a sport in the best acceptation of the word.'[4] You will see that to arrive at this there was no need of a lot of special experiments with *Oenothera lamarckiana* in the Amsterdam Botanical Garden. De Vries could perfectly well have read it in Aristotle – but it does have the value of evidence from someone who scrutinized life for decades and saw its distinctiveness, who saw the organism as a perfected form or as a *message*. De Vries: 'Species are not arbitrary groups between which man here and there draws boundaries the better to survey them: they are sharply distinct, entirely independent beings, restricted in time and space.'[5] Meaning they are defined.

Darwin's stubborn provocativeness (John Bull!) had a beneficial effect on de Vries. It enabled him to claim that natural selection played no part in the shaping of a new form. In this, de Vries was probably wrong: it may not be natural selection as such that creates a mutation, but a mutation most likely needs cramped conditions, overcrowding (Losev would say the 'exaggerated intensification') of life. De Vries for his part took the risk of suggesting periods of time, say 4,000 years, during which species would, as it were, accumulate the energy needed for a mutational leap. What was the purpose of the leap? Just because. Because of sheer exuberance and strength.

Creative activity pays no attention to the prevailing conditions of life: it creates solely in order to form something new; it increases the wealth of forms, but leaves them to cope on their own with the circumstances. One of these forms fortune may favour, others not; fate decides what ultimately is to survive and will, accordingly, be selected to continue the family tree.[6]

Here the final decision rests with fortune and fate. De Vries was in fact mistaken. What he observed was not a mutation but a hybrid. Carl Linnaeus (1707–78) worked out a very clear formula for the emergence of species as hybrids. He established a system for classifying plants and animals that is in use to this day. In the beginning, the Infinite Being, *infinitum Ens*, created classes of plants. Mixing of them during fertilization created genera, and again, *per generationes ambigenas*, after untold generations of cross-breeding fertilization, plant species emerged. Something that argues against this is the reluctance of species to cross-breed.[7]

Two Russian biologists, Andrey Famintsyn (1835–1918), a plant physiologist, and Osip Baranetsky (1843–1905), drew attention in 1867 to a further possible way for the formation of new life forms, symbiosis.[8] In their age of positivist accumulation, it was still necessary to wait for the revolutionary beginning of the twentieth century, when their trend was honed by others. Famintsyn and Baranetsky were working on photosynthesis and osmosis, suffusion or infusing of plants with light, or moisture, for example when the root pressure of a plant causes secretion of water droplets by the leaves. At all events, they discovered that plants absorbed all sorts of extraneous things. A striking case was lichen, which seemed to be a confection of fungus and cyanobacteria. One might have expected that these had become interwoven by accident and would be fighting each other, but Famintsyn and Baranetsky recognized a symbiosis. From this perspective, Famintsyn saw the cell itself as a symbiosis of *several* organisms. This was again that indirect relationship between theory and observation. Famintsyn was wrong in supposing that a particular type of orchid which, while still embryonic, was penetrated by a fungus would be wholly unable to develop without it and could survive only in symbiosis. He was wrong in this instance, but the theory has a certain attraction. Boris Kozo-Polyansky (1890–1957) in the adventurous climate of the early 1920s, suggested that all organisms, including the highest, should be considered confected from lower organisms.[9] A good example was *Convoluta roscofiensis*, a marine turbellaria flatworm with cilia along its body. It is green because of parasitic, single-cell, flagellated green algae attached to it. These supply the worm with starch, and possibly gain something from it in return. The evidence that they are nourishing the worm is that, in the dark, where their green chlorophyll does not function, the worm becomes malnourished and, without their sustenance, soon dies. In light conditions, it lives for over a month.

Kozo-Polyansky proposed indeed that chlorophyll should be considered a separate life form in symbiosis with plants. Chlorophyll's plastids grow into the cell itself, and reproduce from each other rather than from the plant cell, like separate organisms. Chlorophyll in plastids lives in, as it were, incrustations separate from the cells. Similarly, Lorenz Oken (1779–1851) saw infusoria as parts of the organism, primal animals, primal matter (*Urthiere, Urstoff*).[10] Moreover, observing the way the cell nucleus of some orchids moves from one cell to another, Kozo-Polyansky began to consider the nucleus, too, to be an organism separate from the cell and in symbiosis with it. All plants were seen as being composed of microbes. Kozo-Polyansky classed microbes as elementary organisms to the extent that they were not themselves a combination of organisms. They were, so to speak, the atoms of life. These atoms somehow fuse together, and thus every living thing is a hybrid. They form alliances and these separate out and become relatively independent, and so on. Kozo-Polyansky: 'Flora result from the evolution of microbes by means of the formation of consortia and colonies, colonies of consortia, consortia of colonies, and consortia of consortia.'[11]

Ladies and gentlemen, please note that this definition introduces concepts of two orders: colonies and consortia. These are the names of formations that the biologist Boris Kozo-Polyansky observed in his microscope when examining what is called 'life', 'live matter'. They could have been called something else. What Kozo-Polyansky saw in his microscope is what anybody else would see in it. He was investing in his terminology, as in the words '*result from the evolution* of microbes', something the biologist has never observed or never will, because the concept of the meaning of life ('consortium', 'colony', are projecting on to life purposeful formations of human society) and of the origin of life circles around the mystery of life, around something that, as a matter of principle, does not name itself. Kozo-Polyansky was imposing on life a concept of the meaning of the motion of every living thing.

Now, why was this biologist doing that? Was he naïvely unaware that he had been provoked by the mystery of life into promoting a concept that was going to prove controversial? Why can't you just keep to pure observation? Why are you putting on airs? Why do biologists have this uncontrollable urge to bring in, on top of the data obtained from their pure observation, this second layer of meaning, which is clearly not the same as observation?

This interweaving of two completely different orders of speech in biology is prompted by the mystery of life, the mystery of the forest. It is a mystery in which the tree divides into the Tree of Life and the Tree of Knowledge of good and evil, the tree and the Cross. Polarity is a part of life, and our superiority over the biologist is only that we intuit, differing from conventional thinking, that the theoretician *introduces* his theories into practice and that *this* is something dictated by life itself. Plato and Aristotle do not bring the idea and *eidos* into life as the element of wholeness and fullness; life bears within itself a duality. A duality of what, you may ask. You will remember that last year we talked about the Trinity, that first there is *three*, and only after that, three of what?

The Cross, the intersection of perpendicular lines, is the name of this situation. It is more formal and purer than Plato's duo of place and idea, or Aristotle's trio of matter, *eidos*, and incompleteness. Plato's and Aristotle's division, however, has the great merit that – contrary to the popular belief that philosophical terminology is artificial – it applies the words 'species' and 'idea' not to an artificial construct, but to something we see rigidly strengthens the forest. How? By those very words of genus and species. To this day, we have not learned how to be more precise than the classical world. Mendelism is amazement once again at the discovery that the apparent proliferation and rampancy of the forest is contained within a strict framework. It is the same with the human species: individuals can change body and soul to a state of perversity, but even then within themselves, unseen and unnoticed by them, the human species remains invulnerable. All humankind can do to it is terminate it. The species will be gone but not its mystery; the mystery of life itself is something the human species cannot stop. That is, it does not have the buttons to press, the levers of existence which would terminate life. While there is life, there is the polarity of the flexible, adaptable forest and the unyielding nature of the Cross, a geometry.

The attempt by Trofim Lysenko (1898–1976) [a notorious Soviet anti-genetic biologist supported by Stalin, *Tr.*] to use force majeure to crush idealism and to subjugate species, to crush its unassailability in the academy and in people's minds, to knock idealism out of people's heads, did here and there encounter unyielding, incomprehensible, irrational resistance. The species, no matter how they tried to alter the appearance of individual specimens, stubbornly restored itself just as it had been. 'Idealism' seemed to be restored to people's minds automatically.

This happened, even if genetics did not call itself idealism. We are talking about systems that require no apology or justification. They are, however, demanding: to participate in the idea it is not enough to understand and accept it. Indeed, that is completely unnecessary. One has to behave, so to speak, like the idea. Firmness in action, brutality and *wildness*, if you like (humans are not wholly domesticated animals), comes at a price. Something Antonin Artaud sighed for in the twentieth century was the raw, cruel, and rigorous act that remained wholly within its suchness.[12] We have an obligation to remain wild in order to continue nature's strategy. In the sense that a domesticated sheep goes quietly to its doom, its resignation does not contradict wildness. In humans, we can a priori expect alloyed forms, the mixing of the feral and the domestic, to produce cunning. These poles of behaviour can be given different names: conservatism and liberalism, for example. Tameness can degenerate into conformism, and then its opposite, dependent pole also becomes warped into malign brutality. Intuition leads us to follow strange paths.

Strangeness, however, is the standard way in which Sophia operates. This means that the way out for the modern world is ultimately a breaking through of strangeness, of whatever kind it may be. Strangeness is next to holiness, which, we may say, is a wild joy that has discovered the mystery of the Cross. It breaks through where it will, like green shoots through a dead body.

A reminder about natural selection, that is, about death culling life. Death helps life. Natural selection is right in the sense that life has no roadmap, no plan. It never knows what it should do. What is erroneous, however, in the popular understanding of natural selection is the idea that Sophia, divine wisdom, would blunder forwards by means of thousands of trials and errors, waiting blindly for something to turn up out of the play of chance. We can, of course, speak of two principles, those of Wittgenstein and Popper, let us say, and Wittgenstein will be correct to the extent that I would justify his gesture of waving a poker at Popper.

Popper's Darwinism is wrong also in proposing that the development of science (we are becoming increasingly used to St Augustine's treatment of the biblical commandment to 'be fruitful and multiply' as applying primarily to creations of the human mind or, nowadays, to the generations of inventions), the biology of science, if you like, 'develops' by a mechanical working through and realization of every possibility, and it is wrong also in supposing that it is necessary to wait for the verification by the future of what that comes up with. Working through the possibilities and waiting to see what turns up would be tantamount to Sophia passing the initiative to – what? Most likely, to death. In inventiveness, and indeed everywhere else, the features of Sophia are strangeness, suddenness, holiness, ecstasy, paradise, the Cross. This is what I call Wittgenstein versus Popper, or Osip Mandelshtam against Alexey Tolstoy and almost the whole of Soviet literature.

It seems unlikely that anything has changed or ever will change in these methods of Sophia. The present situation with computers changes the configuration of the forest; the computer is like a fire-break, allowing us to see right through every forest. The mass of substance ceases to be profound; it is, as it were, displayed on a surface. Possibly there is beginning to be more geometry in substance. The texture of matter is changing, rather like the transformation of the Sahel region, an arid strip to the south of the Sahara Desert, from the forests and fields it once was into a sandy wasteland.

Nothing has changed in the fact that humanity is part of existence and the world. We can safely represent the computer world as new, wild nature. The strategy of Sophia should be continued under these new, and any other, conditions, within the parameters I have named her steps of intuition. Or, if you like, it makes sense, heuristically it is good, to see today's postmodern world as a jungle. In a jungle, where you can see only a few steps ahead, it is meaningless to say whether it is growing the right way or not. There is no sense, on the other hand, in arguing against the fact that humanity is in a state of sin and degradation. There is no way I can approach the degradation in humanity other than through the degradation in myself, given that I am trapped in the forest. Unlike the primaeval forest, the modern forest includes technology, computer technology, and has the same visibility as an impenetrable forest. It seems, though, that apart from the lack of visibility, the forest has not changed substantially, because it has somehow taken us out of the metric domain and brought us to another, invisible, space. That is why filling up the world with generations of computers, all of which are visible on the surface, changes nothing substantive in the status of the forest.

It seems that visibility hinders the ability to see what is important, that the essence of the forest is non-metric and unplanned. Insight would be, oddly enough, to emerge into the invisible. The myth of Homer is relevant here, a man whose blindness helped him to see what really mattered. I mention the theme of the blind seer only in passing. Also relevant is another important issue which we have no time to go into now, the topic of the mediaeval blindness to landscape and the so-called discovery of landscape in the Renaissance. In mediaeval literature, there are many descriptions of battles and weapons but few of landscapes. In all the Scandinavian sagas, it would seem that only one landscape has been found. This is another example of blindness that is like a discovery. One more note: if we find on the pages of modern poets no technological realia, that is a promising sign. Possibly, just possibly, they are able to see the forest.

Let us return to the landscape of Sophia: the forest, the Cross. The Cross was discovered by Christianity. It always was the life of the forest, the jungle. This is a harsh environment: 'natural selection', the destruction or preservation of species, is the main purpose.

This forest, this jungle, we say, remains. Civilization has become no more humane, no easier for Sophia. Not Popper but Wittgenstein. As Mamardashvili says, what is decisive is not discourse, not terminology, but the steely will of the desperado.[13] The important, interesting predicament is still, as always in the landscape of Sophia, the impossible: humanity's proper place is on the Cross.

In impossibility, out of nothing, substance and life developed from the very beginning. As it was, so it is; the forest has not gone away; we are even now alone in it. The concerns of Sophia are, as a matter of principle, always invisible to the outsider. So-called objective research reveals imaginary laws of nature which are essentially operating instructions, descriptions of skills learned by human beings who do not wait for favours from nature but believe that 'our task is to take them from her'.[14] It needs to be said that Ivan Michurin, when he uttered these words, meant the exact opposite of what they sound like. What he meant was that, without his intervention, there would not exist in nature the 300 varieties of fruit and berries in whose hybridization he had participated.

The forest, depriving us of the long view and removing us from the metric domain, outside of which prescriptive schemes and plans do not work, in return allows us to participate in ourselves, not debilitated by reflection. (Objectivization facilitates control and monitoring of everything that can be controlled and monitored, but at the cost of losing the ability to participate.) Where consciousness with its power of reflection actually belongs, supposedly the supreme function of the brain, is evident from the fact that technology seems to have succeeded in synthesizing consciousness: if a video camera is attached to a television so that what it is shooting is shown on the screen, and then what is happening on the screen is videoed, patterns will appear on the screen, apparently ordered, which can have come neither from the screen nor from the camera or connecting cable. It may be surmised that these are the result of an introspection analogous to human consciousness.[15] Or a mathematization of consciousness. The subject in an experiment, who is not told its purpose, is given a quantity of identical, equal-sized beans and asked to classify them as good or bad. Out of 100 beans, an unprejudiced person will classify 62 as good and 38 as bad. This 62% is a psychological constant.[16]

The fashion for observing comes from being dazzled by appearances, and it is essential to overcome it. Under the surface of every observation, we are inside the forest and embedded in the automaton of Sophia. She decides and acts through us, in us and by using us. She is at once through us and with us: that is, it is not as if we were attached to her by strings and carrying out someone else's work, but neither is it the case that we can do anything by ourselves.

In modern science, we hear voices expressing a departure from past objectification. To quote Grégoire Nicolis and Ilya Prigogine (1989),

> In classical physics, the investigator is outside the system that he observes. He [...] [*Bibikhin*] is the one who can make independent decisions, while the system itself is subject to deterministic laws. In other terms, there is a 'decider' who is 'free', and members of the system, be they individuals or organizations, who are not 'free' but must conform to some master plan. Today, we are getting farther and farther away from such a dichotomy.[17]

This is a typical remark.

Now, how it is typically understood:[18]

> At the present time we are able to distinguish two models of evolution: the finite and the infinite. The infinite model at its simplest infers a progressive asymptotic movement towards a certain goal. Sometimes it is spoken of as an expanding upward spiral. Here the goal of evolution is seen as being outside humankind, which seeks to surpass itself in attempts to advance further. [Finite evolution is a movement as][19] in certain mechanical or hydrodynamic systems: it simultaneously possesses features of chaotic and deterministic motion. The system remains at all times in the vicinity of a closed curve, sometimes called a 'strange attractor'. The presence of the attractor indicates the existence of a target, albeit unattainable, but such that in the process of motion towards it a new quality arises – the fractal nature of movement itself. Here, the goal of evolution, although unattainable, is not

of an external nature, and no special effort needs to be made. We shall in any case end up somewhere.

Here is our expression 'striking it lucky' (*popadanie*) again, the 'closed' nature of the curve corresponds well to our understanding of Spencer's 'fit' as the intuition of appropriateness and sanctification itself. The 'strange attractor', not, of course, within the model of mathematical topology but in its intuiting of the quality of Sophia, is also close to what we have been saying. It could not be otherwise: because everybody has the same thing in mind. But in the description which I read, our landscape, with which we are gradually, piece by piece, becoming more familiar, has again been seen. The rejection of prescriptiveness, of a programme, occurs easily with the introduction of the 'fractal' dimension. Sergey Horuzhy calls this approach in mathematical description an extension of the general situation of postmodernism to science.[20] Along with rejection of the programme goes rejection of effort. Indeed, within the fractal dimension, there is nothing to which effort can be applied. Striking it lucky in nonsense is not something that happens. 'Irrespective of whether evolution has a goal and what its nature might be, we can state that in its process increasing complexity of living organisms occurs.'[21] In this sense, and without any effort, as has been said, 'we will in any case be in luck'. The process of complication takes care of itself and again it has been truly said that this complication is movement of a different order from striving for a goal, and may in any case not be a goal.

We are confirmed in this mood by the fact that the entire constitution of a live, developing organism is encoded in ontogenesis by only 2% of all the links in a molecule of deoxyribonucleic acid – the remaining 98% are conscientiously copied, transferred by heredity, but are not manifest in any of the characteristics of the living organism. Some biologists consider these non-coding 98% to be 'trash'. Within this part, there are probably mutations of some sort from generation to generation, but it is impossible to track them because they have no characteristics.

This discovery fits very well with the smugness of today's class of large data storage devices: they are just that – data storage devices. Perhaps they are for emergency use and need to be preserved, so to speak, packaged (in every sense of the word). They correspond in society, and it does not matter whether we know why, to that 98% of genetic code whose purpose also nobody knows, but precisely because it is packaged, it probably has some important purpose, like a special parcel in the post which nobody is allowed to open.

'We can assume that, in order to ensure some extremely important function is carried out, a constantly replaced and renewable device is employed whose job it is to perform that function, and that device, it would seem, is you and I.'[22] This function, we need to note, is carried out without the application of effort and without the parcel being opened. If we open it and bring out (so far nobody knows how to do that, and the point is that it is best if they do not know) this hypothetical potential into the real world, that will be that. A line of communication stretching across thousands of generations will have been broken. What is in the parcel really does need to be left unopened.

But, then, why not keep everything packaged? Why activate the 2%? That 2% is the entire living organism, mutating or not mutating over the generations. It is needed in order to adapt to the environment, changing, when necessary, along with it, precisely so that the parcel, the 98%, is delivered whatever the circumstances – rather as a package is transported first by van, then by train.

Now, who is the recipient of the parcel? Probably the one who is able to read its contents. That is, we have to wait for the necessary mind, which is even now rapidly developing in the appropriate manner. It will receive the information, that same information which it currently has, only wrapped up. It will unpack it and then it will be clear what needs to be done. It is even possible that the goal will return, clearly spelled out. 'The latest advances in philosophical thought – structuralism and postmodernism – are on the whole insistently demanding precisely such treatment of the elements of culture.'[23]

Until such time as a mind of that stature appears – we are back to our topic – we should not interfere with the automaton we do not understand. Admittedly, the author I am quoting (Sergey Siparov) does not use the word 'automaton', but that is what he has in mind.

Let us take a look at what a designer does when he faces the need to ensure a system will perform a certain function infallibly, with 100% reliability. Increase stability and quality? That will not ensure 100% reliability. A tiny crack in a blank, a random change in the parameters of the environment, could prove catastrophic. Accordingly, in particularly critical situations, an obligatory periodical replacement of one system with an analogous one will be undertaken – an operation requiring human intervention or a special program.[24]

Actually, it is a matter of delivering totally automatic operation, but our author cannot imagine an automaton other than one managed by a human or a program.

Lecture 20, 3 March 1998

If the packet of genetic information that is transmitted from generation to generation and does not advance contains the explanation of the whole history of humankind, its program, as we have read in one philosopher of biology and could read in another, then development, evolution, comes down to a need for the mind to rise to the task of being able to read that. But in fact the mind is already now sufficiently developed and complex to read the packet. It is capable of everything. Accordingly, from this point of view also, no evolution is required, only instruction and schooling.

Calmly turning our back on evolution, we do, incidentally, find ourselves, as we might have supposed, in good company, beginning with Parmenides, Plato, and Aristotle, and in fact all of classical thought. Schopenhauer:

> As the scattered drops of the roaring waterfall change with light-
> ning rapidity, while the rainbow, whose supporter they are, remains
> immovably at rest, quite untouched by that ceaseless change, so every
> Idea, *i.e.*, every species of living creature remains quite untouched
> by the continual change of its individuals. But it is the Idea, or the
> species in which the will to live is really rooted, and manifests itself;
> and therefore also the will is only truly concerned in the continuance
> of the species. For example, the lions which are born and die are like
> the drops of the waterfall; but the *leonitas*, the Idea or form of the
> lion, is like the unshaken rainbow upon it. Therefore Plato attributed
> true being to the Ideas alone, *i.e.*, to the species; to the individuals only
> a ceaseless arising and passing away.[1]

Schopenhauer is considered a critic of Hegel, but there is a general rule: if a thought is genuine, then no matter in which language or to which modernity it spoke, it has the same thing in view. Hegel: 'It is a completely empty thought to represent species as developing successively, one after the other, in time. Chronological difference has no interest whatsoever for thought. The land animal did not develop naturally out of the aquatic animal, nor did it fly into the air on leaving the water.' The human species was not derived from the animal nor the animal from the plant: every organism was immediately the whole thing which it is. (But how? We run to biology, but it tells us nothing.) 'So that even if the earth was once in a state where it had no living things but only the chemical process, and so on, yet the moment the lightning of life strikes into matter, at once there is present a determinate, complete creature, as Minerva fully armed springs forth from the head of Jupiter.'[2] In other words, if you accept the premise of 'the lightning of life', why would you need evolution? It is of no interest.

In Russia, the most notable and important opponent of Darwinian evolution was Lev Berg (1876–1950), a physical geographer and biologist. He was the first person to carry out a physical geographical demarcation zoning of the USSR. He specialized in ichthyology (the anatomy, taxonomy, and distribution of fish), climatology, limnology. In *Nomogenesis, or Evolution on the Basis of Rules*,[3] Berg suggests modifying Darwinism through the introduction of a law of development, but Darwinism is deflated if it can be shown there is already a law governing the development of species. Berg supplied a slightly earlier version of *Nomogenesis* with an epigraph from Goethe: 'There is nothing more germane than the attempts to establish zoonomy and tracing the laws by which the life of organic beings is determined.' The reference to Goethe is not quite appropriate: for Goethe, constants and archetypes are like those 'winnings', those 'fortunate throws of the dice', on the part of nature which we mentioned last time; in Berg, these are laws of development.

Having written that, I pull myself up short: I have said that on the whole I am for Darwin, but here I am expounding his opponent. Overall, I believe Berg loses out to Darwinism because he overlooks the importance of the culminating, concentrating, encapsulating ultimate moment, crucial and critical, in the life of life.

Berg leaves a role to natural selection, but only in order to preserve a norm. Moreover, he has aberrant individuals preserved to a far from trivial extent: not by any means in a way that retains the status quo of a constant natural spread of variations and deviations within a species, *but in the sense that in every generation a large spread appears again and again but is purged and filtered for viability (with Darwinian selection), all the marginal individuals disappear from the scene, and the species tends back to the norm.* Berg quotes [Karl Pearson's][4] research into generations of poppies to the effect that every race is much more a product of its *normal members* than might be expected on the basis of the relative numbers of its individual representatives.[5] The same applies in human society: the dispersion of deviants, degenerates, and alcoholics is great in every generation, but in each subsequent generation, children, on the whole, again begin within the norm. If the number of children in poor health increases, then it is to a lesser extent than among adults. Typically, children are more normal than their parents. The opposite is less common. Attention needs to be paid to Berg's thesis. By itself, natural selection does not change the norm; for that to happen, other factors are needed.[6] The most obvious and predictable is change in the environment. If you continue along this line, we will ask what is meant by 'the environment' and will extend it to include the cosmos. The cosmic environment is plainly changing, but how? The earth's magnetic axis is changing, for instance, and what about changes in radiation, some in connection with the ozone layer?

Berg the biologist and geographer draws attention to simultaneous massive changes: for example, the European spruce which, in the north of Russia and in Siberia, represents a subspecies of *Picea excelsa obovata*. 'Of course the formation of this subspecies did not come about by a single specimen of it appearing somewhere and then conquering the whole of Siberia. No! Under the influence of the Siberian landscape, all the firs in Siberia took the form "*obovata*"' from being just *picea excelsa*.[7] Or geologists themselves made the observation that the shape of the mollusc *Planorbis multiformis* changed in the transition from one horizon of upper Tertiary deposits to another. 'Absolutely all the individual creatures took part in these systematic transformations: nothing supports the view that slight differences in the size or sculpture of the shell had any significance for selection.'[8]

Upper Tertiary deposits in geology date from roughly the period before the appearance of the first human being. If you quiz geologists on how many years the Tertiary Period lasted, they are likely to become flustered: the length of the period is much debated and there is good reason why geologists prefer to talk not of a period but of a sub-era. After the Quaternary Period, they stop counting because that is the latest and the one we live in. A lot is known about the Tertiary Period, which was vastly longer than the Quaternary. Just as in human history the periods become shorter as we approach the present day, so most scholars accord the Tertiary Period tens of millions, in fact about 65 million, years, and our Quaternary Period is counted only in millions: rarely more than 3.5 million. Sometimes the entire Quaternary – that is, the Pleistocene ('for the most part new') Epoch and the Holocene ('completely new') Epoch – are together allowed a total of as little as 600,000 years. In comparison with that, what a lot of space there is in the Tertiary Period and how interesting it appears. If in time the Tertiary Period occupies some 98% of the entire 60–70 million years of the Cenozoic Era, our own Holocene Epoch would drown in the approximately 70-million-year Cenozoic were it not for one detail. And let us not forget that the Palaeozoic Era and the Mesozoic Era both lasted some five times longer than our [Cenozoic, *Tr.*] Era. Indeed, the Palaeozoic Era began more than half a billion years ago. The Cenozoic Era began, following the Mesozoic – note that life serves as the earth's timekeeper more than geology – from the time when the face of the earth as we know it today was formed, with geosynclines, very roughly speaking elongated rafts of the earth's crust which for some reason float on the hotter and more fluid interior of the earth, moving towards each other and, in some places, under the pressure, folding, crumpling without faulting, and forming mountain ranges which we now call, for instance, the Alps, the Caucasus, the Pamirs, the Himalayas, and the Andes also along the Pacific Ocean.

The skin wrinkles in the same way. In some instances, the folding goes upwards and layers from down below are raised which are more ancient. This is an anticline. In the opposite case, the crust is pressed downwards and inwards and this is called a syncline. In an anticline, geologists are presented with strata near the surface that would otherwise have to be excavated from great depths; in a syncline, on the contrary, you dig and dig and everything you find is 'new'.

More important for us perhaps is drastic climate change. Glaciers covered the entire northern third of Europe, Siberia, and, of course, Russia, and for some reason in this environment, amid the snow and ice, human beings turned up. Upper Tertiary deposits occurred during the appearance of the mountain ranges that we know today, a very long time before all the Ice Ages. You will remember the usual way this is described. Let us take Vernadsky as an example:

> Thanks to the discovery of fire, humans managed to survive the glacial period – those huge changes and fluctuations in the climate and biosphere which we are now seeing discovered by scientists in the succession of so-called interglacial periods – of which there were at least three – in the northern hemisphere. They survived them, although at this time a number of other large mammals disappeared from the face of the earth. It is possible that humans contributed to that. The Ice Age has not yet ended and continues to this day. We live in an interglacial period and the warming is continuing – but humans have adapted so well to these conditions that they do not notice the Ice Age. Several thousand years ago, when they already had domesticated animals and agriculture, the Scandinavian glacier melted where St Petersburg and Moscow now stand.[9]

We can regard the snow, to the extent that we still get it in Russia, as a vestige of the last Ice Age. Vernadsky was already seventy-five when he wrote this. He was inclined to move events too far back in the past, placing the origin of life at 2–3 billion years ago, and the emergence of man at several million.[10] A commentator on Vernadsky observes that '[t]he modern species of man, *Homo sapiens*, appeared 40–50,000 years ago, not in Africa but in more northern latitudes of Europe and Asia, probably not without owing something to his ability to adapt to the extreme conditions of the Ice Age.'[11] So then, when moving from one stratum of upper Tertiary System deposits to another, it was observed that the mollusc *Planorbis multiformis* changed radically, without any intermediate forms. The African bee is different and more aggressive. Bees in Abkhazia have a proboscis 0.5 millimetres longer than those in Orlov. For Berg, it is important that all living things change at once (a principal indicator in studies of race).

Berg trusts experiments in the style of the early twentieth century, when discussion of race was topical: great significance was given to the roundness or elongation of the head, which was seen as a way of distinguishing between races, and the measuring of two values: width and length of the skull. On a sample of 6,000 Jews, it was shown that, if they were born in Europe, the width of the skull would be 83% of its length, while if they were born in America, it would be only 81%. That is, in order to develop a longer head, one had only to be born in America. Migrating to America was not enough; that made no difference in comparison with the European parameters. Again, the change was universal. It was dramatic in the first generation, then slower but in the same direction. Jews were convenient because they lived all round the world, and the characteristic parameters of the skull varied everywhere, approximating to the type of the local population.[12] Increased height was similarly of interest and displayed by the Dutch: it could not be ascribed to diet and the cause was not entirely clear. Flexibility of the human body. In the Baltic States, people were blond and blue-eyed. There was a curious kind of mimicry. Byron: 'And as the soil is, so the heart of man.' And not only the heart.[13]

These changes were clearly not hereditary. If returning to one's old homeland, there was massive reversion to the previous state. There are, however, forms (e.g. the fir) which stubbornly maintain phenology. One specialist on the fauna of the Black Sea used to say that he could distinguish Mediterranean oysters in a pile from Black Sea oysters: 'Almost all Black Sea creatures bear a kind of Black Sea "imprint": they are smaller in size (except for some species with more northerly origins), a paler colouration, less pronounced shaping, greater opacity, and so on.'[14]

The totality of the change is manifested also in the fact that the novelty of a particular species when compared with a different one is not in just one organ or another, but total, encompassing the entire build of the animal down to the smallest detail. 'If a swiftly running animal such as an antelope needs long legs, then, firstly, the same variation must simultaneously appear in all four; secondly, simultaneously with the bones *and in the same direction*,[15] the muscles, blood vessels, and nerves must become elongated and all the tissue restructured.' That is what is found from observation. 'To believe that such a set of changes can occur by chance is to believe in miracles.'[16] According to Darwin's theory, it would seem that certain individuals might find they had the successful long legs, but their unchanged neck would now be too short for them to reach the grass, so it would be necessary to wait for individuals who by chance have both long legs and a long neck, enabling them to run away from wolves but still to feed, only then their heart would be too small for the new demands of their circulatory system, and the skin on their bodies would be ill-adapted to their new swiftness.

Here, then, is Berg's main thesis:

We have established two closely related facts. Firstly, natural selection is by no means conducive to individual fortunate deviations but preserves the norm. Secondly, the process of species formation occurs through mass transmutation. These two facts are entirely sufficient to refute selectionism, that is, the doctrine of the selection of randomly useful variations, and to show that evolution is nomogenesis, or the formation of new forms on the basis of rules.[17]

The feature of nature Berg is describing here can be observed by anyone. We have the concept of communal sharing, in the sense of everybody coming together. People who depend on a good crop note during the spring whether the new shoots, for instance of maize, all come up together. If they do, everybody is jubilant: all the grain, as they say, 'looks like it has got together' to germinate at the same time. For people on the land, this is always cause for celebration, and not from some utilitarian chain of reasoning that this means there will be a good harvest – everything can still easily go wrong – but because of how the plants have *behaved*. The seeds might not sprout in unison but then catch up with each other and the crop will still be good, but all the same not as good as if they all came up together. Of course, everything depends on the conditions, whether it is warm after heavy rain. But that there is also on the part of the sown field itself a spontaneous urge, a cooperativeness, a willingness to be equal to the conditions, all together, that is something we can feel. This line of argument can and should be continued: for example, to suggest that the capacity to all pull together improves the prospects of a species in terms of natural selection. But I am going now to break off this thread.

I want to move on to another thesis of Lev Berg. (By the way, his second life was supported by the translation into English in 1926 of his book *Nomogenesis*, which was published in 1922 in St Petersburg.[18] You can also read in English a book by Berg's daughter, Raisa, titled *Acquired Traits*. It was published in 1988 in the USA.[19]) The development of the individual, the 'ontogenesis' (in my opinion, a very unfortunate term), under a so-called law of biogenesis, is held to swiftly recapitulate the main evolutionary stages (phylogenesis) of the entire species to which that individual belongs. The law of biogenesis was formulated by a thirty-year-old German Darwinist, Ernst Häckel, in his two-volume *General Morphology of Organisms* in 1866.[20]

Everything would be straightforward if there were no instances where, on the contrary, individuals have superfluous features or attributes they are not going to develop or need, but which do develop and are needed in groups considered to be at a higher state of development to the group of that individual. A good example is the South African Welwitschia, an ephedra-type plant. It is dioecious, like, for instance, the sandthorn, which is a sign of a 'lower' form of organization, a higher being bisexual, such as the apple.

And here we see in the Welwitschia ... that the male flower, along with six stamens, has a rudimentary ovule. This ovule is infertile but nevertheless provided with a stigma; physiologically it is non-functional but morphologically the flowers of this unique plant are bisexual. What is the significance of this rudimentary pistil which is of no benefit to the plant? It would be comprehensible if this were a legacy from its predecessors, but here we have the rudiment of an organ that will begin to function only in a bisexual angiosperm.[21]

Before we can talk about anticipation of species development, we need a scheme of *how* everything has developed, and there can always be alternative schemes. In the development of an individual specimen (the so-called ontogenesis), we need no scheme to observe this kind of anticipation. The example given by Berg is the ascidian or sea squirt, a marine chordate of the subspecies tunicate. A notochord is a primitive skeletal axis, not yet a backbone. 'Not yet' is our tribute to Darwinism. If we project forward in time, the chordates will become vertebrates, but vertebrates are in fact a third subtype of chordates. The second is cephalochordates and the first tunicates, which have a sac-like body structure. There are over 1,000 species of chordate tunicates, and we might expect, in accordance with Häckel's law, that the larvae of ascidians would not have a notochord while the adults would. In fact, the opposite is true. Adult ascidians, up to 50 cm in length, are living sacs or tunicae, and also classified as marine tunicates, and the adults have no notochord. They are like molluscs, yet ascidian larvae have everything, as if they have every intention of becoming full-blown vertebrates no worse than, say, human beings. They have a notochord, dorsal nervous system, an auditory vesicle, an eye-like organ, gill slits: that is, embryonic ears, eyes, and gills. In other words, everything seems ready for the appearance of a head, and yet no head appears. The notochord and dorsal nervous system, the eyes, ears, and gills, are resorbed as they grow. Does this indicate that ascidians were at one time vertebrates but then turned back and degenerated towards a semblance of molluscs?

It really would be very interesting if it meant that evolution can go backwards, and the myths current in the archipelagos of the Pacific Ocean could prove correct: that the ape is the result of human degeneration.

Berg asked people to refrain from interpreting his thesis along mystical lines: ontogenesis does not necessarily recapitulate phylogenesis but may be a preliminary to it; or the phylogenesis might be ahead of its own time. Transformism is, in a literal sense, 'evolution', the opening out of existing rudiments. There is a *law* of development. Development appears to know where it is going and *why*. To put it crudely, what a creature needs is what it will acquire. Here are two good examples.

One is from Berg. Amphibians, such as the frog, and there are around 3,000 species of amphibians, and also a great many amphibian fossils, as you will have seen, breathe in the larval stage with their gills but, as adults, with their lungs, like we do. What would you say if you saw a fish that had both lungs and gills? There are very few such fish and they are becoming extinct. There is one species in Australia, one in South America, and one [*sic, Tr.*] in Africa. The simplest thing is to conclude that the frog is a fish with a dual breathing system, but no: they belong to completely different groups. The lungfish, in addition to division of the atrium into two ventricles, nasal orifices that open into the oral cavity, and fusion of the elements of the upper jaw to the skull, as in human beings, has a hippocampus in the forebrain like the higher vertebrates, and unlike other fish. That is, in parallel to fish, when the need arose to live also on dry land, everything began to appear that land creatures have, only on the basis of a fish. It is the same situation with the famous similarity of birds to dinosaurs, such as pneumatization of bones apparently connected to the pulmonary air sacs. Birds, however, were not descended from dinosaurs and again, if that were the case, we would have convergence on different foundations. There is even greater similarity between birds and pterosaurs, even to the extent of avian features in the brain structure of the pterosaur Scaphognatus, but again this is not a genetic link. A generalization made by Berg, and not only by him because this is not theory but fact: 'The similarities observed between the two groups of organisms very often turn out to result not from consanguinity of the groups but from independent development in the same direction.'[22] To put it even more succinctly: the differences are primary, the similarities secondary. It is the direct opposite of Darwin: characteristics do not diverge but *converge*. Is this related to the general bulldozer-like levelling and standardization of the environment for living things on earth? I will permit myself a comparison with languages: there used to be more variety but now there is convergence from several directions.

Another example is from Nikolai Vavilov (1887–1943),[23] who so frequently encountered convergence in his work on selection and classification of plants that he considered it possible to *predict varieties*. For example, in 1917 he found a variety of wheat in the Pamir Mountains which was eligulate at the base of the leaf lamina and confidently predicted that a similar eligulate form must exist also in rye. He found it the following year in the Pamirs. *The homologous series* of cultures.

Why does Berg, and indeed everybody else, keep insouciantly talking about 'development'? Not, as we have said, because there are any criteria for development. You have only to start talking about them for everything to become very unclear. But development – that is, movement to a higher level, the rungs of Aristotle's ladder – is seen intuitively, as clear to the naked eye as the difference between the generations in electronics. Quite a different matter is the difference, say, between the system of electronic instruments and synthesizers of a full musical ensemble and Alexander Vustin who, in one of his works, employs only human whistling and the beating of wood against the wood of a piano.[24] In one sense, it is completely clear at first glance to each and every one that in complexity and sophistication the ensemble is absolutely and unquestionably technically superior to Vustin. The superiority of Vustin, no less absolute and unquestionable, over the musical ensemble is by no means as evident, and the main thing is that it is expressed in apocalyptic, prophetic, biblical, or metaphysical terms that science cannot pin down, such as creating something out of nothing, dauntless individuality, again holiness, partaking of the eternal, that is, of youth.

Using the parameter of complexity–subtlety–sophistication, the hierarchical ladder of beings is obvious; it is less obvious using a different parameter, and it is our direct responsibility, the meaning of our lives, to define that parameter. If we are talking about survival, the survival of the human species is linked to meaningfulness, and there is no reason to suppose things are any different for the rest of the living world, except that there we more often talk about a goal. Meaningfulness is no less important *biologically* than bread. *If there is a failure in the supply of meaningfulness, restoring it takes priority over bread; people literally stop eating in order to force truth out of themselves through hunger.* Conversely, the apparent success of adaptation to circumstances, the security of the bread supply in the era of, for example, the *Titanic*, or today's consumer society, is so emphatically not an indication that the human species is on the right path that it seems to indicate the contrary. At all events, when there is a supply of meaningfulness, bread is somehow forthcoming from somewhere, but the reverse does not hold true. Mining for meaning is biologically more important than anything else for human beings, and it is baffling why that does not go for all of us – and what were those winnings of nature that Goethe spoke of but sunlit shafts of meaning? That makes it clear what we have religion, poetry, and philosophy for.

Unfortunately, we do not find in Berg any clear understanding of teleology, purposefulness. (He says, though, that 'Purposefulness is the fundamental attribute of living beings.'[25]) Here his scientific approach is only too casual, and he can talk about purposefulness the way horticulturalists joke about new varieties: 'The most important condition for breeding a new variety is for it to exist already.'[26] The goal is already there; it can be felt. Artificial selection retrieves, as it were, a mislaid form, cleaning off any impurities. Natural selection, on the contrary, works in favour of impure forms.

But see how easy it is to lapse into triviality, and common sense argues against a crude, barbarous understanding of Darwinism along the lines of 'harass living things with extreme conditions and something interesting will pop up'. Nikolai Chernyshevsky needed no specialized biological knowledge when, signing himself 'An old Transformist', he wrote an article in 1888 on 'The Origin of the Theory of the Beneficence of the Struggle for Life': 'The most common form of natural selection is the extinction of superfluous beings from lack of food. Is it in this case only moribund beings that are subjected to starvation? Is this how a farmer would treat his herd? Would he suppose he could improve it by inhibiting reproduction and starving all his animals?'[27]

In this connection, one's thoughts again return to the Neanderthals. In brain size, the structure of their teeth (the roots were shorter and the canines less differentiated from the other teeth), their wider palate, the jaw more interestingly arranged than that of *Homo sapiens*, they were no worse than us. Perhaps our extermination of the Neanderthals was a consequence of a foolhardy belief in the positive nature of struggle and we made a big mistake which we should now try to rectify through religion, which teaches us that 'we wrestle not against flesh and blood, but against principalities, against powers, against the rulers of the darkness of this world, against spiritual wickedness in high places'.[28]

Although only partial, Berg's immunity to the itch of evolutionism frees up his field of vision to see the primordial forms of nature, its brilliant 'finds' (Goethe), acting at every stage, in addition to all related 'origins'. The evolutionist is distracted from pure phenomenology by a schematic obsession with what came out of what, what is developing into what, what is more progressive than what. It is as if someone in the Russian Federation had a chart detailing the absolute progressiveness of everything made or done in the West that blinded them to good quality in our own country.

Berg speaks confidently about physiological parallels between animals and plants.[29] Certain insectivorous plants have an enzyme similar to pepsin to digest animal food. An analogy has been traced between the pitchers of such plants and the gastric mucosa: both contain zymogen, a proenzyme or inactive precursor of an enzyme, thus what the pancreas secretes is not pepsin but pepsinogen, because if biosynthesis produced pepsin, it would digest proteins in the cells producing it and have the effect of a stomach ulcer. Both animal and carnivorous organisms give a chemical signal with an acid for zymogens and proenzymes to be converted to active enzymes. There is a plant whose pepsin dissolves, for instance, the protein in a hen's egg. Digestion produces peptones from partial hydrolysis of protein, which is used in microbiology laboratories as a nutrient medium. Then, in a second stage, this growth medium undergoes further processing. Higher animals have this complex system for digesting proteins, but not all invertebrates do.

Lecture 21, 10 March 1998

Undeterred by the great distance between these things in the evolution-ary scheme, Berg also notes the kinship of plant chlorophyll with animal haemoglobin. Seventy-five years ago, a reaction to distinguish between male and female blood was discovered. The same reaction also works to distinguish between the male and female in dioecious plants, such as sea buckthorn; maple and nettle are also dioecious.[1] The methods of nature are the same in very different contexts.

Berg was a geographer; we have already seen the attention he paid to the geographical changing of forms. The idea is not new. In antiquity, which we choose to call pagan, the power of place was noticed and generally acknowledged, and local gods served to consolidate and sanctify what today is narrowly understood as 'environmental factors'. The earth is a body in the cosmos, and my own feeling is that there is no reason to be dis-missive of the idea of a bond between the cosmos and particular areas of the earth. If the rotation of the earth, the tilt of its axis, the magnetic field, the orbit of the earth and its distance from the sun have been, so to speak, dictated by the cosmos, then why not the attributes of different places? We should not forget that scientific rigour strictly forbids us to fantasize about things we do not know. What I have said can have only a cleansing sense of liberating us from our insistence on confining the attachment of our heart to the soil of the region of our birth to merely climatic or geological factors. We do not know and cannot know what combination of 'factors' contributes to the temperament of a person on, say, the East European Plain. That means we can resort only to observation and more observa-tion. It is not taboo to link the difference between the social and state structures of mediaeval Moscow and Novgorod to the fact that there was once the boundary of a glacier running between them. There was a glacier in Novgorod; there was none in Moscow. At the very least it makes sense to remember that. During elections in France, historians drew attention to a dividing line between supporters of left-wing as against right-wing poli-tics which ran precisely where, during the Roman Empire, there had been a border between two of their provinces. The crucial thing here is to steer clear of conjecture. Only then will our eyes be open to look for continuous, ongoing signals and processes at work in the nature of things where, according to our supposedly scientific concepts, there are no grounds to look for them.

An example, one of many in Berg, of morphological parallelism (from observations by other naturalists): in the mountains of the Samarkand region, a water scavenger beetle is found which differs strikingly in appearance from other such beetles: its whole surface is coarsely muricate, almost completely without lustre, with the pronotum narrowing towards the rear whereas, in all other water beetles, it broadens. In the same area, another water beetle is found, but from a completely different family, not a water scavenger but a diving beetle, with the same unusual feature. Berg supports the observation of A.P. Semyonov, whose 1900 study he is quoting, of a 'tendency in some species, regardless of their genetic proximity, under the influence of the sum of analogous or identical conditions of existence to develop in the same direction, acquiring (progressively or regressively) a set of common characteristics'.[2] In cases like this, I really want to catch the researcher by his coat-tails and tell him to loosen up with all this 'conditions of existence', 'under the influence of the sum of' which the animals live and develop. He should not feel under any obligation to define the conditions under which water beetles change in a particular way in the mountains of Central Asia. Ultimately we do not know why everything is as it is. The causes are just our hypothesis, and a water beetle is not a hypothesis. We would do better to ask *it*. It is better placed to tell us about its environment, and any 'sum of analogous conditions' will always be our own construct. Our Russian people are much affected by the climate of the East European Plain, but they can tell us more about the attributes of the plain than the attributes of the climate can tell us about them.

I would urge: do not be seduced by the simplicity of an explanation, when, for example, species of lizards and beetles and wasps that dig in the sand, moles and desert gophers have adaptations for living in the desert, horn serrations or whiskery feet to use like brushes or brooms, the brushes attached to various parts of their feet or legs. The camel's 'foot with a sole', the beetles with flattened shins, the sand cockroach with spiky shins. All these adaptations are, of course, for pushing sand aside, but not only for that. Later we shall say that the amount of play, of irrational mimicry and multifarious inventiveness in the modifications of animals is just so great that it is not unreasonable to say that living beings go looking for and seek out excuses to exercise their inventiveness. They do so in much the same way an artist, for no obvious reason, may go looking for difficulties, out into the desert to paint landscapes there. What a primitive notion that their environment is as alien to animals as it is to a modern European! That is quite clearly not the case. It is not external or alien to human beings either, only they have yet to work that out.

Berg talks interestingly about such 'aesthetic', playful causes of mutability in his researches into mimicry. I would only take issue with Chernyshevsky, with whom Berg agrees on the subject of morphological parallelism, to make one remark in defence of Darwin. Berg notices a mental similarity in the way of life and instincts which appear to be developed quite independently in such social creatures as termites, ants, bees, wasps, and humans.[3] Termites and ants, by the way, belong to entirely different groups, and yet African termites and South American ants have, clearly independently, invented fungus nurseries, parks, or plantations. Plainly human beings behave in the same way. To create their fungus gardens, South American ants climb trees, cut leaves up there, and bring them down to their nest. The termites on another continent do the same, and also transport the leaves in columns, escorted by soldier ants. The method of cutting the leaves and carrying them back is the same for the ants and termites, but Berg feels obliged to add to this description of ants – or humans? – that the soldiers escorting the worker ants are by no means just on parade. The ants may be eaten by bears, anteaters, badgers, or birds, but their worst enemies are other ants. They are at war every hour of the day, everywhere, singly and anthill against anthill. Typically, each anthill has its own hunting territory. An ant straying into some other ant's domain is immediately attacked. At the border between territories, there is something like a no-man's-land. If adversaries meet, they open their jaws and depart, each back to their own side. If there are insufficient pickings and the nests are too closely packed, groups of ants will attack each other and a war breaks out. 'For some ants, mutual slaughter takes place on a regular basis as part of a work routine for extermination of their excessively proliferating fellow ants.'[4]

We have not the slightest reason to doubt the seriousness of Marikovsky's observations of the ants, but neither have we any way to separate out from them his sense of how life develops, his philosophy of life. It is entirely possible that wars between the ant colonies are not only for the purpose of protecting the territory of one colony against another. Nothing in nature is unambiguous, and we can extend to it what Freud said about the images of the unconscious: 'Keep looking! These images never have fewer than three meanings.' We have no defence against the observing biologist when, as perhaps in the case of the observer of ants, for some reason, maybe thinking about international relations at the time of the Cold War, he is inclined to emphasize the struggle for life.

All description is dependent on the approach being used by the observer. The approach may be modified as the description proceeds, but the description always comes later, it is always preceded by the choice of approach. An additional difficulty is that the approach is not consciously acquired first, so that the guided eye of the researcher, aware of its bias, could then go on to conduct its observation of its 'object'. Invariably, *together* with the attraction of the thing drawing attention to itself, the eyes of the observer somehow just 'naturally' find themselves gazing through those particular lenses, and the pull of the object attracting attention is usually so great that the approach seems just to arrive from somewhere of its own accord. This is effectively a demonstration of Lamarck's principle that when life needs an organ, it creates it. The optic is inseparable from the thing observed, it is a function of it. Let us therefore clarify our claim against the observer of the ants: we are concerned that he is using optics unrelated to what he is observing, that he has a pre-selected grid of coordinates.

Before embarking on the topic of mimicry, for which we shall have to remember what we have said in earlier courses about mimesis, we need to take stock, to make an inventory. Where do we stand and what do we have to hand? We are standing in the forest and would do better, as I said the time before last, to imagine that we never left the primaeval jungle and can see no further than what is immediately around us. The transparency provided by television and computers is illusory, all its perspectives are charted only on an artificial surface. I am going to read from *Infinite in All Directions* by Freeman Dyson, a physicist and biologist born in 1923 in a family of musicians in the United Kingdom who subsequently took American citizenship.[5] (The title of the book is taken from a phrase used by Emil Wiechert. The 'Wiechert–Gutenberg discontinuity' is observed when the speed of seismic waves from an earthquake slows dramatically at a depth of 2,900 km. This results from an almost twofold increase in the density of the earth, presumably at the transition from the earth's mantle to its metallic core. Wiechert said in 1896, 'The universe is infinite in all directions, not only above us in the large but also below us in the small.'[6] When Leibniz says that, we call it metaphysics; when a physicist and chemist does, we are more inclined to believe it because it is 'science'.) I will read from Freeman Dyson:

Sometimes as I listen to the conversations of my young colleagues at Princeton, I feel I am lost in a rain forest, with insects and birds and flowers growing all around me in intricate profusion, growing too abundantly for my sixty-year-old brain to comprehend. But the young people are at home in the rain forest and walk confidently along trails which to me are almost invisible. They have their own discipline, different from the discipline which I was taught forty years ago [Dyson studied under J. Robert Oppenheimer (1904–67) at Princeton, where Nina Braginskaya is now teaching, *Bibikhin*], but still as strict in its way as mine. They are not wandering aimlessly. They are explorers, mapping out the ground, finding the ways that will lead them out of the jungle up to the mountain peaks.[7]

For Dyson, science moves, but not in such a way that the jungle will become less and less dense, or that when the present generation gets out of the jungle to the sunlit peaks, the generation following will not still be in the forest. When I said that we are now, as always, in the jungle, that could be considered to be metaphysics, but when Freeman Dyson says it, we must consider it science.

Let us look around briefly and cursorily at where we stand in this forest. We have already noted that the boundary between physics and biology has gone. The ground beneath our feet has gone completely, because mathematical physics really has despaired of understanding elementary particles comparable in size to the atom, and is devoting major effort to the theory of superstrings.

The distinguishing feature of superstring theory is the postulate that elementary particles are not mere points in space but have metric extension. The characteristic metric dimension is given as a certain combination of the three most fundamental constants of nature: (1) Planck's constant h (named after the German physicist Max Planck, the founder of quantum physics), (2) the speed of light c, and (3) the universal gravitational constant G. The combination, called the Planck length $(Gh/c)\{sup1/2\}$, equals roughly $10\{-33\}$ cm, far smaller than the distances to which elementary particles can be probed in particle accelerators on Earth.[8]

That is, theory – or perhaps superstrings should more accurately be called a hypothesis – has again gone off into the unobservable because, proportionately, superstrings are as small, compared with the size of the atom, as the atom is small compared with the size of the solar system.

A type of theory of particle physics that treats elementary particles as extended one-dimensional 'string-like' objects rather than as the dimensionless points in space-time used in other theories. Superstring theories became popular during the 1980s when Michael Green of Queen Mary College, London, and John Schwarz of the California Institute of Technology showed that certain types of such theories might provide a fully self-consistent quantum theory that describes gravity as well as the weak, strong, and electromagnetic forces. The development of such a unified quantum theory is a major goal in theoretical particle physics, but usually the inclusion of gravity has led to intractable problems with infinite quantities in the calculations. The basic entities in superstring theory are one-dimensional massless strings only 10 {sup -33} cm long. (This distance is the so-called Planck length, at which quantum effects in gravity can no longer be ignored.) The strings vibrate, and each different mode of vibration corresponds to a different particle.[9]

Speaking very approximately, the lack of mass in superstrings is interesting from the perspective of the new interest that physics is showing in the vacuum (the void, the *néant*) and in the fact that for the creation of the world a vacuum, again speaking very approximately, was sufficient. Four-dimensionality, from the viewpoint of the string hypothesis, is an illusion. We need to be talking about ten-dimensionality, if not twenty-six-dimensionality.

If the superstring hypothesis, or theory, begins to work, it will be completely meaningless to talk about the complexity or simplicity or elementariness of the molecules of life: in the depths of each, there will be found just as much of everything as they need. If the idea of the physicist John Wheeler (b. 1911) is correct, the boundary between organic and inorganic will become purely arbitrary. Wheeler and Bohr wrote *The Mechanism of Nuclear Fission* (1939), a seminal treatise that singled out uranium-235 for use in the development of an atomic bomb.[10] It indicates that the structures of physical nature are *not* primary; they are, as it were, semi-statistical generalizations. 'Individual events. Events beyond law. Events so numerous and so uncoordinated that, flaunting their freedom from formula, they yet fabricate firm form.'[11] Wheeler goes on,

> It is preposterous to think of the laws of physics as installed by a Swiss watchmaker to endure from everlasting to everlasting when we know that the universe began with a big bang. The laws must have come into being. Therefore they could not have been always a hundred percent accurate. That means that they are derivative, not primary.... Of all strange features of the universe, none are stranger than these: time is transcended, laws are mutable, and observer-participancy matters.

Wheeler adds, 'The universe is a self-excited circuit.'[12] That means, in our terms, that it is an *automaton*.

Another incursion of physics into biology comes from astronomy. On earth we find craters like those made on the moon by comets, only eroded. Some craters may be hidden in the ocean. A large comet, like that named after Edmund Halley (English astronomer and geophysicist, 1656–1742), which reappears every seventy-six years or so and has a diameter of around 15 km, would leave a crater about 150 km in diameter. There are comets, great agglomerations of ice, of up to 50 km in diameter. A comet one-tenth that size made a crater in the middle of which the town of Nördlingen nestles in Bavaria, surrounded by a perfect circle of hills which were once the edge of the crater. Most important for us are not these changes to the earth's geography but the dust storms after their impact. The limestone in which fossils are found is punctuated by a thin layer of clay which has all the attributes of settled dust. This overlay corresponds in time exactly to the disappearance of a large proportion of fossil remains. Above the clay layer, new and different fossils appear.

Typically, when an elegant theory, to be completely secure, could do with a fact from nature, nature withholds it. Nobody has yet found the crater of the giant comet that caused the biological catastrophe 65 million years ago, which, you will remember, is considered the end of the Mesozoic and beginning of the Cainozoic eras, an important moment that saw the swift and total extinction of the dinosaurs, leaving not a single species, and at the same time of a host of other, especially marine, creatures. Biologists talk about a 'mass extinction'. One hears talk of a constant: biological disasters befall every 26 million years. There is an associated theory of 'comet showers' with the same periodicity. Comets are stored up in the cloud named after Jan Oort (1900–92, Netherlands), who first published about it in 1950.[13] Victor Safronov, a Russian, later suggested that the Oort cloud was the remains of the raw material from which all the planets coalesced.[14]

The detritus that falls on the earth at present, a few meteorites per year, hardly seems sufficient to form a planet in the foreseeable future, so we have to conjecture this constant and suppose that every 26 million years suddenly, within one or two million years, comets shower down like rain from the sky. Let us assume that does happen, that there is this constant. (There is evidence to that effect, although not all biologists and geologists are persuaded.) Then what happens? A body passes close to the Oort cloud and pulls, rips out at least a part of it, or destabilizes the movement of all its comets. The irregular approach of the sun to one or other of the stars would not suffice. There must be some star gravitationally bound to the sun. Two Dutchmen, Piet Hut and Rich Muller, suggested looking for this partner sun 2.5 light-years away, but in which direction? It might not be bright enough to be visible through a telescope. Hut has, however, already given it a name: Nemesis. He assumes it has an elongated orbit, as binary stars often do, and that once in every 26 million years when it is closest to the sun it disturbs the orbits of comets and causes a comet shower. The last period of major extinction of life and formation of craters was about 13 million years ago, so that Nemesis would presently be at its furthest away from us. Hut and Muller named the star Nemesis 'after the Greek goddess who relentlessly persecutes the excessively rich, proud and powerful'.[15] You know, this is a new twist on Darwinism. Nemesis approaches and mercilessly thins out life on earth as a gardener might thin trees, but precisely *adaptation* to the conditions of life on earth means that those who have too comfortably found themselves ecological niches will become extinct! In order to survive the thinning out, it is essential not to have adapted too much, not to have become too specialized, still to be open to change and adaptation. It would seem that human beings, with all their physical vulnerability and lack of adaptation to life in nature in the raw, are best suited to surviving such a situation. As Dyson writes, 'We thrive on ice ages and environmental catastrophes. Comet showers must have been one of the major forces that drove our evolution and made us what we are.'[16]

One further fact from astronomy also extends our forest far beyond the limits of earth, because what I want to say concerns the inventiveness of nature. Its inventiveness is beyond belief: it is insane. Nature, like a conjuror, seems to be performing in front of us, showing us the most fantastic tricks, or rather performing them on itself, like an acrobat putting on a show exclusively for himself. Here is just one example. The brain of a caterpillar is a speck of neurons a few millimetres in length. The migratory monarch butterfly has a program there in accordance with which it eats the leaves of a particular plant, then hangs by its tail, starts pupating, squeezes itself with great difficulty into a rigid chrysalis, emerges from the pupa, dries out, takes to the sky, and flies from America to Mexico, somehow already knowing the several thousand kilometres of its route. How that is recorded in its DNA, how it does this, we are baffled. We would like to know.

Much of this is known, but think about it: let us assume we can compare a living being with a computer. The DN acid is the software, protein is the hardware; the programs, texts, are transmitted by those acids like floppy disks, the servicing of this data chemistry is performed by proteins. But why there are these two in nature is an old question.

Francis Crick was so convinced of the rigidity of this division into twos – two functions, two natures in one nature – that in 1957 he formulated the 'central dogma of molecular biology'. 'The Central Dogma. This states that once "information" has passed into protein *it cannot get out again*. [An impenetrable border! *Bibikhin*.] In more detail, the transfer of information from nucleic acid to nucleic acid, or from nucleic acid to protein may be possible, but transfer from protein to protein, or from protein to nucleic acid is impossible.'[17]

This realization that nature has fantastic capabilities does not seem to require any specialized knowledge. Christiaan Huygens (1629–95), not as an expert in mechanics and optics but simply as a highly intelligent human being, wrote, 'A Man that is of Copernicus's Opinion, that this Earth of ours is a Planet, carry'd round and enlighten'd by the Sun, like the rest of the Planets, cannot but sometimes think, that it's not improbable that the rest of the Planets have their Dress and Furniture, and perhaps their Inhabitants too as well as this Earth of ours.'[18] That is, if life has problems, they are not with its arising, proliferation, and sustenance. With what then are they? With something of the same sort as the problems that bedevil us today: like good and evil.

This is from the very beginning of Huygens's *Cosmotheoros*, which he gave instructions should be printed only after his death. Newton had similar thoughts he had no intention of seeing printed at all, and kept them locked in a big black trunk. His manuscripts about life in the cosmos seem not to have been published to this day and are in the library of the Hebrew University in Jerusalem.

As all regions below are replenished with living creatures (not only the Earth with Beasts, and Sea with Fishes and the Air with Fowls and Insects, but also standing waters, vinegar, the bodies and blood of Animals and other juices with innumerable living creatures too small to be seen without the help of magnifying Glasses) so may the heavens above be replenished with beings whose nature we do not understand. He that shall well consider the strange and wonderful nature of life and the frame of Animals, will think nothing beyond the possibility of nature, nothing too hard for the omnipotent power of God. And as the planets remain in their orbs, so may any other bodies subsist at any distance from the earth, and much more may beings, who have a sufficient power of self motion, move whether they will, place them-selves where they will and continue in any regions of the heaven whatever, there to enjoy the society of one another, and by their messengers or Angels to rule the earth and converse with the remotest regions. Thus may the whole heavens or any part thereof whatever be the habitation of the Blessed, and at the same time the earth be subject to their dominion. And to have thus the liberty and dominion of the whole heavens and the choice of the happiest places for abode seems a greater happiness than to be confined to any one place whatever.[19]

The reason why life most probably is transported all over the universe is because that is more fun, more sociable, more joyful. Joy, bliss, are seen as the purpose of life. Why would life not be omnipotent if even the small corner of it that we see is so awe-inspiring?

Interplanetary spaceships, a lack of imagination when it seems that life must need transportation, relate to a period of positivist scientism which restricted life to the sphere of the visible. But if there is life in the water, in the earth, in the air, why should it not be after its own fashion in space, wherever it fancies? Using inanimate ships is the lot of technology, which lags behind nature (a degenerate automaton). To rise into the air, humans need an apparatus, but a bird is its own apparatus. Life should not be able to move through space only *on* something, but directly, in its own living form. Perhaps Newton laid his manuscripts in that black trunk as a prophecy for the future. Biology and cosmology will converge. Today many notable astronomers are working on the issue of life in space. Francis Crick, who co-modelled the DNA double helix, believes in directed panspermia. Dyson tells us, 'A few years ago I received a letter from him saying, "I am still interested in the idea of Directed Panspermia."'[20]

Panspermia, the idea that microorganisms, spores, are carried by the solar wind or meteorites through the universe is an old idea of Svante Arrhenius, the Swedish physical chemist (1859–1927). When it became clear that direct radiation kills living beings, people began to feel safe and secure in asserting that nothing could either live in space or be transported through the heavens. We, however, are becoming increasingly used to the strange principle that if life needs something, then … *Directed* Panspermia does not necessarily mean that teams of intelligent beings are sending parcels of microorganisms to planets with an atmosphere. The direction here could be of the order of the actions of Sophia, as unbelievable, say, as that a butterfly newly emerged from its cocoon might make a thousand-kilometre flight.

What speaks in favour of life having the ability to scatter itself in the form of a seed of some description to different parts of the galaxy is our repeated experience of an intimate relationship with the stars, an elusive sense of threads stretching out from them. In these conjectures, however, what is vital is not to distort the purity of knowledge, not to lose awareness of our ignorance. We do not *know* how seeds might be transported or whether they are transported in space. Neither, however, do we know for sure that there is no way they could be transported. We will do better to go along with what chemist Michael Polanyi said in 1951–2: 'This universe is still dead, but it already has the capacity of coming to life.'[21] He was speaking of the universe as we observe it.

Mathematics – precisely to the extent to which it is not applied but pure mathematics, not solving set problems but unfolding its harmonies – has succeeded in thus intuiting the structures of what exists. The status of mathematics as a whole tells us about the world, about what exists as a whole. According to an important theorem proved by the twenty-five-year-old Kurt Gödel from Austria in 1931, no matter how you define a finite number of mathematical axioms and procedures (and how could we set an infinite number of axioms?), there will always remain meaningful mathematical expressions that are not deducible or explicable from these axioms. Many people were upset by this; there had been hopes of finding an algorithm to verify or falsify *any* mathematical expression. It transpired there was no such universal algorithm. This means that no development or elaboration of mathematics will exhaust conceivable and meaningful mathematical formulae. If mathematics is as open as that, then, judging by a long since noted parallelism, physics will be also.

Let us note the sole occupation of science, taking into account and trumping all its specialization, in spite of it. As Freeman Dyson has well formulated this, 'I am concerned with the origin of life as a scientific problem, not as a philosophical or theological problem. The problem is to find out what happened.'[22] Note that the question is not whether something has or has not yet happened. That is not what science considers. It begins when it is clear that something challenging has happened. We have the result of what happened and here it is: life. Now that it has happened, we need to understand what happened and how, much as we might set about investigating a crime. What adds spice to the situation is that an extraordinary event is truly a trans-gression, a stepping beyond a limit, beyond a comfort zone; ex-sistence, 'taking a stand outside'. It is like a gift. Imagine someone waking up to find a gift beside them. That is the situation of awakened science. If you like, it has a real a priori to deal with: the human species. Or 'all-is-so'; *So-sein, haecceitas*, the suchness of everything. But there is something wrong with this suchness: with the fact that everything is *so*, something is wrong! It is not quite as it should be. (Or perhaps it is and science is just complicating everything.) We need to work out what is going on, and why we need all this.

Dyson spoke about the rain forest in relation to proliferating particles and theoretical models in modern physics. 'The metaphor is impressionistic, but it is not altogether misleading…. I shall use metaphor again to describe the chemical architecture of life.'[23] Life: jungle, rain forest, but inside is a rigorous distinction. The theory of *two* lives. Emerging from the metric domain was accomplished here long ago. 'Instead of describing nature with mechanical models, physicists now describe it with infinite-dimensional spaces and other even more esoteric mathematical concepts.'[24]

But look at this: the more surely schemes collapse, the more everything proves to be jungle and rain forest, the more distinctly a clear difference emerges between, crudely speaking, nutrition and reproduction, proteins and nucleic acids. What is involved in growth in the organism serves expansion of the living being and not necessarily mere copying, duplication, and backing up for conservation. This is an important distinction. The two processes are so different that a clear question arises as to whether life is one thing or two. That is the extent to which copying and duplicating have been inculcated and become embedded in the process of simple expansion of life and, it is not too much to say, are parasitic on it. Is this not reminiscent of a slave-owning society?

It is interesting that in laboratory experiments (which in the past meant experiments with frogs) it has proved convenient to view these functions separately, to deal with organisms which have been *released from the obligation* of providing themselves with food and are engaged only in replicating themselves. Max Delbrück (b. 1906), who moved in 1937 to the USA, a geneticist and virologist, was awarded the Nobel Prize in 1969 for his work with bacteriophages, bacteria eaters which are now the classical guinea pigs in molecular genetics.[25] These are viruses of bacteria; bacteria are their food. They have virtually nothing in them apart from their reproductive equipment and are hence *almost* a stripped-bare genetic apparatus. A completely bare genetic apparatus is a molecule of ribonucleic acid, RNA. In the German Federal Republic, Manfred Eigen (b. 1927), too, was awarded a Nobel Prize in 1967 for, among other things, observing the in vitro propagation of RNA.[26] In both these cases and others like them we should note that in experiments reproduction and nutrition are somehow independent of each other.

Well familiar with Delbrück's experiments, Erwin Schrödinger (1887–1961) was awarded the Nobel Prize essentially for his contribution to theoretical physics (in parallel with the matrix formalism of Werner Heisenberg). On one occasion, he alarmed Heisenberg by proposing that he might be wrong and demonstrated that quantum leaps can also be viewed as waves and, accordingly, mathematically formalized. Both formalizations subsequently proved to be identical. In 1943, Schrödinger gave an important series of lectures in Ireland on 'What is life?'[27] These were translated shortly afterwards into Russian. He linked the replication, reproduction, and duplication of cells with strict conservation of the original with the quantum-mechanical stability of molecular structures, thereby setting a task for biologists for decades ahead to find out what kind of molecules and structures could deliver that stability. He explained metabolism as the ability of a living cell to extract free energy from the environment in accordance with the laws of thermodynamics. This was the era of structuralism. Structuralism was rife in linguistics and literary studies. Replication clearly interested Schrödinger more than metabolism. This is a negative conclusion: manifest bias in favour of replication. This was in fact true also of Delbrück when he focused his attention on the bacteriophage, a purely parasitic organism in which the metabolic function had disappeared and only the replicative, self-reproducing function had developed. But, it might be argued, this is a degenerative and very specific form of life. Or may it perhaps be the case that *all* life is structured in this way, that it is divided into two functions? We recall Famintsyn and Kozo-Polyansky, who proposed that living organisms should always be viewed as a symbiosis. Is the replicating mechanism parasitic on the substratum, the protein which delivers metabolism? Unquestionably. Does that mean that life is *two* things?

Lecture 22, 17 March 1998

There is a view that early life only expanded and did not replicate. We have already talked about this. The cell would simply divide, both descendant cells receiving equal shares of the composition of the parent cell. That is not observed today: neither in cyanobacteria, which are prokaryotes, otherwise known as Monera, although they do not have a chromosomal apparatus and reproduce asexually by dividing; nor in other prokaryotes which have no distinct cell nucleus, but in which, after cell division, the complete molecular structure of the mother cell is restored in its descendant cells. But if we can now observe *within* a cell molecules delaminating and replicating without the cells replicating or reproducing, then why could not early beings multiply without replication, creating more and more new structures in the course of their expansion – perhaps like in a kaleidoscope? For those living beings, exact self-replication was not the goal. The bias of modern biology towards genetics, when life itself is almost equated with the ability to replicate and copy itself, needs to be corrected. The copying mechanism is parasitic on the metabolic mechanism; it is secondary and, strictly speaking, not essential for life. 'Hosts must exist before there can be parasites. Somebody must eat and grow to provide a home for those who only replicate.'[1]

Another mathematician, John (János) von Neumann (1903–57), from Austria-Hungary, who from 1930 lived in the United States and was a theoretician of automata (*The General and Logical Theory of Automata*),[2] corrected Schrödinger's overemphasis on stable, self-reproducing systems: life is *two* things, metabolism and copying, and, logically at least, they are separate. Only logically? Or did life begin twice, once from proteins, with the protein creatures existing independently for a long time, perhaps mutable like Stanisław Lem's *Solaris*, eating, growing, and developing, before life began a second time and the nucleic acids of creatures came to parasitize the protein creatures?

For the present, that is only a hypothesis. I do not think it will serve us as anything more than a reminder of where we have got to on our progress. The forest has a dual nature, Plato's *khora (receptacle)*, the formless recipient of forms, and the *idea*, the hard, eternal form. We shall get back to philosophy; for now we are making an inventory, browsing the ideas of biologists.

It is argued that the dual structure of life is blindingly obvious from the fact that every organism is divided into hardware and a program, hardware and software. Edward Wilson: 'Each living form [is] ... a product of ... interaction between genes and environment.'[3]

When one reads about the *in vitro* experiments with RNA (the best known in the 1960s by Manfred Eigen, whom we have mentioned, and by Leslie Orgel in the second half of the 1980s), various bits and pieces of Aristotle immediately come to mind, but I will not say which or how. In a protein nutrient medium – the protein serves as a catalyst – the four base nucleotides are dissolved: adenine, guanine, cytosine, uracil (we need not mention sugar ribose), the building blocks, as it were, from which the RNA molecule is formed, the one which in the cells of all living organisms carries out the genetic instructions. One *single* RNA molecule yields in one hour or two, duplicating every two to three minutes, 10^{14} identical molecules.

But what if there is *not a single* RNA molecule in the test tube: that is, there is nothing to copy, although all the necessary nucleotides are in place? There is no sample, but will the RNA components guess how to join up? It takes them a while, and differs at different times, but within two or three hours there will suddenly be an RNA molecule there; the four building brick nucleotides having worked out how to bind themselves chemically. They have been slow, it has taken some time, but once that molecule has appeared it immediately starts to multiply at that same breathtaking speed. Now everything is straightforward, with each new molecule stamping out more of its ilk from the elements. What is even more interesting: the nucleotides do not always join up identically: RNA mutants appear.

So what is this? Spontaneous generation of life from not-yet-life? Not quite. The proteins in the test tube are, after all, extracts of living matter. It is, if you like, micro-cloning, a mini-sheep from a single cell and, moreover, capable of reproduction; the protein catalyst tells the nucleotides what to do. I think this goes against Francis Crick's 'dogma' that once information has gone into a protein it cannot come back out into the nucleic acid. I am not sure what to do about this. Most probably the dogma is correct, judging by how badly and slowly the protein gives the command to the nucleotides to form themselves into a molecule; but not absolutely. The cell is not a dogmatist and will not resist too stubbornly if it has to take on what is clearly the job of something else. However, no one has yet managed to get a self-reproducing molecule without the use of something already alive.

Life is always a symbiosis, that is, a duality. So said Oken, Famintsyn, and, in the nineteenth century, Kozo-Polyansky. That life is dual is also suggested by the symbiosis that Lynn Margulis was interestingly working on. Margulis believes in *global* symbiosis. She seems to have begun publishing only in the 1980s and is best known to journalists because of her Gaia hypothesis that the earth is a live being.

The close interrelation between life and its environment, and its philosophical significance, was noted by the British chemist James E. Lovelock and the American biologist Lynn Margulis. They called this idea of complementary evolution of life and environment the Gaia hypothesis after Gaia, the ancient Greek goddess of the earth. As Lovelock put it, this is 'a new insight into the interactions between the living and the inorganic parts of the planet. From this has arisen the hypothesis, the model, in which the earth's living matter, air, oceans, and land surface form a complex system which can be seen as a single organism and which has the capacity to keep our planet a fit place for life.' The Gaia hypothesis is highly controversial because it intimates that individual species (e.g., ancient anaerobic bacteria, released oxygen into the atmosphere to enable aerobes to breathe, but this was a noble suicide, because some strict, obligate anaerobes can thrive only in the absence of oxygen) might sacrifice themselves for the benefit of all living things.[4]

In favour of the Gaia hypothesis is the question of how the earth has managed to look after itself.

The Gaia hypothesis postulates that the physical conditions of the earth's surface, oceans, and atmosphere have been made fit and comfortable for life and have been maintained in this state by the biota themselves. Evidence includes the relatively constant temperature of the earth's surface that has been maintained for the past 3.5 billion years despite a 25 percent increase in energy coming from the Sun during that period. The remarkable constancy of the earth's oceanic and atmospheric chemistry for the past 500 million years also is invoked to support this theory.[5]

But now, talking about *two* lives, we need to see how Margulis and others continued the idea of symbiosis, which we have so far followed only from Oken to Kozo-Polyansky. According to Margulis also, parasitism and symbiosis have been drivers of progress and increased complexity of cells. Are you remembering that for Famintsyn and Kozo-Polyansky even the nucleus came into the cell from outside? Margulis found clear experimental confirmation for cases to support her view that most of the internal structures of cells did not originate within the cells but are descended from independent living creatures which invaded the cells from outside like carriers of an infectious disease. Her book *Symbiosis in Cell Evolution* summarizes the evidence up to 1981. According to Margulis, the invading creatures and their hosts gradually evolved into a relationship of mutual dependence, so that the erstwhile disease organism became by degrees a chronic parasite, a symbiotic partner, and finally an indispensable part of the substance of the host.[6]

Foreign invasion and a fierce struggle. The cell wants to preserve itself and so does the virus from outside it. *Through disease* a new form is created. It seems likely that the earliest and most successful parasites in cells were the nucleic acids – if it is true that the first living beings were able to eat but had no genetic apparatus.[7]

It is interesting that the parasites, in this hypothesis, actually emerged from proteins themselves, in much the same manner that the RNA molecule which had not been there emerged in Manfred Eigen's test tube. Again, I will not even say how reminiscent this is of Aristotle.

Appearing to support the view that in the early stages of development life was able, at one point, to do without any mechanism of copying is the theory of genetic drift, whose principal author is Motoo Kimura, director of a biological institute near Fujiyama, between Tokyo and Kyoto. This, too, is work that dates from the 1980s. Kimura built a working mathematical model of the behaviour of populations of molecular living beings. He attaches great – perhaps unduly great – value to statistical diffusion, genetic drift of a population, and considers this to be more important for the formation of species than Darwinian natural selection. Perhaps precisely when the mechanisms of strict copying had not yet, conjecturally, become established.

It is important always to bear in mind what the *job* is of scientific biological study of the origin of life, the origin of species, the constitution of organisms, and the structure of the genetic mechanism: it is the work of the researcher as detective, a seeker galvanized by an event, an occurrence. Something has clearly happened and the task is to find out what has occurred and how. We seem already to know *what*: around us is a self-moving automaton, of which we are a part; but this manifest *what* is itself so weird that we ask again and again: what is it? The researcher asks, what is self-movement? How did it arise and how does it work? Edward Wilson: genes are only for procreation of the species, but what is the species for? Life has no purpose. All right, then, life has no purpose, perfectly true, but in itself, as if it has somehow been thrown here from somewhere, perhaps from outer space, it is just so challenging, so glaringly inexplicable, that it is absolutely guaranteed to enthral, like an adventure story or a crime novel, any scientist, and not least Wilson himself. Of course, an event of this magnitude brings with it a different kind of concern: what now? What do we do, how do we behave? As I see it, these are two different and fundamental approaches to consider: some are busy working out what happened; others are thinking about what needs to be done as a result of what happened.

It is not difficult to see how easy, how natural, it is in the midst of all this highly scientific research to lose sight of the main point. And the main point is: why are we so exercised over what happened? The answer – that we are exercised about it because what happened was *us* – is inadequate. While we were originating, we were not there, or we were but do not remember now whether we were and if so how. Why have we only now become self-aware, only now become seriously exercised about what happened and launched this two-pronged science, one aspect of which is examining what happened, while the other is considering what to do now? The answer, which again seems so natural and is generally accepted, which we constantly hear repeated – that then we were children, growing up unaware of anything, but now we are adults who should take responsibility for their further development – is also inadequate. There is no point in all this talk, all these foolish discussions: it is obvious that we will not be able to make things better than they already were when we were not there (or were there but do not remember how). We stumble and err at every step and our most cherished aspiration is to read what is written in DNA and somehow once more be part of that confident, beautiful, infallible world (perhaps not quite as infallible as Goethe thought, but nevertheless enviable and amazing), that success of nature.

At this point, we discover something strange and important: since we have failed to find answers to the riddles posed by nature, we may not be recognizing where and how it is working *today*. Its ways are plainly not those of the scientists investigating it, but it may, unbeknownst to them, be continuing its unrecognized work through them. We are exercised and curious, we research, seeking explanations, and even those who are not curious are affected. People behave, we say, irrationally, insolently, bizarrely, barbarically, and, at the same time, show no interest in investigating nature. We cannot, however, be sure that behaviour we find incomprehensible may not be in response to the demands of nature. To this day we do not know what happened, so we do not know what is happening today. *We should never forget even as we are doing something, even, for instance, studying the ways in which nature acts, that nature is itself doing something in us and through us.*[8]

Science studies the automaton of nature, and there is no reason to suppose that it will not discover its secrets. We do not know, however, whether science itself will then have to change.

Philosophy, poetry, art, music, and religion – we need to seek out within these spheres the things and people who teach how the complete human being should behave towards the automaton of nature, the world we live in; and we have no reason to suppose there is something wrong with what philosophy, music, and religion teach or the way they teach it, rather than that we are just mediocre pupils.

From this two major conclusions follow:

- science may have forgotten to ask why it has lapsed into the approach of the researcher and engineer to what happened;
- science may have forgotten to learn from philosophy and music how to behave towards the automaton.

I shall admit that all this is something I feel strongly about: the automaton as currently used is a giving up in exasperation just like the concept of the limit in modern times: when there was not enough classical patience and endless steadfastness to deal with the infinitely small, we imposed a limit on the paradoxes of Zeno. In the same way, the automaton is a giving up in perhaps analogous exasperation: people could not wait for the *true* automaton to be developed. A replacement for the automaton of the horse, integrated in the 'self-exciting circuit' of the world (John Wheeler, cosmology), is the automobile, dependent on a program and not integrated into the world.

If researchers have something in their hands, they should be able to analyse and understand it. In nature, everything can be analysed, down to what it is made of and what it is for. Job done. An interesting feature of the actions of nature is that failing to work out what things are made of and what they are for results, perhaps, not from ever-increasing complexity but rather from ever-increasing simplicity. Take the origination of life on earth: organic molecules in space become detectable by radio telescopes, and these register their presence in various places in space; geochemists find them in carboniferous meteorites. Right. No problem about where life on earth came from then: it is scattered all over the place, at least in our galaxy. But then we face the question again of how it got there.

In 1982, Alexander Graham Cairns-Smith proposed a theory of the mineral origin of life from clay: microscopic crystals of minerals contained in ordinary clay could serve as initial genetic material without nucleic acids. Crystallites in clay consist of a regular lattice with an orderly arrangement of locations for atoms but an irregular distribution of metals such as aluminium, magnesium, and others. A crystallite in clay has the appearance of a platelet. In nature, this platelet is surrounded by water which has a slurry of elementary organic, carbonaceous molecules. These are not in themselves any rarity. Carbon combines readily with most other atoms, and is found in meteorites. Organic molecules come into contact with the crystallite, which serves as a catalyst, not only for one reaction but several, depending on which atoms are located in the lattice. The crystallite can induce metabolism in organic molecules, and also replicate data it carries within itself, as the organic molecules it has formed peel off from it. That is, it can perform both the functions of RNA. Primordial life on clay, millions of years of protein, and only after that did life originate for a second time in what Cairns-Smith calls a 'genetic takeover', the genetic coup or usurpation when nucleic acids became the replicative apparatus, rather than crystallites in clay, and all that earlier life based on clay was, most probably, eaten. If this theory proves correct, and it has not yet been experimentally verified, what are we to make of the myths about the creation of humans out of clay? They are a visionary dream, our direct mimetic participation in Sophia.

What life came from is thus a mystery not because of the complexity of the phenomenon, which is as simple as cosmic dust or clay; the problem is of the same order as trying to guess what creates the genius in the music of Mozart, which is, after all, much like that of Salieri.[9] Now for the second half of the first question, *how* life works. Again, the difficulty is not in the complexity of its arrangement, because the double helix of DNA has now been discovered and its code read letter by letter. The real mystery is what trick enables the *mechanism* of heredity to remain error-free despite innumerable repetitions. In which part of a molecular structure is the safeguard against 'error catastrophe'? There is a suspicion that nature achieves this not by a mechanism, not through complexity, but more simply. Only how? And in just the same way, we do not yet understand the mechanism of homoeostasis in metabolism, the quasi-stationary equilibrium that ensures that the chemical balance, the percentage content of molecules, in a cell remains unchanged. A cancer tumour is also life, but there homoeostasis has been violated, and if it has not been violated, it is working with unimaginable precision and unfathomable consistency. I look from one year to the next much the same, and yet the atoms in me are different, they will all be replaced and change several times in my lifetime. I eat all sorts of different things, God knows, yet I do not turn into food.

The old understanding, which we find, for example, in Hegel, is that only something akin to fire could provide this quasi-stationary equilibrium. ('Quasi-' because the immutability of an organism is only apparent, and in fact it is pure form consisting of nothing, through which substance flows.) New branches are put on the fire. They have to be replaced if the flame is to remain constant. According to Hegel, the living realm is a realm of fire; subjectivity is *form* rather than something material. 'Animal existence maintains itself in its otherness,' in the substances that pass through this form, through the metabolic mechanism, but which are *not parts* of the living being. What I eat is not part of me! 'Fire releases itself into a multiplicity of members ... the independence of the members is immediately devoured. Animal life is accordingly a Notion developing in space and time.'[10]

So is life fire or notion? In Heraclitus, fire is *logos*. The fire of Heraclitus became the idea in Plato. The idea, as it were, burns in substance, substance flows through it, and the idea, like a tongue of flame, remains the same.

For the flame to remain the same, a lot of fuel needs constantly to be added to the fire. For a basalt cliff to be preserved, its substance needs to be stable. For a living organism to be preserved, on the contrary, an exchange of substance, metabolism, needs to be as intensive as possible. Nutrition, movement, a change of surroundings, are needed to fuel the fire, so there is a paradox: in living beings, the greater the complexity, the simpler. 'Homoeostasis seems to work better with an elaborate web of interlocking cycles than with a small number of cycles working separately. Why this is so we do not know.'[11]

We have already encountered this complexity and this stability of living things when we deliberately did not stray beyond the limits of Aristotle's biology. What we saw then was that genera have key moments when their continuation is in the balance. These are critical, associated with impossibility and a-mechania, and it is by means of this filtration through extremity that the purity and permanence of the genus are safeguarded. For a mechanical automaton, the filter is external. Where is it in a true automaton? In its designer or programmer, a human being. The nature of a true automaton is that it always has to pass through the eye of a needle, through times of extreme stress and risk, like the thousand-kilometre flight of birds and, in all life, the pairing season and giving birth. You will appreciate that this is again not the language of science, and incomprehensible to it. We shall be using both languages, for better or worse. Both are legitimate, and if anyone is able to speak only in one, let them remember that there is another that can render their language meaningless.

This, people say, is one of the inexplicable facts of life, that for its perpetuation what is needed is not simplicity but complexity, indeed chaos or, to put it in our language, it needs the forest; and this, call it 'self-regulation', can be seen both in nature, which until recently, at least in school textbooks, was called inanimate (for quantum mechanics, the electron, although it does not 'enjoy freedom', nevertheless has a degree of choice: it can make unpredictable movements), and in society, the economy, and culture.

The open-market economy and the culturally open society, notwithstanding all their failures and deficiencies, seem to possess a robustness which centrally planned economies and culturally closed societies lack. The homoeostasis provided by unified five-year economic plans and by unified political control of culture does not lead to a greater stability of economies and cultures. On the contrary, the simple homoeostatic mechanisms of central control have generally proved more brittle and less able to cope with historical shocks than the complex homoeostatic mechanisms of the open market and the uncensored press.[12]

Dyson comments on Darwin's final paragraph at the end of *The Origin of Species* and the image of the 'tangled bank' he uses 'to make vivid his answer to the question, What is life?: an image of grasses and flowers and bees and butterflies growing in tangled profusion without any discernible pattern, achieving homoeostasis by means of a web of interdependences too complicated for us to unravel.'[13] This image continues to live; the researcher pictures the primaeval cell as a similar forest, a confused, chaotic microcosm.

Now, is the metabolic system or the replication a true automaton, or are both of them together necessary for the automaton? Well, each individually and both together. We will do well to recall Leibniz, the automaton in the automaton, and down to the finest detail inside, the automaton controlling the automaton, integrated into the automaton of the world which also has no external clockmaker, because he is *inside*.[14]

But alongside this forest, we have already become accustomed to an entirely different image. In Richard Dawkins' book, published not all that long ago,[15] this democracy, this bounteous variety of inventive life, is invaded by a tyranny with harsh demands: the replicative apparatus. Each species is *compelled*, that is, every species as it exists in its individual representatives is a captive, a slave to its genes. It is *obliged* to subject itself to the dictate of heredity, to conduct itself, to develop, to do everything to continue the race. It may seem to it that it is free, it may want that freedom to be enticed by a cornucopia of possibilities, but no matter what the individual does, no matter how the butterfly may rejoice as it flutters among the flowers, its apparent freedom is actually servitude. It has no option but to carry on fluttering, just as the bird free as air has no option but to carry on eating caterpillars. Only genes are free to experiment, if they have a mind to undergo mutation, with different types of behaviour, and individual specimens will have to do what they order. Freedom and slavery trek along side by side, indistinguishable. Moreover, the seemingly free individuals are the slaves, and the seemingly rigid mechanisms are free and do the dictating.

Dawkins cannot abide the tension of this polarity and, at the end of his book, depicts an uprising against the tyranny of the genes, which has lasted 3 billion years, the estimated time since the origination (and already we have to qualify this by saying perhaps the appearance) of life on earth. (Dawkins belongs to the majority of biologists who do not believe in the primordial living cell as a free forest: he equates life with replication.) Only one species has rebelled, *Homo sapiens*. We overthrew the tyranny by inventing symbolic language and culture and can now act against the laws of genetics. For example, they order us to multiply and we enter a monastery. For example, the gene in the course of its experimentation condemns us to death, because it has the idea of introducing congenital haemophilia just to check that it is disruptive, but we, with the aid of medicine, carry on living with haemophilia. We are the first and only species to have broken out of the prison.

But the tyrant pursued us, and this time – staying with Dawkins – inculcated its tyranny straight into the heart of our free, democratic culture in the form of religious dogma: without explanation, we were told not to dare to criticize but just to adhere uncritically to the dogma, and now that, not the gene, is what in a variety of ways puts its stamp on our behaviour. The tyranny of the species ended, the tyranny of the idea began. It would be good if Dawkins recalled that the idea in fact is the species. In his late writings, Losev talked about the cosmos as a tyranny, and quite some slave-owning tyranny at that, ruled over by an icy, cruel idea.[16] Again, the polarity, again two. The cosmos of the ancients is alive for Losev, physical – and subjected to a monstrous, implacable jailer.

The moral Dawkins draws is that humanity has not fought in vain, and if the defeated gene is avenging itself by inveigling its way into our culture in the form of an ideology, we need to rise up again and overthrow selfish replicators, the very rules of language, the conventions of art and science, the inexplicably accepted norms of conduct in food and clothing. We need to seek out every area into which the tyranny has seeped and expel it. We are the descendants of Prometheus. (Incidentally, in connection with the origination of life from clay, it is not only the supreme Godhead who can sculpt; Prometheus can do it too. So, in one of the fables of Hyginus, can the goddess Cura, Care.) We should return to the state of equality that ruled before the tyranny of the genes.

Here, in this curious form, we find a return, intuitive, blindfolded, presented in the form of a crime thriller, to the ideas of Plato, the *eidos* of Aristotle, to our primaeval forest which does not become but is, at one and the same time, the Cross.

Dawkins is being put right: where he sees tyranny and slavery, there is in fact consent. Life has polarities, there are even two lives, but they are like the right and left hands of a pianist playing a contrapuntal invention. The voice of the replicators only seems imperious, and in reality needs the countervailing voice of variation, flexibility, richness, and abundance. And this is being said by scientists. Do you not think that Plato allowed himself something of this sort, but only in his myths, for fun?

The picture of tyrants and slaves is complicated by the garbage in the ruling stratum, the junk DNA. The notion that this part of the apparatus of heredity amounts to 98%, that it is a letter to the future and that we are its couriers, is only one opinion. A more widespread view is that, if this biologically redundant part of the mechanism of heredity really does comprise more than half the nucleic acids, then it does so only marginally, and that in reality it is more like a stowaway taking a ride in us at our expense. It is said that only a crisis economy cannot afford to carry anything superfluous, and that excess baggage dragged along from one generation to the next in the machinery of replication is an indication that it is strong and healthy. That opinion we have heard; another is that, just as civilization drags a lot of rubbish around on its back, like popular or sponsored television programmes, astrology, constantly played background music, and political propaganda, all this junk, so life drags junk around too.

To proceed, I need to recall something said earlier. If scientists are to be allowed to speculate about the inexplicable presence of non-functioning components in the mechanism of life, I would suggest, or rather develop my suggestion, that in everything we do there is a side we know about and manage, and another side which is our mimetic participation in Sophia to the extent that we belong to it. That is, there is a non-functioning side, the one where we work, and a functioning side, where we are truly the automata of life. Where scientists have their own aims, they are like a superfluous burden on the side of their other self which might seem to be serving purity and rigour in a purely formal sense but is, thereby, allowing the voice of nature to be heard through them. Cosmologist Steven Weinberg in *The First Three Minutes* remarks that the conduct of scientists towards what they create can only too easily be irresponsible. It is as if they are not doing what they are doing, do not know what they are doing, what they have in their hands, what it is that is passing through them. 'Our mistake is not that we take our theories too seriously, but that we do not take them seriously enough. It is always hard to realize that these numbers and equations we play with at our desks have something to do with the real world.'[17]

Lecture 23, 24 March 1998

Edward Osborne Wilson (b. 1929, Birmingham, Alabama) is a renowned American biologist recognized as the world's leading authority on ants. He was also the foremost proponent of sociobiology, the study of the genetic basis of the *social behaviour* of all animals, *including humans*.[1] This is again a return to Aristotle's old ascription of humans to the animal kingdom, more precisely to the gregarious or social animals.

We are going to have to talk at unexpected length about ants. I find the journalistic sensationalizing of ever-increasing *organization* very tedious. From censuses to regulations, we seem to be prescribed what is to be done on every day, in every hour, and ultimately in every minute. It is an interring of human biology, which fortunately is very resilient, in building earthworks, and later an immuring of it in iron, in concrete, and now in computers, using teaching, medicine, and administration. It starts with the registration of a birth and leads to a computer database with a file on every human being. It seems unlikely, nevertheless, that all this administrative technology will succeed in fundamentally changing human life. Neither, of course, is it anything new. Ritual in earlier societies could reach equal degrees of sophistication and precision, and 'deliver' an equal or even greater degree of organization. The 'termite state' seems no more than a journalistic cliché to shock and offend by likening humans to ants, with the insinuation that higher human qualities are dying out. But which? Intelligence and will? Perhaps. But those seem always to have been invigorated when it was recognized that everything, including mental processes, was becoming completely mired in causal relationships. The total plotting out of society is perhaps no more than a good, sobering mimesis of the natural interdependence of everything. When it becomes clear that nothing in this perpetual plotting out can actually be relied on and that our need is not, in fact, to devise new and better plotting out, the moral will be not that we should anarchically rebel against it (that has already been tried: there were revolts in the distant past against censuses), but that our task, our concerns, our space, is the realm of the impossible.

When there is this understanding, you can take a more relaxed view of this wall-to-wall technological management of everything, and might even wish it worked more efficiently and in a more discriminating manner. What seems to matter becomes something different, and that is why we are going to be talking a lot about ants. It is this blatant attempt to 'termitize' society, this determination to turn it into an anthill, that reveals the enormous difference between a human being and an ant, which we shall now address.

Observe that no sooner has an underwater school of anchovies proliferated and started enjoying life than cuttlefish, squid, or other cephalopods swim into view. There are hundreds of species of those now, but millions of years ago there were thousands. They target the larger anchovies in the school. For ants and termites, all their toxic chemicals are to no avail against the anteater with its insensitive rubbery snout that sucks them up; or against the myrmecologists with their stoppered glass vial, also sucking up ants for their experiments. In this or some other way, every living species has other species boxing it in, cutting it down, crowding it out, like its own customized nemesis, testing the species, purifying it, and tempering it in battle.

What, then, of our own freedom? We have risen up against the tyranny of our genes, but I hope to show that we are no exception, not alone in our freedom.

Tell me now, how is the human species boxed in, mown down, and culled?

Of course: by war. In the ancient Greek epic, war is there to cull generations of humans, while also tempering and purifying them. Supposedly. It would certainly be absurd to claim the human species faces natural selection in the struggle against tigers and crocodiles. Our race instead goes in for self-selection. This is distinctly odd.

Several things do not add up. Firstly, as we read in Timofeev-Ressovsky, and indeed not only there, war – not every war – effects positive selection. In fact we get something more like *adverse* selection. Wolves, in respect of elk and deer, unquestionably effect positive selection. They do, no doubt, behave abominably, like racists and sadists, but in their neck of the woods they maintain a muscularity and tension that keep life on its toes, nipping its heels, so to speak. In fact, throughout the whole of nature, different species do, one and all, *discipline* each other (to put it mildly). The wolf attacks the deer without giving fair warning and presents no hunting permit explaining the unsustainability of more than fourteen elk per square kilometre of forest.

Before a war among humans, proof of its necessity of one kind or another is presented, primarily, perhaps, for one's own side rather than the enemy, who can be subjected to surprise attack. A country seeks to inflame its countrymen so as to motivate them to fight, and more or less any argument will do.

The reasons are, no doubt, based on instinct no less than those of the wolf and *never* make sense in terms of selection, or of genuinely seeking to improve quality of life. They may cite pacification, the seizing of *Lebensraum* for oneself as a biological species or subspecies, and are always based on ideology. We go to war not in the interests of our biological *species* but for the benefit of an *idea!*

You will be guessing where this is leading. The species is, of course, itself an idea. In the notes I have written as background, there is a quotation from St Paul: 'For we are also His offspring' (Acts of the Apostles, 17: 28). I will say no more.

I return to our first theme, about the *idea*: if we join the army, if we go to war, we do so reluctantly. If willingly, then with a sense of tragic regret, forcing ourselves. It is clear we are the agents of something outside us, something that is more than ourselves, something *higher*. In former times, people would have said, something *godly*.

Alongside the human species, which does not actually purify itself through self-selection, there is a contiguous species, disciplining ours, more powerful, against which there can be no question of human beings prevailing as they might against tigers or microbes, and that is the species of angels, demons, and gods. We live under threat from this species in a relationship of no less harshly rigorous selectivity than all the other creatures we know live with their own neighbouring species.

Ladies and gentlemen, bringing in God and gods to the biological ladder will of course seem to you, in fact should seem to you, like a rather forcible nailing of the world of living things on to a metaphysical scheme, but I am confident of remaining on a scientific level, the only sound level to be on. Judge for yourselves, *how else* are we to name what invades human biology and subordinates it to discipline, organization, order, and law at the dictate – of what? It is as if some organization has determined what is conducive to the development, survival, and improvement of the human species and dictated the necessary laws. With all these laws, as with religious or state ritual, there are always reasons that explain them, and if the ritual is replaced, no fewer new reasons will be found. Even, however, if there are no explanatory reasons, the ritual will be none the milder for it. Akhutin says, we are not altogether a species.[2]

Whether we rebel or not, or call for rebellion, the fact is that the dictate of an idea more powerful than the dictate of species has been released into human society. (The human species is itself an *idea*.) With your indulgence, I will include *gods* in the biological ladder of living beings. No less than ideas they rule humanity, and certainly inflict on humanity through war and revolution everything that, further down the ladder, one species inflicts on another in terms of harsh treatment, discipline, constraint, and selection. *For humankind, gods are a force as real as, or more real and effective than, the idea, in the guise of species, is for other living beings.* Because it is more familiar and easier for us as individuals to understand the human species as our God, it is more difficult and complicated to discern in the fog how other species maintain their continuity, and to recognize that the same mechanism is at work. It is not far-fetched to see the succession, the evolution, of species as a succession of gods (fetishes, totems), a succession of religions, which is never gradual but as abrupt as the succession of species.

Let us count this as an asset: the stabilizing, preserving focal point of a species is the idea, or God (Plato). In this unanticipated manner, the ancient deification of plants and animals is rehabilitated. It seems there will be no escape for us from our strange neighbour and that thus, from a distance, we shall approach Heidegger's quaternion of the world: the earth, the sky, the divinities, and mortals.[3] This opens up such perspectives that it is time for us to leave this landscape for now and get back to our ants.

Starting with the study of ants, Edward Wilson went on to study whole populations. 'He developed the concept of "character displacement", a process in which populations of two closely related species, after first coming into contact with each other, undergo rapid evolutionary differentiation in order to minimize the chances of both competition and hybridization between them.'[4]

Wilson understandably shocked many people by revealing that human society behaves like ant or termite societies. We will have to speak some more about him in connection with ants, but just now I need him so we can complete our excursion into the way science examines how and where life came from, since we are compiling an inventory of biological concepts. At the same time, we shall see how curiously Aristotle's forest recurs again and again, resurfacing only slightly less frequently than Plato's 'idea'. On this occasion, in molecular biology. 'Edward Wilson describes the new picture of the genes in a cell as "a rain forest with many niches occupied by a whole range of elements, all parts of which are in a dynamic state of change".'[5]

To be seeing the primordial cell as a forest, even as a tropical rain forest, a jungle, is to admit that we have lost the plot, lost our way in the quest for where living nature came from and how; because the forest is not the kind of thing to which metric relationships, including causal relationships, can be extended. Matter is indefinite. Science, like a dog, *loses track* of life when it starts looking for where it came from and where it is going. As I have said, this does not mean the problem of the origin of life must be terribly complicated. Perhaps it is quite the contrary: the dog loses track of the squirrel not because the trail has become impossibly difficult but because the squirrel has run up a tree and dogs cannot climb verticals. The dog can only *very accurately* indicate an area within which, on a horizontal plane, the squirrel should be, and indeed is, as it (the dog) runs round the tree.

It may, however, be even more interesting to see how science thinks about where living nature is headed. This second question is, like the first, one that science is reluctant to ask itself, and does so only because to refuse to would be a disgrace. 'Why are you wasting time on something when we do not even know where it is going or why?' 'Why are you engaging in science anyway?' And again, science *very* precisely and unerringly plots on in its metric plane the point to which life is going.

The answer science has to give to the question of where the living world, and indeed nature in general, is going is that it is headed for the heat death of the universe, for destruction, for a black hole, for the ultimate decay of protons, the foundation of the nucleus, the stable part of the atom. Protons will be exhausted after 10^{33} years. They will evaporate into positrons, photons, and neutrinos. Whether or not this is something we want to hear, science cannot tell a lie. Everything in the field it is measuring points unerringly and unambiguously in that direction, just as the dog unerringly identifies the tree up which the squirrel vanished. Here, too, science cannot get it wrong.

Matter *cannot* but wear out. It has nowhere to go. Just as a brick crumbles, so the protons will disintegrate. On the other hand, we can safely predict that technology will progress. The human species will assuredly, if it has hundreds, let alone thousands, let alone millions of years, by the time matter is no longer young and flourishing, long ago have learned to manage its genetics – and here we recall again what Tsiolkovsky had to say about a future humankind that would be transfigured into something light and ethereal.

Even if the universe cools down and weakens terribly, even if atomic nuclei disintegrate, for these new light and airy people created by art and skill, for all their intergalactic journeyings and contacts for their *eternal* existence, it has been calculated, remarkably little energy will be needed. As much as our present sun radiates in eight hours will be sufficient to power a community of these ethereal people comparable in the scope of their culture to ours. And if in the whole galaxy there remains only the energy of one star like our sun, but unscathed, it will be sufficient to power a society with a culture 10 trillion times more extensive than ours. The ethereal human species will establish universal intergalactic links. Perhaps even after the heat death of the universe, humanity will be able to access such an infinitesimal amount of energy. Or it may not, in which case humankind would have to abandon our present bodies, exactly as foreseen by Tsiolkovsky. The crystallographer J.D. Bernal wrote in 1929 of beings

nuclearly resident, so to speak, in a relatively small set of mental units, each utilizing the bare minimum of energy, connected together by a complex of ethereal intercommunication, and spreading themselves over immense areas and periods of time by means of inert sense organs.... Finally, consciousness itself may end or vanish in a humanity that has become completely etherealized, losing the close-knit organism, becoming masses of atoms in space communicating by radiation, and ultimately perhaps resolving itself entirely into light.[6]

You will see from this that science talks more confidently about the future than the past. Nevertheless, the element of uncertainty remains, in that, while humanity undoubtedly could deliver all this, will it in the event have sufficient vigour to support it all? The human species is already weary. Although all it has to do at present is maintain a stable system on the earth, it is already inclined to give up. And in millions of years' time? It is hardly going to have the patience to maintain all these systems of intergalactic contacts.

However odd you may find the idea, we are not confusing separate disciplines but are formally, technically obliged, whether we like it or not, to include in evolution the parameters of boredom and enthusiasm. One biologist complained that there seemed to be no place in Schrödinger's equation for *joie de vivre*. He was referring to that zest without which it would cease to be interesting either to be alive or to study life. If something is not exciting or interesting, people simply stop doing it. Such is the inexorable rule. The ruins of ancient civilizations show what happens when people no longer find it exciting to defend and continue the effort of maintaining them.

Russians have been tending lately to snigger at Tsiolkovsky, but in fact it is he who is increasingly referred to in futurology. He does have a vision that enables us to pass beyond the former dead end, the bad unknowableness of where from, and the bad infinity of where to (and it really is bad infinity when it has been estimated that there will be sufficient energy in any entropic cosmos you can imagine to provide for the *infinite* existence of ethereal humanity). It is Tsiolkovsky who has the principle of 'sensitivity' (or irritability), which, through that wall, now and forever will connect everything in the cosmos, from human beings to the atom. In Tsiolkovsky, the entire universe is linked up, not some time but right now, by one thing: universal sensitivity. Through sensitivity and responsiveness, everything is already in communion with everything else. That is why for Tsiolkovsky the engineering achievements of that future ethereal humanity on its various ethereal islands are essentially needed: to confirm not only that sensitivity and responsiveness are not futile, but also that only they have a future and will have power; that they alone can justify everything and defeat boredom and loss of interest in being.

According to the letter and spirit of Tsiolkovsky, we can confidently assert that the present sensitivity towards everything (he gives the example of the hand on a gauge) is the same sensitivity as is constant and active everywhere, through which everything here and now is connected to everything everywhere and always. Moreover, there is no need to bring in long-range interaction or supersonic speeds: any remote points of space, knowing nothing about each other, know everything about themselves because they are identically connected to sensation.

In the process, everything that is to happen ceases to raise the problem of whether it actually will happen and how it will develop because, in any case, everything will be determined by the continuation of sensitivity. Even the problem of a Creator recedes, whether he created on one occasion or is perpetually doing so, because creativity is coming not from outside but from within, from the essence of matter, which is sensitivity. It is perfectly possible, then, for us to say that God does not at this moment know what is going to happen, but he knows for a certainty that there will be a continuation and further unfolding of sensitivity.

That old conjecture that if there is order (*taxis, kosmos*) there must be a general, and that if there is a clock there must be a clockmaker, overlooks the fact that there is a difference between automatons. Imagine a clockmaker inside his clock and inseparable from its parts. The universe is a clock without a guarantee.

Protons will weary and fall apart, the age of entropy will come and after it the heat death and sundry other deaths, but the solution will not be to seek and obtain, as it were, a new grant, new sources of funding, for the universe, because that new fund will itself have new failure built into it. The solution will be that always, in every situation, there is scope for a stroke of luck, for succeeding, for 'it'. *Sapientia*, from *sapio*, 'I sense,' 'I have taste.' You do not need much to have taste. A beggar can have taste. Remember what Wittgenstein said about the world consisting of only two elements, or even one.[7] Diversity, pluralism – that is already an entropic, doomed situation that cannot support even itself.

But let us get back to ants. I shall first refer to Julian Huxley (1887–1975). Like his brother, the writer Aldous Huxley, and his father, Leonard Huxley, Julian was a British biologist and philosopher [*sic, Tr.*]. Actually his speciality was experimental embryology, but he is best known as one of the founders of the modern synthetic *theory of evolution*. He had been dealt all the right cards: he was the grandson of Thomas Henry Huxley (1825–95), the major propagandist of Darwinism, whom we have quoted above as having said, 'My reflection, when I first made myself master of the central idea of "The Origin", was, "How extremely stupid not to have thought of that!"' No doubt Julian Huxley knew what he was talking about when he said in an article on 'War As a Biological Phenomenon', 'In point of fact, there are only two kinds of animals that habitually make war – man and ants.'[8] Even among ants, war is mainly practised by one group comprising only a few species among the tens of thousands that are known to science. They are the harvester ants, inhabitants of arid regions where there is little to pick up during the dry months. Accordingly, they collect the seeds of various grasses at the end of the growing season. There are wars with heavy losses and the victors carry off the spoils. The wars do not last long: one was observed to last three weeks. The longest on record lasted a month and a half. Huxley emphasizes that war is a rare exception among living creatures, even among human beings.

There is no evidence of prehistoric man's having made war, for all his flint implements seem to have been designed for hunting, for digging, or for scraping hides; and we can be pretty sure that even if he did, any wars between groups in the hunting stage of human life would have been both rare and mild.... As for human nature, it contains no specific war instinct, as does the nature of harvester ants. There is in man's make-up a general aggressive tendency, but this, like all other human urges, is not a specific and unvarying instinct; it can be moulded into the most varied forms. It can be canalized into competitive sport, as in our own society, or as when certain Filipino tribes were induced to substitute football for head-hunting.[9]

For Julian Huxley, war is not good old natural selection, rather the reverse: it is a blight. This does not mean he is against Darwin, and he takes pleasure in quoting his grandfather's praise of *The Origin of Species*. Neo-Darwinism accepts that change results from mutations and comes in leaps and bounds.

The fact that only we and the ants make war is reason enough to study them. William Morton Wheeler (1865–1937) was an 'American entomologist recognized as one of the world's foremost authorities on ants and other social insects. Two of his works, *Ants: Their Structure, Development, and Behaviour* (1910) and *Social Life Among the Insects* (1923), long served as standard references on their subjects.' He collected ants himself, using a device rather like the snout of an anteater. 'He discovered that the social behaviour of ants was among the most complex in the insect world, leading him to use the ant colony as a behavioural analogy for human civilization. His findings were based on firsthand observations of ant species collected from all over the world, including Morocco, the Galapagos, and the Canary Islands.'[10]

After devoting thirty years to the study of ants, he said he still found it completely fascinating and wondered why so few people engaged in it. This despite the fact that he mentions a vast literature on ants: Wheeler's own bibliography, mostly about ants, runs to 467 titles.

Maurice Maeterlinck, whom Wheeler quotes, a symbolist poet, playwright, and essayist, was the first to see the beehive and the anthill as

a single individual, with its parts scattered abroad; a single living creature, that had not yet become, or that had ceased to be, combined or consolidated; an entity whose different organs, composed of thousands of cells, remain always subject to the same central law, although outside it and apparently individually independent. So in the same way is our body an association, an agglomeration, a colony of sixty billion cells which cannot break away from their nest or kernel, and remain, until the destruction of that nest or kernel, sedentary and captive. However terrible, however inhuman the organisation of the termitary may appear, the organisation we carry in ourselves is based on the same design: the same collective personality, the same unceasing sacrifice of the innumerable parts to the whole, to the common good; the same system of defence, the same cannibalism of the phagocytes in the matter of dead or useless cells; the same blind, obscure, dogged toil to achieve unknown ends; the same ferocity, the same specialised processes of feeding, reproduction, respiration, circulation of the blood, etc.; the same complications, the same solidarity, the same appeals in case of danger, the same equilibrium, the same internal police.[11]

This makes me feel very unsettled. If the idea is from biology, is Plato's city as an organism a body not in a metaphorical sense but in the same sense that a living body or an anthill is an organism? That is, without any symbolism, an anthill on a scale we never dreamed of?

Wheeler proposes that 'the organism is neither a thing nor a concept, but a continual flux or process'. It is 'a system of activities, which are primarily directed to obtaining and assimilating substances from an environment, to producing other similar systems, known as offspring'.[12] In this sense, there is nothing metaphorical here: '[T]he animal colony is a true organism and not merely the analogue of the person.'[13]

The ant colony is an individual being. It is widely known that it bands together, but that it resists dissolution is less known, and fierce wars serve to preserve its unitary wholeness. Particular defending soldiers and workers correspond to the tissues of the skin and hair, the muscle and other internal tissues in a person.[14] The ant colony is best compared to foraminiferous *Rhizopoda*, in which the queen represents the nucleus, but winged and possibly conscious. The ability of this nucleus to fly out of the 'organism' does not invalidate the analogy because, as we have seen, the nucleus of a cell can be considered external to it, sometimes migrating from one cell to another. The ant queen immediately discards her wings when she has chosen a site for the future colony and produces wingless progeny. The single flight of the queen – that is, the brief period when she is winged – corresponds to the single movement of a fertilized egg in an organism. Just as *Rhizopoda foraminifera* have sexual and asexual reproduction, so ant colonies can reproduce without the flight of the queen but by simple division.

Now the homoeostasis which distinguishes the organism.

If the worker personnel be removed from a young ant-colony, leaving only the fertile queen, we find that this insect, if provided with a sufficiently voluminous fat-body, will set to work and rear another brood, or, in other words, regenerate the missing soma. And, of course, any portion of the worker or sexual personnel that is removed from a vigorous colony will be readily replaced by development of a corresponding portion of the brood (or, in the case of bees, grubs). On the other hand, if the queen alone be removed, one of the workers will often develop its ovaries and take on the egg-laying function of the queen. In ants such substitution queens, or gynaecoid workers, are not fertilized and are therefore unable to assume their mother's worker- and queen-producing functions. The termites, however, show a remarkable provision for restituting both of the fertile parents of the colony from the so-called complemental males and females. In ants we have a production of fertile from normally infertile individuals.[15]

Plants and animals that live symbiotically with ants are called myrmecophiles and, I am not making this up, 'live amicably side by side'.[16] 'Very striking examples of colonies' restitutional tendency are exhibited when colonies are injured by parasitic myrmecophiles. I shall consider only the case of the peculiar beetle Lomechusa strumosa, which breeds in colonies of the blood-red slave-maker, Formica sanguinea.' (These ants kidnap the larvae of others and force them, when they develop, to serve them.) Though the beetle and its larvae are treated 'with great affection',[17] the latter devour the ant larvae in great numbers, so that

> little of the brood survives during the early summer months when the colony is producing its greatest annual increment to the worker personnel. The ants seem to perceive this defect and endeavor to remedy it by converting all the surviving queen larvae into workers. But as these larvae have passed the stage in their development when such an operation can be successful, the result is the production of a lot of pseudogynes, or abortive creatures structurally intermediate between the workers and queens and therefore useless in either capacity.[18]

*   *   *

[No Lecture 24 was delivered on 31 March 1998. *Tr.*[19]]

Lecture 25, 7 April 1998

It is curious that, if ants treat *Lomechusa strumosa* 'with great affection' and do not suspect or expel it, they are effectively helping it and support-ing life, and that is a case of altruism, of the sacrificial suicide referred to by Lynn Margulis.

Ants chemically castrate their queens and change their sex, half-way at least.

That brings me to thinking about the dark practice of castration, which may have been more common in antiquity than it is now, although it still goes on today. It is not by any means something invented by humans. The *Sacculina* barnacle attaches itself to the belly of the male crab, sinks its suckers into it, and castrates it. The stomach becomes distended and the parasite's soft body penetrates it. In other words, the parasite behaves like a mass of crab roe and the male crab behaves as if it has changed sex and become a pregnant female. These are things in the animal world it is dis-tasteful to talk about. Vladimir Soloviov found them disgusting and intol-erable, but if we look at parasitism through the eyes of Kozo-Polyansky and see all these mutual devourings, enslavements, and castrations as pro-cesses within a single organism, as proposed by Wheeler, who viewed insect communities as *a single organism*, then, according to Maurice Maeterlinck, we can look at our own body and see the same thing, or something analo-gous, happening.

Next. Who is directing all this? What is organizing the anticipatory cooperation or synergy in an anthill or the organism that is a beehive?[1] The Dutch naturalist Jan Swammerdam (1637–80), when he turned to the study of insects, accurately described and illustrated the life histories and anatomy of many species.[2] It was he who called the dominant female insect the 'queen', and she really does enjoy manifest deference in an anthill or beehive. Beehives do, however, seem to be organized less along monarchi-cal lines than in accordance with a kind of communist anarchy, just as in the body there is no ruling cell. We cannot, after all, claim that the brain is in charge because that is more the province of the passions, and they are not in the brain. Perhaps, then, in the mind, but the mind is not the same as the brain.

Who is in charge really is a question worth considering. Who governs the cells in an organism and how? Maurice Maeterlinck spoke of the 'spirit of the hive'. It is pitiless, ruthless towards the well-being and even the life of the winged community. But after all, a *single* bee cannot survive without the hive, so how could it not be willing to sacrifice its life for the hive? All must submit to the spirit of the hive, but it in turn seems to have to submit to a higher duty. The spirit of the hive sees to it that the number of births is proportionate to the number of flowers in its surroundings; the queen herself is forced to leave; she nurtures the rivals who will displace her. The spirit of the beehive decides whether or not a queen born earlier may kill her sisters while they are still in their cells. Then, when the season is coming to an end, the worker bees will kill the entire royal family and everything will be focused on work, building up reserves of honey for the winter. The spirit of the beehive is strict but not miserly; in the plenteous days of summer, instead of working to build reserves, it tolerates the presence in the hive of 300–400 males who really are drones, stupid, absurd, useless, noisy, greedy, dirty, coarse, completely idle, insatiable, and enormous. From these, the queen will make her choice. But then, when the flowers are opening later and closing earlier, the spirit of the hive will one morning issue orders for all the males to be killed instantly.

Worker bees are divided into castes. At different ages, bees make sorties in different ways: nurse bees care for the larvae, all the time next to the queen; domestic bees clean, ventilate, and warm the hive, and accelerate the evaporation of water from the honey by ventilation; other bees work with wax, sculpting honeycomb; chemist bees take care of preserving the honey by inserting droplets of formic acid; bee-packers seal the occupied cells; there are sweeper bees, undertaker bees to take away dead bodies, and, of course, the guardians of the entrance block, who chase away robbers, uninvited visitors, and even, if necessary, barricade the entrance.

Then the spirit of the hive organizes an annual sacrificial day of mass self-immolation to the genius of the 'race': bees which have nicely settled in, just when they are at the peak of their strength and prosperity, suddenly abandon their wealth and home, the fruits of their labours, to the young, who have yet to contribute anything, and swarm. The swarm sometimes perishes, and is in any case always doomed to live in poverty – an act humans find totally baffling.

Where, Maeterlinck asks, does it come from, this spirit of the hive, or of the 'race', that demands heroism from all? How does it know the future? Everything is enigmatic: the intelligence, the destiny, the will, the purpose, the means, the goals. Every last, trivial thing is a mystery. And, moreover, remember that we said the bees are only hirelings, only in the service of flowers and plants. And then we have to talk about the genius of the garden, of the field, the spirit of the forest!

'Entelechy,' people say in bewilderment. It is not that this is a flawed term, but it is empty and meaningless without all its Aristotelian context, and how many people have read and understood all of Aristotle and the connection of his philosophy to his biology? (Incidentally, something that has gone unremarked about Aristotle's transition from 'medicine', i.e. biology, to philosophy is how many such transitions there have been, and for a long time now, since Lamarck's *Philosophie zoologique* [1809] and earlier? Biology inclines people to philosophy today. Aristotle realized that early on, and continued along the path ever more single-mindedly. We are increasingly coming to understand his term *matter, the forest.*)

You can guess what Wheeler thought. The cell as an ant colony of inferior physiological units. For him, *all* organisms are colonies and communities: '[O]ne of the fundamental tendencies of life is sociogenic.'[3] All living things are drawn to other living things, assimilating them or cooperating with them. Symbiosis, inquiline cohabitation, parasitism, xenobiosis. Here we see not so much a struggle for existence as an organism's ability to fit in, to find a compromise, to serve the interests of unity and other organisms, 'to secure survival through a kind of egoistic altruism'.[4] The struggle for survival, yes – but no less, a universal symbiosis, mutual support, as we have seen, all the way to sacrificial, self-sacrificing behaviour.

Let us for a time leave this revealed landscape of neighbours and partners of the human species, of gods. We shall return to it because there is a lot more there for us to see. In particular the piquant proximity of viruses to gods: when we wake up in the morning in a bad mood, we do not know whether it is a new strain of virus or an intimation and premonition of the gods.

The interruption, the analysis that did not happen, can be explained by my inadequacy and a mix-up over the sale of tickets at the Moskovsky Station in Leningrad. The mix-up was deliberately engineered in favour of *insiders*, those working in the station administration, who find it to their advantage because, familiar with the situation, they can more speedily work out what is going on and gain priority in obtaining tickets over outsiders.

The privatized system does not work for the common good; it is against the Gaia hypothesis, according to which all living systems should serve the survival of the earth, even at the cost of self-immolation, as the anaerobes sacrificed themselves by creating an aerobic environment in which they could not exist.

The collapse of the Soviet system, even if it did not mark a complete collapse of our way of life, was at least a partial loss and brings us back to Darwinism and competition among species, whether in absolute parameters or in terms of overall service to Gaia. For a species, the result in either case will be the same: having to leave the stage, to disappear.

To belong to a vanishing species is senseless. It is merely irksome to work at anything when you are up a dead end and, for example, some other civilization is eager to proclaim its merits. The victorious form of life on earth at present is American civilization. Others may consider themselves very important, but even so they will have to announce the fact on American film, or film produced under a US licence, and on a television system invented in America. We are talking here today because the American financial and economic system has been victorious in our country. If this had not been the case, the University would have had a different approach, and our course on the philosophy of biology would have been saying very similar things and adducing the same facts, but there would only really have been one *problem:* how to marshal all these facts and get them to serve the needs of the people's economy, the consolidation of the global socialist system, and the new communist civilization. Our theorizing would have been directed towards resolving that practical task.

We are talking here, indirectly, thanks to the 'new Russians' who hold power.[5] They orientate themselves more or less explicitly by American civilization. As I have said, and as you will certainly agree with me, speaking and acting when you know you are up a dead end is irksome and pointless. There is accordingly really only one alternative to becoming an adjunct to American civilization, only it, too, is unacceptable to us. Here is a typical expression of it: thinking people

> evidently need to occupy the only position worthy of them: that of intellectual opposition ... and in a situation where everybody else has gone mad, remain living carriers of the ideals of human individuality and social justice.... Russia has every right to say to other countries, to the entire world, 'At least I tried to make a dream come true.' Yes, that road came to a dead end, a great intention came to nothing. But if we state that not without regret (the 'not' here seems surplus) and even jubilantly, if we conclude that ideals are always a chimera and start singing the praises of our millionaire saviours, then why was philosophy, religion, or art needed? What did all these Aristotles, Shakespeares, Mozarts, and Belinskys live for? Was it really only so that everyone on earth should live a 'normal' life, a life where you can buy anything, have fun, go on holiday to Australia with the wife?! No. Actually, there was and is some other, higher and precious meaning in human existence. No, actually we will emerge from the madhouse of privatization and the free market, just as we emerged from the madhouse of regimented socialism. That is why, when we talk about the collapse of socialist ideals in their Bolshevik iteration, let us not behave like dwarfs gleefully belittling the corpse of a giant they were incapable of felling. From a grander historical perspective, this is not the destination but only an interrupted flight.[6]

This breaks the rule of phenomenology in speaking not about what is seen, but about what Aristotles, Shakespeares, and Belinskys saw. We do not know what they saw. We cannot answer on their behalf, and they afford us no guarantees.

But if for that reason we do not subscribe to the 'position of the opposition' because it is suspended in thin air, neither do we subscribe to the position of Americanism. We just do not. That is the way things are and there is nothing we can do to change it. We find ourselves nowhere, without recourse. American civilization stands as a defiant, challenging reality in front of us and claims to know the purely methodological secret of survival which we, if we do not partake of it, will *ipso facto* never find.

One of its more disarming aspects is its self-deprecating sense of humour. Here is a typical American parable: the human species has finally completely ruined the earth and flies off to seek a good life on other planets, but there it is just so inhospitable that humankind decides to return to the earth to die. Meanwhile, however, the dinosaurs have resurfaced and brought the earth back to its wonderful, pristine state. 'Give us at least just a bit of the worst land,' the humans say. 'No,' the dinosaurs reply, 'we will give you not a bit but all the earth, only not in private but in communal ownership.'

By the way, it is not impossible that as yet unknown creatures will appear, because the 1 million registered species of living creatures on the earth are only 10% or at most 30% of all the earth's creatures. 'Biology is the study of life, as the naturalist Howard Evans expressed it in the title of a recent book, "on a little known planet".'[7]

Or again, there is a healthy sense of humour in the attitude of American civilization to the human species – that is, to itself, because American civilization has long been assuming responsibility for the whole world, or at least not shifting responsibility for it to others. It sees no political force as providing grounds for hand-wringing resignation. Let us take the discussion of ethics, which shades over into biology and has been taken up by the biologists, which is how Robert Nozick propounds the necessity of vegetarianism.

The most widely discussed alternative theory to Utilitarianism in recent years is set forth in John Rawls, *A Theory of Justice* (1971, repr. 1981). Robert Nozick, *Anarchy, State, and Utopia* (1974), criticizes Rawls and presents a rights-based theory. Another work giving prominence to rights is Ronald Dworkin, *Taking Rights Seriously* (1977).[8]

Human beings justify the eating of meat on the grounds that the animals we kill are too far below us in sensitivity and intelligence to bear comparison. It follows that if representatives of a truly superior extraterrestrial species were to visit Earth and apply the same criterion, they could proceed to eat us in good conscience. By the same token, scientists among these aliens might find human beings uninteresting, our intelligence weak, our passions unsurprising, our social organization of a kind already frequently encountered on other planets. To our chagrin they might then focus on the ants, because these little creatures, with their haplodiploid form of sex determination and bizarre female caste systems, are the truly novel productions of the Earth with reference to the Galaxy. [Ants have a hard-working female colony with terribly few males and, if they run out of them completely that is not a problem because the queen can generate the necessary number of them through parthenogenesis. *Bibikhin*] We can imagine the log declaring, 'A scientific breakthrough has occurred; we have finally discovered haplodiploid social organisms in the one- to ten-millimeter range.'[9]

Humans might find it difficult or impossible to prove they each have unique value.

In other words, just as one part of humanity managed to persuade itself and its adversary and all succeeding generations, as the Greeks of Alexander the Great did, that it had an unconditional right to conquer and oppress, so from a superior level of development the same thing can be shown to all humankind. Or in *more* other words, humanity, as always, just as in the Bible and the times of Homer facing the punishment of the gods, so in America today facing imaginary aliens, looks for excuses, and in *this* respect American civilization does not put itself on an unchallengeably justified higher level in terms of the progress of history, as did Soviet civilization. But, unlike the Soviet version, American civilization has a real, credible chance that (and it does not much matter whether it is right or wrong) if this issue is not solved, it will come out on top in 'natural selection'. This is indicated by the confident, soft way it has of solving the problems it sees itself as facing. It solves the issue of morality by pointing to the fact that American civilization is prepared not to completely annihilate others but to give them a place in a reservation. Each group in the United States has the right to have its own place of worship, its customs, rituals, language, school, newspaper, radio, and television. It is just that these minorities do not have their own language used in administration, government, or legislation. Nationalists say that is worse and that, if they had the choice, they would prefer to have the local administration in their own language (probably because then schooling would automatically be conducted in their language).

American civilization is prepared to recognize the rightness and sanctity of other people's religion and culture. No problem, but it retains the right to dictate the political dispensation. What does that leave for religion? Ants. An American myrmecologist writes that if the ants 'were programmed to eliminate strife between colonies and to conserve the natural environment they would have greater staying power than people, and in a broad sense theirs would be the higher morality'.[10] Moral superiority may be accorded to the ants, but not a say over the political system.

The more so given that human behaviour is dictated by genes. It is a matter of some significance that a set of human genes differs from those of a chimpanzee; the difference is sufficient to explain the differences between human behaviour and that of other animals, given that similar genes explain similar behaviour. For example, ant colonies have such features as age-grading, antennal rites, body licking, a calendar, cannibalism, caste determination, caste laws, colony-foundation rules, colony organization, cleanliness training, communal nurseries, cooperative labour, cosmology, courtship, division of labour, drone control, education, eschatology, ethics, etiquette, euthanasia, fire making, food taboos, gift giving, government, greetings, grooming rituals, hospitality, housing, hygiene, incest taboos, language, larval care, law, medicine, metamorphosis rites, mutual regurgitation, nursing castes, nuptial flights, nutrient eggs, population policy, queen obeisance, residence rules, sex determination, soldier castes, sisterhoods, status differentiation, sterile workers, surgery, symbiont care, tool making, trade, visiting, weather control.[11]

There is no way to prove definitively that cultural behaviour is not dictated by genes. 'Human behavior is ... organized by some genes that are shared with closely related species and others that are unique to the human species. The same facts are unfavourable for the competing hypothesis which has dominated the social sciences for generations, that humankind has escaped its own genes to the extent of being entirely culture-bound.'[12]

The genetic formation of humans took around 5 million years, and a cultural sprint started in the last 10,000 years with, naturally, little or no genetic variation. During this period of history and culture, in effect nothing has happened that was not a consequence of strokes of luck during the millions of years of natural selection. Nothing is happening to the genetic basis of the human species, and it does not give an equal chance to every possible cultural process.

One thing, however, is clear: an individual or group that is able to provide itself a more reliable proliferation in the next generation thereby consolidates and asserts itself. The behaviour may be of any kind. Almost the same castes as we observe among the ants were present in pre-colonial and British India and, to a lesser degree, they persist to this day. More or less common to all humankind, female hypergamy, the 'upward social flow of daughters by marriage to higher ranking men was sanctified by rigid custom and religion'.[13] The Bedi Sikhs, a sub-caste of the Kshatriyas, warriors versed in the Vedas, between Islam and Hinduism, were known as Kuri-Kar, the daughter-murderers. This created a vacuum at the top of society which drew up women from lower castes to the sons of the Sikhs, bringing a dowry, an upward flow of women and wealth. The poorest men in lower castes were left almost without wives. We will be better advised, rather than being angry or surprised, to compare this practice with the complex organization of the ant colony, where both the proportion of females to males and the castes are subordinate to a strict order. In this light, we need to take a fresh look at the destruction of classes by the Russian revolution. There an exclusively moral evaluation of such culling of the human population becomes problematical.

There is a problem also with our so-called free will, or freedom of choice.

'If our genes are inherited and our environment is a train of physical events set in motion before we were born, how can there be a truly independent agent within the brain? The agent itself is created by the interaction of the genes and the environment. It would appear that our freedom is only a self-delusion.'[14]

In fact, we unhesitatingly call the mosquito a small mechanism. 'The whine of a female yellow-fever mosquito is between 450 and 600 hertz (cycles per second). In the laboratory, entomologists have attracted males simply by striking a tuning fork set at these frequencies.'[15] If something organic is placed over the tuning fork, the male will attempt to mate – with what? With a sound which is a sufficient stimulus for it, without any female. He is attuned to the frequency of the sound. The behaviour of the female mosquito is equally inflexible. She seeks out mammalian prey by their warmth or by the odour of lactic acid emanating from the skin. She has two fine stylets with which she penetrates the skin, and one species of mosquito identifies blood by the taste of one of hundreds of constituents of blood, adenosine diphosphate (ADP). Where there is adenosine diphosphate, she knows there is blood. Other similar 'sign stimuli' guide the mosquito to appropriate ponds and smaller bodies of water where she can lay her eggs.

She does nothing else in her life. In the head of this mosquito, there are only 100,000 nerve cells. That is enough to hard-code the mosquito with genes for the few days of her life from birth to the final act of laying eggs. Where here is there room for free will and freedom of choice?

But in what way are humans any different? They have in their head 10 billion neurons, which, of course, is a lot more. We can anticipate that their behaviour will be 100,000 times more complex than that of a mosquito, although in reality it is sometimes not in fact all that much more complex, from birth to death. The huge difference in potential complexity is enough to boggle anyone's mind, but what reason do we have to say that a human being is not a machine, albeit of astounding complexity? One hundred thousand times more complex than a mosquito, but why not just as subject to determinism? No reasons seem to present themselves, other than despair at the prospect of trying to identify causes and aims for us to say that a person acted in a particular way because they *wanted* to. The concept of wanting itself proves to be a biological function. We cannot help remembering with a certain satisfaction that this predicament of completely and utterly predetermined behaviour, the rigidity of the Cross, on which a person can move neither their arms nor their legs, is something we somehow managed to foresee.

There is a big difference between private observation and mass data collection, which has been made possible by modern science and really by it alone. As far as personal traits are concerned, which are usually characterized as 'good' or, on the contrary, 'disagreeable', we find that they are innate. They do *not actually belong* to individuals; their personality is nothing to do with them, it is not *their* personality. The extent to which personality is innate – that is, determined genetically – is systematically underestimated. Research has been conducted on Chinese American children three to five years old. They run, jump, laugh, call to each other, ride bicycles and scooters, but do it all noticeably more quietly than cohorts of European children, and the impression is not of bedlam but of peace and calmness. There is less facial expression, which gives an impression of greater dignity and self-control. Physical movements are more coordinated, there are fewer falls, collisions, and skinned knees, no squealing and shrieking, not even the moral outrage common in children of this age – 'You're naughty!' – no squabbling about ownership, no fights – in fact only good-natured tussling between the older boys. What is this? Centuries of Chinese upbringing or, *on the contrary*, is China the way it is and brings up its children as it does because that is in its genes? The children of Navajo Indians in this respect are even more calm than the Chinese. If a Navajo child is picked up while standing and carried from one place to another, it will rarely paddle with its feet as if walking; if it is sat down, it will lower its head; if placed on its stomach, it will not start crawling. Again, this passivity of Navajo children was noticed long ago and is explained as being due to the fact that Navajo mothers carry their children on their backs squeezed in an upright position into a wooden box. In fact the explanation is probably quite the contrary: it is because Navajo babies are relatively passive that it was natural to carry them in a rigidly fixed position.

But if everything is prescribed genetically, what does the individual human being actually *do*? Edward Wilson, the myrmecologist who is now sixty-nine, in his 1978 book *On Human Nature*, expresses an opinion that I really like. A sense of self adds diligence and meticulousness to the movements of the puppet. I probably like that because it is close to what I have called 'thusness' or simply 'it'. 'The emotional centres of the lower brain are programmed to pull the puppeteer's strings more carefully whenever the self steps onto the stage.'[16]

A widespread fallacy which we will do well to avoid is that a person has some kind of meaningful moral judgement. Plato is more probably right in *Alcibiades I* when he notes that the moral judgement about good and evil that gives an adult politician the energy to act in the cause, naturally, of good against evil is what he already had, very strongly, in his earliest childhood, when he truculently rebuked his playmates for being naughty, bad, and horrid.

Here is a description of the behaviour of a society of hunter-gatherers living in the Stone Age; there are a few dozen of these on earth and they are like extended families, a group of twenty-five individuals occupying and defending a territory for hunting and gathering of 1,000–3,000 km^2, so a rough circle with a diameter of 30–50 km.

The buzz of conversation is a constant background to the camp's activities: there is an endless flow of talk about gathering, hunting, the weather, food distribution, gift giving, and scandal. No !Kung is ever at a loss for words, and often two or three people will hold forth at once in a single conversation, giving the listeners a choice of channels to tune in on. A good proportion of this talk in even the happiest of camps verges on argument. People argue about improper food division, about breaches of etiquette, and about failure to reciprocate hospitality and gift giving.... Almost all the arguments are *ad hominem*. The most frequent accusations heard are of pride, arrogance, laziness, and selfishness.[17]

If they were talking about other groups, especially groups they were at war with, their accusations would be more serious, involving malevolence, slyness, the use of poisons and black magic. In other words, there is a constant grinding, finessing, psyching oneself up to make an effort. When we compare the endless discourse of modern journalism with this constant fault-finding in a primitive society, we find the themes are just the same.[18]

Or again, comparing the observation of modern societies of hunter-gatherers with the behaviour of apes and archaeological evidence, the anthropologist Robin Fox sketches the hypothetical portrait of a hominid who would have had a chance of survival on the basis of that 99% of the history of human genetic evolution that preceded the last 50,000 years of humankind as we know it. Here is the portrait. 'Controlled, cunning, cooperative, attractive to the ladies, good with the children, relaxed, tough, eloquent, skillful, knowledgeable and proficient in self-defense and hunting.'[19] The more pronounced these features, the greater the success in survival and child care. But these are also all features, painstakingly cultivated and propagandized in films, advertising, and on television, of the successful modern American.

Hominids with these qualities, with these genetic elements, could not but catalyse their own development, autocatalysis, faster and faster, until in the end there was almost a vertical takeoff of culture. In a matter of some 10,000 years, everything we see around us today came into existence. Gradually, or by leaps and bounds, the biological development of the human species has proceeded in an oddly unstoppable manner. Over the past two or three million years, every 100,000 years the human brain increased in volume by one cubic inch. It was only some 250,000 years ago that this process stopped and *Homo sapiens* emerged in his present form.

But the chemistry operating in this autocatalysis from the very beginning – genetics – remained exactly the same. A biologist with an up-to-date acquaintance with anthropology and historical anthropology can see quite clearly that modern civilization is simply a *hypertrophied version* of structures that existed previously, in much the same way that the elephant's tusk is a hypertrophied version of a single tooth, or hypertrophy of the frontal bone produces gigantic branched antlers in certain species of deer.

What in the early hunter-gatherers was a modest adaptation to the environment has become a developed and sometimes monstrous form in 'advanced' society. Nevertheless, the direction of growth here, like the growing of a tooth into a tusk, was foreordained: prehistoric human beings had a predisposition towards it.

For example, the hunters of the Kalahari Desert. The upbringing of girls and boys there is identical, the difference is barely perceptible; girls work less with adults (men and women) outside the home, and the occupations of adult women are clearly different from those of men: they gather nuts and fetch water (although men do that too). Then, however, a large hunting family settles down and establishes a village. Already in the first generation gender roles are more clearly defined. Girls stay at home, while boys graze domesticated animals, chasing away monkeys and goats. Previously what a woman had gathered she could keep, unless she chose to make a present of it. It belonged to her; she had equal rights and had self-confidence. Now in the village she is clearly dependent and a characteristic male domination appears. Outside the home, the woman has no voice. Time passes, the change becomes more evident. The hypertrophied gender division is reinforced by custom, ritual, then by the law, and before you know it woman is a chattel to be fought over, traded, sold, and expected to conform to a different morality in relationships. '[T]he great majority of societies have evolved toward sexual domination as though sliding along a ratchet.'[20] Movement of the hands on the clock is in one direction only, and terribly hypertrophied in comparison with the little short movement of a swinging pendulum, but the swing of the pendulum preceded, and had to precede, the movement of the hands on the clock.

But as with the situation of women, look at the hypertrophy of women's fashion in modern society, and of all the features of modern society. Take nationalism. In the Kalahari Desert, the Nyae Nyae !Kung confidently say of themselves that they are completely pure and proper. They forbid themselves to partake of anything that is impure, but another group of the !Kung are repulsive, murderers all of them, and use witchcraft and deadly poisons. In exactly the same way, all civilized national cultures love themselves and consider that their culture in what *really matters* is unquestionably the best, sanctified by God; others may be passable in certain respects, but in what *really matters* they are manifestly worse. Culture works to provide a foundation for this sense of distinction; it writes its ideology and history, and different cultures *invariably* write different histories, in such a way as to confirm the views of their own uniquely good culture.

Now in the broken clock the gearwheel is not spinning, the ratchet has jammed, but what about the spring of the pendulum? It seems not to be moving either, but no! There are just the same oscillations in the spring as before, even if imperceptible, especially if the clock is given a jolt. If we remove the cultural hypertrophy from the surface, we will find beneath it the same genetic mechanisms. They have not gone anywhere. And those masks, the faces that those participating in the culture are obliged to wear during the day, for example women who aspire to a position in society, who aspire to follow the vagaries of fashion. All that will run off, and it will happen not just some day but *right now* in the satraps of civilization, because each such functionary has two faces, one put on for public display and another, perhaps very unsure of itself but responding to some minimal, barely perceptible movement of the pendulum, obeying, as if in a dream, the orders of its genes, has already inclined in its ordained direction, and everything has been transmitted to the ratchet and gearwheel. Support for this overcomplicated system may abruptly cease. The human creature may suddenly, critically, return from the hypertrophied forms to the forms of nature. Self-knowledge, certainly supported by the sum of human knowledge, that great liberator from prevalent stereotypes, should – we are told by enlightened biologists, *must* – elicit that core of *nature* in humankind which is subjected to the hypertrophic norms of civilization. Knowledge and self-knowledge will help us the more precisely to peel away dangerous progress from safe progress and show *what* in human nature needs to be cultivated and what undermined, *what* can safely be enjoyed and what should be treated with caution. Change in human nature must, however, be expected no sooner than we succeed not just in combining and recombining, but in modifying genes, and that means no time soon.

All that applies to any hypertrophied culture also applies to war. A biological predisposition to war in the human species is probably no more than average: hyenas in particular, lions, apes, and langurs, are much more likely than humans to fight to the death among themselves, to eat their young, and even each other. *Cultural* cannibalism, as a ritual in ancient Mexico, is of course hypertrophic. It is thought that in the Valley of Mexico 15,000 people were sacrificed to the gods annually, and then eaten by nobles, their servants and soldiers. A possible explanation is that humans are carnivorous and in Central America there was an endemic shortage of meat.

Biological anthropology, or social biology, rejects Freudian notions of an accumulation in the unconscious of impulses and instincts which periodically find an outlet in war. War is, after all, only one variety of aggressive behaviour. Under the Freudian analogy, with a boiling pot building up a head of steam, war, an effective outlet for the steam, should be replaceable with other kinds of aggression, such as tattoos and other forms of ritualized body mutilation, martial arts, or meting out harsh treatment to deviants. In fact, quite the opposite occurs: *all* kinds of aggression break out simultaneously, again as a kind of autocatalysis.

A topic still little researched is *territorial* war and, more generally, attachment to territory.

Lecture 26, 14 April 1998

We are surrounded by dense forest on all sides, end to end, and what seems to be so personally ours, our thinking, is in no better a position than our actual bodies. The forest has always managed to close around us. In this respect, our efforts to hack our way through the jungle were in vain. Today's big, modern city is again a jungle; science has hacked its way into the macrocosm and the microcosm, but in these new dimensions it always again encounters ready-made formations, so that it seems almost to be putting in an order for what it is going to see. Corresponding to the degree of its refinement and subtlety, in just the right amount for its sophistication and logistics, it encounters sophistication and logistics in nature too. It meets formations of a complexity it is ready to deal with and on the boundaries of what it can handle, invariably glimpsing also the limit beyond which lie 'unanswered questions'.

But of course it is just the same with our thinking. What we always see are its formations, just as when someone wakes they see a finished dream, and hear the ringing of the alarm clock which itself turned into a dream, but what they do not see is the transition from the ringing to what they were dreaming, or the movement from what they were dreaming to the ringing.

What is beyond the reach of science is communication with the double. We are standing next to the double and always find that so interesting, next to the *inter-esse*. Our only important differentness is that we are feeling good because we recognize we are in this interesting situation. And in addition we are comfortable with a situation which seems to obtain whenever any living thing is undertaking anything: it is not too sure what is going to happen next. We learn to be prepared for our inherent unpreparedness, for the fact that in one way or another we are going to be caught out, and what will be decisive (decisive for what? For us, for everything, for anything at all?) will be what we do at the moment we are possessed, captivated.

A 'culture' which does not know, or does not yet know, about the ineluctable unreadiness of living beings to encounters in the forest, but which statistically, perhaps in terms of numbers of publications or the share of on-screen time, is dominant, can be of no help to us whatsoever, not even negatively through its mistakes. It does not even make interesting mistakes, but this 'culture' is perhaps a convenient, neutral background to interesting human behaviour. For example, the behaviour of the hare, which leaps in horror at the sight of the wolf, is interesting, but after all we have been expecting this after his bold performance on the stage.[1] The steady, peaceful hum of placid screen culture is fit only to be the background for something unusual. Science and scientific thinking teach us that actually things are not that simple, and show us exactly how they are not simple.

I will try to understand and explain why science continues to take its bearings from popular culture, adopting its vocabulary and concepts. It is not principally because that culture is actually popular, or because, by using its vocabulary, science is able to attract money to pay for research, but because the culture needs science and asks for its criticism and purification, which makes it natural for science to embed itself in culture. Anything that is connected to that machinery has at the outset no name in it and is proposing something new and unnamed.

But even if that constant, steady cultural background serves for contrast, that is even more true of science. Its purifying, sobering contribution is never enough. Here pragmatic, analytical American thinking has not yet sufficiently crushed the old metaphysics of Europe. It needs to go further. Whether we belong to that American tradition or not, whether we have become part of it too soon or too late, one way or another we need to – 'it's a must, guys'[2] – go to school there and learn its skills. What would be really absurd, though, would be if we made this admirable school of sobriety, with its pragmatic, analytical approach, our model for generating new texts. Now we can never say that the American approach is not for us. On the contrary, whenever we fail to respect the principles, demands, and discipline of pragmatism and analysis, we will see that as a fault and put it right. Let us now honestly admit that our inability to learn the discipline of pragmatism is a failure on our part.

Something that undermines our belief that humankind is something special in nature is the simple fact that many animals, like chimpanzees or ants, behave in a similar way to humans. Are humans markedly different? Well, in the first place, why might not a particular species differ markedly? And in the second place, human beings *en masse*, in most cases, do not differ from animals to their advantage. If, however, you prefer to steer clear of ethical judgement, the distinctiveness can be fundamental, radical, but of such a kind that it makes it pointless to talk of distinctions within life or about life on earth at all. The difference separating the human species from the other animals which it does make sense to talk about is odd, and it is a massive problem. Everything that keeps us busy, that we do and talk about, is an attempt to resolve the human question. To talk in any way definitively about humankind, other than as a burning question, is just that old European trash that needs the broom of American analysis and pragmatism to come and gently, indulgently, sweep it away.

The first thing to sweep away is a particular kind of God, an observer who allegedly created humans free and then left them to fend for themselves in the world, supposedly because he did not want his great love for them to infringe their freedom.[3] That kind of God, the teacher who absents himself from the classroom, greatly annoyed Vasiliy Rozanov.[4] Would a parent, a mother, who saw her baby about to put its hand in the fire calmly let it burn itself so as to learn from experience what sort of thing fire was? Would she not pull it back in time? Would a God who loved people and knew the secret of how they ought to behave really hold back until they managed to work that out for themselves? Would he not intervene and just tell them? Not take them by the hand? It is not particularly interesting to enquire where this unbiblical God was manufactured. The first God in the Bible came and badgered Moses, forced him against his will and beyond his strength to lead the people. He handed down the law and became extremely bad-tempered when the people strayed from it. Anyone who wants to is welcome to investigate the trail, but I must warn you not to suppose this hands-off God is a recent invention. He is a continuation of the ancient tradition of an irascible, jealous god who may know everything but does not intend to share his knowledge with anyone, and has every intention of forcing humans to seek their own way by trial and error.

American pragmatism, while acknowledging God and sweeping away some of his weirder representations, leaves him as empty as the God of the American national religion, the one being referred to when American currency proclaims that 'In God We Trust'. We are under no obligation to accept, along with American pragmatism, the limitations it places on its God, and can confidently say that, if God is real, and if he does indeed regard the human species as his creatures and his children, he will share everything he knows with them. Everything we need to know about coping with the automaton, the living creature that we are ourselves, he has told us, instilled in us, but will, if need be, come after us and say it again, caringly.

Even if it seems risky, it is best to admit honestly that you have been circling round something for so long that you are now spent and incapable of thinking any differently about it. Here is the point: God, about whom it is interesting to think, the real one, not the jealous one, has already told us everything he knows and, moreover, has said it in every way possible and in every language, including the languages of intuition, premonition, and dreams. On this count, we can rest assured, stop trying to construct God, but rather ask whether humans know everything that God knows. Human beings can know a lot but not tell it to anyone, not even themselves, not because they want, like a caring teacher, to give their pupils the freedom to learn by themselves, but because of a different kind of secretiveness and deafness. Humankind remains as unapproachable to itself as its double, and the riddle of the double seems set to remain a riddle, as if it were none of its business. The challenge of American pragmatism, to which we have no option but to respond, compels us to explain, and explain to ourselves, why we are *not* obliged just to consider ourselves a pre-scientific culture whose job is now to catch up. The range of topics we have approached in various ways, the topic of the other, the friend, the other *ego*, the double and twin, the dream, no matter how difficult these topics may be, *concern* us only too much, and matter more to us than pragmatism. We will seek God, if we do, also near to us, as near as if he were our identical twin, and remember Heraclitus, who saw the only difference between men and gods in the fact that the former are mortal and the latter immortal. What is God? He is the human being: not the human being who becomes immortal thanks to modern medicine, but the human who is him yet other than himself. In addition to Heraclitus's articulation of our task, we have the faith of Alexander Pushkin, unambiguous, unembarrassed, unafraid of being called naïve or primitive, a faith

> That there are some the fates find pleasing,
> Angelic friends of man on earth,
> A family of celestial birth,
> Who, dazzling rays of light releasing,
> Will thus enlighten us below
> and bliss upon the world bestow.[5]

We understand this talk of friends to refer to the other us. To face up to the fact that this is in fact our topic is to undertake an obligation, to bind ourselves to a task, which we now do, from this moment on. With thanks to the American pragmatism whose challenge has forced us finally to address what is our primary characteristic.

For now, we are afraid to look but will just get on with it, so let us return to our impenetrable forest and quietly take our place in the midst of the earth's living beings. We can hope for real freedom only when we cease to be afraid of being completely fettered.

We must continue to free ourselves from systems which often seem to have been handed down from the heavens, from somewhere beyond the clouds. Strict borders, red lines, and laws are probably related to the territoriality of all life and the way it defends its territory. We are under no obligation to think that life is part of the landscape; rather the landscape unfolds in different ways, in spaces defined by life. At all events, the boundary belongs to the forest. We long ago took note of the geometry in the forest. Let us look at it again from this angle.

In extant Stone Age-type societies of hunter-gatherers (the men mostly the hunters, the women mostly the gatherers, although the division is not rigid), the rigid division is between your own tribe and other tribes. One society prohibits fishing, hunting, or collecting vegetable food on their territory. Killing the member of another tribe, a neighbour, for picking fruit seems unjustifiably severe, and could even be unwise and have consequences considerably worse than losing part of your territory. There comes into play, however, a rigidity of a different kind than the geography of the forest, and different from rationality and calculation. That member of the neighbouring tribe did not ask permission before gathering. He was sly and dishonest, evil, and because of his innate wickedness rather than to compensate for any harm caused, he must be eliminated as a major threat, as a carrier of the worst kind of evil. In connection with this kind of behaviour, we need to look again at the doctrine of *an eye for an eye and a tooth for a tooth*, which has in it an element of disproportion and a rationale of a different order from standing up for what is good, something that can start out small but must ultimately lead to the 'total eradication of all evil'. The New Testament, on the other hand, speaks of forgiveness, not of an eye for an eye. It takes a different, radical position, while that of Moses is rigidly rational.

The Mundurucú of Brazil are head-hunters, authentic cut-throats, and they, too, have a rigid, uncompromising justification for their raids on *pariwat*, as they call anybody who is not a Mundurucú. (They raid early in the morning after dreams induced by a shaman, cut off as many heads as they can, and carry them off at high speed.) Someone behaving in this way is wise, because a non-Mundurucú is worse than a wild animal, not human. Inside that person, in their intentions, their will and their decisions, their motives and mood, in their 'head', there is so much evil that it is only by severing it, carrying it back home and keeping it there, that the world can be saved from evil.

If the Mundurucú did not rigidly purge nature of evil in this way, population control would be otherwise implemented by famine, so the head-hunters are carrying out a pre-emptive strike. Behind the terrible evil in those heads, which it is so essential to cut off, there lurks a violation of the ecological balance of nature. Accordingly, at this early stage in their development, the Mundurucú are a bit ahead of themselves, saving the earth from the destruction it faces nowadays. In an extreme and unambiguous way, they are acting in accordance with the old maxim that '*Who is not with us is against us.*'[6]

In place of the syllogism 'Population growth will lead to degradation and death by starvation, therefore it needs to be prevented by artificially reducing the population,' the conscious mind moves from reality into a realm where there is good versus evil, where superhuman feats of ingenuity, strength, and courage are needed to exterminate evil. This dogma is then arbitrarily imposed on living beings. The need to impose it is not because evil people have been personally identified, but because there is a need to cull the population. 'There is an innate predisposition to manufacture the cultural apparatus of aggression in a way that separates the conscious mind from the raw biological processes that the genes encode. Culture gives a particular form to the aggression and sanctifies the uniformity of its practice by all members of the tribe.'[7]

Darwinism *avant la lettre* is predisposing human beings towards its inexorability, and long before Darwin's laws of survival can operate, biology cuts in like a frontier boundary. One could argue that a boundary, a limit, a rigidity, is behind the wars of the ants, because the unfamiliar chemistry of a different ant colony hardly seems sufficient to explain the massacres. Obviously, chemistry is only a signal, much as for the head-hunters it is the different language that is the signal, but a small signal is sufficient to unleash the 'we good – you bad' syndrome.

How was this scheme of war invented? The inventor, unaware of his invention, divides himself into his pure self, who cruelly, at the risk of his own life, purifies himself by service and devotion to a sacred, religious cause, a self who knows incontrovertibly what has to be done – and his other self, who knows absolutely nothing about where this cause has come from, or why it is so rigid and demands such complete obedience.

The Mundurucú are only one example, and a straightforward one at that. We see the same thing in a more complex form in all cultures. We need, accordingly, to define culture as almost primarily a weapon of war: *culture serves a military purpose*. Culture has embedded in it an absolute requirement of discipline, obedience, and prohibitions, which invariably includes a consideration expressed with limpid clarity by a member of a warlike tribe: 'We are tired of fighting. We don't want to kill anymore. But the others are treacherous and cannot be trusted.'[8] The difference between 'us' and 'them' may be less than that between us and us; one may feel better inclined towards people on the other side than one's own, but: what one's own side is supposed to be like, must be like, where the border will lie and how it will change, is certainly not encoded in our genes; what is encoded is that there will be a boundary between our side and the others, as is the fact that it will be based on absolute and uncompromising principles.

These principles are manifestly remote from the biological rules, like survival, underlying Darwin's vision. War is waged so emphatically *not* to ensure personal physical survival that when slogans such as 'Give me liberty or give me death', or 'We will die rather than surrender', appear it is clearly time to take cover. The soaring, head-in-the-clouds ideals for which war is waged should not automatically arouse the suspicion that they are indirectly conducive to capturing the best Darwinian strongholds; and it is incumbent upon us to note that those who want to see themselves in this light and behave in this way are certainly reducing their prospects of survival. The presence of an 'other side', which is *always* required, and *never* stopping short of the threat of war, and the fact that war does not as a rule stop short of demanding large, often huge, loss of life, means that in order to preserve their life, people are *obliged to risk* it.

Paradoxically, and this is no mistake, in order to safeguard their lives, humans must pay with them. A lion, on the other hand, will always assess the strength of its would-be prey, and does not psych itself up to attack no matter what the cost. A dog will attack, but that is because humans have trained it to do so. In the case of a suicide bomber, the survival of the human being does not even come into the equation. Soldiers of one species of termites act as walking bombs, their glands and sacs loaded with a single-use fluid. The soldier termite squirts it at the enemy, it instantly thickens and throws the enemy into confusion, but also destroys the soldier, who sometimes literally explodes, the fluid bursting out of him in all directions.

The termites do have a warrior caste, but we have no reports of instances of total mobilization and sacrificial collective suicide in the name of an *ideal* rather than for the safeguarding of the ant colony. For an entire species to be prepared to sacrifice itself for the correct understanding of an idea appears to be the exclusive preserve of the human species.

The strategy of Darwinism extends to all species, but none throw themselves into a state of total mobilization in the service of an ideal that may demand war and may sanction during that war *all* forms of behaviour. Only human religion (understanding religion very broadly, not necessarily even institutionalized, like Marxism-Leninism, but also the dark modern religion of banking, which appears to involve almost no institution other than various forms of roulette wheel) provides such an inexhaustible supply of justifications. A warrior ant as it soldiers into enemy territory will gradually lose heart, its resolve failing until, on completely alien territory, it will become disorientated. A crusader will not be faint-hearted on someone else's territory because religion has sanctioned his extraterritoriality.

There would seem to be no reason to take issue with the notion of a Darwinist origin of the ideal, of worship, religion, and culture as war; an intuited, sensed outcome of fate. Rigorous conditions for survival are projected backwards, as it were, from the future into the present, and dictate extreme, boundary-defending behaviour because sooner or later there is going to be an emergency situation, so why not face it now? Prior discipline before an inevitable encounter. The reconnaissance troops have warned that the encounter is going to be terminal and are constantly probing the depths of the forest. 'History' is even etymologically related to reconnaissance. The initial meaning of ιστορία is investigation, questioning. The history of humanity has turned out as it has, a history of cultures and wars, thanks to history-reconnaissance which gathered sufficient intelligence to make the case for strict, anticipatory discipline.

How has such a complex attuning of humanity been possible? Well, in basically the same way that the lion calculates its leap, or the dolphin, as we read in Aristotle, calculates how deep it can dive on the basis of the limits of the air in its lungs. The reality itself, for example the sight of the bull, directly dictates the parameters of its leap to the lion. Similarly, the reconnaissance of which the human brain is capable dictates the need for discipline to humans.

If culture, primarily the culture of war, is destiny redirected backwards to the present, gathered history, then something that shapes the actions of humans, in addition to these substantive prompts, is a more formal kind of completeness, of fullness. It is something present also in the diving and leaping of the dolphin that Aristotle describes, and in the leaping of the lion.

What we are to call this completeness invariably present in human culture (humans are already behaving as if they were at the boundary, on the brink), I do not know, but invite you to consider that it is associated with the cult of Dionysos, with wine. Wine and fullness: it is a theme that deserves our attention. The founder of the Christian religion began his miracle working by transforming water into wine. The wedding at Cana in Galilee might have flopped because the wine ran out. The wine of the old religion was finished.

It is interesting to compare sex in human beings with this anticipatory aspect of human culture, which always suggests that the final decisive moment of judgement is right now, and provides itself with instant fullness. Modern biology echoes Aristotle's observation that humankind has chosen a strangely circuitous and complicated approach to procreation, as if having forbidden itself more direct methods of proliferation, and having physiologically consolidated the prohibition.

> Sex is central to human biology and a protean phenomenon that permeates every aspect of our existence and takes new forms through each step in the life cycle. Its complexity and ambiguity are due to the fact that sex is not designed primarily for reproduction. Evolution has devised much more efficient ways for creatures to multiply than the complicated procedures of mating and fertilization.[9]

Bacteria simply divide in two, in some species every twenty minutes. Hydras simply produce progeny from parts of their body. Interestingly, there is in human beings an element in their history, entirely healthy, in no way monstrous or even perceived as a deviation from the norm of human reproduction, when reproduction by division suddenly breaks its way through, much like in bacteria. Identical twins are born from the division of a single cell into two within the womb. Nature in these cases, admittedly rare and which humankind could perfectly well get by without, suddenly shows that it is able to perform straightforward, simple reproduction in humans. Theoretically, if there were sufficient space in the womb, reproduction by cell division could proceed ceaselessly. In a sense, as Lucretius Carus put it, for the ancient prokaryotes – of which there were more then than there are now and which reproduced by dividing – the earth itself, to paraphrase him, was just one great womb.[10]

This simple, direct method of reproduction, of which human nature has rather ostentatiously shown itself to be capable, has been displaced. Sex is a difficult, complex, risky undertaking. Aristotle noted that, as if on purpose, the way to give birth has been extended and elaborated. In an abnormal way, and not infrequently fatally, ectopic pregnancy is possible. An engineer might say that the design is recklessly overelaborate, to the extent of making it hazardous. Adjustment of the reproductive system requires such precision that again there is a grave suspicion that getting it perfectly correct is difficult and rare. Aristotle, you will recall, suggests a quite strange combination of moods, different for the husband

and the wife, to get the timing right. More than 2,000 years pass, a book sweeps over Europe like some great revelation and is, in many countries, banned for thirty-five years. The book is *Lady Chatterley's Lover* (1927) by D.H. Lawrence (b. 11 September 1885, Eastwood, Nottinghamshire, Eng., d. 2 March 1930, Vence, France), English author of novels, short stories, poems, plays, essays, travel books, and letters, in which the author emphasizes that the correct setting for a human erotic union is extremely rare. Two souls who are capable of it by chance find themselves in such different positions in society that they have to fight their way to each other through barriers of class and family.

Subsequently, molecular biology has revealed new and alarming facts: the human genetic mechanism is so complex that any mix-up with the chromosomes, or even the slightest shift in the balance of hormones, in the developing foetus will be enough to create abnormalities of physiology and behaviour. In other words, what goes on at the molecular level is at least as complex as the wedding ritual, which, as it were, dramatically re-enacts the behaviour, approach, and mutual selection of the gametes. Just as the smooth proceeding of the wedding ceremony can easily be disrupted, if only because of its complexity, so there can be disruption at the molecular level. We do not need to imagine that, in a creative unconscious mimesis, the wedding ritual is reproducing the physiological complexity of mating, but rather that, intuiting or sensing through empathy the subtleties and precariousness of what is happening at the molecular level, humans hope through strict observance of the wedding ritual to ensure the correct functioning of the physiology, given the endless possibilities of disruption, injury, degradation, and consequences in the form of defective offspring.

So the complexity of human sex confers no advantages in Darwinian terms of survival and, indeed, has disadvantages, requiring all sorts of circumstances. 'There are good reasons for reproduction to be nonsexual: it can be made private, direct, safe, energy-saving and selfish. Why, then, has sex evolved?'[11]

Characteristically, the American biologist replies that this happens for the sake of diversity. If again and again in the progeny of each pair there was no mixing of genes, their offspring would be identical, there would be no diversity, which, of course, would not matter if the environment remained exactly the same, but given the rapid and radical changes that take place on planet earth, diversity gives a chance that someone will be able to adapt.

It is, of course, not necessarily the case that this is the only purpose of bisexual reproduction, but that a living being is seeking something and is interested in a maximum diversity in its attempts is indicated by the polarity of male and female, so striking as if really to maximize the differentiation between the two extremes. Polarity spreads the net wider. The polarity of male and female is a topic in its own right, but here are some facts on how startlingly far apart the poles are. A female in the course of a lifetime will create several hundred reproductive cells, gametes, while a male will generate 100 million during each mating. The female gamete (a very satisfactory word in my opinion, which means marriageable at the molecular level, from γάμος, 'marriage', suggesting that the social ceremony parallels the molecular marriage) is 85,000 times the size of the male reproductive cell. It is a remarkable, and I would say delightful, difference which runs through every level of these beings. I see a connection to the molecular level in such details of human babies as that at six months of age little girls pay closer attention to communicative sounds than to technical sounds, which they are somehow able to discriminate between, while boys at the same age make no such distinction.[12] It is interesting to see how this difference continues and becomes more complex as life progresses. The female of the species is more receptive to communication and personal approaches than the male.

We will do well to leave this infinite region of comparisons and move on. Before we do, however, we have an opportunity to consider further our new obligation, the theme of the twin or double. This is in connection with the old topic of the management of the living automaton. Molecular biology encourages us to look deeper, even in its terminology. A zygote, from the Greek root meaning matrimony, is the name of the link instantly created by the fusion of a male and female gamete, and molecular biology provides a foundation here for a working hypothesis we will find useful as a heuristic device. We shall regard the method of mammalian reproduction, especially in humans, with its characteristic and mysterious complexity so unnecessary for procreation, as being a *ritualization*, on the molecular level a biological ritual of reproduction. Now, without thinking anything and without any guesswork about the strange overcomplication of this ritual, knowing nothing about the molecular level, living beings, birds, mammals, under observable conditions, in the limelight, so to speak, of the stage that is the earth, enact in their mating, and more widely, social rituals, in rivalry, in the ceremony of courtship, of the same or a similar complexity. I will make so bold as to say that *I do not know* which came first and which came second, whether the social ballet is a mimesis of the physiology or the physiological automaton attunes itself, becomes modified and consolidated to adapt itself, to the ritual observed.

We would like to act responsibly here, and do not want this to be just one more lunatic hypothesis. Something tells us that it is possible to prove this. So today I will go no further than raising the issue. Before I formulate it more succinctly, here are a few observations from biology.

The Darwinian explanation of the human peculiarities of sex (the lack of a mating season, which most other mammals have, a time when they are 'on heat'; erotic involvement of almost the entire body; eroticism between individuals of the same sex) – incidentally, if sex is not there for procreation, not there for breeding, the objection to passion for a being of one's own sex, that it does not serve the purpose of procreation, becomes redundant – sex serves, strange as it may sound, not for procreation, or at least not primarily for procreation. Its main aim is something different:

'Genetic diversification, the ultimate function of sex (let us assume), is served by the physical pleasure of the sex act and outranks in importance the process of reproduction.'[13] Human sex, complicated, fraught with risks, finely attuned, is as it is in order to establish and consolidate, to cement links between people.

Without commenting on that opinion, let us nevertheless, in response to this acknowledgement of sexual ecstasy by our biologist, recall Bacchus and Dionysos. Is a sacred madness really required in order to break the chains of so-called natural determinism? Is not intoxication encoded in the very nature of the body, at least of the human body? Does not the belief in iron mechanisms, chains of physico-chemical and biological dependence, date from the age of machinery and the supposed mechanical automaton? Is it really only human culture that has broken out to freedom and joy? Is not the contrary true, that, confused and mechanized, it more often isolates, hems in, the real body made for joy and ecstasy?

Perhaps what is needed is for us to take the view that sobriety and scientific rigour, ecstasy and madness, are equally in tune with the physical chemistry of the body.

Again, is asceticism, the ultimate expression of which is the image of the Saviour on his Cross, or self-sacrifice, supposedly the highest attainment of human culture, not really a recollection and a reminder of what is innate in our biology? We have talked about the self-sacrifice of the warrior termites. The same is true of bees that sting with their entire abdomen to defend the hive: the sting is constructed like a fishhook, and the bee knows that by injecting it there is no way it will be able to recover it; it will remain lodged in whatever has been stung, along with part of the bee's abdomen and all the poison in the sting. Humans are less commonly so altruistic; biologists have rated our altruism as somewhere between that of the sharks, an ancient and utterly selfish species, and the bees. This is why, when we are not manifesting even our biologically determined level of altruism, we have pangs of conscience, vacillation, ambivalence, and feelings of guilt.

This all indicates that the automaton in us is not yet working or has ceased to operate at its full capacity. It seems that our treatment and care of the automaton should not be in terms of inspection and mechanical intervention, but in terms of decorum, ritual, drama, and sportiveness of the individual human and of society. The automaton comes into its own not where its supposed mechanisms are functioning, at the molecular level, but on the level of behaviour. In Provençal culture, the poetry of seekers and troubadours was by no means only a quest for poetic forms, the courtly dancing of the Provençals and Sicilians and of the delectable new Florentine style, the *dolce stil nuovo*, where ecstasy, delight, and joy, on the one hand, and continuation of the race, on the other, were kept chastely separate so that, the researchers tell us, the knight singing in praise of his beautiful lady could never, by definition, marry her. This courtly dancing was not only not a departure from nature, some sublimation of 'physiology', but rather the discovery – in a brief and soon forgotten time, repressed in the wars against the Albigensian heretics – of humankind in its true essence, enacting, setting free, the authentic automaton, an intuiting and restoration of its secret genetic make-up on the physiological and molecular level.

Lecture 27, 21 April 1998

We need to understand the source of our intuitive sense that our behaviour is not completely plotted out according to some agenda and what its significance is if, as we are told by modern biology, genetics is leading us by the nose. 'An enduring miracle', we may say, in the words of the nineteenth-century Russian thinker Pyotr Chaadaev on this subject, and about the long-recognized existence of two parallel categories: the unforgiving, rigid determinism affecting everything and the manifest freedom of everything.[1] 'The coefficient of supplementarity', we can agree with Niels Bohr, who extended his 'coefficient of supplementarity' to include biology, seeing in it two equally plausible ways of explaining, for example, the healing of a wounded whale. On the one hand, there are chemical reactions that naturally, invariably, occur upon contact of blood with damaged tissue and with salt water; while, on the other hand, there is *teleology* – the tendency of a part of the body which has deviated from its state of wholeness to return to a balanced state of integrity.

Since our reading of Wittgenstein, primarily of his *Tractatus Logico-Philosophicus*, we have, you see, been moving towards a different perception of freedom.[2] Firstly, we have come increasingly to respect the living machine, the automaton, at every level of which we see a complexity which even the fantastic modern means of detailed investigation have not yet got to the bottom of; and the refinement of its fine-tuning, from the so-called unity of the genotype to the compaction of a dense genetic program for an entire large organism into a tiny invisible cell.

The unity of the genotype deserves a special, long annotation. It can be discussed in a variety of ways, for example as in the work of Étienne Geoffroy Saint-Hilaire (1772–1844), a

French naturalist who established the principle of 'unity of composition', postulating a single consistent structural plan basic to all animals as a major tenet of comparative anatomy, and who founded teratology, the study of animal malformation. After his appointment as professor of zoology at the University of Paris (1809), he began the anatomical studies that he would later summarize in *Philosophie*

[! Enough! This is more than any theory of probability can explain: the frequency of the connection between biology and philosophy shows there is a link between them to which we should pay attention. *Bibikhin*] *anatomique* (2 volumes, 1818–22). His studies on embryos supplied important evidence for his views on the unity of organic composition among vertebrates, which he now defined in three parts: the law of development, whereby no organ arises or disappears suddenly, explaining vestiges; the law of compensation, stipulating that one organ can grow disproportionately only at the expense of another; and the law of relative position, stating that the parts of all animals maintain the same positions relative to each other.[3]

These three laws were united in Saint-Hilaire's '*loi de balancement*'.

Nowadays, instead of 'balancing', we would talk about homoeostasis, 'any self-regulating process by which biological systems tend to maintain stability while adjusting to conditions that are optimal for survival'.[4] Actually, 'balancing' is more specific, suggesting that if one pan has moved, there is no need to check the other because it will quite clearly have moved in the opposite direction. 'Genetic homoeostasis' has a more specialized meaning: it is the theory, which facts support, that if in the course of evolution any trait becomes dominant and forges ahead, because that is what selection requires, when it reaches its goal, the corresponding population survives and flourishes. The rapidly developing trait then resumes its place and genetic equilibrium is restored. What maintains the balance? Again, something *integral*.

Étienne Saint-Hilaire smoothly extrapolated from the development of the embryo to the development of life in history, and was one of those who paved the way for the adoption of Darwinism. We can see in Darwin a direct terminological link to Saint-Hilaire and his 'correlation of growth'. Darwin writes, 'Correlated Variation. I mean by this expression that the whole organisation is so tied together during its growth and development, that when slight variations in any one part occur, and are accumulated through natural selection, other parts become modified.'[5] This is one of those things in Darwin that his critics tend to overlook. As you remember, Berg objected to Darwin on the grounds that the giraffe needed to do more than extend its neck; it needed to restructure its whole body, and for that another, special round of natural selection would be needed. Here, though, we find in Darwin unapologetic nomogenesis no less than in Berg. Darwin speaks about this even more explicitly when he says, for example, in relation to unintended consequences stemming from *artificial* selection: 'If man goes on selecting, and thus augmenting, any peculiarity, he will almost certainly modify unintentionally[!] other parts of the structure, owing to the mysterious laws [! (We note that Berg himself is less bold in his utterance.) *Bibikhin*] of correlation.'[6] Darwin is aware of the nightmare of breeders, that if they focus on one trait, it may bring with it another, unwanted, feature. 'I do not know of a single intensive selection experiment during the past 50 years during which some such undesirable effects have not appeared.'[7]

Incidentally, in the title of Darwin's famous *The Origin of Species by Means of Natural Selection*, the emphasis is on 'natural', because *artificial* selection, what Aristotle would call 'technical selection', was already known, widely practised, and had been described. Now it was being argued that nature itself actually worked in the same way, also selecting and creating varieties. The only difference was that while breeders obtained varieties within species, nature obtained entire species which were startlingly different. Darwin explained that by the fact that nature had vast amounts of time to perform its selection, not decades but billions of years.

Sergey Chetverikov (1880–1959) was a specialist in evolutionary and population genetics, patterns of selection in populations associated with the dynamics of the evolutionary process, zoogeography, entomology. Like Berg, his work survived the purge of geneticists under Stalin largely by having been published in the West. His 1926 article, in *Zhurnal eksperimental'noi biologii* [*Journal of Experimental Biology*], was translated in 1961 in America. The phenomenon of pleiotropy, 'multiple turning', the 'production by a single gene of two or more apparently unrelated effects'. Pleiotropy was known about before Chetverikov: that is, the gene as a thread that somehow gets woven into all tissues and attributes. (Related incidentally to Wittgenstein's 'family resemblance', where the son clearly resembles his father, but in what way? It is difficult to say: in everything, but elusively. The biologist will say the father's gene has entered and affected everything in different ways.) Chetverikov developed pleiotropy into the concept of the 'genotypic milieu'. The terminology is slightly deceptive. What is being referred to is not the outward environment but the internal milieu, which operates from within on how any gene manifests itself. Individuals are indivisible not only in their soma (the soma, you will recall, is all the cells of an animal or plant with the exception of the reproductive cells), but also in the way any gene they have manifests itself. The gene acts through the medium of an organism that is unique and integral, peculiar to every species and every individual.

There is no reason we should have to talk, as Darwin does, about a *mysterious* law. It is quite sufficient to say that here the mechanism ends and the influence of an indefinable *whole* begins. Ultimately, when people talk of 'genes' and 'genetics' they are referring to the so-called structural genes, on whose presence or absence entirely observable characteristics of an organism depend. But what do the rest of the genes do? The other 50%, or the other 99%? This is currently being researched intensively, and there are authors who already believe it is naïve to talk about 'genes', in the traditional sense, as responsible for something specific.[8] They believe it would be better, at least at the higher levels of organization, to speak of 'regulatory systems' and changes within them.

In favour of the 'unity of the genotype', supported by the 'regulatory system' (the very vagueness of these expressions suggests that biologists are still feeling their way), is, on the other hand, a fact we have already read about in Edward Wilson. When different species, for example of ants, come in contact, they begin to differentiate further, when it would seem simpler for them to merge. An example from Ernst Mayr, who refers to work from the first half of the twentieth century: at the end of the last Ice Age, about 8,000 years ago, the geographical border in Central Europe between two species of crows, the hooded crow and the carrion crow, disappeared. These species had not yet developed isolating mechanisms, like those between donkeys and horses. A male donkey and female horse (more commonly; the reverse is less usual) can successfully produce offspring, mules, but these will not themselves have progeny. Hybrid hooded and carrion crows can have progeny, no problem there, and we might expect that a new crossbred species would inevitably emerge from somewhere in Central Europe. Nothing of the sort. The hybrid belt still extends only 100 miles between the hooded and carrion crows, and deeper into the territory of the hooded crows the hybrid offspring do not survive. Natural selection operates *against* them, and vice versa. The genotype is preserved intact.

In the 1970s, an exemplary study in Denmark showed a similarly narrow hybrid belt between domestic and wild mice. These species, too, seem to have been in close geographical proximity for thousands of years. In effect, the example of the mule described by Aristotle confirms the same situation, except that the narrow hybrid belt there is not geographical (you can ride a mule anywhere) but temporal: it extends to just one generation. 'We also want to know by what mechanisms this unity of the genotype is accomplished.... To be frank, our answers to these questions are still incomplete.'[9]

In the case of the hooded and carrion crows, we might think that the hybrid was not penetrating beyond the zone of direct contact because of an attachment to geographical territory. Against this is the extensive, continent-wide, and even Eurasian distribution of some species. This suggests that, firstly, the crows are indifferent to geographical conditions, and, secondly, there exists a curious further category of species that isolate themselves to an extraordinary degree, so-called insular or colonial population structures. All this militates against the more harmonious and generalized picture presented by Berg, which does of course work for the purpose of showing the flexible settling in of species directly into a given environment by adaptation without any blind mechanism of selection. It fails to show the whole picture. Gophers, moles, and short-tailed mole rats are a well-known example. Gopher experts describe dozens, hundreds, of new subspecies. Perhaps they are complicating matters unnecessarily and these numerous, ostensibly different gopher species are actually all the same? Well, no. As it turns out, molecular biological analysis has revealed differences in the number and structure of chromosomes between the different subspecies of gophers that make it legitimate to classify them as separate species.

There is more. An early fascination with the genetic mechanism led to the view that mutation of a single position indicated a new species. Or, at least, a mutation in several positions, say fewer than ten, was enough to produce a new species of beetle, and all the remaining structure of the molecule that was carrying genetic information would just remain the same. Now people are more inclined to talk about a complete and utter reshuffling of the entire 'balance', to use Saint-Hilaire's term, and the formation of a new chain of the genetic mechanism.

And that is only on the level of genes. So, inside there is a 'genetic revolution' (that term is now in use), and *externally* not only we but the experts see the same familiar sight. An example is a population of fruit flies, *Drosophila pseudoobscura*, in Bogotá, Colombia. These are indistinguishable from the North American and Central American fruit fly. There is not even any behavioural isolation of these Colombian fruit flies. They mate with the North American *Drosophila* (North American fruit flies are defined as coming from north of Guatemala), but females from Bogotá that mate with North American males, like mares mating with donkeys, produce sterile offspring. That is, there is no phenotypic isolation of the *Drosophila* from Bogotá and no behavioural isolation, but there is reproductive isolation. (Compare that, incidentally, with the human species: there is any amount of phenotypic and behavioural isolation, and very striking and eye-catching at that, through colour. There is, however, no reproductive isolation in humankind whatsoever.)

We are talking about unity of the genotype. We need that in order to treat our heredity with more respect. It is not a matter just of the chromosomes we observe under the microscope during cell division, but something like that balance, Darwin's 'mysterious law', the overall chain.

We have no idea *why* what has emerged, both in the particular and in the general balance of formation of species, has developed as it has. What nature has at the back of its mind, what its intention may be, not only eludes us but may, quite possibly, *not exist at all*. Why, for example, does there exist what is called (in German in English texts) the 'structural plan', for example, the fact that the skeleton of all mammals, from elephants to mice, from humans to whales, consists of the same component parts? Why, at least during the stage of embryonic development, do all land vertebrates have four limbs and all insects six? Some dogmatic creationist might say, because that is the *ideal* form. So ideal movement for an insect is possible only with three pairs of legs, while a land vertebrate needs two pairs? That does not seem to make much sense. It seems far more interesting and sensible to say, as Ernst Mayr does, that rather than think about what is convenient for walking, we should look at the chain as a whole. Two pairs of legs are evidently needed for the overall equilibrium of a vertebrate. We do not need to specify which kind needs what, but we do know that to change one attribute introduces instability into the entire chain of the genotype and sets off a strong negative selection against the invading attribute – not because it is harmful, but because of itself it requires too much readjustment. The very complexity of the automaton functions as an inertial system.

Ernst Mayr calls the interfused, chained nature of the genotype, or even the 'total genotype' (referring, for example, to the genotype of insects in general) a 'straitjacket'. Unity of the genotype tends to lock species into their present configuration and make it difficult for them to escape it. May this explain why, for the last half billion years, so few novel life forms have arisen? Everything has remained much as it was. And may the reason why 99.999% of species, lines of evolution, have become extinct not be this stagnation of the genotype which has prevented all these luxuriant species from adapting in time to fast-changing conditions?

These and such other issues as stagnation, inertia, or the balance of the genotype and its structure, which will stubbornly replicate and reproduce itself forever until extinction or revolution, compel us to view the dictate of the species more seriously and respectfully, and conversely to view with more suspicion and less respect efforts to carve out for our own use and convenience some extra little island of freedom from the necessities of nature. We should view with even greater scepticism a confrontation or 'showdown' between culture and the necessities of nature, as if it were the role of culture to harass nature, to seize frontiers and salients from it, to 'exploit' it. It is blindingly obvious that not everything is right in the way human beings are behaving: everybody is agreed on that, and the only reason for all the mistakes is lack of respect for things which deserve more. The prevailing view seems to be that humans have freedom to choose, but keep making the wrong choice. In reality, the choice, the establishing of a frontier, has invariably, as we read last time, already been made. The human being is a borderline creature and, whether it likes it or not, the frontier has been fixed; all that remains is to look and see where it runs. No matter where, no matter how, humans look, they can rest assured that it is their seeing eye that is setting the frontier: the frontier is set in the very act of their looking. It remains for us to look and see where it runs.

It is sobering to have to admit that the frontier belongs to our genetic program. Anyone who is keen to stay in the realm of metaphysics could say that the outlines of existence are charted by *eidos*, but then this supporter of metaphysics will have to, if not accept the new translation of Max Delbrück, physicist and geneticist,[10] and of Ernst Mayr[11] that '*eidos*' = 'genetic program', then have the humility to listen to why that is how it has been translated.

We cannot say that that is just how they have chosen to understand and articulate Aristotle, while we, exercising our freedom of choice, prefer to interpret him differently. There is such a thing as learning, and it is not an activity of consciousness and culture opposed to nature. On the contrary, the genetic program, especially in higher organisms, is primarily what is called an open program, designed for writing into it what has been learned, what has been discovered from experience. For example, the young of birds and mammals are born without a closed program of escape actions to take in the presence of a predator and learn these gradually through the operating of an open program. A baby mouse will not run away from a cat, a lion cub does not eat a mouse, not by mistake or an oversight but because they simply have no appropriate pre-programmed behaviour. But they *do* have a program instructing them to learn this. The *biology* of a fledgeling, baby mouse, or lion cub predisposes them to be subjected to a period of risk when they do not know how to escape or where to escape to. We have no reason to suppose that biology, the program, has not incorporated a similar period of risk and uncertainty for humans and, at the same time, a program for learning. Just like a chick or a mouse, human beings can get it wrong.

The time has now come for us to start making use of the space we have on several occasions prudently left clear, starting a long time ago during the course on 'The Time Is Now' or even earlier, already beginning to suspect that all the prescriptions being offered to us (how to live, behave, work, study) were no longer relevant.[12] In September, when we entered *the forest*, we finally parted company with all prescriptiveness. In the depths of the forest, precepts have no function, unless to tell us to get out of the forest. We had to choose to abandon prescriptiveness or to abandon the forest, so we jettisoned prescriptiveness, rejecting all the precepts on offer. Now that apparent loss we can count but gain. In the place left clear of prescriptiveness, we can now install *eidos*, understood by Max Delbrück as the genetic program, as a kind of prescription from our species, or, better, as the species understood as prescription. To which we should add the observation that the human species is very odd.

Here is an example from the moral code (i.e. the boundary between good and bad, mine and yours), its variability and instruction. The example is taken from myrmecologist Edward Wilson. With the same energy with which societies of hunter-gatherers, now or in the Ice Age, drew the line between those they should support and those closely similar other people whom they should kill, modern baseball fans discriminate with extreme clarity and unambiguousness who ('their side') should be supported, not only by shouting and flag-waving but also by an unwavering willingness to pay for sport, while 'the other side', if they could get on to the field, they would be glad to crush, or at least immobilize. Just that desire is a considerable help. It is more difficult for a team to play 'away', where almost everybody is supporting the opposing team. Now players may leave their team and even go to play for an opposing team; someone coming into their own team may be a foreigner who has been bought in and does not even speak their language. Nothing matters. The home team's reputation does not suffer, and their demarcation from the 'other side' is in no wise weakened. The fan exists in a clean, bright world of combat. 'The substance matters little, the form all.'[13] As Vladimir Vysotsky's character puts it in the Taganka Theatre's rendering of Brecht's *The Good Woman of Szechuan*, respect the form and the content will follow. The substance matters so little that, if the behaviour of their team seems arrogant while the opposing team seem more to their liking, spectators may switch all their sympathies to the other side.

Or another example: a promise is absolute, and the person making it and the person to whom it is made do not even need to talk about that or, if they do, it is a pleonasm: only its unconditional nature, its total sincerity, give it force. On the other hand, you can simply walk away from it and say, 'I am not bound by it.' The situation is inflexible while I am inside it, but agreeing to stay inside it is not inflexible.

The program is inflexible, but can be applied in different ways. What does that point to? The freedom of humans? Or the need for them to learn? Learning is precisely what we do. We do not want just to follow a program, rules which are external to the automaton, or at least not as a first priority, because there is a higher priority. The living automaton is an autodidact and its mission includes not only self-preservation, but also preservation of itself as an autonomous learner.

In the more than 60,000 years since the time of the Neanderthals (in the oldest burials of which, such as in Iraq, seven kinds of flowers have been found, which are believed to have had significance in medicine and the economy, which means they already had ritual and religion), historians of religion have identified some 100,000 human religions. Florensky is probably right that worship is the beginning of culture. In religion, the very air it breathes is the distinction between pure and impure, sacred and profane, sanctification and 'certification'.[14]

Let there, then, be religion, pluralism, and tolerance: any rule is better than no rule. But this 'permitting' of religions is not the only way to treat them. As there are programs and programs, precepts and precepts, the love of sports fans for their team is possible because prior to that there is already within them the element of 'us against them'. Similarly, before the sanctification in accordance with the rules (the charter) of their religion there is a biological holiness towards which, as our reading has told us, Vladimir Toporov was clearing his way. Sainthood 'is cheerfully subordinate to the biological imperatives above which it is supposed to rise', the modern biologist tells us.[15] We concur with his definition of religion: it 'congeals identity',[16] its task is the 'sanctification of identity'. After all, holiness, sainthood as sanction, is precisely recognition of what feels right; the unsanctioned is simply defined as 'what feels wrong'.

We cannot help recalling Parmenides with his definition of being as what is one with itself, but poetry, too, according to Heidegger, is a realm of holiness and healing (*heilig*).[17] We find that all three, religion, poetry, and philosophy, in their very earliest suppositions, point towards *certification*. In all three, we intuit *how to behave towards the automaton*, and the only way of doing so that preserves its *integrity*, including, of course, its learning. In this formal orientation towards the task of maintaining wholeness and holiness, these three ways of dealing with the automaton are in agreement. Science, by virtue of its definition of itself as specialized and professional, finds itself excluded. It is not its purity and rigorousness that excludes and disqualifies it from managing the automaton: it disqualifies itself when it intentionally renounces dealing with the whole.

Needless to say, if religion is understood as a secondary set of commandments, moreover of unknown origin, the 'ethos of science' really will be superior to it. 'If religion … can be systematically analysed and explained as a product of the brain's evolution, its power as an external source of morality will be gone forever.'[18] Well, of course. Something else that is true is that at present science is more interesting than classical literature and philosophy; but we have already conceded that when we approvingly quoted Ionesco to the effect that the technological inventions of our time are more artistic than art; and again just now when we quoted Max Delbrück's translation of '*eidos*' as 'the genetic program'. Or when we said that little will remain of the culture of Old Europe after the pragmatic American broom has swept over it. There is an astringency and freshness in science which the humanities can no longer do without. The provocative formulation of a physicist, I cannot remember who, deserves quotation. It has become almost a commonplace in science and engineering research: theories are not either true or false, they are either elegant or uninteresting.

So, let us learn to care for the automaton in living beings, to care for ourselves. It seems likely that an automaton of such unimaginable complexity will need special care, and not in the sense that we can guess some secret or key as to how to care *even* for the billion differences between cells, but more that we need a 'decorous', respectful approach. The automaton needs to be tuned. There was good reason why today we have been talking about the unity of the genotype not in terms of its individual constituent parts, but on the level of social and personal behaviour. The wrong sort of behaviour causes dysfunction in the automaton and immediately begins to affect its heredity. And vice versa.

My example of Provençal, Sicilian, and Florentine philosophical poetry of the mediaeval Renaissance was, incidentally, as you may have noticed, also an instance of the merging of religion, philosophy, and poetry.

Lecture 28, 28 April 1998

Our excursion into the forest is approaching its end. It began with the fact that the forest takes us out of metric space and away from its framework, and that it burns. In the end, we have found in the forest a different program, the regulatory regime of our genetics and its automaton, working like a computer with hardware and software. The hardware in the organism is the proteins (in a computer it is the processor), and their job is to seize, digest, and make available; their software, their program, regulates how and when these operations are to be performed. The difference between one automaton and another is that for the mechanical automaton freezing may be part of its designer's plan, and when it freezes it needs outside intervention; the living automaton when it crashes also needs an intervention. The difference between them is *where that intervention* needs to come from.

At the end of this course we return to Aristotle, but by now in a different mood. If before we were timid tourists, now we shall return as weary hunters with what we have bagged, and we will boldly ask Aristotle, 'What is going on? You told us (and we nodded obediently) that nature has the principle of motion within itself, but art has it somewhere else. Were you telling us the shark eats itself in order to move, or would we be right in thinking it eats a tuna? And is not the cause of its movement the water, the ocean, its craving for food? In other words, a clearly external cause?' Or to take something closer to home: *our* perplexity. When we, as living beings, lapse into *amekhania*, are we really going to find the way out of our perplexity within ourselves by ourselves? Some people might, but that is hardly going to be the rule. And if we do find the way out of our perplexity within ourselves, which 'ourself' is that going to be? People say, 'After that experience, he changed'; or even, 'He was inwardly reborn'; or 'His crisis left an indelible mark on him.' So can the principle enabling us to recover from our *amekhania* really be inside us?

So-called 'inanimate' nature in Aristotle is brought into movement by the circular motion of the stars, so is the cause of *its* motion really 'within itself'?

Now for art, the cause of whose movement is supposedly external. (We recall that striking example of the chair which, when thrown out into the garden, sprouted not another chair but a tree.) Today automata are capable of manufacturing themselves; and, conversely, can it really be denied that a work of art, a painting or poem, do not have their own force of gravity with which they capture their artist? A poem wants to be heard, and is there to be heard, and calls into existence the poet needed to make it heard.

Aristotle's assertion that the cause of motion is within nature seems extremely odd in view of a simple statistic the palaeontologists and palaeobiologists have calculated, namely that the total of all past and present *species* on earth is 1 billion.

We can adopt as a working definition of species that 'Organisms are grouped into species partly according to their morphological, or external, similarities, but more important in classifying sexually reproducing organisms is the organisms' ability to successfully interbreed.'[1] This second consideration is the more important. We have read about the South American fruit flies that are no different in appearance or behaviour from the North American species, and mate with them but produce sterile offspring. A separate species does not mate with any other species; or if it does mate, it does not produce offspring; or if it does mate and does produce offspring, the offspring are sterile in the first generation; or if it does mate, and does produce offspring, the offspring are able to survive for two or three, but not more, generations before disappearing or developing defectively. In other words: a species is something that does *not* interbreed with any other species.

As of now, just 1 million species have been registered and catalogued on earth. How can living things have the cause of motion within themselves? If that were the case, all those other species would still be moving happily around on the surface of the earth today and not have been reduced to bones and fossils!

In other words, we can forget the idea that life, that nature in general, has the cause of motion within itself. No matter how much we twist and turn Aristotle's definition, the forms of life and of nature never had the cause of motion within themselves. They depend on something other, beginning with the fact that an individual must mate with *another* individual within the species for the motion of the species to continue. And, conversely, technology is moving towards creating, or may already have created, an automaton that has the cause of motion within itself.

To summarize, let us remember Andrey Lebedev's etymology of *hyle* from last September: the forest/wood is associated with burning; it is either burning or it is potentially fuel. If we understand life as fire, then in nature life is conflagrations extinguishing each other, while technology can create an automaton which will not be extinguished, will be constantly refuelled and seek out more fuel for itself. Human civilization learns, and it is not impossible that it will learn to reproduce human beings if other fires do not stop it first. A self-adjusting automaton will appear with a set of instructions calculated to keep it going for eternity. The problem of fine-tuning mood can be solved either by psychotropic regulation or by creating a new human being. The automaton's goal of self-perpetuation will dictate the course of action. Human beings will acquiesce to that goal.

Thought, however, has demonstrated many times that we jettison elements in it at our peril. Marx jettisoned Hegel's idealism and Marxism proved incapable of producing offspring, while *philosophia perennis* marches on. Let us assume that we can no longer make use of Aristotle's distinction between the cause of nature, which is within itself, and the cause of art and technology, which is external. Let us, though, not lose sight of it as a concept and a philosophical exercise. 'Nature has the cause of motion within itself: ἐν αὐτῳ.' The meaning of *somewhere within itself* effectively falls away, and in any case the etymological link is more probably with αὖ, meaning 'once again, afresh, revocably'. Whether it is necessary to return somewhere, or something is to be returned somewhere, is unclear, but that is a step forwards. The supposition is that, if there is revocability, there is a way out, there is dynamism, metabolism, a way back. For Aristotle, turning and returning are primal motion and, moreover, a path to eternity.

Let us suppose that by 'returning' is meant metabolism, restoration of equilibrium, homoeostasis. The real essential of homoeostasis is not, however, the thing that is restored but something else: the act of restoration itself. It is easy to see life, and I recommend that you do, not in terms of the survival of species, of the 'fittest', but in terms of the survival of *stratagems*. It then becomes clearer why Darwinism is so dominant, the struggle between species, survival of the fittest. What was the point of all their adaptation if 99.9% of them became extinct and even those that survived are constantly becoming extinct? Who is the ultimate survivor? The human species will survive, not because it is human but because it is an inventor, on the strength of its inventions and its technology. The generations of technology rapidly succeed each other, displace each other, battle each other so that, again, what triumphs is strategy. Living beings attach themselves to stratagems, ride them, jump off or are thrown off them when, as in the case of humans versus mammoths, humankind finds a better stratagem than the stratagem the mammoths possess. The replacement of one civilization by another has been the replacement of technologies, stratagems, and approaches.

Let us return to my example of migratory birds. Let us suppose that the flock is beginning to feel the cold. It is natural to anticipate that they will gradually migrate somewhere warmer where there is more food, but in fact the flocks do not migrate gradually: they suddenly, all together, relocate thousands of kilometres. They are believed to be guided by the sun, by smell, by the earth's magnetic field, by the pole star. What is decisive is the idea that it will be as warm in southern latitudes as it has been in latitudes further from the equator, so there is a need to migrate, to change their geographical location on the planet. This stratagem of taking wing and physically moving through the air together and over a very long distance, a good guess, a successful idea, may have been suggested to the birds by the worrying sight of the sun sinking lower to the horizon and the idea that it might be possible to move somewhere that phenomenon would not be happening. It may have been prompted by a high-flying bird noticing that the earth slopes, that it is spherical.

This is an insight not dissimilar in kind from the insight of the lion into the force appropriate to its leap, or of the dolphin correlating the air in its lungs with the depth of its dive. The fact that birds are able, or should we rather say (in order not to attribute to them the ability to understand, calculate, to intuit the possibility of such a migration) the fact that there is a drop in temperature, that there is air ready and waiting, inviting the appearance of a means of moving through it on wings, prompts this intuition to arrive. The earth is there, round; there are wings, there is air, there is the changing altitude of the sun. The trick needed is to proceed down the curved surface of the earth until the slanting rays of the sun become vertical. The stratagem is essentially the same as learning to bend the neck to pick a seed of grain up off the ground. The bird sees the sinking of the sun and the sloping of the earth just as the chicken sees the grain. When the flock of birds flies, it is being guided by this stratagem of how to react to the earth; it is being attracted by the earth in just the same way that the beak is being attracted by the grain.

Now that this trick has been devised, as a reward for its having been invented, it has the entire phenomenon of migratory birds existing around it (and all of physiology can be seen as just the same or similar clever guesses at the molecular level). This discovery has *helped itself to* the entire species of migratory birds. They are allocated to it as serfs were allocated to their villages, to such an extent that this technique of flight is inserted into the genetic code of the species. Birds are assigned to this function, much as warrior termites are assigned to the function of defending workers, or as residents assigned to a secret factory are deprived of the right to travel abroad.

Birds so much belong to their migratory behaviour that they *cannot* stay where they are, as other species of birds do. It is so written into their program that young birds that have never flown far will begin to flock in the autumn. The only choice they have is deciding the right day for them all to depart.

We succumb to an optical illusion. We can observe the bird as an object and imagine that everything is focused on it, that somewhere *within it* is the cause of its motion. But no. Actually it is inscribed in the whole linkage of air–climate–geography–astronomy, and is inside an invention, a discovery that can be discerned only with the mind's eye.

In reality, there is no phenotype, no genotype (species): both are only the sum of their functions when they are inventing. 'Be fruitful and multiply!' St Augustine understood: invent![2] Whichever way we turn we see ready-made creatures, but we would do better to look for the intuitions, the design features. That only inventions exist we can see by the ease with which the earth, nature, have dismissed almost a billion species. We can regard these as if mere individual members (Nicholas of Cusa, by way of a digression, viewed whole animal genera as individuals) of a genus, the genus being an invention that worked. Aristotle's 'energy' as a realized possibility.[3]

Lamarckism, which is enjoying something of a comeback, is laughable if interpreted in a primitive way, if we focus on the visible form of an animal and the adaptation of its body to its needs; but it begins to work if we focus not on the behaviour of the living creature but on the living creature as an invention. This, incidentally, fully explains why vertebrates have four legs, or rather we should talk about the 'quadrupedality' and 'vertebracy' of animals living on dry land. They are wedded to this way of moving around and have adapted to it. No one is claiming that 'such-and-such an animal needed four legs to move around and so it got them' in the naïve interpretation of Lamarckism, but that with the appearance of dry land, that ocean of air and vegetation, plants provided an opportunity for the invention of this form of fuelling, of combustion converted into movement, and the spine and legs were attracted to the invention of moving about in space. Of course, movement on dry land, as with any good invention, was accompanied by a host of other discoveries. (Remember Goethe's image of lucky nature at the card table, constantly winning and doubling her stakes.[4])

It is easier to understand their genetic specialization if we think of each species not as serving itself but as being assigned a place within the system of inventions. We can then explain the phenotype by saying that, through its behaviour and place in the invention, the creature orders up its own physiology.

We can similarly approach mimesis in its narrower sense of mimicry. Specifically, we can understand the migration of birds as an imitation of the rotation of the starry sky. The imitation is connected to, entwined with, the intuition that the presence of food is dependent on astronomy. Without any involvement of consciousness, the presence of the star-studded sky, visible, moving overhead and disappearing underfoot, moving through the sky towards the ground, causes the travels of migratory birds as mimesis of the movement of the stars. Birds do not take their bearings from the stars, as ornithologists say, but participate more directly in astronomy: they themselves are stars and the structure of the flock is a mimesis of the constellations.

This is not a conjecture or hypothesis, but more rigorous: if mimicry exists, then some artificial psychological standpoint is needed to prevent it from being extended to everything. In flying creatures, their pneumatic bones are, of course, lighter and therefore better adapted for flight, but *at the same time* this is mimicry, identification with the air by taking it into the bird's innermost essence, into its very bones. By actually breathing with its bones when in flight, the bird can create a vacuum in its skeleton by drawing air out of them with its lungs.

Again it is the easiest thing to *observe* mimicry, for example the similarities between a cuckoo and a hawk.[5] This kind of mimesis, however, is like one creature falling under the influence of another, rather as a piano which no one is playing will start to play if another alongside is being played. It is bound to happen; it cannot not happen, if both pianos have the same strings; and different beings cannot but have the same strings, figuratively speaking, because of the sameness of their substance.

One of the theses of Berg's nomogenesis speaks in favour of the embeddedness of beings in 'operations', in 'energy'. This is his law of convergence, of polyphylesis, that species which, to the eye, belong to the same genus, and are customarily *ascribed* to the same genus, may not in fact belong there. They may have different phylogenesis, different ancestors. It is as if one people of different nations were working in the same factory: they would converge in their habits and even in appearance. Berg: 'Similarities in the form of two forms may represent something secondary, honestly acquired, new; differences, however, are primary, inherited, old.'[6] The fact that very similar-looking gophers should belong to different species becomes more comprehensible when we recall that the overall number of species dropped a thousandfold: that is, it was not just thirty but hundreds of species that were capable of foraging among the roots of meadow plants, so why be surprised that thirty survived? And on the other hand, why would they not become similar, converging to the point where they became indistinguishable from each other, in the light of Berg's polyphylesis, when the engineering and inventiveness of existence in the top layer of the earth's surface made the gophers converge, like the employees of a single company?

Berg has a soft and compromising kind of polyphylesis, but that of Carl Linnaeus, you will remember, was absolute. God created as many species as were needed: '*Species tot numeratur, quot diversae formae in principio sunt creatae.*' 'There are as many species as were created in the beginning.'[7] Berg produces convincing examples: cooking salt and diamonds form cubic crystals, but that does not mean they are related or descended from a common form.

Darwinism, in the latter part of the nineteenth century, faced an alternative evolutionary theory known as neo-Lamarckism. This hypothesis shared with Lamarck's the importance of use and disuse in the development and obliteration of organs, and it added the notion that the environment acts directly on organic structures, which explained their adaptation to the way of life and environment of the organism. Adherents of this theory discarded natural selection as an explanation of adaptation to the environment.[8]

In Soviet neo-Lamarckism, where organisms are only brought in as a random (and easily abandoned) substratum for burnishing the inventions of nature, development is not a problem, except for the purely technical consideration that innovation requires matter, and the more of it there is and the more diverse it is, the better. Matter in this sense is Aristotle's forest as a potential for energy: energy in the sense of some 'brilliant', successful action. You can see that our excursion has not been for nothing. We have not come back to Aristotle empty-handed. For example, we are now able seamlessly to connect to ὕλη its seemingly opposed meanings of *wood* as the living forest and as material, timber. In our neo-Lamarckism, life is material for operations. (We may note in passing that life is something so wonderful that it seems to be of value in itself, which makes it more difficult to see an 'operation' as the goal. '*Whose* operation?' we ask with our customary personalism. We can answer, it is an operation of Gaia. Gaia wants to *be* in 'energy', in *reality. But this is just an aside.*)

Operations require matter: for some complex, for others perhaps not. For this reason, and others, 'increasing complexity' is not invariably the case in evolution. If the material was available, development could even have begun with humankind, a possibility that Berg allows. 'Häckel once derived human beings from the amoeba. Today it is possible, turning the phylogenetic ladder upside down, to defend the view that bacteria and the amoeba derived from man by a process of gradual degradation.'[9] Here Berg is exaggerating a theory of the Russian biologist Dmitry Sobolev.[10] For Sobolev, evolution was a cyclical process, and apes were descended from more nearly humanoid forms. In support of this, Berg adduces a curious fact: the embryo of the gorilla during its prenatal development has a moustache and beard, which then disappears and the baby gorilla when born has, like a human, hair only on its head. In other words, it is not humans, whose embryos have a primal down (lanugo), who are repeating at the embryonic stage the fur covering anthropoids but, on the contrary, the gorilla and chimpanzee, in their embryonic stage, pass through a temporary phase that remains in humans for life.[11] Sobolev believed that primitive mammals were descended from far more specialized reptiles. Echinoderms, too, resulted from degradation. Lungfish, which appeared very ancient and endangered, were descended from far more specialized Palaeozoic fossilized fish.

If we do not believe that greater complexity is of itself a sign of more advanced development, an organism could, for example, be 'assigned' to a successful, effective, vegetative process, and this could be the 'matter' of some other operation involving the same organism. Incidentally, operations and energies do not necessarily need to have a utilitarian purpose: it is enough for energy to be *fascinating*, and there is something captivating in fullness, perfection. For Aristotle, you will remember, energy was the unmoving mover. Max Delbrück and Ernst Mayr, for example, have noted Aristotle's modernity but have, of course, rushed to attach his categories to what is observable, identifying the unmoving mover with the DNA molecule. That is both ridiculous and pointless. The only thing close to the unmoving mover of the real Aristotle is the attractive power of realization, for which there always is scope of one sort or another in matter.

Now I can be even more precise in naming the distinction between true and mechanical automata: it is their adjustment. Living automata adjust themselves to operate optimally. That is something they are drawn to. Artificial automata need to have their optimal mode of operation pointed out to them. True automata do not set themselves the goal of self-preservation and self-reproduction. The ant sacrifices its life for the anthill, the wolf refuses to be domesticated. Mechanical automata might seem similarly to serve an operation and then leave the stage, making way for new generations or, if required to, self-destructing in accordance with their program on completion of an operation. That might suggest that classical Darwinism holds sway in even technological inventions. There are, however, two grounds to doubt that. Life, changing, has accompanied the earth on almost all of its 4 or 5 billion rotations around the sun. The record of generations of technology is very much less and we can already see that if things continue in their present direction, the earth is hardly likely to survive much more than another fifty years. A change in the mood of humankind and a new religion, a new Christianity, is more likely, more credible, than continuing along present lines.

Perhaps the difference is in the kind of operations in which life serves and those performed by technological automata. What is out of the question in the light of this service given by life to energies is that biological engineering might influence the setting of the living automaton: it is invariably dealing with already living matter, and may well be able to extend its possibilities. It may perhaps even enhance the captivation of life by operations, but it is unlikely that, apart from reshuffling living matter, the biological engineer will be able to have any effect on the actual nature of that fascination. The engineer may coincide with the overall movement of life in its focus on an operation and energy, may be able to redirect it in minor ways, but will be unable to alter the direction of movement from possibility, through captivation to realization.

We are coming back to Aristotle, and effectively the course is at an end. His thinking, like modern scientific thinking, 'consciousness', is a creative episode. We are involved in that same captivation by energy, like everything else in nature and, to the extent that we are successful, serve the fullness of realization. That includes our technological inventions, which, as 'operations' and 'energies', come under the heading of the functioning of animals and have no special distinctiveness to them. The only difference is the degree of risk, which is possibly justified by the extremity of the situation. We are aware of that not from observations and calculations, such as the hypothetical date of the crumbling of protons, our collision with a comet, or the cooling of the sun, but through that mimetic prescience (older than consciousness) which draws us in and fascinates us.

We need to look quite nearby for the origins of life and of humankind: in our captivation with the world, no different in us than in any other living thing, and no different today than when everything began. To put it more dramatically, we can say that the ant is created by an ant and the human species creates the human species, with our every step, our every action, although we are as fenced off from our intentional, conscious efforts as nucleic acids are from proteins. For example, the body is drawn in, and cannot but be drawn in, to the enterprise of civilization. The body as matter will be drawn to captivation by energy.

And what of genetics? Trofim Lysenko, who dreamed of making inculcated habits hereditary, was by no means the first: parents, particularly dominant fathers, have always dreamed that their sons will carry on their work; and carry on the sons plainly do, but how and to what end it has never proved possible to program. For all that, the child is always the child, the closest person to the parent. The body remains the closest thing to us, although we have far better understanding of things much further away. Something important, and whether this is true of other creatures it is difficult to say, is that to this day the symbolism of our body, the body's responsiveness to energies, has been more than profound, and positive. No matter how complex the operations, whether the creation of a work of art, or scientific investigation, the body is found to be not merely obedient but ready and waiting to be called upon for effort and something to do.

That is why we feel emboldened, why we have every reason to believe that the body, fundamentally, whether immediately or gradually, but purposefully and holistically, in all its parts, has arisen by being drawn to the same energies as engage and captivate our understanding. It is as if one and the same source creates it and gives it meaning, and it does not seem very important whether the alliance is for a long or a short period.

Leibniz's 'pre-established harmony' between body and soul will need to be understood in a different way: his image of two clocks, identically designed and wound up simultaneously but independently of each other, showing exactly the same time at all times, is a complete impossibility and reminds us that any comparison can only be partially valid. It is, nevertheless, worth considering the circumstances under which the clocks could be perfectly synchronized. If no time at all elapses between winding them up and looking at them; if there is no separation of the clocks; if they are simultaneously close while apart, close but at a distance. These are things that neither biology nor physics contemplates. Logic and mathematics draw attention to the paradoxes of infinity in a formal sense, but a real analysis of what is happening during approaching and moving away can be given only by reflection. Mind consists of the same flashes of energy as distinguish the body.

Not some time, but now, not in books, but in chemistry, more precisely in any successful mental operation which is so close to the body that it fails to see it, everything is created that is created, alive and realized. If I were to stick my neck out, I would even say that the power of proximity is such that if nothing and 'some thing' were givens, then proximity between them would be sufficient for a world to arise. Let that remain an outlandish conjecture.

Our twin, our intimate, physiology has come about in no other way than by a stroke of luck, an auspicious thought which it is not in our power to commission. We need to look for the elements most distant in time and space in what is closest to hand.

We need to understand in a different way also the thesis about imitating nature. Art creates from the outside something nature will register, *if, indeed, it even does.* The main idea and concern of art is therefore not invention for its own sake, but that stroke of luck which the operations of the body recognize and to which they respond.

One more note. Judas is the twin, the contrary, of the doubting apostle, St Thomas, who so inclines to intimacy that he will not believe until he has poked his fingers into the resurrected body. Judas who carries the disciples' moneybag, the means of exchange; Judas the re-ferent and interpreter. The ambiguity with which the Gospel says that he took the money, given the language used in the Gospel, is of no significance, just as cognate words in other Indo-European languages make no distinction between 'taking' and 'carrying'. In the circumstances in which Judas finds himself, in close proximity to the principals and the money, as the taker, the agent, it was simplicity itself, tempting, to help himself. The Last Supper, which he left, was an intimate gathering from which there must be no tale-bearing, no informing. His proximity to the beginning of all that was to come meant he should have kept the greatest distance, but Judas betrayed it with the intimacy of a kiss.

The difficulty of properly understanding Lamarck – that is, essentially, Aristotle – is that he is proposing a direct connection between the operation and its agent (the operation of plucking leaves from high branches, the executor the giraffe with its long neck): the agent needs to reach the highest branches, and he extends his neck much as one might extend a hand. After that lampoon of Lamarck, we need only to add, with a due sense of superiority, that Lamarck did not yet know, of course, about the inaccessibility of nucleic acids, that no amount of complaining by proteins that they were being insufficiently nourished could – as would have seemed only natural – bring about the desired change in the genotype, or even just get the information passed on to the acids. You will recall that information is not transferred from proteins to nucleic acids: there is no mediator to assist. The demise of whole herds of short-necked creatures was not enough to suggest to the genetic machinery that it should think again and reassemble itself. What was needed was for there to be within it, on its initiative, so to speak, a mutation that would subsequently, after many generations, become established through natural, Darwinian selection. August Weismann's discovery of the barrier rigidly dividing the body into somatics and genetics, soberingly, after the anecdotal quality of Lamarckism, brings home the inaccessibility of life to – what? Life itself. The impossibility of direct communication, direct transmission of information from what to what? Strange to relate, from life to life. But with today's post-structuralist, neo-Darwinian mood in biology, the possibility of broadly mimetic interaction between inaccessible sides remains basically underutilized. My example was of the playing of a piano in a locked empty room or, as

Leibniz described it, using identical settings of different mechanisms not in direct contact. Precisely this feature figures very clearly in Lamarckism.

Now some theses. Why was the truthful information given by Judas bad? Not in itself: communicating something you know is not obviously a sin, but in this case it obscured other information. So the technological automaton, the computer, is not by any means bad and dangerous in itself, but only because it obscures the true automaton. In-formation, by the way, is seen by Nicholas of Cusa as instilling *eidos*.[12] A question for next time: are that concept and genetic information similar or are they quite different?

Lecture 29, 5 May 1998

The forest is *overtly* close to us, like flared oil, decomposed forests (mostly floating, planktonic) from the distant past; it is negatively *overt*, in the form of its absence or the disappearance of forests.

The forest is covertly present in our lives as a persistent sense that we were different, for example *hairy*, and that we can be different and that the fact of the matter is that we *are* different. What is indirectly informing this *mythology* is our *biology*.

We belong to the world of life, biology, to a greater extent than we usually think and than we would like to think. Ideology and culture are a diverse *interpretation*, secondary, of a simple law to which *all* life is heir.

The goal of life is not the preservation of life but energy, *en-ergeia*, in the sense of full success.

The goal of life is the species. We, a part of nature, are concerned that the species should have a future. Indeed, for us the species *is* the future.

The difference between the made automaton and the living automaton is that the phase of freezing, crashing, *aporia*, *amekhania* – a fault in the made automaton – for the living automaton is every time an opportunity to look to the future. Only what has passed through impossibility, a-mechania, is redeemed.

The ways of Sophia, the skilful knack of life, are always mysterious.

The way out of a-mechania, the crashing of all mechanisms, is the breaking through of mystery. Next to it is holiness, a wild joy that has seen the mystery of the Cross.

The redemption of life begins when, in *amekhania*, it does not know what can be done.

It is at that moment, when it seems to us that we are cut off from life, abandoned, alone, left to ourselves, seeking and unable to find, a burden to ourselves and wanting an end to ourselves – it is then, and perhaps *only* then, that we fully belong to life, having taken up its Cross. Nobody has promised we will find a way out – we should immediately rid ourselves of illusions – *amekhania* is not a *sufficient* condition for salvation, but a *necessary* one, without which there can, indisputably, be no redemption.

Each time we experience *amekhania*, the failure of the mechanism, the situation is reset to the beginning of everything – with no guarantee that it will miraculously return.

* * *

In terms of the specification, the program, we have ended up with one thing on paper and something else in genetics. Is the same true of information? Indeed it is, and again there is no need for us to innovate: *in-formatio* in the sense of introduction, inculcation of *forma*, the Latin translation of *eidos*, is something we already find in the first philosopher of modern times, Nicholas of Cusa. Somehow, information should be one; but the reality is that information is not accessible to information! Like the automaton to the automaton. Information will be of interest to us where it is interesting: that is, only where it assumes responsibility for taking care of itself. Perhaps we will obtain such solid information as that which is coded in the letters DNA. Information may possibly prove to be a communication, a sharing of success or a contamination with success, across any and all content, but we will come to that later. Looking ahead, we can say that form will not differ in the slightest from the focus on something like fitness. We cannot just look up the answer at the back of our book of exercises, precisely because it centres on light, beauty, and good, which are attractive. As it is now, so it has always been. There are no grounds to suppose that it was not always so and that this attraction alone is too little to account for the formation of the world. That was the topic of today's strange double lecture. Speaking about the forest, we have been drawn into a terrible fight for new meaning. Which is not there.

The term 'ethology' was introduced in 1859 by Étienne Geoffroy Saint-Hilaire, the science of animals' behaviour, mainly in their natural environment (there is good reason for that, namely the effect of being watched by outside observers on the behaviour of animals). Nowadays it mainly examines genetic programming. The first name is that of Konrad Lorenz (1903–89, Altenburg, Austria).[1] How many more times are we going to meet islands of that sunken continent, the Austro-Hungarian Empire? Next, Nikolaas Tinbergen (1907–88).[2] The third name is that of Karl von Frisch (1886–1982).[3]

Sergey Horuzhy's works on ethology have not yet been published. Following in the footsteps of Lorenz and Tinbergen, he speaks of the 'paradigm of delight' in the living world. Life is excess, overflowing, and inclines towards transcendence, as when – a very basic example – if a large egg is placed in a gull's nest, it will prefer to incubate that rather than its own smaller eggs. Horuzhy relates the rapturousness of such German Romantics as Ludwig Tieck (1773–1853), as also the *furore eroico* of the late Renaissance, to this attribute of life.

Ethology is mainly preoccupied with genetic programming, but also observes the phenotype, and there is nowhere better than behaviour to study the decisive power of 'fitness' and success. That is our topic today, together, of course, with the question of where the very possibility comes from of a fitness which is a match for murderous, extreme, and even catastrophic conditions. We come up against situations where something 'might never have happened, but it did' almost before we encounter any content. Accordingly, we have to place 'fitness' alongside that first '*good*' that God saw in the world. We can, and even must, view existence itself as goodness in the sense of success, in the sense of 'How great!', so that there is nothing in existence that is not success.

There is a difference between feeling yourself to be a will achieving set goals (perhaps 'no matter what', 'at all costs'), or an automaton which is a puzzle even to itself, like the animals. But this difference is so marked, so all-embracing in qualitative and quantitative terms, that you begin to wonder whether there *is* a difference in the usual sense between one thing that appears so and another thing that appears so. Is not the difference rather between things seen and things unseen, between dream and reality? One and the same thing if seen in a dream and seen in reality is not one and the same thing, while quite different things seen in a dream and in reality may prove to be one and the same. Between the will of humankind and so-called instinct, or the blind instinct of animals, is not the difference the same, and in fact is not the most interesting thing, the thing that most affects us, when we begin to sense that there is something we are not seeing? Of course (this is just an aside), in our European society, particularly through ethology, the significance of the animal world for society is being restored, a significance which some were perhaps thinking did not extend beyond providing subject matter for children's stories? Ethology is part of biology.

Biology is now the leading science, not because it promises larger litters or the creation of new species. The importance of biology is that it is responding to a high-profile challenge of the *markedness* of life. It is provocatively startling, altogether 'highly improbable',[4] and for its continuation will be requiring things that are incredible, indeed impossible in our system of concepts.

A peak of complexity in a problem is naturally and inevitably accompanied by a scattered distribution. Increased tension near the goal scatters numerous deviations around. The uniqueness and difficulty of the path of life is the reverse side of its improbability. Why is it that in a compact live being the complexity is thousands and tens of thousands of times greater than in the air, water, and soil in the midst of which it is living? Or is all life a bringing into view, into the light, of the invisible complexity of the microcosm? Was the preoccupation of the ancients with the infinitesimal, far from being madness, not an intuition of the complexity of the inscrutable towards which life, on the surface, was pointing?

The distinction between the apparently 6,000-year history of human culture and prehistoric biology dissolves, and in favour of prehistory, because what is recorded in the history books will not outlive culture and civilization and will not register in genetics. Our written information is not destined to become in-formation, while the millions of years of human-kind and the billions of years of life have been indelibly recorded through the mere presence, the heroic achievement, of life. To call that period 'pre-history' is, then, an iniquitous sneer. Organisms, a biologist confidently tells us, are 'historical phenomena'. Max Delbrück: 'Any living cell carries with it the experiences of a billion years of experimentation by its ances-tors.'[5] They are like floppy disks crammed with data, as many as there are cells, billions in every living being. They are like the memory of the most powerful computers, and in every cell there is a book with a record going back a billion years.

Ernst Mayr has depicted the entire history of the earth as occurring in the course of one year. On 1 January, the earth appears; on 27 February, life arrives in the form of prokaryotes,[6] who fill the bowels of the earth with oil and coal, and the atmosphere with oxygen. They carry on from then until 4 September, when the eukaryotes finally appear, the nucleus enters the cell, and separate sexes appear. Single-celled organisms occupied our planet from February to November. On 21 November, the vertebrates arrive; on 12 December, mammals appear; the first apes are born on 26 December, and hominids in the morning of 31 December. Recorded history begins at 23.56.30 hours, or 3.5 minutes before midnight on 31 December, which is now. (And truly, forgive them for they know not what they do. As the clock strikes midnight, we clutch our heads in dismay.) However you look at it, life is something special, 'marked', but its progress has been terrible. Some 999 million *species*, out of a total of a billion, have been turned into imprints on rocks or at best bones, and the same fate faces the survivors: only 20% of the bird species in Europe in the seventeenth century remain. Life came out of improbability, impossibility, and may yet slide back into it on this earth. It has tried inventions and created an unimaginable number of them, but all of them together *may not prove to be enough*. Life is once again in a state of extreme, almost terminal, tension, and there is no reason to think there is anything unusual about that.

Relative success is not enough: life needs *unqualified* success. For the sake of that it tests itself and its inventions to breaking point in terms of endurance, effort, and stress.

The separateness of the programming from the life form carrying it out is fascinating. The history of life is like a stage production in which the director gives the actors no quarter. Ethology studies this closely. Let us look at altruism among animals, many of which show much more than does humankind. We have heard that human altruism is sometimes ranked somewhere between that of the shark and the bees, but altruism has been misunderstood as a kind of self-sacrifice on the part of an individual. Is that what it is, or is something different in play here? A bitch, for example, simply sacrifices herself for her puppies, nursing them, licking them, giving herself to them completely and defending them in case of danger. She is plainly captivated by them, stays close to them at all times, and, if parted from them, begins to pine immediately, whining, eager to get back from a walk, which was certainly not the case before. A few weeks pass and gradually this attachment to the puppies weakens, and she will even appear to shake off a puppy that is still pestering her when it is two months old and she goes off to lie down on her own. This is entirely reasonable. The puppy is naturally becoming more independent and will soon be as steady on its feet as its mother. What is observed, however, does not suggest that the bitch is withdrawing from her puppy in accordance with such common-sense considerations. If previously she was completely captivated by her puppies, devoted to them, finding in them the whole meaning of her life, now she seems almost lost, distracted. While she was on heat, mating, pregnant, giving birth, admiring her new puppies, which she had constantly to lick and feed, it was as if she had jumped on a train and was taking a ride on it, totally absorbed by the succession of major, crucial events. It was evidently not the puppies themselves that were causing this if, about five months after giving birth, she could calmly leave them, but what last time I called an '*operation*'. The bitch had been *carrying out an operation*, or perhaps we should say that an operation took over the bitch, galvanized her, and created meaning for her. That she was captivated was evident also to those around her. Human and animal observers identified these months for the bitch with the enthralling operation she was conducting. The bitch was, if you like, created by the success of the operation. An unseen program, an operation being carried out, had entranced a living creature. Just as migration entrances birds and as, in the human world, an artist is captivated by an idea.

Is the term 'altruism' appropriate here? Would we not do better to talk about captivation by a third force, a dictatorial 'operation', a dictatorial energy to which the 'altruist' deferred as something greater? We need, by the way, to disqualify any altruism in the sense of *do ut des*,[7] which is what we usually observe in humanity; or the so-called altruism of cleaner fish, small fish that accompany large fish and keep them clean and healthy, obtaining leftover food in return.

I see the principle of *luck* and success as universal. If contact with extraterrestrial civilizations is problematical, the community of all being in our immediate part of the cosmos (our own and neighbouring galaxies), if it actually exists, is in a shared effortfulness and joy, not a consciousness. To the extent that we here on earth are absorbed and captivated by our successes, we are in contact with all being in the universe, and may let slip this unity precisely by seeking unity in accordance with certain specified parameters. We are automatically in contact with everything to the extent that we are a success, and inevitably at odds with everyone and everything to the extent that we fail.

What we are talking about here is success not of the individual or of the species but – and this is very important – of the *operation*, of energy as an event. A visual example here: the gorgeous plumage of male birds of paradise does not help them to survive, any more than do the extraordinary antlers of some deer. 'It is quite possible that an excessive development of

certain characters favoured by sexual selection contributed to the extinction of some species.'[8] We wonder what, then, everything is all about, what
the point is, and the answer is always the same: it is the success of what it is
that makes the bird of paradise distinctive, the reason why it is *special* and
draws the eye; it is the success of this extravagant and gorgeous plumage.
It is designed not for the benefit of the bird, indeed it makes life more
worrisome and dangerous for it, but then it is not the bird that creates
the plumage, or, rather, it creates it as an artist creates a work of art, sac-
rificing itself. We could say it is not the bird that makes the plumage but
the plumage that makes the bird, if we could understand and see the significance of how the plumage itself is an achievement, a perfection, which
summons the bird to its creation and to wearing it.

Natural selection is doubtless an optimization, but *there is no parameter
for measuring what is optimal!* We are always able to recognize it with hindsight. We can see that a species was well adapted because we are able to
observe it today. Without resorting to this *ex post facto* teleology, however,
we are left with the purely formal assessment that selection proceeds by
selecting the best, the optimal, the success. We could add, if you like – of
anything, of any operation, any automaton, providing only that it is a
success.

With this we need, at least in part, to link the *commitment* of life to its
programs, its *loyal service*, total reliability. As a side note: we need also to
view the commitment of the old Moscow public servants to their state
from this biological perspective as captivation by a successful operation. In
the same way, it is important that we understand the most straightforward
and succinct definition of Darwinian natural selection: 'If there is herit-
able variation in fitness in a population, evolution ensues automatically.'[9]
The automaton operates here in leaps and bounds of 'fitness', fuelled by
them, so to speak. We defined fitness as viability, *godnost'*, bearing in mind
the etymological link of the word to 'good', and its kinship with intuition.
Now we need to define it more precisely as hitting the target, as being in
luck. Let Plato's understanding of truth and being as the good, in the sense
of giving validity (see Heidegger on Plato's doctrine of truth),[10] remain as
the background to this aspect of our forest.

Fitness, luck, accuracy, being part of a discovery, receiving a tour de
force like the bird of paradise, migrating with the winds, the sun, the stars,
the earth ... the fact that nearly a billion species have become extinct
stops seeming to suggest that life is doomed and that the invitation to be a
winner still stands.

The earth ages and withers, humanity takes a risky move away from religion and a close and reverent attitude to everything, but the law is still not
just any old life but life as burning, as fire, as service. To call here for self-
restraint, for 'respect for all living things', for us to come to our senses, not
to rush towards death, to live and let others live and breathe – such clarion
calls do not know to whom they are addressed, but they are addressed, in
fact, to life, which is essentially fire. It is absurd to expect that life will be

defended by those who do not want life, who want not life but success. It is like trying to persuade someone contemplating suicide of the health benefits of herbal tea, or to learn to love life. Captivation and capture, captivation by capture, wit and wiliness are the only thing that works. Someone who can captivate and be captivated, to capture the world and be captured by the world. Adaptation is essentially capturing the world in both these senses, and not necessarily only here on earth but also more widely. In Darwinism, people are now inclined to talk less of Spencerian fitness and more about adaptation, but the foundation, often unnoticed, remains, that awareness of the world as it is, that awareness of the cosmos, of good order into which it is possible to be integrated. To successfully fit into the world captivates, just as the dolphin is captivated by its diving and soaring. The world is a place where energy, and entelechy in the sense of *per-fectio*, are possible, only we should not see luck and the location of luck as being separate. The world disappears as soon as something ends in failure. The world itself is a stroke of luck, or at least studded, punctuated, marked out by strokes of luck and viability. Under no circumstances should we succumb to cheap teleology, postulating some world in the sky that guarantees success. It is far from clear which came first, the fitness or the world. From the very outset, the world is wholly ordered as luck, as being in luck. It is an incredibly complex laminate of strokes of luck which, in essence, added up to one big piece of luck, one mechanism (or automaton).

If the mechanical automaton did not blind us to the true one, we would see more clearly in any 'operation' a mimesis of the world. Only, we must not understand mimesis as meaning imitation, a kind of copying. We must hear in this word its etymology: measuring out.

I shall be reading today from Nikolaas Tinbergen's *Social Behaviour in Animals*,[11] only I will start with an example or observation of my own. In early spring, several dozen caterpillars gather in a convenient location on a tree and, quite densely packed, clinging to the tree with half their body, start all at the same time rhythmically and energetically swaying the other half in a state of manifest ecstasy and delight such as Horuzhy describes. It seems mildly ridiculous to interpret this demonstration as a collective stretch exercise, though of course it is entirely possible to see it as collective consciousness and a flexing of their power.

This performance also clearly does not have a sexual significance for caterpillars, which have yet to pupate and turn into butterflies. The ecstasy of the collective performance instils a sense of horror, for which one could easily find an explanation in the imagining of how this mass meeting of caterpillars will shortly break up and crawl off over branches and leaves and the state to which they will reduce the poor tree; but that seems like a secondary rationalization of the initial instinctive revulsion, a mirror image of the energy of the collective excitement of living beings. We read in the ageing Edward Wilson's advice, after thirty years of observations, to anyone gazing at ants that the unintentional projection of the observer of ethology's emotions on to what he is observing is a fascinating subject in itself. And indeed, how is the observer not to become involved? Here is Karl Lorenz sitting with his undergraduate and graduate students in front of a large aquarium observing a male instructing the young, forbidding them to swim too far away. The young try to run away, whereupon their father takes an overly freedom-loving child in his lips and draws it back to the nest. Suddenly, very nearby, he spots a tempting worm in the water. What is he to do? The fish stops, deep in thought, then quickly casts aside its baby, swallows the worm, and again quickly takes the baby in its mouth and back to the nest. The observers burst into applause. The poignancy of the situation is that this fish would normally swallow the young of another species immediately after swallowing the worm: it had quickly to overcome the inertia of its eating habits and switch to paternal instincts, which it successfully did.

For the rest of this lecture we are indebted to Nikolaas Tinbergen. The more an ethologist observes living things, the more frankly he will admit to the incompleteness of his observations and explanations of behaviour. In my example of the caterpillars, we can vouch for the ecstasy the caterpillars are experiencing and the revulsion of the observer, but it is less easy to explain what is really causing the protracted, synchronized rhythmical movements of the caterpillars. It is tempting to imagine some prayerful act of worship of the congregation of caterpillars, which is certainly weird enough to match the level of improbability of life. Or again, Tinbergen is observing herring gulls for a long time. At first glance, it may appear that they are coming together in a tight group because they have found somewhere rich in prey. Nothing of the sort: already the flock is flying from one meadow to the next, not because the food has run out in one place or appeared in another, but because one gull has given the signal. Stray gulls fly over and join the flock. What is keeping them all together? It is only too easy to say there is safety in numbers, but caterpillars herding together are asking for trouble from birds.

Tinbergen's descriptions lead not to explanations but to issues. Here he is observing nightingales in April. The singing males have arrived; for the present they are on their own, and each has established his territory, which he delimits with his singing. There the male is, all alone, but suddenly, after a few days, he is with his female. The female has flown *on her own* from the Mediterranean. How has she found the male? It is an achievement, Tinbergen says, no human could ever match. What kind of affects, similar to ours or not, must the male and female nightingales experience when they are reunited after flying thousands of kilometres!

Again, to offer as an explanation that the nightingales need to mate and that is why they have to find each other rather misses the point. Why, in that case, did they have to separate themselves by thousands of kilometres? Why, if one herring gull takes off, do all the others follow suit? Domestic hens, well fed, are standing deep in thought. Suddenly one starts pecking at the ground and all the others start doing the same. 'Sympathetic induction,' Tinbergen says.[12] Human beings behave the same way: one person starts yawning and it proves contagious; one person panics, so do others. Tinbergen is absolutely right. 'It has nothing to do with imitation; the reacting individuals do not learn to perform certain movements by watching others perform them, *but they are brought into the same mood, and react by making their own innate movements.*'[13] We have to say, this is not imitation, this is *mimesis*. Why do starlings sometimes form into flocks thousands strong? And why do we instinctively find the spectacle so exciting? It bewitches *us*, the observers; it induces the same rapture in us. 'It is highly fascinating to see how thousands of starlings, flying round above their roost on a winter evening, turn as if at a command; left, right, up and down. Their co-operation seems so perfect that one forgets the individuals and automatically thinks of them as one cloud, as one huge "super-individual".'[14]

Here all of them are doing the same thing as in my example with the caterpillars. Our bafflement at why they enjoy performing like this, so simply, just to show off their coordination, can reasonably be transferred to an instance where the outside observer finds an easy explanation for the behaviour, but can also overlook the delight, the rapture, at the precise coordination of operations. The blackbird, in common with other song-birds, brings food to the nest. The chicks have been sitting quietly, but as soon as the parent lands on the edge of the nest, they open wide their mouths, which are bigger than their heads. The parent puts a worm in the dreadfully gaping maw of whoever is squawking loudest. The chick swallows it and calms down, but that is not the end of the procedure: '[U]sually the parent waits and looks down into the nest with close atten-tion.'[15] One or other of the chicks in the clump starts shifting about, shakes its stomach, fluffs out the needle-like feathers around its cloaca, and out pops a neat white package of digested food. The parent bird immediately picks it up and swallows it or, if the chicks are older, carries it away from the nest. The adroitness and coordination need to be seen as something that stops this job from being an onerous routine which the parent bird might want to escape from and fly free, and makes it instead a demonstra-tion of a similarly enthralling kind to the starlings' aerobatic display or the bird of paradise's tail fanning; like those starlings, *the blackbird together with its chicks is a single organism.*

The operation or energy which animals are drawn into can be seen as a particular kind of organism (a different meaning of the word here). What is important is the readiness with which individuals, organisms in the usual, observable, sense, connect with and serve the program. The individual itself is also an operation, but here becomes the matter for a dif-ferent operation, collective, if you will, with which the individual connects. Operations, energies, are superimposed one on another.

Automatic responses have a typical, or repetitive, character, or perhaps it is better to say, operations that differ to the point of being quite opposite to each other are linked by a mysterious symbolic unity. The fight posture of a fish observed by Tinbergen, the stickleback, so named, no doubt, for the spines on its back – vertical, head down – is the same as when the male of this species is prodding from above the female, whom he has already brought into the nest, with a vibrating movement to induce her to spawn there. One mode of behaviour, with entirely opposite intentions. Or it may be that, receiving the signal, the creature is feeling its way by trial and error, trying to intuit what is required, decoding differences written into the program. Just as genetics does not program eye colour but a distinctive structure which in a particular milieu, with particular matter, in a particular geographical environment becomes an eye of a particular colour, so, too, genes do not dictate the details of behaviour but only a structure of differences. It makes sense to consider the genetic program along the lines of conscience not dictating 'do this' but suggesting 'no, that's not right'. (For this idea I and not Tinbergen am responsible.)

Anyone who participates in operations is performing them and risks making mistakes, which is why animals pass so easily and swiftly from delight and ecstasy to rapt attention and precision. The operation is perceived as something that *belongs to it*; it never happens, to return to my example of the bitch, that the female, having given birth, fails to enter fully and wholeheartedly into the game of birth. Outside this game, she simply does not exist. Her service here is not in the sense that she will do the job and then go off about *her* business: the collaboration between the individual and the species is total.

We must include among manifestations of delight and ecstasy such things as the amazing colouring of butterflies' wings and the eyes looking out from them. The overstated brilliance of butterflies distinguishes them markedly from caterpillars. The equivalent for our species is drawing attention to oneself in early youth, paying attention to oneself in the mirror and taking an incipient interest in one's clothing. (Before this, teenagers do not care what sort of clothes they wear.) In one's prime, it is dazzling wit as a way of paying, and attracting, attention. We could, and *should*, continue these analogies, for example by likening the behaviour of the caterpillars on parade to military parades.

Now, when we have turned to the question of behaviour, we might say, looking back to our last topic of the impossibility of interbreeding between species, that the main obstacle here is not at the molecular level but on the behavioural level. Offspring are born from the union of a donkey and a horse; on the molecular level, there is no incompatibility, the chemistry is prepared, as it were, to compromise (and here it differs from computer programs, where incompatibility has to be taken more seriously). In technical terms, the union is possible but the glitch appears because the mule is, so to speak, a muddle. Its program is just too complicated and it cannot work out how to behave, it has no initiative, and that is precisely what humans find so convenient about mules.

Lecture 30, 12 May 1998

Which matters more: the particular individual or the biological operation the individual serves? The answer appears to be: the operation. If just two females are left in a pigeon loft, for example, one of them will behave like a male and start courting. Mating behaviour will begin in which *both* females will participate. One of the functions of mating behaviour is to synchronize the rhythms of reproduction, and that is something this couple of two females will achieve; having initiated their unconsummated marriage at different stages of the biological cycle, they will eventually lay their eggs at the same time, and may attempt to hatch them, although, of course, no chicks will be forthcoming. In some way, their behaviour has synchronized the development of the eggs.[1] There is a hypothesis that communal incubation by flocks of birds also leads to synchronization. What, then, we have to wonder, is needed to trigger a mechanism, in this case, of reproduction: only the symbolic presence of a supposed 'male'? A hint? A signal? Is everything already so prepared to launch these operations that even just a slight push will be enough?

It is comical how crude and approximate the dummy of a male stickle-back can be for the female to embark on the mating ritual when she is in season; in fact all that is needed is some rough likeness of an oblong shape, provided it is coloured red underneath (or black in the case of a different species of stickleback). Without that detail, the female shows no interest in the dummy. Something else that helps is painting bright blue eyes on it: the other details are of no importance. (Let us recall the eyes on the butterfly's wings. Altogether the amount of displaying and gazing among animals is such that I am reminded of the words of one artist who said, 'A person is their eyes.') Again, it does not matter whether there is a real nest in the aquarium. A symbolic movement by the dummy, roughly approximating to an invitation to enter an imaginary nest, is enough for the female to start attempting to 'enter' somewhere on the bottom of the aquarium. An equally crude 'female' dummy can have a similar effect on a male, provided only that the dummy has a large stomach.

Does this mean that, like the mosquito programmed to respond to only one of hundreds of elements of blood, the fish acts in response not in fact to an individual of the opposite sex but to signs? The male nudges the female stickleback with his head when she has already entered the nest, but the same effect of inducing her to spawn can be achieved using a vibrating glass rod (to avoid the wrong smell).

So what are specimens seeing if they are not seeing each other in our sense of individuals, if they are in a hurry to perform functions and can easily, amazingly easily, be fooled? A bird needs to see markedly different plumage on a female, since otherwise it might get into a fight, a fight being only a modification of mating behaviour: the two behaviours diverge only at the last moment. Initially what happens is the approaching of another creature of one's own species, in a flock, or for a fight, or for mating. The initial impulse is evidently only to approach a member of one's own species because there is some *business to be transacted* with it (or with oneself, where a female needs to imitate the behaviour of a male). If the female does not have that drastically different colouration to make her look like a male, she needs to indicate her differentness by means of her *behaviour*, by what is called 'female courtship'.

We could adduce many more such examples, and they would all point in the same direction: we are evidently using the wrong categories when we try to read the patterns of animal behaviour; folklore and folk tales anthropomorphize animals. As we try to read their minds, we approximate them to ourselves with an *intimate, familial empathy*, whereas to animals we should apply our also very intimate experience of *bureaucratic, authoritarian, military order*, rigid state and employment regimentation, when what comes *first* is the system, and the individual is expected to conform to it. We call that aspect of life 'inhuman'; we find it repulsive, the figure of the cold official, policeman, team leader. We laugh at all that, call it idiotic, but are nevertheless obliged to put up with it. The lieutenant going to guard a missile with a nuclear warhead has to pass through the requisite number of checkpoints, utter the requisite passwords, and wait for the requisite number of seconds. The sentry at his post must approach, goose-stepping, reply to 'Halt, who goes there?', stand next to the sentry he is replacing without looking him in the face, and make an about-turn.

The formalities have to be observed. The behaviour of animals can be described as a set of steps and actions that animals must be able to perform, and which they should competently, unconditionally, unquestioningly present when those actions are demanded of them through signals. For example, as already mentioned, an animal has ready both aggression and courtship in respect of other individuals; there is a mandatory need to do something (to do nothing, just to walk on by, is also to do something, to perform a pointedly negative act). What exactly should be chosen from the range of actions available is prompted by signals given by the situation and the other individual.

An individual from a different species will most often simply be ignored, treated as just part of the scenery, with certain exceptions which we shall note. There is never an indifferent attitude towards an individual of its own species. One may fight it, attempt to frighten it, or, by mating with it, somehow produce from two bodies an entirely new individual of the same species.

Chemistry and physiology have prepared everything in males and females, and in the spring mating takes priority over food. But they have yet to behave in such a way as to be together at the right time. They can easily not be in that situation. One of the pair might die. There may be other snags. We have already accepted that nature has chosen not to bring the physical chemistry to automatic culmination but has moved the whole business of procreation into an area of risk, complicating matters. We previously, without criticism or discussion, considered both options of the theory of two lives, that genetics was later introduced or tyrannically imposed on simple metabolism, and that both lives always existed together. Now I want to favour the latter view: from the very outset there were two lives.

The polarity between hard and soft was there from the start. We incline to see something aesthetic and free in the behaviour of animals; we find that easier. This makes it all the more necessary to pay attention to the hard side. We are touched by the way the male and female pigeon bring their beaks together. This is so-called *infantile* behaviour on the part of females of many species, a signal they use to avert aggressive behaviour, fighting, on both sides. That is not all. The instinct for infantile behaviour intuits and acts out in anticipation the future feeding of the chicks, which do not yet exist. The male feeds the female like a chick with food it either brings or produces from its crop, and the female thereby stimulates *the male's* future paternal feelings from which the individual can recoil. A snag is possible at this stage too. The female signals his future function to the male.

We find the singing of birds in the spring very affecting, but here again we tend to see only the aesthetics, an optional adornment of the physics and chemistry. That is a mistake. Songbirds *expose* themselves to predators and catchers while simultaneously throwing down a challenge to them in a deadly game. The male nightingale, which begins singing when the female is still in the Mediterranean, a different part of the globe, which is singing to *her*, calling her, his song ringing out over thousands of kilometres, has a transaction with the planet, with astronomy, and has not lost his mind. The male is communicating with the climate, because his singing is caused by the difference between the heat, in the midst of which he was living two or three days earlier, and the damp and coolness; that difference is to be heard in his voice. The male is singing to demarcate his territory, inviting other nightingales to move away, to spread out. In this way, the nightingale is singing *urbi et orbi*, so the whole world can hear. That is why his song is familiar to us, and in this cosmic range is his power. None of that undermines the fact that he is a hard signaller – of territorial limits, of a declaration of intent, summoning his female.

It is clear enough that mating behaviour is the most conspicuous and effective to study. The ritual, differing between species, is clearly linked to differences in the genetic program, the chemistry. The fact we have already noted, that chemistry *permits* the mating of similar species, has an analogy in behaviour. An individual starts out as if it were prepared to mate not only with other species (birds courting the females of other species is no great rarity), but also with the whole wide world: in just the same sexual pursuit as of a female, a butterfly will pursue a beetle, a fly, a small bird, a falling leaf, and even its own shadow on the ground. *Urbi et orbi.* That first signal, the movement of a body of roughly the right parameters, is not, however, followed up by the next confirming and directing signals. The initial movement has a broad focus, but needs to encounter a whole succession of reactions, and is cancelled when, in pursuit, for example, of a female belonging to a different species, a bird meets not consent, signalled, say, by a female landing on the ground, but rather the reaction of it rapidly flying away. That is a malfunction, forcing a correction of the male's behaviour. There is a rethink, a refinement of behaviour. We are likely to miss small signals, like flight at a particular speed or along a particular trajectory.

Or movement towards a fish of a different species. After a first trial approach, no signs of encouragement follow, which there would need to be. A stickleback will offer an invitation to a nest, showing the entrance, then trying to persuade the female by dumb show that she should go into the nest. (Incidentally, squeezing her body through the narrow opening is mimetic role play for discharging the roe from her own body. Then, once the female is in the nest, she needs the further stimulus from the male of his quivering movement.)

This is a rigid system of encouragements and checks; failure at any stage sees the whole operation cancelled; on the other hand, making it through one stage encourages moving on to the next. The nest, about which we will be saying more, is not altogether a structure: blades of grass and twigs are stuck together underwater using a glue which the male discharges from its body, again an anticipation of the release, an actual discharge of its own body, which is the purpose of the nest. The parents will later witness the emergence of the young from the roe and will ensure they remain in the vicinity of the nest, gradually allowing them to move further away from it and leave. So there are three emissions around the nest and the fourth is entry into the nest and emission in there from the stickleback's own body.

Each of the four main stages leading to mating (attract – persuade – appease – synchronize[2]) has its specific signs and signals. There is a clear distinction between stickleback species with a red or a black underbelly, and this signal ensures 'reproductive isolation': an initial winnowing of potential mates occurs on that basis. I say 'signal' rather than 'character-istic', because a characteristic characterizes something, while animal reac-tions, as we shall see, are elicited by precise signals, as if it did not matter in the least whether there was any signaller or bearer of it behind the signal. It is just a signal in an environment, as if the signal itself created the environ-ment, as if there were no individual there. A signal on a crude model works just as well. Any anti-substantialist would be delighted.

Signals work precisely. They are genetically fixed (like the red underbelly, which is very obvious, or the chicks' reaction to the mother bird's beak, which is less obvious) just as rigidly as habitat, food, and the shape of the body. The method by which signals are registered is the same as for the body and the operation: 'fitness' – I see no other way of describing this. Everything in life both takes shape and is fixed by fitness, successes which form into a series and become superimposed on each other. Darwinian selection fixes and confirms strokes of luck. The complex system of mating is one such series of successes.

The individual whom we have in front of us and who seems to be the central figure is actually playing a supporting role in an operation, but the extent to which that is the case is something we need to feel. A female satyr butterfly (which was being closely observed) was seen to be 'courted and seduced' by one male, but mated with another. There was no disruption of the chain, no change in the sequence of actions, it was just that at the moment of orientation another male seized the initiative. By chance one performer was replaced by a luckier one. An example from the human world: a novel by Claude Prosper de Jolyot Crébillon (1707–77), *Les Égarements du cœur et de l'esprit*, *Strayings of the Heart and Mind* (1736–8), describes the simultaneous and equal infatuation of the hero in Paris with two ladies, only, for appearances' sake, presented in a secondary moral framework as a 'straying'. The tenor of the action is a confident return to nature, although, of course, only with an intuitive confidence in the verisimilitude of such a dual attachment, without the underpinning of biology.

An individual comes on stage and leaves the stage. By definition, there can be no bug in the *program*. That it is fail-safe is guaranteed by the necessity of obtaining new members of the same and kindred species. The program is bug-free precisely because it is absolute, maximalist; if you like, impossible. If you set yourself a possible target, people will query why you chose that one and not another. Set yourself a target so fantastic as to be incredible, the immortality of a species, for example, such that it is replicated but never changes, making it immortal, and, strangely enough, such a program will either succeed 100% or fail absolutely. A mere glitch is out of the question. Those executing the program, however, are a different matter. They do so only for as long as they are successful in terms of the program, although they are enthused and captivated by its goal and brilliance.

Behold, a male gull approaches a female, keeping its behaviour, whether aggressive or amorous, as yet unspecified. The female prompts him to choose by adopting the pose of a chick wanting to be fed. Thereby she introduces the topic of feeding. An interesting quirk of all this acting is that, at some point, chicks providing a stimulus for feeding behave like prey. They provoke their parents and take a risk: the parents really will (Tinbergen's observations related to gulls) eat their offspring immediately if they see them dead, having failed to protect them from a sudden attack by other gulls, but having managed to ward off the intruders. (For reasons given below, this is not difficult.) What is the stake in this provocation? Because we have seen that the individual is merely taking a ride on the train of the operation and is replaceable, we can now see that the chick is staking itself, signalling with itself, predicting the right moment in the operation, namely eating, and announcing the topic before the roles have been allocated. What its behaviour is triggering is just food in general, without specifying who is going to do what, the chick to eat the food brought or the father to care enough to bring it. So a child says 'am-am', leaving it to others to clarify who is eating or wants to eat. Deciding is left to whoever wishes, if they do, to be involved in the process. The risk that they, the chicks, will themselves be eaten is balanced by a general confidence that on the whole the operation will go as planned. Similarly, a female, seeing an approaching male who may have aggressive designs, takes a risk and exposes herself submissively, pacifying him with her gesture of infantility.

Conversely, parents sometimes display all the stimuli (signals) to their progeny that should motivate them to flee. Here the topic of pursuit is being enacted, without it being clear who is chasing whom, and again with the danger that they may eat their own offspring, but again with full confidence in the fact that the program (the regulatory regime) includes all the needful corrective signals. We can interpret this acting out by the parents of the role of predator as a *story* being told to the young to prepare them for their future life. Actually it is all much simpler: the adult bird has at the ready, and is enacting, every type of behaviour at its disposal, anticipating and requiring stages of correction.

Just as the female pigeon is willing to adopt the role of male pigeon and act it out, so the baby birds will play the role of prey, their father that of a predator, and a male the role of a female. More to the point, all these different behaviours are proving effective, and ultimately preserve the species and ensure it continues. If we are seeing a species that has survived until today, we know that the individuals, at least in the great majority of cases, have been behaving successfully, in a 'fit' manner.

So-called display, where animals show themselves off, where they strike a pose, is a displaying of successes in the past. Similarly, in order to encourage themselves, sportsmen watch films of their past achievements. There is an awareness here that anything less than brilliant success is failure.

By the way, is it an error if the male, instead of courting a female, attacks her? What can we say? A fight, possessing another's body, victory, is also a sign of 'fitness'.

Altogether the animal, and anything else, after that first great stroke of luck of the successful separation of matter out of the radiation field, the biblical separation of light from darkness, can only continue along the guiding line of success and fitness. So the species, *Homo sapiens*, in the twentieth century has had a succession of unprecedented successes, although there is, of course, the risk that the range of possibilities human-ity has allowed itself may contain a malfunction.

For humankind, everything is more complicated and difficult, although even with birds the complexity of functions is such that the surprise is not how many birds abandon their families and doom their offspring, but how many stay with them. A malfunction is not necessarily a dereliction of duty, for example by males failing to carry out their incubation duties, but can be the contrary, a gull dutifully sitting, say, on an empty nest. We see it in humans, when a mother does not accept the fact that her baby has died and continues to try to look after it, carrying a doll around in its place. The act is correct. The failure is not in the act itself.

It is like a partially sighted driver mistaking one sign for a different one and taking a wrong turn, even though actually making the turn entirely correctly. The significant fact is that an animal will not wait for the signs to be clear. It will prefer to carry out the action, to do the wrong thing rather than do nothing. It finds it easier to make a mistake reading the signs than fail to respond to them in a timely manner. Animals are very conscientious: their main concern is not to leave something undone.

Here is another example of the way in which behavioural, in addition to physiological, stimuli correct actions. If you introduce a chick into the nest of a bird at the beginning of incubation, it will be rejected: the physi-ological clock is not yet ready; but if you do the same thing at the end of the incubation period, even a few days before hatching, the intruder will be accepted. Its cheeping, its characteristic gaping, its open mouth, will be sufficient stimulus to initiate the reaction of feeding. Although the internal physiological clock is not yet quite ready, the clock of external behaviour will override it.

Ethology is ritual, rules, and order. The willingness to feed also comes from within, from the physical chemistry, but needs the behavioural stimuli, the signal of the gaping mouths. If the chicks do not provide it, the parent bird looks at them, then looks around itself in a state of help-less confusion. The idea that it might offer food even to a chick that is not cheeping (which might be precisely because it has been weakened by lack of food) never occurs to a bird. It will wait for those *signals*, of gaping and cheeping, as if *what it is feeding is the signal, as if its duty is not to bring up a chick but to act in accordance with instructions*. But that is the way formal discipline operates. Between strictly carrying out orders, which often, or almost always, proves deadly for a human being (do your duty and to hell with everything else), and reasonable, gentle behaviour, wise and redemp-tive, there is no halfway house: a clean break is always required. Orders are either obeyed or disobeyed. In human society, it usually never occurs to those who issue orders that they might be disobeyed – and they invariably are. If they are disobeyed in the animal world, it is as the result of a mal-function of the kind we have mentioned. To put it crudely, if an individual animal is getting things wrong, it either perishes or errs in the direction of obeying even where there is no strict requirement to do so. Animals are more likely to *see* a strict requirement even where there is none. The general rule is rigid adherence to the program. Behaviour is completely *impersonal*. The actors may malfunction, they may leave the stage, but the program must be fulfilled.

The cuckoo smuggles an egg into the nest of a redstart. The redstart patiently incubates the egg and usually the cuckoo chick hatches out before her own offspring. As mentioned, it heaves an egg or even a redstart chick on to its back and, holding it in place with its rudimentary wings, pushing with its legs and beak, moving backwards, pushes the egg or chick out of the nest or, failing that, to the edge of the nest if it fears it may fall out together with the egg. (Incidentally, the analogous operation of removing its egg from its own nest and transporting it to another bird's nest is performed by the mother cuckoo, following the same pattern.) If the redstart finds its own egg on the edge of its nest, there is no way it will roll it back to the middle of the nest and resume incubating it. It faces the same strict prohibition as all birds do against feeding chicks that are not cheeping! Does that seem unbelievably stupid? No! It is as if birds put their trust in the law and know that an egg cannot move itself from the bottom of a nest to its edge. Accordingly, this must be a foreign object. Forgive me if I liken it to a horrified human mother refusing to acknowledge as her own child a creature with fur and fangs or which immediately starts crawling on four legs.

The redstart's own chicks do not open their beaks as widely or cheep as loudly as the cuckoo. That gets fed first because the order in which food is given is entirely dependent on the loudness of the request (just as in human society grants are given in accordance with the insistence and frequency of applications). The theory is that a hungry chick will cheep loudly, but if it has become too weak to do so it will die of hunger and cold.

By the way, it is hard to believe quite how harsh the framework is within which the animals live. A chick will request food just once or twice before giving up, because otherwise it might attract a predator; only those that live in the hollow of a tree keep cheeping, and not always even then.

We might imagine that this rigidity is only found where the genetic program is operating. But no. The genetic program leaves room for learning from experience. For example, there are many species of the cichlid, an aquarium fish. Some keep the roe in their mouths, which goes on to be a bedroom for the young. These fish eat the young of other species as a matter of course, but distinguish them from their own *not innately but on the basis of experience*: those of their roe that have grown up in their mouths are their own. A perhaps not particularly subtle technique makes it possible to remove the roe after their first mating and replace them with those of a different species. They will then nurture and protect those others, and invariably eat their own; moreover, when they breed a second time and begin to nurture their own offspring, they will eat them too. Having once learned to consider a different species to be their own, they remember what they have learned. A mating couple treated in this manner are, Tinbergen tells us, corrupted permanently.

The rigidity of the rules and the way they are implemented is startling. Konrad Lorenz discovered that the night heron persuades its fledgelings that it does not intend to attack them by giving a graceful nod to the nest's occupants, the offspring and the male or female parent in it. A display is performed on a nearby branch, of its beautiful blue and black cap with the showing of three long white feathers, like a crown on its head, which are usually pressed back on its neck. After bowing, the parent hops from a branch into the nest, where he is joyfully welcomed. Lorenz once managed to position himself on a tree very close to a nest. One of the parents returned and, seeing a human on a nearby branch, assumed an aggressive posture instead of performing the appeasing ceremony of bowing. The fledgelings, which had ceased to be afraid of the peaceable Lorenz, immediately attacked their father. A sentry is under orders to *shoot* if his challenge of 'Who goes there?' is not replied to with the pass-word, *even if he is personally acquainted with the person approaching*. For the sentry, the person approaching does not exist as someone he knows. The heron flying back to the nest does not exist for its family (if that is even the appropriate word) as a familiar figure or an individual, but only as a function, the carrier of a signal or, even more basically, as a signal, a ceremony.

Just the case of the cuckoo is enough to tell us that there is no strug-gle between species: the redstart is not fighting for its species against the cuckoo species. What is taking place is *service*, more or less successful, to programs, mechanisms, operations, regulations, formalities. To put it another way, what we are seeing is a serving by might and main of the *automaton*. The creatures are serving either with their whole body or with their behaviour, to the best of their ability, without knowing why, and they are serving what is achieved by that automaton. Again, they only seem to be serving individuals or the continuation of their species, but given the extinction of the majority of species, they must be serving some other purpose we do not know about. A wild conjecture: is everything gravitat-ing towards the emergence of one exceptional species: the human species? Perhaps, but only in the sense that humans are obliged to prove themselves fit, to find meaning. In this plan, God guarantees only that the possibility of success is not out of the question. There is no evidence that God knows the correct way for humankind to act and is keeping it to himself.

Comparison with human beings leads us to very far-reaching and diffi-cult conjectures. Humans, too, have a ceremony of appeasement (or greet-ing), but it can be neglected, while for the night heron to neglect it is out of the question: the parent heron when it returns *must* execute its graceful nod because otherwise its offspring will rush him as an enemy. Humans also have ceremonies of leave-taking and parting, and they, too, can be neglected. That is not the case for the observed behaviour of aquarium fish. They swim in a zigzag pattern when approaching to relieve their partner who is guarding the offspring, and the partner being relieved swims off rapidly in a straight line. This is evidently so as to *get away* without being followed by the offspring. This could solve a problem which always plagues humans who invariably take too long to say goodbye, but there is a lot here that is new and unclear.

Observers talk about the tediously total obedience of animals, the meticulousness with which the animals observed follow their program as something absolutely sacrosanct. If we are looking for an analogy with humans, it really can only be the performance of sacred rituals. If a parent bird signals alarm, the chicks will cower in the nest and *never dream* of accepting even the most appetizing morsel, seemingly unable to reason that a human who has done them no harm without food is unlikely to do them any harm *with* food. This is not, however, straightforward stupidity: they are strictly, inflexibly adhering to their instructions. Tinbergen made a hide in which to stand and watch the gulls; the chicks got used to it, would come in right to where he was standing and became accustomed to him too. One time, however, the observer impetuously stuck his head out; the chicks paid no attention to him but the parent gull did, and signalled the danger that there was a person in the hide; the chicks naturally immediately obeyed orders, because it was completely impossible for them not to do so, and all ran into the hide and huddled round the observer's feet. In civil defence terms, birds scrupulously take cover when the siren sounds. Bird catchers catch birds not because the birds are stupid, but because they follow the instruction manual, their moves are predictable and are predicted by observant human beings, who can then catch them with their bare hands.

The male will not only never leave a nest where he is incubating eggs, but will not always react even to the ceremony of change when his partner returns. It is the familiar principle that a creature that has committed to a way of doing things would rather, in the ecstasy of obeying orders, prefer to overfulfil its duty than leave it unfinished. In order to replace it on the nest, its partner may have to push it off.

Contemplating the way animals render 'service', we recognize why they so disturb and upset us, almost as if we were looking directly at the sun. They seem to be showing us only too clearly ourselves as we may have been – or could be. Or perhaps indeed are, under the inhuman discipline of a draconian order? Or *will be* in a society for which the so-called totalitarian states, puzzling institutions as yet underresearched, were a trial run, an approach to which is so unexpectedly opened up to us by biology? In animals we get a glimpse of our unknown double or twin.

We observe the ethics of animals with studied impartiality, and *fail to notice what human order is ultimately based on: the same blind naïvety as plants and animals which placidly serve us*, and of children, to the extent that the *populus*, the 'common people', remain child-like.

Let us continue to read, with digressions, Nikolaas Tinbergen's *Social Behaviour in Animals*, first published in 1953. A flock of birds is at once a tool and an operation, an event. Its strength is that it helps to protect; the entire flock is as keen-eyed as its most vigilant bird. But there is in animal society a further reason for staying with the flock, not moving on alone even when that is possible: it becomes 'as one', like a single organism. We should know to look at this in the light of the officiousness of animals. The ideal totalitarian state should be seen as an example of an animal society, and at all events, certainly not of a human family.

Fighting within a species is much more common in the animal world than with external enemies. Animals sometimes have special organs for intraspecific clashes, such as antlers. Combat is not limited to 'reproductive fighting', and in what is said to be fighting over females we need to bear in mind the general constant desire of animals to keep their distance from each other. The need for close bodily contact with another creature of their species comes as a surprise for them, as does the similarity of aggressive and courtship behaviour which they are obliged to discriminate between. In these circumstances, the presence of other males is essential: it enables them to attract aggressive behaviour towards themselves and clarify the distinction from courtship behaviour in relation to females. Again, the intense internal discipline imposed in totalitarian societies comes to mind. In intraspecific fights, we see a lot of mutual correction, such as the regulation of boundary disputes. Most fights are a bluff, a test of nerves, a threat without implementation. The constant squabbling in communal apartments in Russia comes to mind, the cavilling which almost always centred on mutual accusations of improper behaviour. Also the constant watchfulness in primitive societies over morality.

Clearly, states that insist on such unconditional service are aiming to function faultlessly for all eternity. The expression 'official relations', which asks to be applied to such instances as the family attacking the father who omitted the requisite ceremonial gesture when approaching the nest, takes us straight back to the *officium* of ancient Rome, *duty, obligation*, and primarily the sacrosanct duty of a Roman citizen. The Roman republic, pleasingly remote from us, does not look too totalitarian but, closer up, it would. We would be horrified by the harshness and rigidity of the standards, the signs and symbols. The Roman state was conceived, and designed to last, for eternity. According to Cicero, the only thing that could undermine the perpetuity of the state was vice among its citizens. The principles of Roman law remain the basis of modern legislatures.

It is interesting to consider why the internal discipline in even the most authoritarian of human societies will still fall far short of that found among animals.[3] Even more interesting is our curious blindness when observing animals, the reason why we fail to notice in the animal world what in our own everyday lives upsets, shocks, and offends us most of all: the iron law of the state, its formalism, its ritual nature, its bureaucracy, the total indifference to the individual, the inflexibility of norms, the strict 'correction', the repudiation of humane concern, the inhumanity in the sense of disregard for the individual.[4]

Let us return to the constant *self-correction* in animal society. Is this not the purpose of intraspecific clashes which more often than not resolve into aggressive display? Display, the threat posture of birds or fish defending their territory, occurs very frequently, but actual fighting is rare; the possessor of the territory easily repels an aggressor, whose behaviour as he trespasses on someone else's territory betrays his guilty conscience, while that of the defender in his own territory is all righteous indignation. This moral high ground is so powerful that the aggressor is easily put to flight. When, a moment ago full of righteous anger, a bird enters someone else's territory, it suddenly loses heart and flees. But what if a confrontation occurs right on the border? Actual fighting remains a rarity.

The clash of two antagonistic drives within one individual sets off a third: displacement.[5] One gull will begin ostentatiously tearing up the grass in front of another, supposedly in order to build a nest, but with a neurotic intensity not present when a nest is actually being built; or a stickleback in its vertical, upside-down fight posture will start furiously digging the sand, as if to show what will happen to the enemy if it does come to a fight. Curiously, in wading birds, aggressive display suddenly ends when one, right in front of the other, goes to sleep the way herons do, still standing and burying its head in its feathers; domesticated cockerels engage in 'displacement eating', also in an edgy and aggressive manner. Of course, an actual fight can break out, but never immediately, before the *whole gamut of signals has first been gone through*.

It is remarkable that these types of displacement activity are common to all living things. Infantry soldiers during war are observed to have an uncontrollable desire to sleep immediately before facing danger or going on the attack.

Ill-tempered eating – a nervous meal in a restaurant by people facing danger and a menacing situation.

Preening feathers – smoothing your hair, twirling a moustache, scratching your head in a threatening situation.

Let us not forget that animal signals absolutely must be responded to in an appropriate manner; in other words, it will not do for demonstrative gestures to be taken casually or regarded strategically, as mere distracting behaviour. If one cockerel begins pecking the ground in front of another, that is a clear signal that the other one must do likewise; the sleeping posture of an adversary must be reacted to either by waking it up with an alarm cry or by leaving it in peace.

If a red-bellied stickleback appears in the vicinity of another, a defending posture must be adopted to preserve territorial rights and chase it away, which can be done successfully if it is clear to whom the territory belongs. But what if it is not a fish but a dummy? Exactly the same, no matter how crude the model, just as long as it is painted red underneath. Moreover, when a red post office van drove past the window of the laboratory (the experiments were in an aquarium), the fish became nervous and watched its movement closely from inside the aquarium, inclined to aggression. The rules are sacred, just as in Roman law!

Analogously, a robin will assume a fighting posture in reaction to the red colour of a breast. A young robin whose breast is still brown generates no protest, but even a rough bundle of red feathers does. It is important that aggression is evoked not because the bird fails to notice that the bundle of red feathers does not even have a beak, suggesting that the bird is simply short-sighted and stupid, but because the *program reacts not to another individual but to colour*. 'How ridiculous. How idiotic.' But while we laugh at birds, are we overlooking our own reaction to red? Not to red anything but simply to the colour red? Or the reaction in Israel with its fevered religious passions to a Christian Cross, *not to a cross on anyone's chest but simply to the Cross*.

A stickleback of the red-bellied species will react in exactly the same way, not to an individual but to the colour red. In a particular species of woodpecker, the American flicker, the male and female have exactly the same complicated colouring, with alternating black dots and stripes covering their whole body, the only exception being that the male has a so-called moustache, a small black spot at the corner of its beak. A similar black moustache was glued to the female and she was attacked by her own male. When the moustache was removed, he again accepted her. Idiotic, we say, the better to overlook how we ourselves observe formalities in our relationships and how we panic when confronted by physical deformities, or insist that a wife must belong to the same church or the same political party as her husband, that she should walk in the street dressed to match the degree of formality of her husband. The fact that the American woodpecker finds it unacceptable for his mate to have a moustache needs to be seen not as a failure of recognition but as an inflexible, sacred observance of convention, a totemic ritual. American woodpeckers, incidentally, peck ants. We might think this indicates that the bird has insufficient food and has found an alternative source, but no! It is genetically programmed to peck ants. This is a service it performs: it has a special alkaline saliva specifically to neutralize the ants' protective formic acid. Some birds have a waxy cere on their beak. In one species of small parrots, the shell parakeet,[6] the cere is blue in males and brown in females. This is important and closely monitored: females whose cere was painted blue were attacked by males.

Lecture 31, 19 May 1998

There are any number of examples of a strong reaction to signals, colours, and shapes, and of demonstrations of the colour of a person's skin being like the waving of a flag, a sign of war or courtship. Conflict, as in human society, is provoked not by individuals but by signals. Other species are attacked when they *inadvertently* give out a signal of aggression. Thus, the fish in the aquarium were all for attacking the red post office van. There are cases of overt conflict between species, but usually one species passes among others without either seeming to notice the other, as when sparrows hop around among pigeons with no signs of hostility on either side.

The piquancy of the situation is that the woodpecker can perfectly well see that the moustached female is his partner: his objection to her is purely ideological. That animals are perfectly well able to discriminate between individuals is indicated by the fact that in any animal society a 'pecking order' (which initially referred to birds) emerges. First is the dominant male, then a hierarchy in accordance with protocol. All may have exactly the same colouration. In the classroom, the hierarchy of bullying is not only not highlighted by any external signs but also carefully concealed from the teacher, and becomes apparent only briefly when pies are being grabbed in the canteen. The pecking order among animals applies not only to individuals. Among birds, note is immediately taken of which female is paired with which male and she is awarded exactly the same position in the pecking order as her male. You will recall we were talking about human society and the castes of daughter-murderers. There exactly the same thing applies: a woman taken in marriage enters the caste of her husband, but the opposite does not apply.

Signals, colour, gestures, clearly mark the borders of territory and hierarchical differences. Everything is strictly set out and *religiously* observed among animals. The same is true of humans, but for some reason we prefer not only not to emphasize, but even pretend not to notice the minimal but highly distinctive differences in dress, gesture, gait, and facial expression between different income groups. Here it is as if we are embarrassed to make an issue of something to which, on an instinctive level, we scrupulously conform.

We need not delude ourselves that we understand all the reasons for and meanings of such a hierarchy in our society. Let us again look to the animals. The order of official function and the order of actually achieving goals, which is what we tend to notice, are clearly separated. Animals function without considering whether goals are achieved. Alarm calls are given quite independently of whether there is anybody around who might hear them. If there is absolutely no one, a lone bird will emit them nevertheless. Is this more evidence of stupidity? They do not notice there is no one to hear the signal? No, the bird is performing a sacred duty, just as a sentry must act in accordance with the regulations whether there is an officer watching him or not, *just as a priest must perform the liturgy whether anyone has come to the church or not*. Similarly, a German will stop at a red traffic light even if there are no other cars and unlikely to be any within the next half-hour.

A human child has just such a reverent attitude towards signals. When a child anxiously seizes its mother by the hand and pulls her away from a stationary car because 'the driver might turn the headlights on full beam to check them and *blind* us', that is not stupid, not a lack of understanding that 'blind' in this context does not mean depriving someone of sight for the rest of their lives. The child is just employing the unambiguous, non-synonymous, non-interpretive usage of the word that Wittgenstein describes so well.

Another enigmatic, and for us and the whole of modern humanity perhaps most important, distinction in the world is that, as we like to think, humans beat themselves a path to an end whereas an animal religiously and *unthinkingly* observes its ritual. A human being reasons, while an animal is dependent on the reasoning of nature or humans. At the highest level of reasoning, however, humans come back to the holy, the naïve. From here we glimpse the meaning of Aristotle's teleology as purifying, cathartic work on the purpose. The purpose, the goal, in Aristotle's teleology is needed to correct the errors of civilization of modern times – that is, of the last 6,000 years – an epoch that was in full swing when Aristotle was working. The goal as fullness, *en-ergeia*, realization. That is the opposite of 'setting goals' and 'achieving' them in the current 'practical' sense. The opposite of Aristotle's *telos*, these goals are what modern humankind comes barging into the world and nature with, as if the purpose of living beings, which previously they had been fulfilling automatically, was no longer being accomplished and now a conscious effort was needed on the part of humankind because nature is no longer functioning. Human oversight 'needs' to be superimposed on the work of nature. But even as it sets itself conscious targets and achieves them, in some other personal, unintellectual, unarticulated realm humankind continues, as part of the animal realm, not to set goals, which we can interpret as being because it would be disastrous for humankind to know itself.[1] There is still a secret place where humankind continues not to set itself goals and works in accordance with the principle of stimulus and response, understanding the goal as a blessed, all-inclusive fullness.

So, a bird feeds its chick not in order to feed it but because it is cheeping and opening its mouth wide. Both the chick and its parent are acting in accordance with a program. A parent bird cannot be failing to see its own offspring dying, but can calmly watch them starve to death outside the nest. The bird is responding to the nest. Its chicks must be in the nest, otherwise they do not belong to it. That means the bird is responding not to the chick, but to the *nest-plus-eggs-and-chicks*. Here we are reminded that the nest was moulded using the bird's *saliva*. It is a secretion of the bird no less than the egg, and incubation is the bird sitting in equal measure on the eggs and nest. Incubation is continuation, repetition, mimesis, of the process of moulding the nest; the nest is formed not in-order-to but because, as a bird has a beak and claws, so it will build a nest. It is perfectly reasonable to say that birds have a particular kind of beak, wings, and nest; the beak and the nest are replicated in equal measure, so can we not say that the operation of nest-building is just as much part of the bird as its foot?

Just as a bird has wings, so a fish has fins; as a bird has a nest, so has a fish. They seem so different, fish and fowl, but serve the same operation of moving about and procreating. They are a quite different species, class, and family but have intuited the same process. Fish have the idea of nest-building: did they learn it by watching birds?

Fish and birds have that in common, something simple and basic. Their own body has embryos in it, growing, developing, repeating the same process. The bird uses its beak to build a nest from whatever it finds and from its own saliva, as if reporting the nest it has inside itself. The grass that goes into the nest is like its own feathers, the glue of its saliva like its own blood. The nest is built like a homecoming.

'Caring for the chicks.' We can picture a factory for bringing up human babies, a kind of nursery planned along the lines of the kitchen-factories for feeding the community in the USSR in the 1920s. The important thing will be to perform a function in the factory. The bird performs a function. It will fiercely protect its chick while it is alive, but if some enemy raider manages to kill the chick, the parent will lose no time in eating the chick itself. A moment ago it was alive and demanding food, but now, in an instant, it has become food itself.

Is that horrifying? We need to look at the bird from a different perspective: it has been issued a kit consisting of feathers, a beak, gestures, a cry, and behaviour, all rolled into one.

A note: Pushkin saw poets as inhabitants of the world who do not belong in any category.[2] Hölderlin: man lives poetically.[3] This note is not bibliographical but asking a question: what is a poet? The big question is: how many poets are there? Petrarch said there were few: not every generation would have its poet, generations might pass without one. Happy the generation that has a poet. End of note.

Exhibition, display: like flaunting a symbol or a flag. First there was colouration, flaunted by the animal's body, embodied, as it were, in its skin and plumage. When an animal displays its colouration, it is returning to what has already been, to the flaunting of that colouring when the animal was created. The gesture is embedded, innate in its body. It is important not to make the mistake of thinking that the physiology obviously came first, the colouration of the body, and then the display, the flag-waving. The behaviour is, of course, genetically conditioned, but then again, it is carried by individuals, and their existence depends on that behaviour. Let us not rule out the possibility that behaviour, from *tabula rasa*, came first when there was very little or nothing in the way of genetics, and that the body adapted itself to it. Or it might be better to say that, from the very beginning, a very long time ago – that is, since forever – animals, life in general, were a performance, a display, and we cannot say on which level that first appeared, molecular, phenotypic, or behavioural. That beginning is where we need to look. That path will lead us not to 'the beginning of life', but to the display of all displays, the shining light of the world. That is, if you like, what everything mimics, that first mimesis, the display of anything.

Let us agree that it is as if the animal has at its disposal several keys on a keyboard. It is under an obligation to react, although stimuli can produce a variety of reactions. The official requirement is never to fail to react to the signal.

One further example of this ubiquitous mimesis which complicates the definition of primary and secondary. The bird pecks with its beak. The chick primarily pecks at a beak, finding food in the beak of its parent. The beak is the focus, distinctive, something that both pecks and is pecked. To ensure absolute clarity, the beak of certain birds has a red spot on it to show the chick where to peck. Experiments with a dummy beak give biologists grounds to say that the chick is genetically programmed to *peck the beak*. We may say that is only natural, and the pecking is due to sharp, urgent hunger pangs in the chick, as sharp as a beak. Just as hunger pushes the chick, inciting it to action, so the beak is a protruding, piercing part of the body. The beak is strong, at least as strong and persistent and sharp as hunger. There is a lot of beak, there is a lot of food to be eaten, and the chick's encounter with the beak of its parent emphasizes its prominence.

But nothing comes from nothing. The beak is used for pecking because from the outset that is what it is for. The chick uses its beak to peck its way out of the egg. The chick does not come before the beak, which has protruded as a stroke of luck. The male bird uses its beak during the ritual feeding of the female, and subsequently during the feeding of the chicks: does not this point to the return of the beak to itself, to its 'beakiness', its substance, principle, and nature? The beak is used to insert food into the wide-open beak of the chick and seems to have been there from the very beginning, life itself coming forward, like the beak, to meet the teasing challenge of the world.

A bird's beak has just so many uses that, in a sense, the whole bird is one beak sticking out, sniffing, seeking. The beak is the first part to cut through the air, the wings are subservient to it, propelling it, entering into their complex relationship with air and wind. The space flown through is sensed and measured (mimesis is from the same root as *mensura*, 'measure', measurement) in its *immensity* (mimesis is a measuring probe for capturing the world, to the extent that it can be captured – and accordingly in real mimesis the capturing is an embrace, a continuation and expansion of the world), sensed and measured by the beak. Expansion, invasion, capture, not so much even conducted by the beak, as from the beginning, inherent in its compass needle, its targeting, in its *intention*, and from the outset it posits something captured, the atmosphere, its extensive space, but this space itself provokes the beak's capturing efforts, so that the captured is simultaneously the captivating! The capture *of* the world (the objective genitive) is always a capture of the world (the subjective genitive).

But ladies and gentlemen, what has provoked the capturing element of the air and spirit? It was the difference in density between the material substance and the air, which is, ultimately, the convenient separateness of energy and matter in our part of the universe. We are here repeating the first intuitions of Friedrich Schelling, of Lorenz Oken, at the very beginning of the nineteenth century, of Petar Beron in the middle of it, who spoke about the original dissociation of the primal ether. Without abstruse theories, dif-ferentiation is fundamental to everything, that is simple phenomeno-logy. Viktor Molchanov, a Moscow philosopher, has discovered that consciousness begins with distinguishing, only he is mistaken in supposing that this distinguishing between one thing and another is done by consciousness.[4] Prior to consciousness and prior to anything else, there is the making of distinctions, identification: the beak of the divine bird has already pecked through the shell of the world egg and seen the light. Time, movement, and history have been started by the ticking of the global clock, not in the sense that there is measure and rhythm in the first phenomenon, but in the sense that no measure and no rhythm could be adequate to the task of measuring the first e-vent, and that is why the count of time and history will go on eternally. Something has already happened that will never be exhausted by any counting or ratiocination.

When there is such a coiled spring, it does not matter whether all the rest, a beak, comes to pass. There is quite enough *oddity* without it. Living beings are just an episode, one of the adventures of the light.

Animals are embroiled in their faithful service (that animals are faithfully serving is well intuited in fairy tales). In the final analysis, this service is a service at the event of events, through involvement in it. Life, including human life, is involved in these operations, set to work, employed. That is not burdensome for it but gives it greater importance. Display, showing off their dimensions, their scope and colouration, is no less a sign of pride than the posture 'chest out, face up' of soldiers on parade. This parading by animals indicates that they have a job to do from which they should not be distracted.

When a chick pecks a cardboard model of a beak with a red dot (just the outline of a beak is enough, although one with a red mark will get pecked twice as much), it does not matter whether the 'head' of the dummy is painted black or green. The head gets seen; it enters the field of vision, but it is not really necessary: what is needed is the beak and/or a red dot. A parent bird sometimes gets pecked in the eye if it is red, so greatly is the red mark associated with a beak. *At this stage, during feeding*, it does not matter to a chick what the parent looks like or how they otherwise behave, just as long as they have brought food in their beak. It is as if the gods have sent a piece of fish to the chick from heaven. If it was possible just to suspend a red dot in the air, the chick would peck it. This brings us back to the role of colour. The robin displays prominent red plumage on the front of its body. The stickleback displays its red belly. The American woodpecker displays its black moustache. Colour seems even to be the most important element in display. Then there are shapes. They are just there, but they are also deliberately *displayed*; then the calls, the birdsong; then gestures and movements, like the zigzag dance of the stickleback.

The truth of structuralism is that what is crucial is an opposition, the opposition between matter and light. Everybody repeats that, is susceptible to it, bases themselves on it. All other divisions and discriminations are built on that first one – structure on structure. Any operation is a return, a circle, so we can take the view that in reality there is only one structure, division built on the first structure on the structure. Variety comes in because that first division is rich and accommodates any and all discriminations. There is room in it for everything. Life has nowhere to slip into that does not already exist fully fledged.

But: everything that moves-acts-grows has something to start from, somewhere to fit into, in that first dif-ferentiation, but that, to the discomfiture of Molchanov, is not between one thing and another. It is ineffable. Every *return*, accordingly, only seems simple, and in that is the untruth of structuralism and the truth of Umberto Eco, who, in his book *The Absent Structure*, argues that structure only lures and deceives through appearing to be there.[5] It ultimately proves not to exist and we fall into the void.

We are *catastrophically* intent on finding the correct solution, which we are sure is somewhere waiting to be found. The symptom of this is a mortal weariness, to the point of cynicism and vexation, of insolence and breakdown, of provocativeness of the authorities who are primarily and massively feeling the pressure of this mood. They constantly see themselves surrounded by the crowd, with its comprehensive bafflement by almost everything, its bewilderment about what to do about virtually anything, and its tendency to appeal to authorities, civic, academic, medical, sporting, and economic, in the certainty that *they* know. Knowing what every living thing should do is possible only through knowledge that people really do not want to have, knowledge of the way things can be. That is, through knowledge of discipline and orderly routine. A domineering, smug formalism, a rigid knowledge of how everything is meant to be, is vouchsafed only to forms of authority which are impure, mixed together with ideology and dogmatism. This is false knowledge that knows of its falseness through its own inner emptiness, and is exposed at the time of the demise of the leaders of humankind.

In the pure form of totalitarianism, in the discipline of the animal world, in the bureaucratic machinery, the law is very self-assured, the demands uncompromising but never linked to actual knowledge of what there should be and how, or of how people should live their lives. An honest, uncorrupt official or state representative is just as baffled by the phenomenon of our life, society, and state as a homeless, drunken tramp.

Pre-existent, a priori knowledge precedes sought-out knowledge in just the same way that *energeia* (*dunamis*) in Aristotle precedes possibility (*potentia*), and to it every effort and quest return.[6] *Energeia* is best thought of negatively: that it is *not* the development of potentiality. There is almost no limit to what a living being can do; it has so many mechanisms. Fullness, wholeness (another name for energy), can formally be understood as a negative, as negation of *everything presently here* as imperfect. Perfection is something that has never already been achieved, something which will come to be only later, as the result of Darwinian natural selection. Its positive definition as 'beauty' is actually, even on a verbal level, negative: *formosus* is something that has form, and form is something that can be shown, goods in front of you, display. Defining beauty as vivid colour refers us back to light, that abyss from which all *aporia* proceed and in which they reside.

Beauty remains a formal and also elusive criterion both in the automaton, in scientific theory, and in actions. What we would consider a true achievement is hard to define: it is not the straining of every muscle, although it is that also, and not, on the contrary, relaxation. We can no longer say, now when we understand that life is service, that the goal is life itself, and it is absurd to say that it is not life.

Konrad Lorenz reminds us of the strangeness of this situation, which he calls contemporary. It might be more accurate to call it present, our actual position, because we are getting glimpses of something no one has ever seen before. It is an uncomfortable, difficult situation. Lorenz suggests names for the 'great becoming', *großes Werden*, this calls for, and these names are traditional: 'creativity', 'unity'. He quotes Teilhard de Chardin, '*créer c'est unir*', and that, too, is a return to an old thesis that unity and being are interchangeable, *esse et unum convertuntur*.[7]

Unfortunately, where Lorenz and many others fail, relying on the support of counting and accounting mechanisms, is in believing that unification is recombination. 'Observe,' says Lorenz (it is not his example, and the train of thought is typical of modern times),

> that if we integrate a capacitor into a simple direct current circuit, the current will not immediately achieve the rated voltage; initially it will go into charging the capacitor. If we integrate an induction coil

into the circuit the voltage will, on the contrary, immediately be as rated, and then fall. If we then connect both a capacitor and a coil, a new attribute, not previously present in the system, will appear: oscillation.[8]

I fear this is typical behaviour of looking for something lost where the light is brightest. Combining things is something modern humans find very easy, and it enables them to do an *unimaginable* number of things. This, however, is the unimaginable nature of bad infinity. There is nothing *wesensmäßig*, essentially, new here, the network oscillation is not primary. Characteristically, piling on the complexity is mistaken for rising to a higher level, as if everything is not already suffocating enough. There is more contact with this *Neuwerden*, this innovation, in ecstasy, or even in madness and despair. Neither growing life from something lifeless, nor the appearance of human beings out of the ape, is major news after the peeling apart of light and matter. Although, of course, intuiting a space – a strange land – where beginnings and ends are hidden is insufficient to immediately move to participation in creating a world.

Nobody anywhere, in heaven or earth, knows what exactly is needed now, or what state of redemption all creation should slip into. This is something not even superintelligent aliens can know. The likelihood is, however, that they understand no worse than we do that, as Dostoevsky put it, beauty will save the world. That is, something that is not the result of combinations. There are frequent spasms of thought, which is still trying to find combinations of something to free it from its own constructs (like Münchhausen trying to pull himself out of the swamp by his own hair). We need to include among these efforts the theory of self-organization and the attention being paid to fractals in geometry; these are attempts to formalize a retreat, from the generalizations that result when living reality is fed into mathematical models, to this same reality. These efforts are evinced by a growing suspicion that, after having generalized everything, science is left holding nothing. The suspicion is that science has been trying to draw water with a sieve.

Phenomenological rigour called for a return to images of reality, not by further complicating abstractions which had already been leading away from it, but by reconsidering the concepts with which science had allowed itself to perpetrate the schematization, beginning with the concept of the *limit*. All that is new in the new approach is the attention being paid to the challenging, elusive age-old reality; apart from that, development continues of the toolkit of computer technology.

That a human being is an animal, *ein Tier*, Lorenz, after all the attention he has paid to animals, cannot dispute. What he will not allow is for anyone to say that a human being is '*eigentlich nur ein Tier*', no more than an animal. That, he says, would be '*eine zynische und wertblinde Blasphemie*', 'a cynical blasphemy blind to values'.[9] That sounds humane and politically correct, but it is not risk-free, because it leaves the listener expecting that humane complacency will, with the same confidence that it makes the pronouncement, be able to go on to demonstrate just how exactly a human being is more than an animal. But all the tools at the disposal of the humanists enable them only to sort through once again and summarize their constructs in the hope that qualitatively new knowledge will emerge from the complexity. A despair blind to values is preferable in this respect to the prospect of salvation through the bad infinity of rationalism. It is not mistaken in thinking that nobody anywhere knows what needs to be done; its only mistake is perhaps in predicting that success is fundamentally impossible. Life is an accumulation of strokes of luck, and if you are now out of luck, that is not necessarily always going to be the case for everyone else.

The sad habit of combining things on the off-chance that something may work out also defines the way we look at life. Between human beings and those simple, naïve animals and birds there are the primates, the apes. Konrad Lorenz is observing an orangutan which is looking at a banana it cannot reach.[10] Disappointed, it appears to lose interest. It looks vacantly at a crate, then at the flat, empty floor underneath the bunch of bananas. Suddenly, there on the empty floor, the orangutan *visualizes* the absent *crate* and itself standing on it. The ape gives a cry of joy and rushes, somersaulting in an access of delight, to put the world to rights. The crate needs to go where the orangutan pictures it, right under the bananas. According to Lorenz, the orangutan has acquired spatial imagination and soon it will be time for a human to appear.

The ape's insight seems an achievement in comparison with the world of birds, which would *never* visualize an egg that is lying on the edge of the nest as lying on the empty floor of the nest. They will never picture an egg in that emptiness if it is not already there, or make the connection between what is after all their own egg on the edge of the nest and the one that is *missing* from the security of the nest. The bird seems dull, frozen in some icy state of stagnation and millenia-long immobility. Is that right? Do birds not have spatial imagination?

Actually, they do, and in spades. They have spatial imagination on a planetary scale. Birds feel with their wings; they feel the way their body glides through the air; they see the sloping horizon and sense – the south! They cannot see it with their eyes, the place they will fly to, from which they are absent but where they are *going to be*! It is certainly not 'spatial intuition', '*räumliche Einsicht*', that distinguishes the orangutan from birds, but the *degree of their seriousness in respect of the world*. The bird seriously moves itself around the planet. If you were to move the axis of the earth's rotation, the result would be the same as what the bird is doing when it migrates. If the bird were able to move the axis, it wouldn't, because it has already taken the weight of the planet on itself. It moves the planet with the motion of its wings, remaining the focus, shifting the atmosphere with the motion of its wings, and with it the land and sea.

Never thinking, as if because she lacks hands or proper legs (because a bird is virtually without arms or legs), to roll her own egg back into the warm nest, allowing it to grow cold, the bird with her rigidity seems to be calling on the world order to continue on its way. She is inflexibly connected to it through her non-intervention. She is connected to it precisely because she comes into contact with the whole only by sticking her beak into it, the pointedness of the beak drawing her into it, movement as swift as an arrow. She absorbs it into her movement.

The orangutan, and later the human, on the contrary moves the crate and brings everything into motion with its hands, which the bird does not have. It moves it and then will be left standing beside an upturned crate. Even after the banana has been picked, the crate will stand there like, ultimately, the upturned globe with its tilted axis. *Is Lorenz right that the essential difference in an ape, and later a human, is spatial imagination, and later thought?* Lorenz himself talks after this about the errors of civilization. The bird, conducting itself stupidly, did not use its mind and did not work out what was going on; the orangutan, using its mind, is left with a crate on the floor of its cell. What is the orangutan going to do with this crate, where is he going to move it to and why? The bananas are no longer hanging down; he has picked them. Humans have wasted all the oil. What is the orangutan going to do now with the crate in the middle of his cell? What are humans going to do with the drilling rigs, the subsiding ground, the nuclear waste?

The first real difference between the human being who drills for oil, and the bird which does not, all becomes just rather too problematical. More interesting seems to be the difference between the human being who is an animal and the human being who is not, if there is such a person. The driller on an offshore rig and Jacques Cousteau are more or less level pegging in terms of their mental development and technological backup. The real achievement at this level of scientific equipment proves somehow not to be the quantity and complexity of what gets moved around in nature but, on the contrary, the ability, if there still is any, to return to the mode of the bird, accommodating the planet within oneself, retaining one's place and role on the planet. That is, the thinking that is of value is *not* the ability to put things together, but returning to the cosmos, and above all taking on itself all the unresolvedness, the unresolvability, of life.

All discussion of the difference between humans and animals pales beside the fact that we find each person is two, just as we have found that we have not one but two lives and that, moreover, the same person both throws crates about and returns everything to its proper place. Humans are dual, a twin, a double, alien to themselves. It is not that the combiner, the fixer, in the human must be destroyed, but that it should, on the contrary, win, but only after it has repudiated sly calculation and accepted the rule of law. Both are one and the same person. The problem is that the twins *as twins* cannot know or understand anything. Their twin identity is established too early for them to notice it. One and the same person scatters incorrigible business dealings over the planet, and also clears up the mess.

Remarkable as ethology is in its field investigations and juxtapositions, it is, like any other science, contingent upon its cultural background. What Lorenz, together with all modern thinking, says about the behaviour of the animals being dictated by their genome, while humans are managed by their brain, and a collective brain at that, just does not seem to be true.[11] This is clearly a more complex, but not necessarily a higher, life form. The essence of human beings is rather that, *in spite of* their brain, in spite of the piling up of system upon system, they can nevertheless be in nature and relate to it in both senses of the word, not only in one. To put it another way: the nub of the matter is the ability of technology to *imitate* nature, in the sense not only of mere imitation but also of mimesis. Humankind endures where it *preserves* in its species the ability to live a poor life, with no rights to speak of, without arms or legs (after Wittgenstein).[12]

Lorenz is right, of course, when he says that having invented the bow and arrow, or now the computer, humankind is as unlikely to lose them, even though they are acquired characteristics, as it is to lose any organ in its body of comparable *Arterhaltungswert*, or value in enabling the species to survive. But in itself, the increase of fruits of the intellect guarantees nothing. Since a return to understanding that the purpose of life is unknown, and an understanding that the enigma (the prominence, the exposure, the specialness) of all life is a problem for the future, right now I would say that the really significant, distinctive biological feature of humankind is not conceptual thinking and objectification, but despair and nihilism right in the midst of plenty and relative prosperity.

The difference between humans and the animals is better not claimed to be speech, the creation and interpretation of texts, but Wittgenstein's ability to distinguish between *saying* and *showing*.[13] Real success is a strange thing: it cannot be called anything other than successful. That is, it and everything about it cannot be said; it must be shown or it is not real.

The old names for success – unity, wholeness – continue to fit, but only if they are heard in their entirety: unity as uniqueness, wholeness as wholesomeness and healing. The new names, *system, equilibrium*, no longer have that alluring edge, and they are problematical. Equilibrium. But craziness can be redemptive, as in Don Quixote.

Mind. But the supreme faculty in humans, as in animals, is instinct, religion, fear of *everything*, precisely because a human can impinge on everything.

I prefer to speak of two humans, the twin and the double (*not*, I repeat, in the sense that one is good and the other bad, but from the standpoint that one does not know the other) rather than, like Lorenz, speaking of the degeneration of humankind. Because how can Lorenz not see that with the theme of degeneration we are again losing the human being, who slips away? Lorenz himself says that with successful adaptation in one direction, having secured major energetic and material benefits, living beings may neglect to fulfil other requirements towards life. He mentions an example we have already encountered: the parasitic *Sacculina carcini*, which emerges from the egg as a typical barnacle with all the expected parts of its body, but is parasitic on the shore crab, attaches itself to its stomach, and no longer needs them. It dispenses with its eyes, legs, and body articulation and becomes a sack-like creature, degenerating to the level of a fungus that grows through the body of its host.

The other symptoms of human degradation enumerated by Lorenz are actually not exclusive to humans because animals degenerate in exactly the same way. The feature of modern civilization that appals Lorenz, whose extreme alarm pushes him over the brink into naïvety, is that the degenerating masses are not only unaware of being diseased but, on the contrary, also consider themselves to be prospering, vital, and enjoying life as never before. This is also not an exclusively human trait. The clothes louse becomes so complacent, as a result of an overabundance of warmth and food, that, unlike fleas and cockroaches, it ceases to flee from danger, compensating by fecundity for the decline in its population caused by attempts at extermination by its host. Likewise, 'the rise, resulting from domestication, of behaviour orientated towards food and reproduction and, at least in respect of the latter, a characteristic fall in selectivity'. Again there is nothing specific to humans in this because permissiveness, '*bedrohliches Symptom des Verkommens*', a baleful symptom of decline, is not confined to humans. '*In der für Haustiere so typischen Weise verschwinden die feineren Verhaltensmuster der Paarbildung, während der Kopulationstrieb überwuchert. Feinere erotische Verhaltensweisen, wie zum Beispiel der Vorgang des Sich-Verliebens und der Werbung, gelten überhaupt nicht als sexuell.*' 'In the manner so characteristic of domestic pets, the finer forms of mating behaviour disappear, while the instinct for coition dominates. The finer erotic forms of behaviour, like falling in love and courtship, are not even regarded as sexual.'[14]

Since this '*rasch um sich greifende Absinken*', 'rapidly spreading contagion of degeneration',[15] this adverse selection, which we heard about a considerable time ago, is not a specifically human disaster, all these alarming observations are irrelevant because they apply to all living beings and are, not to put too fine a point on it, not our problem. On the contrary, if all living things are on the slide, it is only natural that humankind, too, will be on the slide. If we wanted to find reasons why humankind, as opposed to all other life forms, does not have the right to succumb to the natural path of self-seeking, pleasure, and well-being, we would need first to *find* human beings. Lorenz quotes Wilhelm Busch:

Climbing calls for graft and crawling,
Never loosening your grip.
The good Lord is forever hauling,
The Devil waits for you to slip.[16]

Well then, let God carry on hauling, that is up to him; it is his job. Humans, elusive, slip away into their skills. They are not personally to blame: living things in general are guilty of degeneration. *Should* humans take responsibility for the whole world? Why? The purpose of life is unclear. Comparing us with other life forms leads in one way or another to the *mission* of truth, of directness. Not to the theoretical problem of truth, but to the *task* of truth and justice.

Let us return to animal behaviour. The chick of a herring gull, choosing between the dummies on offer, will invariably go for the beak with a red dot. The red dot indicates the goal, the beak, and the dot is exactly where the chick needs to peck. Did this dot arise through natural selection? Did dots appear randomly on different parts of the parent gull's body as the result of mutation but were of no significance for the species, but when a spot migrated to the beak it proved so useful that out of the entire species only inheritors of this mutation survived? The explanation is clearly far-fetched. According to Berg, and he is right, the dot on the beak was con-solidated by natural selection, but natural selection had nothing to do with how it got on the beak. It is easier and more straightforward to explain it by the fact that the beak was a sufficiently important event for an impor-tant place on it to be marked in some way. It is not particularly convincing to say that the chick's reaction to the red dot is genetically conditioned. It is the same situation as with eye colour: there are no black-coloured eyes in the genetic program; there is a grid of prohibitions and permissions which, as an organism develops, determines choice in favour of a particular solu-tion. There is primarily a multi-layered concentration, fed in from various directions, a targeting of the targeting, the focusing on an intrusive, target-ing part of the body.

Now, something about the clear distinction between the formal and the personal in animals. In the example where the male chases away the female which has a painted moustache, the formal program prevails. The male does have a personal attitude towards the female, and he again accepts her after the moustache has been cleaned off. Personal recognition is a differ-ent system, and the animal operates now in accordance with one and now in accordance with the other. As in human society, personal relations are one thing, official relations another. Differences in dress, manners, and language are one thing, the transition to a personal level is something else. These two systems can, however, become mixed, as in the case of bullying and domination in the Russian army, which is an attempt to formalize per-sonal relationships, to suppress the personal.

Sparrows are good at recognizing each other but we are less good at distinguishing between them.

An example of moving from the official level of signalling to the unoffi-cial is the way clothing, manners, and language made it easy to differentiate castes before the revolution; after the revolution, a secret hierarchy became more marked but less visible when, for example, Person No. 1 was poorer than anyone else.

Some notes about colour: its importance cannot be overstated. Colour perception is difficult. It seems that birds and insects perceive the shorter wavelengths better; for them, red is infra-yellow, i.e. black; ultra-violet is a separate colour. Plants know this and have long been coordinated with the insect eye. You will find there are almost no pure reds, while there are many blues and violets; and among these, where we see one colour, animals and insects may see more.

Lecture 32, 26 May 1998

In this and other courses, we have been proceeding by a series of prohibitions: we must not think this or believe that. There is some truth in the suggestion that when you look for a criterion of knowledge, you find ignorance. The encyclopaedic scope of our ignorance, the knowledge in respect of everything that 'things are not quite that simple and not quite as we thought', is an equally valid measure of knowledge in science, philosophy, and the art of living.

On a path less trodden, it is always a pleasure to find someone to quote, someone to shelter behind. Let us read from the conclusion of Tinbergen's *The Study of Instinct*: 'Man is an animal. He is a remarkable and in many respects a unique species, but he is an animal nevertheless.'[1] Note: his enormous differences seem not entirely to be *his* differences; they are linked in complex ways to the other animals in a manner we do not really understand, and in which there is probably no less service to something than we see in other animals. 'In structure and functions of the heart, blood, intestine, kidneys, and so on, man closely resembles other animals, especially other vertebrates. Palaeontology as well as comparative anatomy and embryology do not leave the least doubt that this resemblance is based on true evolutionary relationships.'[2] This remains true even if the time connection is reversed, from present-day humans to the animal: all the more do the animals show us ourselves 'unpacked' as what we are. 'Man and the present-day primates have only recently diverged from a common primate stock.'[3]

Study of the similarities of ethos between animals is only beginning; it consists almost entirely of lacunae. It is believed that only the lower reflexes, like jerking back a hand or foot from fire, are common to all higher animals; human behaviour is the province of psychology and ethics based on the presumption that only humans have a real soul and morality. We lack an integral science (it did not develop after Aristotle, for whom it seemed natural) that studies the behaviour of human *and* all other living beings on an equal footing. 'One of the main reasons for this is the almost universal misconception that the causes of man's behaviour are qualitatively different from the causes of animal behaviour.'[4]

Tinbergen's use of 'causes' here is ambiguous. Let us rather look at his examples to see what he has in mind. The 'misconception' he refers to is the characteristic feature of people to feel they are different, special. I am fairly sure there has never been anyone like me before: I am not like everybody else, unique in the world. Our family is unique. It is only in our village that people don't talk funny, like those folks in the next village. Only Russians have an inborn sense of morality. This is ubiquitous, universal. People will clutch at anything as a sign that they are exceptional. A random example: Wittgenstein's returning of the human species to biology: 'Language is part of our organism.' The translator naturally comes to the rescue, translating the human species from biology into cultural institutions: 'Language is part of our organization.'[5] The example is clear to see: consciousness is given major or crucial significance; it directs and governs. What consciousness is *for* is a puzzle. We remember Wittgenstein's image of the driver who, to make his truck move faster, pushes the steering wheel forward.

'Somehow it is assumed that when, in investigating behaviour, one climbs higher and higher in the hierarchical structure, ascending from reflexes or automatisms to locomotion, from there to the higher level of consummatory acts, and to still higher levels, one will meet a kind of barrier bearing the sign "Not open to objective study; for psychologists only."'[6] Tinbergen politely gives the name of non-objective research to the dreamy imagining of consciousness, the activity of conveniently ordering concepts and carrying out operations with vocabulary as the control centre, first, of an exceptionally aware individual, and subsequently, on his advice, of the whole of society.

'Some psychologists even assume that emotions like hunger somehow take part in the objective causation of behaviour. In this assumption, there is a real conflict between psychology and ethology.'[7] Psychology steers well clear, in its conceptual apparatus and its terminology, of anything inaccessible to consciousness. *In actual fact*, and *if they are really starving*, humans will do things they themselves find unexpected and incomprehensible, and the ordinary 'feelings of hunger' will most likely go away. 'Food-seeking behaviour' may or may not be accompanied by feelings of hunger and does not depend on them but directly on biology: for example, on contraction of the muscles of the stomach wall. Conversely, it is possible to feel hungry without actually being hungry. Humans resort to food-seeking behaviour not because they decide to do so as a result of feeling hunger. Feeling hungry is only one rather mysterious component of hungry behaviour which ultimately reorganizes the entire body. When food-seeking behaviour begins, most usually only during its early stages, there is a feeling of hunger. If it is not there to give me a signal of how I need to behave, then what is it for? When we start asking questions of that kind, it is best not to probe too far, but to be amazed at our confidence that we can and need to discover *reasons*, as if everything in us must be for a reason. Perhaps we feel hungry for no reason, just because, like singing, dancing, the mood we are in. 'When the food-seeking drive is aroused, the subject experiences hunger.'[8]

The instinctive food-seeking drive often conflicts with reason. This is a rare phenomenon in normal Western society. But everyone who has lived through periods of real starvation – a condition common enough outside the Western world, that has touched western Europe just long enough to make its significance clear to us – knows how relatively weak reason is when it is up against really powerful instinctive motivation.[9]

Powerful, crucial things pass through and unsettle human beings – as powerful as the millions and billions of years compressed into their bodies – so that we can only gaze in amazement at ourselves. This power is not conspicuous or obtrusive and can perhaps be noticed only by chance. A human observing the mating behaviour of animals, their display, is surprised to note that something of the sort seems to be familiar from human behaviour, their own and that of others, but a strange feeling, rather like Soloviov's embarrassment, keeps us from looking soberly and open-eyed at our kinship with or, more honestly, total similarity to the animals.[10]

Mating behaviour in man.... Now every individual among us who has the habit of self-observation, and who has not forgotten his youth, knows how often the urge has driven him 'blindly', 'against better judgement', to obey it, when there was a conflict between better judgement and drive. Falling in love changes one's entire outlook upon one's surroundings. Criminologists teach us that the number of crimes, even of serious ones like murder, committed in obedience to the instinctive urge to show off before a female is astonishingly high. Quite different, but from our standpoint equally significant, are murders due to sexual rivalry.[11]

These cases are complicated, both to observe and to understand: there is too much interweaving in them. Here are some more straightforward cases: displacement activities, displacing fight or flight in conflict situations – like scratching behind your ear in a fraught, difficult situation. In birds – ducks, for example – the same movement is seen in straightening or touching neck feathers with the beak. In a broader sense, to start smoothing or grooming oneself in a disturbing, threatening situation is an innate characteristic human beings share with the entire animal kingdom. 'In women it mostly takes the form of adjusting non-existing disorder of the coiffure, in the man it consists of handling the beard or moustache, not only in the days when men still had them but also in this "clean-shaven" era. Further, it is striking that displacement scratching can be observed regularly in primates.'[12] Fighting, war, and flight we shall omit, but just as flight or hiding is almost always the first and commonest reaction among living beings in general and also among humans, so moroseness and unsociability, inner emigration and 'dissent', and 'going ape' are all instances of flight, so common that for many people in the course of their day their main reaction is a complex accumulation of escape behaviours. We usually forget that we are intimidated, we forget the fear and are so accustomed to our evasive, distracting manoeuvres that we no longer notice them. The same, however, is true of animals.

It is only too easy to evoke escape tendencies. In the most clear-cut cases these are easily inferred, for overt escape behaviour can rarely be mistaken. But even a weak activation of the escape drive inhibits other behaviour, and it requires sharp observation and considerable experience with a given species to detect slight signs of inhibition through fear. This is not astonishing when we realize how many people fail to recognize even rather obvious expressions in their fellow-men, and also how much more difficult it is to recognize such expression in species other than our own.[13]

In women, combing their hair in front of the mirror, the conscious mind can readily discern the intention: that is, something the mind can understand, the deliberate performance. It is said the woman's aim is to be liked and therefore, etc. It is said mockingly that the activity has little rationality, or that indeed it does little to improve her appearance and only increases tension. When no stereotypical intent can be attributed, the mind goes into overdrive or comes to a standstill. Similarly, when a dying person is already profoundly unconscious, they may start making movements as if trying to tidy up something on their body. This is displacement activity of the same order as a bird preening in a conflict situation, and at the same deeply unconscious level.

My example of the cockerels furiously pecking grain as displaced fighting has an analogous displacement activity against nervous strain in the abundant consumption of food in old Moscow and, indeed, in the demonstrative eating in restaurants in modern Moscow, which is also caused by stress and fear. We must probably also classify nosepicking as a profound, hereditary displacement activity against stress, which is also embarrassing and which is observed in similar situations in apes.

Another innate displacement activity in man seems to be sleep. In low intensities, in the form of yawning, it is of common occurrence in mild conflict situations. Just as in some birds (avocet, oystercatcher, and other waders) actual sleep is an outlet in situations where the aggressive instinct and the instinct of escape are simultaneously aroused. Reliable and trained observers, among them Professor P. Palmgren of Helsingfors, have told me that in situations of extreme tension at the front, just before an actual attack, infantrymen may be overcome by a nearly insurmountable inclination to go to sleep. Sleep, as is known from Hess's experiments, is a true instinctive act depending on stimulation of a centre in the hypothalamus. It is also in line with other instinctive acts in that it is the goal of a special kind of appetitive behaviour.[14]

Just as yawning is a displacement activity, so, evidently, is a reluctance to get up in the morning. Foot soldiers who desperately want to sleep before a mortally dangerous operation get woken up. A beautiful, similar case is described in 'In Praise of Poetry' by Olga Sedakova, who senses that what happened to her was something universally human but which, it would seem, is common to all living beings.

I had no direct reason to take my leave of life, and I think I was even rather sad about that. There was only one way I wanted to do this: by jumping off a mountain.... So here I am, having climbed to a high place and walked to the edge. The sun was high, the mountains deserted. I woke up when the sun was setting and had forgotten why I was here. My only thought was that I needed to get down to the town before it was dark. Last year's grass was aflame on the slopes. I ran into the hotel in singed clothing.... A village girl who had poisoned herself with some extract or other told me she had experienced the same stupor: she had brought the bottle to her lips and fallen asleep until dawn. Then it was as if someone had prodded her, and she drank it all down before the rest of the house woke up. 'I drank it like water,' she said. This is probably a common occurrence. Only nobody prodded me.[15]

Without realizing it, a person will yawn from stress, or, in the Garden of Gethsemane, sensing the approach of terrible danger, will fall asleep. Consciousness is needed in order to understand the real causes, and to correct the errors of consciousness itself. I am going to leave that puzzle now without trying to disentangle it: consciousness is needed in order to correct the error, and the error is consciousness itself in the first place.

Just as animals display themselves to each other, so, it seems, they have no objection to having their lives inspected. That is the reverse side of their curiosity. The ethologist is surprised how close birds, once they realize he is not dangerous, allow the observer to approach.[16] This is an addition to what we have said above about eyes and mimesis.

Another aspect of this willingness to be observed is, no doubt, the allure of other living creatures. We have already heard about the growing enchantment ants exercised over a myrmecologist, and the same can be true of the bee:

Its sustained flight, its powerful sting, its intimacy with flowers and avoidance of all unwholesome things, the attachment of the workers to the queen – regarded throughout antiquity as a king – its singular swarming habits and its astonishing industry in collecting and storing honey and skill in making wax, two unique substances of great value to man but of mysterious origin, made it a divine being, a prime favourite of the gods, that had somehow survived the golden age or had voluntarily escaped from the Garden of Eden, along with poor fallen man, for the purpose of sweetening his bitter lot.[17]

As in the olden days, so today. Just as Wheeler had not tired of observing ants after thirty years, so Tinbergen emphatically assures us that, after hundreds of observations of his herring gulls, he continued to make new discoveries about their behaviour. The title of his book, *Social Behaviour in Animals*, has a resonance that this is also about *our* society, directly relevant to us. Through his observations, he is personally involved in what is most interesting in the society of his birds.

For bird work one has to get up early. Most birds show a maximum of activity, particularly of reproductive behaviour, in the hours round sunrise. A second, but lower, maximum falls in the evening. It is best to arrive an hour before sunrise, and stay till three or four hours after sunrise, when the activity wanes. Once you get used to being in the field early, you will like it much better than getting out later when the sun has already climbed high, the dew has evaporated, and the scenery has become dry, colourless, and dull. Further, the more promptly one reacts to the alarm clock, the easier it is.[18]

The founder of modern ethology came to an accommodation with this desire of animals to be looked at. Konrad Lorenz kept his animals in a kind of semi-captivity, so that they drew him into their lives: 'They court or fight him, or try to make him join them when they move about.'[19] To enter the life of animals in such a way as not to upset them, remembering that they for their part are very aware of the human observation and change their behaviour flexibly, that is what is essential, the whole trick.

The trick is, to insert experiments now and then in the normal life of the animal so that this normal life is in no way interrupted; however exciting the result of a test may be for us, it must be a matter of daily routine to the animal. A man who lacks the feeling for this kind of work will inevitably commit offences just as some people cannot help kicking and damaging delicate furniture in a room without even noticing it.[20]

And how could one not be captivated? We may possibly be the last generations to observe this challenging, worrying spectacle of the life of which we partake. It is possible that with us the chain of life with its billions of years of history will be broken. We have already basically exhausted the fossil oil and coal, and even, to a large extent, natural gas. Soon it will be the turn of oxygen. Compared with the earth's history, this has happened in an instant of time, but in every generation life has been at risk. The worry of the present moment is not the risk, which has always been one and the same, but the expectation of those living in this link of the chain of life, in this generation, that they will find the secret of fitness, of success, of being, of fullness, of property, success, and goodness – since otherwise they will have failed.

Why is our body *ours*, even though it has been created and defined by random events of the millions of years of our history and the billions of years of the history of other living beings? The simple answer is that there is no problem. It is for the same reason that language is *ours*. Because all those layers that have cumulatively created our body and language, each of those events, has been a stroke of luck, existence of the same kind that we recognize as our own. The creation of our body has been an accumulation of strokes of luck. That is why our body and our language help us: no matter how much we rely on them, no matter how we develop them, they will reveal what we need, what is wholesome. A collective of billions of living beings worked together with us to create us, and at every turn, in every link, everything might have broken off, and every time *they* managed not to be broken, and accordingly we, too, continued.

When it is said, 'symbolically', as is popularly believed, in Psalm 51, 'that the bones which thou hast broken may rejoice', these are no *symbolic* bones, but the real bones, the hard patient substratum which was the essential precondition for *any* behaviour of *all* our ancestors, and con-firmed in that behaviour and formed a skeleton.[21]

Behaviour could be orientated on the strictness of the laws of light, the steely stars (*sidera*). What here is a symbol of what? The broken bones are a symbol of humility, because they are like the earth, like the deepest, most immovable element of the earth: the rocks over which the soil lies, the bones of the earth. The earth is resigned because everything tramples it, but it will remain when life is gone. Life returns to it. What remains longest of life is what is most of the earth. With these musings we are making a standard mythological, symbolic move (or perhaps poetic, metaphorical), searching for some idea, of humility in this case, some appropriate, tangible, material, observable, and palpable expression. We are constructing a metaphorical, intellectual category, exploiting images, as they say, rooted in something, perhaps in artistic vision, or the unconscious, or at the level of archetypes of the mind.

Now, perhaps, after our excursion into the forest, we will not need the circuitous detour through consciousness or the subconscious, either in the case of these words of the psalm, or ever. Not through consciousness but more directly. Life through protrusion, through measuring existence, through probing intention, has absorbed into itself, as it could, what it could. Bacteria and invertebrates in their own way, and the creatures moving freely on dry land, across the earth in their way, in the oceans of water and of air in the only way they could, unable to do otherwise, had to take the earth on to themselves and into themselves, to include it in the form of bones, a skeleton. In order to move over the land, they had to become like a different cosmic body in relation to it, to separate from the land and then take off from it, directly or through the medium of air or water. The earth is our equal, directly or through the medium of air or water. They move over the earth like a replica of the earth itself, like a cast (and in this sense we must understand the moulding of man from clay as the moulding of a second earth), like its mirror image. They (that is, we) absorbed the earth, not somehow through the reflecting action of consciousness, but directly, with our body, with the parts of the body.

The difference between humans, all life in general, and the earth dissolves. Ultimately, we all live within the same nature. It transpires there is no difference, save in particulars, between human and animal society. For example, the distinction between the personal and the official is just the same. Ethology, when it develops, will attain the serene Aristotelian level of moral assessment of courage, wisdom, and virtue or, on the contrary, of wickedness, malice, and indolence, of human and animal alike. Indeed, ethology is already beginning to do so, with Konrad Lorenz, who sees the same vices in civilization and animals, primarily but not solely domestic pets; and with Nikolaas Tinbergen, who, in agreement with Lorenz, condemns the degeneracy of the male herring gull that refused to replace the female on its nest and proved unworthy of deserving offspring.

Here it is good to remember that human beings constantly discuss everything, write things down, become *conscious* of them, while animals do not. But what exactly do humans describe and become conscious of? We should not be in too much of a hurry to say anything and everything in the world. The point is that a person does not come immediately to see the world: for example, to begin to see the living thing in himself and others. Even there it is necessary to break through the clutter of consciousness. Humans understand and describe first of all what they themselves build, their own constructs. This is such a universal rule, so normal, that there have even been attempts, such as by Ernst Cassirer, to present it as a law: a human is able to comprehend, to understand, only what he has himself created.[22] This is not true, but is worth thinking about. Here we need to recall a thesis Hannah Arendt proposed for the modern world and which, independently, was proposed also by Werner Heisenberg: humans in the modern age encounter everywhere and invariably, even in the study of nature, in their theories and discoveries, only themselves.[23] Heidegger objected that, on the contrary, humans now never encounter, never see, never find themselves any more.[24] Let us, however, not be distracted by this tangle of questions and note only the truth that humans primarily remember, become aware of, make sense of, record and store in libraries, mainly, and perhaps exclusively, what they themselves create and construct.

Then the difference between humans and the other forms of life comes down to the fact that other life forms record themselves only in the genetic program, whereas humans do things that do not get recorded in the genetic program and need to be inscribed on paper, clay, or some other medium. Life, including humans to the extent that they are not self-conscious, that they are just a living being, do not need to record anything because it remains within a strange Sophia, within her auto-maton. Humans need to make their own record because they transgress the law, making constructs that nature will not adopt and consolidate. The memory of their initiatives and constructs is called 'consciousness', 'culture'. Consciousness has the same derivation as conscience. We return to what makes them indistinguishable: the consciousness of the con-science of trans-gression, of overstepping nature. Where to? Into the void, exploiting the fact that the void is there and lets them in.

Precisely because of the way human constructs are balanced in the void, the problem of good and evil arises. What humans create, construct, in the void has meaning only if their technology is able to imitate nature: that is, to intuit, to succeed as being, fullness, and richness. The purpose of the construction must be good and evil, otherwise what is the point of it? The void that allows in human creativity is trackless. There are no 'laws of history', no gods to indicate safe, established paths. What gets mistaken for the laws of history is either the continuing working of nature in the midst of the constructs of humans, or the patterns of inertia that attend any motion, meaningful or meaningless. To hope that somewhere 'in all this', in the whole enterprise of culture, there is any meaning above and beyond what we manage to find or implement in it is completely idiotic: no more sensible than the behaviour of the individual in Heraclitus who would build houses with his own hands and then start asking what he had built about its and his own meaning.[25] 'I have no meaning, so I will build something that one of my many skills enables me to, and perhaps that will be my meaning.'

Under these circumstances, the study of animal societies is not only no less valuable than studying human society, but is dealing with a pure form of something that carries over into human society (the restaurant banquet as a furious pecking at grain under the nose of another cockerel). The only difference is that in human society it is not just complicated by the interweaving of extraneous elements but, more alarmingly, tangled and made sinister to the point where it seems impossible it will ever be disentangled. Studying animals also gives us a direct and edifying lesson in humility, service, and courage. We should not see our human world as some kind of gain for nature. Where could that something come from if not from nature itself?

Is there in humanity anything that is unambiguously good? Yes, there is thinking, poetry, heroism – but these are terribly difficult and rare, and analogous to what we find among the animals whose lives are lived constantly at the extreme limit of effort and on the brink of starvation and extinction. In the present age, humans are cast into a state of bewilderment and *amekhania*. Culture is an already vast memory of human transgression, a record which every new revolution wants to delete but which every time is restored by conscience, which is itself, we recall, the notification of a crime. Is there within culture the possibility of a return to nature, to Sophia, to the true automaton? Of course there is. It is the most natural thing in the world and indubitably possible at all times. Everything that humans have made has always been, in its way, good, only not always unconditionally so. Usually, indeed, dubitably and conditionally, and in need of new words to confirm it and make it memorable.

Using the same means of assembly and construction, humans can equally well demolish and deconstruct, only in the course of difficult, unsparing disassembly they are likely to find themselves veering towards new construction. Then, of course, there is the question of how, using which means, the dismantling is to be carried out and who is going to conduct it if the human remains undeciphered. A human, from their bones to their hair, can be read like a book, as layers of events laid down over *billions* of years that have absorbed all life. That is why, when sometimes during a discussion on religious and philosophical matters there is mention of supposed horizontal and vertical dimensions, it is not only senseless but also comical to have in mind some sort of chart of a vertical and a horizontal, when these concepts continue in cultural memory to represent life getting to its feet, head uppermost. This upright posture was in turn a measuring of height using a human's own body and a pointing to the stars (to the stars, note, not to the sun, because the bee with its six legs and the birds flying horizontally turn towards the sun).

The human species is a book that has taken billions of years to write, and since it worked out how to *get to its feet* another 5 million years or so, some 150,000 generations, have passed. All those generations firmly remembered their deeds and misdeeds by rote, *par coeur*, in their hearts, while the last 100 generations have somehow been permitted to separate and deposit the memory of their deeds in libraries and museums.

The poignancy of our present moment is not that with our generation, after 150,000 human generations and perhaps 100 million animal generations, everything looks like going horribly wrong. Everything could, on the one hand, have gone horribly wrong with any generation; and, on the other, Gaia is a persistent entity that has many times replaced her puppets. The poignancy of our moment is that, irrespective of whether or not we will become, for some future life, a distant past that existed millions of years ago, for us, as for that future life, as for life in all times past, the task in the unique conditions of our present day, where everything is constantly in flux and everything is new, is to find *meaning*, if only in nihilism and despair. It is not that we are in despair because everything is so bad, but everything is so bad because we have despaired. Despair is always at its peak when life is at its most prosperous. The mistake is in what we see as prosperity. Perhaps we have a wrong understanding of pro-sperity, and should re-de-fine it to mean that our actions should lead to the good. Perhaps the criteria need every time to be redefined, created, even. That is not easy.

The purpose of life is not life. Let us return to Aristotle, whom we so regrettably had to leave on 25 November. Everything we have said since then in our excursions through new writers can be seen as preparation for a thorough reading of Aristotle's biology and of Aristotle in general, and here is why.

We stopped at that time at 741a in *De generatione animalium*: why, if all matter is present in the feminine principle, we still need the *live*. The so-called wind eggs have life; they are not dead, not monsters. This life is only vegetative, and for moving, animal life, with parts, its motion would be impossible without 'feeling', *aesthesis*. In a way, I have already said this: the animal is *intended* to walk on land. Its destiny is to be related to the earth, to relate to the earth, to be, unlike a plant, which is rooted in the earth and cannot survive if uprooted from it, a second kind of living. (Throughout antiquity, the earth was seen as alive and sentient, which opens up the huge topic of pre-Socratic *biology*, which is at the same time ontology.)

But we will come to grief in Aristotle on that aesthesis which the male principle imparts and will need something to which I now invite you: a study of Aristotle's aesthetics. This will call for a complete reviewing of the problem of aesthetics and, for a start, we will have to dismiss the nonsensical belief that in Aristotle aesthesis, feeling, is something inferior to the excellence of ('scientific') cognition.

I shall read you Akhutin on aesthesis, from an article being published in the next issue of *ARKhE*. Akhutin suggests forgetting for the time being or, preferably, forever about 'sensualisms' with their belittling of feeling.[26] Knowledge *is* perception, aesthesis

in the sense of direct and simple (immediate and irreducible) *grasping, identification, discernment*, all at the same time, here and now. We are talking ... about the form of *total knowledge*. ... How (and what) something that exists proves to be, manifests itself as, is perceived as being is one and the same thing. What exists is what was found to exist in the world that revealed itself when humans found themselves in it, when they opened their eyes.... This *foundation* is akin to Parmenides' de facto identification ... of attentiveness and being.... Aesthesis is that in which and through which what exists is revealed to each person (transpires) and by which each person is drawn into what exists (finds their way there). It is the element of their *mutual involvement*.

The male principle, or rather the encounter between male and female necessary for a moving (historical) living being, begins with what in ethology is called 'display'. And this presentation is, of course, nothing new after the show which was developed by space with the expansion of the stage of light and matter. This cosmic event programmed also the male-female performance that led to aesthesis, the first moment of attentiveness and assimilation of everything not by consciousness but by the body, the whole being.

We are at the trifurcation of three roads. One, which was open to us from the very beginning but which I kept quiet about, is the pre-Socratic biology of the cosmos; the second is a serious, close reading of Aristotle; and the third is a return to the law of all life, to religion and service. In the autumn, when the harvest is being brought in, we shall decide which of these roads to take, or whether to embark on a completely new one.[27]

Glossary

Amekhania – A notion widespread in the ancient Greek literature, particularly in lyric poetry and tragedy. It was much discussed among classicists in the late Soviet period. *Amekhania*, literally the lack of means to act, is a condition of helplessness, of a certain ethical paralysis. It is a negative trait attributed by the Greeks to their heroes. In Bibikhin (who follows Heidegger with his *'pantoporos aporos'*), the term takes on a positive tonality. In contrast with modern activism, the Greeks valued moments of immobility because through them they found themselves immersed in the world, captivated by it. Something larger than themselves was acting through them at that time. In *The Woods*, *amekhania* is virtually synonymous with 'the Cross'. The Cross is a religious symbol, but here it is also understood as a branching out of possibilities in the forest, a standstill.

Attention (mindfulness) – A key concept for Bibikhin. It is the way that the world and its facts impinge upon us, concern us, before we consciously control them. In this sense, against the modern fixation on the ego, the world precedes consciousness within consciousness itself. We are 'late for the event of the world', says Bibikhin, and this should teach us humility.

Automaton – This notion stems from Aristotle, who understood it not in the modern 'automatic' sense but as a spontaneous, self-initiated action (as opposed to destiny, *tyche*). Bibikhin boldly juxtaposes the ancient automaton with modern technology, demonstrating the almost complete inversion that happens to the meaning. Even more boldly, he links the automaton to Sophia, the Russian theological concept denoting the existential, corporeal nature of Spirit. In his voluminous reading of Wittgenstein, Bibikhin understands automaton as a 'shift in aspect', or a shift of *Gestalt*, which happens playfully, unpredictably. It is a mechanical element built into nature itself, and responsible for its capacity to de-centre and liberate.

Captivation (zakhvat) – Engagement, participation in historical movements of the world, which are not initiated by the subject but happen to it 'in advance', in a state of unconscious *attention*, and are even constitutive for the subject. The philosophical precedent of this notion is perhaps 'enthusiasm', but there are important differences. Captivation, obviously linked to *being taken*, is at the origin of knowledge as well as of taking possession and property, and thus acquires an ambivalent, reversible character: who possesses what – the subject the object, or the object the subject? Here the philosophical parallels are with Heidegger, who often, if not thematically, speaks of the *'greifen'* implicit in *Begriff* (the concept), but the greater proximity is with Carl Schmitt's notion of the *'Nahme'*, the original taking of land, in *The Nomos of the Earth*, of which Bibikhin was most probably ignorant.

Consecration, sanctification (osviashchenie) – A sanction, symbolic permission, a yes which, to Bibikhin, is the core of any religious attitude. Sanction emerges in response to a fullness and completeness that is characteristic of life, and is often expressed by the root *'sviat'* (the saintly), but the latter is usually overflowing, more than complete, and requires an eschatological full stop given by a subject. Bibikhin associates this symbolic act with the masculine gender. Parallel to this place in the history of philosophy is Hegel's notion of a sovereign, as well as more generally his construction of language.

Fitness (godnost') – A phenomenon responsible for the evolution of life. A success, which depends on luck, a fortunate combination of organs which remains in memory and determines form *(eidos)*. *Godnost'* is associated with correctly *guessing (ugadyvat')*.

Law (zakon) – Against our usual philosophical disdain for legality (as the sphere of the posited), or a naïve belief in its rationality, Bibikhin takes law seriously and shows in the present volume that human law, with its harsh rigorousness, mimics the cosmic law. While history and life are obviously free and fluid, there is something in them that is of an extremely *harsh*, tyrannical nature.

Prior discipline, latter discipline – Two major strategies of dealing with event. We are always late for the event. One approach, characteristic of the West, consists of anticipating an event, just in case, and establishing a firm law. Another, characteristic, for example, of Russia, is latter discipline, which is based on a sober awareness that it is in any case impossible to catch up with the event: hence an anarchic passivity with regard to power, and intense mobilization at the last moment.

Sanction, sanctity – Sanctity derives from sanction. Sanction is a human, and divine, capacity to say yes to things. The act is immaterial, does not add anything substantial to facts, but produces value.

Suchness, being thus (haecceitas) – A concept developed by the mediaeval philosopher Duns Scotus in the sense of an existential and situational definition of a thing as unique. It contrasts with *quidditas*, 'whatness', which speaks to a thing's generic characteristics, its place in the whole. Scotus attributed the need for *haecceitas* to our finite capacities of understanding, but in twentieth-century existentialism, and in Bibikhin, the notion acquires an unequivocally positive meaning. This is the path to seeing the 'things themselves', in their bare being an *event*.

Ultimate, the (prede'lnoe) – The borderline situations or events which mobilize humans for extreme exertion, and also open them to intuition of the transcendental.

Wood(s) – The main subject of the present volume. The element of wilderness which is both an underlying substratum ('matter') and an enclosing milieu of human existence. Wood as the forest is an aspect of the world, taken in its impenetrability, in reference to early humans who lived in the forest and cleared their space in its midst. Experientially, forests produce a vertiginous effect on us akin to drugs and cause *amekhania*. The forest is also the element of life, and as such cannot be reduced to matter; it contains form and matter at the same time and embodies their very relationship.

The World (mir) – An amalgam of Heidegger's notion of the world, Losev's 'cosmos', and the Russian historical notion of the world as a human community (*mir*). The world is a horizon of totality, required for understanding, but is also a measure of scale, ambition, and beauty qua *effect*.

Compiled by Artemy Magun

Notes

[AM] indicates notes by the editor, Artemy Magun.

Introduction

Compiled from the final report to the Russian Academic Foundation for the Humanities on the *Les (Hyle)* research project, September 1999. [*O.E. Lebedeva, compiler*]
1 Konstantin Eduardovich Tsiolkovskii (1857–1935) was a Russian and Soviet rocket scientist and a pioneer of astronautical theory. Tsiolkovskii combined technological expertise with an adherence to the philosophy of Russian cosmism. [*AM*]
  Vladimir Ivanovich Vernadskii (1863–1945) was a Soviet scientist who worked in the fields of radiogeology, geochemistry, and biochemistry. He was one of the leading scientific thinkers of Russian Cosmism and is most famous for his book *The Biosphere*, tr. David B. Langmuir (New York: Copernicus, 1997), which challenged conventional views of Earth's history. [*AM*]
2 Lev Berg (1876–1950) was a prominent Soviet biologist and geographer who proposed an evolutionary theory in opposition to the views of Darwin and Lamarck. [*AM*]
3 Karl Pearson (1857–1936) was a British biologist and mathematician and one of the founders of biometrics. He was an ardent supporter of selectionism. The research referred to is his investigation of the heritance and inheritance of the Shirley poppy. Karl Pearson, 'Cooperative Investigations on Plants: I. On the Inheritance of the Shirley Poppy', *Biometrika*, no. 2, 1910, pp. 56–100; Karl Pearson, 'Cooperative Investigations on Plants: III. On Inheritance in the Shirley Poppy: Second Memoir', *Biometrika*, no. 4, 1906, pp. 394–426. [*AM*]
4 'Flourishing complexity' is a notion outlined by Konstantin Leontiev (1831–91) defining a period central to a triune process of development of social organisms. The first stage of the process, defined as 'primary simplicity', is the birth of a social organism, while the third, called 'secondary mingling simplification', is its death. 'Flourishing complexity' is the middle stage, the actual life of a social organism, which is characterized by multiple complex tendencies, immanent contradictions, and so on. Konstantin Leontiev, *Vizantizm i slavianstvo* (Moscow: Dar, 2005). [*AM*]

356 Notes to pp. 4–12

5 Charles Darwin, *The Origin of Species by Means of Natural Selection*, 6th edition (London: John Murray, 1876), ch. 10, p. 265. [*Tr.*]
6 Lev Berg, *Nomegenez ili evoliutsiia na osnove zakonomernostei* (Petrograd: Gosudarstvennoye izdatel'stvo, 1922), ch. 1, p. 21. [*Tr.*]

Lecture 1, 2 September 1997

The lecture course on Wood (*Hyle*) was delivered in the Philosophy Faculty of Moscow State University in 1997–8. This publication has been prepared from the surviving notes. I wish to thank everyone who has helped me prepare the text of the lectures for publication: Konstantin Chamorovskii, Anatolii Akhutin, Aleksandr Mikhailovskii, Egor Ovcharenko, Vardan Airapetian, Vladimir Gurkin, Ol'ga Sedakova, and El'fira Sagetdinova. [*O.E. Lebedeva*]
1 See Vladimir Bibikhin, *Vitgenshtein: smena aspekta* (Moscow: IFTI sv. Fomy, 2005). [*Russian editors*]
2 'Great is Russia but there can be no retreat, for behind us lies Moscow.' A phrase traditionally attributed to a Soviet officer, Vasilii Klochkov, who is thought to have uttered it during fighting by the 'twenty-eight Panfilov soldiers' during the 1941–2 battle for Moscow. The source for this is an article by Aleksandr Krivitskii (*Krasnaia zvezda*, 22 January 1942), and sceptics claim that it was in fact he who coined the phrase. Unlike Hitler, Napoleon did capture Moscow in 1812. [*Tr.*]
3 See '*ὕλη*' in Henry George Liddell and Robert Scott, *A Greek–English Lexicon* (*http://www.perseus.tufts.edu/hopper/text?doc=Perseus:text:1999.04.0057:entry =u/llh*). [*Tr.*]
4 Italian, see *https://www.matematicamente.it/storia/Sintini-decifriamo_leonardo. pdf* carta 3B foglio 34 2. English, see *The Codex Hammer of Leonardo da Vinci*, tr. Carlo Pedretti (Florence: Giunti Berbèra, 1987), p. 26 (sheet 3B, folio 34 recto). [*Bibikhin, Tr.*]
5 *Philologus*, 138, 1994, 1, pp. 24–31. A scholarly journal published since 1846. [*Bibikhin*] Andrei Lebedev, 'Orpheus, Parmenides or Empedocles? The Aphrodite Verses in the Naassene Treatise of Hippolytus' *Elenchos*', *Philologus*, vol. 138, no. 1 (1994), pp. 24–31. See Hippolytus *Refutatio omnium haeresium*, ed. Miroslav Marcovich (Berlin: de Gruyter, 1986), ref. v. 8, l. 43, p. 164 (ll. 225–31) = Hippolytus (Antipope), *Refutatio omnium haeresium*, ed. Paul Wendland (Leipzig: J.C. Hinrichs, 1897), p. 97, ll. 2–8. [*AM, Tr.*]
6 Genesis, 3: 1ff. [*Russian editors*]
7 Deletion by the original editors 'for formal reasons'. [*Tr.*]
8 Lev Nikolaevich Tolstoi, 'Pozhar', in *Sobranie sochinenii*, 22 vols (Moscow: Khudozestvennaia literatura, 1982), vol. 10, pp. 25–6. [*Bibikhin*]
9 'This poet [René Char] ... told me that the uprooting of the human that is taking place there will be the end, unless poetry and thought reach a position of power without violence.'. '*Der Spiegel* Interview with Martin Heidegger', in *The Heidegger Reader*, ed. Günter Figal, tr. Jerome Veith (Bloomington: Indiana University Press, 2009), supplement 1, [pp. 313–33], p. 325. [*Russian editors, Tr.*]
10 Lebedev, 'Orpheus, Parmenides or Empedocles?', p. 31. [*AM*]
11 See Jean-Paul Sartre, *Nausea*, tr. Richard Howard (New York: New Directions, 2013), ch. '6 p.m.'. [*Tr.*]

12 Vasilii Belov (1932–2012) was a Soviet and Russian writer, a master of so-called 'village prose'. See Belov, *Kanuny* (Moscow: Sovremennik, 1978), part 1, XIV. [*AM*]
13 See *Xenophanes of Colophon: Fragments*, ed. J.H. Lesher (Toronto: University of Toronto Press, 2001), fragment 28; Thales, *Texts of Ancient Greek Philosophy*, ed. Daniel Graham (Cambridge: Cambridge University Press, 2010), pp. 29ff. [*AM*]
14 In 1967, Desmond Morris, a psychologist and television presenter, published a book titled *The Naked Ape: A Zoologist's Study of the Human Animal* (New York: McGraw-Hill). [*Bibikhin*]
15 It is an incorrect argument that we only have experience of our present-day selves, bare but clothed, and have none of ourselves as naked and hairy beings. The experience of having a hairy body is curiously familiar to us if only because when we are born the boundary between the brow and the head hair is blurred. A smooth covering of hair disappears from the brow after birth. A legacy of earlier hairiness is still present in the sense of shame we feel when naked. That shame is so innate and invariably present that Vladimir Solov'ev based a system of ethics on it. [*Bibikhin*]
16 See William Faulkner, *The Sound and the Fury* (New York: W.W. Norton, 2014). [*Tr.*]
17 See Michel Foucault, *Madness and Civilization: A History of Insanity in the Age of Reason,* tr. Richard Howard (London: Vintage, 2013). [*AM*]
18 Bernhard Welte (1906–83) was a Professor of Christian religious philosophy in Freiburg. His project was to achieve an understanding of Christian faith through phenomenology and metaphysics. [*AM*]
19 See Martin Heidegger, *Being and Time*, tr. John Macquarrie and Edward Robinson (New York: Harper, 2008). See 'Care, Concern, Solitude', in Michael Inwood, *A Heidegger Dictionary* (Malden, MA: Blackwell, 1999), pp. 35–7. [*AM*]
20 Palamism is a theological current in Eastern Christianity based upon the teachings of Georgii Palamas (c.1296–1359). [*AM*]

Lecture 2, 9 September 1997

1 The book *Otkrovennye rasskazy strannika dukhovnomu ottsu svoemu* was written by an unknown author. The narratives were copied on Mount Athos by Hegumen Paisii, abbot of the Cheremiss monastery of the Kazan Diocese and published under the aegis of that monastery. A fourth edition was published in Moscow in 1884. The narratives were twice reprinted abroad by YMCA Press in Paris and it may have been this edition that Bibikhin used. References in the present volume are to *The Way of a Pilgrim and The Pilgrim Continues His Way*, tr. Reginald M. French, 2nd edition (London: SPCK Classics, 1954, reissued 2012). This was first published in the UK in 1931. [*Russian editors, Tr.*]
2 See Alla Selawry, '1. Moliashchiisia predstoit Bogu', in *Neprestanno molites'! O molitve Iisusovoi* (Munich: Bratstvo Prep. Iova Pochaevskogo, 1990) (*https://omolenko.com/imyaslavie/selavry.htm*). [*Tr.*]
3 Ilarion (c. 990–c.1055) was a metropolitan of Kiev in mediaeval Rus. He held his post during the Great Schism of the eleventh century between the Catholic and Eastern Orthodox churches. [*AM*]
4 See Ol'ga Sedakova, 'Hilarion, the Metropolitan of Kiev', in Neil Cornwell,

ed., *Reference Guide to Russian Literature* (London: Fitzroy Dearborn, 1998). [*Russian editors*]

5   Rousseau's essay 'A Discourse on the Sciences and Arts' won a contest held by the Academy of Dijon for responses to the question 'Has the Restoration of the Sciences and Arts Contributed to the Purification of Morals?' See Jean-Jacques Rousseau, *The Social Contract and Discourses*, tr. G.D.H. Cole (London: Everyman, 1993). [*Russian editors, Tr.*]

6   *The Way of a Pilgrim*, p. 57. Page references hereafter are given in brackets in the text. [*Russian editors, Tr.*]

7   Igumen Valaamskogo monastyria Khariton, *Umnoe delanie. O molitve Iisusovoi* (Serdobol': Sortavalassa Oy Raamattutalon, 1936), as related by Alla Selawry, 'Neprestannaia umnaia molitva', tr. from German in *Neprestanno molites'! O molitve Iisusovoi* (Moscow: Lara, 1992), p. 37. [*Russian editors*]

8   Alla Selawry, '4. Nadezhnyi kliuch k molitve', in *Neprestanno molites'!* (1990). [*Tr.*]

9   Ibid. [*Tr.*]

10 Ibid. [*Tr.*]

11 Bibikhin's italics. [*Russian editors*]

12 *Neprestanno molites'!* (1992), p. 130. [*Bibikhin*] Also mentioned in *The Way of a Pilgrim*, on p. 54. [*Russian editors, Tr.*]

13 Bibikhin's italics. [*Tr.*]

14 Bibikhin's italics. [*Tr.*]

15 See Vladimir Bibikhin, *Uznai sebia* (St Petersburg: Nauka, 1998); *Vitgenshtein: smena aspekta*. [*Russian editors*]

16 Bibikhin's italics. [*Russian editors*]

17 Source not established. [*Tr.*]

18 Bibikhin's italics. [*Russian editors*]

Lecture 3, 23 September 1997

1   Religion meant connection only in the primitive Christian imagination of Lactantius. The true etymology is *re-lego*, from '*legere*', respect for heritage, awe. [*AM*]

2   Vasilisk of Turov (d. 1824) was an Orthodox monk who lived in the wilderness in Siberia. He was canonized as a saint by the Russian Orthodox Church in 2004. Zosima Verkhovskii (1768–1833) was an Orthodox schema monk (from the Greek word σχῆμα – image) who founded two convents. [*AM*]

3   Arsenii Troepol'skii (1804–70) was an Orthodox spiritual writer of the Hesychast tradition. [*AM*]

4   Ignatii Brianchaninov (1807–67) was a theologian of the Russian Orthodox Church. He was canonized as a saint in 1988. [*AM*]

5   Feofan the Recluse (1815–94) was a bishop, theologian, and a saint of the Russian Orthodox Church (canonized in 1988). [*AM*]

6   *Neprestanno molites'!*, p. 143. [*Russian editors*]

7   Palama, *Triady I*, 1, 7. [*Bibikhin*] See Sv. Grigorii Palama, *Triady v zashchitu sviashchenno-bezmolvstvuiushchikh*, tr. Vladimir Bibikhin (St Petersburg: Akademicheskii proekt, 2014), p. 15. [*O.E. Lebedeva*]

8   *The Way of a Pilgrim*, p. 251. [*Tr.*]

9   This section is not in the English translation of *The Way of a Pilgrim*

being used. See *Otkrovennye rasskazy strannika dukhovnomu svoemu ottsu,* 'Prilozheniia. Tri kliucha ko vnutrennei molitvennoi sokrovishchnitse i svia-tootecheskie nastavleniia o molitve', section B 1: 'Izrecheniia Isikhiia presvitera Ierusalimskogo', part 4, 'Vnimanie - chtoby vsegda derzhat' ...' (*http://www. hesychasm.ru/library/strannik/txt05.htm*). [*Tr.*]

10 This is one philosophy which is always only too much in evidence. There is another: 'Why did I prefer vain reputation above all else? ... Why did I not love the fair fragrance of the divine prayers and psalms, not bow my head before the bishops? Why did I shun, not the world, but the holiness of the heavenly way of life, angelic philosophy and never-waning glory?' Archmandrite Mikhail (Kozlov), *Zapiski i pis'ma* (Moscow: Bogoroditse-Rozhdestvenskii Bobrenev monastyr' Moskovskoi eparkhii, 1996), p. 53. He signs his letters 'Makarii Kozlov, a sinful pilgrim', or just 'Makarii Kozlov, pilgrim'. [*Bibikhin*]

11 *Otkrovennye rasskazy,* 'Prilozhenie (glavnye raznochteniia iz pervogo kazan-skogo izdaniia 1881 goda i afonskoi panteleimonovskoi rukopisi No. 50/4/395)', n.2, 'Iz vsekh molitv ...'. (*http://www.hesychasm.ru/library/strannik/txt09.htm*). [*Tr.*]

12 *The Way of a Pilgrim,* p. 246. [*Tr.*]

13 Vladimir Solov'ev (1853–1900) was a great Russian religious philosopher, poet, and mystical writer. See Solov'ev, *Sophia, God and a Short Tale About the Antichrist: Also Including At the Dawn of Mist-Shrouded Youth,* ed. and tr. Boris Jakim (New York: Semantorn, 2014). [*AM*]

14 *Otkrovennye rasskazy,* 'Prilozhenie', section A 4, 'Nastavlenie Ignatiia i Kallista', 'Vedai i to chto ...'. [*Tr.*]

15 Ibid., section B 1, 'Izrecheniia Isikhiia Presvitera Ierusalimskogo', part 15, 'Dolzhno vseuserdno peshchis' o sokhranii ...'. [*Tr.*]

16 Bibikhin's italics. [*Tr.*]

17 *Otkrovennye rasskazy,* 'Prilozhenie', section B 2, 'Izrecheniia Filofeia Sinaiskogo', part 7, 'Vsiakii chas i vsiakoe mgnovenie ...'. [*Tr.*]

18 Psalms, 16: 8. [*Tr.*]

19 See Heidegger, *Being and Time.* See 'Angst', 'Boredom', and 'Fear', in Inwood, *A Heidegger Dictionary,* pp. 15–18. [*AM*]

20 Y.M. Lotman and B.A. Uspensky, *The Semiotics of Russian Culture,* ed. Ann Shukman (Ann Arbor: University of Michigan Press, 1984). [*AM*]

Lecture 4, 30 September 1997

Conclusion of Lecture 3 of 23 September 1997. [*Bibikhin*]

1 See *Timaeus* in: *Plato, Timaeus. Critias. Cleitophon. Menexenus. Epistles,* tr. R.G. Bury, Loeb Classical Library 234 (Cambridge, MA: Harvard University Press, 1929). The reference is to pp. 49–51. [*AM*]

2 The reference is to Bibikhin's lecture series on 'Property (the Philosophy of Ownership)', delivered in the Philosophy faculty of Moscow State University over three semesters in spring and autumn 1993 and spring 1994. [*Russian editors*]

3 Pavel Florenskii (1882–1937) was a notable theologian and priest of the Russian Orthodox Church. He was also a philosopher, mathematician, and inventor. [*AM*]

4 See Heraclitus, *The Art and Thought of Heraclitus: An Edition of the Fragments*

with Translation and Commentary, ed. Charles H. Kahn (Cambridge: Cambridge University Press, 1981), fragment LXXXVIII, p. 69. [*AM*]

5 See Nicholas of Cusa, *Learned Ignorance or Docta Ignorantia*, tr. Jasper Hopkins (Minneapolis: Arthur Banning, 1985). [*AM*]

6 Plato, *Timaeus*, 56b. [*AM*]

7 'Ἀγεωμέτρητος μηδεὶς εἰσίτω' this injunction was said to be engraved on the gates of Plato's Academy. [*AM*]

8 Vladimir Bibikhin, 'Tochka (otryvok iz kursa "Pora"). Tochki – Puncta', in *Ezhekvartal'nyi katolicheskii zhurnal, posviashchennyi problemam religii, kul'tury i obshchestva*, nos 3–4 (2) (Moscow: IFTI sv. Fomy, 2002), pp. 74–103; see also Bibikhin, *Vitgenshtein: smena aspekta*. [*Russian editors*]

9 Nikolai Kuzanskii, *Sochineniia*, 2 vols (Moscow: Mysl', 1979–80). [*Bibikhin*]

10 See David Hilbert, *The Foundations of Geometry* (North Charleston, SC: CreateSpace, 2016). [*AM*]

11 English-language source not identified. [*Tr.*]

12 Nicolai Hartmann, 'Zur Lehre vom Eidos bei Platon und Aristoteles', in *Kleinere Schriften* (Berlin: de Gruyter, 1957), vol. 2, p. 136. [*Russian editors*]

13 Plato, *The Epinomis; or, The Philosopher*, *Plato in Twelve Volumes*, tr. W.R.M. Lamb (London: Heinemann, 1925), vol. 9, 992a. [*Tr.*]

14 Platon, *Sochineniia*, eds Aleksei Losev and Valentin Asmus, 4 vols (Moscow: Mysl', 1990), vol. 3 (2), p. 638. [*Russian editors, Tr.*]

15 Nicolai Hartmann, *Platos Logik des Seins* [Plato's Logic of Being] (Berlin: de Gruyter, 1965), pp. 21–8. [*Russian editors, Tr.*]

16 Ibid., p. 10. '*Die Theorie des "Timaios" stellt, inhältlich betrachtet, eine Synthese von Atomistik und Ideenlehre dar, wie man sie bei der natürlichen Gegensatzstellung dieser beiden Lehrbegriffe eigentlich für unmöglich halten sollte. Eine gründliche Untersuchung des geschichtlichen Themas, das hier vorliegt, fehlt bis heute noch. Die klassische Geschichtsschreibung der Philosophie in den letzten hundert Jahren hat hier eine jener zahlreichen Lücken, die eine Folge ihres mangelnden philosophischen Problemverständnisses sind.*' Hartmann, 'Zur Lehre vom Eidos', p. 136. [*AM*]

17 The reference is to the ancient Greek *sorites* (paradox), 'The Heap'. The moment when a handful of elements becomes a 'heap' is indeterminate. The paradox is attributed to Eubulides of Miletus. See: Roy A. Sorensen, 'Sorites Arguments', in Kim Jaegwon, Ernest Sosa, and Gary S. Rosenkrantz, eds, *A Companion to Metaphysics* (Hoboken, NJ: Wiley, 2009), p. 565. [*AM*]

18 See Plato, *Parmenides* (Indianapolis: Hackett, 1996), 144a–b. [*AM*]

Lecture 5, 7 October 1997

1 *Encyclopaedia Britannica*, s.v. 'Christianity: Relics and Saints' (*https://www.britannica.com/topic/Christianity/Relics-and-saints*). [*Tr.*]

2 See 'Yggdrasil (Ygg's Steed)', in John Lindow, *Norse Mythology: A Guide to Gods, Heroes, Rituals, and Beliefs* (Oxford: Oxford University Press, 2002), pp. 319–22. [*AM*]

3 Ossip Zadkine (1890–1967) was a Russian-born avant-garde French sculptor and artist. [*AM*]

4 Pavel Florenskii, *Filosofiia Kul'ta* (Moscow: Mysl', 2004). The ontology of the Cross is the central topic of this 1922 lecture course. [*AM*]

5 *The Metaphysics of Aristotle*, tr. John H. M'Mahon (London: George Bell, 1884). [*Tr.*]
6 Aristotle, *On Coming-to-Be and Passing-Away*, tr. Harold H. Joachim (Oxford: Clarendon Press, 1922), book 2, part 1 (329a). [*Tr.*]
7 Aristotle, *Physics*, tr. Robin Waterfield (Oxford: Oxford University Press, 2008), book 1, 190b 20–5. [*AM*]
8 Aristotle, *Physica*, tr. R.P. Hardie and R.K. Gaye, in *The Works of Aristotle*, ed. W.D. Ross (Oxford: Clarendon Press, 1930), vol. 2, book 1, ch. 7.

Lecture 6, 14 October 1997

1 Arsenii Chanyshev (1926–2005), Soviet philosopher. Taught from 1955 in the Department of the History of Foreign Philosophy in the Philosophical faculty of Moscow State University. [*Russian editors, AM*]
2 Martin Heidegger, *Phenomenological Interpretations of Aristotle*, tr. Richard Rojcewicz (Bloomington: Indiana University Press, 2001). [*Tr.*]
3 See Vladimir Bibikhin, *Rannii Khaidegger* (Moscow: IFTI sv. Fomy, 2009), lecture I.12. [*Russian editors*]
4 Vladimir Bibikhin, *Chtenie filosofii* (St Petersburg: Nauka, 2009), p. 142. [*Russian editors*]
5 *Physica*, 184a, 14. [*Tr.*]
6 Aleksei Losev, *Istoriia antichnoi estetiki. Aristotel' i pozdniaia klassika* (Moscow: Iskusstvo, 1975), p. 59. [*Russian editors, Tr.*]
7 Sophia (Greek Σοφία) is a personification of the divine wisdom in Judaic and Christian religions. In Russian Orthodox philosophy, starting with Vladimir Solov'ev, Sophia is a core philosophical and theological category which can be approximately described as the existential *facticity* of the Holy Spirit. [*AM*]

Lecture 7, 21 October 1997

1 'Science does not think in the sense in which thinkers think.' Martin Heidegger, *What is Called Thinking?* tr. J. Glenn Gray (New York: Harper, 1976), p. 134. [*AM*]
2 Adam Mickiewicz, *Forefathers' Eve* [*Dziady*], tr. Charles Kraszewski (London: Glagoslav, 2017), e-book 439.2/570. [*Russian editors, Tr.*]
3 Ibid.
4 Plotinus, *Enneads*, ed. Lloyd P. Gerson, tr. George Boys-Stones et al. (Cambridge: Cambridge University Press, 2017), I, 8.14, 44–50. [*AM*]
5 Osip Mandelstam, 'Midnight in Moscow', in *The Moscow and Voronezh Notebooks: Poems 1930–1937/Osip Mandelstam*, tr. Richard and Elizabeth McKane, introduced by Victor Krivulin (Tarset: Bloodaxe, 2003). [*AM*]
6 See Nikolai Gogol, 'The Nose', in *Diary of a Madman and Other Stories*, tr. Ronald Wilks (Harmondsworth: Penguin Books, 1987 reprint), pp. 42–70.
7 'Pier Paolo Pasolini, who had worked as a scriptwriter for Fellini, achieved international recognition for *Il Vangelo secondo Matteo* (*The Gospel According to St Matthew*, 1964), a brilliant semi-documentary reconstruction of the life of Christ with Marxist overtones. Pasolini went on to direct a series of astonishing, often outrageous, films that set forth a Marxist interpretation of history

362 *Notes to pp. 83–95*

and myth: – *Edipo re* (*Oedipus Rex*, 1967), *Teorema* (*Theorem*, 1968), *Porcile* (*Pigsty*, 1969), *Medea* (1969), *Salò* (1975) – before his murder in 1975.' Robert Sklar and David A. Cook, 'History of the Motion Picture', *Encyclopaedia Britannica*. [*Russian editors, Tr.*]

8 See Anatolii Akhutin, 'Otkrytie soznaniia (Drevnegrecheskaia tragediia i filosofiia)', *Povorotnye vremena* (St Petersburg: Nauka, 2005), pp. 142–93. [*Russian editors, Tr.*]

9 *The Pilgrim Continues His Way*, in *The Way of a Pilgrim*, pp. 186–7. [*Tr.*]

10 Aristotle, *De anima*, tr. R.D. Hicks (Cambridge: Cambridge University Press, 1907), book 2, ch. 1, pp. 51–2. [*Tr.*]

11 Aristotle, *Generation of Animals*, tr. A.L. Peck (London: Heinemann, 1943), book 2, ch. 5, p. 207. [*Tr.*]

12 The mass inability to have children, despite their prosperity and high educational level, of women in, for example, Germany is very well known. The cause of their infertility, it has been established, is not men. The men are in full working order, but unable to have children. Woman here is in a *different* situation. [...] [*Bibikhin*] The remainder of Bibikhin's footnote appears to have been omitted from the Russian publication. [*Tr.*]

Lecture 8, 28 October 1997

1 Heinz Happ, *Hyle. Studien zum aristotelischen Materie-Begriff* (Berlin, New York: de Gruyter, 1971). [*Russian editors*]

2 '*Man fragt sich, warum diese stets bekannten Einzelzüge der aristotelischen Hyle nicht schon längst das klischeehafte Bild von der „passiven" Hyle korrigiert haben, ja wie es überhaupt zu diesem Bild kommen konnte.... Die Hyle des Aristoteles ist eine Metamorphose des „vorsokratischen" Materie-Prinzips, den aristotelischen Problemstellungen anverwandelt und in neue Zusammenhänge hineinverwoben, aber voll ungebrochener Kraft.*' Ibid., p. 775. [*Russian editors*]

3 See Shmuel Sambursky, *Physics of the Stoics* (London: Routledge, 1959). [*AM*]

4 Happ, *Hyle*, p. 777. [*Russian editors*]

5 Aristotle, *De caeolo*, tr. J.L. Stocks, in *The Works of Aristotle*, ed. W.D. Ross (Oxford: Clarendon Press, 1930), vol. 2, book 1, ch. 9, p. 875. [*Tr.*]

6 What Bibikhin is referring to here is unclear. The volume of the Russian translation of 'On Heaven' in Aristotle, *Sobranie sochinenii* (Moscow: Mysl', 1981), vol. 3, pp. 263–368, was not edited by Losev, and the Russian word is 'matter', not 'mother'. However, the identification between mother and matter is common for Losev's own philosophical texts, such as *Dialektika mifa* (Moscow: Mysl', 2001). Aristotle himself compares matter to a woman, in *Physics*, 1, 9. [*AM*]

7 Geoffrey Bennington and Jacques Derrida, *Jacques Derrida*, tr. Geoffrey Bennington (Chicago: University of Chicago Press, 1993), p. 206. [*Tr.*]

8 See Vladimir Solovyov, *The Meaning of Love*, tr. Jane Marshall, tr. rev. and ed. Thomas R. Beyer, Jr (Hudson, NY: Steiner Books, 1985). [*AM*]

9 Epigraph to *Jacques Derrida*, p. v. [*Tr.*]

10 P. 207 of the English translation. [*Tr.*]

11 Ibid., p. 98. [*Tr.*]

12 Derrida abbreviates 'St Augustine' to 'SA'. In another book, *Glas*, he uses the same abbreviation for '*savoir absolu*', Hegel's absolute knowledge, as he imme-

diately reminds us in *Circonfession*, p. 54. SA sounds the same in French as *ça*, the translation of Freud's 'Id'. Moreover, because Bennington's text should, in theory, be explaining all of Derrida, as is fully discussed in the text on the grey background, '*savoir absolu*' relates also to it. [*Bibikhin*]

13 *Jacques Derrida*, English, pp. 56–8. [*Tr.*]
14 Ibid., p. 118. [*Tr.*]
15 Ibid., p. 87. [*Tr.*]
16 Ibid., pp. 71–2. [*Tr.*]
17 *Jacques Derrida*, French, p. 77. [*Tr.*]
18 French, p. 66; English, p. 66. [*Tr.*]
19 French, p. 104; English, p. 108. [*Tr.*] 'Algic' from the Greek *algos*, pain. [*Russian editors*]
20 English, p. 115. [*Tr.*]
21 Ibid., p. 121. [*Tr.*]
22 French, p. 132. [*Tr.*]
23 English, pp. 145–6. [*Tr.*]
24 French, p. 149; English, p. 158. [*Tr.*]
25 English, p. 155. [*Tr.*]
26 French, p. 157; English, pp. 167–8. [*Tr.*]
27 French, pp. 202–3; English, pp. 217–18. [*Tr.*]
28 English, pp. 268, 270. The quotation is from St Augustine, *Confessions and Enchiridion*, tr. Albert C. Outler (Philadelphia: Westminster Press, 1955), book 13, ch. 34, section 49. [*Tr.*]
29 French, pp. 248–9; English, p. 268. [*Tr.*]
30 English, p. 272. [*Tr.*]
31 Ibid., p. 273. [*Tr.*]

Lecture 9, 4 November 1997

1 *Jacques Derrida,* English, p. 305. [*Tr.*]
2 Ibid., pp. 305–6. [*Tr.*]
3 Ibid., p. 306. [*Tr.*]
4 Aristotle, *Historia animalium*, tr. D'Arcy Wentworth Thompson, in *The Works of Aristotle*, ed. W.D. Ross (Oxford: Clarendon Press, 1910), vol. 4. [*Tr.*] Actually even the root in 'history' is the same as in knowledge, or what nowadays we might call intelligence, gathering information about the situation in the world. History was initially contemporary and only later ancient, contributing to understanding of the contemporary world. [*Bibikhin*]
5 Aristotle, *Magna moralia*, tr. St George Stock, in *The Works of Aristotle*, ed. W.D. Ross (Oxford: Clarendon Press, 1925), vol. 9, 1187b. [*Tr.*]
6 *Jacques Derrida*, English, p. 75. [*Tr.*]
7 See Parmenides, *The Fragments of Parmenides*, tr. A.H. Coxon (Las Vegas: Parmenides, 2009), fragment V, p. 58. [*AM*]
8 Aristotle, *Ethica Nicomachea*, tr. W.D. Ross, in *The Works of Aristotle*, ed. W.D. Ross (Oxford: Clarendon Press, 1925), vol. 9, 1141b. [*Tr.*]
9 Ibid. [*Tr.*]
10 Aristotle, *Historia animalium*, book 1, part 1, 488a, 20–4. [*Tr.*]
11 The Russian translation by Vladimir Karpov reads differently: 'Further, there are domesticated and wild animals; some are such always, as man and the mule

are always domesticated, the leopard and wolf always wild; others can be easily domesticated, like the elephant. Or otherwise, all genera which are tame can also be wild, for example, horses, oxen, pigs, sheep, goats and dogs.' Aristotle, *Istoriia zhivotnykh*, tr. V.P. Karpov (Moscow: RGGU, 1996), p. 75 (15). [*Tr.*]

12 See Fyodor Dostoevsky, *The Brothers Karamazov*, tr. David McDuff (London: Penguin, 2003), part 2, book 5, ch. 5. [*AM*]

13 Charles G. Darwin, *The Next Million Years* (London: Hart-Davis, 1952). [*Bibikhin*]

14 *Historia animalium*, book 1, parts 9–10. [*Tr.*]

15 Ibid., book 1, part 15. [*Tr.*]

16 Ibid., book 2, part 1. [*Tr.*]

17 Ibid., book 4, part 7, end. [*Tr.*]

18 Ibid., book 4, part 8. [*Tr.*]

19 Ibid. [*Tr.*]

20 Ibid., book 4, part 9. [*Tr.*]

21 The passage continues, 'Viviparous quadrupeds utter vocal sounds of different kinds, but they have no power of converse. In fact, this power, or language, is peculiar to man. For while the capability of talking implies the capability of uttering vocal sounds, the converse does not hold good. Men that are born deaf are in all cases also dumb; that is, they can make vocal sounds, but they cannot speak. Children, just as they have no control over other parts, so have no control, at first, over the tongue; but it is so far imperfect, and only frees and detaches itself by degrees, so that in the interval children for the most part lisp and stutter' (536b, 1–9). [*Tr.*]

22 Tertullian, *The Apology for the Christians*, tr. T. Herbert Bindley (Oxford: Clarendon Press, 1890), ch. 17. [*AM*]

23 See Jacques Derrida, *Writing and Difference*, tr. Alan Bass (London: Routledge, 2002). [*AM*]

Lecture 10, 11 November 1997

1 See Ludwig Wittgenstein, *Tractatus Logico-Philosophicus*, tr. D.F. Pears and B.F. McGuinness (London: Routledge, 2001), statement 4.002, p. 22. [*AM*]

2 Aristotle, *Ethica Nicomachea*. [*Tr.*]

3 *Magna moralia*, book 1, part 1. [*Tr.*]

4 *Ethica Nicomachea*, book 1, part 2. [*Tr.*]

5 See Fyodor Tyutchev, 'Silentium!', tr. Vladimir Nabokov (*https://culturedarm. com/silentium-by-fyodor-tyutchev/*). In another translation, 'A thought, once uttered, is a lie', Fyodor Tyutchev, *Selected Poems*, tr. John Dewey (Gillingham: Brimstone, 2014). [*AM*]

6 *Historia animalium*, book 4, part 9. [*Tr.*]

7 Ibid., book 1, part 1. [*Tr.*]

8 Ibid., book 8, part 1. [*Tr.*]

9 See Viktor Molchanov, *Razlichenie i opyt: fenomenologiia neagressivnogo soznaniia* (Moscow: Modest Kolerov i 'Tri kvadrata', 2004). [*Russian editors, Tr.*]

10 See Karl Löwith, *Martin Heidegger and European Nihilism*, ed. Richard Wolin, tr. Gary Steiner (New York: Columbia University Press, 1998). [*AM*]

11 *Historia animalium*, book 4, part 10. [*Tr.*]

12 Ibid., book 4, part 5. [*Tr.*]

13 Ibid., book 5, part 14. [*Tr.*]
14 Ibid., book 5, part 15. [*Tr.*]
15 Aristotel', *Istoriia zhivotnykh*, tr. Viktor Karpov (Moscow: RGGU, 1996), p. 470. [*Bibikhin*]
16 *Historia animalium*, book 5, part 15. [*Tr.*]

Lecture 11, 18 November 1997

1 A lecture course 'Truth (the Ontological Foundations of Ethics)', read over three semesters (autumn 1998, spring and autumn 1999) in the philosophical faculty of Moscow State University, was announced as a continuation of the courses 'Principles of Christianity' and '*Hyle*'. To date it has not been published. [*Tr.*]
2 *Historia animalium*, book 5, part 19. [*Tr.*]
3 Ibid., book 5, part 22. [*Tr.*]
4 These are the so-called transcendentals of being as defined in mediaeval Scholastic thought: the higher qualities which transcend all categories and are inseparable from being itself. [*AM*]
5 See Georg W.F. Hegel, *Lectures on the Philosophy of History*, tr. John Sibree and Ruben Alvarado (Cambridge: Cambridge University Press, 1998), p. 88. [*AM*]
6 See John Pint, 'How to Quell a Killer-Bee Attack: BeeAlert Available in Mexico', *The Guadalajara Reporter*, 6 December 2018 (*https://theguadalajarareporter. net/index.php/columns/columns/john-pint/52777-how-to-quell-a-killer-bee-attack -beealert-available-in-mexico*). [*AM*]
7 *Historia animalium*, book 9, part 40. [*Tr.*]
8 Ibid. [*Tr.*]
9 See Aristotle, *Politics*, tr. Ernest Barker, rev. Richard Stalley (Oxford: Oxford University Press, 2009), book 4. [*AM*]
10 *Historia animalium*, book 9, part 40. [*Tr.*]
11 Ibid. [*Tr.*]
12 Merab Mamardashvili, *Lektsii po antichnoi filosofii* (Moscow: Agraf, 1999), p. 50. [*Bibikhin*]
13 *Historia animalium*, book 9, part 40. [*Tr.*]
14 Ibid., book 9, part 43. [*Tr.*]
15 Ibid., book 9, part 47. [*Tr.*]
16 Ibid., book 9, part 48. [*Tr.*]
17 Ibid. [*Tr.*]
18 Ibid., book 9, part 49. [*Tr.*]
19 Apparently a slip of the pen. This is in fact the tenth book. [*Tr.*]
20 Aristotle, *History of Animals, Books VII–X*, tr. D.M. Balme (Cambridge, MA: Harvard University Press, 1991), book 10, part 5. Ross's edition of *Historia animalium* does not include what this edition gives as book 10. [*Tr.*]
21 *History of Animals*, book 10, part 6. [*Tr.*]
22 Ibid., book 10, part 7. [*Tr.*]

Lecture 12, 25 November 1997

1 *Historia animalium* (tr. Wentworth Thompson), book 6, part 17. [*Tr.*]
2 Ibid., book 6, part 18. [*Tr.*]
3 Ibid. [*Tr.*]
4 Ibid. [*Tr.*]
5 Potions, medicine, poison. [*Russian editors*]
6 *Historia animalium*, book 6, part 22. [*Tr.*]
7 Yiannis G. Papakostas, Michael D. Daras, Ioannis A. Liappas, Manolis Markianos, 'Horse Madness (Hippomania) and Hippophobia' (*https://hal.archives-ouvertes.fr/hal-00570821/document*). [*AM*]
8 *Historia animalium*, book 6, part 18. [*Tr.*]
9 Ibid., book 6, part 19. [*Tr.*]
10 It is unclear which dictionary Bibikhin used. The standard Max Fasmer mentions but rejects the previously dominant reference to *kob'* (augurium), mentions *skoba* in passing, but accepts the connection to the Lithuanian words *kabeklis*, a hook, and *kabeti*, to hang. Max Fasmer, *Etimologicheskii slovar' russkogo iazyka* (Moscow: Progress, 1986), vol. 2, p. 267. [*AM*]
11 The quotation is in fact not from book 7 but from *Historia animalium*, book 6, part 3. [*Tr.*]
12 Ibid., book 7, part 3. [*Tr.*]
13 See Fyodor Dostoevsky, *A Writer's Diary*, tr. Kenneth Lantz (Evanston, IL: Northwestern University Press, 2009), note from October 1876, I. [*AM*]
14 *Historia animalium*, book 7, part 10. [*Tr.*]
15 Ibid., book 7, part 4. [*Tr.*]
16 Aristotle, *De generatione animalium*, tr. Arthur Platt, in *The Works of Aristotle*, ed. W.D. Ross (Oxford: Clarendon Press, 1910), vol. 5. [*Tr.*]
17 Ibid., book 2, part 5. 'The reason is that the animal differs from the plant by having sense-perception; if the sensitive soul is not present, either actually or potentially, and either with or without qualification, it is impossible for face, hand, flesh, or any other part to exist; it will be no better than a corpse or part of a corpse. If then, when the sexes are separated, it is the male that has the power of making the sensitive soul, it is impossible for the female to generate an animal from itself alone, for the process in question was seen to involve the male quality.' [*Tr.*]
18 Ibid., book 1, part 1. [*Tr.*]
19 *De generatione animalium*, book 1, part 2. 'The male and female principles may be put down first and foremost as origins of generation, the former as containing the efficient cause of generation, the latter the material of it.... By a male animal we mean that which generates in another, and by a female that which generates in itself; wherefore men apply these terms to the macrocosm also, naming Earth *mother* as being female, but addressing Heaven and the Sun and other like entities as *fathers*, as causing generation.'
20 Ibid., book 1, part 3. 'With regard to the difference of the spermatic organs in males, if we are to investigate the cause of their existence, we must first grasp the final cause of the testes. Now if nature makes everything either because it is necessary or because it is better so, this part also must be for one of these two reasons. But that it is not necessary for generation is plain.... It remains then that it must be because it is somehow better so.'

21 Ibid., book 1, part 21.
22 Ibid. [*Tr.*]

Lecture 13, 2 December 1997

1 Anatolii Akhutin, *Poniatie 'priroda' v antichnosti i v Novoe vremia: 'Fiusis' i 'Natura'* (Moscow: Nauka, 1988), pp. 33ff. Page references to the text are given in round brackets. [*Russian editors, Tr.*]
2 Giordano Bruno, *Cause, Principle and Unity*, ed. and tr. Robert de Lucca (Cambridge: Cambridge University Press, 1998, reprint, 2003), p. 83. [*Tr.*]
3 Ibid., p. 84. [*Tr.*]
4 'The themes of the dignity and excellence of man were prominent in Italian humanist thought and can be found clearly expressed in Giovanni Pico della Mirandola's influential *De hominis dignitate oratio* (Oration on the Dignity of Man), written in 1486. In this work Pico expresses a view of man that breaks radically with Greek and Christian tradition: what distinguishes man from the rest of creation is that he has been created without form and with the ability to make of himself what he will. Being without form or nature he is not constrained, fated, or determined to any particular destiny. Thus, he must choose what he will become. (In the words of the 20th-century existentialists, man is distinguished by the fact that for him existence precedes essence.) In this way man's distinctive characteristic becomes his freedom; he is free to make himself in the image of God or in the image of beasts.' *Encyclopaedia Britannica*, 1994–8, s.v. 'Giovanni Pico della Mirandola', *Britannica* CD 98.
5 '[S]uch Untowardness is found to be in all Creatures, biting, tearing, worrying, and hurting one another, and such Enmity, Strife, and Hatred, in all Creatures; and that every x Thing is so at odds with itself, as we see it to be not only in the living Creatures, but also in the Stars, Elements, Earth, Stones, Metals, in Wood, Leaves, and Grass, there is a Poison and Malignity in all Things; and it is found that it must be so, or else there would be no Life, nor Mobility, nor would there be any Colour nor Virtue, neither Thickness nor Thinness, nor any Perceptibility or Sensibility, but all would be as Nothing.' Jacob Böhme, *Three Principles of the Divine Essence*, tr. John Sparrow (North Charleston, SC: CreateSpace, 2016), preface, paragraph 13. [*AM*]
6 Jacob Böhme, *Aurora*, ch. 1, part 2. Online at *http://www.archive.org*. Search for JacobBoehmesAurora-electronictext-edition [2009]. [*Bibikhin, Tr.*]
7 Ibid., ch. 1, parts 4–8, 12. [*Tr.*]
8 Ibid., parts 15–18. [*Tr.*]
9 See above, Introduction, note 1. [*AM*]
10 The source of this quotation is, predictably, the *Encyclopaedia Britannica*, according to Renée-Marie Croose Parry, *The Political Name of Love* (n.p.: New European Publications, 2007), p. 253, n. 7. [*Tr.*]
11 *Encyclopaedia Britannica*, s.v. 'Tsiolkovsky'. [*Tr.*] See above, Introduction, note 1. [*AM*]
12 Konstantin Tsiolkovskii, 'Zhivaia Vselennaia', *Voprosy filosofii*, no. 6, 1992, pp. 135–58. [*Bibikhin*]

Lecture 14, 9 December 1997

1 See Daniel H. Shubin, *Konstantin Eduardovich Tsiolkovsky: The Pioneering Rocket Scientist and His Cosmic Philosophy* (New York: Algora Publishing, 2016). [*AM*]

2 V.N. Toporov, *Issledovaniia po etiologii i semantike*, vol. 3, book 2: 'Indiiskie i iranskie iazyki' (Moscow: Iazyki slavianskih kul'tur, 2010), pp. 296–7. [*Bibikhin*]

3 Mikhail Bakhtin, *Rabelais and His World*, tr. Carly Emerson and Michael Holquist (Indianapolis: Indiana University Press, 1984), pp. 328–47. Bakhtin (1895–1975) was an influential Russian and Soviet literary theorist and philosopher. [*AM*]

4 V.N. Toporov, 'Ideia sviatosti v drevnei Rusi: *vol'naia zhertva* kak podrazhanie Khristu. "Skazanie o Borise i Glebe"', *Russian Literature*, vol. 25 (1989), pp. 1–102. [*Bibikhin*] Quotation is from pp. 42, 46–7. Vladimir Nikolaevich Toporov (1928–2005) was a prominent Soviet and Russian linguist, one of the founders of the Tartu–Moscow Semiotic School. [*AM*]

5 See Ol'ga Sedakova, 'Pokhvala poezi', *Sochineniia* (Moscow: NFQ, 2001), vol. 2, pp. 71–2. [*AM*]

6 Handwritten notes by Vladimir Bibikhin at the end of the lecture: 'What does that leave us? The forest, hairiness ... Now: a pity they are no more. But there is: the Cross in tobacco, etc. The living? We are drowning in it ... The active agent ... Holiness is joyfulness, but immediately a break, dismay, *amekhania*. Joyful holiness is the first religion. But, the pendulum-swing of *amekhania*, of the Cross. Joy of the Cross? That is *difficult*, need to expand on this. It is by no means a negligible force.' [*Russian editors*]

Lecture 15, 16 December 1997

1 Vladimir Bibikhin, *Sobstvennost'* [*Property*] (St Petersburg: Nauka, 2012); *Mir* [*The World*] (St Petersburg: Nauka, 2007); *Chtenie filosofii* [*Reading Philosophy*] (St Petersburg: Nauka, 2009); *Vitgenshtein: smena aspekta* [*Wittgenstein: Change of Aspect*]. [*Russian editors, Tr.*]

2 See Vladimir Bibikhin, *Iazyk filosofii* [*The Language of Philosophy*], 3rd edition (St Petersburg: Nauka, 2007); *Uznai sebia* [*Know Thyself*]; *Pora: Vremia–bytie* [*Time is Now: Time–Being*] (St Petersburg: Vladimir Dal', 2015). [*Russian editors, Tr.*]

3 Vasilii Rozanov, *O sebe i zhizni svoei* (Moscow: Moskovski rabochii, 1990), p. 542. [*Bibikhin*]

4 Francis Crick, *Of Molecules and Men* (Seattle: University of Washington Press, 1966), p. 12. [*Bibikhin*]

5 Some sections of this lecture appear in the author's introduction, which is based on a report submitted by the author to the Russian Academic Foundation for the Humanities on his *Les (Hyle)* research project. [*Tr.*]

6 See above, Introduction, note 4. [*AM*]

7 Darwin, *The Origin of Species*, ch. 10, pp. 264–5. [*Bibikhin, Tr.*]

8 Lev Berg, *Trudy po teorii evoliutsii. 1922–1930* (Leningrad: Nauka, 1977), p. 21. [*Bibikhin, Tr.*]

9 Ibid., p. 20. [*Bibikhin*]
10 Lucretius, *De Rerum Natura*, ed. William Ellery Leonard (London: E.P. Dutton, 1916). [*Tr.*]

Lecture 16, 23 December 1997

1 Nikolai Timofeev-Ressovskii (1900–81) was a Soviet biologist. See N.V. Timofeev-Ressovskii, N.N. Vorontsov, and A.V. Iablokov, *Kratkii ocherk teorii evoliutsii* (Moscow: Nauka, 1977). [*AM*]
2 G.V. Derzhavin, *Stikhotvoreniia* (Leningrad: Sovetskii Pisatel', 1957), p. 360. [*AM*]
3 'The most sorrowful lyrical feeling develops to the music of victory.' See Sedakova, 'Pokhvala poezii', after p. 71. [*Tr., Russian editors*]
4 Source not identified. [*AM*]
5 See Vladimir Solovyov, 'Ideia sverkhcheloveka', in *Mir Iskusstva*, no. 9 (1899) (*http://russianway.rhga.ru/upload/main/12_Solovyev2.pdf*). [*AM*]
6 Quoted in Bibikhin, 'Iskusstvo i obnovlenie mira po Ezhenu Ionesko', in *Samosoznanie kul'tury i iskusstva XX veka* (Moscow–St Petersburg: Universitetskaia kniga, 2000), p. 485. [*Russian editors, Tr.*]
7 Ibid., p. 486. [*Russian editors, Tr.*]
8 Ibid., p. 506. [*Russian editors, Tr.*]
9 Ibid., p. 492. [*Russian editors, Tr.*]
10 Ibid., p. 494. [*Russian editors, Tr.*]
11 John Wheeler [Dzh. Uiler], 'Kvant i Vselennaia', *Astrofizika, kvanty i teoriia otnositel'nosti*, ed. Edoardo Amal'di (Moscow: Mir, 1982), p. 546. [*Russian editors, Tr.*]
12 See Erwin Schrödinger, *What is Life?* (Cambridge: Cambridge University Press, 2012). [*AM*]
13 Akhutin speaks of the 'opening of consciousness' in his published texts (see above, Lecture 7, note 8). To him, tragedy is a cultural form which opens up the human being to truth. From this it logically follows that there is such a thing as an unopened, closed consciousness. [*AM*]
14 See Vladimir Voeikov, *Vitalizm: mozhet li on sluzhit' issledovatel'skoi programmoi? Biofilosofiia* (Moscow: IFRAN, 1997). [*Bibikhin*]
15 German, '*Achsenzeit*': the period in world history between 800 and 200 BCE when all the most important religions and philosophies which now shape culture were born. The concept was introduced by Karl Jaspers. See Jaspers, *The Origin and Goal of History*, tr. Michael Bullock (London: Yale University Press, 1965), pp. 1–22. [*AM*]

Lecture 17, 10 February 1998

1 Viktor Toporov, *Sviatost' i sviatye v russkoi dukhovnoi kul'ture*, 2 vols (Moscow: Gnosis, 1995–8). [*AM*]
2 Romans, 8: 22. [*Tr.*]
3 It is unclear what the mathematical reference here is. It may be to the discipline of topology. [*AM*]
4 Proclus ('Prokl'), *Nachala fiziki*, tr. and ed. Svetlana Mesiats (Moscow:

Greko-latinskii kabinet Iu.A. Shichalina, 2001). Cf. Albertus Ritzenfeld, *Procli Diadochi Lycii institutio physica* (Lipsiae: in aedibus B.G. Teubneri, 1912). *[AM]*

5 Proclus, *Nachala fiziki*, p. 102. *[AM]*

6 Viktor Pelevin (b. 1962) is a widely recognized Russian fiction writer. Among his novels which have been translated into English are *Homo Zapiens* (London: Penguin, 2002) and *The Clay Machine Gun* (London: Faber, 2002). *[AM]*

7 Sergei Averintsev, "'Akh, moi milyi Avgustin!'", *Argumenty i Fakty*, no. 3, 1998 (*http://www.aif.ru/archive/163779*6). *[Bibikhin, Tr.]*

8 The 'superfluous man', in Russian *'lishnii chelovek'*, is a character type whose frequent recurrence in nineteenth-century Russian literature has made him a national archetype. He is usually an aristocrat, intelligent, well educated, and informed by idealism and goodwill, but incapable, for reasons as complex as Hamlet's, of engaging in effective action. Although he is aware of the stupidity and injustice surrounding him, he remains a bystander. *Encyclopaedia Britannica*, s.v. 'Superfluous Man'. *[AM]*

9 See s.v. *'Nevozmozhnyi'*, in *Tolkovyi slovar' Ozhegova* (*https://gufo.me/dict/ozhegov/невозможный*). *[AM]*

10 See Henri Poincaré, 'Science and Hypothesis', in *The Foundations of Science: Science and Hypothesis, The Value of Science, Science and Method* (New York: Science Press, 1913). *[AM]*

11 'Why is there something rather than nothing? For nothing is simpler and easier than something.' 'Principles of Nature and Grace Based on Reason', in G.W. Leibniz, *Philosophical Essays*, ed. and tr. Roger Ariew and Daniel Garber (Indianapolis, IN: Hackett, 1989), p. 210. *[AM]*

12 Berg, *Trudy po teorii evoliutsii*, p. 45. *[Bibikhin]*

13 Ibid., p. 46. *[Bibikhin]*

14 Ibid. *[Bibikhin]*

15 See Merab Mamardashvili, *Lektsii po antichnoi filosofii* (Moscow: Agraf, 1997), p. 17. *[Bibikhin]*

16 Lev Berg, *Teorii evoliutsii* (St Petersburg: 'Academia', 1922), p. 16. *[AM]*

17 Darwin, *The Origin of Species*, p. 49. *[Tr.]*

18 'On the Reception of *The Origin of Species*', in Francis Darwin, ed., *The Life and Letters of Charles Darwin* (London: John Murray, 1888), vol. 2, p. 197. *[Tr.]*

19 Immanuel Kant, *Idee zu einer allgemeinen Geschichte in weltbürgerlicher Absicht*, A 394–5. 'The Natural Principle of the Political Order Considered in Connection with the Idea of a Universal Cosmopolitical History', in *Kant's Principles of Politics, Including His Essay on Perpetual Peace [1784]*, ed. and tr. William Hastie (Edinburgh: T. and T. Clark, 1891) (*http://oll.libertyfund.org/titles/358#Kant_0056_39*). *[Tr.]*

20 Ibid. (*http://oll.libertyfund.org/titles/358#Kant_0056_46*). *[Tr.]*

Lecture 18, 17 February 1998

1 See Victor Pelevin, 'Prince of Gosplan', in *A Werewolf Problem in Central Russia and Other Stories*, tr. Andrew Broomfield (New York: New Directions, 1998). *[AM]*

2 'Anthropic principle, in cosmology, any consideration of the structure of the universe, the values of the constants of nature, or the laws of nature that has

a bearing upon the existence of life.' *Encyclopaedia Britannica*, s.v. 'Anthropic Principle'. [*AM*]

3 Lucretius, *De Rerum Natura*. [*AM*]

4 Petrarch, 'An Excursion to Paris, the Netherlands, and the Rhine', in James Harvey Robinson, ed. and tr., *Petrarch: the First Modern Scholar and Man of Letters*, 2nd edition (London: Knickerbocker Press, 1914), pp. 301, 303. [*Bibikhin, Tr.*]

5 Ibid., p. 303. [*Tr.*]

6 Denis Diderot, 'Letter on the Blind for the Use of Those Who See', in *Diderot's Early Philosophical Works*, ed. and tr. Margaret Jourdain (London: Open Court, 1916), p. 113. [*Bibikhin, Tr.*]

7 Quoted in Margaret Jourdain, 'Introduction', in ibid., p. 11. [*Tr.*]

8 Sarah Austin, tr. and ed., *Characteristics of Goethe*, 3 vols (London: Effingham Wilson, 1833), vol. 1, p. 59. [*Tr.*]

9 See Denis Diderot, *Thoughts on the Interpretation of Nature and Other Philosophical Works*, tr. Lorna Sandler (Manchester: Clinamen, 2000). [*AM*]

10 Lucretius, *De Rerum Natura*, 5, 416–31. [*Tr.*]

11 Quoted in Berg, *Trudy po teorii evoliutsii*, p. 60. [*Bibikhin*]

12 Ibid., p. 65. Bibikhin's italics. [*Tr.*]

13 *Sovetskii entsiklopedicheskii slovar'* (Moscow, 1982), s.v. 'Lamarkizm'. [*Russian editors*]

14 J.B. Lamarck, *Zoological Philosophy*, tr. and ed. Hugh Elliot (London: Macmillan, 1914), p. 119. [*Tr.*]

15 Ibid., pp. 119–20. [*Tr.*]

16 See above, Lecture 7, note 4. [*AM*]

Lecture 19, 24 February 1998

1 Berg, *Trudy po theorii evoliutsii*, p. 72. [*Bibikhin*] Lamarck, *Zoological Philosophy*, p. 124. [*Tr.*]

2 *Sovetskii entsiklopedicheskii slovar'*, s.v. 'Lamarkizm'. [*Russian editors*]

3 [Letter to Moritz Wagner, 13 October 1876], in *The Correspondence of Charles Darwin* (Cambridge: Cambridge University Press, 2016), vol. 24: *1876*, p. 315. [*Tr.*]

4 Hugo de Vries, *Species and Varieties: Their Origin by Mutation*, ed. Daniel Trembly MacDougal, 2nd edition (London: Kegan Paul, Trench, Trubner, 1906), pp. 549–50. First published in 1904. [*Tr.*]

5 Quoted from *Berg, Trudy po teorii evoliutsii*, p. 75. [*Tr.*]

6 Ibid. [*Bibikhin*]

7 Ibid., pp. 76–7. [*Bibikhin*]

8 See A.S. Famincyn (Famintsyn), 'Die Symbiose als Mittel der Synthese von Organismen', *Plant Biology*, vol. 38, no. 2, 1912, pp. 435–42. [*AM*]

9 See Boris M. Kozo-Poliansky, *Symbiogenesis: A New Principle of Evolution*, ed. Victor Fet and Lynn Margulis, tr. Peter H. Raven (Cambridge, MA: Harvard University Press, 2006). [*AM*]

10 See Lorenz Oken, *Die Zeugung* (Saarbrücken: Dr Müller, 2011). [*AM*]

11 Berg, *Trudy po teorii evoliutsii*, p. 79. [*Bibikhin*]

12 See Vladimir Bibikhin, 'Poet teatral'nykh vozmozhnostei', *Res cogitans*, no. 3 (Moscow, 2007). [*Russian editors*]

13 See Mamardashvili, *Lektsii po antichnoi filosofii*, Lecture 12. [*AM*]

14 The quote belongs to Ivan Michurin (1855–1935), a Russian and Soviet botanist. See I.V. Michurin, *Itogi shestidesiatiletnykh rabot* (Moscow: ANN SSSR, 1950), p. 10; see English translations of Michurin's works: I.V. Michurin, *Vegetative Hybridization and Mentors* (Honolulu: University Press of the Pacific, 2005). [*AM*]

15 Martynas Yčas [M. Ichas], *O prirode zhivogo: mekhanizmy i smysl* (Moscow: Mir, 1994), quoted in Sergei Siparov, 'Teleologiia evoliutsii', *Silentium*, no. 3 (St Petersburg, 1996), p. 67. [*Bibikhin*] Although apparently translated by A.S. Antonov and Elena Godina, no English-language publication of this work has been identified. [*Tr.*]

16 This is an experiment by a Soviet-American psychologist, Vladimir Lefebvre. *A Psychological Theory of Bipolarity and Reflexivity* (Lewiston, NY: Edwin Mellen, 1993). See also Alexey Stakhov, *The Mathematics of Harmony* (Singapore: World Scientific Publishing, 2009), p. 121. [*AM*]

17 Quoted in Siparov, 'Teleologiia evoliutsii', p. 60. [*Bibikhin*]

18 Ibid., p. 68. [*Bibikhin*]

19 Apparently added by the Russian editors. [*Tr.*]

20 Sergey Horuzhy is an influential Russian philosopher and theologian, a mathematician by first training. He was a close friend of Bibikhin. Here we are probably dealing with an oral remark. [*AM*]

21 Siparov, 'Teleologiia evoliutsii', p. 67. [*Bibikhin*]

22 Ibid., p. 69. [*Bibikhin*]

23 Ibid., p. 70. [*Bibikhin*]

24 Ibid., p. 67. [*Bibikhin*]

Lecture 20, 3 March 1998

1 Arthur Schopenhauer, *The World as Will and Idea*, 6th edition, tr. Richard Haldane and John Kemp (London: Kegan Paul, Trench and Trübner, 1909), vol. 3, pp. 274–5. [*Bibikhin, Tr.*]

2 I am quoting Berg, who is quoting I.I. Lapshin, *Zakony myshleniia i formy poznaniia* [*The Laws of Thinking and Forms of Cognition*] (St Petersburg: Bezobrazov, 1906), p. 119. [*Bibikhin*] The present translation is quoting from *Hegel's Philosophy of Nature*, tr. A.V. Miller (Oxford: Clarendon Press, 1970), pp. 20, 284. [*Tr.*]

3 Lev Berg, *Nomogenez, ili evoliutsiia na osnove zakonomernostei* (Petrograd: Gosudarstvennoe izdatel'stvo, 1922). [*AM*]

4 Name inserted by O.E. Lebedeva. [*Tr.*]

5 Berg, *Trudy po teorii evoliutsii*, p. 83. [*Bibikhin*]

6 Part of the paragraph is quoted in the author's research report which forms this volume's introduction. [*Tr.*]

7 Berg, *Trudy po teorii evoliutsii*, p. 84. [*Bibikhin*]

8 Ibid., p. 86. [*Bibikhin*]

9 Vladimir Vernadskii, *Razmyshleniia naturalista. Nauchnaia mysl' kak planetnoe iavlenie* (Moscow: Nauka, 1977), p. 29. [*Bibikhin*]

10 Prokaryotes are now believed to have appeared 3.5 to 4 billion years ago. In the text quoted, Vernadskii appears to be talking about the appearance not of *Homo sapiens* but of hominids (about 1.9 million years ago). *Wikipedia*, s.v. 'Prokaryotes', '*Homo sapiens*'. [*Tr.*]

11 See Vernadskii, *Razmyshleniia naturalista*, p. 157. See Irina Ivanova, ed., *Geologicheskii vozrast iskopaemogo cheloveka* (Moscow: Nauka, 1965). [*Bibikhin*] Compare with 'The earliest fossil evidence of early *Homo sapiens* appears in Africa around 300,000 years ago.' *Wikipedia*, s.v. '*Homo sapiens*'. Early modern humans appear to have migrated from the Middle East to Europe around 50,000 years ago. K. Kris Hirst, 'Why Don't We Call Them "Cro-Magnon" Anymore?', *Thought.Co*, 14 November 2019 (*https://www.thoughtco.com/we-dont-call-them-cro-magnon-170738*). [*Tr.*]

12 Berg, *Trudy po teorii evoliutsii*, p. 243. [*Bibikhin*]

13 Ibid., p. 245. [*Bibikhin*]

14 Ibid., p. 249. [*Bibikhin*]

15 Bibikhin's italics. [*Tr.*]

16 Berg, *Trudy po teorii evoliutsii*, p. 86. [*Bibikhin*]

17 Ibid., p. 87. [*Bibikhin*]

18 Berg was denounced in 1931 for his 'complete unwillingness to recant his objectively wholly harmful theoretical principles', and moved out of genetics. Kaprun M. Mitropol'skii, 'Ne priroda a Berg pytaetsia odurachit' studentov', *Leningradskii universitet. Ezhedekadnaia gazeta*, no. 15 (68), 18 March 1931, p. 3. Quoted in *Wikipedia*. [*Tr.*]

19 Raisa Berg, *Acquired Traits: Memoirs of a Geneticist from the Soviet Union*, tr. David Lowe (New York: Viking, 1988). [*Bibikhin*]

20 Ernst Häckel, *Generelle Morphologie der Organismen* (Berlin: George Reimer, 1866). Another well-known book of his is *Die Welträthsel. Gemeinverständliche Studien über Monistische Philosophie* [*The Enigma of the World*] (Bonn: Emil Strauss, 1899). [*Bibikhin, Tr.*]

21 Berg, *Trudy po teorii evoliutsii*, p. 87. [*Bibikhin*]

22 Ibid., p. 91. [*Bibikhin*]

23 A distinguished geneticist arrested on false charges in 1940 and given a death sentence which was commuted to twenty years' imprisonment. He died in prison in 1943. [*Tr.*]

24 Alexander Vustin (1943–2020) was a Soviet and Russian composer and a friend of Bibikhin. [*AM*]

25 Berg, *Trudy po teorii evoliutsii*, p. 101. [*Bibikhin*]

26 Ibid., p. 129. [*Bibikhin*]

27 Ibid., p. 132. [*Bibikhin*]

28 Ephesians, 6: 12. [*Tr.*]

29 Berg, *Trudy po teorii evoliutsii*, p. 218. [*Bibikhin*]

Lecture 21, 10 March 1998

1 Berg, *Trudy po teorii evoliutsii*, p. 218. [*Bibikhin*]

2 Ibid., pp. 249–50. [*Bibikhin*]

3 Ibid., p. 261. [*Bibikhin*]

4 Pavel Marikovskii, *Nasekomye zashchishchaiutsia* (Moscow: Nauka, 1978), p. 27. [*Bibikhin*]

5 Freeman Dyson, *Infinite in All Directions* (New York: Harper & Row, 1988). [*Bibikhin*]

6 Ibid., p. 36. [*Bibikhin*]

7 Ibid., p. 6. [*Bibikhin*]

8 In English in Bibikhin's notes. *Encyclopaedia Britannica*, s.v. 'The Very Early Universe: Superunification and the Planck Era'. [*Tr.*]
9 In English in Bibikhin's notes. A quotation from *Encyclopaedia Britannica*, but precise location not found. [*Tr.*]
10 *Encyclopaedia Britannica*, s.v. 'John Archibald Wheeler'. [*Tr.*]
11 John Archibald Wheeler, *Frontiers of Time* (Austin: University of Texas Press, 1978), p. 13. [*Bibikhin*]
12 Quoted from Dyson, *Infinite in All Directions*, pp. 52, 53. [*Bibikhin*]
13 See Jan Oort, 'The Structure of the Cloud of Comets Surrounding the Solar System and a Hypothesis Concerning its Origin', *Bulletin of the Astronomical Institutes of the Netherlands*, vol. 11, no. 408, 1950, pp. 91–110. [*AM*]
14 See Victor Safronov, *Evoliutsiia doplanetnogo oblaka i obrazovanie zemli i planet* (Moscow: Nauka, 1969). [*AM*]
15 Richard Muller, *Nemesis, the Death Star* (London: Mandarin, 1990), p. 114. [*Tr.*]
16 Dyson, *Infinite in All Directions*, p. 32. [*Bibikhin*]
17 Francis Crick, 'On Protein Synthesis', in *Symposia of the Society for Experimental Biology* (Cambridge: Cambridge University Press, 1958), vol. 12, p. 153. [*Bibikhin*]
18 *The Celestial Worlds Discover'd: or, Conjectures Concerning the Inhabitants, Plants and Productions of the Worlds in the Planets*, 2nd rev. edition (London: James Knapton, 1722), book 1, ch. 1, pp. 1–2. [*Tr.*]
19 As quoted by Frank Edward Manuel, *The Religion of Isaac Newton* (Oxford: Clarendon Press, 1977), pp. 99–102. [*Bibikhin*] (*https://en.wikiquote.org/wiki/Isaac_Newton*). [*Tr.*]
20 Dyson, *Infinite in All Directions*, pp. 50–1. [*Bibikhin*] On p. 51, Dyson goes on to qualify this by adding, 'Directed panspermia is only a hypothesis on the wilder fringe of speculation.' [*Tr.*]
21 Ibid. [*Bibikhin*]
22 Ibid., p. 54. [*Bibikhin*]
23 Ibid., p. 55. [*Bibikhin*]
24 Ibid. [*Bibikhin*]
25 The Nobel Prize: 'Max Delbrück' (*https://www.nobelprize.org/prizes/medicine/1969/delbruck/biographical/*). [*Tr.*]
26 The Nobel Prize: 'Manfred Eigen' (*https://www.nobelprize.org/prizes/chemistry/1967/eigen/facts/*). [*Tr.*]
27 See Schrödinger, *What is Life?* [*AM*]

Lecture 22, 17 March 1998

1 Dyson, *Infinite in All Directions*, p. 63. [*Bibikhin*]
2 John von Neumann, 'The General and Logical Theory of Automata', in L.A. Jeffress, ed., *Cerebral Mechanisms in Behaviour: The Hixon Symposium* (Oxford: Wiley, 1951), pp. 1–41. [*Bibikhin*]
3 Edward O. Wilson, *On Human Nature* (Cambridge, MA: Harvard University Press, 1978), p. 17. [*Bibikhin*]
4 *Encyclopaedia Britannica*. CD version. [*Tr.*]
5 See the *Britannica Guide to Climate Change, 2008*. [*Tr.*]
6 Dyson, *Infinite in All Directions*, p. 68. [*Bibikhin*]

7 In the manuscript, this paragraph has an exclamation mark against it. [*Russian editors*]
8 The automaton, self-moving, αὐτὸς μέμαα, has most likely the same etymology as the Latin *motio, motor.* [*Bibikhin*]
9 Antonio Salieri (1750–1825) was an Italian composer widely recognized across Europe. He is also renowned for his ambiguous and dramatic relationship with Mozart, which has been the subject of much controversy. Bibikhin's reference is to Pushkin's play *Mozart and Salieri* where Pushkin compares a genius to a hard-working artist. See Alexander Pushkin, *Mozart and Salieri: The Little Tragedies* (Chester Springs, PA: Dufour Editions, 1987). [*AM*]
10 Bibikhin appears to be quoting from the German original (Hegel, *Vorlesungen über die Philosophie der Natur*, para. 337). A published English translation reads: 'Fire releases itself into members, and is ceaselessly passing over into its product, which is ceaselessly led back to the unity of subjectivity, so that there is an immediate absorption of its independence. Animal life is therefore the Notion displaying itself in space and time.' See Hegel, *Philosophy of Nature*, tr. Arnold V. Miller (London: Routledge, 2013), vol. 3, section 3, Organic Physics (Organics), § 337, ll. 28–37, p. 13. [*Bibikhin, Tr.*]
11 Dyson, *Infinite in All Directions*, p. 88. [*Bibikhin*]
12 Ibid., p. 91. [*Bibikhin*]
13 Ibid., p. 92. [*Bibikhin*]
14 Gottfried Leibniz, *Monadology*, tr. Lloyd Strickland (Edinburgh: Edinburgh University Press, 2014), para. 64. [*AM*]
15 Richard Dawkins, *The Selfish Gene* (Oxford: Oxford University Press, 1972). [*Bibikhin*]
16 This applies for instance to Losev's 'Social Nature of Platonism', in *Ocherki antichnogo simvolizma i mifologii* (Moscow: Mysl', 1993), pp. 530–620. The argument is tricky, though, because Plato is, to the Russian Orthodox Losev, a pagan, and the attribution of tyranny to Plato's cosmos, from this point of view, is not a surprise. Losev's view of Plato's social teaching as harsh is shared by Bibikhin himself in his *Aleksei Fedorovich Losev. Sergei Sergeevich Averintsev* (Moscow: Institut Sv. Fomy, 2006). [*AM*]
17 Steven Weinberg, *The First Three Minutes* (New York: Basic Books, 1977), pp. 131–2. [*Bibikhin*]

Lecture 23, 24 March 1998

1 Edward Wilson is not to be confused with Robert Wilson, who, together with Arno Penzias, in 1965 discovered background radiation in the universe, a broad-spectrum, diffuse electromagnetic radiation which can come from any-where. There is also cosmic microwave background radiation believed to be left over from a time when the universe was different, extremely hot and dense, and indeed so hot and dense that it exploded at speeds much greater than the speed of light. *Encyclopaedia Britannica*, s.v. 'Edward O. Wilson'. [*Bibikhin, Tr.*]
2 Anatolii Akhutin's constant and fundamental belief is that in no way do human beings belong to a 'genus': by their very essence, as a basic principle; each individual is their own entire human genus, to the extent that they succeed in giving birth to themselves again and again. [*Russian editors*] This particular thought appears to have been communicated orally. [*AM*]

3 See Martin Heidegger, 'The Thing', in *Poetry, Language, Thought*, tr. Albert Hofstadter (New York: Harper, 2016). [*AM*]
4 *Encyclopaedia Britannica*, s.v. 'Edward O. Wilson'. [*Tr.*]
5 Dyson, *Infinite in All Directions*, p. 96. [*Bibikhin*]
6 Quoted in ibid., pp. 112–13. [*Bibikhin*]
7 According to Wittgenstein's *Tractatus*, the world is composed of objects united into configurations. This can also mean that the world consists of objects, and that relations among them are not, properly speaking, elements. [*AM*]
8 Julian Huxley, *On Living in a Revolution* (London: Chatto & Windus, 1944), p. 76. [*Bibikhin*]
9 Ibid., p. 83. [*Bibikhin*]
10 *Encyclopaedia Britannica*, s.v. 'William Morton Wheeler'. [*Tr.*]
11 Maurice Maeterlinck, *The Life of the White Ant*, tr. Alfred Sutro (New York: Dodd, Mead, 1927), pp. 151–2. [*Tr.*]
12 William M. Wheeler, *Essays in Philosophical Biology* (Cambridge, MA: Harvard University Press, 1939), p. 5. [*Bibikhin*]. William M. Wheeler, 'The Ant-Colony as an Organism', *Journal of Morphology*, vol. 22 (1911), Philadelphia: Wistar Institute of Anatomy and Biology, p. 308. [*Tr.*]
13 Wheeler, *Essays*, p. 7. [*Bibikhin*]. Wheeler, 'The Ant-Colony', p. 310. [*Tr.*]
14 Wheeler's text reads, 'The most general organismal character of the ant-colony is its individuality. Like the cell or a person, it behaves as a unitary whole, maintaining its identity in space, resisting dissolution.... This resistance is very strongly manifested in the fierce defensive and offensive cooperation of the colonial personnel.... The colonial soma, moreover, may be differentiated as the result of a physiological division of labor into two distinct castes, comprising the workers in which the nutritive and nidificational activities predominate, and the soldiers, which are primarily protective. Here, too, the resemblance to the differentiation of the personal soma into entodermal and ectodermal tissues can hardly be overlooked.' Wheeler, 'The Ant-Colony', p. 312. [*Tr.*]
15 Ibid., p. 319. [*Tr.*]
16 Ibid., p. 318. [*Tr.*]
17 Ibid., p. 319. [*Tr.*]
18 Ibid. [*Tr.*]
19 Note by Bibikhin for a lecture on 31 March 1998, which was cancelled: 'Deities do not present hunting permits, just like wolves. Things to ponder: only when well away from gods; as deer can play only in the absence of the wolf. But contemplate without gods? Brave hare. All culture, journalism, newspapers ... – are a defence against the gods. Is science also part of the system of defence? More like a slithering into a vegetative soul, while retaining a sense of guilt towards God. Why war is impure: a mixture.' [*Russian editors*]

Lecture 25, 7 April 1998

1 Wheeler, *Essays*, p. 21. [*Bibikhin*]. 'The Ant-Colony', p. 320. [*Tr.*]
2 *Encyclopaedia Britannica*, s.v. 'Jan Swammerdam'. [*Tr.*]
3 Wheeler, 'The Ant-Colony', p. 324. [*Tr.*]
4 Ibid., p. 325. [*Tr.*]
5 'New Russians' refers to a business elite formed during Russia's transition to a market economy in the early 1990s. In common usage, the term has derogatory

connotations, as this social group engaged in an exuberant and often inappropriate display of wealth and social status. [*AM*]

6 Abdusalam Guseinov, *Iazyk i sovest'. Izbrannaia sotsial'no-filosofskaia publitsistika* (Moscow: IFRAN, 1996), pp. 123–4. [*Bibikhin*]

7 Edward O. Wilson, *On Human Nature* (Cambridge, MA: Harvard University Press, 1978; repr. 2004), p. 15. [*Tr.*]

8 *Encyclopaedia Britannica*, s.v. 'Ethics'. [*Tr.*]

9 Robert Nozick, as paraphrased in Wilson, *On Human Nature*, pp. 17–18. [*Bibikhin, Tr.*]

10 Ibid., p. 23. [*Bibikhin*]

11 Ibid., pp. 22–3. [*Bibikhin*]

12 Ibid., p. 32. [*Bibikhin*]

13 Ibid., p. 40. [*Tr.*]

14 Ibid., p. 71. [*Bibikhin*]

15 Ibid., p. 55. [*Tr.*]

16 Ibid., p. 75. [*Bibikhin*]

17 Richard Borshay Lee, *The !Kung San*, quoted in Wilson, *On Human Nature*, p. 85. [*Tr.*]

18 Ibid. [*Bibikhin*]

19 Quoted in ibid., p. 86. [*Bibikhin*]

20 Ibid., p. 92. [*Bibikhin*]

Lecture 26, 14 April 1998

1 This is probably an allusion to the Soviet cartoon *Nu, pogodi!* [*Just You Wait!*], where a hare and a wolf act out situations reminiscent of the American Tom and Jerry cartoons. The hare often performs on stage, where he is caught unawares by the wolf. [*AM*]

2 In English in the original. [*Tr.*]

3 This is a widespread theology of freedom, although it has not been supported by any great theologians. For a recent and clear pronouncement on the doctrine in Orthodoxy, see Alexander Shmeman, 'Bog svobody i problema zla', in *Besedy na Radio Svoboda* (Moscow: Pravoslavnyi Sviato-Tikhonovskii Gumanitarnyi Universitet, 2009) (*https://foma.ru/bog-svobodyi-i-problema-zla.html*). [*AM*]

4 Vasilii Rozanov, 'Svoboda i vera' [*Vestnik Evropy*, 1891], in *Sobranie sochinenii* (Moscow: Respublica; St Petersburg: Rostok, 2009), vol. 28. [*AM*]

5 Alexander Pushkin, *Evgenii Onegin* (St Petersburg: Drofa Plius, 2010), ch. 2, section 8. [*AM*]

6 This is a rephrasing of Christ's words from Matthew, 12: 30, of which Stalinist-era Bolsheviks as well as George W. Bush were particularly fond. [*AM*]

7 Wilson, *On Human Nature*, p. 114. [*Bibikhin*]

8 Ibid., p. 119. [*Bibikhin*]

9 Ibid., p. 121. [*Bibikhin*]

10 Lucretius, *De Rerum Natura*, 5.809. See the discussion above in Lecture 18. [*AM*]

11 Wilson, *On Human Nature*, p. 122. [*Bibikhin*]

12 Source not identified. [*Tr.*]

13 Wilson, *On Human Nature*, p. 137. [*Bibikhin*]

Lecture 27, 21 April 1998

1 See Petr Chaadaev, 'Filosoficheskie pis'ma', in *Sobranie sochinenii*, 2 vols (Moscow: Nauka, 1991), vol. 2, letter 3. [*AM*]

2 Bibikhin's course of lectures on Wittgenstein was delivered in the autumn semester, 1994, and the spring semester, 1995; his course 'Logika Vitgenshteina' was delivered in the autumn semester, 1996. See Vladimir Bibikhin, 'Logiko-filosofskii traktat *Vitgenshteina*', in *Filosofiia na troikh* (Riga: Rizhskie chteniia, 2000); Bibikhin, *Vitgenshtein: smena aspekta*. [*Russian editors*]

3 *Encyclopaedia Britannica*, s.v. 'Étienne Geoffroy Saint-Hilaire'. [*Tr.*]

4 Ibid., s.v. 'Homoeostasis'. [*Tr.*]

5 Ch. Darwin, *On the Origin of Species by Means of Natural Selection* (London: John Murray, 1959), p. 143. [*Bibikhin*] Darwin, *The Origin of Species*, p. 114. [*Tr.*]

6 Darwin, *The Origin of Species*, p. 9. [*Tr.*]

7 Quoted from Ernst Mayr, *Toward a New Philosophy[!] of Biology: Observations of an Evolutionist* (Cambridge, MA: Harvard University Press, 1988), pp. 242, 424–5. [*Bibikhin*]

8 For a similar argument, see Paul Rabinow, *French DNA, Trouble in Purgatory* (Chicago: University of Chicago Press, 1999). [*AM*]

9 Mayr, *Toward a New Philosophy of Biology*, p. 427. [*Bibikhin*]

10 Max Delbrück was born in 1906, and since 1937 has been living in America. [*Bibikhin*] He had in fact died in 1981. [*Tr.*]

11 Ernst Mayr was born in 1904, and since 1931 has been living in America. [*Bibikhin*] He has since died, in 2005. [*Tr.*]

12 Bibikhin, *Pora: Vremia–bytie'*. [*AM*]

13 Wilson, *On Human Nature*, p. 164. [*Bibikhin*]

14 Ibid., p. 183. [*Bibikhin*]

15 Ibid., p. 166. [*Bibikhin*]

16 Ibid., p. 188. [*Bibikhin*]

17 '[P]oets sing the healing whole in the midst of the unholy'; 'Holiness can appear only within the widest orbit of the wholesome. Poets who are of the more venturesome kind are under way on the track of the holy because they experience the unholy as such.' Martin Heidegger, 'What Are Poets For?', in *Poetry, Language, Thought*, pp. 137, 138. [*AM*]

18 Wilson, *On Human Nature*, pp. 200–1. [*Bibikhin*]

Lecture 28, 28 April 1998

1 *Encyclopaedia Britannica*, s.v. 'Species'. [*Tr.*]

2 'But the power of human generation refers to the process of mental conception; this we see in the fruitfulness of reason. Therefore, we believe that to both of these two kinds it has been said by thee, O Lord, "Be fruitful and multiply." In this blessing, I recognize that thou hast granted us the faculty and power not only to express what we understand by a single idea in many different ways but also to understand in many ways what we find expressed obscurely in a single statement.' St Augustine, *Confessions and Enchiridion*, book 13, ch. 24, section 37. [*AM*]

3 See Nicholas of Cusa, *Learned Ignorance*, book 2, pp. 126, 171 (Latin); 95, 126 (English). [*AM*]

4 See above, Lecture 18, note 8. [*AM*]
5 Namely, the Russian saying, 'to exchange a cuckoo for a hawk', meaning 'out of the frying pan into the fire'. [*Tr.*]
6 Berg, *Trudy po teorii evoliutsii*, p. 280. [*Bibikhin*]
7 *Philosophia botanica*, 1751. [*Bibikhin*]
8 *Encyclopaedia Britannica*, s.v. 'Evolution'. [*Tr.*]
9 Berg, 'Zakonomernosti v obrazovanii organicheskikh form', in *Trudy po teorii evoliutsii*, p. 331. [*Bibikhin*]
10 Dmitrii Sobolev, *Nachala istoricheskoi biogenetiki* (Kharkov: Gosudarstvennoe izdatel'stvo Ukrainy, 1924). [*Bibikhin*]
11 Berg, *Trudy po teorii evoliutsii*, p. 339. [*Bibikhin*]
12 The word '*informatio*' is used by Nicholas of Cusa in *De Beryllo* in the sense of educational formation: 'On Intellectual Eye-Glasses', in Nicholas of Cusa, *Metaphysical Speculations*, tr. Jasper Hopkins (Minneapolis: Arthur Banning, 1998), pp. 791–838, cit. p. 813 [47]. More broadly, here and in *Learned Ignorance*, he describes the work of intellect as consisting of imposing forms (*eide*) on matter and thereby incorporating it, so that some commentators see him (and Neoplatonism in general) as a source of the modern notion of 'information'. [*AM*]

Lecture 29, 5 May 1998

1 'Austrian zoologist, founder of modern ethology, the study of animal behaviour by means of comparative zoological methods. His ideas contributed to an understanding of how behavioural patterns may be traced to an evolutionary past, and he was also known for his work on the roots of aggression.' *Encyclopaedia Britannica*, s.v. 'Konrad Lorenz'. [*Bibikhin, Tr.*]
2 Tinbergen was a 'Dutch-born British zoologist and ethologist'. *Encyclopaedia Britannica*, s.v. 'Nikolaas Tinbergen'. [*Bibikhin, Tr.*]
3 'Karl von Frisch was a zoologist whose studies of communication among bees added significantly to the knowledge of the chemical and visual sensors of insects. He shared the 1973 Nobel Prize for Physiology or Medicine with Konrad Lorenz and Nikolaas Tinbergen.' *Encyclopaedia Britannica*, s.v. 'Karl von Frisch'. [*Bibikhin, Tr.*]
4 Mayr, *Toward a New Philosophy of Biology*, p. 5. [*Bibikhin*]
5 Quoted in ibid., p. 27. [*Bibikhin*]
6 Single-cell organisms without a nucleus. [*Bibikhin*]
7 Giving in the expectation of something in return. [*Russian editors*]
8 Mayr, *Toward a New Philosophy of Biology*, p. 105. [*Bibikhin*]
9 Ibid., p. 117. [*Bibikhin*]
10 Martin Heidegger, 'Plato's Doctrine of Truth (1931/32, 1940)', in *Pathmarks*, tr. Thomas Sheehan (Cambridge: Cambridge University Press, 1998), pp. 155–82. [*AM*]
11 Nikolaas Tinbergen, *Social Behaviour in Animals. With Special Reference to Vertebrates*, 2nd edition (London: Chapman and Hall, 1964). [*Bibikhin*]
12 Ibid., p. 17. [*Bibikhin*]
13 Bibikhin's italics. [*Russian editors*]
14 Tinbergen, *Social Behaviour in Animals*, p. 18. [*Bibikhin*]
15 Ibid., p. 19. [*Tr.*]

Lecture 30, 12 May 1998

1 Tinbergen, *Social Behaviour in Animals*, p. 26. [*Bibikhin*]
2 Ibid., pp. 36ff. [*Bibikhin*]
3 Omission in the original publication. [*Tr.*]
4 Marginal note by Bibikhin: 'Right is wrong!' In Russian 'right' also has the meaning of law, justice. [*AM*]
5 Tinbergen, *Social Behaviour in Animals*, p. 75. [*Bibikhin*]
6 Ibid., p. 69. [*Bibikhin*]

Lecture 31, 19 May 1998

1 'Know Thyself' (*Uznai sebia*) is the title of one of Bibikhin's lecture courses (St Petersburg: Nauka, 1998). [*AM*]
2 'Poety – sverkhkomplektnye zhiteli sveta.' Oral remark by Pushkin, conveyed by P.L. Yakovlev in his 'Vospominaniia', ed. I.A. Kubasov, *Russkoe slovo*, no. 7, 1903, p. 214. [*AM*]
3 Friedrich Hölderlin, 'In Lovely Blue', in *Hymns and Fragments*, tr. Richard Sieburth (Princeton: Princeton University Press, 1984), pp. 249–51. [*AM*]
4 See Viktor Molchanov, *Razlichenie i opyt. Fenomenologiia neagressivnogo soznaniia* (Moscow: Modest Kolerov i 'Tri kvadrata', 2004). [*AM*]
5 See Umberto Eco, *La estructura ausente* (Barcelona: Lumen, 1978). [*Tr.*]
6 These appear to be confused. The sentence should perhaps read: 'Pre-existent, a priori knowledge precedes sought-out knowledge in just the same way that actuality (*energeia*) precedes potentiality (*dunamis*) in Aristotle and to it every effort and quest return.' [*Tr.*]
7 'Which amounts to an admission that to create is to unite.' Pierre Teilhard de Chardin, 'Comment je crois', in *Oeuvres de Pierre Teilhard de Chardin* (Paris: Seuil, 1969), vol. 10. [*Tr.*]
8 Konrad Lorenz, 'Zivilisationspathologie und Kulturfreiheit', in Ansgar Paus, ed., *Freiheit des Menschen* (Graz: Styria, 1974), pp. 147–85. [*Bibikhin*] The exact page reference has not been identified. [*Tr.*]
9 Ibid., p. 154. [*Tr.*]
10 The reference is to Wolfgang Köhler's experiment showing 'insight' in apes. See Praveen Shrestha, 'Insight Learning' (*https://www.psychestudy.com/behavioral/learning-memory/insight-learning*). [*AM*]
11 Lorenz, 'Zivilisationspathologie', p. 159. [*Bibikhin*]
12 Bibikhin is referring to Wittgenstein's thought experiment where a leg is anaesthetized but may nevertheless 'feel' pain. See Ludwig Wittgenstein, *Philosophical Investigations*, tr. G.E.M. Anscombe (Oxford: Blackwell, 1986), paras 411–12. Cf. *Vitgenshtein:smena aspekta*, p. 238. [*AM*]
13 Wittgenstein, *Tractatus Logico-Philosophicus*, statement 2.172, 4.022 passim. [*AM*]
14 Lorenz, 'Zivilisationspathologie', p. 182. [*Tr.*]
15 Ibid. [*Tr.*]
16 '*Aufsteigend mußt du dich bemühen,/ Doch ohne Mühe sinkest du./ Der liebe Gott muß immer Ziehen,/ Dem Teufel fällt's von selber zu.*' Ibid., p. 184. [*Tr.*]

Lecture 32, 26 May 1998

1 Nikolaas Tinbergen, *The Study of Instinct* (Oxford: Clarendon Press, 1950, repr. 1969), p. 205. [*Bibikhin*]
2 Ibid. [*Bibikhin*]
3 Ibid. [*Bibikhin*]
4 Ibid. [*Bibikhin*]
5 The reference is to a Russian translation by Maria Kozlova: 'Logiko-filosofskii Traktat [*Tractatus Logico-Philosophicus*]', in Liudvig Vitgenstein, *Filosofskie raboty* (Moscow: Gnosis, 1994). In statement 4.002, Kozlova translates 'Organismus' in '*Die Umgangssprache ist ein Teil des menschlichen Organismus ...*' not as the obvious '*organizm*' but as '*ustroistvo*' (constitution). 'Everyday language is a part of the human constitution' (p. 18). Bibikhin is objecting to the word not being translated as 'organism'. [*AM*]
6 Tinbergen, *The Study of Instinct*. [*Bibikhin*]
7 Ibid., p. 206. [*Bibikhin*]
8 Ibid. [*Bibikhin*]
9 Ibid., p. 208. [*Bibikhin*]
10 Vladimir Solov'ev, 'Opravdanie dobra. Nravstvennaia filosofiia', in *Sobranie sochinenii*, 2 vols (Moscow: Mysl', 1988), vol. 1, part 1, chs 1–2. Solov'ev claims there that the key difference between humans and animals is embarrassment. He speaks of his embarrassment when observing certain aspects of animals' behaviour. [*AM*]
11 Tinbergen, *The Study of Instinct*. [*Bibikhin*]
12 Ibid., p. 210. [*Bibikhin*]
13 Tinbergen, *Social Behaviour in Animals*, p. 137. [*Bibikhin*]
14 Tinbergen, *The Study of Instinct*, p. 210. [*Bibikhin*]
15 Ol'ga Sedakova, 'Pokhvala poezii', *Volga*, no. 6, 1991. Also in Sedakova, *Proza* (Moscow: NFQ/ Tu Print, 2001), p. 58. [*Bibikhin*]
16 Tinbergen, *Social Behaviour in Animals*, p. 133. [*Bibikhin*]
17 W.M. Wheeler, *Social Life among the Insects* (New York: Harcourt, Brace, [1923]). [*Bibikhin*]
18 Tinbergen, *Social Behaviour in Animals*, pp. 133–4. [*Bibikhin*]
19 Ibid., p. 136. [*Bibikhin*]
20 Ibid., p. 138. [*Bibikhin*]
21 See Psalms, 51: 8, 'Make me to hear joy and gladness; that the bones which thou hast broken may rejoice.' [*Tr.*]
22 See Peter E. Gordon, *Continental Divide: Heidegger, Cassirer, Davos* (Cambridge, MA: Harvard University Press, 2012). [*AM*]
23 See Werner Heisenberg, *Across the Frontiers*, tr. Peter Heath (Woodbridge, CT: Ox Bow Press). [*AM*]
24 See Gordon, *Continental Divide*. [*AM*]
25 See Heraclitus, *The Art and Thought of Heraclitus*, ed. and tr. Charles H. Kahn (Cambridge: Cambridge University Press, 1981), fragment CXVII, p. 81. [*AM*]
26 See A.V. Akhutin, 'Chtenie *Teeteta*', *ARKhE: trudy kul'turologicheskogo seminara*, no. 3, 1998, pp. 129–33. The article was republished in A.V. Akhutin, *Povorotnye vremena* (St Petersburg: Nauka, 2005). See there Bibikhin's note, 'Po povodu "Chteniia *Teeteta*"': 'Akhutin's study of aesthesis is timely and essential in order to displace the invalid formulation "sensation–opinion–science–

Sophia", claimed to correspond to the classical hierarchy of cognition.' Ibid., p. 199. [*Russian editors*]
27 In 1998–9, Bibikhin gave a course of lectures on 'Truth' (*Pravda*). [*AM*]

Index